CAMBRIDGE UNIVERSITY PRESS

Computer Science

for Cambridge International AS & A Level

REVISION GUIDE

Tony Piper

CAMBRIDGE
UNIVERSITY PRESS

Shaftesbury Road, Cambridge CB2 8EA, United Kingdom

One Liberty Plaza, 20th Floor, New York, NY 10006, USA

477 Williamstown Road, Port Melbourne, VIC 3207, Australia

314–321, 3rd Floor, Plot 3, Splendor Forum, Jasola District Centre,
New Delhi – 110025, India

103 Penang Road, #05-06/07, Visioncrest Commercial, Singapore 238467

Cambridge University Press is part of the University of Cambridge.

It furthers the University's mission by disseminating knowledge in the pursuit of education, learning and research at the highest international levels of excellence.

www.cambridge.org
Information on this title: www.cambridge.org/9781108737326

© Cambridge University Press & Assessment 2020

This publication is in copyright. Subject to statutory exception and to the provisions of relevant collective licensing agreements, no reproduction of any part may take place without the written permission of Cambridge University Press.

First published 2016
Second edition 2020

20 19 18 17 16 15 14 13 12 11 10 9 8 7

Printed in Great Britain by Ashford Colour Ltd.

A catalogue record for this publication is available from the British Library

ISBN 978-1-108-73732-6 Paperback

Cambridge University Press has no responsibility for the persistence or accuracy of URLs for external or third-party internet websites referred to in this publication, and does not guarantee that any content on such websites is, or will remain, accurate or appropriate. Information regarding prices, travel timetables, and other factual information given in this work is correct at the time of first printing but Cambridge University Press does not guarantee the accuracy of such information thereafter.

Cambridge International copyright material in this publication is reproduced under licence and remains the intellectual property of Cambridge Assessment International Education.

Cambridge Assessment International Education bears no responsibility for the example answers to questions taken from its past question papers which are contained in this publication.

Exam-style questions and sample answers have been written by the authors. In examinations, the way marks are awarded may be different. References to assessment and/or assessment preparation are the publisher's interpretation of the syllabus requirements and may not fully reflect the approach of Cambridge Assessment International Education.

Cambridge International recommends that teachers consider using a range of teaching and learning resources in preparing learners for assessment, based on their own professional judgement of their students' needs.

....

NOTICE TO TEACHERS IN THE UK

It is illegal to reproduce any part of this work in material form (including photocopying and electronic storage) except under the following circumstances:
(i) where you are abiding by a licence granted to your school or institution by the Copyright Licensing Agency;
(ii) where no such licence exists, or where you wish to exceed the terms of a licence, and you have gained the written permission of Cambridge University Press;
(iii) where you are allowed to reproduce without permission under the provisions of Chapter 3 of the Copyright, Designs and Patents Act 1988, which covers, for example, the reproduction of short passages within certain types of educational anthology and reproduction for the purposes of setting examination questions.

DEDICATED TEACHER AWARDS

Teachers play an important part in shaping futures. Our Dedicated Teacher Awards recognise the hard work that teachers put in every day.

Thank you to everyone who nominated this year, we have been inspired and moved by all of your stories. Well done to all of our nominees for your dedication to learning and for inspiring the next generation of thinkers, leaders and innovators.

Congratulations to our incredible winner and finalists

WINNER

Ahmed Saya
Cordoba School for A Level,
Pakistan

Sharon Kong Foong
Sunway College,
Malaysia

Abhinandan Bhattacharya
JBCN International School Oshiwara,
India

Anthony Chelliah
Gateway College,
Sri Lanka

Candice Green
St Augustine's College,
Australia

Jimrey Buntas Dapin
University of San Jose-Recoletos,
Philippines

For more information about our dedicated teachers and their stories, go to

dedicatedteacher.cambridge.org

CAMBRIDGE UNIVERSITY PRESS

Brighter Thinking
Better Learning

Contents

AS Level Content

Chapter 1	Information representation	1
Chapter 2	Communications	17
Chapter 3	Hardware	31
Chapter 4	Processor fundamentals	42
Chapter 5	System software	60
Chapter 6	Security, privacy and data integrity	74
Chapter 7	Ethics and ownership	83
Chapter 8	Databases	89
Chapter 9	Algorithm design and problem solving	106
Chapter 10	Data types and structures	117
Chapter 11	Programming	130
Chapter 12	Software development	154

A Level Content

Chapter 13	Data representation	168
Chapter 14	Communication and internet technologies	180
Chapter 15	Hardware and virtual machines	187
Chapter 16	System software	204
Chapter 17	Security	223
Chapter 18	Artificial Intelligence	233
Chapter 19	Computational thinking and problem solving	251
Chapter 20	Further Programming: fundamentals of practical coding	284
Chapter 21	Further Programming: imperative	300
Chapter 22	Further Programming: object-oriented	330
Chapter 23	Further Programming: files and file processing	346

Glossary	435
Acknowledgements	438
Index	439

Introduction

Fundamental to the current syllabus is that you the learner should approach the qualification in an open-minded way. It includes five key concepts to help students develop a deep understanding of the subject and make links between different aspects. The key concepts for Cambridge International AS & A Level Computer Science are:

- Computational thinking
- Programming paradigms
- Communication
- Computer architecture and hardware
- Data representation and structures

For more information on the key concepts, please refer to the Cambridge International AS & A Level Computer Science syllabus.

If you have previously studied for the IGCSE Computer Science qualification, then this syllabus is a natural progression to further your knowledge. If you decide to follow the qualification with study in higher education then this qualification will give you the breadth of knowledge for a confident start point for further study.

The programming content should bring out the creativity in you. There is no better feeling for the computer scientist than a program which works where you can stand back and think "I created that ... and it works!". As your programming and related skills base grows you will gain in confidence to solve bigger and more complex problems.

Computer Science is a technical subject, therefore you must become a master at using the correct vocabulary. The glossary at the end of the book lists the essential vocabulary.

Information representation

Chapter 1

Learning Objectives:

- Understand the binary, decimal and hexadecimal number systems and Binary Coded Decimal (BCD)
- Understand the one's complement and two's complement representation used for positive and negative integers
- Perform binary addition and subtraction of integers
- Use the terms for the naming of large binary and large decimal numbers
- Understand how characters are represented using:
  - The ASCII system, including the extended character set
  - Unicode
- Bitmaps
  - Understand how data in a bitmap is encoded and the different bitmap file formats
- Calculate a bitmap image file size
- Understand the limitations of a bitmap image
- Vector graphics
  - Understand how a drawing is constructed by selecting shapes or objects from libraries
- Describe applications where bitmaps or vector graphics would be used
- Sound
  - Understand how sound data is encoded
  - Understand the effect of sampling rate and sampling resolution
- Understand the need for compression techniques for all of the above media and text files, and the terms run-length encoding (RLE), 'lossy' and 'lossless'

1.01 Number systems

Humans use the base 10 number system.

Computers use digital data in the form of electrical signals. Digital data is represented as **bits**.

Data values, such as numbers and characters, need more than a single bit. Most PCs store data as 8-bit patterns called **bytes**.

Any number system is founded on a **base**, for example, denary is base 10. The largest number used in any position will be one less than the number base. Each position has a **place value** and this depends on the number base.

Binary number system

Binary is the 'base 2' number system.

This is summarised in the following table:

System	Base	Possible digits	Place values				
Binary	2	0, 1	etc.	2^3	2^2	2^1	Unit
				1	1	0	0

Table 1.01 Binary – base 2.

To convert the binary number 1100 to a denary number, you write it as:

$(1 \times 8) + (1 \times 4) + (0 \times 2) + (0 \times 1) = 12$.

You can add a suffix to the binary number to make it clear that it is binary, i.e. 1100_2.

Hexadecimal number system

Hexadecimal is the 'base 16' number system.

System	Base	Possible digits	Place values				
Hexadecimal	16	0, 1, 2, 3, 4, 5, 6, 7, 8, 9, ~~10~~, ~~11~~, ~~12~~, ~~13~~, ~~14~~, ~~15~~ A, B, C, D, E, F	etc.	16^3	16^2	16^1	Units
					2	A	C

Table 1.02 Hexadecimal – base 16.

The digits allowed in base 16 extend past 9, so you replace 10, 11, 12, 13, 14 and 15 with a letter. For hexadecimal you use the characters A to F as shown in Table **1.2**.

To convert the hexadecimal number $2AC_{16}$ to a denary number, you write it as:

$(2 \times 256) + (A \times 16) + (C \times 1) = (2 \times 256) + (10 \times 16) + (12 \times 1) = 512 + 160 + 12 = 684$.

Hexadecimal is a shorthand representation for a binary code. Applications where hexadecimal is used include:

- assembly language programming to represent instructions in the program code
- graphics packages to represent colour codes
- program code to represent characters.

Conversion between different bases

Worked example 1.1

Convert 69_{10} into binary.

Table **1.3** shows you how to divide the number repeatedly by 2 and record the remainders. You find the answer, 1000101_2 by collecting these remainders, starting *at the bottom*. Try to remember this, as it is not obvious.

	÷2	remainder
69	34	1
34	17	0
17	8	1
8	4	0
4	2	0
2	1	0
1	0	1
		= 1000101_2

Table 1.3 – Convert denary to binary.

Worked example 1.2

Convert $1000\ 1100_2$ into denary.

You need to use the place values (2^0, 2^1, 2^2 etc).

1	0	0	0	1	1	0	0

$= 1 \times 2^7 + 0 \times 2^6 + 0 \times 2^5 + 0 \times 2^4 + 1 \times 2^3 + 1 \times 2^2 + 0 \times 2^1 + 0 \times 2^0$

$= 128 + 0 + 0 + 0 + 8 + 4 + 0 + 0$

$= 140$

Progress check A

Convert these numbers to denary:

a 0100 0001

b 1010 1010

c 1111 1111

Progress check B

Write the 8-bit binary for the integers 3_{10}, 31_{10} and 96_{10}.

You might need to add 1, 2 or 3 zeros to the left side of the binary number so that each **nibble** is complete. Hence, you will write 10101 as 0001 0101.

Conversion between binary and hexadecimal

One approach would be to convert the binary number into denary first; but there is a more direct way:

Worked example 1.3

Convert 0111110101011111_2 into hexadecimal.

Divide the binary number into nibbles:

        0111   1101   0101   1111

Write the denary for each nibble:

        7   13   5   15

Convert to hexadecimal: 7   D   5   F

Written as $7D5F_{16}$ or 7D5F hex

(Programmers who are used to working in hexadecimal or binary will often skip the denary step).

The method can be used in reverse to convert from hexadecimal to binary.

Worked example 1.4

Convert 1C9 Hex to a binary number that is to be stored as two bytes.

	1	C	9
Hexadecimal	1	12	9
Binary	0001	1100	1001 = 1 1100 1001$_2$

'Stored as two bytes' means this will be stored as a 16-bit binary pattern.

0	0	0	0	0	0	0	1	1	1	0	0	1	0	0	1

The convention is to label the bit on the right-hand side as position 0.

Using 16 bits, bit position 0 is the **least significant bit**, and bit position 15 is the **most significant bit**.

Conversion between hexadecimal and denary

Worked example 1.5

Convert from hexadecimal to denary.

For hexadecimal > convert to binary > convert to decimal.

78 hex > 0111 1000$_2$ > 120$_{10}$

The opposite of the above example is to convert from denary to hexadecimal.

Worked example 1.6

To convert 93$_{10}$ to hexadecimal:

It is easiest to convert the denary number to binary first – then to hex.

93$_{10}$ > 0101 1101$_2$ > 5D hex

Worked example 1.7

Convert 93$_{10}$ to hexadecimal – this time we shall not convert the denary number to binary first.

93 = 5 × 16 + 13

13 must be written as D, so the hexadecimal is:

5D hex

Progress check C

Convert these hexadecimal numbers to denary:

a   89 hex   b   206 hex

Convert these hexadecimal numbers to 12-bit binary representations:

c   3F hex   d   1EA hex

e   CAB hex

Magnitude of numbers

The size of a file on the computer could be several thousand or several billion bytes. Hence, you need a notation to state the number concisely.

If you are counting in denary, then 1000 bytes is referred to as 1 kilobyte and 1,000,000 bytes is referred to as 1 megabyte.

However, the computer is more used to working with base 2.

In this case, 1 kibibyte is 1024 bytes (1024 is 2^{10}) and 1 mebibyte is 1,048,576 bytes (1024 × 1024 or 2^{20}).

Other multiples are in common use as the size of computer storage devices and memory continues to increase. The table below summarises the terms used.

Denary		Binary	
kilobyte	1000 (10^3) bytes	kibibyte	1,024 (2^{10}) bytes
megabyte	1,000,000 (10^6) bytes	mebibyte	1,048,578 (2^{20}) bytes
gigabyte	1,000,000,000 (10^9) bytes	gibibyte	1,073,741,824 (2^{30}) bytes
terabyte	1,000,000,000,000 (10^{12}) bytes	tebibyte	1,099,511,627,776 (2^{40}) bytes

You can remember these easily because they are increasing by a multiple of 1000 in the case of denary or 1024 in the case of binary, each time.

Denary		Binary	
kilobyte	1000 bytes	kibibyte	1024 bytes
megabyte	1000^2 bytes	mebibyte	1024^2 bytes
gigabyte	1000^3 bytes	gibibyte	1024^3 bytes
terabyte	1000^4 bytes	tebibyte	1024^4 bytes

Progress check D

File A has a file size of 2 kibibytes. File B has a file size of 2.1 kilobytes.

Which file has the larger file size?

Two's complement representation

Programs will need to use both positive and negative integers.

We are going to use a representation called two's complement.

Two's complement has a negative place value for the most significant bit.

For two's complement representation using a single byte (eight bits), the place values are as shown.

−128	64	32	16	8	4	2	1

Worked example 1.8

Convert the following denary numbers to 8-bit two's complement binary numbers.

a 56 = 32 + 16 + 8

−128	64	32	16	8	4	2	1
0	0	1	1	1	0	0	0

b −125 = −128 + 3 = −128 + 2 + 1

−128	64	32	16	8	4	2	1
1	0	0	0	0	0	1	1

c −17 = −128 + 111 = −128 + 64 + 32 + 8 + 4 + 2 + 1

−128	64	32	16	8	4	2	1
1	1	1	0	1	1	1	1

TIP

Note the method for the negative numbers. You need to start with 1×-128 and then work out what positive number to add to it as shown in b and c opposite.

1.02 Addition and subtraction of binary integers

The numbers will use two's complement.

All the examples below show each number stored with eight bits.

Addition

> **TIP**
>
> Using one's complement will show an alternative method to use for negative integers.

Worked example 1.9

Adding two positive integers (+31) + (+69)

+31	0	0	0	1	1	1	1	1	
+69	0	1	0	0	0	1	0	1	+
			1	1	1	1	1		This row shows the 'carry bit' from each addition
Answer	0	1	1	0	0	1	0	0	This is +100 denary

Worked example 1.10

Adding a positive and a negative integer (+56) + (−12)

+56	0	0	1	1	1	0	0	0	
−12	1	1	1	1	0	1	0	0	+
	1	1	1	1					This row shows the 'carry bit' from each bit addition
Answer	0	0	1	0	1	1	0	0	This is +44 denary

Worked example 1.11

Adding two positive integers (+114) + (+38)

+114	0	1	1	1	0	0	1	0	
+38	0	0	1	0	0	1	1	0	+
	1	1			1	1			This row shows the 'carry bit' from each bit addition
Answer	(1)	0	0	1	1	0	0	0	This is −104 denary

The pattern is not the answer that we expected, of +152.

The problem is that the correct answer is outside the range of numbers that it is possible to represent using 8-bit two's complement.

The range possible is: smallest number −128 and largest number +127.

Similarly, if you calculate (−106) + (−23), it would not show a correct answer of −129.

In both of these examples, **overflow** above has occurred in the most significant bit position.

One's complement and two's complement

> **Worked example 1.12**
>
> Express −27 denary in one's complement and two's complement.
>
> $+27_{10} =$ $0001\ 1011_2$
>
> The one's complement is $1110\ 0100$
>
> Now add 1 to this $1110\ 0101\ +$
>
> Gives the two's complement $1110\ 0101 = -27$
>
> So starting with the positive number (+27), the one's complement can be used to work out the two's complement for −27.

Subtraction

You can do a subtraction by either doing a binary subtraction or turning the calculation into an addition.

> **Worked example 1.13**
>
> Binary subtraction of 56 and 19.
>
> Calculate +56 − 19
>
> | +56 | 0 | 0 | 1 | 1 | 1 | 0 | 0 | 0 | |
> |---|---|---|---|---|---|---|---|---|---|
> | +19 | 0 | 0 | 0 | 1 | 0 | 0 | 1 | 1 | − |
> | | | | | | 1 | 1 | 1 | | This row shows the 'carry bit' from each bit subtraction |
> | Answer | 0 | 0 | 1 | 0 | 0 | 1 | 0 | 1 | This is + 37 denary |

Worked example 1.14

Subtraction - by adding the two's complement

Calculate +59 − 19

This is the same as if you calculate (+56) + (−19).

+56	0	0	1	1	1	0	0	0	
−19	1	1	1	0	1	1	0	1	(+)
	1	1	1	1	1				This row shows the 'carry bit' from each bit addition
Answer	0	0	1	0	0	1	0	1	This is +37 denary

Progress check E

Show the binary calculations.

a   (+13) + (+78)

b   (+90) − (+92)

Binary Coded Decimal (BCD)

This is an alternative binary representation that can be used for a positive denary integer. It does not use place values.

Each denary digit in the sequence is represented as a group of four binary digits (a nibble).

Worked example 1.15

Represent the denary integer 571 in BCD.

  5   7   1

0101   0111   0001

So, 571 denary is 0101 0111 0001 in BCD.

Applications of BCD

BCD is used in electronics systems where a string of digits is used to represent some value. BCD has the advantage that a given number is easily scalable by a factor of ten. To multiply the number by ten simply add a group of zero bits to the least significant end. This calculation is much simpler than multiplying a two's complement number by ten.

Progress check F

Write the denary number 184 in BCD.

1.03 Representing characters

All characters must be stored as numbers.

The character set will include upper case letters, lower case letters, the number digits and all the punctuation and other characters found on a standard QWERTY keyboard.

A coding system such as **ASCII** or **Unicode** will be used.

Each character will be encoded with a different number.

ASCII (American Standard Code for Information Interchange)

The ASCII coding system uses a 7-bit code to represent each of the characters. A selection of the codes is shown in the table below:

\multicolumn{6}{c}{ASCII code table (part)}
Character	Denary	Character	Denary	Character	Denary
<Space>	32	I	73	R	82
A	65	J	74	S	83
B	66	K	75	T	84
C	67	L	76	U	85
D	68	M	77	V	86
E	69	N	78	W	87
F	70	O	79	X	88
G	71	P	80	Y	89
H	72	Q	81	Z	90

The characters with codes 0 to 31 are called control characters. If you use them in a program, they will cause some effect – such as a 'bleep' (ASCII code 7).

For example, ASCII code 12 causes the paper in the printer to be ejected.

The maths tells us that 7-bits makes 128 different codes possible (with binary codes 0000000, 0000001, …, 1111111).

The computer stores all ASCII codes as a byte (8-bits).

Extended ASCII character set

Consider if all eight bits of the byte were to be used. The number of different characters that could then be represented increases to 256. This is called the extended character set.

Agreement was reached with a standard, called ANSI as to what all the character codes below 128 would represent.

But different standards emerged as to how the codes 128–255 would be used. This caused problems as different countries used a different standard.

This was the reason for the introduction of a new universally recognised character set called Unicode.

Unicode

Unicode provides a unique number for every character. This number will be recognised as the same character on different platforms, and in different programs and languages.

Different standards exist for Unicode - UTF-8, UTF-16, UTF-232 and others. UTF-8 is the most widely used on the WWW.

UTF-8 uses one byte for the first 128 characters, called code points (the upper and lower case letters, number digits, etc). The first 128 code points are encoded as a single byte. Up to 4 bytes are used for other characters. The first 128 Unicode code points have the same encoding as the 8-bit ASCII character codes.

Unicode codes have the format:

`U+0041`. This is the code for character A. The U+ indicates 'Unicode' and the digits are the hexadecimal code to be used. Note, this confirms that this code is the same as the ASCII code.

All data that is to be used by programs, for example, an email message or web page, must specify the encoding method used.

For a typical webpage, the HTML tag would be:
`<meta http=equiv="Content-Type" content="text/html; charset = utf-8">`

1.04 Graphics

Bitmapped image

A bitmap graphic is a rectangular grid built up from a number of **pixels**.

Each pixel will be a particular colour and each pixel's colour will be stored as a binary number.

The contents of the bitmap file will be this sequence of binary colour codes, each representing a single pixel in the rectangular grid.

The table shows the various **encodings** used for bitmaps.

The number of bits used to encode a single pixel is called the **bit depth**.

The number of possible colours that can be used is called the **colour depth**.

Type of encoding	Bit depth	Colour depth	Explanation
Monochrome	1 bit	2	Only two colours (Black and white). One byte stores eight pixels.
16 colour	4 bits	16	One byte stores two pixels.
256 colour	8 bits (1 byte)	256	One byte stores one pixel.
24-bit colour or 'Tru-colour'	24 bits (3 bytes)	2^{24} i.e. 16,777,216	Millions of different colours are possible.

The **file header** data will include the width and height, measured in pixels, the type of encoding and other data, such as a date stamp.

Bitmap calculations

Worked example 1.16

A bitmapped image has a width of 100 pixels and a height of 50 pixels. The file header uses 60 bytes. The image is encoded as a '256 colour' image. Calculate the file size (in kilobytes).

Number of pixels = 100 × 50 = 5000

Each pixel is stored with one byte ... so

Bytes used for the pixel data = 5000

Total file size = pixel data + the file header = 5000 + 60 = 5060 bytes = 5.06 kilobytes

The general formula is:

File size (in bytes) = (Width in pixels × Height in pixels × Bit depth) + Header bytes

Worked example 1.17

An image has a width of 2048 pixels and a height of 128 pixels. The file header uses 100 bytes. The image is saved as a '24-bit colour' image. Calculate the file size (in kibibytes).

Number of pixels = 2048 × 128

Each pixel is stored with 3 bytes ...

Bytes used for the pixel data is = 2048 × 128 × 3 = 786432

Total file size in bytes = Pixel data + the file header = 786432 + 100 = 787532 bytes

File size = 787532 / 1024 = 769 kibibytes

Progress check G

A bitmap file is encoded as a 16-colour image and has size 1024 × 64 pixels.

Calculate how many kilobytes will be used to store the pixel data.

TIP

The question asks for the amount of storage needed for the pixel data, not the file size.

Image resolution and screen resolution

The clarity with which a bitmap image is viewed on a monitor screen will depend on two factors: **Image resolution** and **screen resolution**.

Vector graphics

A **vector graphic** is made up from a number of drawing objects. A vector graphics program, such as Microsoft Visio or CorelDRAW, comes with a vast number of different objects organised into groups or 'shape libraries'. Examples include 'Basic shapes' (rectangle, circle, straight line) and 'Computer shapes' (various peripherals, computers as shown in Figure 1.01).

You could construct a network diagram of the computers in your classroom using computers. You could use the computer object, from the 'Computers' shape collection/library, cable runs: using straight line objects, from the 'Basic shapes' collection/library and workbenches: using rectangle objects from the 'Basic shapes' collection/library.

Figure 1.01 shows a typical vector graphics session. The user has started to draw a network diagram. Objects are organised into groups of shapes. The creator has selected a straight line from the 'Connectors' group and an LCD screen from the 'Computer' group.

Objects have **properties**. These properties determine the size and appearance of each object and they are held in a **property list** (which can also be called a drawing list). If an object is resized, its properties are simply recalculated. If this can be done without the resized object losing any of its definition, the object is said to be **scalable**. The screenshot shows the current size and position properties for the LCD monitor object.

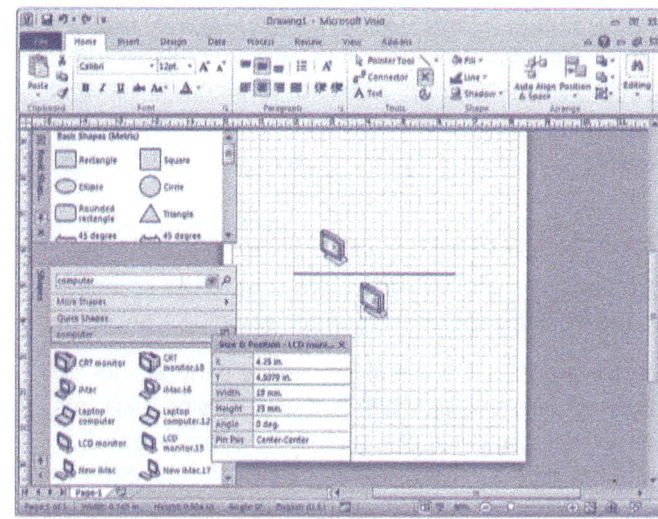

Figure 1.01 Vector graphic software.

Progress check H

A vector graphic drawing contains a circle object.

Name four properties stored for a circle object.

Scalable Vector Graphics File (SVG format)

Files in this format use an XML-based text format to describe how the image should appear. Text descriptors are used to describe the features of the graphic. Therefore an SVG file can be scaled to different sizes without losing quality.

This is why website and print graphics are often built using images that have the SVG format. They can be resized as appropriate, for different future designs.

Bitmap or vector graphics?

Bitmaps have drawbacks in that they tend to have a large file size and if you attempt to over-enlarge a bitmap with image editing software, individual pixels might become visible. This is called 'the staircase effect' or 'pixellation'. Figure 1.02 shows the ladybird before and after it has been enlarged.

Figure 1.02 Enlarged bitmap.

Vector graphics have the advantage that changing the size of any object will not affect the quantity of the object's appearance, as all vector objects are **scalable**. Also, many object libraries for specialist drawings are available.

Applications of bitmapped and vector graphics

Bitmaps are useful when you are capturing a scanned image from a paper document or scanning a photograph.

Vector graphics are useful for making general line-drawing diagrams or when you are drawing diagrams for specialist applications, such as flowcharting and networking diagrams.

You might need a diagram that you have created using vector graphics software for inclusion in a word processor document. When completed, it must be exported in one of the universally recognised file formats.

1.05 Sound

Sound is an analogue signal and generates **analogue data**. The characteristics of the sound received are determined by its frequency and amplitude. A sound can be analysed as a collection of frequencies. If they are closely related (or there is only one) they will impart a sense of pitch, like a musical note. Otherwise they might be perceived as noise. The amplitude of a sound is a measure of its power and is perceived as loudness.

The computer can only store **digital data**. To be saved as data on the computer, the sound signal must be

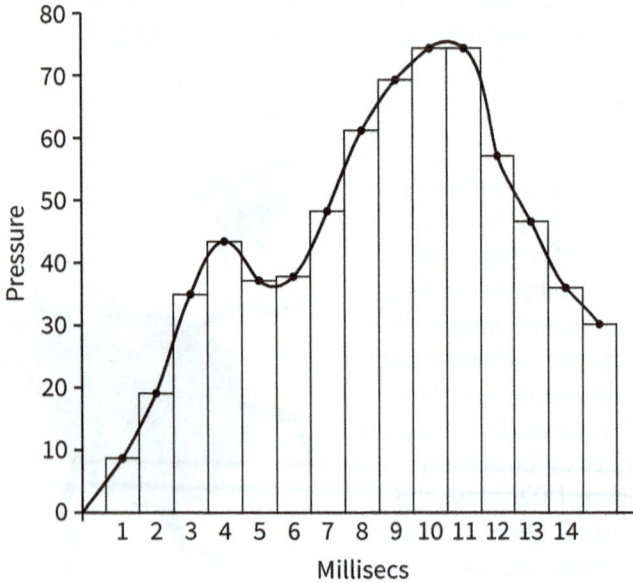

Figure 1.03 A sound wave.

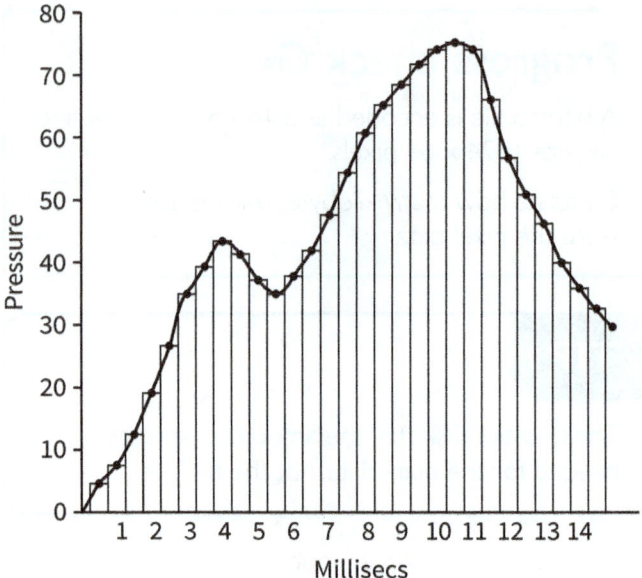

Figure 1.04 Changing the sampling rate.

converted from an analogue to a digital value. This is done using hardware called an **analogue-to-digital converter (ADC)**.

Sound signals are sampled at set time intervals. These sample values are the binary values that encode the sound file.

Accuracy of the sound file

The issues that affect the sound **accuracy** and the file size are the sampling resolution: which is the number of bits used to encode each sampled value and the sampling rate; which is the frequency with which samples are taken i.e. how many sampled values per second. The effect of increasing the sampling rate and/or increasing the sampling resolution will be to increase the file size.

The graph in **Figure 1.03** illustrates the sampling rate. Samples are being taken every 1 millisecond, i.e. 1000 samples per second.

This example uses only 8 bits to store each sample. **Figure 1.05** shows the sampled data values stored in main memory from memory location 300 onwards.

Consider the second recording of the same sound wave in Figure **1.04**. This time the sampling rate is doubled. There are 2000 samples taken every second (or 1 sample every 0.5 miliseconds).

It follows from the two recordings that if samples are taken more frequently, the accuracy of the sound wave will increase and if a larger number of bits is used to encode each sample, the sound resolution will increase.

Memory location	Sample data	
	Analogue sound value *	Digital data (stored in memory)
300	8	0000 1000
301	20	0001 0100
302	35	0010 0011
303	44	0010 1100
304	38	0010 0110
305	38	0010 0110
306	48	0011 0000
307	61	0011 1101
308	64	0100 0000
309	75	0100 1011
310	75	0100 1011
311	57	0011 1001
312	45	0010 1101
313	36	0010 0100
314	29	0001 1101

*The sampled values are shown as integers for simplicity.

Figure 1.05 Sample data stored in memory.

Progress check 1

A sound file was recorded with a sampling rate of 10 samples per millisecond.

Calculate how many sampled values are stored for this file, which has a playback length of 13 seconds.

1.06 Compression techniques

Compression techniques will encode data in a way that results in fewer bytes for the file.

Why use compression?

Sound files tend to have a large file size. The necessity to transfer files across the internet is widespread. The smaller the file size, the less time it will take to complete a file transfer. In the following sections, we will look at three different ways to compress images, and then look at ways to compress other file types.

Run-length encoding (RLE) and bitmaps

Consider a bitmapped file of a photograph where over half of the pixels have the same value representing the blue sky. An alternative to storing perhaps 300 consecutive pixel values is to save a single copy of the pixel value together with the number of occurrences of the value in the 'run'. This is **run-length encoding (RLE)**. This way we have reduced the number of pixels used to store this portion of the graphic from 300 to a very small number.

Consider a 30 × 4 pixel, 256-colour image. Rows 1 to 4 are shown. The image has three different colours - coded in the diagram as w, r, g.

Progress check J

Calculate the encoded RLE for rows 2, 3, and 4 of the image in Figure 1.05.

Lossless encoding

By using RLE, the original bitmap can be re-created exactly when the data is read from the compressed bitmap image file. There is no loss of quality of the image, that is, it is lossless. Other techniques do exist which produce a lossless image but are outside the scope of this syllabus.

The first row of pixels in the table at the bottom of the page is encoded: 9w2b2w4b4g9w

Assuming each number is stored as a single byte, the first line will be stored using 14 bytes (compared to the original 30). This is a very effective compression.

Lossy encoding

Lossy techniques are based on two concepts that exploit the limitations of the human eye. One of these is that an image that has a large background can encode the background pixels with a lower resolution. The other is that, for colours such as blue, to which the human eye is less sensitive, a lower resolution can be used.

w	w	w	w	w	w	w	w	w	b	b	w	w	b	b	b	b	g	g	g	g	w	w	w	w	w	w	w	w	w
w	w	w	w	g	g	g	g	g	b	b	b	b	b	r	r	r	r	r	r	r	w	w	w	w	w	w	w	w	w
w	w	w	w	w	w	w	w	w	w	w	w	w	w	w	w	r	r	r	r	r	r	w	w	w	w	w	w	w	w
w	w	w	w	w	w	w	w	w	w	w	w	w	w	w	w	w	w	w	w	w	w	w	w	w	w	w	w	w	w

Lossy compression techniques have the disadvantage that there can be a slight loss in the quality of the image when displayed.

Compression of a sound file

There are many file formats for audio data and most of these are a form of lossy compression. For sound data, the compression technique will lessen the dynamic range between the loudest and quietest parts of an audio signal. This is done by boosting the quieter signals and attenuating the louder signals. The sound engineer will use sound editing software with features to do this.

The most popular compressed audio format is MP3. The trick therefore is always to accept a trade-off between a lossless file format, for example .WAV, that is used to encode a purchased CD, and a format such as MP3, that has a much smaller file size. The smaller file size is a must for the audio to be made available from music sharing providers such as Spotify and Apple Music.

MP3 compression uses a combination of digital technology and the science of aural perception, psychoacoustics. The technique removes data bits from the original digital file that are considered to be essentially inaudible. These bits can include frequencies beyond the normal threshold of human hearing.

Note that there is a similarity here between techniques used for audio compression and for image compression. They both exploit the limitations of the human senses; the eye for image perception and the ear for perceived sound quality.

Compression of a text file

A **text file** is made up of a sequence of character codes, so how can you compress these?

Each ASCII character code is exactly 8-bits, so you would encode a text file containing the text HELLO WORLD as a string of 11 characters × 8 bits = 88 bits, before you make any attempt at compression.

A technique for text files must be 'lossless'.

You can't use any of the techniques that are used for bitmaps, sound and video, with text files.

A special method called **Huffman compression** using 'Huffman trees' was devised to do this.

The method is as follows: The whole file is scanned and the frequency of each character recorded. From this data a tree structure (the Huffman tree) is built, where each character is coded with fewer than 8 characters. The Huffman tree is stored in a translation table which is subsequently used to de-compress the file.

You don't need a detailed knowledge of the method.

Past paper questions

1. a Convert the following binary number into hexadecimal: 10111000 [1]

   b Convert the following denary number into BCD format: 97 [1]

   c Using two's complement, show how the following denary numbers could be stored in an 8-bit register:

   i 114 [1]

   ii −93 [1]

Cambridge International AS & A level Computer Science 9608 paper 11 Q1 June 2015

2 a Six computer graphics terms and seven descriptions are shown below.

Draw a line to link each term to its correct description.

Term **Description**

- Bitmap graphic
- Image file header
- Image resolution
- Pixel
- Screen resolution
- Vector graphic

- Measured in dots per inch (dpi); this value determines the amount of detail an image has
- Picture element
- Image made up of rows and columns of picture elements
- Image made up of drawing objects. The properties of each object determine its shape and appearance
- Specifies the image size, number of colours, and other data needed to display the image data
- Number of samples taken per second to represent some event in a digital format
- Value quoted for a monitor specification, such as 1024 x 768. The larger the numbers, the more picture elements will be displayed

[6]

b i A black and white image is 512 pixels by 256 pixels.

Calculate the size of this image in kilobytes (KB) (1 KB = 1024 bytes).

Show your working. [2]

ii Give a reason why it's important to estimate the file size of an image. [1]

Cambridge International AS & A level Computer Science 9608 paper 11 Q8 November 2015

3 a Convert the following denary integer into 8-bit binary: 55

| | | | | | | | |

[1]

b Convert the following Binary Coded Decimal (BCD) number into denary: 10000011 [1]

c Convert the following denary integer into 8-bit two's complement: –102 [1]

| | | | | | | | |

d Convert the following hexadecimal number into denary: 4E [1]

Cambridge International AS & A level Computer Science 9608 paper 11 Q2 June 2016

4 A group of students broadcast a school radio station on a website. They record their sound clips (programmes) in advance and email them to the producer.

  a Describe how sampling is used to record the sound clips. [3]

  b The students use software to compress the sound clips before emailing them.

   i Choose a method of compression (lossy or lossless) and justify your choice.

      Students also email images to the radio station for use on its website.

      These are compressed before sending using run-length encoding (RLE).

   ii Explain what is meant by run-length encoding. [3]

   iii The following diagrams show :

   - The denary colour code that represents each colour
   - The first three rows of a bitmap image

Colour symbol	Colour code (Denary)
B	153
W	255

	0	1	2	3	4	5	6	7	8	9	10	11	12	13	14	15
0	B	B	B	B	B	B	B	B	B	B	W	W	W	B	B	B
1	B	B	B	B	B	B	B	B	B	W	W	W	W	W	W	B
2	B	B	B	B	B	B	B	W	W	W	W	W	W	W	W	W
...																
95																

Show how RLE will compress the first three rows of this image. [2]

Cambridge International AS & A level Computer Science 9608 paper 11 Q4 June 2016

Communications

Learning Objectives:

- Understand the benefits of networking
- Understand the characteristics of a LAN and a WAN
- Explain the client-server and peer-to-peer models
- Understand thin-client and thick-client and their differences
- Understand the network topologies bus, star, mesh and hybrid topologies
- Understand cloud computing
- Understand the differences between wireless and wired networks
- Describe the hardware used in a LAN
- Describe the role of a router in a network
- Understand Ethernet and the issue of collisions
- Understand bit streaming
- Understand the difference between the World Wide Web and the internet
- Describe the hardware needed to support the internet
- Explain the use of IP addresses
  - The format of IPv4 and IPv6 addresses
  - use of subnets
  - The difference between a public and private IP address
  - The difference between a static and dynamic IP address.

2.01 Benefits of networking

Networking will allow for:

- certain hardware devices to be shared by many computers, for example, a shared printer or scanner
- specialist applications such as email
- access to an Intranet that is available to all employees of a company
- good work practices such as:
  - file sharing. All employees have common access to important company documents. The company will only have stored a single copy of each document. When a document requires editing, it will need changing in one place only.
  - easy communication between users
- access to files from any workstation
- centralisation of administration and security
  - updating software once only on a central server
- use of a global wide area network – a huge factor in how the company does business
- use of the internet and other networks by individuals, making available a wealth of services and resources.

Local Area Networks (LAN) and Wide Area Networks (WAN)

Characteristics of a Local Area Network (LAN)

A LAN will be a private network. A LAN would be appropriate for a home computer system or for a small enterprise business. The geography of the LAN will range from a single room to a single site.

A typical LAN will have a number of workstations (computers). Each computer on the LAN will have access to shared resources. The LAN will be 'scalable' – more computers can be connected to the LAN. The communication method will be either wired or a wireless network. A larger LAN will have specialist servers that carry out one role only - for example an email server.

A larger LAN will have specialist servers that carry out one role only, for example an email server.

Characteristics of a Wide Area Network (WAN)

A WAN is a network of connected computers (or other networks) which communicate over a wide geographical area; for example, within a town, region, country or even globally. Various methods of communication are used to make this possible including the use of the public telephone network, leased telephone lines or satellite communications. The internet is an example of a WAN.

Client-server model

A client computer application will access various resources and services provided by a server.

The tasks done by the server are varied, but the process is always that (1) the client software makes a request to the appropriate server, (2) the processing of the request is carried out on the server and (3) the results of the request are sent back to the client computer.

Below are listed some common applications:

- File server: All software and user data files are stored on the server
- Domain controller server: The server is used for the management of user accounts: IDs and passwords. The client computer software will send a log-on request to the server. The request is processed on the server, which will grant access if the user ID and password are recognised.
- Email server: The server is used for the sending and receiving of emails, and their storage. A 'sent email' is sent to the server for processing and forwarding to the **Internet Service Provider**. When the client computer requests 'receiving email' a request is sent to the email server, which will access the server of the email provider.
- Print server: The server is used for the management of print jobs from the network client computers.
- Database server: The server provides a Database Management System.
- Web server: The server is used for the management of the pages from the company's website(s).

Note that you usually name the server after the application that it performs.

Peer-to-peer networking

Traditional peer-to-peer file sharing and file downloading do not have a single central server. All computers i.e. **peers** are able to act both as a client (receiving files from another 'peer' source) and as a server (providing files to other 'peers').

Instead of having one server that many clients access, a peer-to-peer network operates with each peer storing some of the files. Each peer can therefore act as a client and request a file from another peer or it can act as a server when another peer requests the download of a file.

Client server

Benefits

- Different servers can provide for a wide range of services.
- Provides for the central storage of all files and documents.
- Security – including the administration of user accounts – is centralised.

Drawbacks

- Initial set-up costs for the server and the client workstations will be high.
- A server-based network requires the use of a specialist network operating system.
- If the server fails then the work of all users is affected.

Peer-to-peer (P2P)

Benefits

- No dedicated server is required.
- Additional computers can join the P2P network easily.
- Each computer can act as both a provider and receiver of resources.

Drawbacks

- The system by its nature is 'de-centralised' and so will be difficult to administer.
- There is less control over the identification of malware from other computers in the network.

Thin-client and thick-client

There are two different ways in which the client and the server work together.

Thin-client computing

The resources of the client computer will be very limited, with limited processing power, memory and data storage. In this arrangement, the user at the client computer requests an application to run on the server, the client sends input data to the server when the server requests it and then the client receives the output from the application.

Essentially the server is doing all the work. The role of the client is only to provide the server with input, then receive and display the final output.

Thick-client computing

The resources of the client computer are more extensive, with greater processing power, memory and data storage. In this arrangement, the client has the applications software installed locally and the client accesses the server for data needed by the application, for example, data from a database. The client is able to process this data locally and the results are displayed.

Alternatively, the client might have to first download the application software from the server and then proceed as above.

2.02 Network topologies

For any form of communication to take place, there will be: a sender, a receiver and the transmission medium, for example, copper cable, the data or 'message' and the protocol used.

The type of communication can take various forms such as simplex mode where data flow is one-way only, half duplex where data can flow either way but not simultaneously and full duplex where simultaneous both-ways data flow is possible.

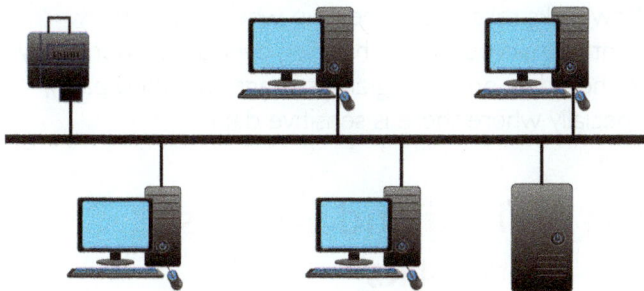

Figure 2.01 Single segment bus network.

When a message is sent it can be as a unicast (which is a one-to-one communication), a one-to-all communication, (an example of which could be broadcast radio and television) or a multicast (which is one-to-many or can be many-to-many destinations, for example, a group transmission).

> **TIP**
>
> Care is needed with the use of the term node. It is also used later in Chapter 19 to describe an item of data.

> **Progress check A**
>
> A user on a LAN sends an email. Is this an example of unicast or multicast communication?

Bus topology

Early LANs used a bus topology that was a single cable segment with several computers and peripherals connected onto the cable. Each device is called a **node**.

> **TIP**
>
> The terms simplex, half-duplex and full-duplex are not required for this syllabus.

A bus network uses a multicast broadcast. A node will send a data packet in both directions along the cable. The message is received by all other nodes, but only retained by the node that recognises itself as the recipient.

If the signal reaches the end of the cable, it will bounce back and collide with another signal on the cable. Terminators stop this happening. The cable segment will be fitted with two terminators.

Star topology

In a star topology, each node has a point-to-point connection to the central device. Transmission is duplex and messages from the central device could be unicast, multicast or broadcast.

Note that, like a bus network, if one of the nodes fails, this will not affect the performance of the network. The exception to this is the central device, which must not fail.

The nodes will be computer workstations, peripheral devices and one or more servers.

You can use the central device to connect this star network to other remote networks including the internet.

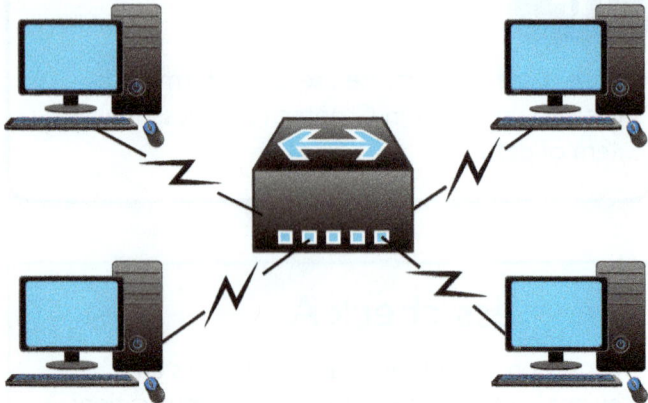

Figure 2.02 Star topology.

Mesh topology

Every node has a dedicated point-to-point connection to every other node.

Transmission is duplex and messages could be unicast, multicast or broadcast. The internet is an example of a mesh network.

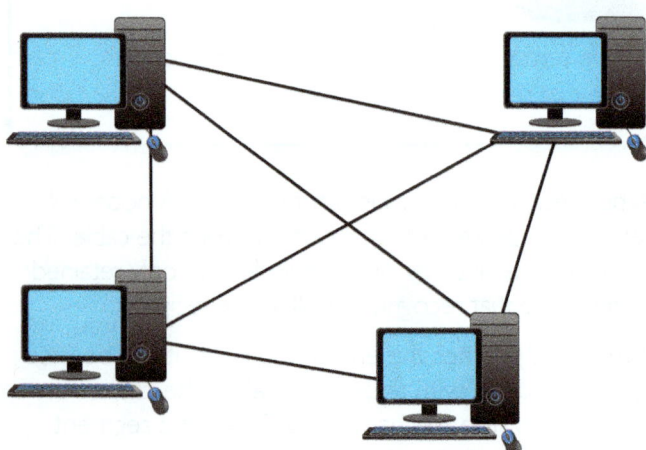

Figure 2.03 Mesh network.

Hybrid topology

There are inter-connected networks that mix different topologies and/or protocols. An example would be a star network whose central device connected to one other star network and a bus network.

2.03 Cloud computing

Cloud computing is based on the principle of a central shared resource. A third party will provide the facility. The 'cloud' will provide for some form of service (usually paid-for), data storage and high-level 'services' that are made available to the user's computer and software.

Public and private clouds

A public cloud is openly available and likely to be free-of-charge. A private cloud is a paid-for resource.

Gmail is an example of a public cloud where all the responsibility for security and data storage is with Google. Apple Music is an example of (private) cloud computing. This is a subscription service. There is a large pool of data available (the music files), the service is provided by the third party (Apple) and the user will need software on their PC/tablet/smartphone to use the service.

Benefits and drawbacks of cloud computing

The benefits of cloud computing are:

- Cost effective: the user receives a developed, tried and tested facility at an affordable price
- Capital expenditure on both hardware and software can be avoided: capital expenditure is replaced by a lower level of operational costs
- Flexibility of access: users can access the facility on any device, using a web browser from anywhere
- Improved centralised **security of data**.

Drawbacks relate to ownership where a company might be nervous about handing over the responsibility for their data processing and storage to a third party, especially where there is sensitive data.

2.04 Wired and wireless networks

In wired networks, all of the devices are connected by cables. In the early days this was done using a

T-connector into the network interface card of the computer. Modern buildings are now wired with a cabling infrastructure and connections are made from each device into a patch panel/hub on the wall.

Wireless networks are networks without wires where the communication medium must be some form of communication using waves from the **electromagnetic spectrum**, for example, **radio waves**, **microwaves** or **infrared**.

The issues you have when choosing the medium are whether the waves penetrate through objects such as a thick wall of a building, whether there will be interference with the messages, the amount of bandwidth available, whether the signal can be accurately guided in a particular direction and whether **attenuation** takes place and the signal might weaken and then need some form of **repeater**.

Copper cable

Copper cabling comes in different forms, for example, twisted-pair, coaxial or fibre-optic.

Twisted-pair

A twisted-pair is a pair of copper cables, twisted together. It is designed to cancel out electromagnetic interference.

Twisted-pair is available in several specifications. The simplest is made up of two insulated copper wires surrounded by the external insulation. One of the Ethernet networking standards uses a cable with four twisted-pairs called Cat-5 which supports a maximum cable segment length of 100 metres.

All forms of copper wiring suffer from a loss of signal strength as the cables get longer. A shielding screen is used either as a return path for the signal or as a form of screening to eliminate various forms of electromagnetic interference.

Coaxial

Coaxial cable has a central single strand wire that is insulated from the outer multi-strand wire mesh braided around the central insulation.

Coaxial cable is also available in a number of specifications.

The most widely used bus networking standard for the physical layer (see the discussion of protocols that follows) is called Ethernet. This has developed standards based on the transmission speeds called 10BASE-T (transmits at 10Mb/sec), 100BASE-TX (100 Mb/sec) or 1000BASE-T (1000Mb/sec, i.e. 1 Gb/sec).

Uses of coaxial cable include the connection between a radio or television receiver/sender and the arial, computer network connections and cable television connections.

- An advantage of coaxial cable is that electromagnetic interference from other metal objects in close proximity is unlikely to affect the signals.
- A bus network uses either twisted pair or coaxial cabling.

Fibre-optic cable

Up to 24 glass strands are grouped into a single cable. A signal is transmitted along a single strand as a modulated light beam, using pulses of light. Because the medium for communication is light, rather than electrical signals, the data should be free of interference and also less susceptible to unauthorised access.

Fibre optic has many advantages over copper wire. In particular, the signals will be free from any interference, they will not suffer from a loss of strength (attenuation) and the cabling does not suffer from corrosion.

Typical applications include any form of long-distance communication including telephone communication, internet communications and networking.

Telecommunications and the Electromagnetic spectrum

All forms of telecommunications include some form of electromagnetic wave acting as the signal carrier. Then a form of modulation of the signal makes the carrier wave vary. Modulation makes the carrier wave change to represent different signals and hence different data.

If two humans communicate by talking, the carrier is a sound wave and the range of frequencies possible with a sound wave limits the possible signals. The same is true for electromagnetic communication. Each form will have a range of frequencies that are possible with corresponding benefits and drawbacks that make them suited to particular applications.

Radio waves

Radio waves have the largest range of wavelengths and include AM-radio (around 400 m), television (40 m) and FM-radio (around 4 m).

Radio waves are used for receiving television signals (sent from the TV broadcaster radio mast) via the domestic antennae and for sending/receiving of mobile phone communication.

Microwaves

Microwaves have wavelengths measured in centimetres.

Compared with infrared and visible light, microwaves have the benefits that microwave energy can penetrate haze, light rain and snow, clouds and smoke. For this reason, satellites that capture pictures of the Earth use microwave communication.

Satellite communication

Artificial satellites orbiting the Earth provide telecommunications between the satellite and receiving/sending stations.

Applications are numerous and varied, for example: satellite radio and television broadcasting, photography of the Earth (see earlier section on microwaves), satellite-based internet, satellite phones and military communications.

Wireless

Communication can use radio, microwave or infrared frequencies. The term 'wireless' has come to be used to describe any form of data communication that is 'without wires'.

WiFi is the term for the industry standard IEEE.802.11. WiFi hotspots are now popular, for example, as a way of attracting custom to a cafe.

The range of applications of wireless communication is now widespread and includes communication for a local area network and the use of smartphones and other portable devices.

2.05 Hardware to support a LAN

Switch – Switched Ethernet

With a switch, the full bandwidth is available to all communications between a sender node and receiver node. The switch must maintain an address table containing the MAC address for each device connected to it. The connection is a full-duplex one allowing the sending and receiving of data simultaneously.

Server

This was discussed earlier when describing a client-server model of operation.

Network Interface Card (NIC)

Each computer must be fitted with a Network Interface Card (NIC). This allows the computer to communicate with the network.

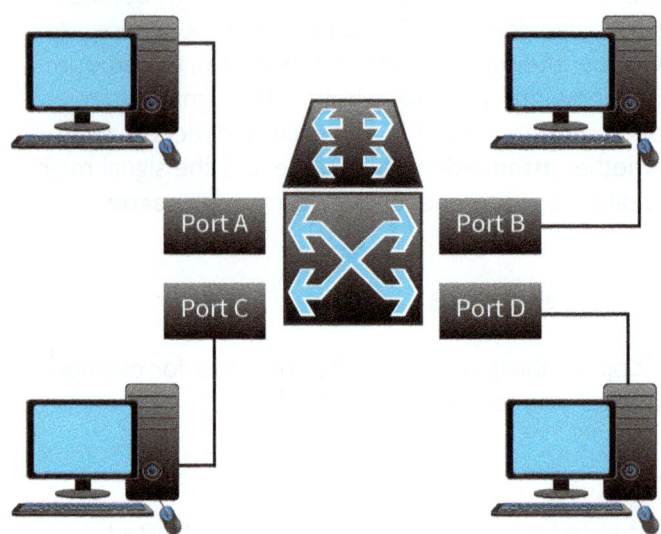

Figure 2.04 A 4-port Ethernet switch.

Wireless Network Interface Card (WNIC)

The WNIC is a hardware device that connects a device to a wireless network. On a PC, the device will either be a card inside the box or will be provided for with a USB stick. The PC uses a small antenna to make a radio wave communication.

Wireless Access Point (WAP)

Hardware which provides access to a particular wireless network. This may be used anywhere including the home, an office or public place all with the aim that users who have a wireless enabled device (PC, tablet or smartphone) can get access to the wifi network.

Cables

Cables are used for a wired network.

Bridge

A bus LAN can be made up from more than one 'cable segment'. You then need hardware to direct packets from a node on one segment to a destination node on a different segment. A hardware device to do this is called a **bridge**.

Repeater

Signals travelling a large distance might suffer from attenuation, i.e. loss of strength. The signal can be boosted at various points on the communication path. The hardware to do this is called a repeater.

The role of a router

The task of a hardware **router** a is to receive data packets from a sending device and then route each packet to its destination address. The router must maintain **routing tables** that show the best possible path for the data packet. The packet might need to be re-directed many times before it reaches its destination.

Routers are used to facilitate the communication of data packets between sub-nets of a LAN, to connect a **private network** to a public network such as the internet and for the Domain Name Service for the World Wide Web (Discussed later in section 2.08).

> ### Progress check B
> Your business currently uses two stand-alone PCs in the same room. List the minimum hardware needed to change to a bus network with internet access.

> ### Progress check C
> Describe what changes are needed if the computers are on the ground and second floor.

2.06 Ethernet

The most widely used bus networking standard is Ethernet. This has developed standards based on the transmission speeds called 10BASE-T (transmits at 10 Mb/sec), 100BASE-TX (100 Mb/sec) or 1000BASE-T (1000 Mb/sec i.e. 1 Gb/sec).

The electrical signal is broadcast along the cable and will be received by the destination device.

Each message is sent from one device as an Ethernet frame. Each Ethernet frame is made up of the **MAC address** of the source, destination MAC address and the 'payload' data. Frames can vary in size with up to 1500 bytes of data.

In the Bus topology section, we saw that collisions can occur.

Carrier Sense Multiple Access/ Collision detection (CSMA/CD)

CSMA/CD is the Ethernet's strategy to avoid collisions.

These are the stages in the process of attempting to send an Ethernet frame:

- The sending device will 'listen' to the communications line before attempting to transmit
- If the line is not in use, i.e. 'No carrier sensed', then the device will transmit immediately
- More packets are then transmitted with a short time delay between each transmission
- If the line is in use, i.e. 'Carrier sensed', then the device will wait until the line is later sensed as idle
- The device will listen on the line to check for no collision of the packet. If a collision is detected the device will:
  - stop sending
  - jam the line (to make other devices aware they are unable to use the line).

The letters describe the key points of the strategy: CS (Carrier sense) which is the strategy of attempting to send a data packet if the medium is idle, MA (Multiple access) which is the strategy needed when each node is competing for the communications line and CD (Collision Detection) which is the strategy of not attempting to send more packets if a collision is detected.

Collisions

Collisions are detected by a voltage change at a node.

When a collision is detected, the jamming signal will effectively notify all nodes of the collision and all nodes should delay before attempting a new transmission.

2.07 Bit streaming

The quality of the broadband connection will determine the speed at which data is transmitted. Speeds are given for an 'upload' transmission rate and a 'download' transmission rate.

A bit stream is a sequence of bits, representing a stream of data. The sequence of bits will be transmitted continuously over a single channel. The speed of transmission is the **bit rate**. The bits are transmitted serially, one after the other as a sequence of bytes. The bytes could be any form of digital data, for example, text characters, pixels from a picture, a video clip or a sound file.

Real-time bit streaming

Satellite channels in the UK now have the facility to allow a subscriber to watch live television on a device such as a personal computer, tablet or smartphone.

The device will need the appropriate software or app. The communication channel will be a wireless connection or a 3G/4G connection for a smartphone or tablet.

The BBC in the UK provides the same facility, called BBC iPlayer, for the viewing of (some) live television programmes, and a service for 'listening live' to its radio broadcasts.

Other examples of live streaming would include: a video call on a mobile device or the images from close-circuit TV cameras carrying out security surveillance on (perhaps) an airport.

On-demand bit streaming

Providers call this a 'catch up' service. Programmes/broadcasts that the user missed when it was originally broadcast are available to be viewed at a later date.

Providers such as the BBC/satellite TV providers and other content providers such as Netflix offer a large selection of films that can be provided 'on demand'.

Issues with bit streaming

The most common problems are about the connectivity of various devices, the software to provide the service and the quality of the service.

The delivery of the content to the user might be subject to a pause in the picture or sound before it then resumes. The reason for this is that the bitstream will be directed into a storage area on the device. This is called a buffer.

An issue with this is whether the communication channel can deliver the bit-stream at a sufficiently high rate. Broadband providers suggest this requires a download speed of 3 Mbps or higher.

A further issue is whether the software can process and display the content of the buffer at a high enough speed. The two key factors here will be the speed at which data is retrieved from, for example, the hard disk and the specification of the processor.

> ### Progress check D
>
> You have a subscription to a music streaming service and each day they offer you suggested new albums that are available.
>
> When you decide to play one of the albums, is this 'real-time' or 'on-demand' bit streaming?

2.08 The World Wide Web and internet

The internet

The internet is a global communication infrastructure that links together computers and networks.

It forms a collection of connected internets. All network traffic is made up of packets of data with a source address and destination address. There will be a large number of available paths for the transmission of any data packet.

The communication methods used are various, including wired, radio and satellite communications.

The internet is an open network. Access to it is provided by companies called Internet Service Providers (ISPs).

The internet allows anyone to access, retrieve, process and store all manner of information in a digital format including voice, video, documents and images.

The World Wide Web (WWW)

The WWW is made up of web pages, made available from web servers. The page content is viewed on a device with web browser software.

The WWW has changed the way we teach and learn, research information, buy and sell products and communicate globally with others.

Uniform Resource Locator (URL)

A 'resource' on the WWW could be a web page, an image, a video clip, sound file, a PDF document or many other types.

Each resource is identified (and therefore found by users) with its URL, for example:

http://www.e-Publishing.com/A_Level/Bin/Syllabus.pdf

The component parts of this URL indicate:

www – the resource is on the World Wide Web.

e-Publishing.com – the company is using this domain name.

A_Level/Bin – the resource is stored in the folder A_Level with sub-folder Bin.

Syllabus.pdf – the filename of the document.

Domain Name Service (DNS)

A web browser requests a resource using the URL. Somewhere on the internet, the IP address must be 'looked up' from the URL. This is the role of the Domain Name Service (DNS, also known as Domain Name System).

Once the IP address is known, it is the function of routers to route the data packets to the requesting device.

Because maintaining a central list of domain names and IP address mapping would be impractical, the lists of domain names and IP addresses are distributed throughout the internet in a hierarchy of authority. The DNS database resides on a hierarchy of special database servers.

At the top level of the hierarchy, root servers store a complete database of internet domain names and their corresponding IP addresses. The internet employs 13 root servers that have become somewhat famous for their special role. Maintained by various independent agencies, the servers are aptly named A, B, C and so on up to M.

Most lower level DNS servers are owned by businesses or Internet Service Providers (ISPs). For example, Google maintains various DNS servers around the world for the management of the google.com, google.co.uk and other domains. Your ISP also maintains DNS servers as part of your internet connection setup.

There is probably a DNS server within close geographic proximity to your access provider that maps the domain names in your internet requests or forwards them to other servers on the internet.

When a client web browser requests a resource with the URL, a piece of software called the DNS resolver (usually built into the network operating system) first contacts a DNS server to determine the resource's IP address. If the DNS server does not contain the mapping, it will forward the request to a different DNS server at the next higher level in the hierarchy. Further forwarding of the request might be needed before the URL is resolved.

2.09 Hardware to support the internet

The Public Switched Telephone Network (PSTN)

The Public Switched Telephone Network creates a dedicated line or circuit between two end-points. It was originally designed for two-way voice communication.

Each use of the network requires a 'call setup' in which a connection or circuit is established between the two end-points. The PSTN is an example of circuit switching.

Dedicated lines

A business might prefer to use a communication line that is dedicated for use by its computers only. This facility must be purchased from a telephone company.

A dedicated line has the advantages that it provides consistently high data transfer speeds for both upload and downloads, it provides high and consistent bandwidth and that bandwidth does not drop at peak times.

This enables a dedicated line to carry phone calls, allow lots of staff to connect simultaneously to their work computers from home and carry video transmission without buffering and signal degradation.

A modem

If data is sent over the PSTN there is a problem, as the computer uses digital data, but the PSTN uses analogue data.

A hardware device is therefore needed at either end of the communication line.

The PC must convert digital signals to analogue data to use the PSTN. At the receiving end, a second modem converts the analogue data to digital data. After this, a server might process the digital information.

A wireless network will also use modems. The wireless modem will convert between digital data and radio waves.

Cell phone networks

The land mass is divided into areas called cells, hence the term 'cell phone'. At least one transceiver or base station serves each cell. The cells are usually hexagonal in shape and the base station for each cell uses a different frequency range to that of any of its neighbouring cells.

The most common usage of a cell network is a mobile phone network. This provides for communication from a portable mobile phone to a base station with radio waves. Radio waves travel in straight lines. For this reason, a large land mass might need to be divided into smaller cells to avoid a 'line-of-sight' signal interruption.

Radio waves broadcast in all directions and are least affected by obstacles.

2.10 IP addresses and networks

IP address

'IP' stands for **internet protocol**.

Many local area networks use the TCP/IP protocol. This is discussed in Chapter 14.

On a network, each device has a unique IP address.

There are two different systems in use: IPv4 and IPv6 IP addressing.

Internet Protocol version 4 (IPv4)

All Version 4 IP addresses (ipV4) are 32 bits and so they are encoded as four bytes. An IPv4 address is written as four numbers written in 'dotted decimal notation' i.e. four decimal numbers, for example, 168.13.11.27

Progress check E

In theory, how many different IPv4 addresses are possible?

A typical network **topology** is shown in Figure **2.05**. The network has three segments that are connected using two routers. There is a third router that provides the connection to the internet.

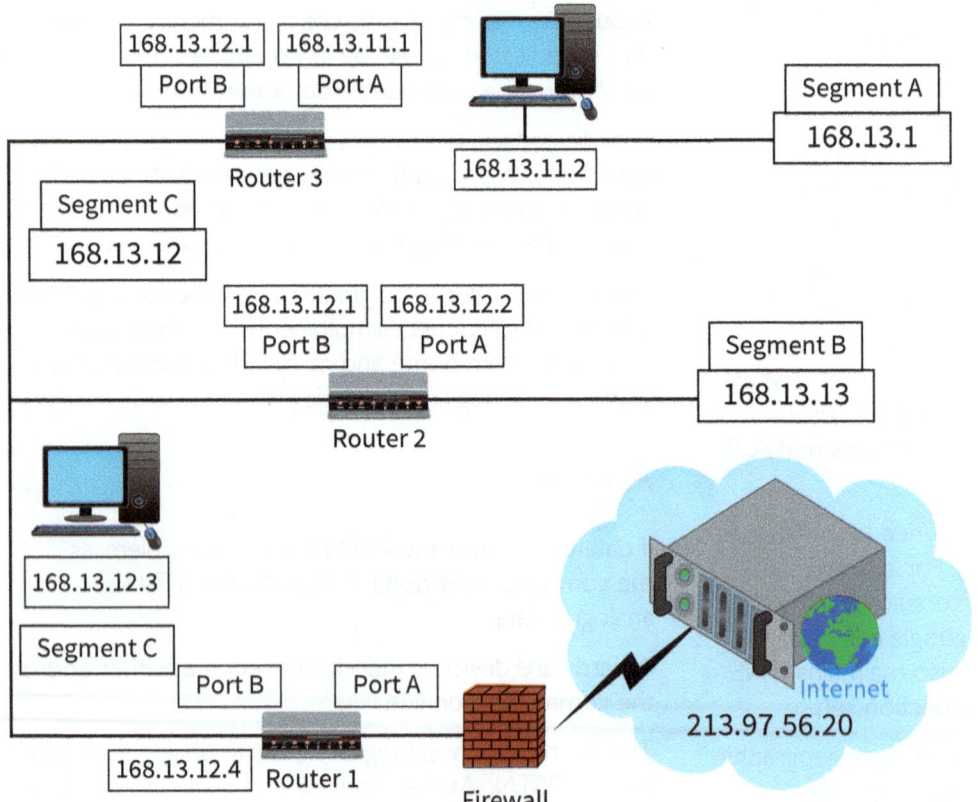

Figure 2.05 Three segment LAN using IP addressing.

This can be summarised as:

Segment	Devices	Network ID – Starts with …
A	Computer X	168.13.11
B	Computer Z	168.13.12
C	Intranet server and Computer Y	168.13.13

Table 2.01 LAN segments and IP addresses.

| Address type | IP v4 address | | | | | Description |
| | Network ID | | Host ID | | | |
	Bytes	Bits	Bytes	Bits		
Class A	Byte 1	8	Bytes 2, Byte 3, Byte 4	24		Starts with a 0 bit
Class B	Byte 1 and Byte 2	16	Byte 3 and Byte 4	16		Starts with bits 10
Class C	Byte 1, Byte 2 and Byte 3	24	Byte 4	8		Starts with bits 110

Table 2.02 IP address classes.

Each network class therefore has a different capacity to address networks and hosts.

This use of IP v4 addressing for a segmented network has the first two bytes to identify the network, the third byte to identify the segment and the fourth byte to identify the device.

There are three ranges of IP addresses - Class A, Class B or Class C - that have been reserved for use on private networks.

> **Progress check F**
>
> Another computer is to be added to segment C.
> Explain why the IP address 168.13.11.229 is unsuitable.

IPv6 addressing

The simple problem with IPv4 addresses is that as more and more networks use the internet, we will exhaust the different numbers that are possible using 32 bits. IPv6 is intended to eventually replace IPv4.

IPv6 uses eight groups, each with four hexadecimal digits. This is an IPv6 address: 2001:0db8:85a3:0000:0000:8a2e:0370:7334.

Note there are differences in the way the IP address is written. One difference is that IPv4 writes denary numbers, whereas Ipv6 uses hexadecimal. The other difference is that IPv4 separates the numbers with a full stop, whereas IPv6 uses a colon.

> **Progress check G**
>
> How many bits are used for an IPv6 address?

Good news! There are various ways in which the numbers of digits can be reduced and the IPv6 address still recognised. Here are some examples.

IPv6 address	Explanation
68E6:7C48:FFFE:FFFF:3D20:1180:695A:FF01	No simplification possible
72E6:::CFFE:3D20:1180:295A:FF01	:0000:0000: has been replaced by ::
72E6:0:0:CFFE:3D20:1180:295A:FF01	Each 0000 is replaced by a single zero digit
6C48:23:FE:FFFF:3D20:1180:95A:FF01	Leading zeros omitted from 00FF and 095A

Table 2.03 IPv6 address simplification.

> **Progress check H**
>
> Write this IPv6 address in a simplified form.
> 118A:77FF:000F:0000:342B:00DC:0000:11CC

TIP

The format of IPv6 addresses is complex and you do not need to know it for this course.

Private and public IP addresses

Blocks of IP addresses have been reserved for private network use. These are the groups with the first denary numbers 10 …, 172 …, and 192.68 … .

A public router would ignore any IP address from these ranges. Two branch offices that are to communicate must have the private IP address encapsulated within a packet that uses a public IP address recognised across the internet.

This means that several devices on a LAN that use different private IP addresses will communicate across the internet using a single public IP address. In Figure **2.05** the two computers each have a different private IP address but will communicate over the internet using the same public IP address.

This technique is called Network Address Translation (NAT).

> ## Progress check I
>
> What is the network identifier for the Figure **2.05** LAN?
>
> What is the identifier for the segment containing the intranet server?

Values 0 and 255 are not used for device numbering, so the implication is that a maximum of 254 devices can be connected to any segment of the LAN.

The security of private IP addresses will be the responsibility of the network management of the LAN. Outsiders accessing the LAN over the internet will have no knowledge of particular private IP addresses for a recipient device – only the public IP address of the router for this LAN.

The allocation and security of public IP addresses will be managed by the ISP. If a user does not want a recipient to know their public IP address then the user can install Virtual Private Network (VPN) software. This effectively hides the IP address from the provider of a resource. This can be used for illegal access to a resource. A user living in another country (country X) may not be allowed legally access media content from (say) the UK. If the user attempts to access the media server using their normal IP address the recipient can recognise that this IP address belongs to country X. Running VPN software which makes first a connection to a UK-based server will disguise the true location of the user.

Subnetting

When a device sends a data packet, a router receives it. If the packet is for a destination device on the same segment, for example Computer Y sending data to the intranet server, then the router will work out that this IP address is on the same segment.

This is done using a subnet mask, that uses an AND bitwise operator. Bit operators are discussed in Chapter 4 under the heading 'Bit manipulation'. The 'mask' is used to blank out various parts of the 32 bits. Depending on the mask used, either the network ID or the Host ID part of the IP address can then be found.

Here is an example of the use of IP addressing:

A user, at Computer Z on a LAN sited in London, is loading data to a web server situated in the United States. The web server has, for example, a known IP address 213.86.69.07

These are the stages when data is routed from Computer Z to the WWW web server:

1. Use a mask to find the segment. This establishes that the destination address is not on this segment.
2. A data packet is sent to Router 1 and Router 2.
3. Router 1 will identify, using a mask, that the IP address is outside of this LAN so it forwards the packet to the gateway.
4. The gateway will calculate the network ID of the packet. From this it will decide to which router it should be directed. The router will be one of a hierarchy of routing paths.

    At each 'hop' the router will decrement the 'time to live' value of the packet.
5. The packet will be directed to several routers using the routing tables stored at each router.

Static IP address and dynamic IP address

A static IP address is one that is never changed.

Any connection is made to the internet by the company or individual's Internet Service Provider (ISP). They will have millions of clients and so it is impractical to allocate every client their own static IP address.

When the user requests access to the internet, the ISP will allocate a dynamic IP address – that is, the ISP allocates an address only when it is needed.

Past paper questions

1. a Telephone calls can be made by using:

   - conventional telephones (using the Public Service Telephone Network (PSTN) system) over a wired network
   - a computer, equipped with speakers and microphone, connected to the internet

   Put a tick (√) in the correct column to match each description to the appropriate communication method.

Description	Conventional telephone using PSTN	Internet based system
Connection only in use whilst sound is being transmitted		
Dedicated channel used between two points for the duration of the call		
Connection maintained throughout the telephone call		
Encoding schemes and compression technology used		
Lines remain active even during a power outage		

   [5]

   b Distinguish between the internet and the World Wide Web (WWW). [3]

   c Name the hardware device that is being described:

   i   A device that transfers data from one network to another in an intelligent way. It has the task of forwarding data packets to their destination by the most efficient route. [1]

   ii A device used between two dissimilar LANs. The device is required to convert data packets from one protocol to another. [1]

   iii A device or software that provides a specific function for computers using a network. The most common examples handle printing, file storage and the delivery of web pages. [1]

Cambridge International AS & A level Computer Science 9608 paper 11 Q5 June 2015

2. a The table shows four statements about IP addresses.

   Tick (√) to show which of the statements are true.

Statement	True (√)
The IP address consists of any number of digits separated by single dots (.)	
Each number in an IP4 address can range from 0 to 255	
IP addresses are used to ensure that messages and data reach their correct destinations	
Public IP addresses are considered to be more secure than private IP addresses	

   b Consider the URL:

   http://cie.org.uk/computerscience.html [2]

   i   Give the meaning of the following parts of the URL. [3]

   http:

   cie.org.uk:

   http:

ii Sometimes the URL contains the characters %20 and ?.

Describe the function of these characters.

%20:

?: [2]

Cambridge International AS & A level Computer Science 9608 paper 11 Q3 November 2015

3 A company operates a chemical plant, which has a number of processes. Local computers monitor these processes and collect data.

The computers transfer these data to a central computer 50 km away. A telecommunications company (telco) provides cables.

Engineers at the telco had to decide which type of cable to use. They considered the use of either copper cable or fibre-optic cable.

State two benefits of each type of cable. Each benefit must be clearly different. [4]

Cambridge International AS & A level Computer Science 9608 paper 11 Q6 November 2015

4 Access to World Wide Web content uses IP addressing.

a State what IP stands for. [1]

b The following table shows four possible IP addresses.

Indicate for each IP address whether it is valid or invalid and give a reason.

Address	Denary/Hexadecimal	Valid or invalid	Reason
3.2A.6AA.BBBB	Hexadecimal		
2.0.255.1	Denary		
6.0.257.6	Denary		
A.78.F4.J8	Hexadecimal		

[4]

c Describe two differences between public and private IP addresses. [2]

Cambridge International AS & A level Computer Science 9608 paper 11 Q7 June 2016

Hardware

Chapter 3

Learning Objectives:

Computers and their components:

- Understand the basic hardware components of any computer system
- Describe the operation of hardware devices:
  - Input: Microphone
  - Input/output: Touchscreen (Resistive and Capacitive technology, virtual headset)
  - Output: Speakers, laser printer, 3D-printer
  - Storage: Magnetic hard disk, solid state memory, optical disc
- Understand the differences between the various types of memory used as ROM and RAM
- Understand monitoring and control systems and their differences
- Understand the role of sensors and actuators in their operation.

Logic gates and logic circuits:

- Draw and use the truth table for the logic gates: NOT, AND, OR, NAND, NOR, XOR
- Construct a truth table from:
  - A problem statement
  - A logic circuit or expression
- Construct a logic expression from:
  - a problem statement
  - a logic circuit
  - a truth table.

3.01 Computers and their components

Figure 3.01 summarises the components of a computer system.

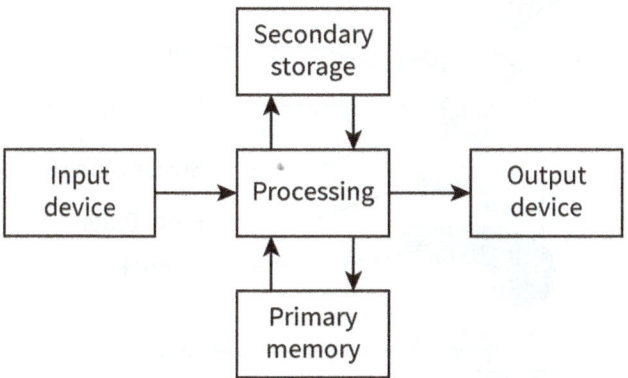

Figure 3.01 Typical computer system.

On a typical PC computer, the system would consist of input (keyboard and mouse/trackpad), output (monitor), secondary storage (the hard disk or solid state memory), primary memory (memory chips on the motherboard) and processor (the microprocessor on the motherboard).

The secondary storage may be made up of more than one device. A second or third device could be removable, such as a pen drive or second hard disk.

Embedded systems

As its name suggests, an embedded system is a computer system that is 'embedded' inside some appliance like a washing machine. Any embedded system has three components:

- Hardware: circuits on a motherboard (processor and memory chips) with a simple interface to allow the user to communicate
- Application software
- Real Time Operating system (RTOS): that supervises the application software and any user input.

The major advantage of an embedded system is its simplicity – it has been specifically designed to perform a specific function.

They are contained on a single chip called a microcontroller and so can be very cost effectively mass produced.

A potential drawback is that recent systems could provide a security risk. Embedded systems in household devices can now communicate data using a wifi connection over the internet. A recent application has been a device sited near the front door of a house which can communicate data when an attempted delivery is made to the house.

3.02 Operation of hardware devices

Laser printer

The laser printer uses a laser beam and a rotating mirror to draw an image of the page on a photosensitive drum. It converts the image on the drum into an electrostatic charge that attracts and holds toner. It rolls electrostatically charged paper against the drum. The charge pulls the toner away from the drum and onto the paper. Heat is then applied to fuse the toner to the paper. Finally, the electrical charge is removed from the drum, and the excess toner is collected.

By omitting this final step and repeating only the toner-application and paper-handling steps, the printer can make multiple copies.

3D printer

Forget printers and paper! A 3D printer builds an object from polymer resin.

The computer must have a (digital) 'blueprint' of the object that it will copy.

The blueprint is produced either with a 3D-scan of the existing object, or using 3D-modelling software to produce a new design/blueprint.

A 3D printer builds up a 3D model one layer at a time, from the bottom upward, by repeatedly printing over the same horizontal plain. The method is called **fused depositional modelling (FDM)**.

The printer calculates – from the stored 3D CAD drawing – the sequence of two-dimensional, cross-sectional layers. Each layer is then printed in sequence. Molten plastic is ejected from a fine nozzle which moves precisely under computer software control.

The printer deposits a layer of molten plastic or powder and fuses them together and to the existing structure with adhesive or ultraviolet light.

The type of plastic used (called **thermoplastics**) must be such that it melts when heat is applied and solidifies when it cools down. The process will add more and more layers of the resin until complete. When the final layer is added, the resin is hardened using adhesive or ultraviolet light.

Microphone

A microphone is an input device. Sound is a wave in a medium such as air. We hear different sounds due to the changes in the frequency and amplitude of these waves.

A microphone responds to the varying pressure of the sound wave and outputs an electrical signal that is normally analogue. There are several different technologies used to achieve this. One of these is called a dynamic microphone and works as follows. The sound wave hits a diaphragm. The diaphragm moves and this causes a magnetic coil to move. The movement of the coil creates an electric current.

Speakers

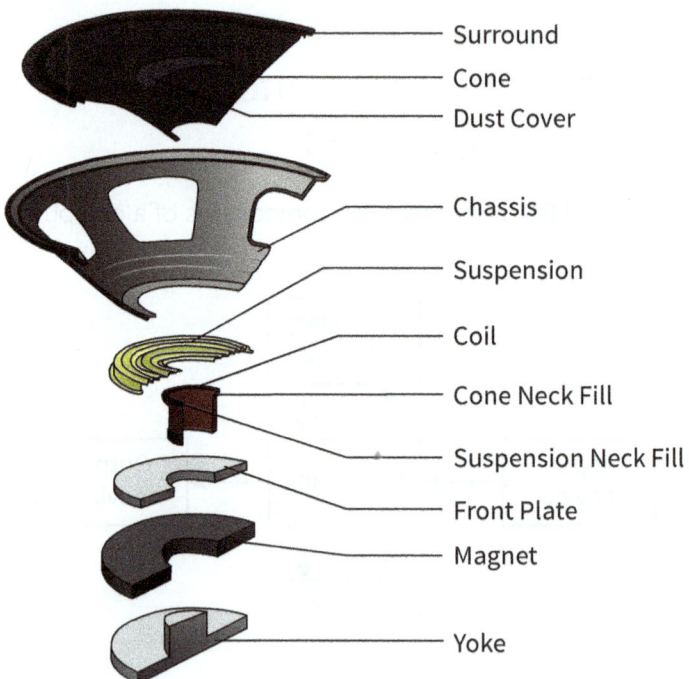

Figure 3.02 Loudspeaker construction.

A speaker is an output device.

It takes an electrical signal and translates it into physical vibrations to create sound waves. The key components of a loudspeaker are a diaphragm, a voice coil and a permanent magnet. The diaphragm or cone at the wide end is connected to a circular suspension and at the narrow end to the voice coil.

A magnet on the end of the voice coil interacts with an electromagnet. Changing the polarity of the current sent to the electromagnet will cause the magnet on the coil to move. It is these very fast changes in the movement of the diaphragm or coil that produce sounds. The movement of the coil causes the air in front of the cone to vibrate. The movement determines the frequency and amplitude of the sound wave produced.

> **TIP**
>
> A speaker does the exact reverse of what is done by a microphone.

Magnetic hard-disk

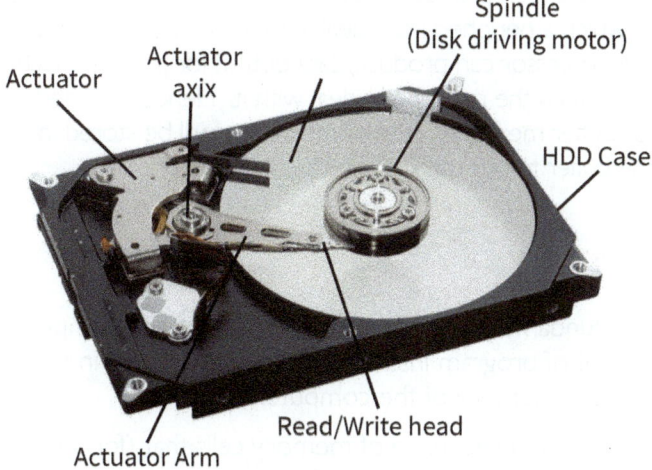

Figure 3.03 Hard disk platters.

Hard disks are used for **secondary storage**/memory.

> **TIP**
>
> Hard disks are spelt with a K in the USA and with a C or a K elsewhere. All forms of optical discs are spelt with a C.

A hard disk has one or more platters made of aluminium or glass. The surface of a platter is ferrous oxide, which can be magnetised. The platters are mounted on a central spindle and the entire mechanism contained inside a sealed aluminium box.

The disk is rotated at high-speed. Each platter of the disk has a read/write head mounted on an arm positioned just above the surface. The arm moves between the outer and inner tracks of each platter at very high speed. Electronic circuits control the movement of the arm (and hence the heads).

The surface of each platter is divided into concentric tracks and each track will be divided into a basic unit of storage called a block. The data contained in a block, typically 512 bytes, is the basic unit of storage that can be read/written with a single read/write. Data is encoded as a magnetic pattern for each block.

Three factors determine the performance of a hard disk, the data transfer rate, the seek time and the capacity of the disk. The data transfer rate is the number of bytes per second that can be read from the disk and transferred to the processor. The seek time is the time that the disk will take to position the head assembly onto the required track and rotate until the required block is under the head. This is called the latency time. The capacity of the disk is a key factor when purchasing a computer. A capacity measured in terabytes is now common for a PC.

Solid state (flash) memory

Solid state (flash) memory has many advantages over magnetic disk storage. In particular, it has no moving (mechanical) components, it is typically more resistant to physical shock, it makes no noise and it has lower access times and latency. See the section which follows on Electronically Erasable Programmable Read Only Memory (EEPROM).

Optical disk reader/writer

This is a **secondary memory** device. This is the general term given to all formats of CD and DVD storage. The basic disc is made from plastic. The plastic is coated with a layer of aluminium. The disc has a surface arranged in a long spiral. The spiral is a sequence of bumps and pits (lands) that encode the digital data.

The reading of the bumps and pits is done with a laser beam. The laser beam passes through the CD's polycarbonate layer. The laser light is reflected from the aluminium layer. The light is received by an opto-electronic device. The electronics in the player/recorder device interprets the changes in light patterns as data bits.

Touchscreen

A touchscreen acts as both an input and output device and is widely used for tablets and smartphones. Some touchscreens make use of resistive technology and others make use of capacitive technology.

Resistive technology

The hardware consists of a normal glass panel, covered with a conductive and a resistive metallic layer. The two layers are separated by spacers. An electric current runs through the two layers while the touchscreen is switched on. When a user touches the screen, the two layers make contact in that exact spot. The user presses on the screen. The screen bends so that two conductive layers touch at a precise spot. Software calculates the exact point of contact from the change in the electrical field. The co-ordinate data is then understood and actioned by the OS.

Capacitive technology

The glass panel has a layer over it that can store an electric charge. Changes in electric charge are measured by circuits located at each corner of the glass panel. When the user touches this layer, charge is transferred to the user so the charge on the capacitive layer decreases. The processor inside the device calculates, from the relative differences in charge at each corner, exactly where the touch event took place. The processor relays that information to the touchscreen driver software. From the calculated coordinates, the OS will take appropriate action.

Virtual headset

This is an output device worn on the head that gives the user a 'virtual reality experience'. It is used by gaming applications and for a simulation of some real-world experiences.

Figure 3.04 Virtual headset.

The headset will have stereo sound, embedded head movement sensors and separate image projection received by each eye. A VR headset must be able to respond very fast with a rendered display in response to changes to various inputs. The Graphics Processing Unit (GPU) is responsible for this.

Rendering issues are reduced if the headset is fitted with eye-tracking hardware and software.

The virtual reality screen has to stretch a single display across a wide field of view (for the typical user this is 110 degrees). The quality of the lenses in the headset will determine this. Fresnel lenses are commonly used in virtual reality headsets as they are light and compact.

3.03 Data storage and memory

Buffers

A **buffer** is a temporary storage area. The type of memory will be some form of **RAM** memory (see below). A buffer is needed when the speed at which the processor can produce data is much faster than the speed at which a peripheral can deal with the data. For example, the processor can produce data output for printing much faster than the printer can deal with it. Hence the need for buffer memory in the printer. Data will be stored in the buffer temporarily, immediately before printing.

Memory

The fundamental model of the Von Neumann computer is a set of program instructions and data stored in the primary memory of the computer.

Memory is a sequence of memory cells that (for a PC) each contain a byte (8 bits). Each memory cell has a unique memory address.

Random access memory (RAM)

The processor will directly access any memory location if it knows its address.

Memory will be formed from either SRAM or DRAM memory chips (see later). The contents of RAM memory are retained as long as the power supply to the computer remains. The contents are lost when the computer is powered off.

Read Only Memory (ROM)

'Read only' implies the memory is written to once and its contents are permanently retained. The stored data can then be read many times. **ROM** is typically used on a PC to store the **boot program code** and in an embedded system, to store the program code for the machine's various washing programmes.

Static RAM (SRAM)

SRAM is one form of RAM. Each bit of data is stored using the state of a six transistor memory cell. SRAM is more expensive to produce (than DRAM) but it provides faster access (than DRAM) and requires less power (than DRAM).

An application of SRAM is for **cache memory** for the CPU.

Dynamic RAM (DRAM)

DRAM stores each bit of data using a single transistor and a capacitor. This hardware comprises a DRAM memory cell. The capacitor holds a high or low charge (to represent 1 or 0). The transistor acts as a switch that lets the control circuitry on the chip read the capacitor's state of charge or change it. DRAM is less expensive to produce (than SRAM). See the other comparison points shown above for SRAM.

DRAM is the predominant form of main memory used in modern computers.

Programmable ROM (PROM)

This is memory that can be written to once only, using a device called a 'programmer'. This process is sometimes called 'burning' the memory chip. The term comes from the process where individual fuses on the chip are blown out or burnt.

Electronically Erasable Programmable ROM (EEPROM)

Before EEPROM, there were EPROMS where the code on the chip could be changed many times. This effectively makes the chips 'reuseable'. This required that the contents were first deleted using ultraviolet light.

The contents of an EEPROM can also be changed many times. The existing contents still have to be deleted first but this is done with an electric current. The change to the contents can be done with the memory chip in situ. EEPROMs store small amounts of data but allow the data to be easily changed.

Applications include their use in microcontrollers and for remote keyless security systems. Flash memory is constructed as an EEPROM chip. It has a grid of columns and rows. There is a cell made up of two transistors at each intersection.

A thin oxide layer separates the two transistors. One of the transistors is known as a floating gate, and the other one is the control gate. The floating gate's only link to the row, or **wordline**, is through the control gate. As long as this link is in place, the cell has a value of 1. To change the value to a 0 requires an electronics process called process called Fowler-Nordheim tunnelling, the details of which are not required for the syllabus.

3.04 Monitoring and control systems

A **monitoring system** that is carried out by a computer system is what it says, a system designed to 'watch' or monitor some state external to the computer system. A house fitted with a burglar alarm system is a monitoring system. The input(s) to the computer system would be data from sensors to detect the presence of an intruder. Movement will be detected by the **sensor** which will send a signal to the computer system. This signal would be interpreted by software and could trigger the sounding of an alarm, or display on-screen some warning message.

In this and other examples, the process is 'automatic monitoring', meaning there is no human interaction in the monitoring process.

Other examples of monitoring systems are pollution or weather monitoring systems where data readings from the sensors are fed back to the computer system remotely and then processed by software to produce (say) temperature/wind speed graphs or a car dashboard display showing the temperature outside the car.

Control system

Control systems are either 'event-driven' or 'time-driven'.

In an event-driven system, the controller, in response to some event, will alter the state of the system.

Examples of this include (1) when a robot loads a part into a work area and the part is sensed as present, (2) when the level of liquid plastic in the hopper of an injection moulding machine is monitored for replenishment by a sensor, and (3) when parts moved along a conveyor are counted via an optical sensor.

Some control systems are 'time-driven'. The controller will take action either at a specific point in time or after a certain time has lapsed.

Examples of this include (1) when a factory buzzer sounds a bell at specific times of the day to indicate the start of shift, start and end of the break period and end of the shift, (2) when a paint spraying operation is carried out for a certain length of time and (3) when the agitation cycle in a washing machine is set to operate for a certain length of time before the controller stops this phase of the wash cycle.

All process control systems have the following in common:

- The process involves the continual measurement of data from sensors – **input variables** such as temperature, pressure and flow rate
- The processing of the data by software takes place, followed by a decision to take action when some critical condition is reached
- The actuation of devices such as a values, switches or an output warning light takes place.

Sensors

A sensor is a transducer whose purpose is to sense (that is, to 'detect') some physical property of its environment. Sensors are used, for example, for the detection of: temperature, pressure, an infra-red beam or sound.

For example, a temperature sensor could be a thermocouple. This sends an electrical signal through an **analogue-to-digital converter**, which produces a digital value that is processed by computer software.

> **TIP**
>
> A sensor never does any processing.

> **Progress check A**
>
> Name an application for each of the following sensor types:
>
> a   Pressure
> b   Temperature
> c   Wind speed/flow
> d   Light intensity

Actuators

An **actuator** is a motor that controls a piece of mechanical equipment. It is operated by a source of energy, typically an electric current, hydraulic (fluid) pressure or pneumatic (air) pressure.

The energy that drives the actuator originates as the output from computer software, which is receiving data from sensors.

> **Progress check B**
>
> Name an application for each of the three types of actuator.

Feedback

A **control system** uses feedback. The way in which this takes place is that input is received from sensor(s), the input data is processed by software, output(s) from the system are produced and new data is collected from the input sensors.

The whole process forms a continuous feedback loop.

3.05 Logic gates and logic circuits

Logic circuits are constructed from logic gates.

AND gate

An AND gate has two or more inputs and a single output. The table shows the four possible combinations of input with the output each produces. This is called a truth table.

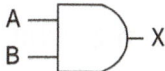

Figure 3.05 AND gate.

Input		Output
A	B	X
0	0	0
0	1	0
1	0	0
1	1	1

Table 3.01 AND gate truth table.

The AND gate produces a 1 output only when both inputs are 1.

OR gate

An OR gate has two or more inputs and a single output.

Figure 3.06 OR gate.

Input		Output
A	B	X
0	0	0
0	1	1
1	0	1
1	1	1

Table 3.02 OR gate truth table.

> **TIP**
>
> An AND and OR gate can have several inputs but you only need to focus on those with two at this level.

NOT gate

Sometimes called an inverter, a NOT gate has a single input and single output.

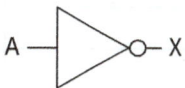

Figure 3.07 NOT gate.

Input	Output
A	X
0	1
1	0

Table 3.03 NOT gate truth table.

XOR (EOR) gate

An exclusive OR gate has two inputs and a single output.

Figure 3.08 XOR gate.

Input		Output
A	B	X
0	0	0
0	1	1
1	0	1
1	1	0

Table 3.04 XOR gate truth table.

NAND gate

A NAND gate follows the same logic as an AND gate followed by a NOT gate.

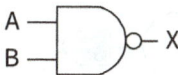

Figure 3.09 NAND gate.

Table 3.05 NAND gate truth table.

Input		Output
A	B	X
0	0	1
0	1	1
1	0	1
1	1	0

NOR gate

A NOR gate follows the same logic as an OR gate followed by a NOT gate.

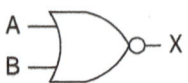

Figure 3.10 NOR gate.

Input		Output
A	B	X
0	0	1
0	1	0
1	0	0
1	1	0

Table 3.06 NOR gate truth table.

Construct a logic circuit

The starting point for constructing a circuit could be either a logic expression (expressed in words)

X = 1 when (A OR B) = 0 AND (B OR C) = 1

or a simplified logic expression

X = NOT (A OR B) AND (B OR C)

The equivalent circuit is as follows:

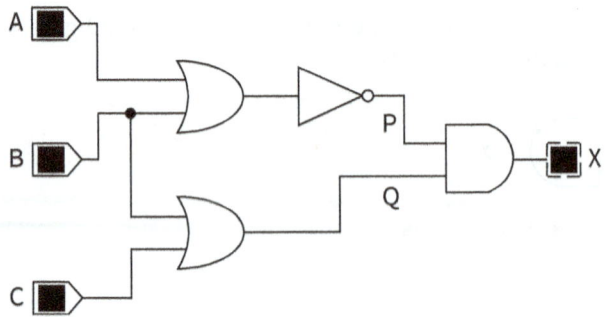

Figure 3.11 Constructing a circuit.

Progress check C

Draw the logic circuit for the logic expression:

X = (A AND B) AND NOT(A OR B)

Constructing a truth table from a circuit

The maths says that an expression with three inputs will need eight rows for the truth table. The truth table **Table** 3.07 shows all possible combinations of input and the output each produces.

TIP

A good idea is to label some intermediate points in the logic circuit (in Table 3.07 we have used P and Q) and calculate the bit value at these intermediate points.

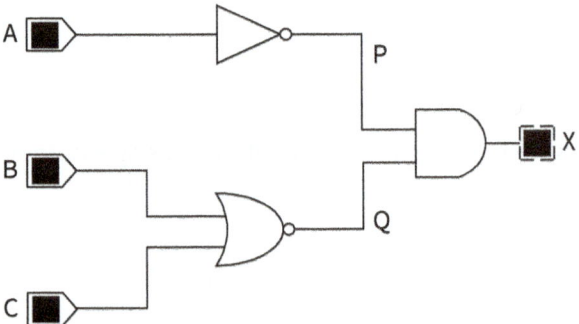

Figure 3.12 Circuit.

Before starting we have added two intermediate points: P and Q. Tracing each row carefully gives the information in the following table:

Inputs			Intermediate		Output
A	B	C	P	Q	X
0	0	0	1	1	0
0	0	1	1	1	1
0	1	0	1	1	1
0	1	1	1	1	1
1	0	0	0	0	0
1	0	1	0	1	0
1	1	0	0	1	0
1	1	1	0	1	0

Table 3.07 Corresponding truth table.

Progress check D

Draw the truth table for the circuit shown.

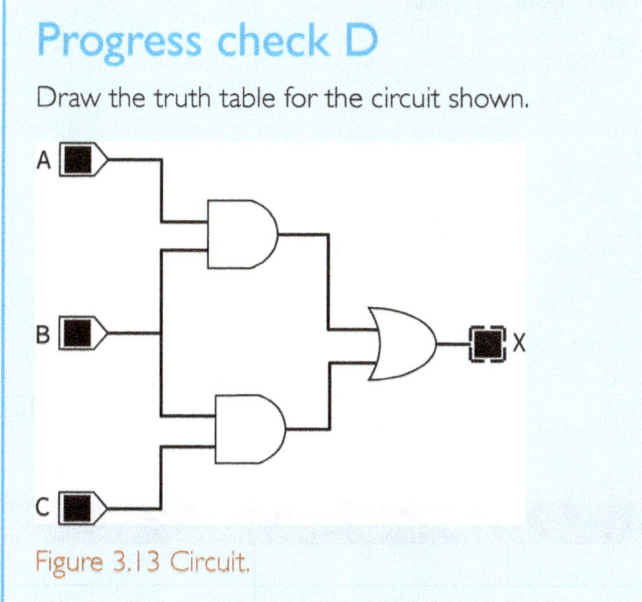

Figure 3.13 Circuit.

Progress check E

Write the logic expression for the same circuit.

TIP

We will study logic expressions and circuits again in the A Level content. It will use Boolean Algebra to simplify expressions. This is not needed for AS Level.

Constructing the logic expression from a given truth table

Study the truth table for a circuit with two inputs (A and B) and output X.

Inputs		Output
A	B	X
0	0	1
0	1	0
1	0	0
1	1	1

Table 3.08 Given truth table.

This is expressed as: X=1 when (A=0 AND B=0) OR (A=1 AND B=1)

X= (NOT A AND NOT B) OR (A AND B)

Progress check F

Draw the circuit for this expression.

Past paper questions

1. A system is monitored using sensors. The sensors output binary values corresponding to physical conditions as shown in the table.

Parameter	Description of parameter	Binary value	Description of condition
P	Oil pressure	1	Pressure >= 3 bar
		0	Pressure < 3 bar
T	Temperature	1	Temperature >= 200 °C
		0	Temperature < 200 °C
R	Rotation	1	Rotation <= 1000 revs per minute (rpm)
		0	Rotation > 1000 revs per minute (rpm)

The outputs of the sensors form 1 the input to a logic circuit.

The output from the circuit, X, is 1 if any of the following three conditions occur:

either   oil pressure >= 3 bar and temperature >= 200 °C

or   oil pressure < 3 bar and rotation > 1000 rpm

or   temperature >= 200 ° and rotation > 1000 rpm

a   Draw a logic circuit to represent the above system.

[5]

b   Complete the truth table for this system.

P	T	R	Workspace	X
0	0	0		
0	0	1		
0	1	0		
0	1	1		
1	0	0		
1	0	1		
1	1	0		
1	1	1		

[4]

Cambridge International AS & A level Computer Science 9608 paper 11 Q7 June 2015

2   A motor is controlled by a logic circuit. The circuit has inputs (0 and 1) from three sensors R, T and W. The motor is switched off when the output from the logic circuit is 1.

The following table shows the three sensors and the conditions being monitored.

Sensor	Description	Binary value	Condition
R	Rotation	0	Rotation < 4000 rpm
		1	Rotation >= 4000 rpm
T	Temperature	0	Temperature >= 90 °C
		1	Temperature < 90 °C
W	Water flow rate	0	Water flow rate >= 50 litre/min
		1	Water flow rate < 50 litre/min

The output, X, is 1 if:

Temperature >= 90°C and rotation >= 4000 rpm

Or

Temperature < 90°C and water flow rate >= 50 litre/min

a Draw a corresponding logic circuit.

[5]

b Give a logic statement corresponding to the logic circuit in part (a). [2]

c Complete the truth table for this system.

| INPUT | | | Workspace | OUTPUT X |
R	T	W		
0	0	0		
0	0	1		
0	1	0		
0	1	1		
1	0	0		
1	0	1		
1	1	0		
1	1	1		

[4]

Cambridge International AS & A level Computer Science 9608 paper 11 Q5 November 2016

3 A Personal Computer (PC) has a number of input and output devices.

   a i Name three components of a speaker. [3]

      ii Explain the basic internal operation of a speaker. [4]

   b i The user is considering the purchase of a removable device for secondary storage.

        Name one suitable device. [4]

      ii Describe two possible uses for this device on a home Personal Computer (PC). [2]

Cambridge International AS & A level Computer Science 9608 paper 11 Q5 November 2017

Chapter 4

Processor fundamentals

Learning Objectives:

CPU architecture:

- Name and describe the role of the special purpose registers in the CPU
- Name and describe the role of the data bus, address bus and control bus
- Describe CPU design factors that influence the performance of the computer
- Name and describe typical ports and peripherals connected to a PC
- Understand the relationship between machine code and assembly language
- Understand the role of the Special Purpose registers in the Fetch-Execute cycle.

Assembly Language:

- Understand the syllabus instruction set
- Describe the F-E cycle with 'register transfer' notation

- Understand the different modes of addressing
- Understand that various instructions available are organised into groups
- Write a simple assembly language program using the syllabus instruction set
- Understand and use symbolic addressing
- Understand how the Boolean operators are used for 'bit-wise' operations
- Use program instructions
- Understand how to test for a particular bit position
- Carry out shift operations
- Understand the use of bit manipulation for the monitoring/control of a device.

4.01 Central Processing Unit (CPU) Architecture

Figure **3.01** at the beginning of the previous chapter showed the CPU at the centre of any computer system. The Central Processing Unit (CPU) on the microprocessor chip does the 'processing' execution of any program code it is given.

General purpose registers

A **register** stores data after a calculation or a datum has been retrieved from primary memory. The data value may represent an address.

We will shortly learn that the assembly language programmer can put data values in the accumulator register. We shall soon learn that for our practical work we shall consider a computer system with one general purpose register called the Accumulator (ACC).

Note that the syllabus document has the Accumulator under the heading 'Special Purpose Registers'. The reason for this that we only have one such register. It is strictly a general purpose register.

Special purpose registers

As the name suggests, these are registers that carry out a 'special job'. Some registers are accessible to assembly language program instructions but other registers are not accessible and you should think of them as 'buried inside' the microprocessor circuits. The role of each special purpose register is described here.

> **TIP**
>
> In practice, a processor will have several general purpose registers. The syllabus specifies only one called the **accumulator (ACC)**.
>
> Assume also that each memory location stores a byte.
>
> We will describe program instructions/data being 'fetched' from the primary memory and then '**executed**'.

Program counter

The processor must know the address of the first instruction of the program. The program counter (sometimes abbreviated to PC) register stores the memory address of the next instruction to be 'fetched' (from memory). After each current instruction is processed, the PC contents must be incremented. See Figure **4.01** that follows.

Memory Data Register

When a data value or a program instruction is fetched from memory, its value is temporarily stored in the Memory Data Register (MDR). See Figure **4.01**.

Memory Address Register

Whenever a memory cell is to be accessed, its address must be known. The address about to be used is held in the Memory Address Register (MAR). See Figure **4.01**.

Index Register (IX)

The IX stores an integer number that will be used to change an address value.

Current Instruction Register

When a program instruction is fetched, it is stored in the Current Instruction Register (CIR). It is the task of the processor to make sense of it and execute it. See Figure **4.01**.

Status Register (Also called the Flag Register)

All of these special purpose registers deal with an entire byte.

The Status Register is different. Each of the eight bits indicates (or 'flags') whether something happened when the last instruction was executed.

Individual bits could be named and used to indicate:

- Carry: following an arithmetic shift operation, this is set to 1 if a carry occurred
- Zero: following a 'compare' instruction, this is set to 1 if True, 0 if False
- Negative: following an arithmetic operation, this is set to 1 if a negative result
- Overflow: following an arithmetic operation on a two's complement number, this is set to 1 if the result was out of range

Each bit position will be set to 0 if the event did not occur and to 1 if the event did occur.

What does a program look like?

A computer program is a sequence of program instructions that you will load into the primary memory when the program is to be executed. The processor will process these instructions in sequence. It will also store data that is needed by the program, in the primary memory.

Every memory location will have an address.

Different components working together

Inside the processor, an Arithmetic Logic Unit (ALU) performs calculations on the data, a control unit fetches, processes and then executes each instruction held in primary memory. The computer system has input and output devices connected. Buses connect components together.

The Immediate Access Store (IAS)

This describes the role played by the internal (or main) memory of the computer system. In the execution of most programs data will be read from here and other values stored and retained here.

Buses

A bus is a communications channel made up of several lines.
Figure **4.02** shows the buses that connect components and how input/output devices are connected to the computer system.

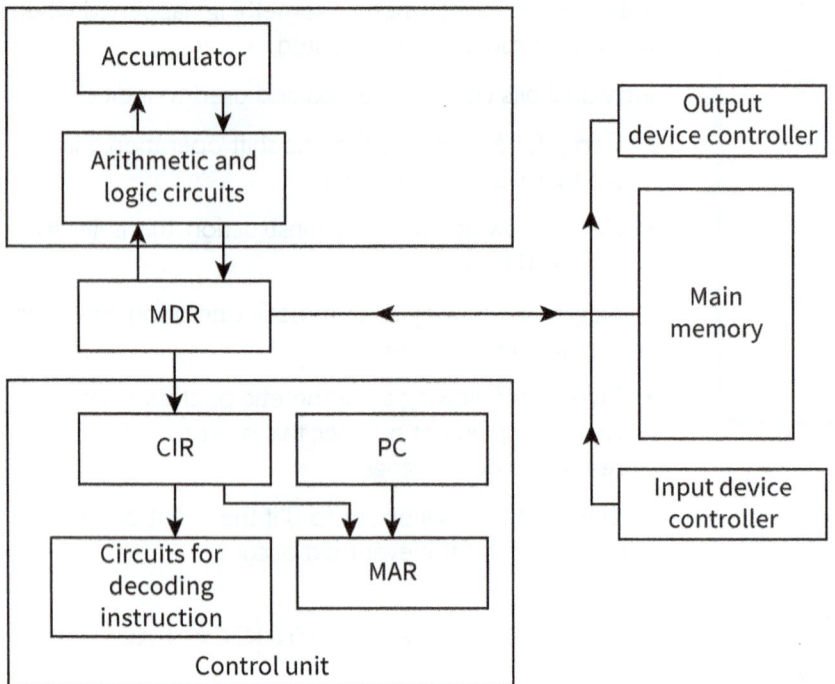

Figure 4.01 Inside the processor.

Address bus

Consider a program instruction to 'read' a value from a memory location. Before the program reads from memory, it first loads the address bus with the address value. The address bus only carries address values. The address bus is unidirectional – values are only ever loaded onto this bus.

Data bus

When the read operation takes place, the data bus transports the value from the memory location into the Memory Data Register (MDR) inside the processor. The data bus is bi-directional. For example, it will be used to perform both 'memory read' and 'memory write' operations.

Control bus

The control bus has a number of lines that are each dedicated to sending or receiving a particular signal. In the 'read operation' described above, one line would be used to send a signal to the control unit in the processor to indicate that the 'read operation has now completed'.

Other control signals indicate that:

- the user presses the 'reset' button
- a memory write operation has completed
- an input/output operation has completed

an interrupt has been received (Interrupts are discussed later in this chapter).

> ### Progress check A
> An address bus has 16 lines. Calculate how many different addresses are possible.

These three buses together are called the system bus.

There are some points in Figure **4.02** that will help to make sense of how the processor executes a sequence of instructions.

The Memory Data Register (MDR) is connected directly to main memory. It is a temporary store for the data value read/written.

The Arithmetic and Logical Unit is where instructions that require some form of arithmetic or logical operation are processed.

The 'processor' should be considered the Control Unit and ALU working together.

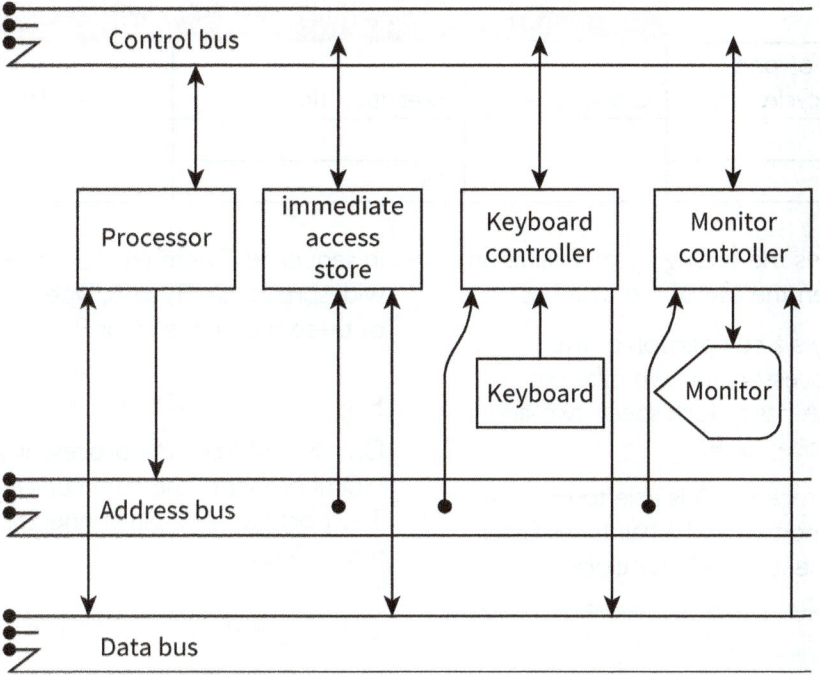

Figure 4.02 The three buses

Factors that affect performance

Processor type and cores

Modern processors are much more complex than shown in Figure **4.01**. A processor can have many **cores**, which means there is more than one processor on the microprocessor. Each core is able to carry out the range of program instructions. Each core will use the buses and the input/output infrastructure.

Different cores enable instructions to be processed in parallel and so increase the overall performance of the computer. 'Quad-core' processors are now common in PCs and mobile devices.

Cache memory

Cache memory is a small amount of fast memory, placed between the processor and primary memory and/or placed between primary memory and the disk

Cache memory is designed to make data transfer speeds faster.

A program might frequently use certain data values. A good technique would then be to load these data values from the disk into cache and keep them available to the processor from the cache memory.

Bus width

The number of lines determines the size of the binary pattern that can be carried on the bus.

Binary arithmetic shows that a bus with 8 lines would give numbers that range from:

0000 0000 to 1111 1111

i.e. 256 different numbers.

Hence, an address bus with eight lines would only be able to address 256 different memory locations.

Similarly, a data bus with 8 lines would be able to transfer binary values ranging from

0000 0000 to 1111 1111.

(Internal) Clock speed

The processor has an internal clock that synchronises activity. Each different program instruction has a stated number of clock cycles that it takes to execute that instruction.

This stated number of clock cycles for each instruction in the processor's **instruction set** never changes. However, it might be possible to reduce the time taken (in say microseconds) for one clock cycle. This is called 'over-clocking'.

Different processor instructions take a different number of clock cycles to execute. Compare the following. An instruction to increment a value in the accumulator register would take few clock cycles whereas an instruction that has to access a location in primary memory and then copy the value to the accumulator would take many more clock cycles.

	Time for one clock cycle (μs)	Instruction 1		Instruction 2	
		Clock cycles	Execution time	Clock cycles	Execution time
Processor A	2	3	6	12	24
Processor B	5		15		60

This is because it involves the setting up of a value on the address bus and then the use of the data bus.

The following table shows a comparison of the performance of two processors for two different instructions. Processor A has a clock speed two-and-a-half times faster than Processor B.

The conclusion is that Processor A is able to execute the same program around two and a half times faster than Processor B because it has a faster clock speed.

> ## Progress check B
>
> Processor C has its processor clock speed set to 3 microseconds per cycle. One of the instructions in its instruction set takes 12 clock cycles. Calculate the time taken to execute this instruction.

Ports and peripherals

At least one input device and one output device must be connected to any computer system. This will be through one of a number of ports found on the case of the computer. A 'port' is a hardware connection, used to provide the input or output of data to or from a device.

Common ports on a PC are shown in Figure **4.02**:

Port	Input	Output
Universal Serial Port (USB)	√	√
VGA		√
HDMI		√
Ethernet ('network')	√	√

Table 4.01 List of PC ports.

Universal Serial Bus (USB)

The connection is made by means of a bus that connects a port on the computer case to the processor. A PC will have more than one USB port. Each port can connect to a device. The USB bus allows bi-directional data transfer, for example, it can read and write to the connected USB external disk drive. The word 'serial' means that data bits are transferred along a single line, in sequence. There are now several USB standards in widespread use: Type A, Type B and a 'micro-USB'. All of these have either 4 or 9 pin connectors.

High Definition Multimedia Interface (HDMI)

Data is sent from the processor to the connected HDMI monitor. The communication is unidirectional. The port has a 19-pin connector, hence the HDMI bus has 19 lines.

Video Graphics Array (VGA)

VGA was the standard port and bus used for screen output before the increased use of HDMI. The port is unidirectional.

4.02 Assembly language

A processor is designed to carry out a number of different **program instructions**. This is called the instruction set.

Each instruction will be made up of two parts, **the op code**, for example, 'add the number that follows, to the accumulator (ACC) contents' and **the operand**, for example: 58 (the number to be added).

Both the op code and the operand are encoded as a binary patterns. They are stored in memory as bit patterns.

If the program instruction is expressed as a binary or hex pattern, it is called **machine code**.

> ### TIP
>
> We must always be careful with the operand. If it is a number, we must be clear whether it is the actual number the instruction wants, or is it the contents of a particular memory location?
>
> In the example above #58, the 'hash' symbol makes it clear we use the actual number.
>
> 58 would mean 'use the contents of the memory location with address 58'.

However, it is much easier to understand if the program instructions are written in a 'shorthand' way, called assembly language. Using, the example above:

Program instruction   'add the operand number to the contents of the ACC'

Machine code   0110 0000 (0011 1010)

Assembly language   ADD #58

> ### Progress check C
> Study the program instruction example above.
>
> Check that the machine code binary pattern (circled) is number 58.

Groups of instructions

The syllabus uses a fictitious processor with a single general purpose register called the accumulator (ACC), an index register (IX) and an instruction set with 32 instructions that fall neatly into groups.

> ### TIP
> You do not need to memorise assembly language instructions.

Data movement

	Op code	Operand	Explanation
1	LDM	#n	Immediate address. Load the number n to ACC. (The hash makes clear it is a number)
2	LDD	\<address\>	Direct addressing. Load the contents of the location at the given address to ACC
3	LDI	\<address\>	Indirect addressing. The address to be used is at the given address. Load the contents of this second address to ACC
4	LDX	\<address\>	Indexed addressing. Form the address from \<address\> + the contents of the index register.
5	LDR	#n	Immediate addressing. Load the number n to IX
6	MOV	\<register\>	Move the contents of ACC to the given register (IX)
7	STO	\<address\>	Store the contents of ACC at the given address

Input and output of data

	Op code	Operand	Explanation
8	IN		Key in a character and store its ASCII value in ACC
9	OUT		Output to the screen the character whose ASCII value is stored in ACC

Arithmetic operations

	Op code	Operand	Explanation
10	ADD	\<address\>	Add the contents of the given address to ACC
11	ADD	#n	Add the denary number n to ACC
12	SUB	\<address\>	Subtract the content of the given address from ACC
13	SUB	#n	Subtract the denary number n from ACC
14	INC	\<register\>	Add 1 to the contents of the register (ACC or IX)
15	DEC	\<register\>	Subtract 1 from the contents of the register (ACC or IX)

Unconditional jump, Conditional jump and Compare instructions

	Op code	Operand	Explanation
16	JMP	<address>	Jump to the given address
17	CMP	<address>	Compare the contents of ACC with the contents of <address>
18	CMP	#n	Compare the contents of ACC with number n
19	CMI	<address>	Indirect addressing. The address to be used is at the given address. Compare the contents of ACC with the contents of the second address
20	JPE	<address>	Following a compare instruction, jump to <address> if the compare was True
21	JPN	<address>	Following a compare instruction, jump to <address> if the compare was False

	Op code	Operand	Explanation
22	END		Return control to the operating system

Modes of addressing

Immediate addressing

In this case, it is not really an 'address'. The operand is a number. See instructions 1 and 5.

The operand could be given as a decimal, binary or hexadecimal number, denoted with:

LDM #59	no prefix to the number indicates 'decimal'
LDM #&3B	'hexadecimal' number
LDM #B0100 0001	'binary' number

Direct addressing

In this case, the operand is the address of the memory location. See instructions 2 and 7.

Indirect addressing

In this case the operand is a 'forwarding address'. Look at this location to find the second address where the data is found. See instructions 3 and 19.

Indexed addressing

Indexed addressing uses the Index register. The address to be used is formed from the number in IX added to the operand address. See instruction 4.

Relative addressing

Note that there is no instruction in our instruction set above that uses relative addressing.

For relative addressing, the address to be used is an 'offset' from the address containing the first instruction of the program. For example, the program is loaded to a block of memory locations starting at address 100. The instruction is 'LOAD +16'. The instruction will load the contents of address 116 to ACC.

> **Progress check D**
>
> Note that some of the instructions do not have an operand.
>
> List these instructions.

4.03 Sample assembly language programs

All of these instructions are best illustrated with some example programs.

Program 1

Op code	Operand
LDM	#13
ADD	#7
STO	103
END	

Registers		Memory address
IX	ACC	103
Not used	Empty	Empty
	13	
	20	
		20

Trace table

Note that this uses only immediate addressing.

A trace table is a way of 'tracing' and checking what happens after each instruction is executed.

Program 2

Op code	Operand
LDD	100
SUB	101
STO	102
END	

Register		Memory address		
IX	ACC contents	100	101	102
Not used	Empty	63	20	Empty
	63			
	43			
				43

Trace table

Note that Program 2 uses direct addressing.

Program 3

Op code	Operand
LDM	#26
STO	120
LDD	130
ADD	120
STO	131
LDI	140
ADD	131
STO	150
END	

Register		Memory address				
IX	ACC	120	130	131	140	150
Not used	Empty	Empty	12	Empty	150	72
	26					
		26				
	12					
	38					
				38		
	72					
	110					
						110

Trace table

Note that Program 3 uses immediate, direct and indirect addressing.

Program 4

Op code	Operand
LDX	200
ADD	200
INC	ACC
INC	ACC
STO	201
END	

Register		Memory address		
IX	ACC	200	201	202
2	Empty	21	Empty	16
	16			
	37			
	38			
	39			
			39	

Trace table

Note that Program 4 uses indexed addressing.

Program 5

Op code	Operand	Register		Comment
		IX	ACC	
		Not used	Empty	
IN			65	The user keys in 'A' – ASCII code is 65
INC			66	
INC			67	
INC			68	
OUT				Character 'D' is shown on the screen
END				

Trace table

Note the input and output to/from the program.

Program 6

	Op code	Operand	Register		Comment
			IX	ACC	
			Not used	Empty	
100	IN			48	The user keys in '0' – ASCII code is 48
101	OUT				Characters '0','2','4','6','8' are shown on the screen
102	INC			49 51 53 55 57	
103	INC			50 52 54 56 58	
104	CMP	#58			
105	JNE	102			
106	END				

Trace table

Note that the program code must know the address (100) where the first instruction is loaded.

It uses a 'compare' instruction and returns to address 102 five times. This is a program containing a loop. We will study loops in **pseudocode** in detail in Chapter 11 Section 11.2.

Progress check E

LDM #&5A

  STO 201

What decimal number is stored at address 201 ?

Progress check F

LDM #B01000001

DEC

STO 201

What decimal number is stored at address 201 ?

4.04 The Fetch-Execute (F-E) cycle

We now know what a program looks like. It is a sequence of program instructions (and possibly data values) stored in a continuous block of memory.

We have shown the programs Program 1 to Program 6, in assembly language. What is actually loaded into memory is the machine code equivalent of each instruction.

> **TIP**
>
> Although called the 'fetch-execute cycle', there are really <u>three</u> stages: 'fetch-<u>decode</u>-execute'.

The fetch-execute cycle describes how any program, once it is loaded into memory, will be executed using the special purpose registers.

To execute a program, the steps are:

Stage	Register transfer notation
Fetch the next instruction …	
The Program Counter (PC) is loaded with the address of the next instruction to be fetched	
The contents of the PC are copied to the Memory Address Register	MAR ← [PC]
The contents of the PC are incremented (ready for the next fetch)	PC ← [PC] + 1
The address given by MAR is located, and the contents of this address copied to the Memory Data Register	MDR ← [[MAR]]
The contents of MDR are copied to the Current Instruction Register	CIR ← [MDR]
Decode …	
The op code and operand parts of the instruction are identified and the instruction executed.	
Execute the instruction …	

The second column describes the steps using **register transfer' notation**. [PC] denotes 'the contents of the Program Counter'. The 'assign' operator (similar to that used for assignment statements in pseudocode later) denotes that the register on the left is 'given the value which follows'.

Interrupts

An **interrupt** is generated when, for example, (1) a printer sends a message that it is out of paper, (2) a program attempts to divide by zero in a calculation or (3) the user presses the 'Reset' button.

When an interrupt is received by the CPU, the computer system must identify the source of the interrupt signal and run appropriate program code to deal with the event. This is called the **Interrupt Service Routine (ISR)**. Then the computer system must return to the processing of the program, at the point reached when the interrupt was received.

In order that the processor can return to the current program at a later stage, the data stored in all the registers must be saved. This is done on a special area of memory called the **stack**.

Every different cause of an interrupt will have its own ISR program code available to be run when required.

The processor hardware must have a way of recording when an interrupt occurs. Two different ways to do this could be to use one of the bits in the Status Register to flag the interrupt, or (preferably) to maintain a register, called the Interrupt Register. We have 8 or 16 bits available, so each bit could be used to flag (identify) one of the possible interrupt sources.

Interrupts and the fetch-execute cycle

You could add a step into the F-E cycle to manage interrupts. Before the next program instruction of the current program is fetched, the processor looks to see if an interrupt has occurred. So, the F-E cycle now has four stages, i.e. (1) test for interrupts, (2) fetch the next instruction, (3) decode the instruction and (4) execute the instruction.

4.05 Bit manipulation

There are further instructions in our processor's instruction set, namely the logical operators: AND, OR and XOR and also the instructions that 'shift' a pattern of bits to the left or right.

	Label	Op code	Operand	Explanation
23		AND	#n	Bitwise AND operation of the contents of ACC with n
24		AND	<address>	Bitwise AND operation of the contents of ACC with the contents of <address>
25		XOR	#n	Bitwise XOR operation of the contents of ACC with n
26		XOR	<address>	Bitwise XOR operation of the contents of ACC with the contents of <address>
27		OR	#n	Bitwise OR operation of the contents of ACC with n
28		OR	<address>	Bitwise OR operation of the contents of ACC with the contents of <address>
29		LSL	#n	Bits in ACC are shifted logically n places to the left. Zeros are introduced on the right-hand end
30		LSR	#n	Bits in ACC are shifted logically n places to the right. Zeros are introduced on the left-hand end
31	<label>:	<op code>	<operand>	Labels an instruction
32	<label>:		<data>	Gives a symbolic address <label> to the memory address with contents <data>

At the machine code level, and also in assembly language, these instructions operate on two numbers on a 'bit by bit' basis, called a 'bitwise' operation.

Shift instructions

In a real processor's instruction set there will be many instructions to shift a bit pattern.

The pattern can be shifted:

- to the left a stated number of places
- to the right a stated number of places
- using a type of operation called a '**cyclic shift**'
- using a type of operation called an '**arithmetic shift**'
- using a type of operation called a '**logical shift**'

The syllabus that you are studying uses only two instructions for a logical shift.

Logical shift

A logical shift uses one of the bit positions (labelled C) in the Status Register. C is the label for bit 7 in the Status Register. This bit is called the Carry Flag.

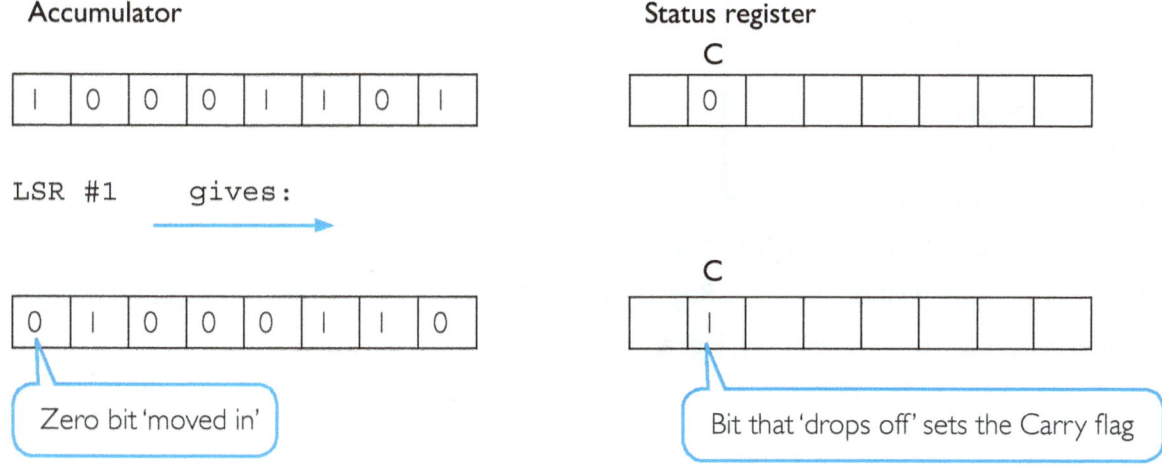

This is the first use we have seen of the Status Register. C is set to 1 if the 'dropped off' bit is a 1. The positions on the left are filled with zero bit(s).

A left logical shift works in the same way. C might/might not be set. Positions on the right are filled with zero bits.

Progress check G

The accumulator contains the two's complement integer +52 denary.

`LSR #3` is executed.

Write the binary for the ACC contents before and after the instruction. What denary number is now in ACC?

Logical Right Shift

Bit positions on the left hand side of the Accumulator are filled with zero bits.

"One place right logical shift".

`LSR #1   gives:`

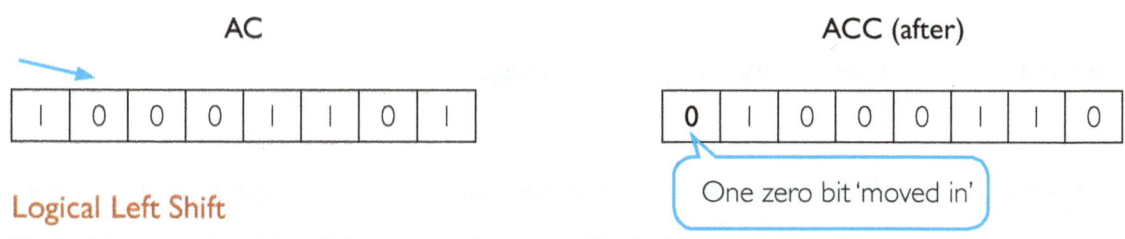

Logical Left Shift

Bit positions on the right of the Accumulator are filled with zero bits.

"Three place left logical shift".

`LSL #3   gives:`

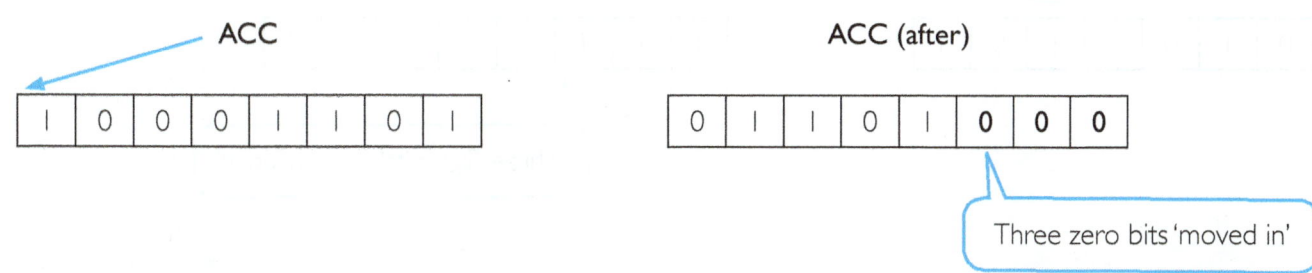

> **TIP**
>
> The Carry bit in the Status register may or may not be involved with a shift operation.

In the syllabus document – shifting and their assembly language:

- There is no mention of any involvement of the Status Register and its Carry bit. This therefore has been omitted.
- Assembly language instructions are only shown using logical shifts

Cyclic Right Shift

Bits which are shifted out of the right hand side are re-cycled into the empty positions created on the left.

"Two place cyclic right shift".

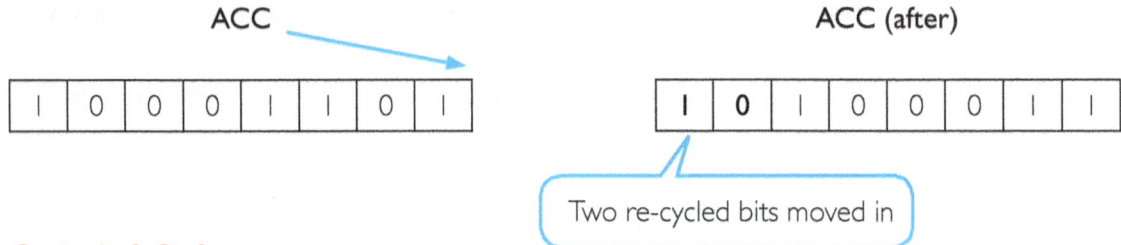

Cyclic Left Shift

Bits which are shifted out of the left hand side are re-cycled into the empty positions created on the right.

"Three place cyclic left shift".

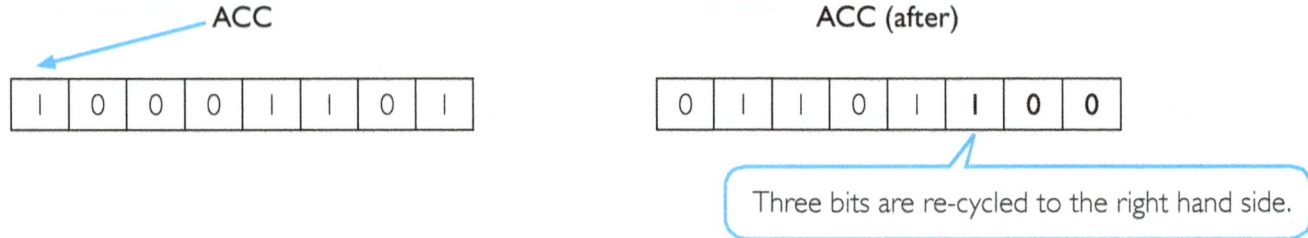

Arithmetic Shift

Arithmetic shifts assume that the original value is representing a signed integer.

Arithmetic right shift

Note the sign of the most significant bit (bit 7). Bits are shifted out of the right hand side. The gap(s) on the left are filled with the original bit 7

"Arithmetic right shift three places".

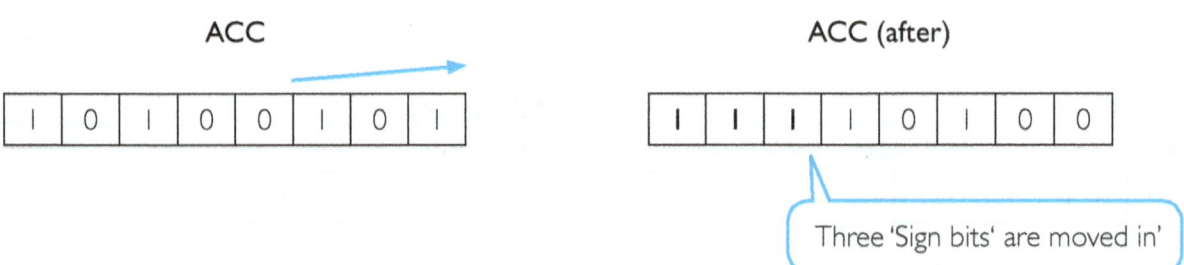

Arithmetic left shift

Bits are shifted out of the left hand side. The gap(s) on the right are replaced with zero bits.

"Arithmetic left shift four places".

ACC

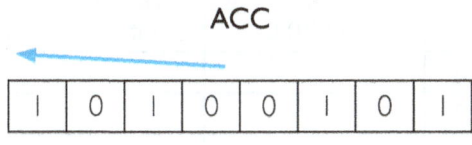

| 1 | 0 | 1 | 0 | 0 | 1 | 0 | 1 |

ACC (after)

| 0 | 1 | 0 | 1 | 0 | 0 | 0 | 0 |

Four Zero bits 'moved in'

Note: This arithmetic left shift does not preserve the sign of the number. The original number was negative, but the shifted pattern shows a positive number. This is where the Carry bit in the Status Register could be used to keep track of the sign of the number.

Boolean operators

In all of the following examples we shall assume there is a bit pattern in the accumulator that is operated on by a bit pattern labelled **NUM**.

Make yourself familiar again with the truth tables studied in Chapter 3 Section 3.05.

AND Operator

Input		Output
0	0	0
0	1	0
1	0	0
1	1	1

ACC | 0 | 0 | 0 | 1 | 0 | 1 | 0 | 1 |
NUM | 1 | 0 | 1 | 1 | 1 | 1 | 1 | 0 | AND
ACC | 0 | 0 | 0 | 1 | 0 | 1 | 0 | 0 |

The result for each bit position is obtained using the truth table for the AND operator.

OR Operator

Input		Output
0	0	0
0	1	1
1	0	1
1	1	1

ACC | 0 | 0 | 0 | 1 | 1 | 1 | 0 | 1 |
NUM | 1 | 0 | 1 | 1 | 0 | 1 | 1 | 0 | OR
ACC | 1 | 0 | 1 | 1 | 1 | 1 | 1 | 1 |

The result for each bit position is obtained using the truth table for the OR operator.

XOR Operator

Input		Output
0	0	0
0	1	1
1	0	1
1	1	0

ACC | 0 | 0 | 0 | 1 | 0 | 1 | 0 | 1 |
NUM | 1 | 0 | 1 | 1 | 1 | 1 | 1 | 0 | OR
ACC | 1 | 0 | 1 | 0 | 1 | 0 | 1 | 1 |

The result for each bit position is obtained using the truth table for the XOR operator.

Labels

You can use a label to address a memory cell as an alternative to using the actual address number.

Program 8 uses two labels – PATTERN and ANSWER.

Program 8

Address	Label	Op code	Operand
150		LDM	#B01011100
151		AND	PATTERN
		STO	ANSWER
152			
153	PATTERN:	01001001	
154	ANSWER:		
155		END	

Registers	Memory address	
ACC	153	154
Empty	01001001	Empty
01011100		
01001000		
		01001000

Trace table

The program has been loaded into memory starting at address 150. Two labels have been used:

Address 152 has symbolic address (or label) `PATTERN`.

Address 154 has symbolic address `ANSWER`.

4.06 Matching and masking

Matching

The Program 9 below tests for a 'match'.

Is the value stored at location `IMHERE` 79? Output 'T' if True or 'F' if False.

The method is to load the contents of `IMHERE` to ACC, subtract 79, do a compare operation then if the ACC contents are zero output T, otherwise output F.

Program 9

Address	Label	Op code	Operand
150		LDD	IMHERE
151		SUB	#79
152		CMP	#0
153		JPE	OUT_TRUE
154		JMP	OUT_FALSE
155	IMHERE	#79	
156			
157	OUT_TRUE:	LDM	#84
158		OUT	
159		JMP	FINISH
160	OUT_FALSE	LDM	#70
161		OUT	
162	FINISH:	END	

Registers		Memory
ACC	Status Register C bit	Address 155
Empty	0	79
79		
0		
	1	
84		

Note, the program has the memory location numbers shown but the program does not use them. It use labels instead, for example for the conditional and unconditional jump instructions. The compare instruction (at 152) sets the C flag in the Status Register if True.

The ASCII codes used are 'T' = 84 and 'F' = 70.

Masking

The logical operators are used for the operation of 'masking out' (or blanking out with zeros) certain bit positions.

'Mask out' bit positions 1, 3, 4 and 6 of the ACC contents.

	7	6	5	4	3	2	1	0
ACC	0	0	0	1	0	1	0	1

The method is to form an 'AND mask' with, zero bits in the positions to mask out and with 1 bits in the positions to retain the original content.

	7	6	5	4	3	2	1	0	
ACC	0	0	0	1	0	1	0	1	
MASK	1	0	1	0	0	1	0	1	AND
ACC	0	0	0	0	0	1	0	1	

The result is that masked positions are all set to zero and retained positions are unchanged.

Setting an individual bit position

ACC contains the ASCII code for upper case character 'K'.

The program will change the code to lower case 'k'.

ASCII code for K is 75.

ASCII code for k is 107.

The difference between upper and lower case is always 32.

The bits patterns are:

	7	6	5	4	3	2	1	0
K	0	1	0	0	1	0	1	1
k	0	1	1	0	1	0	1	1

The program will change the bit in position 5 from 0 to 1.

	7	6	5	4	3	2	1	0
K	0	1	0	0	1	0	1	1
OR	0	0	1	0	0	0	0	0
k	0	1	1	0	1	0	1	1

The OR operator does this with 1 in the position to 'set' to 1 and 0s in all other positions (which are unchanged).

> ## Progress check H
>
> A memory location NUMBER stores a number. It must have its bit 5 position set to 1 and saved. Write the three assembly language instructions to do this.
>
> | | 7 | 6 | 5 | 4 | 3 | 2 | 1 | 0 |
> |---|---|---|---|---|---|---|---|---|
> | NUMBER: | 0 | 0 | 0 | 0 | 0 | 0 | 0 | 0 |

Bit manipulation to monitor/control a device

There is nothing new here. You could use a special register. Each individual bit position shows the current state of a connected device. For example, bit 5 of the register could show whether or not an actuator that drives a motor is currently switched on or off.

Past paper questions

1. Five modes of addressing and five descriptions are shown in the diagram.

   Draw a line to connect each mode of addressing to its correct description.

   Mode of addressing

   - Direct
   - Immediate
   - Indexed
   - Indirect
   - Relative

   Description

   - The operand is the address of the address of the value to be used
   - The operand is the address of the value to be used
   - The operand is the offset from the current address where the value to be used is stored
   - The operand plus the contents of the index register is the address of the value to be used
   - The operand is the value to be used

   [4]

Cambridge International AS & A level Computer Science 9608 paper 11 Q3 June 2015

2. a Explain how the width of the data bus and system clock speed affect the performance of a computer system. [3]

   b Most computers use Universal Serial Bus (USB) ports to allow the attachment of devices.

   Describe two benefits of using USB ports. [2]

   c The table shows six stages in the von Neumann fetch-execute cycle.

   Put the stages into the correct sequence by writing the numbers 1 to 6 in the right-hand column.

Description of stage	Sequence number
The instruction is copied from the Memory Data Register (MDR) and placed in the Current Instruction Register (CIR)	
The instruction is executed	
The instruction is decoded	
The address contained in the Program Counter (PC) is copied to the Memory Address Register (MAR)	
The value in the Program Counter (PC) is incremented so that it points to the next instruction to be fetched	
The instruction is copied from the memory location contained in the Memory Address Register (MAR) and is placed in the Memory Data Register (MDR)	

   [6]

Cambridge International AS & A level Computer Science 9608 paper 11 Q8 June 2015

3   a

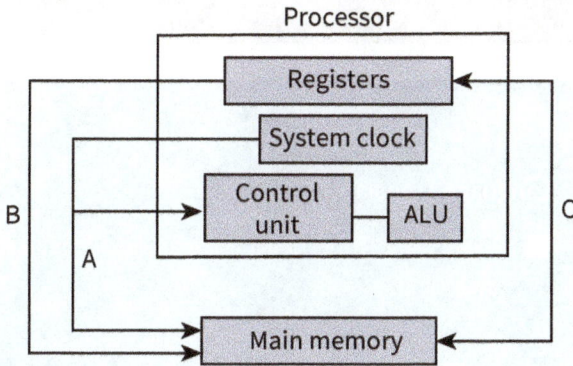

The diagram shows a simplified form of processor architecture.

Name the three buses labelled A, B and C. [3]

b   State the role of each of the following special purpose registers used in a typical processor: [4]

Program Counter

Memory Data Register

Current Instruction Register

Memory Address Register

Cambridge International AS & A level Computer Science 9608 paper 11 Q2 November 2015

4   a   Describe how special purpose registers are used in the fetch stage of the fetch-execute cycle. [4]

    b   Use the statements A, B, C and D to complete the description of how the fetch-execute cycle handles an interrupt.

A	The address of the Interrupt Service Routine (ISR) is loaded to the Program Counter (PC).
B	The processor checks if there is an interrupt.
C	When the ISR completes, the processor restores the register contents.
D	The register contents are saved.

At the end of the cycle for the current instruction ……………………… .

If the interrupt flag is set, ………………………, ……………………… and ……………………… .

The interrupted program continues its execution. [3]

Cambridge International AS & A level Computer Science 9608 paper 11 Q3 June 2016

Chapter 5: System software

Learning Objectives:

Operating system:
- Explain the need for an operating system (OS)
- List and explain the management tasks carried out by the OS
- Describe the role of some utility software
- Understand the need for program libraries
- Understand the benefits to the developer offered by Dynamic Link Library (DLL) files.

Language translators:
- Understand the need for translator software, including:
  - An assembler for assembly language
  - A compiler for high-level language code
  - An Interpreter for high-level language code
  - A partially compiled and interpreted solution such as Java
- List and justify the benefits of a compiler compared with an Interpreter and vice-versa
- Describe the features of an Integrated Development Environment (IDE).

5.01 Operating system

The need for an operating system

The computer hardware is completely unusable without an operating system (OS).

Management tasks carried out by the operating system

The computer system has the following resources that must be managed by the OS:

- Primary memory: Do we have enough memory to load another program?
- Secondary storage: Is there sufficient hard disk space to save a file?
- Processor: If a number of programs are concurrently loaded, how does the OS decide which gets the next use of the processor?
- Input/Output devices: Are they working? Are they recognised by the various applications programs in use?

> **Progress check A**
>
> Is the operating system classified as system software or applications software?

The file system

When the power to the PC is turned on, the computer goes through a process called **booting-up**. Switching on the power triggers the running of a small program stored in ROM. On a PC this is called the **BIOS (Basic Input-Output System)**. The BIOS will identify all the peripheral input and output devices. It runs the boot loader software. The boot loader software was described earlier in Chapter 4.

This program will contain the start address of the operating system stored on the hard disk, so the boot process will load the operating system from secondary storage.

The disk may be divided into **logical drive** areas called partitions. A new PC might already come with partitions. These could include, for example, Drive C: for all the operating system and application program files, Drive D which is then intended for the user's data files.

As additional devices are available, CD/DVD drive, flash memory stick, etc, each device will be allocated a logical drive letter.

The **file directory** is what the user sees. The file directory will show a list of all the files stored, their name, date and time last saved, file size and other information.

You studied the construction of a hard disk in Chapter 3. A block is the amount of data that can be read/written in a single write/read operation and a block will consist typically of four contiguous sectors. A block forms the basic **file allocation unit** that is allocated to files.

When the user gives the instruction to save a file, the operating system has to decide which file allocation units are to be used to store this file. The OS will manage this by maintaining a list of all the unused file allocation units, recording which allocation units have been used to store each file on the hard disk. When the user deletes a file, the allocation units for that file are returned to the list of available allocation units.

The **File Allocation Table** (FAT) is a map of the usage of all the file allocation units.

Primary memory

The processor must manage the available memory space. For example, what happens when a program finishes its execution? Is there sufficient free memory to load a new program?

The memory manager software tracks where in primary memory the program and its data are currently stored.

Consider just one program loaded into primary memory. Remember, the operating system is itself a set of program modules and so primary memory is also needed for the OS.

This strategy however of (operating system + one process only) is wasteful on memory. On a modern PC there is sufficient memory available to load several processes into memory at the same time.

Various strategies can be used for the allocation of the available primary memory and this will be discussed in Chapter 16.

User interface

The user interface hides the complexities of the hardware from the user. That is, it makes using the computer as easy as possible for the user.

The interaction for the user will be very different for the different types of interface.

One kind of interface is the **command line interface**. It will need the user to action events by keying in one-line commands. The user must have a detailed knowledge of the available commands.

Another kind of interface is the **graphical user interface (GUI)**. This will be very different. The user must use a pointing device such as a mouse or trackpad, or, for a touch-screen, a stylus or finger, to point to icons or text on the screen.

Process management

Modern PCs have sufficient primary memory to allow several programs to be loaded into memory currently. An instance of a program executing is called a **process**.

Consider a session where four simultaneous file downloads are taking place. There are four processes running, each using the (same) file-download software. The OS is said to be **multitasking**. It must decide how to make the most efficient use of the computer system in managing these four processes and any others that are currently running.

Security management

The OS is responsible for keeping the computer system secure from any attempted usage by unauthorised users. A system of user accounts with passwords addresses this. Increasingly biometrics are being used to gain access to a computer system or device.

Management of hardware for Input/Output

A traditional desktop PC would have a monitor for output and communication with the user, a scanner for the capture (input) of images, a printer for hard copy output and speakers for the output of sound.

All of this hardware must be managed by the OS. We would not want two programs trying to print at the same time.

Applications software, for example, the word processor, must interact with the hardware in order to receive data from input devices (the user typing at the keyboard) and to send its result to output devices (the text displayed on the monitor screen). It is the task of program code in the OS to manage this.

Particular peripherals will need special software loaded when they are to be used. These are called, **drivers**. When a new device is connected to the computer, the driver software for that device must be installed.

> **Progress check B**
>
> List the five resources that are managed by the operating system of the computer system.

5.02 OS utility software

Disk formatter

You studied the construction of a hard disk in Chapter 3.

> **TIP**
>
> The list of possible utility software is huge, but you only need to know about those covered here.

The particular file format will be dictated by the operating system being used. The Windows Operating system has now used a 20-year-old file system called NTFS. The particular file format used will determine the maximum individual file size which is possible and also the maximum drive size of any partitions. In new fille system called NTFS was designed to replace the FAT32 file system.

Formatting a disk is the process of preparing the disk for use with the operating system's file storage system.

Formatting will delete all existing data on the disk.

Other types of storage such as flash memory cards and flash drives come pre-formatted.

Virus checker

The term 'malware' is short for 'malicious software' and is commonly used to describe a vast range of threats. Malware is any software that is designed to cause some form of malfunction of the computer system, loss of data or unauthorised access. A **virus** is software that is designed to install its own code without permission in a computer system and is certainly intended to cause harm and thus falls within the category of malware.

Virus checker software is installed and run to identify any threats to the running of the computer and to 'quarantine' any suspicious files.

New viruses are found on a daily basis, so the **virus database** must be continually updated.

Defragmentation software

When data is written to a hard disk, the OS will decide which file allocation units are to be used. A 'best case' is that the units used are on as few tracks as possible. This requires the least number of movements of the read/write heads and so results in a faster overall speed in the writing/reading of a file.

However, a large file might use blocks that are scattered all over the surface of the disk. The result will be that the file takes a long time to load, as many read operations are required. The file is fragmented across the disk.

The user can periodically run a utility program called a 'de-frag' that will attempt to reorganise the allocation units used so that the blocks are spread across fewer tracks.

A secondary advantage of this process should be to create larger contiguous regions of free space.

Disk contents analysis

Loss of the data on a hard disk is the worst case scenario for a user! A disk might report that the computer is unable to read data from the disk. Software is available that will attempt to offer a solution by retrieving the data from the disk. 'Disk recovery' is a service offered by various commercial providers.

File compression

Compression techniques for use with image, sound and video files were discussed earlier in Chapter 1, Section 1.6.

Compression software takes the original file contents and processes the bytes in such a way that a new version of the file is produced, which takes up less bytes.

Back-up software

Regular backups should be taken of the data on any computer system. This safeguards against computer failure, in particular of the secondary storage.

To make the backup you need to make a copy of the file(s) and then verify the backup copy. That is, compare byte by byte the data on the original medium and the copy on the backup device.

You will then need software available to restore the backups if and when this is needed.

5.03 Program libraries

Most programmers write programs in a high level language, such as Visual Basic.Net, Java or Python. The programming language will include all of the essential keywords and other syntax that make up the language. In addition to the basic features of the language, specialised coding features will be available to use, from **program libraries**. The programmer will need to specify in their code that a particular library is required. New libraries will be made available with new releases of the programming environment software and might also be available from third party suppliers. Users may also produce their own libraries.

The program libraries will be very varied, ranging from libraries that provide basic input/output to other very specialised applications such as interfacing to the controller of a particular piece of electronics.

Having program libraries available makes program design and coding easier and faster for the developer.

Dynamic Link Library (DLL) files

A DLL file is executable code that is only loaded into main memory when required by an executing process. Consider a user who is word processing. The spell-checker might be required after 20 minutes of a session, so it will be loaded to memory only when it is needed.

Also, efficient code-sharing can be enabled. The code in a DLL can be shared among all the processes that use that DLL.

Consider a DLL with the program code to perform a spell-check. This DLL might be used by word processing, presentation software and spreadsheet applications. The DLL occupies a single place in physical memory.

Consider when changes are to be made to the presentation and spreadsheet software. This new code can be written and compiled without the need to consider changes to the existing DLL spell-checker code.

5.04 Language translators

Assembler software

We wrote some assembly language in Chapter 4.

The assembly language instructions each have a **machine code** (binary) equivalent.

The assembly language code must be first translated to machine code for the computer to understand it. This translation is done by software called an **assembler**. Sometimes, the programming language is also called 'assembler'. The assembler software used must be for the appropriate processor instruction set. There are several different processors that might be used inside a PC and they have variants, for example, 32-bit or 64-bit processors. The programmer might have to ascertain, for example, which one of the Intel family of processors is being used: x 86, 80386, 80486, etc. The developer must be clear that the assembler software used is for the correct instruction set.

The original assembly language program (written by the programmer) is called the **source code**.

The translated machine code is called the **object code**.

The assembly process for a 'two-pass' assembler

Every assembly language instruction has a machine code for that instruction. For example:

Assembly language	Machine code
LDD <address>	0000 0010

Op Code table		
Opcode (mnemonic)	Operand	Opcode (binary)
LDD	<address>	0000 0010
LDI	<address>	0000 0101
STO	<address>	0000 1111
OUTCH		0000 1000
JPE	<address>	1000 0000
JPN	<address>	1000 0001
CMP	<address>	1000 0010
JMP	<address>	1000 0010
INC	<address>	0000 1011

Figure 5.01 Op code table (some instructions only).

To carry out the assembly process, the assembly software must have the **op code table** available and will create an address table called the **symbol table**.

Every assembly language op code and its machine code equivalent needs to be in the op code table. The symbol table contains all the labels used and the actual memory address or relative address.

Most assemblers are two-pass assemblers. To complete the symbol table and produce the final machine code, the assembly language source code must be scanned twice.

Table **5.01** shows the op code table (some entries only) that will be used as a lookup table.

The first pass finds labels, enters each one in the symbol table and (if known) enters their address alongside the label.

How is it done? Consider now the translation of the program shown in Figure **5.02**.

The assembly process will take the source code assembly language program (on the left) and produce the machine code/object code (on the right).

On completion of the first pass, the symbol table has the entries shown in Figure **5.03**.

Note that some labels are first entered with the absolute address not known at this stage, for example, `Value`.

Other labels will have the absolute address known the first time that address is found, for example, `StartProg`.

Assembly language

Label:		
StartProg:	LDI	Here
	CMP	Value
	JPE	EndProg
	OUTCH	
	LDD	Here
	INC	ACC
	STO	Here
	JMP	StartProg
EndProg:	END	
Here:		50
		65
		74
		65
		90
Value:		32

Machine code

0000 0101	0000 0101	(+9)
1000 0010	0001 0000	(+14)
1000 0000	0000 1000	(+8)
0000 1000		
0000 0010	0001 1001	(+9)
0000 1011		
0000 1111	0001 1001	(+9)
1000 0010	0000 0000	
1111 1111		
0011 0010		
0100 0001		
0100 1010		
0100 0001		
0101 1010		
0010 0000		

Figure 5.02 Sample program to illustrate the assembly process.

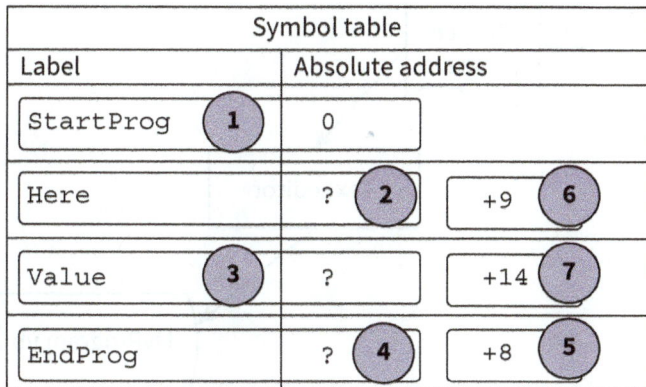

Symbol table	
Label	Absolute address
StartProg ①	0
Here	? ② +9 ⑥
Value ③	? +14 ⑦
EndProg	? ④ +8 ⑤

Figure 5.03 Entries to the symbol table during translation.

The circle labels shown the sequence in which the data is entered to the symbol table. For example:

① The label `StartProg` is entered and its absolute address is known.

② The label `Here` is entered but its absolute address is not yet known. It can be worked out on the second pass.

On the second pass now that all the addresses used are recorded, the complete machine code program can be produced. As shown on the right of Figure **5.02**

Progress check C

This program was studied in Chapter 4.

Address		Label	Op code	Operand
Relative	Actual			
0	150		LDM	#B01011100
+1	151		AND	PATTERN
+2	152		STO	ANSWER
+3	153			
+4	154	PATTERN:	#B01001001	
+5	155	ANSwER:		
+6	156		END	

Figure 5.04 Assembly language program about to be translated.

Show how a two-pass assembler would build the symbol table and machine code by completing these tables, numbering the order in which the entries are made.

Object file	

Symbol table	

Figure 5.05 Machine code file and symbol table.

Op Code table		
Opcode (mnemonic)	Operand	Opcode (binary)
LDM	<address>	1000 1000
STO	<address>	0000 1111
AND	#n	1000 1100
END		1111 1111

Table 5.02 Op code table.

Translation of high level languages

Programmers will normally write programs in a high-level language. If the programmer is using Visual Basic the program will be translated by a Visual Basic translator. Similarly, a Python program will need a Python translator. There are two types of translator software for high-level languages: compiler and interpreter. The original high-level language program is called the source code.

Compiler

A compiler translates a source code program written in a high-level language into object (or machine) code. The original program is said to be 'compiled'.

1. The programmer writes the program code with **text editor** software
2. Load the compiler software with this source code
3. The compiler scans the code
4. Any **syntax errors** found?
5. If 'yes':

    The developer must make changes to the source code
    Go to Step 2
6. If 'no':

    Produce the machine code program file
7. The program has been successfully compiled and saved

The cycle is repeated until the compiler finds no errors and the final executable machine code file is produced.

Things to note about the compilation process are that once the machine code file has been produced, the compiler software is no longer needed and the source code program is no longer needed.

You can only run the program file after it has been successfully compiled and the machine code file produced.

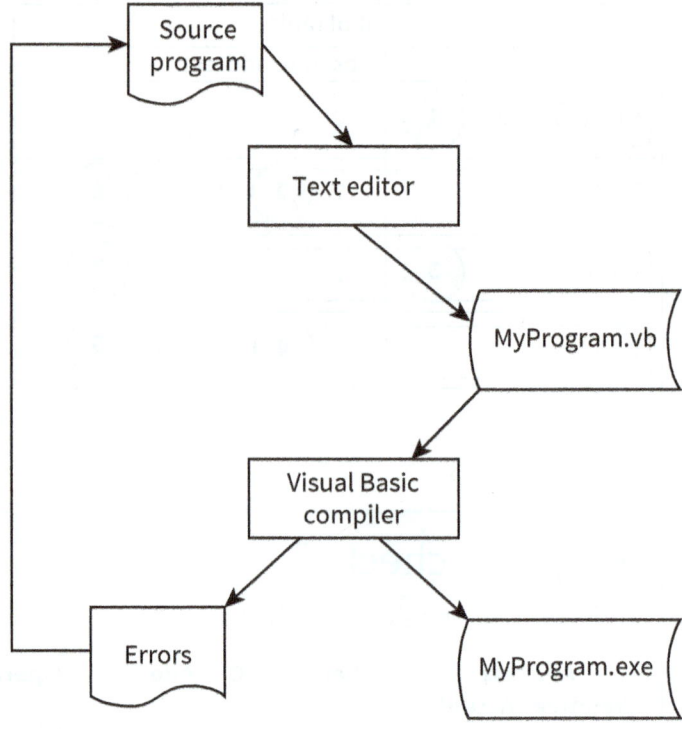

Figure 5.06 The compilation process.

Progress check D

The flowchart to show the assembly process would be similar to Figure **5.06**.

Draw the flowchart.

Interpreter

The process is entirely different to a compilation. The program is said to be 'interpreted'.

1. The interpreter analyses the next statement
2. if no **syntax errors:**
3. execute the statement
4. Go to Step 1
5. if an error was found in the statement:
6. Stop execution of the program

    Make changes to the source code

The interpreter looks at each program statement in turn. If it finds a syntax error, the program stops execution. If the statement has no error, it is executed and the interpreter moves on to the next statement.

Benefits and drawbacks of compilers/interpreters

Benefits of a compiler	
Compiler	Interpreter
Compiler creates object code, i.e. the executable file. Compiled programs will execute faster.	Interpreted code will execute slower as every statement has to be analysed before execution.
The compiler software is not needed at runtime.	The interpreter must be present in primary memory every time program execution is attempted.
Once compiled, no further translation is needed.	Every time the program is executed, it has to be interpreted.
If the program contains loops, a compiler will need to translate this section of code once only.	An interpreter must translate the statements in a loop on every iteration.

Table 5.03 Benefits of a compiler.

Benefits of an interpreter	
Compiler	Interpreter
	Makes for easier debugging.
The whole program must be completed before the code is compiled.	Allows an attempted execution of the program at any stage in its development.
Execution cannot be started until we have a successful compilation (of the entire source code).	Allows for testing of the parts of the program before all the code is written.

Table 5.04 Benefits of an interpreter.

Hybrid translation – Java

Java is a platform independent language, which means that you can run a Java program on any platform, hardware and operating system, without any modification.

Java uses a two-step translation process. Firstly, Java source code is compiled (using the javac compiler). This produces a form of intermediate code called 'bytecode'. Then this bytecode is executed by software called the Java Virtual Machine (JVM).

The current version of JVM uses a technique called Just-in-time (JIT) compilation to compile the bytecode to the native instructions understood by the CPU.

5.05 Features of an Integrated Development Environment (IDE)

The following illustrations are generated using the Visual Basic.NET IDE. You might prefer to wait until you have done some program coding in your chosen language before studying this section.

In section 5.04 where we studied translator software, the programmer used a text editor to create the program code and then a compiler or interpreter to translate the source code.

Modern software is available that allows all the stages of the program creation, translation and testing to be carried out by the same software. This software is called an **Integrated Development Environment (IDE)**.

The text editor

The text editor has features that help with the creation of the source code.

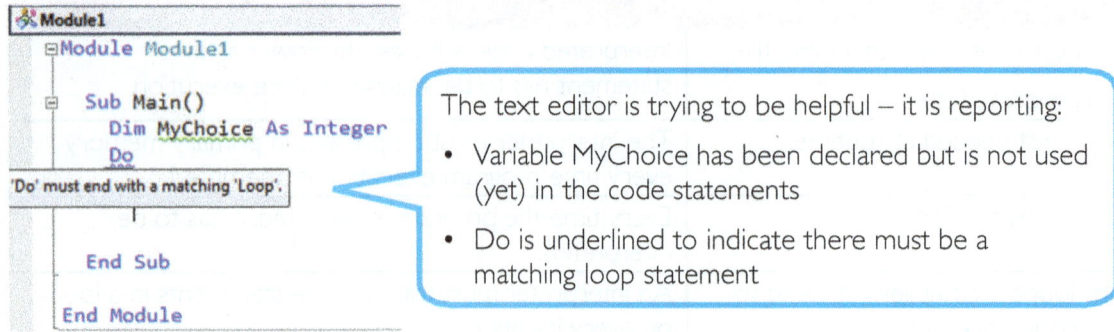

Figure 5.07 Matching syntax.

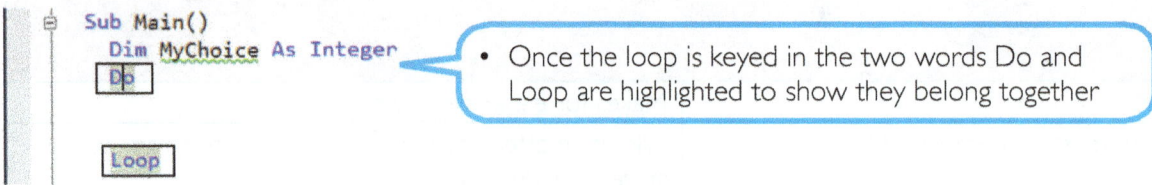

Figure 5.08 Matching blocks.

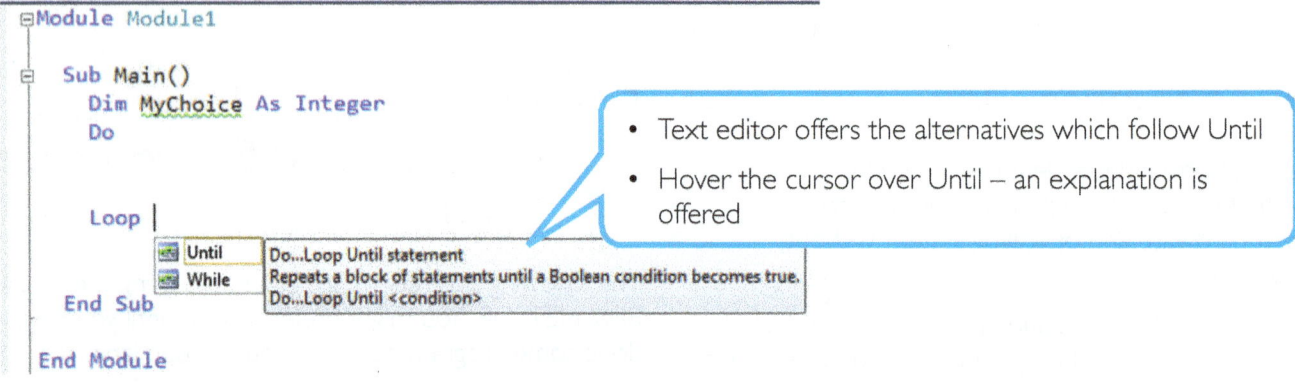

Figure 5.09 Context sensitive prompts.

These features are called context sensitive prompts.

```
Module Module1
   Sub Main()
      Dim MyChoice As Integer
      Do
         Call DisplayMenu()
         Console.Write("Choice ? ")
         MyChoice = Console.ReadLine
         If MyChoice = 1 Then Call MyProcedure1()
         If MyChoice = 2 the call MyProcedure2
      Loop Until MyChoice = 3
   End Sub
```

- The entire statement is underlined – 'Then' has been misspelt

Figure 5.10 Syntax check - Misspelt keyword.

Viewing the code

The editor has several **prettyprint** features that you can see in Figure 5.11. Language keywords are shown in blue. The text to be displayed as part of a `Console.Writeline` statement is shown in red.

Viewing part of the code

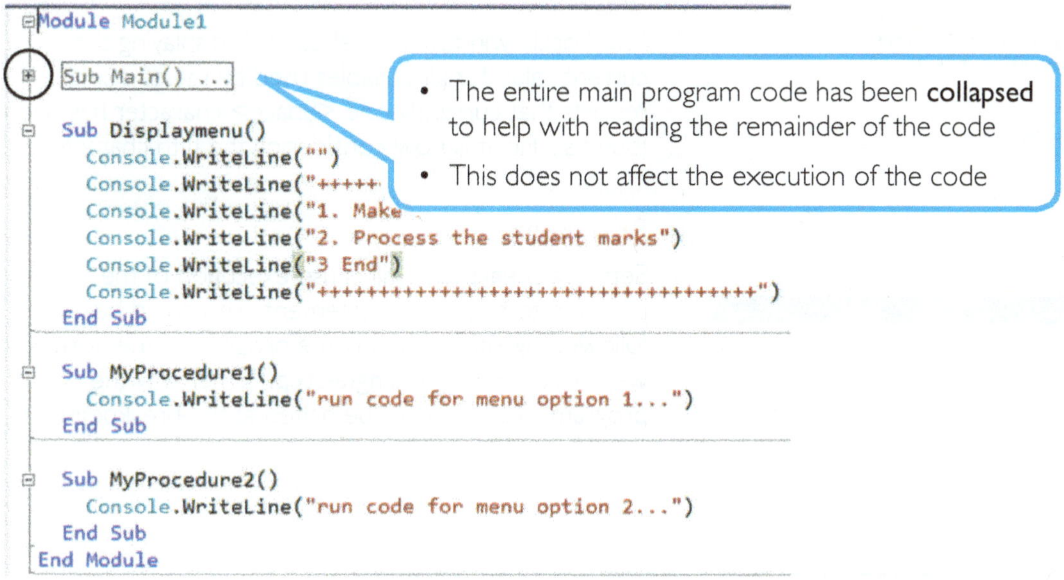

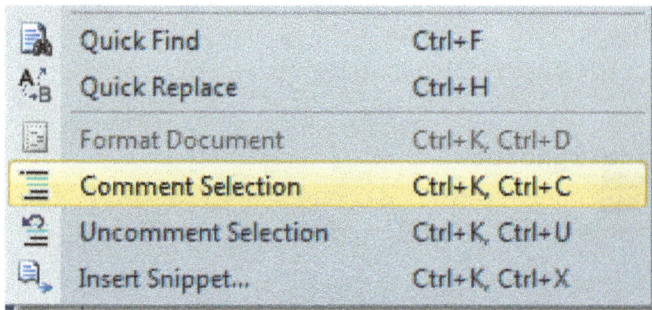

Figure 5.11 Collapsing blocks of code.

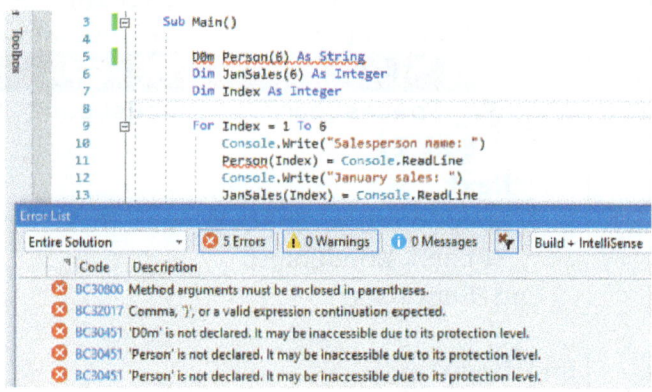

Figure 5.12 'Commenting out' statements.

The programmer may choose to 'Comment Out' a selection of the code. This way the code will not execute, as the selected statements are treated as comments (only).

Running the program

The user has attempted to run the program and it has been refused. This is because the user has spelt the keyword 'Dim' incorrectly and also, later in the code it also reports that the `Person` variable has not been declared.

Figure 5.13 Compile error – Syntax error.

Debugging features

The programmer is able to 'single-step' through the execution of the program.

```vb
Function CountWords(ThisString As String) As Integer
    Dim i As Integer
    Dim SpacesCount As Integer
    Dim WordCount As Integer
    SpacesCount = 0
    For i = 2 To Len(ThisString) - 1
        ' the first and last characters are ignored
        If Mid(ThisString, i, 1) = " " Then
            SpacesCount = SpacesCount + 1
        End If
    Next
    WordCount = SpacesCount + 1
    Return WordCount
End Function
```

Name	Value	Type
CountWords	0	Integer
i	5	Integer
SpacesCount	1	Integer
ThisString	"the royal family"	String
WordCount	0	Integer

Figure 5.14 Reporting the value of variables.

The screenshot shows the program part-way through its execution.

The highlighted line is the statement that has just been executed.

Reporting variables

The 'Locals' window (Visual Basic) is displaying the current value for all variables used by the code. It reports that currently one <Space> character has been found so far. It is now considering the fifth character.

Breakpoints

Setting a breakpoint will cause execution of the program to halt at this statement. This could be followed by either running the program in the normal way or continuing to **single-step**. Either way the program execution will be halted at the breakpoint.

```vb
Function CountWords(ThisString As String) As Integer
    Dim i As Integer
    Dim SpacesCount As Integer
    Dim WordCount As Integer
    SpacesCount = 0
    For i = 2 To Len(ThisString) - 1
        ' the first and last characters are ignored
        If Mid(ThisString, i, 1) = " " Then
            SpacesCount = SpacesCount + 1
        End If
    Next
    WordCount = SpacesCount + 1
    Return WordCount
End Function
```

Figure 5.15 Use of a breakpoint.

Report window

The user has set a breakpoint and is checking that the correct value for the expression `len(ThisString) - 1` is calculated as 13.

```
Function CountWords(ThisString As String) As Integer
    Dim i As Integer
    Dim SpacesCount As Integer
    Dim WordCount As Integer
    SpacesCount = 0
    For i = 2 To Len(ThisString) - 1
        ' the first and last characters are ignored
        If Mid(ThisString, i, 1) = " " Then
            SpacesCount = SpacesCount + 1
        End If
```

```
Immediate Window
? len(ThisString) - 1
13
```

```
file:///C:/___CUP Book/Section ...
text string ? united nations
```

Figure 5.16 Reporting the value of an expression.

This is the report window (Visual Basic.NET calls it the 'Immediate Window').

Past paper questions

1   A game program is written which can be either interpreted or compiled. The table shows five statements about the use of interpreters and compilers.

Tick (✓) to show whether the statement refers to an interpreter or to a compiler.

Statement	Interpreter	Compiler
This translator creates an executable file		
When this translator encounters a syntax error, game execution halts		
The translator analyses and checks each line just before executing it		
This translator will produce faster execution of the game program		
Use of this translator makes it more difficult for the user to modify the code of the game		

[5]

Cambridge International AS & A level Computer Science 9608 paper 11 Q11 November 2015

2 Three examples of language translators and four definitions are shown below.

   Draw lines to link each language translator to the correct one or more definitions.

   Language translator　　　　　　　　　　　　　**Definition**

   | Compiler |

   | Assembler |

   | Interpreter |

   - The software reads the source code and reports all errors. The software produces an executable file.
   - The software reads each statement and checks it before running it. The software halts when it encounters a syntax error.
   - The software translates a high-level language program into machine code for the processor to execute.
   - The software translates low-level statements into machine code for the processor to execute.

   [3]

Cambridge International AS & A level Computer Science 9608 paper 11 Q2b and c November 2016

3 a i   Explain why a computer needs an operating system. [2]

      ii Give two key management tasks carried out by an operating system. [2]

   b New program code is to be written in a high-level language. The use of Dynamic Link Library (DLL) files is considered in the design.

      Describe what is meant by a DLL file. [2]

Cambridge International AS & A level Computer Science 9608 paper 11 Q2 November 2016

4 A small company produces scientific magazines. The owner buys some new desktop computers. The computers are used to store thousands of colour images (diagrams and photographs). All the computers have internet access.

   Name three utility programs the company would use on all their computers. Describe what each program does.
   [6]

Cambridge International AS & A level Computer Science 9608 paper 11 Q7a November 2016

5 The program below is to be translated using a two-pass assembler.

The program now starts with a directive which tells the assembler to load the first instruction of the program to address 100.

Label		
	ORG	#0100
StartProg:	LDV	#CountDown
	CMP	Num1
	JNE	CarryOn
	JMP	Finish
CarryOn:	OUTCH	
	LDD	CountDown
	DEC	
	STO	CountDown
	JMP	StartProg
Finish:	LDM	#88
	OUTCH	
	END	
CountDown:		15
		32
		51
		67
Num1:		32

On the first pass of the two-pass process, the assembler adds entries to a symbol table.

The following symbol table shows the first eleven entries, part way through the first pass.

The circular labels show the order in which the assembler made the entries to the symbol table.

Symbol table

Symbolic address		Absolute address				
StartProg	(1)	100	(2)			
CountDown	(3)	UNKNOWN	(4)			
Num1	(5)	UNKNOWN	(6)			
CarryOn	(7)	~~UNKNOWN~~	(8)	104	(11)	
Finish	(9)	UNKNOWN	(10)			

Explain how the assembler made these entries to the symbol table. [3]

Cambridge International AS & A level Computer Science 9608 paper 11 Q4c November 2017

Chapter 6
Security, privacy and data integrity

Learning Objectives:

Data security:

- Explain the difference between the terms: security, privacy and integrity of data
- Understand the need for both security of the computer system and its data
- Describe security measures to protect a computer system
- Distinguish between measures which are suitable for a stand-alone and/or network system
- Describe threats resulting from the use of a network and the internet
- Describe measures used to restrict threats
- Describe measures to protect the security of data.

Data integrity:

- Distinguish between data verification and data validation
- List, describe and apply methods for data validation checks
- Describe data verification for data entry
- Describe data verification for data transfer.

6.01 Data security

You need to distinguish between threats to the entire computer system and threats to the information/data stored.

> **TIP**
> The terms security, privacy and integrity are often confused, so you need to take care with them.

> **TIP**
> Most of the issues that follow apply to both stand-alone and networked computer systems.

Security of the computer system

Also called 'cybersecurity'.

Security of computer systems is an ever-increasing issue as computer systems are increasingly complex.

Measures to protect security

User accounts

Access to the computer system should only be possible with a valid User ID (that is a user 'account') and the required password.

General authentication with passwords

Authentication means 'proving that you are who you say you are'.

A user who attempts to log on as user TonyP is insufficient for authentication as user IDs are generally public. If user TonyP is the only person with knowledge of his password, then use of the password establishes authentication and says, 'This must be TonyP.'

The company might have a minimum requirement as to what is acceptable as a password. Users must follow the company policy about the choosing and changing of passwords.

Here are some examples of password requirements:
- a password might have to consist of a mixture of upper case, lower case and digit characters
- be at least eight characters

- cannot be a password that has previously been used
- users are forced to change their password every (say) 30 days
- users are encouraged not to use 'memorable data' for their password, for example, their pet's name or birthday.

The computer system might generate a log of all user usage, record all unsuccessful attempts at logging-on and record attempted log-ons. In particular, the computer might record attempts to log-on at unusual times of the day, such as outside the normal working hours or at a terminal that the user is not permitted to use.

A security measure might be, for example, to disable the user account and/or terminal after (say) three wrong passwords have been entered.

General authentication using biometric techniques

The use of biometrics includes fingerprint scanning and retina scanning. Biometrics are used to access certain computers or rooms to establish the authenticity of the user.

General authentication using digital signatures

Digital signatures can be used when sending an email. The additional of a digital signature to an email establishes that the email was indeed sent from the proposed sender.

Terminal restrictions

On a network, access for users can be restricted to the use of certain terminals only. For example, call-centre staff are only authorised to log on from terminals in certain rooms.

The network OS could record any attempts by a user to log on at a terminal at which they do not have permission.

Firewalls

A **firewall** is a system designed to prevent unauthorised access to a **private network**. Firewalls can be implemented with either hardware or software, or a combination of both.

All messages entering or leaving a private network pass through the firewall. It examines each message and blocks those that do not meet security checks.

A firewall allows remote access to the private network through secure **authentication certificates** and logins.

A hardware firewall is typically found in a **broadband router**. A software firewall is installed on the computer and can be customised to set up the protection features required. A software firewall will protect your computer from outside attempts to control or gain access to the computer.

Network threats

Malware – virus

Viruses are clearly a threat to the computer system and/or data. A virus is a self-replicating program designed to do harm to the computer system.

Virus checking software was covered in Chapter 5, Section 5.01.

> **TIP**
>
> The use of digital signatures is covered again in Chapter 17, Section 17.04.

Malware – spyware

Spyware might or might not be malicious software. Spyware is introduced onto a computer without the knowledge of the user. The software will collect information about the use of the computer and relay this back to the originator. A common form of spyware is a 'key-logger' which records the sequence of key presses made by the user. For example, a malicious use would be the gathering of the keystrokes for a user's password.

Corporate spyware

An example of a non-malicious use of software is the installation of software by the company to monitor the work practice of the user. Checkout operators at a point-of-sale terminal in a supermarket could have their performance monitored.

Hackers

A hacker is a person who gains unauthorised access to a computer system with intent to either do harm to the system, for example, to shut the system down or to gather data from the system, for example, to gather the payment card data of customers.

Phishing

Phishing is the sending of an email to an individual with the appearance that it has come from a reputable company known to the recipient. The email will contain a link that directs the user to a bogus site designed to capture personal information that can later be fraudulently used.

Pharming

This is the practice of a user clicking on a link that has been tampered with to re-direct the user to a bogus site. If the user proceeds, they will enter data that is then captured and made available to the unintended recipient.

Pharming targets many users at the same time using the sending of bulk emails.

The security of data

Any of the techniques used to protect the computer system must also contribute to the protection of the data stored.

The techniques described below specifically safeguard data.

Encryption

The original data file has all the data bytes changed in some way by applying an **encryption algorithm**. The file is then transmitted to some recipient. The encrypted file is meaningless unless the receiver knows the decryption key (or cipher) and the encryption algorithm needed. The decryption key and algorithm can change the encrypted file back to its original state.

An example of this is: A text file has (say) 6 added to the ASCII value for each character.

The file starting with characters CPT2, etc. would be encrypted as IVZ8, etc. and unless the decryption key of 'take the ASCII value for each character and subtract 6' is known, it will be very difficult to decrypt the file.

This is a very simple example of encryption and one that would not be very robust in practice. The decryption could easily be worked out by trial and error or simply by an inspired guess.

Access rights to data: authorisation

The user has been **authorised** to use certain files/programs.

> **TIP**
>
> Do not confuse the terms 'authorisation' and 'authentication'. They are different.

There is an example of authorisation in Chapter 8, Figure **8.06**. It shows that different groups of users of a database, i.e. general public, junior clerk, manager, group manager, each have different access rights to certain files.

When working with database software, SQL commands are used to implement authorisation: user groups are created and each user group is then granted various **permissions**, for example, read only, read and write, etc, to certain features.

Password protection of files

Individual files can be password protected. Microsoft Office software can have a password set for access to a document, spreadsheet or database.

6.02 Data integrity

Integrity in everyday English means that a set of rules or standards are followed. In computing, **data integrity**. Data integrity is the maintenance of, and the assurance of the accuracy and consistency of, data over its entire life-cycle. Data integrity is a critical aspect to the design, implementation and usage of any system which stores, processes, or retrieves data.

Later when we study database design (Section 8), referential integrity is essential for preserving data integrity.

> **TIP**
>
> Do not use the word 'correct' to describe integrity. A data value can be sensible (that is it has integrity) but might be incorrect.
>
> For example, an employee workplace code could be stored as 'London' which is a valid code, but this employee's workplace is actually 'Paris'. So the data does not have data integrity, despite 'London' being a 'correct' data value.

Data validation

When data is input, validation checks can be made using software. The validation checks will be made with program code.

Check digit

An extra digit character is added to an important field, for example, an employee code.

Assume an employee code was 3675 and will have an extra calculated digit added to the right. This character is the check digit.

One method is as follows:

The original digits are multiplied by 'weights', for example, 1, 2, 3 or 4.

Employee code	Multiplier	Calculation
3	1	3
6	2	12
7	3	21
5	4	20
	Total:	56 / 11 gives remainder 1
	Check digit:	= 1

If the check digit is calculated as 10, then it is encoded as 'X'.

Therefore, the complete employee code above is: 3 6 7 5 X

The data entry software would know the calculation used for the check digit, and so can check the integrity of an employee code when it is entered.

Note that the checking software will never know what is wrong with the number, only that it must be an error.

> ### Progress check A
>
> The code 94372 is invalid.
>
> Using the algorithm shown above, what check digit would the software calculate for this employee code?

'From a list'

There is a list of data values. These are the only possible valid values.

An example of this is where the first two characters of a product code are always selected from the list:
EL: electrical
CO: consumables
HA: hardware

Range check

A number value must be within a certain range.

To illustrate this, suppose a program's main menu offers six choices: 1, 2, 3, 4 and 5, and 6 to exit. The number input by the user must be an integer in the range 1 to 6. Any other input from the user is invalid and will be refused.

Limit check

This is similar to a range check, but the allowed value must be less than an upper limiting value.

For example, a football team records its results. Each match is given a number. The team never plays more that 50 matches in a season.

Format check

A code follows a certain format.

An example of this is: All product codes start with a two upper case letters, followed by four digit characters.

For example: EL9623   is a valid product code

C8432 and   are invalid product codes
CK268

Length check

The length of the data value, i.e. the number of characters, is fixed.

In the above example, all product codes are exactly six characters.

Presence check

A field must contain a value. It cannot be left blank.

In Chapter 8 the SQL data definition language uses the syntax NOT NULL as part of the attribute definition. This means the data value cannot be left blank.

For example, when entering the data for a customer order, a product code must be present.

Uniqueness check

The data value for an attribute cannot be repeated for other records.

For example, all product codes in the products file must be different.

Existence check

The check is typically done to validate that a filename or an email address does exist.

Progress check B

A gym is to design a web form for application for membership.

These are some of the fields the applicant will complete:

- Family name
- Forenames
- Date of birth (members must be over aged 18 and under 80)
- Address
- Email address
- Membership type: A – Adult, J – Junior, S – Senior citizen
- Type of membership required (F – Full, L – Limited to certain times of the day)
- Number of times likely to visit the gym in any one week
- Have you been a member of a gym before?

Consider validation checks that could be used for data capture on the web form.

Draw up a table as shown in Table 6.01 and tick any appropriate checks for each attribute.

Attribute	From a list	Range	Format	Length	Presence	Check digit
Family Name						
Forenames						
DateOfBirth						
Address						
Email						
MemType						
NoOfVisits						
Before						

Table 6.01 Validation checks summary.

Tools for data entry and validation

The user enters data by typing in characters at the keyboard or making selections from a list provided.

The program constructs web forms by using standard controls, for example, using a text box for text entry, making a single selection from a group of radio buttons, making one or more selections from a group of check boxes and making a single selection from a drop-down list.

The choice of what controls to use for what data value is an important design consideration for the form. These controls can be programmed to carry out data validation. Check boxes and radio buttons will show the list of permitted values only on the form. Drop-down lists when selected, only display the list of permitted values. Text boxes will be used, where a length check, of (say) exactly 6 characters is made when the user tries to submit the data. A second check may be made to check for a particular format only, for example, all upper-case characters and no punctuation characters.

Data verification for data entry

A visual check can be made. The task is to key in the information of the new gym member's paper form to a web-form on the computer.

We key in the customer name, pause to read the characters from the screen, and compare with the name on the document.

We have carried out a **visual check**, and this is the simplest form of data verification.

We can use **double entry**. Verification here means the user will have to enter the data value twice. For double entry, the user keys in the data value, the software blanks out the first entry, the software asks the user to key in the customer name a second time, it checks if the two entries match and, if not, the user is asked to start again.

> **Progress check C**
>
> Where have you been asked to carry out double entry data verification?

Data verification during data transfer

In Chapter 5 we used the term 'verification' when describing making a backup copy of files.

The backup process does a verification check between the original data and the copy made. The contents of the two files are checked byte-by-byte to check that they match exactly.

Parity check

Parity is a check on the validity of individual characters codes in a file when it is read/written.

For example, all ASCII codes have a seven-digit code to represent a character.

'A' is coded as 65 denary, i.e. $100\ 0001_2$.

But all computers store data in 8 bits, i.e. a byte.

So, an 8th bit is added to the 7-bit ASCII code at the most significant end.

This extra bit can be used to check the validity of the byte. The bit is called the **parity bit**.

The system will work on either **even parity** or **odd parity**.

Assume for the following example that odd parity is used. This means the total number of '1' bits must be an odd number (1 or 3 or 5 or 7).

For character 'A' above, the parity bit is 1, making the complete code 1100 0001.

The inclusion of the '1' parity bit makes the total number of '1' bits in the byte an odd number (in this case 3).

Assume bit 3 had been corrupted and the data was sent as 1100 1001, then the 'odd parity system' would know that this code must be in error, as it has an even number (4) of '1' bits.

A **parity block check** can be used. For this, a parity check can be made on a *group* of bytes transmitted in sequence.

A parity block is calculated from a rectangle made up of rows for each data byte. Another parity check is made on each column and stored in a **parity byte**, shown in the diagram in the final row.

An example of this is: There are four data bytes, followed by a parity byte.

1	1	0	0	1	1	0	1
0	0	1	0	0	0	0	0
1	0	1	1	1	1	0	0
1	1	0	0	0	0	1	0
0	1	1	0	1	1	0	0

Parity byte

Figure 6.01 Data bytes and parity byte.

> **Progress check C**
>
> Study Figure **6.01** and explain how to check: the final column of parity bits and the bit values in the parity byte.

Case 1: Assume that there was an error in the bytes transmitted. The error is the bit marked in Figure **6.02**.

1	1	0	0	1	1	0	1
0	0	1	0	0	0	0	0
1	0	**0**	1	1	1	0	0
1	1	0	0	0	0	1	0
0	1	1	0	1	1	0	0

Column 3 has an error
– using odd parity, the parity block bit should be 0

Figure 6.02 Parity block with a single error.

This error will mean the receiving software calculates the parity bit for this byte as 1, but it was received as a zero. So there must be an error. Also, the parity byte calculation will show an error in the third column. The software can therefore conclude that the error must be the highlighted bit and so will change this from the received 0 to a 1.

Progress check D

A data transfer sends four data bytes followed by a parity byte. The system uses even parity.

0	0	0	0	1	1	1	1
1	1	1	0	0	0	0	0
1	0	1	1	0	0	0	1
0	1	1	1	1	0	0	0
0	0	1	1	0	1	1	0

Figure 6.04 Parity block.

Circle the bit errors which have occurred when the above five bytes are received.

Will the receiving software be able to identify where the error(s) occurred?

Case 2: Two of the bits received from one of the data bytes were in error: Figure **6.03**.

1	1	0	0	1	1	0	1
0	0	1	0	0	0	0	0
1	0	1	**0**	1	1	0	**1**
1	1	0	0	0	0	1	0
0	1	1	0	1	1	0	0

Odd parity is being used

There is an error in columns 4 and 8

The total number of 1 bits is (0 and 2) which is even.

Figure 6.03 Parity block with two errors.

Byte 3 passes the parity check for the byte, but the issue is that it is the parity bit itself that is one of the errors.

The parity byte will show that there is an error in columns 4 and 8, as in both these columns the column check is showing an even number of '1' bits.

Checksum check

A checksum is a validation check used when data is transmitted. A checksum check is carried out on a complete block of data within a file, when it is read/written.

In Chapter 3 we studied the construction of a hard disk. Data is stored as blocks. A block could be made up of 1024 continuous bytes. The final byte contains the checksum. Each byte in the block could be interpreted as a number (even though in fact it could typically be a byte from a sound file…).

The checksum figure is calculated as the total of the number values of the previous 1023 bytes. This checksum number is stored as the final byte in the block.

When the data block is read/written, the checksum figure is calculated by the communications software. This calculated number is compared with the stored checksum value in the final byte. If they do not match, then a 'file read/write' error will be reported.

Worked example

Consider the following simplified example where a block is made up of 8 bytes – Byte 7 stores the checksum.

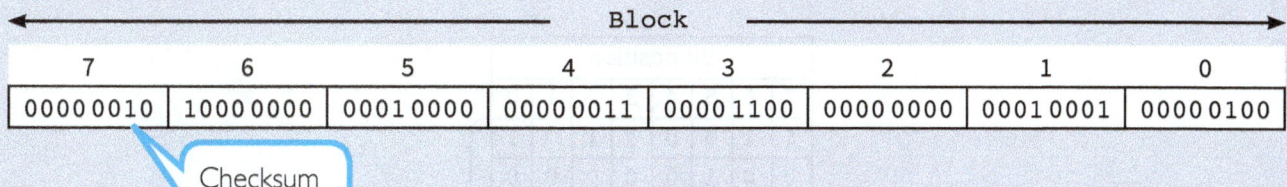

This block of data from the file is read to primary memory from the disk.

Checksum calculation:

Byte number	6	5	4	3	2	1	0	Total
Number	128	16	3	12	0	17	4	180
								1011 0100

Checksum byte: 1011 0100 which matches with the calculated checksum value.

Conclusion: The block of data has been successfully read with no errors.

Past paper questions

1. a Give a brief description of the terms validation and verification. [2]

   b Data are to be transferred between two devices. Parity checks are carried out on the data.

   Explain what is meant by a parity check. Give an example to illustrate your answer. [4]

Cambridge International AS & A level Computer Science 9608 paper 11 Q9 November 2015

2. a Explain the term computer virus. [2]

   b A virus checker has been installed on a PC.

   Give two examples of when a virus checker should perform a check. [2]

Cambridge International AS & A level Computer Science 9608 paper 11 Q10 November 2015

3. Employees using some new computers receive training. At the end of the training, each employee completes a series of questions.

   Three answers given by an employee are shown below.

   Explain why each answer is incorrect.

   a 'Encryption prevents hackers breaking into the company's computers.' [2]

   b 'Data validation is used to make sure that data keyed in are the same as the original data supplied.' [2]

   c 'The use of passwords will always prevent unauthorised access to the data stored on the computers.' [2]

Cambridge International AS & A level Computer Science 9608 paper 11 Q7c November 2016

4   A computer receives data from a remote data logger. Each data block is a group of 8 bytes. A block is made up of seven data bytes and a parity byte.

Each data byte has a parity bit using odd parity. The parity byte also uses odd parity. The following table shows a data block before transmission. Bit position 0 is the parity bit.

Bit position							
7	6	5	4	3	2	1	0
1	1	0	0	1	1	0	1
0	0	1	0	0	0	0	0
1	0	0	1	1	1	0	A
1	1	0	0	0	0	1	0
1	1	0	0	0	0	1	0
1	1	0	0	0	1	1	B
0	0	0	0	0	0	0	0
0	1	1	0	1	1	0	0

Data bytes (rows 1–7) ← Parity byte (row 8)

a   i   Describe how the data logger calculates the parity bit for each of the bytes in the data block.   [2]

ii   State the two missing parity bits labelled A and B.

iii Describe how the computer uses the parity byte to perform a further check on the received data bytes.   [2]

Cambridge International AS & A level Computer Science 9608 paper 11 Q5(a) June 2017

Ethics and ownership

Chapter 7

> **Learning Objectives:**
> - Understand the need for ethical behaviour as a computing professional
> - Understand the need for ethical behaviour in a given workplace situation
> - Understand the purpose of copyright legislation
> - Understand the different types of software licensing
> - Free Software Foundation, Open Source Initiative, shareware and commercial software
> - Show understanding of artificial intelligence (AI).

7.01 Ethics

The term ethics is not restricted to computing and the use of computers.

Ethics are the moral principles that guide a person's behaviour.

In our context this is ethics that applies to the computing workplace. Employers will draw up a Code of Conduct about what behaviour is expected. Some of these will have a moral dimension. Others will amount to little more than common sense guidelines about the way the employees behave.

Ethics and the role of the computing professional

Computers have an all-pervading role in industry, government, medicine, education, entertainment and society at large.

Computing professionals are involved at all stages of a project: the analysis, specification, design, development, maintenance and testing of software systems.

Because of their roles in developing software systems, software engineers have significant opportunities to do good, cause harm or to influence others. Software engineers must commit themselves to making software engineering a beneficial and respected profession.

BCS Code of Conduct

Computer professionals are encouraged to join a professional body. There are two professional bodies: The British Computer Society (BCS) – also known as the Chartered Institute for IT – and The Institute of Electrical and Electronic Engineers (IEEE).

Becoming a member of a professional body requires you to follow a code of conduct expected by the organisation. This will be summarised in a formal document that you must sign.

The British Computer Society has a published code of conduct that includes individual responsibilities in the workplace, guidelines for the use of the internet in the workplace, guidelines for the use of use of internal and external email, what is considered misuse of equipment and other resources, what is considered unacceptable behaviour and rules about the use of sensitive data.

An employee who does not adhere to these guidelines could expect disciplinary action. Some behaviour and actions could be the subject of legal action.

The code of conduct contains eight principles related to the behaviour its members. These principles identify the ethical framework in which individuals and groups operate.

The list of eight principle headings will impact on all aspects of the developer's work irrespective of their precise job role.

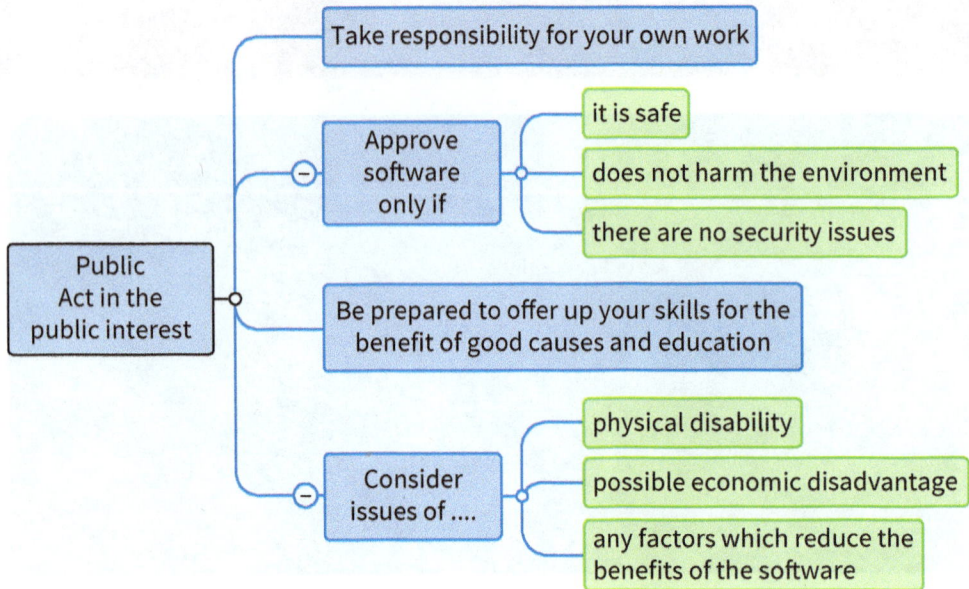

Figure 7.01 IEEE ethics principles – Responsibility to the public.

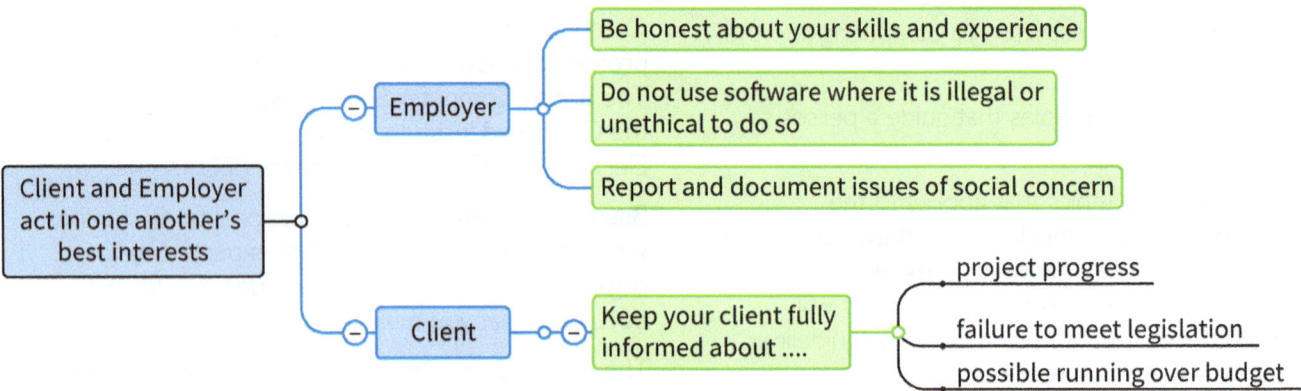

Figure 7.02 IEEE ethics principles – Responsibility to the Client and Employer.

Figure 7.03 IEEE ethics principles – Other six principles.

The expansion boxes illustrate some specific actions/safeguards to be implemented.

Typical software-developer workplace-scenarios

Much of software design and coding is done as teamwork where each member of the team will have a collective responsibility to other team members. This includes the sharing of expertise and the recognition of the contribution made by other team members to the team's work.

The analyst will need to spend a considerable amount of time in the client's workplace and should be respectful of rules and procedures that are in place for the client's employees.

> ### Progress check A
> Business A is a software house that is developing software for Business B. It is expected to take six months to develop and install.
>
> List a number of ethical issues the Manager at Business A should consider when communicating with Business B.

7.02 Software licensing

A licence defines the rights and obligations that the author of the software grants to the licensee. The granting of a licence does not assume that a charge has been made for the software.

When you buy a commercial software package you are not buying the software; you are buying the right to use the software. The software company owns the software.

Free Software Foundation (FSF)

'Free' is not intended to mean 'free of charge'. The philosophy of the organisation is that 'free' means the user of the software is free to run the software, copy the software, distribute the software to other users and study the code and change and improve the software. The user is encouraged to make their improvements available to other users and this might be a condition of the licence.

The philosophy is designed to encourage a programmer/developer community.

The flagship software of the FSF is GNU, a Unix-like operating system. GNU is a collection of many programs; applications, libraries, developer tools and games. The program is a Unix-like operating system that allocates machine resources. GNU is typically used with a kernel, called Linux. This combination is the GNU/Linux operating system. GNU/Linux is used by millions, though many just call it 'Linux'.

The name 'GNU' is a recursive acronym for 'GNU's Not Unix'. GNU is pronounced as one syllable: g'noo.

Open Source Initiative

An open source licence grants the right to copy, modify and redistribute the source code.

These licences might also impose obligations. These obligations might be that modifications to the code that are distributed must be made available in source code form or that an author attribution must be made in documentation for the open source code.

The Open Source Software Institute is a membership-based, non-profit organisation.

Organisations involved in OSS development include the WordPress Foundation (WordPress), the Apache Software Foundation (OpenOffice and Apache web server), the Linux Foundation (Linux OS) and the Mozilla Foundation (Firefox web browser).

There are advantages and disadvantages with the use of open source software.

The advantages are (1) that start up costs of adopting the software are nil, (2) that there is no supplier lock-in, (3) that you have the freedom to do what you want with the software, (4) that there are open standards that support and encourage collaborative development and (5) that there is simplified licensing where there are a large number of users of the software.

The disadvantages are that it might be difficult to get support and that some proprietary formats such as Microsoft's .doc, .docx, xls and xlsx file formats are so widely used that other formats might be less acceptable for business.

Shareware

Shareware is software that is distributed free usually on a trial basis and often with the understanding that the user might need to pay for it later. Some software developers offer a shareware version of their program with a built-in expiry date: for example, after 30 days the user can no longer get access to the program.

Other shareware (sometimes called 'liteware') is offered with certain capabilities disabled as an inducement to buy the complete version of the program at a later date.

Commercial software

Software is purchased for business under an end-user licence agreement. The licence sets out how the software can be used.

The agreement will usually prohibit certain things such as making unauthorised copies of the software and passing them on, selling your licence to someone else, using it on more than a certain number of computers and attempting to **reverse engineer** the code.

Commercial software is sold without access to the source code. The intention is that, without this code, neither you nor any other software supplier can make changes to the software package.

Commercial software is made available under a number of different types of licence. 'Shrink-wrap' licences are usually for one installation of the software, i.e. 'off-the-shelf' software purchased either online or from a retail store. 'Per-user' licences are common where software might be in use by more than one user simultaneously. The licence is for a specified maximum number of users. 'Site licences' are much less restrictive. They allow an unlimited number of users from the same organisation to use the software.

Some licences terms might require software activation. This allows the supplier to check that the software is installed on just one PC. Re-activation will be required if the software is installed on a different PC.

> ### Progress check B
> A software licence from The Free Foundation makes the recipient at liberty (or 'free') to do what?

Copyright law

In the UK there is legislation regarding the use of material on the internet. It is subject to similar copyright conditions as for other types of media, for example, printed material such as newspapers, magazines and books.

It is recommended that only a single copy of material is downloaded, the copy is erased when the purpose for which it has been made has ended and consent of the copyright holder should be sought for any large scale use of material.

If material is to be put in a report where evidence is to be presented that was produced by someone else, the permission of the copyright holder must be sought and full acknowledgement given to the source.

In recent years, the software industry has taken determined action to protect its rights. In the UK, the Federation Against Software Theft (FAST) has undertaken a number of successful legal actions.

7.03 Artificial intelligence (AI)

Artificial intelligence (AI) is not new. Artificial intelligence is a branch of computer science that aims to create intelligent machines. It has become an important part of the technology industry.

We could all make a list of the human traits that we consider contribute to intelligence, for example, visual-spatial awareness, creativity, inter-personal skills, linguistic, logical, seeing relationships, learning and many others.

Artificial intelligence for the computer is much more than being able to simulate human behaviour.

While definitions of AI have been around since the 1960s and are ever changing, there is general agreement that the attempted definitions are concerned with performance that is measured in comparison either to human performance or to some ideal performance, called rationality or 'doing the right thing'.

Definitions are also are either concerned with human thought processes/reasoning or with the behaviour of the system.

Many applications in use today are powered by AI:

- music recommendations made to me from my music streaming applications, such as Apple Music or Spotify
- the identification of email spam
- Google translation
- the voice-controlled home 'intelligent assistant' such as Amazon's Alexa or Apple's Siri
- driverless cars and drones

High-frequency trading by machines has replaced much of the decision-making by human traders.

Research associated with artificial intelligence is highly technical and specialised. Imitating the human traits of 'common sense', reasoning and problem-solving is difficult and some of these traits are difficult to imitate in machines. Some, however are possible based on the availability of previous data. A music streaming service can record what genre of music I play frequently and what artists. Recommendations then would seem to be based on 'more of the same'.

Two factors have fuelled recent interest in AI. One of these is the explosion in the availability of vast amounts of data, '**big data**' and in particular data about persons and their behaviour. The other is the widespread availability of increased computing power to process this data.

This claim is from Eric Schmit, the former Chairman of Google, at a conference in 2010:

'We have had an explosion in data. Every two days now we create as much information as we did from the dawn of civilization up until 2003'.

Knowledge engineering is a core part of AI research. Machines can often act and react like humans, but only if they have abundant information relating to the world. Artificial intelligence must have access to objects, categories, properties and relations between all of them to implement knowledge engineering. Knowledge engineering has evolved through the development of programming languages such as Lisp and Prolog and their availability to reason from given facts and rules. Applications called 'Expert Systems' are also long-established.

Applications of AI

Activities for which artificial intelligence is designed include:
- Speech recognition
- Learning
  - AI can provide the tools for more individualised and tailored learning. If software were able to record a student's performance in some on-screen exercise, then the future sessions could be tailored based on their previous responses.
- Healthcare
  - today, hundreds of people die daily simply because of a wrong diagnosis. Using AI, a diagnosis can be made which is more accurate than a health professional
  - For example, deep learning (discussed in Chapter 18) is already on its way to analysing irregular heart rhythms from an ECG better than a cardiologist
  - Google's AI algorithm recently identified diabetic blindness slightly better than an ophthalmologist
  - trends in epidemics, due to 'big data', can be mapped and predicted
- Robotics
  - Robots require intelligence to handle tasks such navigation and the manipulation of an object
- Climate change
  - For example, using AI to control street traffic lights can help reduce car emissions
  - Power usage can be optimised and regulated based on demand
  - Supplementing computer vision with AI can map the Earth's surface to track deforestation, predict water shortages, and warn about other geographical changes and make natural disaster predictions

  Home energy efficiency with a 'smart home manager' installed

- Military applications
  - In the U.S., President Donald Trump is suggesting a 'Space Force' to assure American dominance in space, using AI.

The impact of AI – Social, economic and environmental

The use of automated machines that are computer controlled has been widespread for over 30 years. Robotics is a major area for the manufacturing industries. When they were introduced, there was a heated debate about what would be their social impact. Would they result in job losses? Would they create a different category of jobs?

The same debate is now being heard about AI.

As AI technologies become more widespread and in everyday use, it raises concerns about possible negative impacts on jobs, personal privacy and the economy. A pessimistic forecast from experts is that 'about half of our jobs will be taken over by automation and robotics within the next 15 years'.

In medicine, not only will diagnosis become increasingly accurate, but also the accessibility of these AI enabled devices more accessible.

The all-pervasive nature of AI enabled machines means they will have a high social impact.

The climate change initiatives clearly will have an environmental impact.

By offering new software tools for entrepreneurs, AI might also create new lines of business that we can't predict at present.

The examples stated at the start of the section tell us we are already interacting with AI as an everyday activity.

The possibilities of AI are endless. Its future will be created by us, and it will influence the choices we make and the actions we take. AI technology has the potential to become the most influential human innovation in history.

Hence, there should always be appropriate safeguards in place to ensure that AI systems are intentional, intelligent, and adaptable without sacrificing the important qualities that define us as humans.

Past paper questions

1. Raj has joined a software company as a trainee programmer. He was given the company's Code of Conduct document during his induction training. The handbook has a section headed 'Ethical Behaviour'.

    a   Describe what is meant by ethics. [2]

    b   Raj is assigned to work as a new member of a development team.

    In his first week, Raj feels uncomfortable working with one of his colleagues. He is unfamiliar with the programming language used by the team. Next week he will be working on one of the company's clients with a colleague. Raj is very nervous about working in an unfamiliar workplace.

    Raj has a review with his manager after his first three weeks.

    The Code of Conduct document was produced by the Human Resources section. It closely follows the ACM/IEEE Software Engineering Code of Ethics that uses these eight key principles:

Public	Client and Employer	Product	Judgement
Management	Profession	Colleagues	Self

    There are issues Raj will want to raise with his manager.

    - Describe two of these issues.
    - State the key ACM/IEEE principle this comes under.
    - Suggest what action should be taken to demonstrate ethical behaviour.

    Cambridge International AS & A level Computer Science 9608 paper 11 Q6 November 2017

2. A team of software engineers is developing a new e-commerce program for a client. State three of the principles of the ACM/IEEE Software Engineering Code of Ethics. Illustrate each one, with an example, describing how it will influence their working practices. [6]

    Cambridge International AS & A level Computer Science 9608 paper 11 Q6 June 2016

Chapter 8: Databases

Learning Objectives:

Database concepts:

- Describe the limitations of files for data storage
- Describe the benefits of using a relational database
- Use the relational database terminology
- Produce a data model from a given specification
- Draw an entity-relationship diagram to document the model
- Demonstrate understanding of the normalisation process
  - Explain why a given design may/may not be in third-normal form
  - Produce an amended design to change it from unnormalised to a normalised solution.

Database Management System (DBMS):

- Show understanding of the features provided by DBMS software
- Describe the software tools found within DBMS software.

Data Definition Language (DDL) and Data Manipulation Language (DML):

- Understand and use the SQL commands for the DDL
  - Create a database: CREATE DATABASE
  - Create a table: CREATE TABLE
  - Change a table definition: ALTER TABLE
  - Add a primay key to a table: PRIMARY KEY
  - add a foreign key to a table: FOREIGN KEY
- Understand the data types available in SQL and apply these for a given database design
  - CHARACTER, VAR, BOOLEAN, INTEGER, REAL, DATE, TIME
- Write SQL scripts for queries where data is stored in at most two tables using the syntax:
  - SELECT, FROM, WHERE, ORDER BY, GROUP BY, INNER JOIN, SUM, COUNT, AVG
- Write SQL scripts to modify data:
  - add a record: INSERT INTO
  - update a record: UPDATE
  - delete a record: DELETE FROM.

8.01 Database concepts

File based approach

Before the development of database software, a database application would have been programmed and constructed using one or more flat files.

First, the record structure is designed. For example, for a customer database the **fields** would be customer name, contact person, address, town and account customer? (Yes/No).

A major limitation of using flat files is that the **record structure** is fixed.

Consider if after using the file for some time, we then wanted to add another field. This would require a lot of work. The file would have to be re-designed and the program code would need to be amended to access the file.

Relational database

Relational database software is based on the concepts that data will not be duplicated and the data design will be stored separately from the programs that access the data.

Program - Data independence

The database software stores not only the data itself but also a definition of the database(s) in a **data dictionary**. **Program-data independence** is the separating out of the data definition (as accessed by application programs) from the programs that access the data.

8.02 Relational databases

The terminology

Some 'thing' about which data is recorded, for example, a customer, a product, an order, is referred to as an **entity**.

A **Table** is the implementation of the data for an entity using relational database software.

A **Tuple** is the data for one row in a table.

An **Attribute** is one of the data items about which data is recorded, for example, a customer table could include the three attributes customer name, address and town.

A **Data dictionary** is a feature of database software. It contains a description of all the tables, queries and reports that make up the database design.

Primary key

It is a fundamental rule of relational database design that every tuple in a table must be unique. This can be that there is an attribute that will 'do this job' for us. For example, for the `CUSTOMER` table, all of the customer names are different, so use `CustomerName` as the primary key for the `CUSTOMER`.

Alternatively, we could add a reference number attribute to ensure that all of the tuples are different. For example, `ProductID` is the primary key for the table `PRODUCT` and `OrderNo` is the primary key for table `ORDER`.

Note that there could be more than one attribute that would act as the primary key. Each of these attributes is said to be a **candidate key**, i.e. a contender for the primary key.

Table notation

The following notation describes three table designs. The attribute underlined indicates the primary key.

CUSTOMER(<u>CustomerName</u>, CustomerAddress, CustomerTown, ContactPerson, AccountCustomer)

PRODUCT(<u>ProductID</u>, Description, TypeOfItem, RetailPrice, InStock)

ORDER(<u>OrderNo</u>, OrderDate, CustomerName, ProductID, Quantity)

Secondary key and indexing

Indexing is used to make data retrieval faster.

Part of the table design process will be to decide which attributes need to be indexed. For example, if we frequently search for a customer name, good design would be to index the customer name attribute.

Any attribute that is indexed (and is not the primary key) is called a **secondary key**.

For example, in the `ORDER` table we frequently search on customer name, but not the quantity. Hence we should index the `CustomerName` attribute. `OrderNo` is the primary key and so this attribute is already indexed.

The database software updates the list of indexes every time the data in the order table is changed.

A table can have any number of secondary keys, but every index has to be updated when the database data changes. The updating of the indexing data will take a lot of processing time, so there is a trade-off between the processing and time taken to keep the indexes up-to-date. You should also consider the fast data retrieval times (for example, when running a query) that indexing provides.

> ### Progress check A
>
> You are designing a table to store student data for a school admin system.
>
> The table will include the following attributes:
>
> `StudentNumber, StudentName, Form, Address, YearEntered`
>
> a   Which attribute(s) will be the primary key(s)?
>
> b   Suggest one attribute that should be set up as a secondary index. Explain your choice.

Relationships

A link between two tables is called a **relationship**.

Relationships are of three kinds:

- 1-to-1: which are rare and exist probably only because the two tables were created at different times
- 1-to-many: the most common type of relationship

Note: The two relationships for this order processing scenario are both 1-to-many.

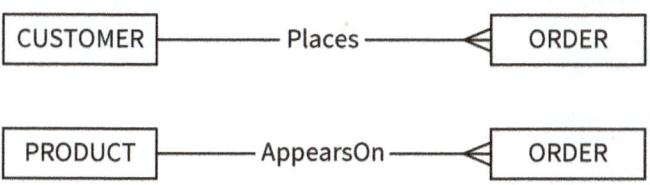

Figure 8.01 Two 1-to-many relationships.

- Many-to-Many: We could have added a third relationship to our E-R diagram which shows:

    'Many customers will purchase many products'.

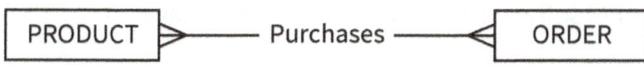

Figure 8.02 A many-to-many relationship.

> **TIP**
>
> It is not possible to directly implement a many-to-many relationship with relational database software. A relationship stated as many-to-many is always implemented with an intermediary table and then two one-to-many relationships from the original tables.

If the designer has started with this many-to-many relationship, the strategy must be to re-design by introducing the third table ORDER with two 1-to-many relationships (as shown in Figure **8.01**).

Foreign key

How are relationships formed?

The primary key attribute in the 'one side' table will link to (the same) attribute in the 'many side' table. This attribute in the 'many side' table is called the **foreign key**.

In our order-processing data table, over a period of time, one customer will place many orders.

Primary key `CustomerName` (in the `CUSTOMER` table) will link to foreign key `CustomerName` (in the `ORDER` table).

Many customers will order the same product from the company, so one product is present on many orders.

Primary key `ProductID` (in the `PRODUCT` table) links to foreign key `ProductID` (in the `ORDER` table).

Referential integrity

The data stored in the tables must obey all of the relationships that exist.

For example, referential integrity would be violated if there were a customer name in one of the `ORDER` table tuples that was not present in the `CUSTOMER` table.

> **Progress check B**
>
> What would cause referential integrity to be violated between the `PRODUCT` and `ORDER` tables?

Entity-relationship (E-R) diagram

The entities and the **relationships** can be shown on an entity-relationship diagram.

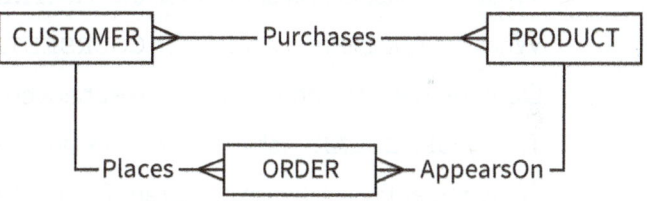

Figure 8.03 E-R diagram with all relationships.

The entities have a name. The relationship line shows the **degree of the relationship**. Each relationship has a name, i.e. 'Places', 'AppearsOn', 'Purchases'.

> **TIP**
>
> Some designers will show each relationship as a separate E-R diagram. We did this earlier in Figure **8.01** and Figure **8.02**.

Progress check C

Consider this scenario:

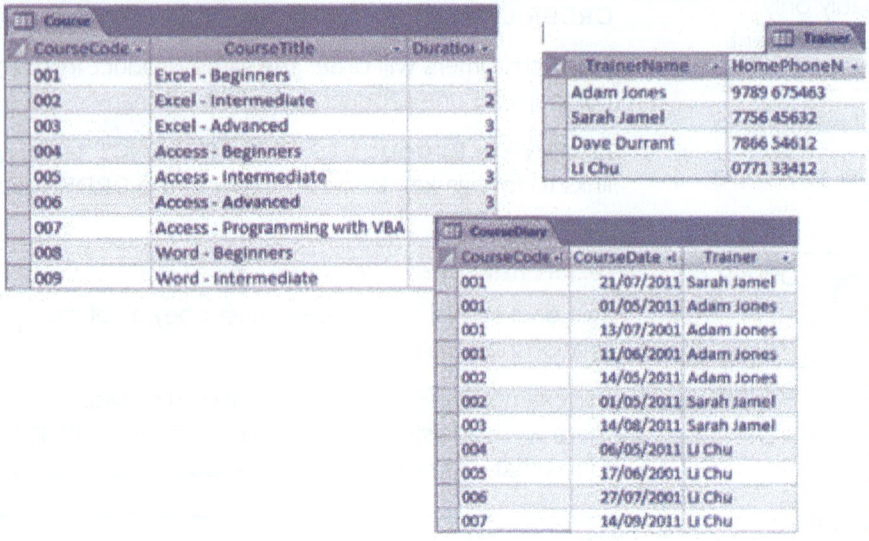

Figure 8.04 Training courses scenario.

A training agency offers courses in software skills for popular PC software. Courses run for 1 to 5 days.

Each course is delivered by one trainer. Courses offered are shown in table `Course`. Each course is available many times throughout the year and this course schedule data is stored in table `COURSEDIARY`.

a   What attribute is used for the primary key of table `COURSE`?

b   Suggest two other attributes which the company might store about each trainer.

c   What is a suitable primary key for the `TRAINER` table?

d   What is a suitable primary key for `COURSEDIARY`?

e   Describe two relationships which exist between the tables `TRAINER`, `COURSE` and `COURSEDIARY`.

f   The `COURSEDIARY` table has two foreign keys. What are they?

g   Draw the entity-relationship diagram for this scenario.

Normalisation process

When designing the database tables/relationships, we must ask the question; 'How do we know we have a design that will not result in **duplicated data**?'

There is a **normalisation** process in which there are three formal rules, called First, Second and Third Normal form (1NF, 2NF and 3NF) that are used to check the design.

A fully normalised set of tables will contain no **redundant data**.

Consider the PROGRESS CHECK C scenario:

A firm encourages its staff to attend training courses. Each course has a unique course title and duration from 1 to 5 days. Some courses are offered more than once on different dates.

Employees have a `StaffID` and their name recorded. Data is recorded showing all courses attended by each employee.

First Normal Form (1NF)

1NF states that '**There should be no repeated groups of attributes**'.

STAFF(<u>StaffID</u>, StaffName, CourseTitle1, Date1, Duration1,
    CourseTitle2, Date2, Duration2, CourseTitle3, Date3, Duration3, etc.)

StaffID	StaffName	CourseTitle	SessionDate	Duration
037	Polly Searle	Managing People	12/03/2022	2
		Health and Safety 1	19/04/2022	1
		Health and Safety 2	23/12/2022	2
067	Will Harris	Health and Safety 1	19/04/2022	1
		Excel Stage 1	03/03/2022	2
184	Neal King	Marketing Stage 1	05/06/2022	2
		Excel Stage 1	03/03/2022	2
		Customer Care	10/05/2022	1

Table 8.01 STAFF table design – Not 1NF.

This table design has the group of attributes; CourseTitle, Date and Duration repeated, and so the table is NOT in 1NF.

Some designs will illustrate this with a diagram that shows the course attendances being repeated for a single employee.

Solution? Create a new table. Store the course attendances individually for each employee.

Include a foreign key to link back to the original STAFF table.

> Foreign key to link back to the STAFF table

STAFF(<u>StaffID</u>, StaffName)

  STAFF-RECORD(<u>StaffID</u>, <u>CourseTitle</u>, CourseDate, Duration)

This new design assumes that the course title is unique, that a particular course can be offered on more than one date and that a member of staff never attends the same course more than once.

Note, the table STAFF-RECORD requires a composite primary key of (<u>StaffID</u> + <u>CourseTitle</u>)

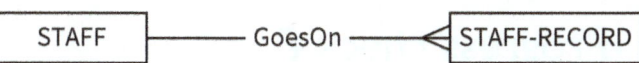

Figure 8.05 Relationship.

Second Normal Form (2NF)

2NF states '**The non-key attributes in the table must be dependent on knowing all of the primary key**'.

So, for tables that have a single value primary key, the table MUST be in 2NF.

Table STAFF therefore must be in 2NF.

But consider:

STAFF-RECORD(<u>StaffID</u>, <u>CourseTitle</u>, CourseDate, Duration)

Primary key (is a composite key) of StaffID + CourseTitle

There are two non-key attributes, CourseDate and Duration.

But, CourseDate and Duration will be known from knowing <u>only</u> the CourseTitle (i.e. only part of the primary key).

Hence table STAFF-RECORD is not 2NF.

Solution? – Create a new table

Remove Duration and CourseDate and create a new table COURSE-SESSION.

STAFF(<u>StaffID</u>, StaffName)

STAFF-RECORD(<u>StaffID</u>, <u>CourseTitle</u>, Date)

COURSE-SESSION(<u>CourseTitle</u>, <u>CourseDate</u>, Duration)

But there is now an issue with the COURSE-SESSION table.

It has a composite primary key and the duration will be known from knowing just the course title. Hence table COURSE-SESSION is NOT in 2NF.

Solution? Create a new table COURSE.

STAFF(<u>StaffID</u>, StaffName)

STAFF-RECORD(<u>StaffID</u>, <u>CourseTitle</u>, Date)

COURSE(<u>CourseTitle</u>, Duration)

COURSE-SESSION(<u>CourseTitle</u>, <u>CourseDate</u>)

Third Normal Form (3NF)

Like 2NF, third normal form is concerned with non-key attributes.

3NF states 'There must not be a dependency between any non-key attributes'.

An example of this is where all four tables have only one or no non-key attributes. Therefore there cannot be non-key attributes that are dependent. So, all four tables are in 3NF.

Consider if we had stored more data items in the STAFF table because the company has a single location in each of a number of different cities. We will add the City, CityAddress, Country attributes

STAFF(<u>StaffID</u>, StaffName, City, CityAddress, Country)

But if we know the city we shall know the country and the address. Therefore, we have two non-key attributes (CityAddress and Country) that are dependent on a third non-key attribute (City).

Solution: Create a new table LOCATION.

We must then retain a foreign key of City in the STAFF table to give:

STAFF(<u>StaffID</u>, StaffName, City)

LOCATION(<u>City</u>, CityAddress, Country)

You should now check these final table designs to confirm all five tables are in 1NF, 2NF and 3NF.

STAFF(<u>StaffID</u>, StaffName, City)

LOCATION(<u>City</u>, CityAddress, Country)

STAFF-RECORD(<u>StaffID</u>, <u>CourseTitle</u>, Date)

COURSE(<u>CourseTitle</u>, Duration)

COURSE-SESSION(<u>CourseTitle</u>, <u>CourseDate</u>)

> **TIP**
>
> When an attribute appears in more than one table, use the following notation, for example:
>
> STAFF.StaffID and STAFF-RECORD.StaffID to make clear which table the attribute refers to.

Progress check D

a   Complete Table 8.02 to summarise all the foreign keys in this final design.

State the table each foreign keys links back to.

| Foreign key | Links to |
Table - Attribute	
STAFF.City	LOCATION.City

Table 8.02.

b   Draw the E-R diagram.

Progress check E

Which of these are true statements?

a   'There must be no repeated group of attributes' – this is Second Normal Form.

b   'Non-key attributes' means those which are not part of the primary key.

   c   Both 2NF and 3NF are concerned with non-key attributes.

   d   A table with a composite primary key using two attributes must be in 2NF.

   e   A table with a single attribute primary key must be in 2NF.

Progress check F

All students have a tutor. Tutors are referred to by the three characters taken from their name (first initial and first two letter of surname) which must be unique to each student. For example tutor Will Smythe has initials WSM. All tutors have their own separate tutor room.

`STUDENT(StudentID, StudentName, TutorName, TutorInitials, TutorRoom)`

a   Which of these are true statements?

   i   The primary key of a student is `StudentID`.

   ii   The table is not in 3NF since `TutorName`

      is dependent on `TutorInitials`.

   iii   The table is not in 3NF since `TutorRoom` is dependent on `TutorInitials`.

   iv   The table is not in 3NF because it has a single attribute primary key.

b   Consider this new design:

`STUDENT(StudentID, StudentName, TutorInitials)`

`TUTOR(TutorInitials, TutorName, TutorRoom)`

   i   What attribute in `STUDENT` acts as a foreign key?

   ii   Describe the relationship between these two tables.

8.03 Database Management Systems (DBMS)

A DBMS is software which enables the definition, creation and querying of a large collection of data. The software also provides features for the maintenance of the data including:

- backup
- security
- interrogation of the data, i.e. with SQL queries
- controlled access to the data, i.e. with **views** which are only available to certain database users

All aspects of the use of the DBMS software will be administered by a Database Administrator (DBA).

Software tools found within a DBMS

One of these tools is a 'developer interface'. The database designer must have the ability to create all the basic objects, tables, queries, etc., that make up the database. Other features will be actioned from a command line interface.

Another tool is the '**query processor**'. Some users with competent computing skills would design their own SQL queries to extract information from the database.

Figure **8.06** shows a company where different staff are using the three available databases.

Data modelling and the logical schema

The **logical schema** is the basic relational database data design, made up of the table designs and any relationships. The process of producing the logical schema is called **data modelling**. Modelling produces the database description - tables, relationships, etc. - for what is happening in the real world.

Data dictionary

The **data dictionary** is a repository of all the information about the basic database design and all objects that have been created for its use, for example queries, views and reports.

Concurrent access to data

The same data is available to several terminal users. The DBMS software will control 'multi-user access' to the data with techniques such as record locking and file/table locking.

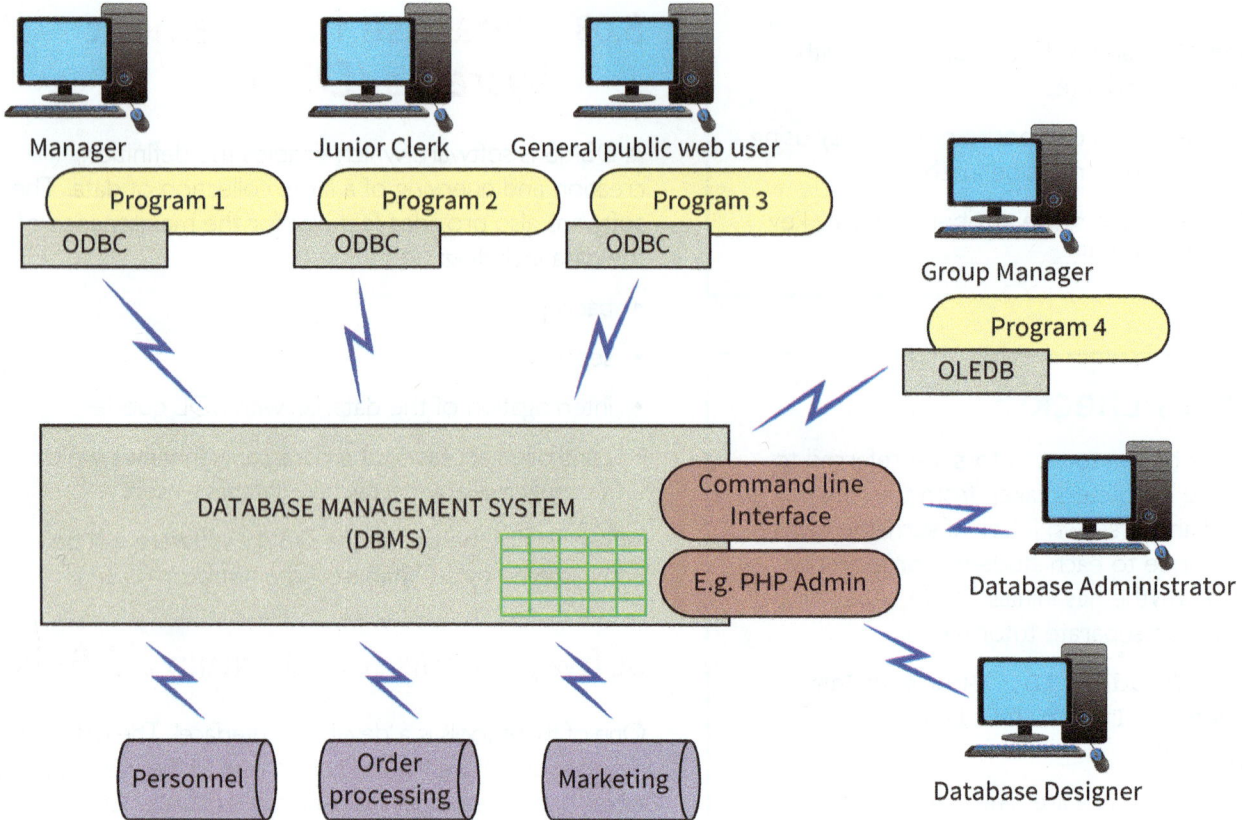

Figure 8.06 Business DBMS in action.

Database locking

A lock may be applied to the entire database, preventing activity from all other users. Total locking like this is used when the entire database is involved in some activity such as rebuilding the indexes or deleting data marked as deleted.

Table locking

A less severe lock is **table-level locking**. Other tables can still be accessed. However, as many transactions involve more than one table, this can also result in severe delays when one of the required tables is locked.

Record locking

What must be done to avoid two different users attempt to concurrently update the same tuple?

Locking individual records will cause the least delay and will prevent the second user gaining access to this record. The DBMS software must lock a row (only) of a table (i.e. a tuple), and report to the second user that they should perform their update later.

Queries are produced quickly

The DBMS has a facility called a 'query processor' that lets the user quickly create a new query. The user writes the query in SQL (see later) or, alternatively, the screen that the user sees is visually designed with a 'Query By Example' feature. The user will pick the table to be used in the query used from a visual pick list. Then similarly, pick from a list the attributes they want to see reported in the query.

Writing a SQL query, or using the query by example feature is generally a quick process. Compare this to the alternative of creating a new program to query the database that would take a lot longer and the user would need programming skills.

> **Progress check G**
>
> Which of the following would be contained in the database's data dictionary?
>
> a   The list of attributes used for all tables
> b   Detail for all attributes – name, data type – does it have a secondary index?
> c   The customer data
> d   The results for all queries
> e   Query descriptions

Data integrity

Database management systems must offer excellent validation support. The DBMS uses its data dictionary to perform validation checks on data entered into the database. Validation checks are set up at the table design stage, and are effective every time a reference is made to that item of data including application programs which access data in that table.

Compare this to a 'file based approach', where the validation checks have to be coded. Every time that data item is used, the validation checking code would have to be present in the program code.

Data security

'Backup' is a centralised task administered by the Database Administrator (DBA).

Since all data is centrally held within the DBMS, strategies for controlling the security are much easier to implement than with a file based approach.

A **database backup** saves a database to a file on a hard disk or other storage medium. To protect a database from power failure, disk crash, or other potential data loss, the DBA will regularly backup the database. Backup and database maintenance are designed to improve database performance, perform garbage collection of space occupied by deleted records, i.e. remove any deleted files (this reduces the database size) and create a stable snapshot of the database for archiving purposes.

'**Access rights**' to particular tables/views can be created by the database designer. This allows particular individuals/groups of users only access to certain data.

See Figure **8.06**, where we would expect the different groups of users to have a very different access to the data. For example the Database Administrator would be the only person able to create new tables and make other changes to the logical schema.

Read again the points made earlier about concurrent access to data. These various levels of locking are effectively a security feature.

Access to the database delivered by high-level language programs

Other users, such as the Manager, Junior Clerk and others in Figure **8.06** will not have a high-level of computing skills. Applications programs must be written to perform tasks to carry out their job role. For example, the Junior Clerk has to enter the data for a new employee. This will be done using a program that displays a web form into which the data is entered. What the applications program must do is connect to the database and generate the appropriate SQL to save the data. Technologies have developed, such as OBDC (Open Database Connectivity) to do this. Other companies such as Microsoft have developed their own variants of this such as OLEDB.

Duplicated data

Study again the logical schema for our staff training database.

```
STAFF(StaffID, StaffName, City)
LOCATION(City, CityAddress, Country)
STAFF-RECORD(StaffID, CourseTitle, Date)
COURSE(CourseTitle, Duration)
COURSE-SESSION(CourseTitle, CourseDate)
```

Study the `STAFF-RECORD` table. We did not store the `DURATION`, `CourseTitle` is sufficient.

- Study the `STAFF` table. We did not store any other data about the location, `City` is sufficient.

    A golden rule of relational database design is to **avoid unnecessary duplicated data**.

    If data does become duplicated then some of it will be redundant.

8.04 Data Definition Language (DDL) and Data Manipulation Language (DML)

The industry standard for both the Data Definition Language (DDL) and Data Manipulation Language (DML) is Structured Query Language (SQL).

Modern database software will provide 'point-and-click' features for the user, to design the database and the writing of queries. Behind the scenes the software is processing the user actions with SQL scripts.

Data Definition Language (DDL)

The DDL is used for the creation of the database, table design, creation of relationships and any changes to the table designs.

The DML is used for the creation of queries and for basic maintenance of the data (add, delete and amend data records).

We will use the training records database – `TRAINING` - used earlier in the chapter. The data model for this database was:

`STAFF(StaffID, StaffName, City, Department)`

`LOCATION(City, CityAddress, Country)`

`STAFF-RECORD(StaffID, CourseTitle, CourseDate)`

`COURSE(CourseTitle, Duration)`

`COURSE-SESSION(CourseTitle, CourseDate)`

Create the database
`CREATE DATABASE TRAINING;`

The command could have additional parameters to give a user name and password required to access the database.

Attribute data types
We must define the 'type of data' that will be assigned to each of the table attributes.

Data type	Explanation
CHARACTER	An unspecified number of characters
VARCHAR(n)	A string of characters of fixed length n
BOOLEAN	True or False value
INTEGER	Positive or negative whole number
REAL	Number data which might have a fractional part
DATE	In the format MM/DD/YYYY
TIME	In the format HH:MM

Create a table definition
```
CREATE TABLE STAFF
  (
  StaffID     : VARCHAR(6),
  StaffName   : VARCHAR(40),
  Department  : VARCHAR(10),
  City        : VARCHAR(30),
  ) ;
```

Alter a table definition
Add an attribute.

The number of years service for each member of staff is to be recorded.

`ALTER TABLE STAFF`

`ADD YearsService INTEGER ;`

Delete an attribute.

The department is to be deleted from the staff data.

`ALTER TABLE STAFF`

`DELETE Department ;`

Change the data type for an attribute

The StaffID is to be stored as an integer (not string).

`ALTER TABLE STAFF`

`MODIFY StaffID INTEGER ;`

Add the primary key to a table

The primary key can be stated when the table is first created.

```
CREATE TABLE LOCATION
  City NOT NULL,
  City         : VARCHAR(30),
  CityAddress  : VARCHAR(40),
  Country      : VARCHAR(30),
  PRIMARY KEY (City)
  );
```

> NOT NULL says the attribute cannot be left blank.

Or, if the primary key is added at a later stage:

```
ALTER TABLE LOCATION
ADD PRIMARY KEY (City) ;
```

Adding a foreign key to a table

Again the foreign key(s) can be stated when the table is first created:

```
CREATE TABLE COURSE-SESSION
   (
   CourseTitle : VARCHAR(50) NOT NULL,
   CourseDate  : DATE NOT NULL,
   PRIMARY KEY (CourseTitle, Date),
   FOREIGN KEY (CourseTitle) REFERENCES COURSE(CourseTitle)
   );
```

> The 'NOT NULL' can be included with the data type

Or, if the foreign key is added at a later stage:

```
ALTER TABLE COURSE-Session ESSION
FOREIGN KEY (CourseTitle) REFERENCES COURSE(CourseTitle)
```

Data manipulation language (DML) for queries

The keywords used in a query are:

`SELECT, FROM, WHERE, ORDER BY, GROUP BY, INNER JOIN.`

Display all attributes for cities in India.

```
SELECT *
FROM LOCATION
WHERE Country = 'India' ;
```

Display the city name for all cities in the UK.

```
SELECT City
FROM LOCATION
WHERE Country = 'UK' ;
```

Display the Staff Ids for all staff who attended the Excel Stage 1 course on the 13th May 2022.

```
SELECT StaffID
FROM STAFF-RECORD
WHERE CourseTitle =
'Excel Stage 1' AND CourseDate = #13/05/2022# ;
```

> The logic of the query requires the **AND** operator.
>
> # is used to enclose a date value.

Display the cities where the company has offices - alphabetically by city.

```
SELECT City
FROM Location
ORDER BY City
```

Display the cities where the company has offices – grouped by country.

```
SELECT City
FROM Location
GROUP BY Country
```

Queries - needing data from two tables

What if the same query as above required the staff <u>name</u> rather than ID to be displayed?

The name is stored in the `STAFF` table and there is a relationship between `STAFF-RECORD` and `STAFF`.

Note: the table name is now added in front of the the attribute name, using the 'dot notation'.

The `INNER JOIN` keywords select all tuples from both tables where there is a match between the columns in both tables.

```
SELECT STAFF.StaffID, Staff.StaffName
FROM STAFF-RECORD INNER JOIN STAFF
WHERE STAFF-RECORD.CourseTitle =
'Excel Stage 1'
        AND STAFF-RECORD.CourseDate = #13/05/2022# ;
```

Query Functions

The following three functions are available to use in a query. They all take an attribute name as **parameter**. The function acts on several tuples returning a single value.

The following are examples of their use and so are called **aggregate functions**.

Count and display the number of members of staff

```
SELECT COUNT (*)
FROM STAFF
```

Calculate and show the average number of years service for all the members of staff.

```
SELECT AVG(YearsService)
FROM STAFF
```

Calculate the total number of hours training done by the staff member with ID = 89

```
SELECT SUM(Duration)
FROM STAFF-RECORD
WHERE StaffId = 184
```

Data manipulation for data maintenance

Inserting a new record, deleting an existing record and updating a record is called '**data maintenance**'.

Insert a record

Add the new staff record with the data shown.

```
INSERT INTO STAFF
(StaffID, StaffName, City)
VALUES ('050091', 'Rankin', 'London');
```

Delete one or more record(s)

Staff member 060078 has left the company.

```
DELETE FROM STAFF
WHERE StaffID = '060078' ;
```

> This will cause referential integrity problems – there might be records in the `STAFF-RECORD` table which will also require deleting.

Amend one or more record(s)

The Excel Stage 1 course has now been changed from a 1-day to a 2-day course.

```
UPDATE COURSE
SET Duration = 2
WHERE CourseTitle = 'Excel Stage 1';
```

Progress check H

Study the following scenario:

Bands are registered with an agency.

An agency will have several artists and bands on its books. A band/artist never has more than one agent.

Bands go 'on tour'. Concerts that are 'one offs' are rare, and the band will indicate the maximum number of gigs which they intend performing on any tour. A tour therefore consists of one or more gigs.

The promoter tends to use the same set of venues. Each venue has recorded: venue name, location (for example, Paris) and capacity.

Each band's tour gigs are booked into a venue. The same venue may be booked for a sequence of tour dates if the promoter is anticipating a high demand for tickets.

The following data model is produced:

`BAND(BandName, AgentName)`

`AGENT(AgentName, AgentAddress, AgentContactName)`

`BAND-TOUR(BandName, TourName, StartDate, FinalDate, MaxNoOfGigs)`

`BAND-TOUR-CONCERT(BandName, TourName, GigDate, VenueName)`

`VENUE(VenueName, Capacity, Location)`

Complete the tables showing the primary key and any foreign keys for each table. The first entry is done for you.

Table	Primary key	Foreign Key(s)
BAND	BandName	None
AGENT		
BAND-TOUR		
BAND-TOUR-CONCERT		
VENUE		

Progress check I

Draw the Entity-relationship (E-R) diagram for the data model.

Progress check J

Write SQL queries for the following:

a   Display a list of all band names which use agent Maximum Exposure.

b   Display a list of all the band names which go on tour on or after 01/01/2022.

c   Display a list of tour names which start after 01/06/2022 and have more than ten tour concerts.

d   Display a list showing band name, tour name and venue for all tours which have a concert in Paris.

e   Display a list of all concerts date and venues for the 'Back to the future' tour in ascending date order.

Past paper questions

1   A clinic is staffed by several doctors. The clinic serves thousands of patients. Each day and at any one time, there is only one doctor in the clinic available for appointments.

The clinic stores patient, doctor and appointment data in a relational database.

a   i   Underline the primary key for each table in the following suggested table designs.

```
PATIENT(PatientID, PatientName, Address, Gender)
DOCTOR(DoctorID, Gender, Qualification)
APPOINTMENT(AppointmentDate, AppointmentTime, DoctorID,
PatientID)
```
[2]

   ii   Complete the following entity-relationship (E-R) diagram for this design.

[2]

b   The doctors are concerned that many patients make appointments but do not attend them. Describe the changes to the table designs that could be made to store this information. [2]

Cambridge International AS & A level Computer Science 9608 paper 11 Q7 November 2017

2   A database has been designed to store data about salespersons and the products they have sold. The following facts help to define the structure of the database:

- Each salesperson works in a particular shop
- Each salesperson has a unique first name
- Each shop has one or more salespersons

- Each product that is sold is manufactured by one company only
- Each salesperson can sell any of the products
- The number of products that each salesperson has sold is recorded

The table `ShopSales` was the first attempt at designing the database.

FirstName	Shop	ProductName	NoOfProducts	Manufacturer
Nick	TX	Television set Refrigerator Digital camera	3 2 6	SKC SP HKC
Sean	BH	Hair dryer Electric shaver	1 8	WG BG
John	TX	Television set Mobile phone Digital camera Toaster	2 8 4 3	SKC ARC HKC GK

a   State why the table is not in First Normal Form (1NF). [1]

b   The database design is changed to :

`SalesPerson(FirstName, Shop)`

`SalesProducts(FirstName, ProductName, NoOfProducts, Manufacturer)`

Using the data given in the first attempt table, (`ShopSales`), show how these data are now stored in the revised table designs.

Table: `SalesPerson` [2]

FirstName	Shop

Table: `SalesProducts`

FirstName	Shop	ProductName	NoOfProducts	Manufacturer

[3]

c   i   A relationship between the two tables has been implemented.

    Explain how this has been done. [2]

ii Explain why the `SalesProducts` table is not in Third Normal Form (3NF). [2]

iii Write the table definitions to give the database in 3NF. [2]

Cambridge International AS & A level Computer Science 9608 paper 11 Q9 June 2015

3 A hospital is divided into two areas, Area A and Area B. Each area has several wards. All the ward names are different.

A number of nurses are based in Area A. These nurses always work on the same ward. Each nurse has a unique Nurse ID of `STRING` data type.

[A-NURSE]>————————————<[A-WARD]

a Describe the relationship shown in the diagram. [1]

b A relational database is created to store the ward and nurse data. The two table designs for Area A are :

`A-WARD(WardName, NumberOfBeds)`

`A_NURSE(NurseID, FirstName, FamilyName, ..........................)`

i   Complete the design for the `A-NURSE` table. [1]

ii Explain how the relationship in part (a) is implemented. [2]

c In Area B of the hospital, there are a number of wards and a number of nurses.

Each Area B ward has a specialism.

Each Area B nurse has a specialism.

A nurse can be asked to work in any of the Area B wards where their specialism matches with the ward specialism.

The relationship for Area B of the hospital is :

[B-NURSE]>————————————<[B-WARD]

i   Explain what the degree of relationship is between the entities `B-NURSE` and `B-WARD`.

ii The design for the Area B data is as follows :

`B-NURSE (NurseID, FirstName, FamilyName, Specialism)`

`B-WARD (WardName, NumberOfBeds, Specialism)`

`B-WARD-NURSE (.........................................................)`

Complete the attributes for the third table. Underline its primary key. [2]

iii Draw the relationships on the entity-relationship (E-R) diagram.

[B-NURSE]   [B-WARD]

[B-WARD-NURSE]

[2]

d   Use the table designs in part (c)(ii).

   i   Write an SQL query to display the NurseID and family name for all Area B nurses with a specialism of 'THEATRE'. [3]

   ii Fatima Woo is an Area B nurse with the nurse ID of 076. She has recently married, and her new family name is Chi.

       Write an SQL command to update her record. [3]

       UPDATE

       SET

       WHERE

Cambridge International AS & A level Computer Science 9608 paper 11 Q1 June 2017

4 a   Five descriptions and seven relational database terms are shown below.

       Draw a line to link each description to its correct database term.

Description

- Any object, person or thing about which it is possible to store data
- Dataset organised in rows and columns; the columns form the structure and the rows form the content
- Any attribute or combination of attributes that can act as a unique key
- Attribute(s) in a table that link to the primary key in another table to form a relationship
- Attribute or combination of attributes that is used to uniquely identify a record

Database term

- Secondary key
- Candidate key
- Entity
- Foreign key
- Primary key
- Table
- Tuple

[5]

b   Explain what is meant by referential integrity. [3]

Cambridge International AS & A level Computer Science 9608 paper 11 Q1 November 2016

Chapter 9: Algorithm design and problem solving

> **Learning Objectives:**
>
> **Computational thinking skills:**
>
> - Understand what is meant by:
>   - Abstraction
>   - Decomposition and stepwise refinement
>   - Pattern recognition
>   - An algorithm
> - Document a task using:
>   - Structured English
>   - A program flowchart.
>
> **Algorithms:**
>
> - Understand and apply the three basic constructs:
>   - Sequence
>   - Selection
>   - Iteration
> - Understand and write the pseudocode used for these constructs.

9.01 Computational thinking skills

Computers are used to solve problems. Understanding the problem is a key skill. Before a possible computer solution can be considered, the problem itself must be fully understood. Once the problem is understood, possible solutions can be considered that a computer solution could implement.

Computational thinking is <u>not</u> programming. Programming tells a computer what to do and how to do it. Computational thinking enables you to first work out exactly what to tell the software solutions to do.

Abstraction

What makes computer science different?

All the natural sciences deal with the world 'as it is'. The task of the physicist is to understand how the world works by applying the laws of physics, not to invent a world in which these laws apply.

The computer scientist must create abstractions of real-world problems that can, through an interface, be understood by computer users and can be represented, by a programmer inside the computer.

Abstraction in the real world

Consider doing the family washing.

Using the machine is a good example of abstraction.

You need to know how to use your washing machine to complete the wash.

You need to provide water, provide washing powder, provide dirty washing, switch it on and select the wash programme.

You don't need to know how the washing machine works internally or the ideal temperature of the water.

Someone else did all the designs for that and created a washing machine that now acts as an abstraction and hides all the detail of the wash process.

To use the machine, the user must know how the interface to the machine works. These parameters are needed: water, washing powder, dirty washing and the wash programme.

You just interact with a simple interface that doesn't require any knowledge about the internal implementation of the machine.

Figure 9.01 Washing machine interface.

A second example is to consider a part of the London bus map.

The design of this bus map fits with the basic ideas of abstraction.

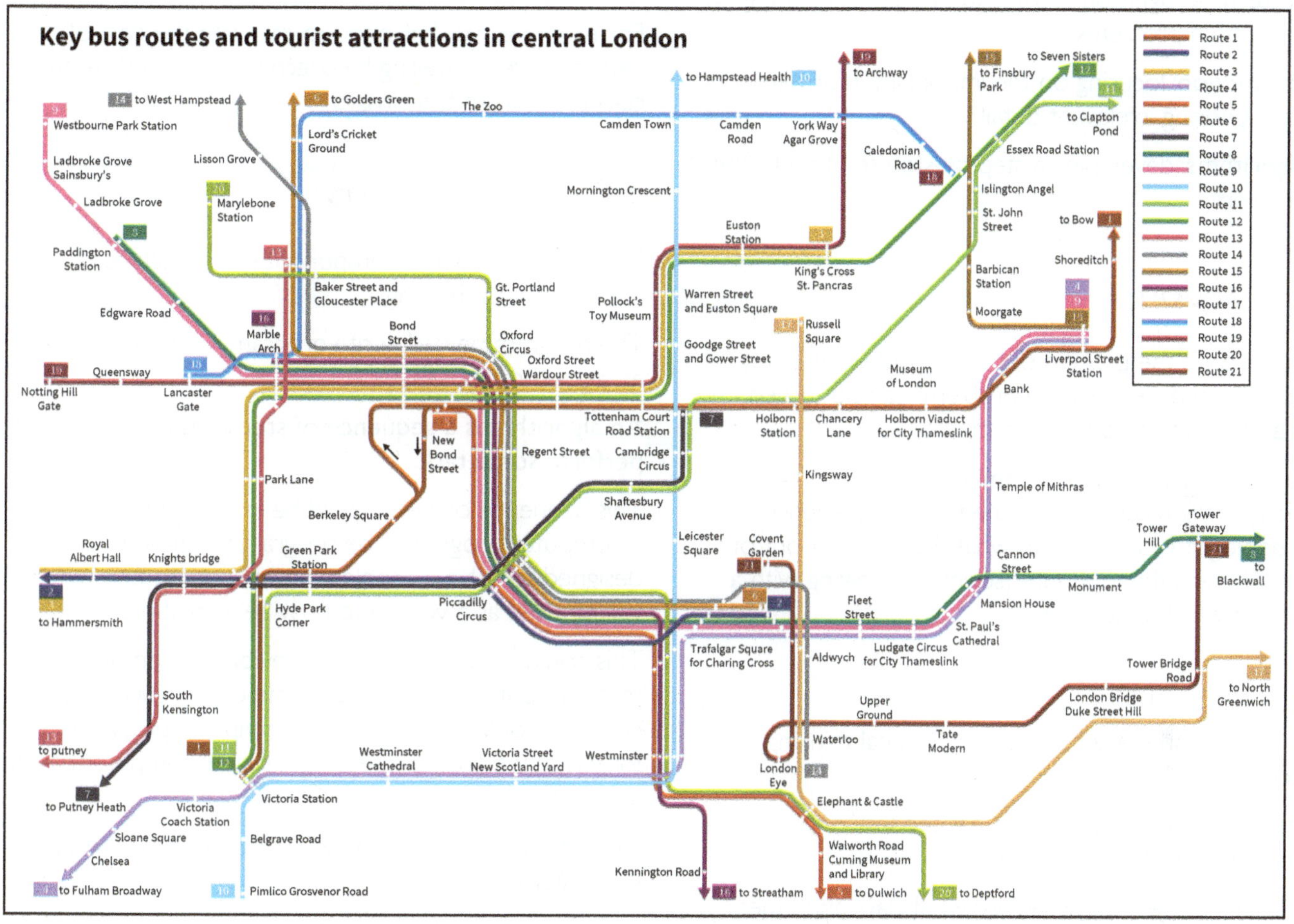

Figure 9.02 London buses route map.

We do not need to know the exact road geography of the routes. The roads and parks are not the exact shapes shown. It need not be drawn accurately to scale.

There is a paradox here. Mere mention of the word 'abstract' tends to imply that something is more difficult to understand, for example, abstract algebra. Sets and group theory *are* more demanding than Year 7 algebra, but, in actual fact, abstract for the computer scientist is intended to hide unwanted detail and thus simplify our understanding.

TIP

Abstract art is often meant to be a work that represents something but only has limited detail about the real world object. Compare this with our computer science definition where we will 'strip out' any unwanted detail.

Computational thinking

Consider when a computer system is to be designed. The analyst will be bombarded with a mass of information and data from several people involved with the problem.

Computational thinking has four key cornerstone techniques:

- **decomposition**: breaking down a complex problem or system into smaller, more manageable parts
- **pattern recognition**: looking for similarities among and within problems
- **abstraction**: focusing on the important information only, ignoring irrelevant detail
- **algorithms**: developing a step-by-step solution to the problem.

Abstraction

Abstraction is the process of filtering out what is not important, in order that the problem can be turned into a working computer system.

Abstraction is what makes computer science fundamentally different from the traditional sciences. The geologist is dealing with what they see in front of them whereas the computer scientist is dealing with a model of what is required.

Decomposition

Decomposition is a second computational thinking principle.

Consider a club secretary who has the task of planning a trip to a museum 50 km away.

The issues to be considered are what days and times the museum is open, how much it will cost, what members of the club want to go and how to get there.

We have broken down or decomposed the problem of 'Planning the museum trip' into a number of sub-tasks.

Further decomposition will be needed before we arrive at a solution.

- How much will it cost?
    - Are there special prices for a large group?
- What members of the club want to go?
- How will we get there?
    - If the number of takers is over 10, investigate the cost of a coach and calculate the cost for each member.
    - Otherwise check which members are willing to drive and calculate the cost for each member.

Pattern matching

Once some decomposition has been done, the designer looks for patterns within the sub-tasks.

For example, we shall need to calculate the cost of getting there. Travelling by coach will incur a different calculation from travelling by cars.

9.02 Algorithms

These are the fourth component in our picture of computational thinking.

The programmer will write program code that follows an algorithm.

An algorithm is a sequence of steps designed to perform some task.

This 'sequence of steps' could be implemented as a computer program. The program will have been designed to solve a problem and the computer system will be used as a vehicle to provide a solution.

This could be a task that has previously been done manually, but with the aid of some device such as a calculator or was done using a computer program, but for which we are now seeking a better computer-based solution.

Consider a variety of applications which are done by a computer program:

- The printout of utility bills
- The issue of utility bill reminders for bills which have not been paid on the due date
- The control of an industrial process
- The simulation of some industrial process
- All of the common data processing applications – stock control and management, order processing and tracking, accounting and resource management

For all of these applications, there is a clear problem to be solved for which the computer system is used to provide a solution.

What are the underlying algorithms?

The algorithms to solve the problem will be designed from a detailed knowledge of the operation of the application. For example, we know that bills are sent out every three months and a payment reminder is sent when the payments becomes 30 days overdue.

> ## Worked example 9.01
>
> Consider the task of repairing a puncture on a bicycle. A computer solution will not be used to solve the problem, but the underlying steps make up an algorithm.
>
> The following is what we might say if we 'think aloud' the process.
>
> Check, are all tools and materials available?
>
> IF 'no' then:
>
> > Delay the task
> >
> > STOP
>
> IF 'yes' then:
>
> > Remove the wheel
> >
> > Remove the inner-tube
>
> Check, is there major damage?
>
> IF 'yes' then:
>
> > Buy a new inner tube
>
> IF no then:
>
> > Inflate the tube to locate the leak
> >
> > Apply glue and a patch
> >
> > Inflate the tube to re-test
>
> If 'still leaking' then:
>
> > Purchase new inner tube
>
> If 'no leak' then:
>
> > Re-assemble

Structured English

Structured English provides a more formal way to document the stages of the algorithm.

```
PROCESS RepairPuncture
Start:  JobDone ← "NO"
    IF 'all tools are not available'
      THEN
          Delay the task
          GOTO End
      ELSE
          Remove the wheel
          Remove the inner-tube
    ENDIF
    IF 'there is  major damage'
      THEN
            Buy a new inner tube
            GOTO Delay
      ELSE
          Inflate the tube to
          locate the leak
          Apply glue and a patch
          Inflate the tube to re-test
    ENDIF
    IF 'still leaking'
      THEN
            Purchase new inner
            tube
            GOTO Delay
      ELSE
          Re-assemble
          JobDone ← "YES"
          GOTO End
    ENDIF
Delay:  Purchase new inner-tube
    IF JobDone ← "NO"
      THEN
            GOTO Start
    ENDIF
End:
ENDPROCESS
```

In the structured English:

- Three labels (`Start`, `Delay` and `End`) have been used to mark particular steps in the algorithm. This is exactly the same as the use of labels in our assembly language programming in Chapter 4 Section 4.02.
- When a decision has to be made the keywords `IF – THEN – ELSE – ENDIF` have been used
- Indentation and the use of blank lines ('white space') have been used to indicate which steps belong together
- The complete process has been given an identifier name `RepairPuncture`.

The process is marked with a clear `STARTPROCESS` and `ENDPROCESS`.

> **TIP**
>
> The layout of algorithms has consistently used: a font (`Courier New`) that is different to the main text; indentation and whitespace; CAPS for the keywords (`IF`, `THEN`, etc.) and proper case for the identifiers, for example, JobDone.

> **TIP**
>
> The algorithm has used a GOTO keyword to jump to a particular step in the algorithm.
>
> For a high-level language, when we met the various loop structures in Section 11.2 the use of GOTO was avoided. The use of GOTO is considered bad programming practice as it encourages 'spaghetti-like' algorithm design.
>
> For assembly language (Chapter 4, Section 4.02) the `JMP <address>` instruction is the equivalent of a GOTO statement. In assembly language programming this GOTO structure is often unavoidable.

Identifier names

Choosing identifier names is a big issue for the programmer. Sensible and meaningful names should be used. An identifier RepairPuncture is preferable over R or RP. The programmer may need to re-visit the design several months later and so a good initial choice of names will make the design more readily easier to understandable.

There will always be a trade off between clear descriptive names but not names which are excessively long.

We have used several identifier names, `RepairPuncture` for the whole process, `JobDone` to indicate whether or not the process has been completed and `Start`, `Delay` and `End` to label a step in the algorithm.

9.03 Three basic constructs

All problems that can be documented as a sequence of steps can be coded using the three basic constructs:– sequence, selection and iteration.

Sequence

The steps that make up the algorithm must be carried out in sequence.

Selection

A decision has to be made. A question is asked ,'Are all the tools available?'

This is called **the condition**. The result of the condition is always either TRUE or FALSE. The algorithm carries out a different set of steps for the TRUE and FALSE conditions.

Iteration

'Iterated' means 'repeated'. Iteration will occur in an algorithm design when a block of steps is repeated. This is done in program code with the use of a **loop** structure.

9.04 Methods and tools for design

Stepwise refinement

In the design, one of the steps is stated as `Re-assemble`.

This single step could be expanded, i.e. we could use **stepwise refinement**.

`Re-assemble` consists of:

```
Replace the inner tube
Replace the tyre
Replace the wheel
Inflate the inner tube
```

Program flowchart

A flowchart can be used as an alterative to a structured-English description of an algorithm design.

A program flowchart uses the following symbols:

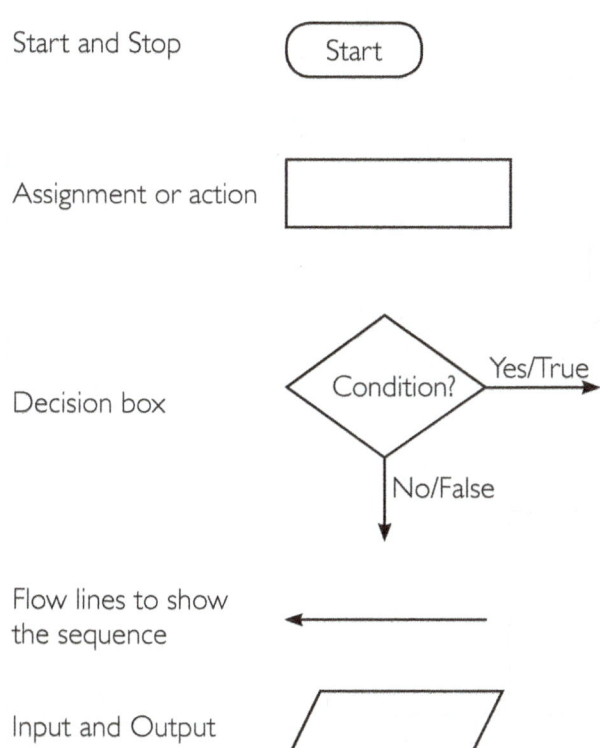

The `RepairPuncture` problem did not require any input from the user or outputs. Most tasks, and so programs, <u>will</u> perform both input and output.

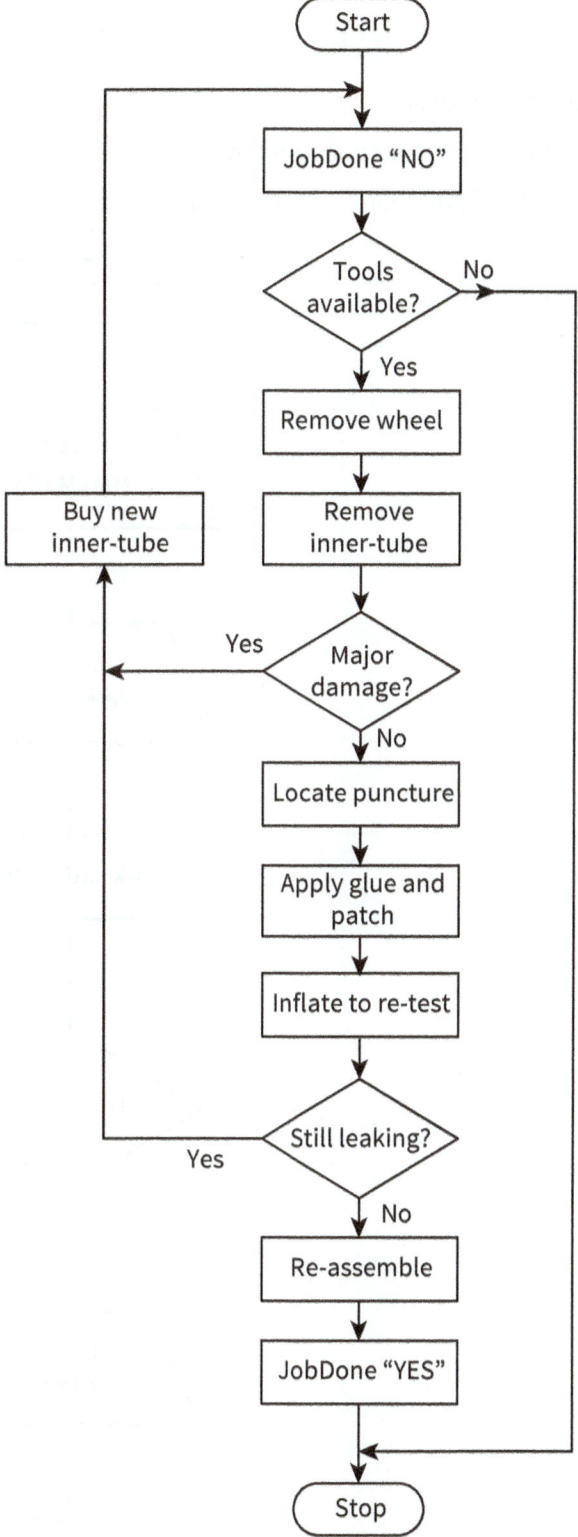

Figure 9.03 'Repair puncture' flowchart.

Progress check A

Study the flowchart.

a What is the output when the user keys in 70, followed by 90?

b What is the output when the user keys in 65, followed by 85?

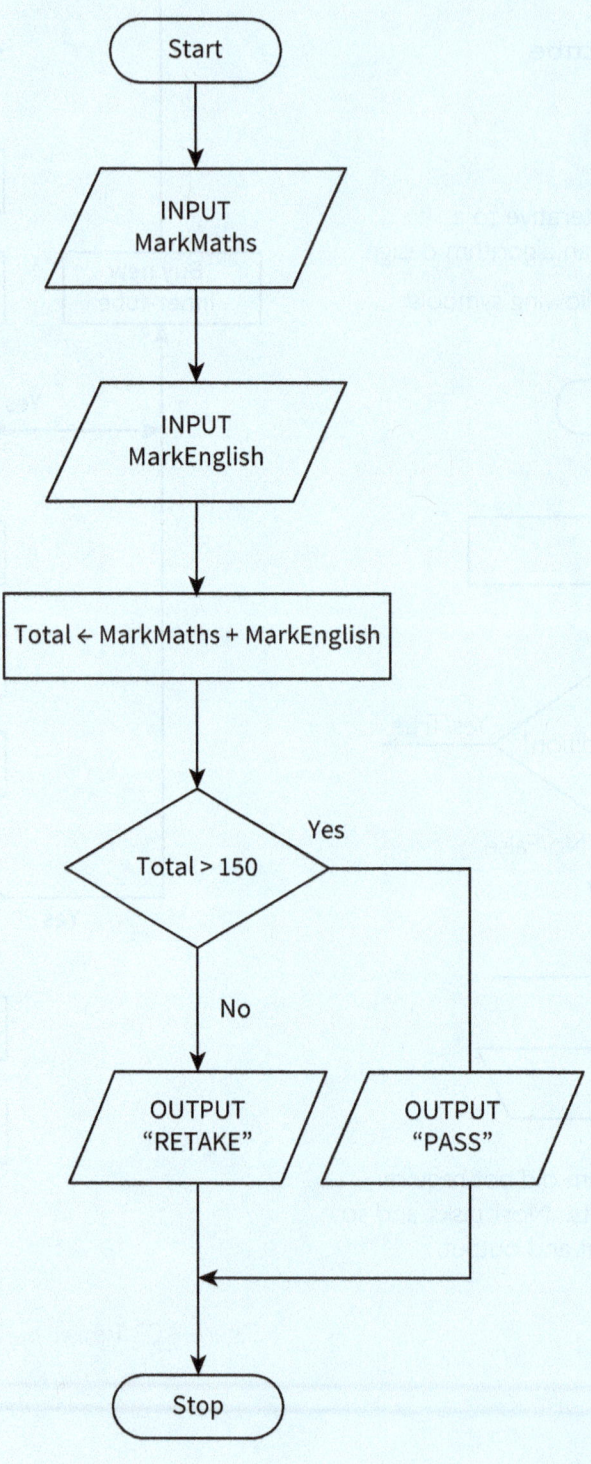

Figure 9.04.

Pseudocode for the problem description

> ### Worked example 9.02
>
> A garage buys used cars and then aims to sell the vehicles at a profit. The garage has to decide the selling price.
>
> The garage will record data for the price paid, the date the vehicle was first registered (i.e. when new) and the mileage.
>
> A program is to be written to calculate the proposed selling price.

Algorithm design stages: Input – Processing – Output

The **Input** will be the three data items about the car.

The **processing** will calculate the selling price as follows:

- The price will drop by 5% for every month in age.
- This calculated price is called the 'Provisional Sell Price'.
- An adjustment may be made to this figure based on the mileage of the vehicle.
- Normal monthly mileage is 1000 km. If the car's actual monthly mileage is less that this, the Provisional Sell Price is increased by 5%.
- The Provisional Sell Price is now called the 'Sell Price'.

The output from the program is the Sell Price and Profit.

An Identifier table

Many data items are either input or calculated. Identifier names are summarised in an identifier table.

Identifier name	Description
`PricePaid`	Original price paid
`RegDate`	Purchase date
`Mileage`	Car mileage when purchased
`NormalMileage`	The expected car mileage based on the age of the car
`ProvSellPrice`	The calculated selling price
`SellPrice`	The final selling price, adjusted if necessary
`Profit`	Sell Price – Price Paid

The // symbol denotes a 'comment'

```
01  // Input the data for this car
02  INPUT PricePaid
03  INPUT RegDate
04  INPUT Mileage

05  // Calculate the proposed
    selling price
06  Months ← TodaysDate - RegDate
07  // The calculated value on the
    right is 'assigned' to
08  // The Months variable on the left
09  NormalMileage ← Months * 1000
10  ProvSellPrice ← PricePaid *
    0.95 ^ Months
11  // A 5% reduction is 0.95
12  // "*" means "multiply" and "^"
    means "to the power of".
13  // This is code for a
    mathematical equation:
14  // ProvSellPrice ← Price Paid ×
    0.95Months
15  IF Mileage < NormalMileage
16     THEN
17        SellPrice ← ProvSellPrice
    * 1.05
18   // A 5% increase
19     ELSE
20        SellPrice ← ProvSellPrice
21  ENDIF
22  Profit ← PricePaid - SellPrice
23  OUTPUT SellPrice, Profit
```

As this is pseudocode it is displayed using the `Courier new font`.

Several identifiers have been used to represent data items.

The lines of the pseudocode have been numbered (for easy reference only).

Like the Structured English used earlier, the pseudocode has used a number of 'keywords'. These are, `INPUT` – `OUTPUT` – `IF` – `THEN` – `ELSE` – `ENDIF`.

The symbol ← has been used for 'assignment'. Line 06 is read as 'The Months value is calculated by subtracting the RegistrationDate value from the TodaysDate value'.

> ## Progress check B
> Draw the flowchart for the car price calculator algorithm.

> ## Progress check C
> An investor inputs an amount to invest. The value of the investment increases by 10% each year. Stop the process when the investment has doubled in value. Output the number of years this has taken.
>
> Complete the labels A, B, C and D in the flowchart.
>
>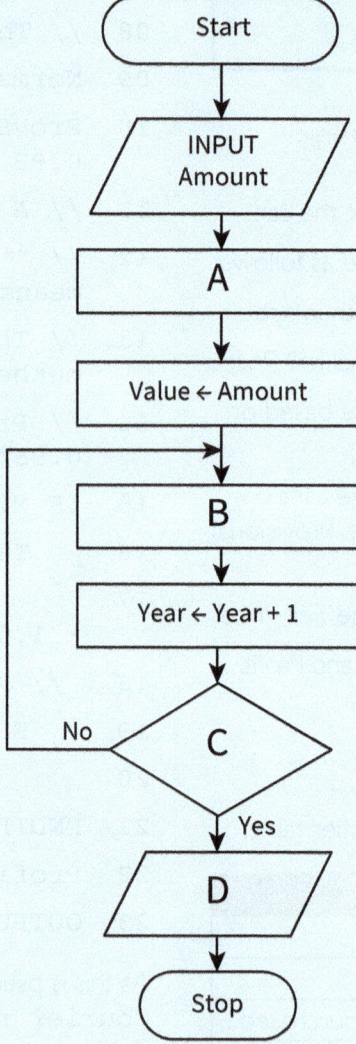
>
> Figure 9.05.

Past paper questions

1. A program is to be written to calculate the discount given on purchases.

   A purchase may qualify for a discount depending on the amount spent. The purchase price (`Purchase`), the discount rate (`DiscountRate`) and the amount paid (`Paid`) is calculated as shown in the following pseudocode algorithm.

   ```
   INPUT Purchase
   IF Purchase > 1000
       THEN
           DiscountRate ← 0.10
       ELSE
           IF Purchase > 500
               THEN
                   DiscountRate ← 0.05
               ELSE
                   DiscountRate ← 0
           ENDIF
   ENDIF
   Paid ← Purchase * (1 - DiscountRate)
   OUTPUT Paid
   ```

   The algorithm is also to be documented with a program flowchart.

   Complete the flowchart by:
   - Filling in the flowchart boxes
   - Labelling, where appropriate, lines of the flowchart

   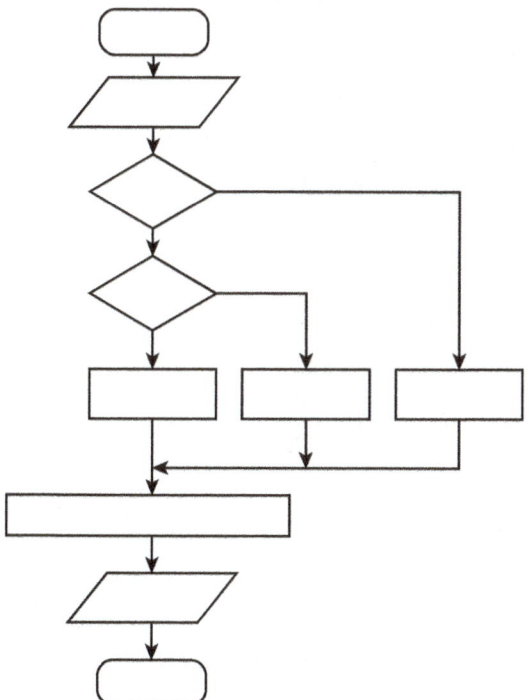

   Cambridge International AS & A level Computer Science 9608 paper 21 Q4 November 2015

   [6]

2. A programmer wants to write a program to calculate the baggage charge for a passenger's airline flight.

Two types of ticket are available for a flight:

- Economy class (coded E)
- Standard class (coded S)

Each ticket type has a baggage weight allowance as shown below. The airline makes a charge if the weight exceeds the allowance.

Ticket type	Baggage allowance (kg)	Charge rate per additional kg ($)
'E'	16	3.50
'S'	20	5.75

The program design is to be amended. The value input by the user for the ticket type is to be validated. Part of the amended flowchart is shown below.

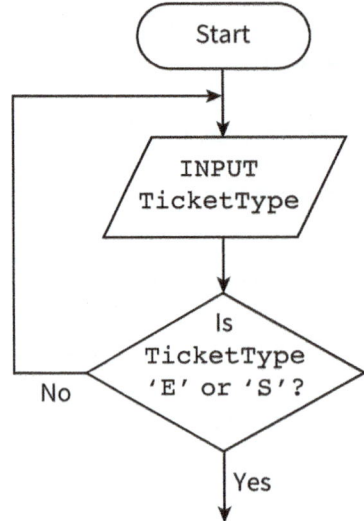

Write pseudocode to use a pre-condition loop for this validation. [3]

Cambridge International AS & A level Computer Science 9608 paper 21 Q1c November 2016

Data types and structures

Learning Objectives:

Data types and records:
- Understand and use the standard pseudocode data types
- Write and use a 'record' data type.

Arrays:
- Use one or more one-dimensional arrays for a problem
- Use a two-dimensional array for a problem
- Use the terminology associate with arrays
- Write pseudocode for an array description.

Files:
- Understand the need for text files
- Write pseudocode for open, close, read and write for a text file.

Introduction to Abstract Data Types (ADT):
- Understand the operation and applications for:
  - A stack
  - A queue
  - A linked list
- Describe (not write pseudocode) how an item is inserted and deleted from each of these data structures.

10.01 Data types and records

Standard data types

The computer system or, more precisely, a programming language, or applications software such as a spreadsheet, needs to distinguish between different types of data. When writing pseudocode, your algorithm will need to make clear the **data type** intended for all **identifiers** used.

This was done in Chapter 9 by showing the data type in an Identifier table. This shows the identifier name chosen by the programmer, the appropriate data type and a description of what this identifier will store in the program.

A `DECLARE` pseudocode statement is used and this is called a **declaration statement**.

We are already familiar with using an identifier name for some data item in the problem. `PurchaseDate` could be the identifier name chosen by the programmer. The data type appropriate for this identifier is `DATE`.

The declaration statement for this identifier is:

```
DECLARE PurchaseDate : DATE
```

Boolean

Pseudocode data type `BOOLEAN` is either TRUE or FALSE.

Some data have only a TRUE or FALSE value, for example, is a customer allowed credit?, or is the vehicle taxed?

```
DECLARE CreditAllowed : BOOLEAN
DECLARE VehicleTaxed : BOOLEAN
```

Date and Time

Psuedocode data type: `DATE`.

```
DECLARE RegistrationDate : DATE
```

Numbers

The programming language must distinguish between different types of number.

Integer

Pseudocode data type **INTEGER**.

This is a positive or negative whole number.

Identifier	Data type	Description
`Mileage`	`INTEGER`	The car mileage when purchased

Or,

`DECLARE Mileage : INTEGER`

Real

Pseudocode data type: **REAL**.

Numbers that have a fractional part are called real numbers.

`DECLARE AverageDailyRainfall : REAL`

Character

Pseudocode data type: **CHAR**.

A single character. Some data values will take the form, gender: 'M' for male, and 'F' for female, for example, or fuel type: 'P' for petrol, 'D' for diesel, 'E' for electric.

`DECLARE Gender : CHAR`

`DECLARE FuelType : CHAR`

String

Pseudocode data type: **STRING**.

A string is a sequence of characters from the character set.

Ali Harris

14 The High Street

9876

This name and address could be stored by a program as three separate strings.

`DECLARE ClientName : STRING`

`DECLARE AddressLine1 : STRING`

`DECLARE AddressLine2 : STRING`

> **TIP**
>
> The syllabus will use the following convention with pseudocode:
> - Double quotes ("Petrol") to contain a string value
> - Single quotes ('P') to contain a single character value.

Progress check A

Explain why 8, "8" and '8' will be treated differently by a computer program.

Progress check B

Revisit the gym member data in Chapter 6, PROGRESS CHECK B.

What data type would be used for each of the following data items?

`FamilyName`
`Forenames`
`DateOfBirth`
`Address`
`Email`
`MemType`
`NoOfVisits`
`MemberBefore`

Record structure

A record is a set of related data items. The items can be of different data types.

Worked example 10.1

A banking ATM transactions application stores bank ID, account number, date of the transaction, time of the transaction, type of transaction (withdrawal or PIN services), the amount withdrawn and the ATM identifier from where the transaction was made.

These seven data values together form the data for a single transaction.

The record type pseudocode description for this data is:

```
TYPE Transaction
    Bank_ID          : STRING
    AccountNumber    : INTEGER
    TransactionDate  : DATE
    TransactionTime  : INTEGER
    TransactionType  : CHAR
    Amount           : REAL
    ATM_ID           : INTEGER
ENDTYPE
```

Note, the use of indentation in the record definition.

Code to handle a transaction would have an identifier of this type, declared as follows:

```
DECLARE ThisTransaction : Transaction
```

Using the record data structure, individual data items use the dot notation as follows:

```
ThisTransaction.BankID ← "C86952"
ThisTrasaction.AccountNumber ← 4568890
```

This reads as The `BankID` value for `ThisTransaction` is assigned the value "C86952"

10.02 Arrays

An **array** is a data structure in a program that uses the same identifier name for several data values.

We use an array for a collection of items of the same date type, for example, an array of string values or an array of integer values.

In practice, arrays might sometimes contain more than one data type, but you can assume for this syllabus that the items will be of a single data type.

One-dimensional array

Worked example 10.2

A garage sells cars and stores data for the number of cars sold in each month of the year. The array will have identifier `MonthlySales`. We need to store 12 values.

The array can be visualised as shown.

In Figure 10.01 the number shown to the left of each value is called the array **index**.

The lower bound of the array is 0, i.e. the lowest index. The upper bound of the array is 11, i.e. the highest index. `MonthlySales[0]` is 19. `MonthlySales[3]` is 7.

It could be drawn as a horizontal table and have exactly the same meaning.

MonthlySales

0	1	2	3	4	5	6	7	8	9	10	11
19	3	4	7	8	12	14	6	6	8	9	2

Figure 10.02 1D array.

MonthlySales

0	19
1	3
2	4
3	7
4	8
5	12
6	14
7	6
8	6
9	8
10	9
11	2

Figure 10.01 1D array.

Progress check C

a How many sales were made in February?

b In which month were the most cars sold?

This array is a **one-dimensional (1D) array**. The meaning of this will become clear when we examine a two-dimensional array.

Each position is called an **element** of the array.

Two-dimensional (2D) array

Some datasets can be visualised as a two-dimensional table.

Worked example 10.3

Six employees are sales staff. We record the number of sales made by each employee over 12 months.

Sales

	0	1	2	3	4	5	6	7	8	9	10	11
0	0	0	0	3	4	0	0					
1	1	12	12	6	7	8	9	18	8	12	11	6
2	2	4	5	1	2	3	11	6	7	2	3	1
3	11	12	3	4	6	7	1	2	6	7	11	4
4	1	0	0	8	0	0	1	1	2	3	4	
5	0	0	1	2	3	4						

Figure 10.03 Sales data grid.

Each row represents a salesperson and each column represents a month.

This dataset will be represented as a **two-dimensional (2D) array**. The 2D array has identifier name `Sales`, with two subscript numbers. The convention is to denote the row number with the first subscript and the column number using the second subscript.

Note that this is opposite to the (x, y) order used in coordinate geometry!

So the order is rows, then columns.

Assigning values to the array

```
Sales[2, 6] ← 11
Sales[5, 3] ← 2
```

And similarly for all other values in the grid.

> ## Progress check D
> **a** How many sales were made in April by the salesperson with array subscript 3?
> **b** What array cell stores the 18 sales made by person 2 in August?

> ## Progress check E
> A program will store data for 203 employees. Their date of joining and name is recorded.
> What data structure(s) could be used?

An array of records

Consider the bank transaction data studied in Worked Example 10.01. If up to 2000 transactions were recorded, a data structure that could be used is an array of records.

Identifier	Data type	Description
`BankTransaction`	`ARRAY[0..1999] OF Transaction`	Array storing the data for many transactions

Note: the 'OF' should be read as "of data type `Transaction`". Data would be written to the array as follows:

`BankTransaction[0].BankID= "C86993"`

`BankTransaction[0].AccountNo = 4569932`

and similar statements for the other data items.

Similar statements for other transactions using a different array index.

Data would then be read as follows:

`ThisBankID = BankTransaction[0].BankID`

`ThisAccountNo = BankTransaction[0].AccountNo`

> **TIP**
>
> Visual Basic and Java both have arrays BUT Python does not. The data structure in Python is called a list.
>
> The practical programming for this is covered in Chapter 21.

Linear search

This refers to searching a collection of items for a particular value where the dataset is stored as an array. This is covered in Chapter 11.

Bubble sort

This refers to sorting a collection of items into a particular order where the dataset is stored as an array. This is covered in Chapter 19.

10.03 Files

Why do we need files?

Data stored in primary memory, including data in arrays, will be lost when a program ends.

Most applications will require some data to be permanently saved. The data is then available to the program the next time it is run.

The AS syllabus coverage of files is restricted to the use of a **text file**. The file will have an identifier name. Text files are usually given the file extension .txt.

Both of the files which follow are storing data for four employees.

Each file stores the name, data of birth, salary grade and number of years' service.

```
File1.txt
Adam Smith 12/04/1998 A 3
Jules Ahmed 04/12/1987 A 4
Mary Simmons 09/11/1996 B 1
Adam Jones 09/07/1976 C 11
```

```
File2.txt
Adam Smith
12/04/1998
A
3
Jules Ahmed
04/12/1987
A
4
Mary Simmons
09/11/1996
B
1
Adam Jones
09/07/1976
C
11
```

Figure 10.04 Two possible text file organisations.

For `File1.txt` the programmer has decided to store the data for each employee as a single line of text. Each of the data items is separated by a <Space> character.

For `File2.txt` each data item is stored on a new line in the file.

Any program that is to use one of these data files must be clear about the **file organisation** used.

Number digits, such as values for years' service, will be treated as a string value when they are read from the file. The program must then convert this string to an integer.

Pseudocode for text files

Opening a text file

The use of the file must be made clear by stating the **file mode**. When we create a new file or read data in an existing file it must be 'opened'.

The file mode is either **READ** for reading line(s) of text from a file, **WRITE** to write line(s) of text to the file or **APPEND** to add a line of text to the end of existing file.

Note that we can only read or write data to a file in the same 'opened' session.

Writing to a text file

Consider the following problem:

The programmer uses the `File1.txt` structure to write the first line to the file.

The employee data has been assigned to an identifier `EmployeeString` with **STRING** data type.

```
EmployeeString ← "Adam Smith 12/04/1998 A 3"
OPENFILE "File1.txt" FOR WRITE
WRITEFILE "File1.txt", EmployeeString
CLOSEFILE "File1.txt"
```

> Writes the string stored by `EmployeeString` to the file `File1.txt`

Note that the file must be 'opened' at the start of the session and finally 'closed'. The file name is repeated in the `WRITEFILE` statement, since a program might be using more than one text file. The program code for this design will create a new file `File1.txt` with one line of text.

Progress check F

```
OPENFILE "Products.txt" FOR WRITE
WRITEFILE "Products.txt", "Screwdriver"
WRITEFILE "Products.txt", "Hammer"
WRITEFILE "Products.txt", "Saw"
CLOSEFILE "Products.txt"
```

What would be the final result after running this as program code?

> **TIP**
>
> If the program were run a second time, the original file `File1.txt` would be overwritten, i.e. none of the original data would be preserved.

Progress check G

```
OPENFILE "Products.txt" FOR WRITE
WRITEFILE "Products.txt", "Screwdriver"
OPENFILE "Products.txt" FOR WRITE
WRITEFILE "Products.txt", "Hammer"
OPENFILE "Products.txt" FOR WRITE
WRITEFILE "Products.txt", "Saw"
CLOSEFILE "Products.txt"
```

What would be the final result after running this as program code?

Reading from a file

The file must be opened at the start of the session, with file mode `READ` and then closed when it is no longer in use.

We will assume that we have already run the program code for the writing of the Adam Smith employee data. The `File1.txt` file contains one line of text.

```
DECLARE EmployeeString : STRING
OPEN "File1.txt" FOR READ
READFILE "File1.txt", EmployeeString
CLOSE "File1.txt"
OUTPUT EmployeeString
```

> The `READFILE` statement reads one line of text (a string) from the file `File1.txt` and assigns the text to indentifier `EmployeeString`.

This would display:

```
Adam Smith 12/04/1998 A 3
```

10.04 Introduction to Abstract Data Types (ADT)

What is an ADT?

An abstract data type is a collection of data items together with operations that act on that data, called 'behaviours'.

When we study Object-Oriented Programming (OOP) we will see that an abstract data type is implemented as a class.

Stack

A stack is a dynamic data structure that operates on the principle, **'last item added will be the first to leave'**.

This is often abbreviated to LIFO: 'Last In – First Out', or FILO: 'First In – Last Out', turned the other way around, but meaning the same.

> **TIP**
>
> You need to be confident about using an array which either starts with index zero or one. The discussion which follows uses a lower bound of one.

To implement a stack

Store the values in an array: lower bound 1 and upper bound **N**. A pointer indicates the position of the item that is currently at the 'top of stack' (TOS) position.

Figure **10.05** shows the stack after the three items 106, 57 and 44 are added in that order.

- The first item to leave will be 44
- If no items have left, the next new item will be stored at position 4.

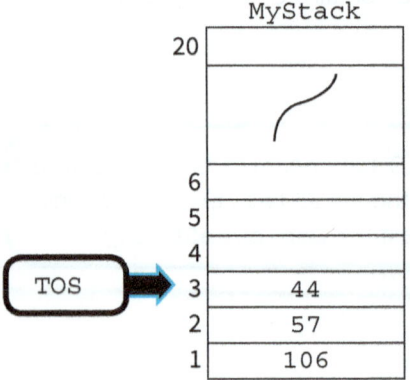

Figure 10.05 Items added to a stack.

Stack – insert an item

Inserting an item to a stack is called a 'push' to the stack.

The algorithm is straightforward:

Check that the stack is not full

If space is available:

    Increment the stack pointer TOS.

    TOS ← TOS + 1

    Input the new item `NewItem`

    Add the new item at position TOS

    `MyStack[TOS]` ← `NewItem`

Stack – delete an item

Removing an item from the stack is called a 'pop' from the stack.

Check that the stack is not empty. If not:

    Output the item at position 'top of stack'.

    Decrement the stack pointer TOS

    TOS ← TOS - 1

> **TIP**
>
> These are a 'pseudocode' statements to describe what happens. The syllabus says "you will not be required to write pseudocode for these structures …"
>
> You would however be expected to understand a given description such as this one.
>
> The same follows for the discussion of a queue and linked list which follows.

Queue

A queue is a data structure that operates on the principle: **'First item added will be the first to leave'**. It is abbreviated to FIFO: 'First In – First Out'.

> **TIP**
>
> When explaining how a stack/queue behaves, do not simply answer LIFO/FIFO, you need to say in words what the acronym stands for.

To implement a queue

Store the values in an array, lower bound 1 upper bound **N**.

The queue is controlled by *two* pointers. A 'head' pointer points to the item that is currently at the head of the queue. A 'tail' pointer points to the item that is currently at the rear of the queue.

A new item is always added to the end of the queue.

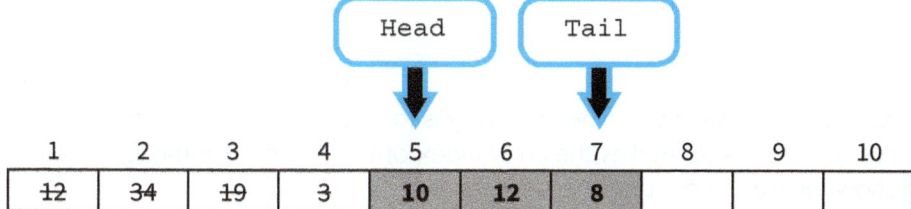

Figure 10.06 Items added and removed on a queue.

Progress check H

Draw the array and pointers for the initially empty `MyQueue` queue.

Progress check I

In Figure **10.06** an item is about to leave the queue:

a   Which item is this?

b   What pointer change is required?

A new item is to join the queue.

c   How will the algorithm know the position at which to store the value?

Queue – Insert an item

This is straightforward because the item to insert is always at index position `Tail+1`. The value is `MyQueue[Tail+1]`.

Queue – delete an item

This is also straightforward because the item to delete is always at index position `Head`. The value is `MyQueue[Head]`.

The stage will soon be reached where, once three more items have joined the queue, the queue will run out of space.

Queue – insert an item

Consider the queue `MyQueue` which has 10 cells. The current state of the queue below shows seven items have joined the queue, four (1 to 4) have already left, the current queue occupies cells 5 to 7 and the position where a new item will be added next is `Tail + 1`.

The solution is to make the queue behave as a **'circular queue'**. Once the `Tail` pointer reaches value 10 and a new value is to be added, `Tail` will be re-set to index 1.

The queue data structure is re-visited at A Level in Chapter 19.

Linked list

A linked list is a data structure consisting of a set of **nodes**. Each node consists of the **data value** and a **link pointer** to one of the other nodes. The purpose of the linked list structure is to link the nodes in some particular order, for example alphabetical order.

Visualise the linked list data

Start: 3

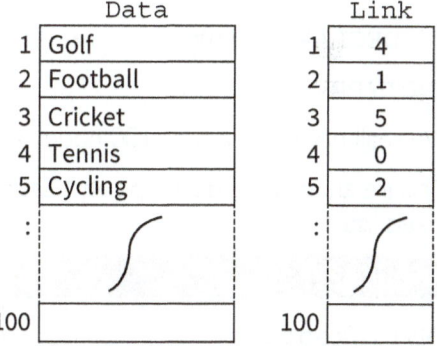

Figure 10.07 Items added to the linked list.

Figure **10.07** shows the data values stored in the arrays. Figure **10.08** shows the conceptual linked list that is created by the link pointers. The node that is the end of the linked list has its pointer set to zero to denote 'end of list'.

There is some detail needed here. The program would need to know at this stage that the next available 'free' array position is 6.

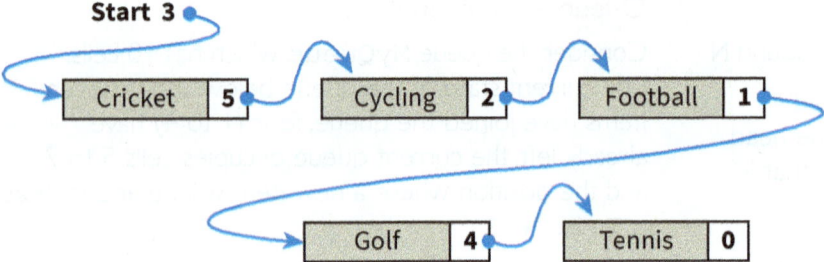

Figure 10.08 Conceptual linked list.

To implement a linked list

Solution 1 to this problem is store the data using two 1D arrays. The first array is for the data values and the second array is for the link pointers. A 'Start' pointer is needed, defined as the array index of the first item in the list. A 'next free position' index pointer is needed to show where the next new value is stored.

The identifier table is:

Identifier	Data type	Description
Data	ARRAY[1..20] OF STRING	The data value for the nodes
Link	ARRAY[1..20] OF INTEGER	The link pointer value for the nodes
Start	INTEGER	The index of the node which is at the start of the linked list
NextFree	INTEGER	The index of the node where the next new value will be stored

Table 10.01

Solution 2 to this problem is to create a 'record' data structure consisting of the data for one node, its data and link value. A 'Start' pointer is needed, i.e. the array index of the first item in the list. A 'next free position' index pointer is also needed, i.e. the array index for the next new value to be stored.

```
TYPE   LinkedListNode
    DECLARE DataValue : STRING
    DECLARE Link      : INTEGER
ENDTYPE
```

We shall have as many as 100 node values, so:

Declare an array of data type `MyLinkedList` that uses our data type `LinkedListNode` to implement the linked list.

Identifier	Data type	Description
MyLinkedList	ARRAY[1..100] OF LinkedListNode	The data values for the nodes

> ### Progress check J
>
> The following values join a linked list data structure in the order shown. The linked list arranges the cities in alphabetical order:
>
> LONDON, AMSTERDAM, NEW DELHI, DHAKA, SINGAPORE and NEW YORK.
>
> Show the visual state of the linked list.

Linked list – insert an item

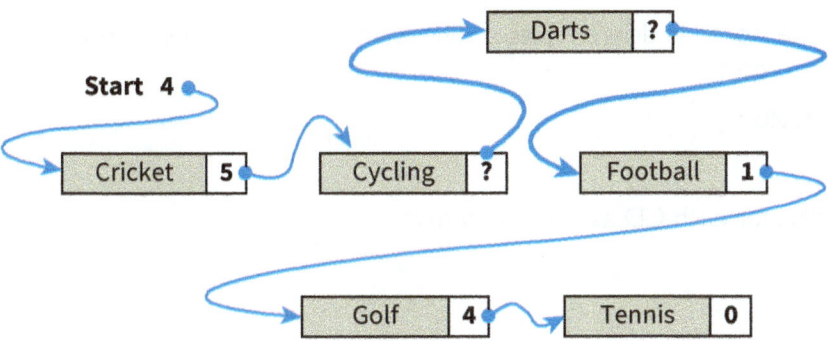

Figure 10.09 Item added to a linked list.

Insert algorithm is as follows:

Traverse the list until we find the first node (Football) that is greater than the insert item (Darts). This establishes that the new item is to be inserted between Cycling and Football.

The new value becomes part of the linked list by storing the data value (Darts) at the next free position (6) and adjusting the link pointers. Here, the Darts pointer will be the current Cycling pointer and the Cycling pointer will be 6.

There are special cases that must be considered: the linked list could be empty or the new node could become the new start of the list.

Linked list – delete an item

Consider the original items. The task is to delete Golf from the linked list.

A change is made to the pointers as shown in Figure 10.10.

The algorithm will be:

Input the item to delete.

Traverse the list until found.

Make the pointer change.

Note that the pointer of the previous node (Football's pointer) will now point to the node (Tennis) pointed to by the deleted item.

A special case will be when the item to delete is the first in the list.

The linked list data structure is re-visited in the A Level syllabus in Chapter 19.

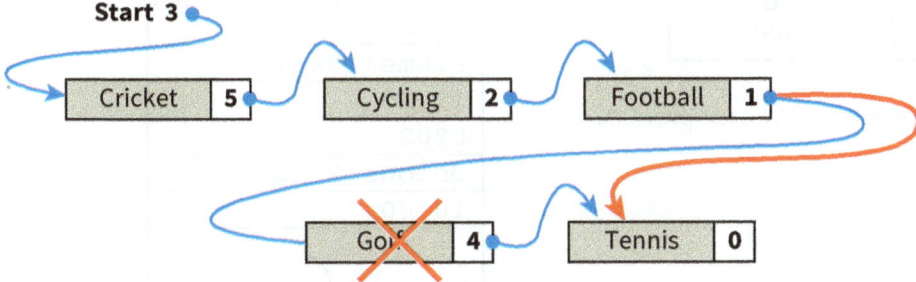

Figure 10.10 Delete an item in the diagram.

Past paper questions

1 Toni has a large collection of jazz CDs that are stored in different places. She wants to record where the CDs are stored. She decides to write a program to do this.

The program must store the data in a file, `MyMusic`

  a i Why is a file needed? [1]

      ii `MyMusic` is a text file with the data for each CD as one line of text.

        Data for a typical CD are:

        Title: Kind of Green

        Artist: Miles Coltrane

        Location: Rack1-5

        The line will be formed by concatenating the three data items.

        For the example above, the line stored will be:

        `Kind of GreenMiles ColtraneRack1-5`

        Describe a problem that might occur when organising the data in this way.

        Describe a possible solution. [5]

Cambridge International AS & A level Computer Science 9608 paper 22 Q5a June 2016

2 A company maintains a file of product data. Ahmed is to write a program to add a new product and search for a product based on the structure diagram shown:

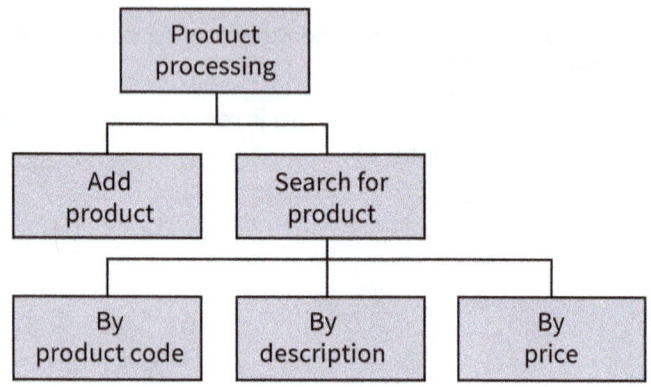

The program records the following data for each product:

- Product code
- Product description
- Product retail price.

The text file **PRODUCTS** stores each data item on a separate line, as shown in the table.

File Products
0198
Plums(10kg)
11.50
0202
Onions(20kg)
10.00
⁄
0376
Mango chutney(1kg)
02.99
⁄
0014
Mango(10kg)
12.75

The program uses the variables shown in the identifier table.

Identifier	Data type	Description
PRODUCTS	TEXT FILE	Storing the code, description and retail price for all current products.
PCode	ARRAY[1 : 1000] OF STRING	Array storing the product codes.
PDescription	ARRAY[1 : 1000] OF STRING	Array storing the product descriptions.
PRetailPrice	ARRAY[1 : 1000] OF REAL	Array storing the product retail prices.
i	INTEGER	Array index used by all three arrays.

a The first operation of the program is to read all the product data held in file **Products** and write them into the three 1D arrays.

Complete the pseudocode below.

OPEN ....

   i ← 1

WHILE ....

   READFILE ("PRODUCTS", ...)

   READFILE ("PRODUCTS"', ...)

   READFILE ("PRODUCTS", ...)

   ....

   ....

ENDWHILE

CLOSE "PRODUCTS"

OUTPUT "PRODUCT FILE CONTENTS WRITTEN TO ARRAYS" [5]

When Ahmed designed the PRODUCTS file, he considered the alternative file structure shown below.

File PRODUCTS

0198 Plums (10kg)	11.50
0202 Onions (20kg)	10.00
0376 Mango chutney (1kg)	02.99
0014 Mango (10kg)	12.75

b State one benefit and one drawback of this file design. [2]

Cambridge International AS & A level Computer Science 9608 paper 21 Q4c November 2016

Chapter 11

Programming

Learning Objectives:

Programming basics:

- Understand that data is represented by variables and constants
- Use pseudocode for:
  - the declaration of variables and constants
  - the assignment of variables and constants
- Evaluate arithmetic expressions
- Use built-in functions in pseudocode.

Constructs:

For all of the following, understand the pseudocode to implement:

- Use selection in a task
  - IF construct (four variants)
  - CASE construct
- Use iteration in a task
  - 'count controlled' loop
  - 'post-condition' loop
  - 'pre-condition' loop
- Understand the pseudocode for a linear search
- Understand the pseudocode for a bubble sort.

Structured programming:

- Understand and use the terminology used with procedures and functions
- Understand the need for procedures
  - Code a procedure with pseudocode
  - Understand the difference between passing parameters 'by value' and 'by reference'
- Code a function using pseudocode.

11.01 Programming basics

We already have some of the fundamentals required for writing program code.

In **pseudocode** we have made up identifier names to represent data items, for example, `CustomerName`, `MyStack`.

Identifiers must be declared before they are used, using the pseudocode keyword `DECLARE`.

Identifier names

Always use meaningful identifier names. Meaningful variable names make the code easier to follow and understand. Your code might be worked on by other programmers or you might return to a program some months later.

Try to adopt your own consistent style for names, for example, `AverageRainfall` and not `averagerainfall`.

The names you choose need to be meaningful without being too long.

> **TIP**
>
> The syllabus document 'Pseudocode Guide for Teachers' states that the examination papers will use: 'Mixed case (or 'camelCase') with upper case letters indicating the start of a new word', for example
>
> `NumberOfPlayers`
>
> or
>
> `numberOfPlayers`.
>
> Some other guidelines tend to be universal: names should not start with a digit character; names do not contain <Space>s; and the 'dash' character is not used though the underscore ("_") is acceptable.

> **Progress check A**
>
> Which of the following identifier names conform to the recommended style?
>
> ```
> 1FaultTotal
> NoOfFaults
> Number Of Faults
> NumberofFaults
> Number_Of_Faults
> Number-Of-Faults
> ```

In Chapter 10 we have already written a declaration statement and drawn up an identifier table for documenting the identifiers needed in a problem.

Variables and constants

Variables

A variable is the representation of a data value that is required by the problem.

A memory location is used to store the data value.

The variable name or identifier, decided by the programmer, is the label for this memory location.

The value stored by a variable may change during the execution of the program.

Constants

If you are confident that the data value will not change, then it should be declared as a constant. This will help to prevent accidental changes later. By studying the nature of the task, the programmer will make the decision to use either a constant or a variable.

Declaration of variables

Most programming languages insist that all variables and constants are declared before they are used within the program code. Such languages are said to be **strongly typed languages**.

In program code, the particular language might allow a variable to also be initialised with a value.

For variables in pseudocode programs, we shall keep the two issues - declaration and assignment - separate.

Declare the variable as a separate statement, then, assign it a value at a later stage in the program.

Examples of declarations are:

```
DECLARE CustomerName      : ARRAY [1..2000] OF STRING
DECLARE NumberOfAccidents : INTEGER
DECLARE HasFullLicence    : BOOLEAN
DECLARE LicenceType       : CHAR
```

Assignment – Variables and constants

Constants

The declaration of a constant and the assignment of the value is done with a single statement:

`CONSTANT Pi = 3.142`

Note: In pseudocode the data type can be implied, for example, Pi must be storing a `REAL`.

Variables

`CustomerName ← "Harrison"`

`NumberOfAccidents ← 0`

`HasFullLicence ← TRUE`

Note: The use of the **assignment operator** and not the 'equals' sign.

Input from the keyboard

A value will be keyed in and immediately stored as a variable.

`INPUT CustomerName`

Assumes `CustomerName` has earlier been declared as a STRING.

Output to the console

The value to be output will be the current value of a variable.

```
OUTPUT CustomerName
```

Pseudocode syntax allows for a mixture of text and one or more variables in the output.

```
OUTPUT "The customer name is: ", CustomerName
```

Arithmetic expressions

The task carried out by the program could require the calculation of some value. This will use the maths arithmetic operators (+, -, *, / and ^) in an assignment statement.

The Logical operators - **AND**, **OR** and **NOT** - can be used in pseudocode logic statements.

Here are some examples:

Using the **NOT** operator:

```
IF CustomerName = NOT("Harrison")
```

Note there is an alternative to this using the arithmetic operators -

```
IF CustomerName <>"Harrison"
```

Using the **AND** operator:

```
IF NoOfAccidents >=1 AND NoOfAccidents < 3 THEN ...
```

This selects all drivers who have had one or two accidents.

Using the **OR** operator:

```
IF LicenceType = 'A' OR LicenceType = 'C' THEN ...
```

The logic could be more complex and require the use of brackets:

```
IF (LicenceType = 'A' OR LicenceType = 'C') AND NoOfAccidents = 0 THEN ...
```

Worked example 11.01

The basic premium for car insurance is calculated with a reduction for each year the driver has been accident free.

```
INPUT AccidentFreeYears
BasicPremium ← 550
PremiumPaid ← BasicPremium * 0.95 ^ AccidentFreeYears
OUTPUT "Adjusted premium is: ",PremiumPaid, "dollars"
```

Progress check B

These pseudocode statements each have an error. What is the error?

a   `PayRate : REAL`

b   `PayRate = 9.90`

c   `YearsEmployed * 5.50 ← PayRate`

       Why would you criticise this programmer's statement?

d   `tp ← basicpay + Opay + bonus`

Built-in functions

Built-in functions are those that are available to the programmer as part of the programming language.

They fall into groups for specific uses. One group is **string handling functions**, for example, to return (see next section) the number of characters in a string. Another group is **maths functions,** for example, to return the integer part of a real number. There are many, many others.

Using the terminology for functions

A function has an identifier name. It takes as input one or more **parameters/arguments** or none at all and it returns a calculated value.

An example of this is:

```
ThisLength ← LENGTH("Footballer")
```

In this example, the name of the function is `LENGTH`, it returns the number of characters in the string, i.e. 10 to variable `ThisLength` and so, in the program statement, 10 is assigned to the `ThisLength` variable.

The definition for the `LENGTH` function would be shown as:

`LENGTH(<StringValue>) RETURNS INTEGER`

`<StringValue>` is called the argument of the function and the definition states the data type of the value to be returned (`INTEGER`).

String and character handling functions

Description	Function syntax	Returns
Return the single character at position `Pos` in the string `Str`	`Str(Pos:INTEGER)` This assumes the first character is position 1.	CHAR
Returns N characters from the start of the string `Str`	`LEFT(Str:STRING, N:INTEGER)`	STRING
Returns N characters counting backwards from the end of `Str`	`RIGHT(Str:STRING, N:INTEGER)`	STRING
Returns N characters starting at position `Pos` in `Str`	`MID(Str:STRING, Pos:INTEGER, N:INTEGER)`	STRING
Change all characters in `Str` to upper case	`TO_UPPER(Str:STRING)`	STRING
Change all characters in `Str` to lower case	`TO_LOWER(Str:STRING)`	STRING
Concatenate (join together) two strings	`String1 & String2` & is an operator (not a function)	
The next functions use or return a single character:		
Returns the character having the ASCII value of `ThisInteger`	`CHR(ThisInteger:INTEGER)`	CHAR
Returns the ASCII value for `ThisCharacter`	`ASC(ThisCharacter:CHAR)`	INTEGER
Returns the lower case character for `ThisCharacter`	`LCASE(ThisCharacter:CHAR)`	CHAR
Returns the upper case character for `ThisCharacter`	`UCASE(ThisCharacter:CHAR)`	CHAR

Table 11.01 String/character built-in functions using pseudocode.

Functions with numbers

Description	Function syntax	Returns
Convert a string value to a number	`STRING_TO_NUM(ThisString : STRING)`	REAL
Truncating a number – this means the whole number part only. Note: this might be different to 'rounding' the number	`INT(ThisReal:REAL)`	INTEGER

Table 11.02 Number built-in functions using pseudocode.

Progress check C

Use the Table 11.01 and 11.02 built-in functions.

State the value returned by these function calls when:

```
a ← "slow down"
b ← "NOT VERY FAST"
c ← 901.63
d ← "42.96"
```

1. LEFT(a, 4))
2. TO_UPPER(RIGHT(a, 4))
3. LEFT(b, 3)
4. MID(b, 5, 6)
5. MID(a, 6, 2) & RIGHT(b, 4)
6. LCASE(LEFT(a, 4) & "/" & RIGHT(b, 4))
7. STRING_TO_NUM(d) + 1
8. INT(STRING_TO_NUM(d) - 2)

> **TIP**
>
> Referring to built-in functions, the syllabus states 'Any functions not given in the pseudocode guide will be given. String manipulation functions will always be given'.

11.02 Constructs

IF structure

A task might ask a question where a different route is taken through the code depending on whether some **condition** is TRUE or FALSE.

There are many variations of the **IF** structure.

IF – THEN – ENDIF

Worked example 11.02

In an examination, the grade is a PASS for a mark of 40 and above.

```
INPUT Mark
IF Mark >= 40
    THEN
        OUTPUT "PASS"
ENDIF
```

IF – THEN – ELSE – ENDIF

Worked example 11.03

The grade is a PASS for a mark of 40 or above, otherwise the program reports a FAIL.

```
INPUT Mark
IF Mark >= 40
   THEN
       OUTPUT "PASS"
   ELSE
       OUTPUT "FAIL"
ENDIF
```

Nested IFs

Worked example 11.04

A grade is now awarded as follows:

Mark	Grade awarded
Under 40	FAIL
40 and under 75	MERIT
75 and over	DISTINCTION

The logic could be structured with a sequence of three separate **IF statements**.

```
INPUT Mark
IF Mark < 40
   THEN
       OUTPUT "FAIL"
ENDIF
```

Drawing boxes helps us to see where each IF statement begins and ends

```
IF Mark >= 40 AND Mark < 75
   THEN
       OUTPUT "MERIT"
ENDIF
```

(Continued)

```
IF Mark >= 75
    THEN
        OUTPUT "DISTINCTION"
ENDIF
```

An alternative is to use **nested IF** statements. This means we have one IF statement sitting inside another.

```
INPUT Mark
IF Mark < 40
    THEN
        OUTPUT "FAIL"
    ELSE
        IF Mark >= 40 AND Mark < 75
            THEN
                OUTPUT "MERIT"
            ELSE
                OUTPUT "DISTINCTION"
        ENDIF
ENDIF
```

This last example raises the question, what if there are many more alternatives?

> **TIP**
>
> Read carefully through the four IF structure examples. Note the indentation that has been used.

Case structure

If there are many alternatives, use a **case structure**.

Worked example 11.05

A grade is awarded as shown by the table below.

Mark	Grade Awarded
Under 40	FAIL
40 and under 50	E
50 and under 60	D
60 and under 70	C
70 and under 80	B
80 and over	A

(Continued)

```
INPUT Mark
CASE OF Mark
    <40                 : OUTPUT "FAIL"
    >=40 AND <50        : OUTPUT "E"
    >=50 AND <60        : OUTPUT "D"
    >=60 AND <70        : OUTPUT "C"
    >=70 AND <80        : OUTPUT "B"
    >=80                : OUTPUT "A"
ENDCASE
```

The CASE structure can have a final case:

```
OTHERWISE :   <statement>
```

Flowchart to illustrate the Case structure

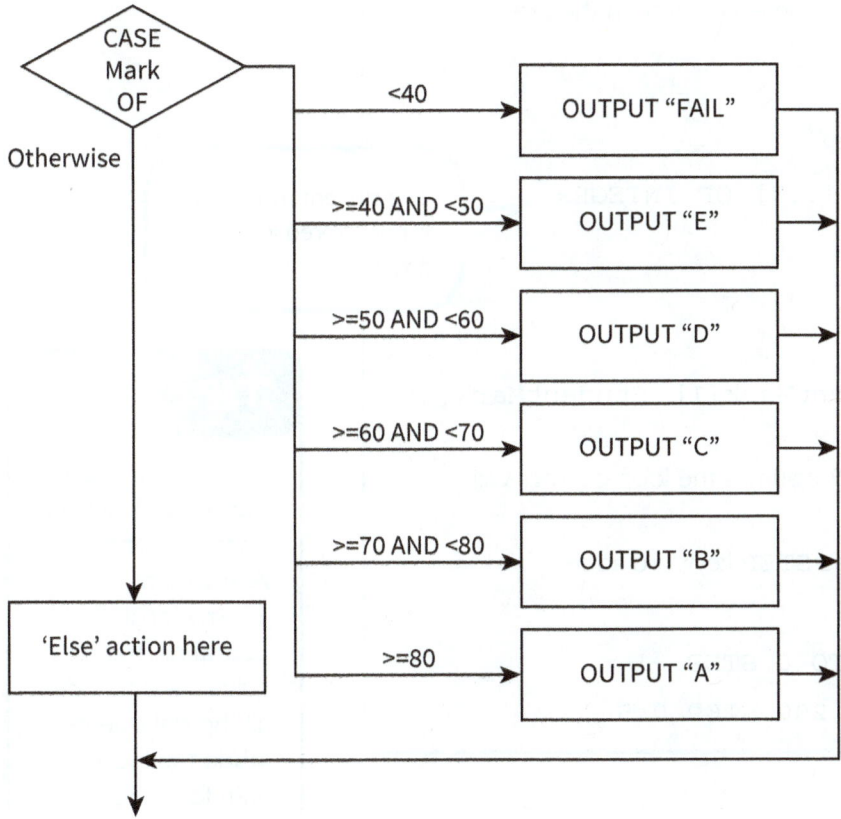

Figure 11.01 Flowchart using the Case structure.

Iteration and loops

If something is 'iterated', it is repeated. If a program has a loop, the code inside the loop will be iterated or repeated.

Pseudocode (like most high-level programming languages) has three alternative structures for a loop: the count controlled loop, the post-condition loop and the pre-condition loop.

Count controlled loop

The pseudocode keywords are `FOR` and `NEXT`.

We use this structure when we know, by the nature of the problem, the number of iterations to be made. The pseudocode will require an integer variable to act as the **loop counter**. After each iteration the value of the loop counter is incremented.

Worked example 11.06

Process the exam marks for seven students.

```
DECLARE Index            :INTEGER
DECLARE StudentMark      :INTEGER
FOR Index ← 1 TO 7
    INPUT StudentMark
NEXT Index
```

> On the first iteration `Index` has value 1
> On the second iteration it has value 2, and so on

This code works but it is of little use because on each iteration the previous student mark keyed in will be overwritten.

Consider this pseudocode:

```
DECLARE Index            :INTEGER
DECLARE StudentMark      :ARRAY[1..7] OF INTEGER
FOR Index ← 1 TO 7
    INPUT StudentMark[Index]
NEXT Index
```

> The student mark data is now stored in an array

Now the seven marks are stored as `StudentMark[1]`, `StudentMark[2]`, etc.

The statement `FOR Index ← 1 TO 7` assumes the loop counter will increment in steps of +1.

A different increment can be stated with the `STEP` keyword added.

Examples:

```
FOR TemperatureValue ← 100 TO 0 STEP -1
FOR TemperatureValue ← 0 TO 200 STEP 0.5
```

TIP

In the Pseudocode Guide For Teachers from Cambridge Assessment International Education, the guideline is to indent all the statements inside the loop with four <Space> characters.

Progress check D

Write pseudocode to output the seven student mark values from the array.

A 'post-condition' loop

The pseudocode keywords are **REPEAT** and **UNTIL**.

Use this loop structure when the number of iterations cannot be predicted. A condition will test for another iteration at the *end* of the loop. This is called a 'post-condition' loop.

```
REPEAT
    <statement(s)
UNTIL <condition>
```

Note, with the condition at the end, the statements inside the loop will be executed at least once.

> ## Worked example 11.07
>
> The number of students is not known. Marks are to be keyed in and stored in array **StudentMark**. The program terminates when a mark of -1 is entered.
>
> ```
> Index ← 1
> REPEAT
>     INPUT NextMark
>     StudentMark[Index] ← NextMark
>     Index ← Index + 1
> UNTIL NextMark = -1
> ```
>
> Note: The final -1 value is also stored.

> ## Progress check E
>
> Write pseudocode to output the student mark values from the array.

A 'pre-condition' loop

The pseudocode keywords are **WHILE** and **ENDWHILE**.

Similar to a Repeat-Until loop but here the condition comes at the *start* of the loop.

```
WHILE <condition>
    <statement(s)>
ENDWHILE
```

Note, if the condition is false the first time, then the statements inside the loop are never executed.

> ## Worked example 11.08
>
> Consider the same problem: the input and storage of an unknown number of student marks.
>
> ```
> Index ← 1
> INPUT NextMark
> WHILE NextMark <> -1
>     StudentMark[Index] ← NextMark
>     INPUT NextMark
> ENDWHILE
> ```
>
> Note: The final -1 value is not stored.

> ### TIP
>
> When a problem design requires a loop, do we know how many iterations?
>
> If you do know how many iterations, use FOR-NEXT.
>
> If you don't know how many iterations, use either REPEAT-UNTIL or WHILE-ENDWHILE.

11.03 Problems that use these constructs

Linear search

We shall now use arrays and loops to carry out a linear search.

> ### Worked example 11.09
>
> A program stores 20 names in a 1D array. The user inputs the name to be found.
>
> The program will output the array position in which the item is found, or the message, 'Name NOT FOUND'.
>
> The algorithm required is a **linear search**. Consider the first item in the array, then the second, etc. Stop searching when the item is found, or when we reach the end of the array.
>
> The variables needed are:
>
> | Identifier | Data type | Description |
> | --- | --- | --- |
> | Name | ARRAY[1:20] OF STRING | The name data |
> | Index | INTEGER | Index position in the surname array |
> | SearchName | STRING | The requested name |
> | IsFound | BOOLEAN | Flags whether or not the requested name has been found |
>
> Table 11.03 The required variables.
>
> ```
> INPUT SearchName
> IsFound ← FALSE
> Index ← 1
> REPEAT
>     IF Surname[Index] = SearchName
>         THEN
>             IsFound ← TRUE
>             OUTPUT "Surname was FOUND - at position", Index
>         ELSE
>             Index ← Index + 1
>         ENDIF
> UNTIL (IsFound = TRUE) OR (Index = 21)
> IF IsFound = FALSE
>     THEN
>         OUTPUT "Surname was NOT FOUND"
> ENDIF
> ```
>
> The loop choice above is a **REPEAT - UNTIL** loop, as we might not need to consider all items in the array. Note: the algorithm will only find and report the *first* occurrence of the requested surname.

How many comparisons?

When carrying out a linear search, if there are N values in the dataset, on average the program will have to compare N/2 values in the array before the required item is found.

Bubble sort

The method requires that the data values are stored in an array. The algorithm we shall develop could be used to sort either string, integer or real number values.

MyArray

1	2	3	4	5	6	7	8	9	10
23	12	4	11	56	2	51	17	8	20

Figure 11.02 Bubble sort data.

The bubble sort algorithm is as follows:

Compare adjacent items starting with cells 1 and 2, i.e. compare 23 with 12.

If the first item is larger then swap the items in the array. So, `MyArray[1]` now stores 12 and `MyArray[2]` stores 23.

Repeat, comparing adjacent items until finally we compare `MyArray[9]` with `MyArray[10]`.

1	2	3	4	5	6	7	8	9	10
12	4	11	23	2	51	17	8	20	56

Figure 11.03 Bubble sort data.

This is called **one pass** up through the data items.

At this point we are certain that the largest value is in the final array position.

We now start the second pass. This time the final comparison made will be items with subscripts 8 and 9.

The third pass will do a final comparison between items 7 and 8.

The 9th pass will compare items 1 and 2 only.

This suggests that if the array has an upper bound of N (N data items) then the total number of passes needed is (N-1).

Swapping two items

This needs some thought. If we action

MyArray[1] ← MyArray[2]

MyArray[2] ← MyArray[1]

the result is that both array cells will then contain the same value.

The solution is to use a temporary variable to store one of the values.

Temp ← MyArray[1]

MyArray[1] ← MyArray[2]

MyArray[2] ← Temp

Identifier	Data type	Description
MyArray	ARRAY[1:10] OF INTEGER	The array storing the data items
Temp	INTEGER	Stores one of the data values when a swap is made
Pass	INTEGER	Loop counter for the outer loop
UBound	INTEGER	The upper bound of the array
i	INTEGER	Index value for the array
Swapped	BOOLEAN	Set to FALSE at the start of each pass. Set to TRUE when a swap occurs.

Table 11.04 Bubble sort identifier table.

```
Pass ← 1
REPEAT
    Swapped ← FALSE
    FOR i ← 1 TO ( UBound - Pass)
        // the comparisons loop
        IF MyArray[i] > MyArray[i + 1]
            THEN
                // swap
                Swapped ← TRUE
                Temp ← MyArray[i]
                MyArray[i] ← MyArray[i + 1]
                MyArray[i + 1] ← Temp
        ENDIF
    NEXT
    Pass ← Pass + 1
UNTIL (Pass = UBound) OR (Swapped = FALSE)
```

> The **outer REPEAT loop** starts a new pass

> The **inner FOR loop** repeats the comparison of adjacent items

> Note: The use of boxes drawn onto the pseudocode can help to visualise where each loop starts and ends

Check: The first iteration of the outer loop (`Pass=1`) uses i values 1 to (10-1) i.e. 9 for the inner loop. `Swapped` is used to check after each pass whether any values were swapped on that pass. If there were no swaps, the list must already be in order and so no more passes are required.

Progress check F

Use the bubble sort algorithm to sort the array `Animal` into alphabetical order.

Draw up and complete a trace table with the following headings. Add as many rows as necessary.

Pass	i	UBound	Swapped
1	1	4	FALSE

Animal				
1	2	3	4	5
CAT	ANT	COW	RAT	BEE

Table 11.05 Bubble sort trace table.

You will need around 10 blank rows for the trace table.

Were the items sorted before all possible iterations of the outer loop?

11.04 Structured programming

Procedures

In Chapter 9 Section 9.01, we have already stated that it is good practice to design the algorithm for our problem using the idea of sub-tasks that are designed and later coded separately.

Procedures (and functions) are called **subprograms** or **subroutines** and fit with the idea of using a modular approach to both the problem design and coding.

Consider any application where the user is continually presented with a main menu and (say) three menu choices are available.

Procedures make possible the writing of a block of code once, which can be repeatedly executed when the program executes.

A procedure has an identifier name. It is a block of pseudocode statements. It is good practice to indent the statements inside the **PROCEDURE** markers.

The pseudocode syntax to define a procedure is:

```
PROCEDURE <identifier>
    <statement(s)>
ENDPROCEDURE
```

The pseudocode syntax to use or 'call the procedure' is:

```
CALL <identifier>
```

Worked example 11.10

Consider a program that presents a main menu of three choices to the user.

Study the pseudocode. You will see that it has been designed using three procedures.

When the menu is displayed, the `DisplayMenu` procedure is called.

If the user selects option 1, the program runs the `MyProcedure1` code.

Similarly, Option 2, calls the `MyProcedure2` code.

```
01      // Main program
02      DECLARE MyChoice  :  INTEGER
03      REPEAT
04          CALL DisplayMenu
05          INPUT MyChoice
06          IF MyChoice = 1
07              THEN
08                  CALL MyProcedure1
09              ELSE
10                  IF MyChoice = 2
11                      THEN
12                          CALL MyProcedure2
13                  ENDIF
            ENDIF
14      UNTIL MyChoice = 3
15      // end main program
```

> Here is where the three procedures are **defined**

(Continued)

```
16
17      PROCEDURE   DisplayMenu
18          OUTPUT "1. Make available the student marks"
19          OUTPUT "2. Process the student marks"
20          OUTPUT "3. End"
21          OUTPUT "Your Choice ? "
22      ENDPROCEDURE
23
24      PROCEDURE MyProcedure1
25          <statement(s)>
26      ENDPROCEDURE
27
28      PROCEDURE MyProcedure2
29          <statement(s)>
30      ENDPROCEDURE
```

Here is where the three procedures are defined

The `DisplayMenu` **procedure header** has no parameters. There are no brackets after the identifier name. Remember that almost all of the built-in functions that we studied earlier had at least one parameter.

Progress check G

a   List the statement numbers where a procedure has been <u>defined</u>.

b   Give the line number where procedure `DisplayMenu` is <u>called</u>.

c   How many times will procedure `DisplayMenu` be called when the program is executed?

Procedures with parameters

Worked example 11.11

Consider a dataset of 200 kitchen stock item prices. The values are stored in a 1D array `KitchenPrice`.

A program is to display all product prices after imposing a 15% increase.

The code is straightforward:

```
FOR Item ← 1 TO 200
    KitchenPrice[Item] ← KitchenPrice[Item] * 1.15
    OUTPUT KitchenPrice[i]
```

(Continued)

NEXT Item

This could be coded as a procedure `PriceIncrease` as follows.

We will pass the name of the array and its upper bound to the procedure through the procedure header.

```
01      // Main program
02      // KitchenPrice array has the 200 prices stored
03
04      CALL IncreasePrice(KitchenPrice, 200)
```

Arguments

Procedure header/interface

```
10      PROCEDURE IncreasePrice(PriceArray : ARRAY OF REAL, UBound : INTEGER)
11          DECLARE Item : INTEGER
12          FOR Item ← 1 TO UBound
13              PriceArray[Item] ← PriceArray[Item] * 1.15
                OUTPUT PriceArray[i]
14          NEXT Item
15      ENDPROCEDURE
```

There are several things to note here. The procedure header/interface has two **parameters**. The variable `Item` is now only used inside the procedure so it is declared as a **local variable**. That means its **scope** is only inside procedure `IncreasePrice`.

`PriceArray` and `UBound` used in the procedure code are the identifiers shown as parameters.

What is the benefit of using parameter passing?

Worked example 11.12

Consider a second array of 550 electrical goods prices stored in array `Electrical`.

The 15% price increase could be done using the same `IncreasePrice` procedure.

The procedure call to do this is:

`CALL IncreasePrice(Electrical, 550)`

The use of procedures, with parameter passing, is a tool to produce **re-usable program code**.

> **Progress check H**
>
> What change(s) would need to be made to the pseudocode to allow the percentage price increase to be varied?

Passing values by reference or by value

The issue is that when the procedure code is run and the increased prices are calculated, will these increases change the price values in the array <u>back in the main program</u>?

Passing values by value

Only <u>copies</u> of any data items are passed as parameters. Following the call to the procedure, when control passes back to the main program the values of the data items used as arguments are unchanged.

Passing values by reference

This is the opposite. It the values change as a result of running the procedure code, their value remains in that changed state when control returns to the main program. This happens because the procedure header is passed as **an address (pointer)** to the memory location where each of the argument(s) is stored.

Which mechanism is to be used is made clear by adding the syntax `BYVALUE` or `BYREF` before each parameter.

If neither is stated, then the passing of parameters is assumed to be 'by value'.

Consider the case where a permanent price increase is required. The function header would now become:

```
PROCEDURE IncreasePrice(BYREF
PriceArray : ARRAY OF REAL,
            BYVALUE UBound : INTEGER)
```

`UBound` was passed 'by value' as we know its value will not be changed by the procedure call.

Functions

We have studied the built-in functions that are provided as part of a high-level programming language. The programmer can also code their own **user-defined functions**. This is a misleading term as it really means 'programmer-defined' functions.

Functions will use the same terminology as for procedures so we have already learnt the terminology that we need.

A function has a function header with an identifier name, a specified data type, parameters (none, one or more) and it always returns a single value

As an example, consider a trivial example of a function to accept two integers and return their sum.

The steps in designing the function are to firstly decide on its identifier name, for example, `AddTwoIntegers`. Then decide on the parameters, `Num1` and `Num2`, both of data type `INTEGER`. Its data type will be to return an `INTEGER`.

```
FUNCTION AddTwoIntegers(Num1 :
INTEGER, Num2 : INTEGER) RETURNS
INTEGER

    DECLARE Answer : INTEGER

    Answer ← Num1 + Num2

    RETURN Answer

ENDFUNCTION
```

The function would then be used in a program as follows:

```
// declaration statements not shown
INPUT FirstNum
INPUT SecondNum
MyAnswer ← AddTwoIntegers(FirstNum,
SecondNum)
OUTPUT MyAnswer
// the function returns a value
// to variable MyAnswer
```

Worked example 11.13

Design a function to calculate how many words are in a string input by the user.

The method is to count the number of <space> characters in the string.

We will avoid any special cases where the string could start or end with a <space>.

Figure 11.04 Pseudocode implemented with program code.

> **TIP**
>
> Note the comment lines in the program.
>
> However, the use of the variable `SpaceCount` and the statement `RETURN SpaceCount` is intended to make the code easier to understand.

```
// declaration statements not shown for main program
OUTPUT "Text string ? "
INPUT MyString
WordCount ← CountWords(MyString)
OUTPUT WordCount
FUNCTION CountWords(ThisString : STRING) : INTEGER
    DECLARE i           : INTEGER
    DECLARE SpacesCount : INTEGER
    DECLARE WordCount   : INTEGER
    SpacesCount ← 0
    FOR i ← 2 TO (LENGTH(ThisString) - 1)
        // the first and last characters
        are ignored
        IF MID(ThisString, i, 1) = " "
            THEN
                SpacesCount ← SpacesCount + 1
        ENDIF
    NEXT i
    WordCount ← SpacesCount + 1
    RETURN WordCount
    // these two lines could have been coded as:
    // RETURN SpaceCount + 1
ENDFUNCTION
```

There are several ideas here from earlier work:

- The use of the two built-in functions:
  - `LENGTH`
  - `MID`
- The FOR – NEXT loop structure
- Local variables `i`, `SpacesCount` and `WordCount`
- Calculating a running total: `SpacesCount`

Function for use with file handling

In pseudocode we will use a built-in function, `EOF`, to test for the end of a file when it is open for reading.

```
OPEN "MyFile" FOR READ
REPEAT
    <statement(s)>
UNTIL EOF("MyFile")
CLOSEFILE "MyFile"
```

> Note it follows all the rules for any function:
> - Identifier name   EOF
> - Parameters?   one parameter, the file name
> - Return value   TRUE or FALSE

Worked example 11.17 that follows make use of EOF.

11.05 Examples of efficient pseudocode

Worked example 11.14

This is an example of counting values from an array.

Read an unknown number of values from array `Values`. Some of the values are 'ON' and some are 'OFF'. The final value in the array is 'X'.

Count the number of ON values.

```
ONCount ← 0        // Variable stores the number of "ON" values
Index ← 1          // Index value for the array
REPEAT
    If Values[Index] = "ON"
        THEN
            ONCount ← ONCount + 1
    ENDIF
    Index ← Index + 1
UNTIL Values[Index] = "X"
OUTPUT "The number of ON values is : ", ONCount
```

Progress check 1

Draw up a formal identifier table for the pseudocode above.

Worked example 11.15

A user inputs an unknown number of words at the keyboard. Input ends when 'END' is keyed. The program counts the number of words which started with letter 'P' (it could be a capital or lower case 'p').

```
PCount ← 0
INPUT NextWord
WHILE NextWord <> "END"
    FirstLetter ← LEFT(NextWord, 1)
    IF FirstLetter = "P" OR FirstLetter = "p"
        THEN
            PCount ← PCount + 1
    ENDIF
    INPUT NextWord
ENDWHILE
OUTPUT "The number of Ps was : ", PCount
```

TIP

Calculating a total will be needed in many of the programs that you write.

The technique is to store the total with a valiable `ThisTotal`. You initially assign value 0: `ThisTotal ← 0`.

Then, whenever `NextValue` is added, `ThisTotal ← ThisTotal + NextValue`

Worked example 11.16

This is an example of using a 2D array.

Six employees are sales staff. We record the number of sales made by each employee over 12 months.

Sales

	1	2	3	4	5	6	7	8	9	10	11	12
1	0	0	0	3	4	0	0					
2	1	12	12	6	7	8	9	18	8	12	11	6
3	2	4	5	1	2	3	11	6	7	2	3	1
4	11	12	3	4	6	7	1	2	6	7	11	4
5	1	0	0	8	0	0	1	1	2	3	4	
6	0	0	1	2	3	4						

Figure 11.05 Data for 2D array.

Calculate the total number of sales made.

The approach is to calculate the total for numbers in row 1, then repeat for row 2, etc.

The numbers are stored in 2D array `Sales`.

```
TotalSales ← 0
FOR Row ← 1 TO 6
    FOR ColumnNumber ← 1 TO 12
        TotalSales ← TotalSales + Sales[Row, Column]
    NEXT Column
NEXT Row
OUTPUT TotalSales
```

Worked example 11.17

This is an example of using files and finding the largest value.

The file Takings.txt contains the daily takings at a shop for a 14-day period. Each figure is stored on a new line in the file.

Write pseudocode to read the values from the file. Output the largest figure and the corresponding day number.

Identifier	Data type	Description
NextValue	STRING	The current figure read from the file
Biggest	STRING	The current largest takings figure
BiggestDayNumber	INTEGER	The day number with the biggest takings
Counter	INTEGER	The day number

Table 11.06 Example 4 identifier table.

```
OPEN "Takings.Txt" FOR READ
Biggest ← 0
Counter ← 1
REPEAT
    READFILE NextValue
    ThisNumber ← TONUM (NextValue)
    IF ThisNumber > Biggest
        THEN
        Biggest ← ThisNumber
        BiggestDayNumber ← Counter
    ENDIF
    Counter ← Counter + 1
UNTIL EOF("Takings.txt")
CLOSEFILE ("Takings.txt")
OUTPUT BiggestDayNumber, Biggest
```

Something to note is that the pseudocode uses built-in functions.

`EOF( )` tests for 'has the end of the file been reached?'

The built-in function `TONUM()` changes the string value read from the text file to a number.

Exam-style questions

1. A program displays a menu with choices 1 to 4. The code to display the menu is written as the procedure `DisplayMenu`

   a Pseudocode which uses this procedure is:

   ```
   CALL DisplayMenu
   REPEAT
       OUTPUT "Enter choice ( 1 .. 4)"
       INPUT Choice
   UNTIL Choice >= 1 AND Choice <= 4
   ```

      i Describe what this pseudocode will do. [3]

      ii State why a loop is required. [1]

   b The following pseudocode is a revised design.

   ```
   CONSTANT i ← 3
   CALL DisplayMenu
   NoOfAttempts ← 0
   REPEAT
       OUTPUT "Enter choice (1 .. 4)"
       INPUT Choice
       NoOfAttempts ← NoOfAttempts + 1
   UNTIL (Choice >= 1 AND Choice <= 4) OR NoOfAttempts = i
   ```

      i Give the maximum number of inputs the user could be prompted to make. [1]

      ii State why this algorithm is an improvement on the one given in part (a). [1]

Cambridge International AS & A level Computer Science 9608 paper 22 Q2a, b June 2015

2. A company wants a program to output the total monthly sales for one of the selected websites. The programmer codes a function with the following function header:

   `FUNCTION MonthlyWebSiteSales(ThisMonth : INTEGER, ThisSIte : CHAR) RETURNS INTEGER`

   The function returns the total number of bicycles sold for the given month and website.

   The function will use the following:

Identifier	Data type	Description
ThisMonth	INTEGER	Represents the month number e.g. 4 represents April
ThisSite	CHAR	Coded as: • X for website X • Y for Website Y

a   Give the number of parameters of this function. [1]

b   Some of the following function calls may be invalid.

Mark each call with:

- A tick (√) for a valid call
- A cross (x) for an invalid call

For any function calls which are invalid, explain why.

Function call	Tick or cross	Explanation (if invalid)
`MonthlyWebSiteSales(1, "Y")`		
`MonthlyWebSiteSales(11, 'X', 'Y')`		
`MonthlyWebSiteSales(12, 'X')`		

[3]

Cambridge International AS & A level Computer Science 9608 paper 22 Q5c June 2015

3   A program is to simulate the operation of a particular type of logic gate.

- The gate has two inputs (TRUE or FALSE) which are entered by the user.
- The program will display the output (TRUE or FALSE) from the gate.

The program uses the following identifiers in the pseudocode below:

Identifier	Data type	Description
InA	BOOLEAN	Input signal
InB	BOOLEAN	Input signal
OutZ	BOOLEAN	Output signal

```
01      INPUT InA
02      INPUT InB
03      IF (InA = FALSE AND InB = FALSE) OR (InA = FALSE AND InB = TRUE)
        OR (InA = TRUE AND InB = FALSE)
04         THEN
05            OutZ ← TRUE
06         ELSE
07            OutZ ← FALSE
08      ENDIF
19      OUTPUT OutZ
```

a   The programmer chooses the following four test cases.

Show the output (OutZ) expected for each test case.

Test case	Input		Output
	InA	InB	OutZ
1	TRUE	TRUE	
2	TRUE	FALSE	
3	FALSE	TRUE	
4	FALSE	FALSE	

b   The selection statement (lines 03 – 08) could have been written with more simplified logic. [4]

Rewrite this section of the algorithm in pseudocode. [3]

Cambridge International AS & A level Computer Science 9608 paper 21 Q3a, b November 2015

4   Use the data in Figure 11.05.

```
FOR SalesPerson ← 1 TO 6
    FOR MonthNumber ← 1 TO 12
        TotalSales ← TotalSales + Sales[SalesPerson, MonthNumber]
    NEXT MonthNumber
NEXT SalesPerson
OUTPUT TotalSales
```

Amend this pseudocode so that the output is the six salesperson numbers, their total and the final total.

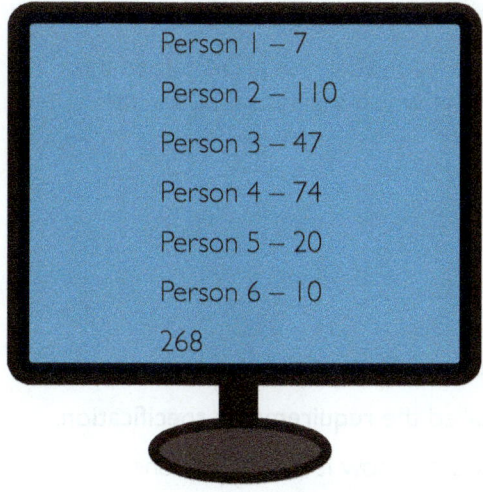

Figure 11.05

[5]

Chapter 12: Software development

Learning Objectives:

Program development life cycle:
- Understand the purpose and stages of the development life cycle
  - analysis, design, coding, testing, deployment and maintenance
- Understand the need for different approaches
  - waterfall, iterative, Rapid Application Development (RAD).

Program design:
- Use a structure chart
  - Derive the equivalent pseudocode
- Use a state-transition diagram.

Program testing and maintenance:
- Identify different types of program errors
  - syntax, logical and run-time errors
- Understand different approaches to program testing
- Understand a test strategy
- Draw up suitable test data for a test plan
- Understand the need for program maintenance
  - perfective, adaptive and corrective
- Suggest amendments to an existing program to enhance functionality.

12.01 Program development life cycle

The purpose of a development life cycle is to give clarify to all the stakeholders involved in the project as to their involvement. Staff need to be aware of their role and especially the time frame in which their contribution falls.

Developing new software is an expensive task.

It is largely 'labour intensive', requiring the skills of computing specialists.

Analysis

The first task is to establish exactly what is required. Analysis is essentially 'finding out'.

Once this is completed, the requirements are written down in a document called the **requirements specification**.

The requirements specification document defines what the software should do, not how it should be done.

Figure 12.01 shows ways in which this information will be gathered.

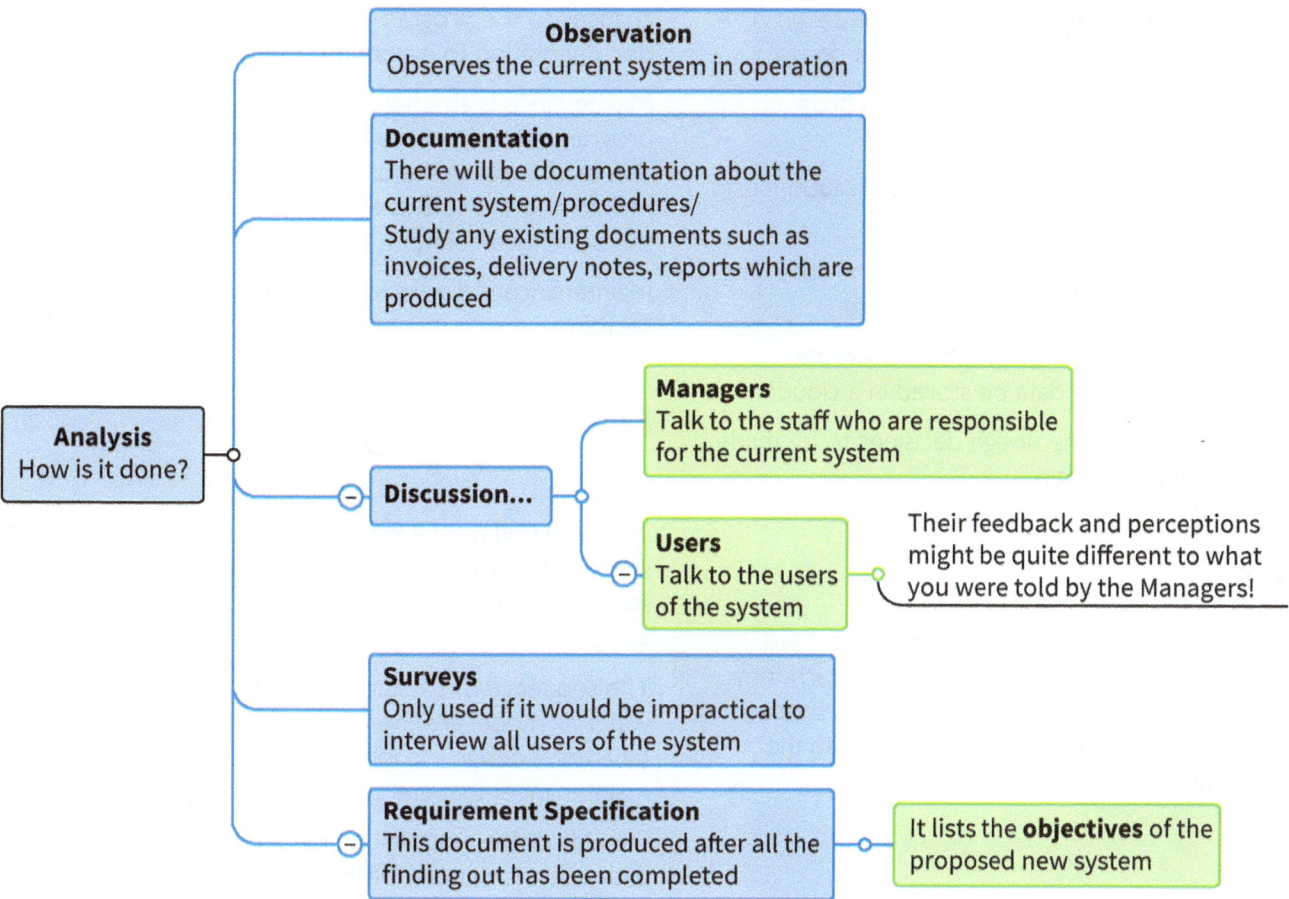

Figure 12.01 Analysis stage.

Design

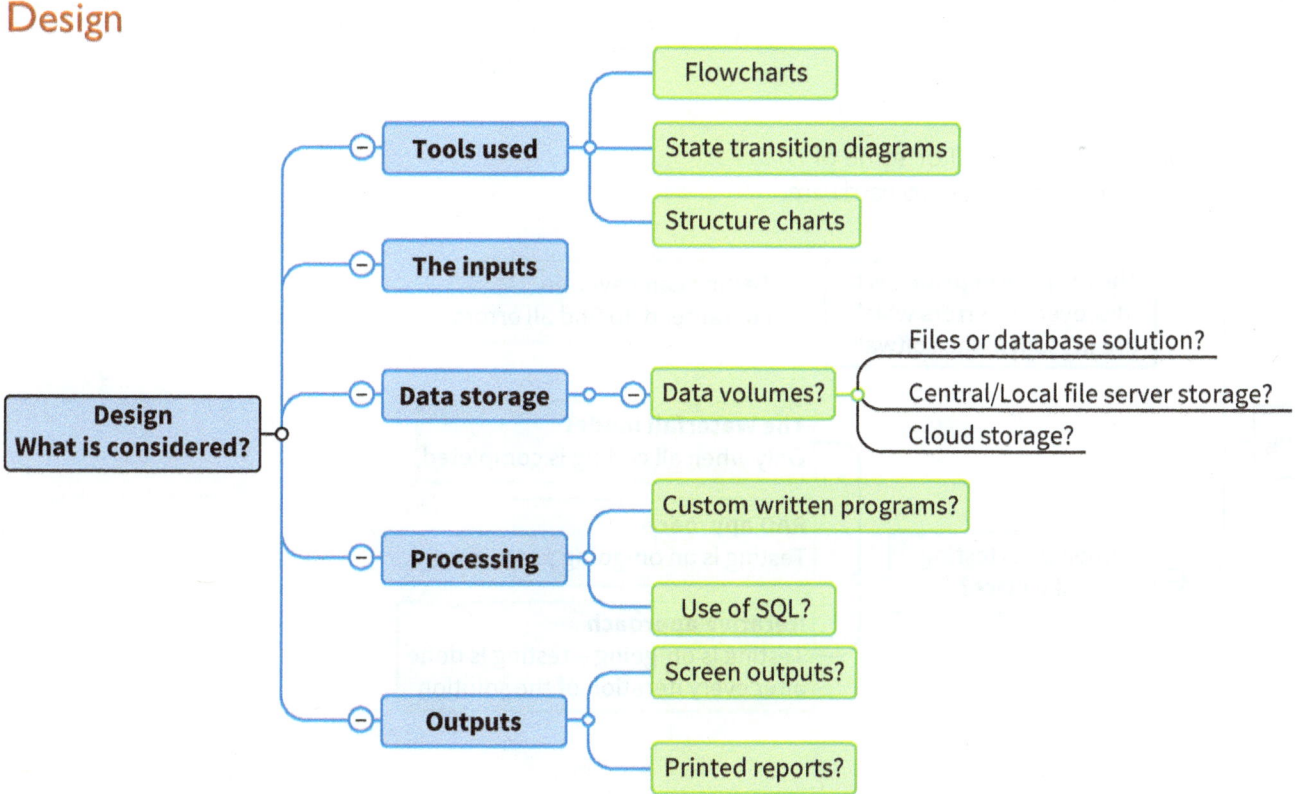

Figure 12.02 Design stage.

The nature of the problem will influence the design. The following questions are useful in planning the design.

Is this a bespoke 'stand-alone' program, or a program which is intended for mass sales?

Is the solution to be web-based as the application must be remotely available?

Is there a large volume of data? If so, then the core data storage would be done with DBMS software.

Is the data storage to be local on a server on the business premises, or will data be stored in a cloud?

These are just some of the design decisions to be made before any coding can begin.

Coding

Coding is done by programmers. Programmers will each have a specialist high-level language in which they are very competent. It is a design decision to choose the language the programmers will use to write the program code.

Testing

There are different life cycle models, waterfall, RAD and iterative. These are discussed in the next section.

Maintenance

Maintenance changes will require all or some of the following actions: making changes to hardware, changes to the program code and/or changes to documentation to support its operational effectiveness.

Maintenance is an on-going process. Software programs remain in use until they become obsolete due to changes in the user's needs, or the cost of maintaining the software becomes too high to match the benefits received in return.

Maintenance is discussed again later in the 'Testing' section.

Different life cycle models

Waterfall

The **waterfall model** emphasises a logical progression of steps to be taken in sequence, much like the cascading steps down a waterfall that has several plateaus down its path.

The sequence of six stages to be followed for the waterfall model are the traditional six stages cycle (analysis – design – coding – testing – deployment - maintenance) that are done in strict sequence.

Benefits of the waterfall model are that it is a clear pathway, it is suitable for large scale projects with large teams, it forces a planned approach where every stage of the project can be monitored, it allows for design changes at an early stage (before coding starts) and a clear 'time line' can be drawn up for the complete project.

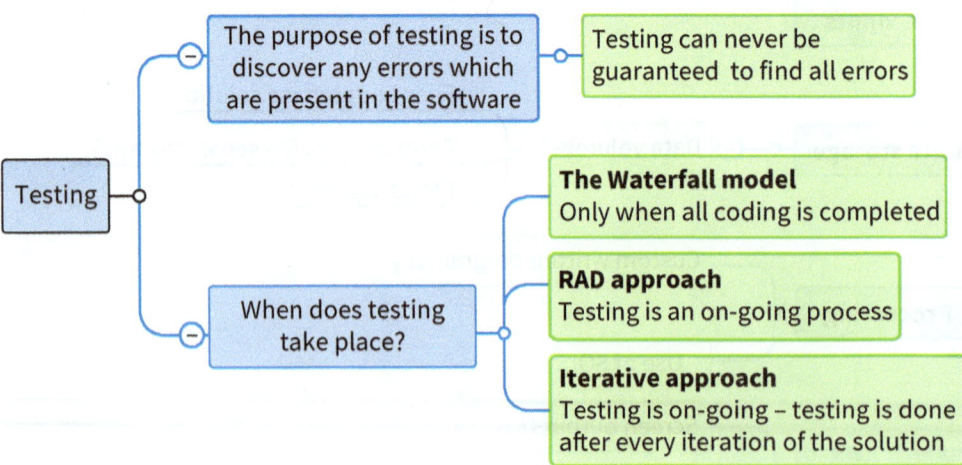

Figure 12.03 Testing stage.

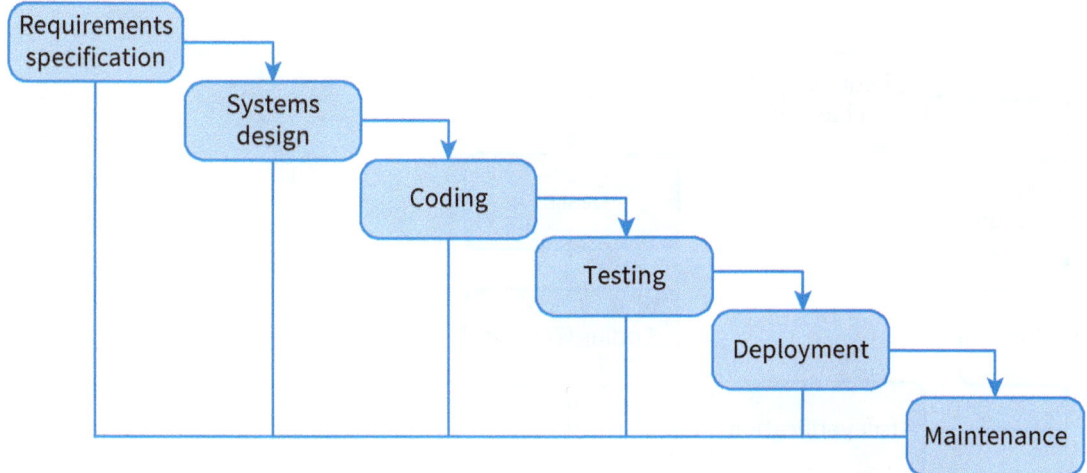

Figure 12.04 Waterfall model of the development life cycle.

Drawbacks of the waterfall model are that there is a lack of adaptability across stages and that it is difficult to adjust to late user feedback. Feedback that is provided late into the development cycle can often be too little, too late. Changes at this late stage will be costly and time-consuming for both the development team and the client. Further drawbacks are that there is a delayed testing period. Testing is not integral to earlier stages. Most bugs will not be discovered until very late into the process. Testing is not seen as integral to coding.

Rapid Applications Development (RAD)

The RAD model is a sharply contrasted alternative to the typical waterfall development model.

The designers and programmers work together at a very early stage of the project.

Feedback from the users comes from the use of a 'live' system, is a continual process and allows for initial modeling and for prototypes to be created.

Prototypes of parts of the system are seen as more useful than a detailed overall design document.

Design, coding and testing is seen as an integrated process and iterative process (not separate stages as in the waterfall model). Errors are likely to be picked up at an early stage.

Benefits of the RAD approach are that progress on the project is more measurable, code is generated quickly, RAD encourages developers to produce re-useable components (this is discussed further with Object-oriented programming (OOP) in Chapter 20), relevant user feedback during development is invaluable, and if required, the code can be quickly changed to alter the system.

A drawback of the RAD approach is that it is difficult to use with large scale projects because parts of the system may be quickly changed and the changes will need to be conveyed to several developers when the changes impact on their work.

Further drawbacks are that it demands frequent user contact and involvement (the team must be able to communicate with users on a frequent basis) and skilled developers are required because RAD techniques require a more varied skill-set across the development team.

Iterative

The **iterative** model is a cyclic process. It produces an initial, simplified implementation, then it follows incremental development where each iteration produces enhancements.

The solution will become progressively more complex with more features until the final solution is reached.

Benefits of the iterative model are that each new iteration of the software is referenced with a version number, each iteration should be a quick process and result in a shorter development time. So when problems arise with the latest iteration it is a quick process to **roll back** to use the previous iterated solution.

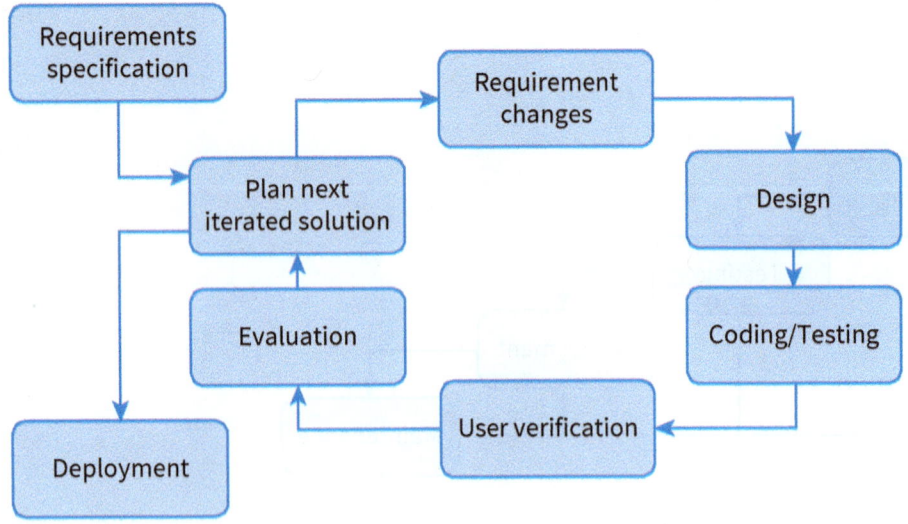

Figure 12.05 Iterative model of the development life cycle.

One drawback of the iterative model is that it generates pressure for continual user involvement (as with RAD). Each new iteration will require testing and feedback from users for it to be thoroughly evaluated.

A further drawback is that users will tend to continually suggest new features, for example, requests to add features to the next iteration that were not in the original requirements specification.

12.02 Program design

Structure chart

A structure chart is a design method used when the problem divides into sequential stages or process. Each process is represented as a box. The programmer must document on the diagram the data items which are needed for each stage and data items which are then passed on to subsequent stages.

The following worked example first describes the process stages using structured English which we are already familiar with.

> ### Worked example 12.01
>
> Consider again the car salesman problem from Chapter 10.
>
> A first description of the problem could be in structured English:
>
> 1   INPUT the price paid, registration date, mileage
> 2   CALCULATE selling price
> 3   CALCULATE profit
> 4   OUTPUT selling price, profit.
>
> We will make up an identifier name for each process. Each of them (input, calculate and output) needs data. These data items are called parameters. Later, each process will be implemented with program code as a procedure.
>
> The breaking down of the problem into procedures and the passing of data values into each procedure can be shown using a structure chart.

(Continued)

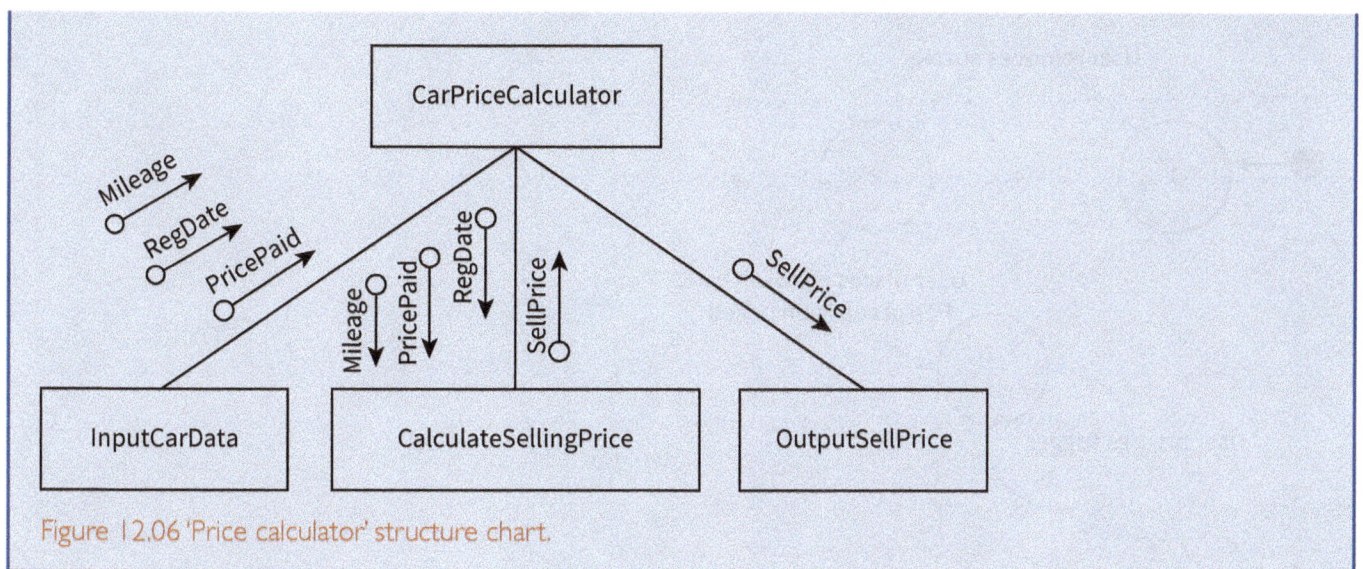

Figure 12.06 'Price calculator' structure chart.

Derive the equivalent pseudocode

Each stage will be designed as a procedure so, the pseudocode becomes:

```
InputCarData(PricePaid: REAL,
RegDate : DATE, Mileage : INTEGER)

CalculateSellingPrice(PricePaid :
REAL, RegDate : DATE, Mileage :
INTEGER)

OutputSellingPrice(SellPrice : REAL,
Profit: REAL)
```

State-transition diagram

A state-transition diagram is used to demonstrate the behaviour of some part of the problem.

We shall see in the A Level syllabus that the object may be implemented as a 'class'. Methods will be coded that transform the object from one state to another.

A state-transition diagram has only two elements, a circle (or rounded box) to represent **each possible state** of the object and connecting arrows to indicate a **transition** from one state to another.

A label on each connecting arrow indicates the **activity** that causes the state transition.

A state-transition diagram always has an **initial state** of the object.

Worked example 12.02

Consider a 'self service' petrol pump that is to dispense petrol.

The diagram shows three possible states:

1 Idle
2 Ready to dispense
3 Dispensing.

The arrows are each labelled with the activity that causes the change of state.

(Continued)

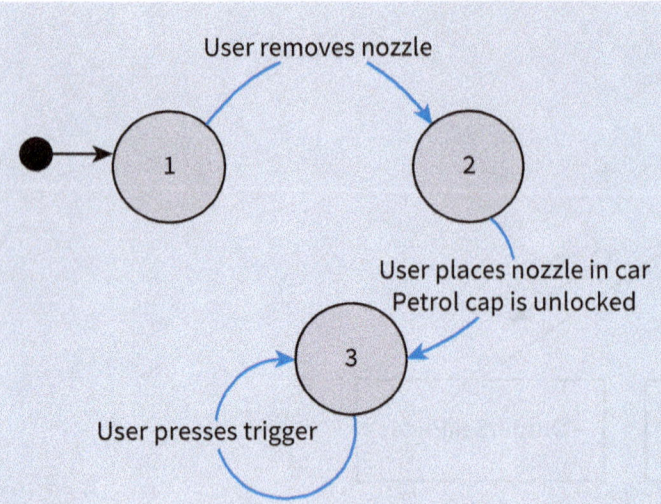

Figure 12.07 State transition diagram for use of a petrol pump.

Each connecting line is labelled with the **event** which acts as the trigger to cause the change of state, a **guard** and the action that results from the event.

The minimum labelling of a connecting line is the event or trigger.

A state can have a self-transition that is a transition that returns to itself. In the example, the user is continually pressing the nozzle of the pump and the petrol pump machine is remaining in the 'Dispensing' state.

The diagram might show a final state, indicated by: ⟶◉

A state-transition diagram can have more than one end state.

Progress check A

A connecting door between two rooms is always in one of three states, open, closed or locked.

Assume the door is initially locked.

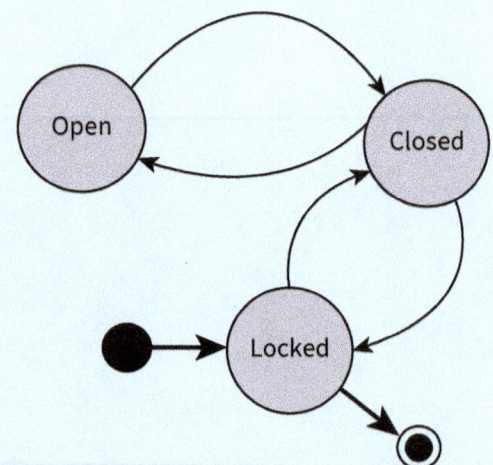

Figure 12.08 Show start and final states.

Complete the diagram and label the connecting transitions with the event that causes the transition. At the end of each day, the door is locked.

Worked example 12.03

An ATM machine is used by bank customers. The main menu is shown after the bank card is inserted by the user - The screen prompts for the PIN. A correct PIN then displays the main menu. After three incorrect PIN attempts the card is retained.

    MAIN MENU

1. Withdraw cash
2. Enquire about their account balance
3. Return card.

After a cash withdrawal or a balance enquiry, the main menu is again displayed.

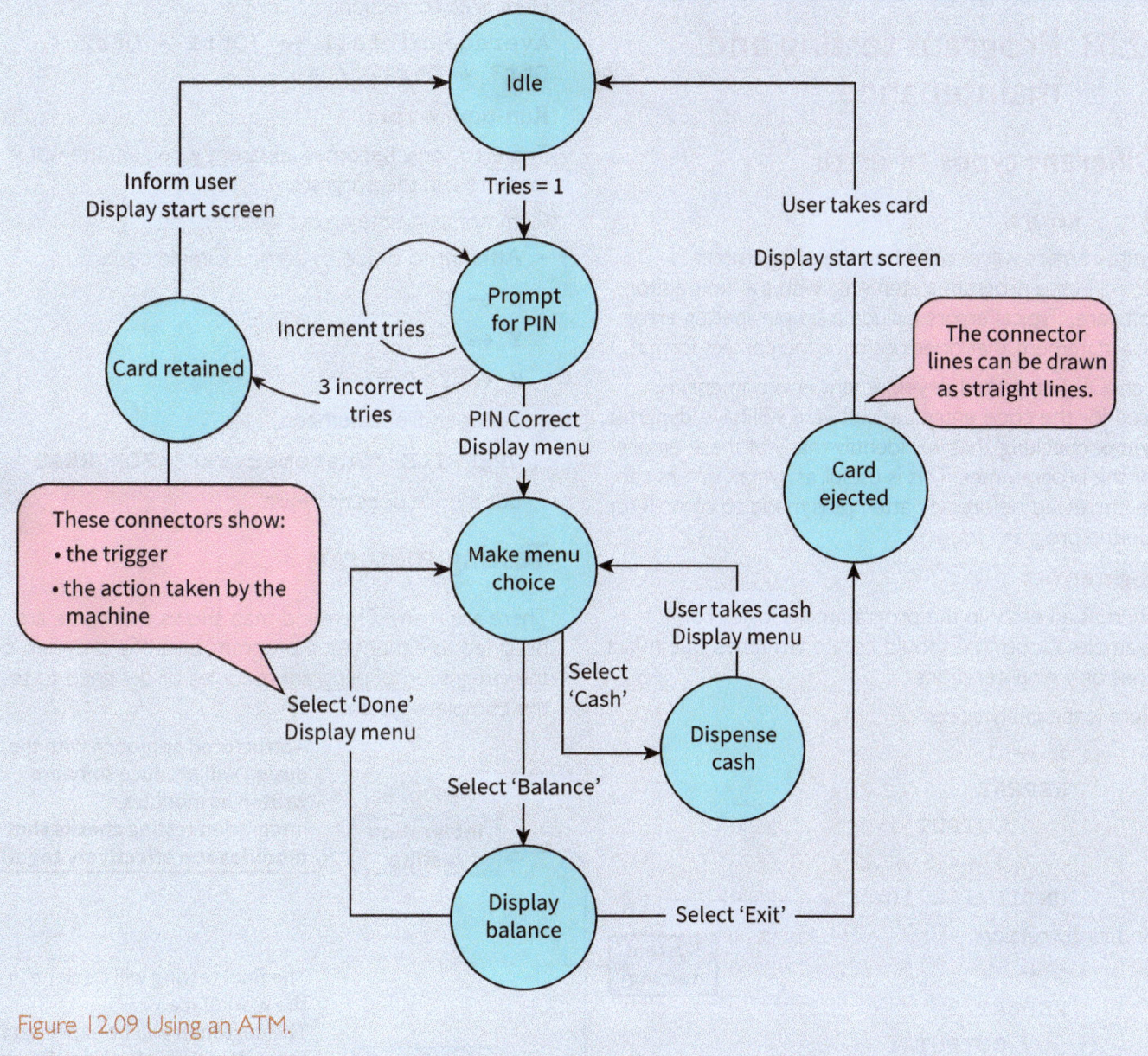

Figure 12.09 Using an ATM.

> ### Progress check B
> A college plans to offer a course. The course is initially advertised, then students enrol. The course can take a maximum of 10 students and is closed when 10 enrolments have been reached. There is a possibility that the course could be cancelled, either before or after any enrolments have been taken. If it is cancelled after there are enrolments, students are contacted to inform them.
>
> Draw the state-transition diagram with the states advertised, enrolling, cancelled and closed.

> ### Progress check C
> There is an alternative change to the pseudocode that would also result in ten iterations. What is this alternative version?

Here is another example: An arithmetic expression has been incorrectly written and the value calculated is incorrect:

```
AverageRainfall ← Qtr1 + Qtr2 + Qtr3 + Qtr4 / 4
```

This calculates an incorrect value for the quarterly average.

Here is its correction:

```
AverageRainfall ← (Qtr1 + Qtr2 + Qtr3 + Qtr4) / 4
```

Run-time errors

The error only becomes apparent when an attempt is made to run the program.

Common run-time errors include:

- Attempt to divide by zero. Example code:
  ```
  X ← 0
  Y ← 13
  Z ← Y / X
  ```
- An 'open file' statement:
  ```
  OPENFILE "Customer.txt" FOR READ
  ```
  but the file does not exist.

12.03 Program testing and maintenance

Different types of error

Syntax errors

Syntax errors will occur when the programmer is keying in the program statements with the text editor software. Typical errors include a simple spelling error or a statement that does not have the correct format.

If an IDE (integrated development environment) is used for the code entry, the software will have '**dynamic syntax checking**' that will identify many of these errors for the programmer. This is useful, as syntax errors can be corrected before any attempt is made to compile or run the program code.

Logic errors

There is an error in the programmer's logic. For example, a loop that should iterate ten times, but in fact does only nine iterations.

Here is the faulty code:

```
i ← 1
REPEAT
    OUTPUT i
    i ← i + 1
UNTIL i = 10
```

And its correction:

```
i ← 1
REPEAT
    OUTPUT i
    i ← i + 1
UNTIL i = 11
```

Testing methods

There are many. The mind-map shows that some are designed to either test a program, part of a program or the integration of program modules or designed to test the complete system.

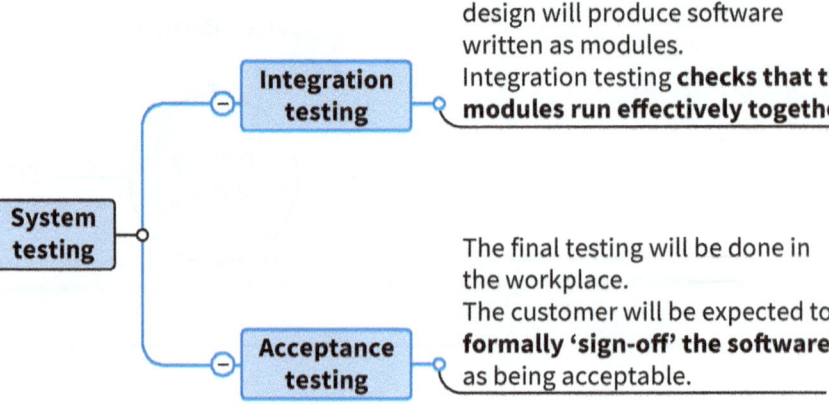

Figure 12.10 System testing.

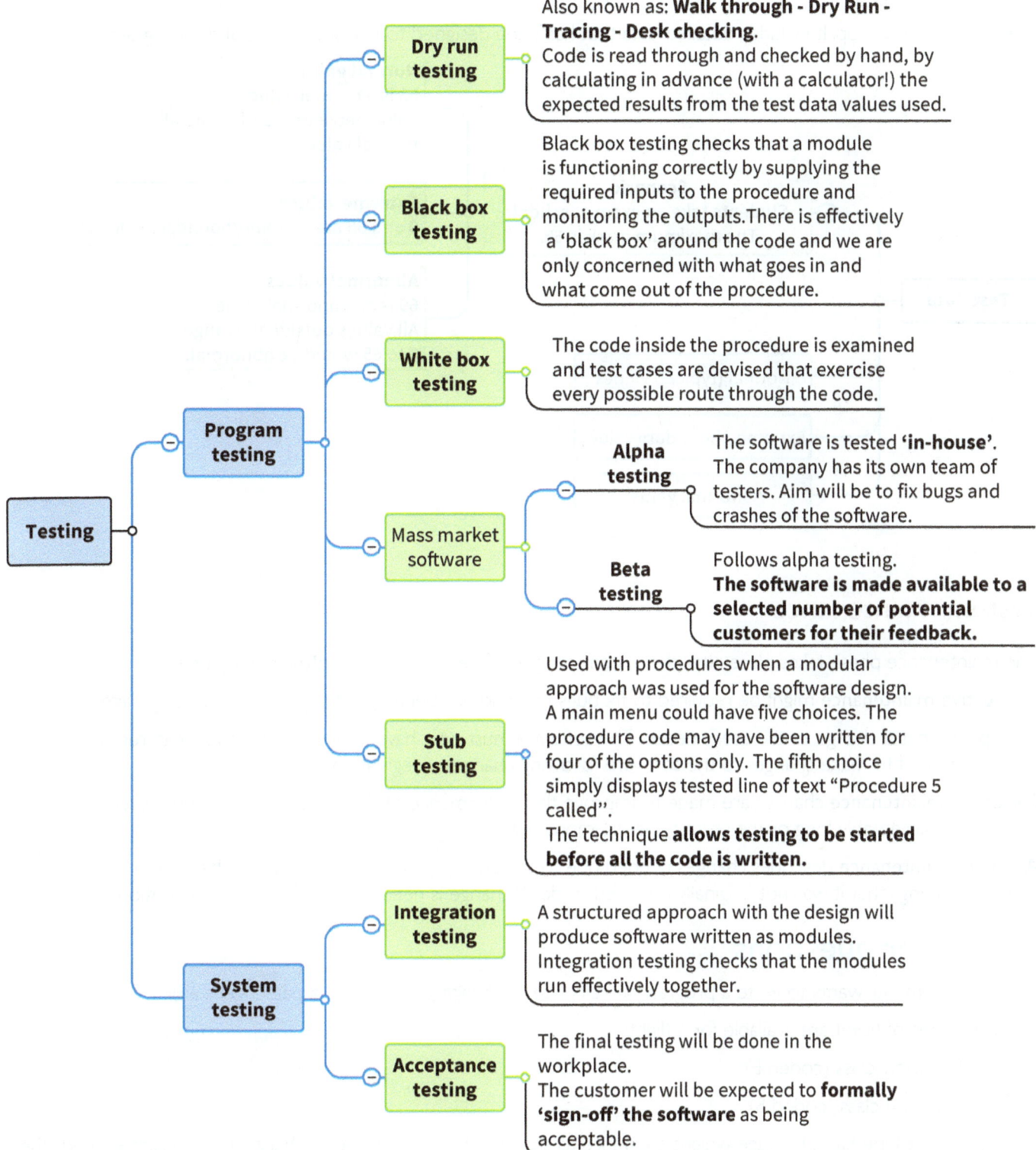

Figure 12.11 Program testing.

Choosing test data

A test plan is drawn up. It includes detailed data that has been designed to test some part of the program.

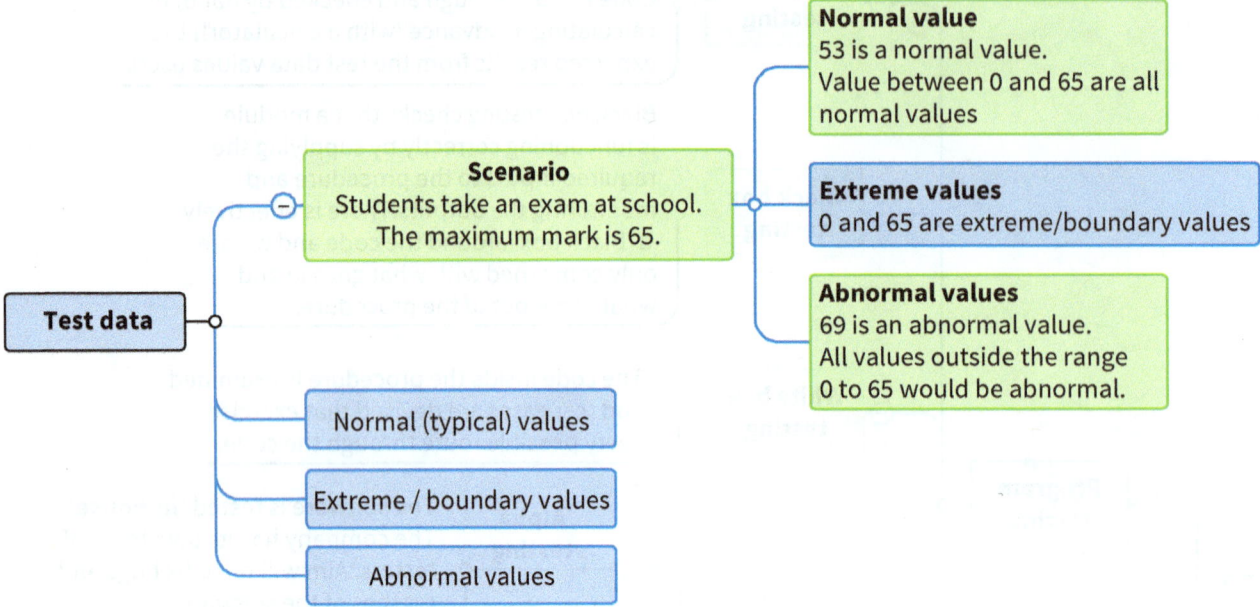

Figure 12.12 Test data.

System maintenance

The maintenance phase takes place after the system/programs are in use. This is **after deployment**.

Corrective maintenance might be required to fix bugs that had not been found at the formal testing stage.

Perhaps there is a change to the user's needs. The software must now have additional/amended features. The user might be forced to make changes to the software following changes in legislation.

Perfective maintenance changes are made to improve the performance of the system. For example, user response times are unacceptably long or the security needs improving.

Adaptive maintenance describes changes needed due to the changing needs of the system. The system must now be able to do things that it was not originally designed to do. A change is needed to the system specification.

Past paper questions

1. A programmer wants to write a program to calculate the baggage charge for a passenger's airline flight.

    Two types of ticket are available for a flight:

    - Economy class (coded E)
    - Standard class (coded S)

    Each ticket type has a baggage weight allowance as shown. The airline makes a charge if the weight exceeds the allowance.

Ticket type	Baggage allowance (kg)	Charge rate per additional kg ($)
'E'	16	3.50
'S'	20	5.75

    The programmer needs data to test the flowchart.

Complete the table of test data to show five tests.

TicketType	BaggageWeight	Explanation	Expected output
E	15		

[5]

Cambridge International AS & A level Computer Science 9608 paper 21 Q1b November 2016

2   A user can lock a safety deposit box by inputting a 4-digit code. The user can unlock the box with the same 4-digit code.

There is a keypad on the door of the safety deposit box. The following diagram shows the keys on the keypad.

1	2	3
4	5	6
7	8	9
R	0	Enter

Initially, the safety deposit box door is open and the user has not set a code.

The operation of the safety deposit box is as follows:

A   To set a new code the door must be open. The user chooses a 4-digit code and sets it by pressing the numerical keys on the keypad, followed by the Enter key. Until the user clears this code, it remains the same. (See point E)

165

B   The user can only close the door if the user has set a code.

C   To lock the door, the user closes the door, enters the set code and presses the Enter key.

D   To unlock the door, the user enters the set code. The door then opens automatically.

E   The user clears the code by opening the door and pressing the R key, followed by the Enter key. The user can then set a new code. (See point A)

The following state transition table shows the transition from one state to another of the safety deposit box:

Current state	Event	Next state
Door open, no code set	4-digit code entered	Door open, code set
Door open, code set	R entered	Door open, no code set
Door open, code set	Close door	Door closed
Door closed	Set code entered	Door locked
Door locked	Set code entered	Door open, code set
Door locked	R entered	Door locked

Complete the state-transition diagram.

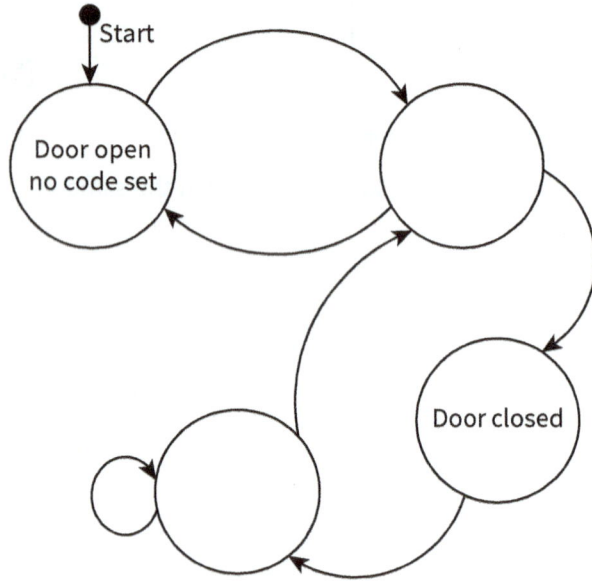

[3]

Cambridge International AS & A level Computer Science 9608 paper 43 Q1a November 2016

3   To code a 'Search by product code' procedure, Ahmed draws a structure chart showing the different stages.

The procedure uses the variables shown in the identifier table.

Identifier	Data type	Description
SearchCode	STRING	Product code input by the user
ThisIndex	INTEGER	Array index position for the corresponding product
ThisDescription	STRING	Product description found
ThisRetailPrice	REAL	Product retail price found

You can assume that before the procedure is run, all the product data is read from file **PRODUCTS** and then stored in three 1D arrays as described in the table below

Identifier	Data type	Description
PRODUCTS	TEXT FILE	Storing the code, description and retail price fot all current products
PCode	ARRAY[1:1000] OF STRING	Arry storing the product codes
PDescription	ARRAY[1:1000] OF STRING	Array storing the product descriptions
PRetailPrice	ARRAY[1:1000] OF REAL	Array storing the product retail prices
i	INTEGER	Array index used by all three arrays

Label the structure chart to show the input(s) and output(s).

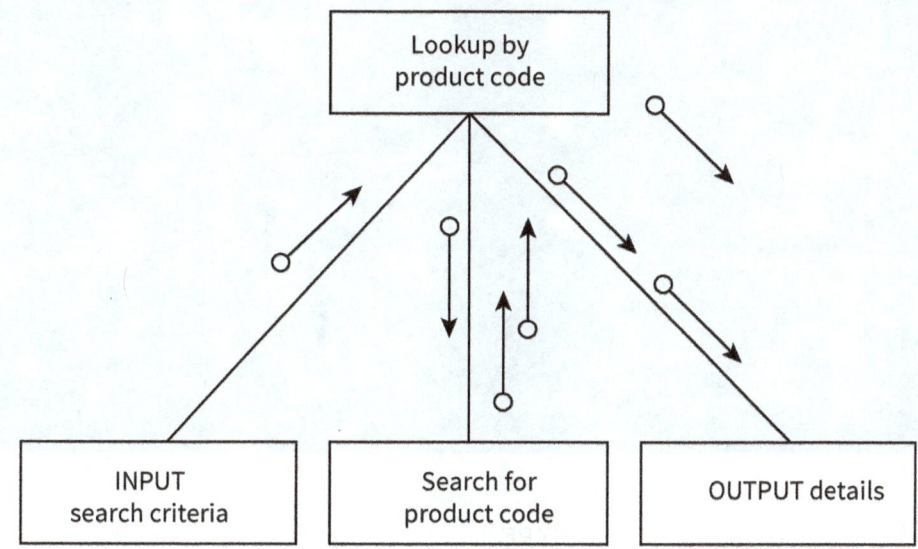

[4]

Cambridge International AS & A level Computer Science 9608 paper 21 Q4d November 2016

Chapter 13

Data representation

Learning Objectives:

User-defined types:
- Define and use (in pseudocode) user-defined types
- Define and use (in pseudocode) composite data types
- Choose an appropriate user-defined type for a given problem.

File organisation and access:
- Understand serial, sequential and random file organisation
- Understand sequential and direct access file access
- Understand how a hashing algorithm can be used to access data in a sequential/random file.

Floating-point numbers:
- Understand and use two's complement form
- Describe the format of a floating-point representation of a real number
- Understand and use normalisation
- Understand how overflow and underflow can occur
- Understand that a floating-point representation can be an approximation
- Understand that, as a consequence, the representation can have rounding errors.

13.01 User-defined data types

The programmer is the 'user' in this context as they are about to be a user of their particular programming language. The term 'programmer-defined' perhaps would have been better!

A user-defined data type will be designed and used by the programmer where the nature of the problem has data which is more complex than those represented by the simple data types, integer, string, etc.

The two-stage process will be to firstly define the new data type and then to use in their program data items of that type.

Non-composite types

Enumerated types

An enumeration is an ordered listing of all the items in a collection.

In pseudocode, give the type an identifier name and list the data values that form the type.

```
TYPE
    DECLARE DaysOfTheWeek = (Sunday,
    Monday, Tuesday, Wednesday,
    Thursday, Friday, Saturday)
ENDTYPE
```

A variable is then declared of this type.

```
DECLARE ThisDay : DaysOfTheWeek
```

Note that the possible enumerations are not string values and so no delimeter is used.

We can then process the `DayOfTheWeek` variable.

```
ThisDay ← Thursday

IF ThisDay = Saturday OR ThisDay = Sunday
    THEN
        OUTPUT "It's not a work day"
    ELSE
        OUTPUT "It's a work day"
ENDIF
```

> ### Progress check A
>
> Products are classified as category A, B, C or D.
>
> a Define an enumeration type `ProductCode`.
>
> b Assign the value C to variable `ThisProductCode`.

Pointers

The purpose of declaring an array is to reserve memory for the storage of the data. This is potentially wasteful as we could reserve storage space that never gets used.

`Order[1..2000] OF STRING` reserves 2000 storage spaces.

Pointers are designed to overcome the need to reserve memory in advance.

This is called, **dynamic memory allocation** and memory will be allocated as and when required.

In this example this would be when the data for a new order is saved to the array.

Pointers are used to access data which is dynamically created at run-time.

A pointer is a variable that stores the address of a variable.

Instead of the *data*, the pointer contains the *address* of the data.

To implement this use the declaration:

`DECLARE OrderPointer : ^Order`

This notation is read as:

`^Order` is a pointer data type, pointing to data of type `OrderPointer`.

Composite types

Sets

Assume we wish to create a set of integers that are the possible menu choice values.

Consider the case where we want to check the validity of user input. Using a standard IF statement will be very long-winded:

`IF Choice=1 OR Choice=2 OR Choice=3 OR Choice=4 OR Choice = 5 THEN ….`

Instead, the set of valid values can be given a single identifier name:

`DECLARE MenuChoice : SET OF (1,2,3,4,5)`

By using this 'SET' data type, the IF structure can be replaced by:

`IF Choice IN MenuChoice`

Other examples are:

`DECLARE SweaterSize : SET OF (XXLarge, XLarge, Large, Medium, Small)`

`DECLARE Title : SET OF (Mr, Mrs, Ms, Miss, Dr)`

> ### Progress check B
>
> a Define a set data type `ShoeSize`. Values are 38, 39, 40, 41, 42, 43, 44.
>
> b Write a selection statement that implements:
>
>   If variable `ThisSize` is 44 then output the message 'OUT OF STOCK'.

Records

The data for many applications consists not of a single data value, but of several data values of different types. We have already used this record data type in Chapter 10.

Classes/objects

The use of classes and objects is the basis of the object-oriented programming paradigm. This is discussed extensively in Chapter 19 Section 19.01.
A class is the blueprint from which actual objects (called instances) will be created.

Designing user-defined types for a given problem

> ### Progress check C
>
> Data is to be stored for nurses who work in a hospital:
>
> - The Nurse ID for that hospital – a five digit code
> - The family name
> - First names
> - The date the nurse first registered with the Nursing and Midwifery Council
> - Whether or not the basic Health and Safety course has been completed
> - The ward name on which the nurse is based
>
> Design a user-defined data type for the nurse data.

13.02 File organisation and access

We have already studied a text file in Chapter 10.

A text file consisted of several lines of text. Processing the file involved opening the file for reading, reading the lines of text in sequence and outputting the text and then closing the file.

We now need to consider how a file is used to store data.

File organisation methods

Serial organisation

Records are written to the file in chronological order. A file of bank transactions would have a chronological order and a new transaction to be added would be appended to the end of the existing file.

For many data files, where there is no chronological aspect, the data items simply appear in no particular order - only the order in which they were created in the file.

> ### Worked example 13.01
>
> A file stores a list of animals and the words used for their young, the female and the male.
>
> Study Figure 13.01. The records are in no particular order, so the file is said to have serial organisation. In this situation, records can only be read from the file in the order in which they have been stored.
>
> ```
> "nightingale", "chick", "hen", "cock"
> "bear", "cub", "sow", "boar"
> "goat", "kid", "nanny", "billy"
> "octopus", "fry", "hen", "NA"
> "camel", "calf", "cow", "bull"
> "aardvark", "cub", "sow", "boar"
> "elephant", "calf", "cow", "bull"
> "red deer", "calf", "hind", "stag"
> "ant", "larva", "queen", "drone"
> "goose", "gosling", "goose", "gander"
> "alligator", "chick", "NA", "NA"
> "zebra", "foal", "mare", "stallion"
> "tiger", "cub", "tigress", "tiger"
> ```
>
> **Serial file organisation** — The records are in no particular order
>
> Figure 13.01 Serial file organisation (with delimiters).

TIP

There are many variations in the precise encoding used for file contents. The file in Figure 13.01 has speech marks to **delimit** each datum and then a **comma separator** for each datum. Figure 13.02 that follows uses a different encoding.

Sequential organisation

A possible improvement is as follows: Records are ordered, for example, stored in animal name order. The file is then said to have **sequential organisation** with animal name chosen as the **key field**.

key field (animal name)	field (young)	field (female)	field (male)
ant	larva	queen	drone

```
aardvark, cub, sow, bear
alligator, chick, NA, NA
ant, larva, queen, drone
bear, cub, sow, boar
camel, calf, cow, bull
elephant, calf, cow, bull
goat, kid, nanny, billy
goose, gosling, goose, gander
nightingale, chick, hen, cock
octopus, fry, hen, NA
red deer, calf, hind, stag
tiger, cub, tigress, tiger
zebra, foal, mare, stallion
```

Sequential file organisation

Animal name is the **key field** – the records are in animal name order.

Figure 13.02 Sequential file organisation.

Random organisation (using a record key)

Random file organisation allows **direct access** to a particular record in the file and for records to be written and read to/from the file in the same **file session**.

The file is opened in RANDOM mode.

The user will allocate each record a **record key number**. The record **key number** is used to with a **hashing function** to calculate the **address** where this record is to be stored.

File access methods

Sequential access for serial and sequential files

Study both Figure 13.01 (Serial organisation) and Figure 13.02 (Sequential organisation).

A major limitation of both serial and sequential organisation is that the data values can only be read from the file in sequence (i.e. sequentially).

In the serial file, the 'goose' data can only be read after the preceding six animals have been read. In the sequential file, the 'zebra' data can only be read after all the other 13 animal records have been read.

This is a major drawback when using data files with serial or sequential organisation.

Fixed length data values

An alternative technique for file organisation is to store each data line with a fixed length.

```
aardvark     cub       sow      boar
alligator    chick     NA       NA
ant          larva     queen    drone
bear         cub       sow      boar
camel        calf      cow      bull
elephant     calf      cow      bull
goat         kid       nanny    billy
goose        gosling   goose    gander
nightingale  chick     hen      cock
octopus      fry       hen      NA
red deer     calf      hind     stag
tiger        cub       tigress  tiger
zebra        foal      mare     stallion
```

Figure 13.03 Fixed length records.

This has a possible benefit as follows.

Each animal's data above takes up 37 bytes. This means that the 4th data line in the file will start with byte number $3 \times 37 + 1 = 112$. File access methods provided by certain programming languages can make use of this. This will involve positioning a **file pointer** to a certain byte position in the file.

Direct access to a sequentially organised file

This is only possible if the file has been created with fixed length records. The data will then work in conjunction with an **index file**.

The index file contents would be stored in main memory so there would be fast access to the value of 'goat' and its index position in the main file. The software will then set up a file pointer positioned at byte number $7 \times 37 + 1 =$ byte 260 in the main file.

Key field	Index
aardvark	1
alligator	2
ant	3
bear	4
camel	5
elephant	6
goat	7
goose	8
nightingale	9
octopus	10
red deer	11
tiger	12
zebra	13

Find Goat →

```
aardvark     cub       sow        boar
alligator    chick     NA         NA
ant          larva     queen      drone
bear         cub       sow        boar
camel        calf      cow        bull
elephant     calf      cow        bull
goat         kid       nanny      billy
goose        gosling   goose      gander
nightingale  chick     hen        cock
octopus      fry       hen        NA
red deer     calf      hind       stag
tiger        cub       tigress    tiger
zebra        foal      mare       stallion
```

Figure 13.04 Direct access to a sequentially organised file.

Direct access to a random file

A single record is retrieved (directly) from the file by simply using its known record its known record key and hashing the disk address. This is the record key that was used when the data was written to the file.

Hashing algorithms

Hashing is a clever way to calculate this record key number from one of the known data items.

Worked example 13.02

A file of people's names is to be created. The record key is to be hashed from the name. It is estimated that the file will eventually contain 500 names.

A hashing function calculates the key number, from the surname.

The hashing calculation used here is as follows:

Surname: PIPER	ASCII code
P	80
I	73
P	80
E	69
R	82

Total: 384
Divide by 503 … Remainder: 384

503 is chosen because it is the first prime number greater than the anticipated number of records.

Issues with any hashing functions are that they should generate an appropriate range of keys. Two different names could 'hash' to the same key number and the implication is that the data for the first record that used this key will be overwritten.

(Continued)

We need to have a strategy for dealing with this second issue. A solution is as follows:

Generate the key number and if there is already a record with this number then search the file in sequence after this key for the first unused position. Then write the data in this unoccupied position in the file.

The hashing function can be given an identifier name, and expressed as:

```
KeyNumber ← MyHashingFunction(<name>)
```

Choosing a file organisation and access method

A summary of what is possible is shown in Table 13.01:

File Organisation	Sequential access	Direct access
Serial	✓	✗
Sequential	✓	✗
Sequential + Index file	✓	✓
Random	✓	✓

Table 13.01 File organisation and access summary.

The key issue in deciding what organisational method to use is the question: Do we need fast access to individual records?

Consider the following scenarios:

1. A product file with 2000 items is to have each price increased by 5%.

   Since all records have to be accessed, we can process them in sequence.

   Therefore:

   Organisation: serial or sequential.

   Access: sequential.

2. An orders file has thousands of new orders from customers added each day. Customer Services are always receiving queries from customers about a particular order.

   We need fast access to individual orders.

   Therefore:

   Organisation: Random, with the order number as the record key.

   Access: Direct access, using the record key.

> **TIP**
>
> Python: The hash table data structure is essentially what the Python programming language implements as a data structure called a **dictionary**.
>
> Visual Basic: This has two variations: a data structure called an ArrayList and a second data structure called a HashTable. Like the Python dictionary, the HashTable stores two values. A key is used to access the data and the data value.
>
> Please note that you need to be able to produce program code using these 'language specific' data structures.

> **Progress check D**
>
> A bank maintains a file of all the accounts held at the branch.
>
> The bank is always answering enquiries from customers about their account balance.
>
> a Describe why random file organisation should be used.
>
> b State what should be used as the record key.

13.03 Real numbers and normalised floating-point representation

The format of binary floating-point real numbers

Computer programs will use not only integer numbers, but also numbers that might have a fraction part, i.e. real numbers.

A number can be represented in 'standard form'.

Consider 1987.381

This can be expressed as $\qquad 1.987381 \times 10^3$

or $\qquad 0.1987381 \times 10^4$

Floating point representation uses the same approach, except we must use an exponent with base 2.

For our **floating-point format**, we express the first part, called the **mantissa**, as a fraction and then calculate the appropriate **exponent**.

Very small numbers are also possible: 0.000876 is expressed as $0.876 \times \frac{1}{10^3} = 0.876 \times 10^{-3}$

Hence for the range of numbers we will want to represent, any number can be expressed as fraction $\times$ 10^{Exponent}, where both the fraction and the exponent can be positive or negative.

Since we store numbers in a computer system using base 2 (binary), the same principles can be followed using 2 instead of 10:

$$\text{Number} = \text{Fraction} \times 2^{\text{Exponent}}$$

This is called floating-point format:

$$\text{Number} = \text{Mantissa} \times 2^{\text{Exponent}}$$

Hence, we can express any real number in floating point form by stating the mantissa (usually in two's complement) and the exponent (usually in two's complement).

The only issue then is how many bits are available for the mantissa and exponent.

Convert binary floating-point real numbers into denary

Worked example 13.03

A floating-point number uses 8 bits for the mantissa and a 4-bit exponent (both in two's complement).

The place values for the mantissa and exponent are shown below.

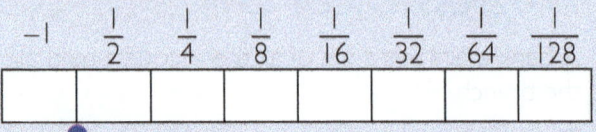

Note carefully the place values for the mantissa.

Worked example 13.04

-1	$\frac{1}{2}$	$\frac{1}{4}$	$\frac{1}{8}$	$\frac{1}{16}$	$\frac{1}{32}$	$\frac{1}{64}$	$\frac{1}{128}$	-8	4	2	1
0	1	0	1	1	1	0	0	0	1	0	0

Mantissa: $\qquad$ $1/2 + 1/8 + 1/16 + 1/32 = +23/32$

Exponent: $\qquad$ $+4$

Denary number: $\qquad$ $+23/32 \times 2^{+4} = +23/32 \times 16$

$\qquad\qquad\qquad\qquad = +11.5$

Worked example 13.05

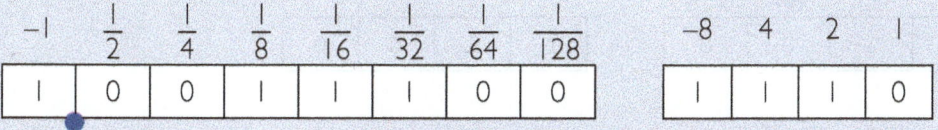

Mantissa: $-1 + 1/8 + 1/16 + 1/32 = -25/32$
Exponent -2
Denary number: $-25/32 \times 2^{-2} = -25/32 \times 1/4$
                 $= -25/128$

Convert a denary real number into its floating point representation

Example, for a positive number

Using the format in Worked example 13.05, what is the representation for 11 ½ ?

$11\ ½ = 23/2$

We need to multiply the numerator and denominator by the power of 2 that can create the fraction closest to 1.

$23/2 = 23/2 * 16/16$
$ = 23/32 \times 16$
$ = (16/32 + 4/32 + 2/32 + 1/32) \times 2^{+4}$
$ = (1/2 + 1/8 + 1/16 + 1/32) \times 2^{+4}$
$ = $ 01011100 for the mantissa and 00000100 for the exponent.

Example, for a negative number

Using the format shown, what is the representation for –5 ½ ?

$-5\ ½ = -11/2 \times 8/8$
$ = -11/16 \times 8$
$ = (-1 + 5/16) \times 2^{+3}$
$ = (-1 + 4/16 + 1/16) \times 2^{+3}$
$ = (-1 + 1/4 + 1/16) \times 2^{+3}$
$ = $ 10101000 for the mantissa and 00000011 for the exponent.

Progress check E

Using an 8-bit mantissa and exponent, write the representation for:

a 17 ¾   b 3 $^3/_{16}$ c –9$^1/_2$

Normalised floating-point format

There is more than one possible representation for a number using floating point representation.

These examples use an 8-bit mantissa and 4-bit exponent.

Consider Pattern 1.

–1	$\frac{1}{2}$	$\frac{1}{4}$	$\frac{1}{8}$	$\frac{1}{16}$	$\frac{1}{32}$	$\frac{1}{64}$	$\frac{1}{128}$		–8	4	2	1
0	1	0	0	1	0	0	0		0	0	1	1

$+9/16 \times 2^{+3} \qquad = 4.5$

Alternatively – Pattern 2.

–1	$\frac{1}{2}$	$\frac{1}{4}$	$\frac{1}{8}$	$\frac{1}{16}$	$\frac{1}{32}$	$\frac{1}{64}$	$\frac{1}{128}$
0	0	1	0	0	1	0	0

–8	4	2	1
0	1	0	0

= (1/4 + 1/32) × 2^{+4}

= +9/32 × 2^{+4} = 4.5

Hence, both Pattern 1 and Pattern 2 are correct representations for the number 4.5.

In Pattern 2 we have made the mantissa smaller by a factor of 2, but then doubled the exponent.

This raises the question, how do we decide which representation to use?

The reasons for normalisation

The form to use is called the **normalised representation**. Normalised form is the form that will ensure that the maximum accuracy of the number is preserved, for example, Pattern 1 was the normalised form.

For a bit pattern in its normalised form, we study the mantissa. For all positive numbers, the mantissa must start (in binary) with the digits 01. For all negative numbers, the mantissa must start with the digits 10.

> **TIP**
>
> Do not confuse the term 'normalised' used here with 'Normal Forms' used in database modelling.

> **Progress check F**
>
> These are three normalised floating-point form numbers, each of which has an 8-bit mantissa and an 8-bit exponent.
>
> A   01110000 00000001
>
> B   10001000 00000111
>
> C   10100000 10001001
>
> a Explain how you recognise that all three numbers are in normalised form.
>
> b Calculate each denary number, by working out the mantissa, the exponent and the denary number.

If a real number is not represented in its normalised form then there will be the risk that a **loss of accuracy** might result. The examples that follow on underflow and overflow, explained below, illustrate this.

Changing the allocation of bits to mantissa and exponent

First, we discuss what range of numbers are possible for our 8-bit mantissa and 4-bit exponent.

The following shows four of the extreme cases :

	Mantissa (two's complement)	Exponent (power of 2)	Denary number	
1	0111 1111 +127/128	0111 +7	+127	For 1 and 2. The mantissa starting 01 … confirms this is a positive number.
2	0100 0000 +64/128 = +1/2	1000 –8	+1/512	
3	1000 0000 –1	0111 +7	–128	For 3 and 4. the mantissa starting 10 … confirms this is a negative number.
4	1011 1111 –67 /128	1000 –8	–67 /32768	

More bits for the mantissa gives *more accuracy*.

More bits for the exponent allows a *greater range of numbers* to be represented.

Underflow and overflow

Underflow occurs if the number is too small to be represented by the bits available. Overflow occurs when we attempt to represent a large number which cannot be represented due to the number of bits used for the mantissa and exponent.

Worked example 13.06

Assume a real number is represented with a 5-bit mantissa and 5-bit exponent. The place values are:

-1	$\frac{1}{2}$	$\frac{1}{4}$	$\frac{1}{8}$	$\frac{1}{16}$		-16	8	4	2	1

If we attempt to represent the small number $+\frac{1}{2^{21}}$

the lowest value for the exponent we can represent is -16

So, $+\frac{1}{2^{21}} = \frac{1}{2^5} \times \frac{1}{2^{16}} =$ which is represented by:

This bit cannot get stored – It will be lost

-1	$\frac{1}{2}$	$\frac{1}{4}$	$\frac{1}{8}$	$\frac{1}{16}$	$\frac{1}{32}$	-16	8	4	2	1
0	0	0	0	0	1	1	0	0	0	0

So, the conclusion is that, using a 5-bit mantissa and 5-bit exponent, the number is too small to be represented. Instead it shows up as zero and we have **underflow**.

Worked example 13.07

Consider the largest positive number that can be represented.

-1	$\frac{1}{2}$	$\frac{1}{4}$	$\frac{1}{8}$	$\frac{1}{16}$		-16	8	4	2	1
0	1	1	1	1		0	1	1	1	1

This is the denary number +3720. Any attempt to represent a larger number than this will fail. The result will **overflow** into the leftmost position, converting the positive result into a negative one. The opposite can also occur.

Progress check G

Show the working for the calculated largest value of +3720 using a 5-bit mantissa and 5-bit exponent.

A binary representation may be an approximation

The representation of $+4\frac{1}{2}$ we considered earlier would be:

-1	$\frac{1}{2}$	$\frac{1}{4}$	$\frac{1}{8}$	$\frac{1}{16}$		-16	8	4	2	1
0	1	0	0	1		0	0	0	1	1

This calculates correctly as +4 ½ and is in its normalised form.

An alternative attempt could have been:

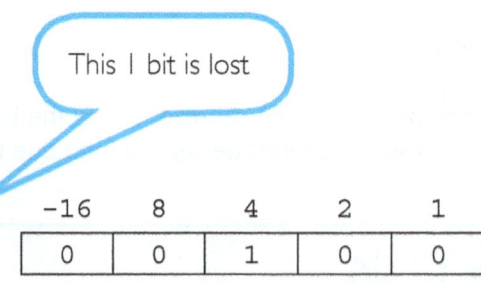

This 1 bit is lost

-1	$\frac{1}{2}$	$\frac{1}{4}$	$\frac{1}{8}$	$\frac{1}{16}$		-16	8	4	2	1
0	0	1	0	0	1	0	0	1	0	0

We have made the mantissa smaller by a factor of 2 and increased the exponent accordingly.

The least significant 1 bit in the mantissa is now lost. The bit pattern then calculates to:

¼ × 2^{+4} = 4

The conclusion is that there has been a **loss of accuracy** with this alternative (un-normalised) representation. We have introduced a **rounding error**.

Past paper questions

1 Data types can be defined in a programming language.

The data type `StudentRecord` is defined by the code:

```
TYPE StudentRecord
    DECLARE StudentID            :   INTEGER
    DECLARE StudentFirstName     :   STRING
    DECLARE StudentSurname       :   STRING
    DECLARE StudentDOB           :   DATE
    DECLARE StudentCourse        :   ARRAY [1:10] OF STRING
ENDTYPE
```

A variable, `CollegeStudent`, is declared with code:

`DECLARE CollegeStudent : StudentRecord`

  a Write a pseudocode statement to assign 6539 to the `StudentID` of `CollegeStudent`.

  b The type definition for `StudentRecord` is changed.

   i Students can take six courses from: Computer Science, Engineerng, Science, Maths, Physics, Chemistry, Music, Drama and English Language.

   Rewrite **one** line from the type definition of `StudentRecord` to implement the change.

   DECLARE   [2]

   ii The values for the field `StudentID` must be between `1` and `8000` inclusive.

   Rewrite **one** line from the type definition of `StudentRecord` to implement the change.

   DECLARE   [1]

  c A programmer is asked to write a program to process the assessment data for each student. Students sit one exam for every course they take.

  A composite data type, `StudentAssessment`, need to be defined with the following three fields:

- a student assessment code (a unique code of three letters and two digits)
- the marks for the six exams
- the average mark of the six exams.

    i   Write pseudocode to define the data type `StudentAssessment`.
        [4]

    ii Data about all students and their assessments are stored in a file that uses random organisation. The `StudentID` is used as the key field.

        The program allows a user to enter data for a new student.

        Explain how the program adds the new data to the file. [3]

Cambridge International AS & A level Computer Science 9608 paper 32 Q1 June 2018

2   In a particular computer system, real numbers are stored using floating-point representation with:
- 12 bits for the mantissa
- 4 bits for the exponent
- two's complement form for both mantissa and exponent

    a   Calculate the floating-point representation of +2.5 in this system. Show your working.

        Mantissa   **Exponent**

        [3]

    b   Calculate the floating-point representation of -2.5 in this system. Show your working.

        Mantissa   **Exponent**

        [3]

    c   Find the denary value for the following binary floating-point number. Show your working.

        Mantissa   **Exponent**
        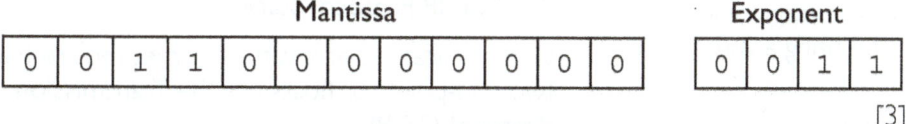

        [3]

    d   i   State whether the floating-point number given in **part c** is normalised or not normalised. [1]

        ii Justify your answer. [1]

    e   The system changes so that it now allocates 8 bits to both the mantissa and the exponent.

        State two effects this has on the numbers that can be represented.

        1

        2   [2]

Cambridge International AS & A level Computer Science 9608 paper 31 Q1 November 2016

Chapter 14

Communication and internet technologies

Learning Objectives:

Protocols:

- Understand the term protocol and the difference between a connected and connectionless communication
- Understand the role of each layer in the TCP/IP protocol stack
- Understand a number of different application protocols.

Circuit switching and packet switching:

- Understand circuit switching
- Understand packet switching
- Justify the benefits and drawbacks of each
- Understand the function of a router in packet switching
- Understand how packet switching is used for internet communications.

14.01 Protocols

A **protocol** is a way of communicating.

Communication between a computer and a device must start with some form of connection.

For example, a computer about to send data to a printer sends a signal asking 'Are you ready?' and then the printer sends back an acknowledgement signal.

This is a 'connection required' form of communication. The computer and printer might be using a wired or a wireless connection.

There are other protocols that are 'connectionless', i.e. they do not require a connection to be confirmed before communication can start.

A protocol stack

The protocol is built up in layers, with one layer 'stacked' on top of the previous layer. Each layer is responsible for some part of the communication.

TCP/IP protocol suite

Applications that use the internet for communication are client-server applications. The communication requires a connection to be made between the two 'end-points'. The client will initiate some form of communication to/from the server. The server is simply waiting for requests from applications, for example, a web browser, on client computers.

The communication uses a collection of protocols that work together, called the **TCP/IP Protocol Suite**. The different protocols that are needed are built up, one upon another, in a particular order. This is referred to as the **TCP/IP Protocol Stack**.

Communications across the internet require that the two end-points or **hosts** use the **Transmission Control Protocol (TCP)**.

Layer	
Application	Software applications; web browser – e-mail client – FTP for file transfer
Transport	TCP
Internet/IP layer	IP
Network/Link	At the network cable (e.g. Ethernet) or wireless

FIG 14.01 TCP/IP protocol stack.

Application layer

The application software will 'package up', i.e. organise, the 'core data' that is to be transmitted. For an email client this is the email text content. For a web browser, this will be the text content, the tags and, if present, JavaScript (or other language) code. For file-transfer client software, it will be the file bytes to be downloaded. Each application will have its own 'application protocol' for the way this core data is packaged.

These application layer protocols can be summarised.

Application	Application protocol	Name origin	Port number
Email – receiving	POP3	Post Office Protocol version 3	110
	IMAP	Interactive Message Access Protocol	143 or 993
Email – sending	SMTP	Simple Mail Transfer Protocol	25
File transfer (e.g. for downloads)	FTP	File Transfer Protocol	20 or 21
Web browser	HTTP	Hypertext Transfer Protocol	80

Table 14.01 Application protocols.

The software (e.g. the web browser or email client) will use the appropriate applications protocol (see Table **14.01**) and also the 'software **port**' to direct the data on to the next layer, the Transport layer. This is discussed below.

Transport layer

The TCP (Transport Communication Protocol) layer sets up a bi-directional connection between the two hosts and maintains this connection. There will be a software process, the TCP software, running on each **host** with this task.

The task of the TCP software is to monitor any errors that occur, monitor data packets and to organise the data packets received into a format that the client or server application is expecting.

If packets are not received, the TCP software will instigate their re-transmission.

IP addresses

Remember that data is being sent across the internet and that the internet identifies each host using an IP address.

But the destination of a data packet also needs its port number.

Socket = IP address and Port number.

TCP is not the only available transport protocol. User Datagram Protocol (UDP) is a connectionless protocol, less reliable than TCP, but faster because there is no checking.

Internet (or Internet Protocol) layer

An IP packet consists of the header section + the data section. The **header section** has 14 data items. These include:

Progress check A

a What do the initials TCP and IP stand for in the TCP/IP protocol suite?

b Write, in order, the four layers of the TCP/IP protocol suite.

c State three different protocols that would be used at the application layer.

	Description
Length	The length of the header (Multiples of 32-bits)
The version	An IPv4 packet will store the value 4.
Source IP address	
Destination IP address	
The 'time to live' value	Designed to stop a packet being continually passed from one router to another without ever reaching its destination. It behaves as a 'hop count' – the value in the header is decremented every time it is passed to a new router. The packet is 'killed' when the count reaches zero and a message is sent to the source IP address. A typical trace route allows up to 30 hops before the packet is killed.
Checksum	Checks the integrity of the header data.
Total packet length	The data section (and so the length of the packet) can be a variable size.

Table 14.02 IP packet header contents.

The network/link layer

Receives packets from the internet layer and adds hardware addresses. For a Local Area Network using Ethernet, this hardware address is called a **MAC address (media access control address)**. Manufacturers of devices are allocated their own range of numbers from which individual hardware devices are each given a unique MAC address. Using Ethernet, the final packaging of packets for sending across the cable is called an **Ethernet frame**. Figure 14.02 shows a typical Ethernet frame contents as data is sent from a client web-browser to a web server.

Network layer – Ethernet frame

Source address (Client): 0D:00:F6:11:1F:C7

  Internet (IP) layer

  Source IP address (Client): 168.127.56.3
  Destination IP address (Server): 226.37.58.11

  Transport (TCP) layer

  Source port (Client device): 1047
  Packet sequence number: 1
  Destination Port number (server): 80

    Application layer

    DATA BYTES: (say) 56, 89, F3, etc.

Figure 14.02 The packaging of an Ethernet frame.

> ## Progress check B
> a   Explain what is meant by the terms: IP address, socket and port number.
> b   Explain the relationship between them.

14.02 Application protocols

Some of these were summarised earlier in Table 14.01.

The following are general points that apply to all application protocols. They all use the client-server model. The server is not aware of any particular client computers, it is continually 'listening' for requests. The client and the server communicate once a socket is established.

HyperText Transfer Protocol (HTTP)

The HTTP protocol consists of request messages and response messages. For example, a HTTP server listening on port 20 receives the client request message. The server responds with a typical message.

An example of a response line that you might have seen is:

> `HTTP/1.0 404 Not Found` – The requested resource does not exist

Consider this typical sequence in Worked example 14.01 in the use of HTTP.

> ## Worked example 14.01
>
> The web browser requests the web page MyFile.html which is stored at domain MyDomain.com in folder MyFolder.
>
> 1. The user keys into the address bar of the browser:
>
>   `http://www.MyDomain.com/MyFolder/MyFile.html`
>
> 2. This will open a socket on the client and connect to port 80 of the `MyDomain` host web server.
>
> 3. The text string is received by the server:
>
>   `GET /MyFolder/MyFile.html HTTP/1.0`
>
>   `From: tonypiper@hostname.com`
>
>   `User-agent: Internet Explorer 12`
>
> 4. The server will respond with the text stream:
>
>   `HTTP/1.0 200 OK`
>
>   `Date: Friday 13 April 2019 12:00 GMT`
>
>   `Content-Type: text/html`
>
>   `Content-length: 1208`
>
>   `<html>`
>
>   `<body>`
>
>   `<h1>It has to be - hello world<h1>`
>
>   `etc.`
>
> 5. The text is sent to the client using the open port 80 connection.
> 6. This is rendered by the client web-browser and displayed.

File Transfer Protocol (FTP)

File Transfer Protocol (FTP) is used to transfer files from one host to another.

All of the file to be downloaded is obtained from a single source, a FTP server.

Two applications of FTP are the provision of software and other files to download from a remote FTP site and the updating of website pages.

In the case of the updating of website pages, a complete mirror copy of the website is held on a client computer. The files are stored on a local server on the client. Changes to web pages are made on the local server so that the links, etc. can be thoroughly tested. The local server files are then be uploaded to the 'live' website using the FTP client software.

POP3 (Post Office Version 3) and SMTP (Simple Mail Transfer Protocol)

These are popular email protocols, SMTP (for the sending of a mail message) and POP3 (for receiving email).

Consider that a client computer sends an email message to one or more intended recipients.

If it uses SMTP, then the client email software knows the address of the email server (the server is continually listening for incoming mail messages), the protocol to be used for sending (i.e. SMTP), and so the port number (25) to which it must be directed.

When transferred, the message is saved on the email server in the different mailboxes.

If the client computer uses POP3 then when the recipient next loads their email client software, this software knows the server to be contacted, the protocol to be used for receiving mail (i.e. POP3) and the port number (110). Their mail server is contacted. Any messages are delivered from the server.

IMAP

An alternative protocol to POP3 for receiving email.

Emails and sent messages are stored on the server.

IMAP has the benefit that mail can be received by several devices in different locations.

BitTorrent

BitTorrent is a communications protocol for **peer-to-peer networking**.

Traditional peer-to-peer file sharing had a single source providing files to many recipients, i.e. 'single source – multiple mirrors'. BitTorrent does things differently.

BitTorrent client software allows a user to join a '**swarm**' of hosts. Participants upload or download files to/from each other simultaneously. The final download is made up of file segments that originated from a number of different sources who are all members of the swarm.

A user who wants to make a file available for upload creates an identification file called a **torrent descriptor file**. Its availability is then advertised by email or notification on a web page. The descriptor file contains meta-data about the file to be made available. The computer acts as the **initial seeder** by making the torrent descriptor file available to potential users.

The descriptor file is then given to other BitTorrent nodes that act as peers or **leeches**.

A download is instigated at any peer by connecting with the seed requesting the file.

A file to be made available is divided into segments or pieces. When a peer receives a piece of the file it can then act as a distributor of this piece of the file to others in the swarm. This is the fundamental idea of BitTorrent; the task of distributing the file is shared by a number of peers.

Features of the BitTorrent client software are that it must keep a log of which pieces it has successfully received and so can be made available to other peers and which pieces are still to be received.

A download can be paused at any time, which makes the approach well suited to the transfer of large files.

Once a peer has received all the pieces of the file, it then becomes a **seeder**.

What files are available to download?

Torrent files are advertised for download on websites. A peer downloads the descriptor file. The descriptor file contains the data about the tracker. The **tracker computer** monitors the identity of all peers who are currently members this torrent file's swarm. The list will initially only show the initial seeder. With this information, potential peers can start the download.

> ## Progress check C
> Explain the following terms connected to the BitTorrent protocol: tracker computer, seeder and swarm.

14.03 Circuit switching and packet switching

Circuit switching

Circuit switching enables communication between two network nodes or end-points via a dedicated communications channel or circuit. The link guarantees communication at a constant bit rate.

The earliest example of circuit switching was the analogue telephone network. A connection from the calling telephone established a connection to the telephone exchange. Dialling the number instigated the connection request. In the early days, the connection to the recipient of the call was then established by a telephone operator plugging a copper cable into a 'patch panel' to make the connection between caller and recipient via the exchange. The connection was retained for the duration of the call and then released when the telephone call hung up.

Even if no data exchange is taking place, the connection remains until released. The connection remains protected from other potential users of the network.

Packet switching

Data is transmitted as packets or **datagrams**.

These packets are then transported through the network independently of each other. They might well take different routes between the two end-points, and so arrive in a non-sequential order.

On the internet, it is the task of **routers** that support the **Domain Name Service** to decide the route taken by packets.

Each packet consists of 'header data' + the 'payload'. The header will be the information shown in Table **14.02**.

The IP and Ethernet protocols are both examples of a 'connectionless communication'. Each datagram must contain the source and destination address in its header.

At the destination, the packets must be re-assembled using each packet's sequence number.

The role of a router

The task of a hardware router is to receive data packets from a packet-switched network and then route each packet towards its destination address. The router will maintain **routing tables** that suggest a best possible path for the packet's destination IP address. The packet might need to be re-directed many times (to other routers) before it reaches its destination.

Routers are a key component of the provision of the **Domain Name Service** for the World Wide Web. A router can also be used to monitor data packets on a segmented Local Area Network. Look back to Figure **2.03** in Chapter 2.

For the home computer user, the router is the hardware supplied when the user signs up for their internet connection to be provided by a particular **Internet Service Provider (ISP)**. The router is constantly passing data between the home PC and the internet.

Feature of transmission	Packet switching	Circuit switching
A dedicated channel does not need to be setup before transmission takes place	✓	
Single communications path		✓
Guaranteed communication channel once established		✓
Different routes are possible for data transfer	✓	
Data is sent as a single stream		✓
Bits/bytes arrive in the correct sequential order		✓

Past paper questions

1. a Explain what is meant by circuit switching. [2]

   b There are many applications in which digital data are transferred across a network. Video conferencing is one of these. For this application, circuit switching is preferable to the use of packet switching. Explain why this is so. [3]

   c A web page is transferred from a web server to a home computer using the internet. Explain how the web page is transferred using packet switching. [3]

Cambridge International AS & A level Computer Science 9608 paper 32 Q3 November 2015

2   The TCP/IP protocol suite can be viewed as a stack with four layers.

   a   i   Complete the stack by inserting the names of the three missing layers.

Transport

   ii   State how each layer of the stack is implemented. [1]

   b   A computer is currently running two processes:
   - Process 1 is downloading a web page.
   - Process 2 is downloading an email.

       i   Describe two tasks that the transport layer performs to ensure that the incoming data is downloaded correctly. [4]
       ii Name a protocol that will be used by Process 1. [1]
       iii Name a protocol that will be used by Process 2. [1]

Cambridge International AS & A level Computer Science 9608 paper 33 Q5 November 2016

3   The TCP/IP protocol suite is used on the internet.

   a   The table has statements about transmitting data across the internet.

   Put a tick (✓) in each row to identify whether the responsibility belongs to TCP or to IP.

Responsibility	TCP	IP
Correct routing		
Host to host communication		
Communication between networks		
Retransmitting missing packets		
Reassembling packets into the correct order		

   [5]

   b   Identify two other internet protocols. State a use for each protocol. [4]
   c   State the name of the TCP/IP layer that uses IP addresses. [1]
   d   Emails are transmitted across the internet using packet switching and routing tables.
       i   Give four items of data in an IP data packet. [4]
       ii Describe two benefits of using packet switching. [4]
       iii Give two items of data stored in a routing table. [2]

Cambridge International AS & A level Computer Science 9608 paper 32 Q4 June 2018

Hardware and virtual machines

Learning Objectives:

Processors, parallel processing and virtual machines:

- Understand the difference between a Reduced Instruction Set computer processor and a Complex Instruction Set computer processor
- Understand the differences between the four processor architectures:
  - SISD, SIMD, MISD and MIMD
- Show understanding of the consequences of massively parallel computers
- Understand the concept and potential uses of a Virtual Machine (VM).

Boolean algebra and logic circuits:

- Write a given logic expression using Boolean algebra
- Write a Boolean algebra expression from a given truth table
- Produce the truth table for a half-adder circuit
- Produce the truth table for a full-adder circuit
- Show understanding of a flip-flop (SR and JK).

Simplify a given Boolean algebra expression using:

- Identities
- De Morgan's law
- Draw up a Karnaugh map for a given logic expression
- Simplify a logic expression using a Karnaugh map.

15.01 Processors and parallel processing

Reduced instruction set computers (RISC)

The home is likely to have many devices with **RISC-based processors**. These include Nintendo, Xbox, PlayStation and many televisions and smartphones and other embedded systems. However, the desktop PC and laptop computer are likely to have a non-RISC processor. The reason for this is that moving to a new RISC instruction set in the processor would mean that all the existing software would no longer work.

In Chapter 1.4 we assumed the processor architecture had only one general purpose register, the Accumulator.

Complex Instruction Set Computers (CISC)

PC processors have around eight general purpose registers with several hundred machine instructions in the instruction set.

The large number of instructions are matched closely to the hardware of the processor and the structures used in high-level language program code.

A CISC instruction set means that instructions can be of different lengths. Instructions such as `OUT` have no operand and would need only a single byte. Most other instructions have an operand and will occupy at least two bytes.

Different numbers of clock cycles are used to execute instructions. For example, an instruction such as `DEC ACC` might require only two clock cycles whereas an instruction using indirect addressing might take 12 clock cycles.

> **Worked example 15.01**
>
> Assume the CISC instruction set has a 'multiply' instruction.
>
> Consider `MULT NUM1,NUM2`
>
> `NUM1` and `NUM2` are the address labels used for two memory locations.
>
> The instruction will: load the value of `NUM1` to a register, multiply the register contents by the contents of address `NUM2` (The answer is now in ACC) and then copy the contents of the register back to address `NUM1`.
>
> The approach taken with a RISC processor is different.
>
> There will be separate instructions for the 'load' stage, the 'calculation' stage and the final 'store' stage. Table **15.02**, which follows, shows the detail of this with five stages.

Differences between CISC processing and RISC processing	
CISC	RISC
Limited number of general purpose registers	Large number of general purpose registers
The number of clock cycles taken by instructions vary	Each instruction takes exactly one clock cycle
Instructions are variable length (e.g. take up 1,2,3, etc. bytes)	All instructions have a fixed byte size
Instructions are in the hundreds ….	Very reduced number of instructions
and include specialised instructions hard-wired into the control unit	
Extensive use made of cache memory	Instructions and data held in RAM

Table 15.01 CISC v. RISC.

Pipelining

The term 'pipeline' is in everyday use. If you had three pieces of homework to complete you would say, 'I have three homeworks in the pipeline'. You can only work on one homework at any time but you might keep switching between the different tasks.

This analogy holds for our computing definition of **pipelining**. The fetch-execute cycle in Chapter 4.04 executed the program instructions in sequence.

CISC computer, instruction execution

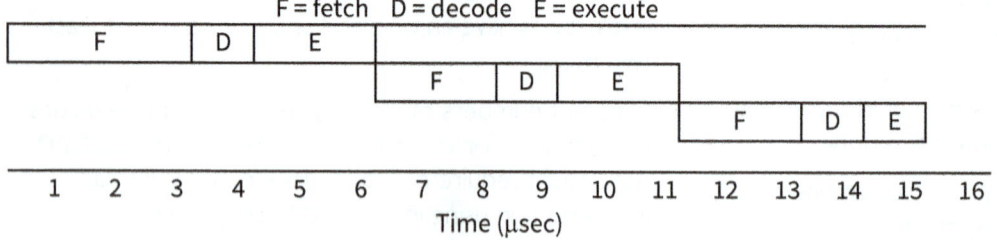

Figure 15.01 CISC processor - sequential fetch-decode-execute.

Note the sequential nature of execution. Instruction 2 is not fetched until instruction 1 has completed its execution.

The instructions each take a different number of clock cycles for their fetch-decode and execution.

Instruction 1 takes 6 μs, Instruction 2 takes 5 μs and Instruction 3 takes 4 μs.

Pipelining does not have the requirement that instruction 1 is completed before execution of Instruction 2 can be started.

All RISC processors will use some variation of the following five basic steps.

Stage	Action
1	Fetch the instruction from memory
2	Decode the instruction
3	Execute the instruction or calculate an address
4	Access an operand in memory – memory read/write
5	Write the result to a register

Table 15.02 RISC instruction sequence.

Problems with pipelining

Two issues will cause a pipeline to stall: a data dependency between instructions and a branch instruction.

What is data dependency?

Here is the first example of this.

A program contains the following sequence of instructions:

```
ADD R3,R1,R2  //add the contents of
registers R1 and R2 and store the
result in register R3
ADD R5,R3,R4
```

This will cause a data dependency.

The stages for pipelining the two instructions are as follows:

- When Instruction 2 is at its second step (Table **15.02**) the processor will read the value in R3 and R4.
- Instruction 1 is one step ahead, so
  - at this time the contents of R1 and R2 are being added, but not yet written to R3.
- Therefore the second instruction is unable to read the R3 value it needs.
- The pipeline must be stalled.

One technique for dealing with data dependent instructions is for them to be identified by the compiler. The compiler will then attempt to re-order the instructions.

Here is the second example of a pipelining problem. It is caused by Branch instructions.

```
LOOP: ADD R3,R1,R2
      // add R1 to R2 and store in R3
      ADD R6,R4,R5
      // add R4 to R5 and store in R6
      JPE R3,R6,LOOP
      // compare R3 and R6 - if equal,
                jump to address LOOP
```

The issue is the same here as in Example 1:

- The third instruction has to know the values in registers R3 and R6.
- But these values are not known
  - neither instruction 1 or instruction 2 has yet written the values R3 and R6 to the registers.
- This will cause the pipeline to stall.

Interrupt handling on CISC and RISC processors

We have already covered **interrupts** in Chapter 4 for a CISC processor. The fetch-execute cycle had additional stages added 'to check for interrupts before the next instruction is fetched'.

The system will use **vectored interrupts**. Every device is assigned a device number. Each number corresponds to a bit position in an **interrupt register**. Hence when one of the bits is set the processor will know the source of the interrupt.

Once the interrupt is received, the state of all registers must be saved and the appropriate **interrupt service routine (ISR)** code executed.

The use of interrupts on a RISC processor is no different. The same definition for an interrupt holds:

'A signal sent to the processor to indicate that an event has occurred that needs its attention'.

Processing architectures

The concept of parallel processing means the architecture has more than one processor.

The syllabus lists four architectures.

1 Single instruction, single data (SISD)

The computer system has one processor with one data source that is working on a single program. The overall task will be coded as a sequence of stages.

SISD is not parallel but sequential processing.

2 Single instruction, multiple data (SIMD)

In this situation, several programs are all executing the same program code. There are several processors, each with its own local cache memory. Each processor is processing data from a different source.

This makes it possible to have a single program instruction that performs the same action simultaneously on several data items.

This will be an appropriate architecture for problems that need to do an analysis of a large dataset using the same criteria.

> ### Worked example 15.02
>
> An example is the inverting of an RGB bitmap image.
>
> The algorithm must iterate through each pixel integer value and perform the inversion calculation. This fits exactly with the **SIMD** definition. It is a single operation on many data values.
>
> SIMD is sometimes called **array processing** or vector processing.

3 Multiple Instruction, Single Data (MISD)

Many processors perform operations on the same data value. The data may be one value from an array.

One architecture for **MISD** is the parallel input of data values through a network of processor nodes. The nodes (whose behaviour is programmable with software) will merge or sort the data values into a final result.

The MISD architecture is in effect a collection of SISD units.

This approach is called **systolic arrays** and is an example of a **massively parallel computer system**.

This architecture is often referred to as a 'supercomputer'.

Benefits of this approach are that all of the data and intermediate results are contained within the processor array. There is little use of data transfers along buses or access to main memory.

MISD is well suited to applications such as artificial intelligence, **pattern matching** and image processing.

4 Multiple Instruction, Multiple Data (MIMD)

MIMD architecture has a number of processors that function independently and simultaneously on different data values.

15.02 Virtual machines

A virtual machine is the **emulation** of a computer system using software.

The role of a virtual machine

Virtual machines are classified depending on the degree to which the target machine is copied.

System Virtual machines (full virtualisation)

This emulates a completely different computer system by emulating the functioning of a different target operating system (the 'guest OS').

The VM software provides an emulated hardware platform that is different from the host computer's instruction set.

> ### Worked example 15.03
>
> Consider a PC user with these requirements.
>
> The computer is running Operating system X (the 'host OS').
>
> Requirement 1: A number of applications programs have been purchased to run under operating system X, including the two applications A and B.
>
> Requirement 2: She is also keen to have experience of using a different operating System Y. Applications C and D are only available to run under operating system Y.
>
> Requirement 3: The user is keen to find out about a new beta version release of operating system X.
>
> How is it done?
>
> Requirement 1: No need for any new software. Applications A and B run using the host OS, operating system X.
>
> *(Continued)*

Requirement 2: Virtual Machine software (V1) must be installed. Operating system Y (operating system Y) is installed and operating system Y will run under V1.

This meets the need that the user wants to have experience of the different operating system Y.

Requirement 3: The beta operating system X is treated as a completely different OS. The Virtual Machine software (V1) must be installed. The beta operating system X software is installed and the Beta operating system X will run under V1.

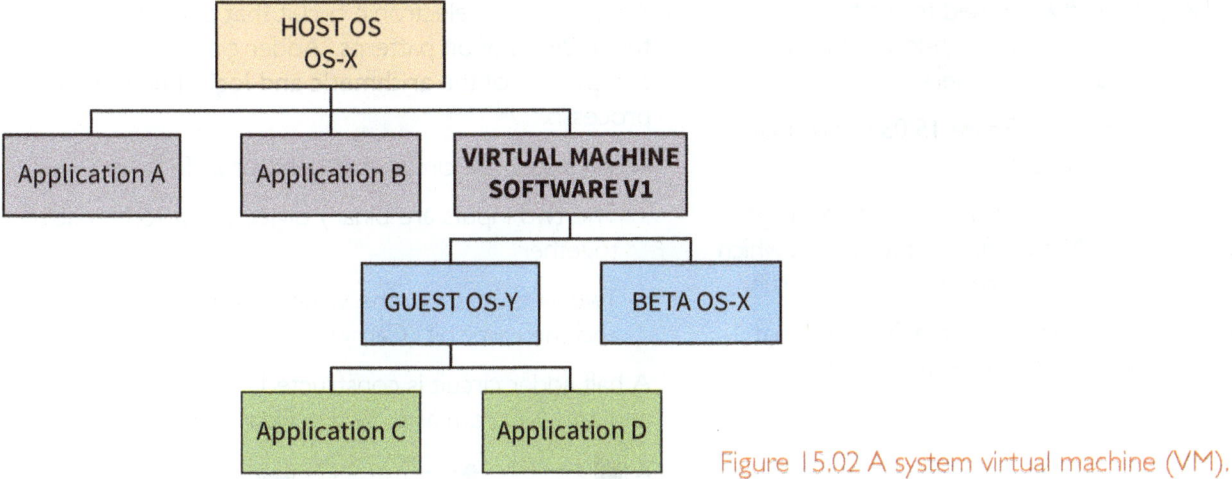

Figure 15.02 A system virtual machine (VM).

Figure 15.02 shows the software configuration for the three user requirements we started with.

The running of applications programs A and B requires no virtual machine.

The trial operating system OS-Y must be run under the virtual machine software. Applications C and D can only be run under OS-Y.

The user has decided not to install the beta version of OS-X yet as the host OS. Therefore, it must be run under the Virtual machine software.

Process virtual machines (application virtual machines)

These also execute as a single application process under the host operating system software.

A program can then be run under the VM which is platform independent.

Process VMs are implemented using an interpreter.

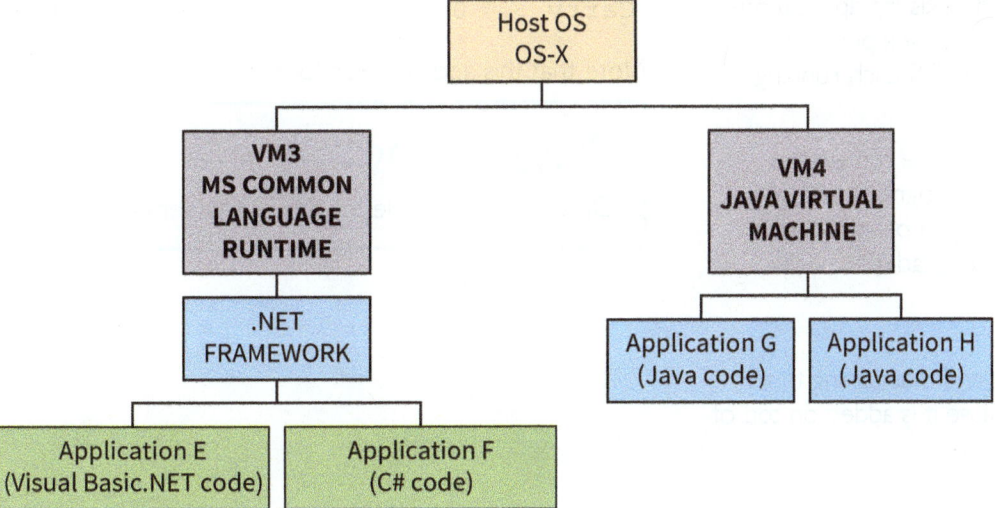

Figure 15.03 A process Virtual Machine.

This type of VM is used by Java Virtual Machine and by Microsoft VM.

In the case of Java Virtual Machine the Java software is installed on the computer and application programs designed to run in this VM environment are then runnable.

In the case of Microsoft VM (the Common Language Runtime), which is the basis of the Microsoft.NET framework, this is the software used to support program code written in several high-level languages, Visual Basic.NET, C# and many others.

The software configuration in Figure 15.03 shows that two virtual machines are installed.

One of them is VM3 and is the MS Common Language Runtime supporting the Microsoft.NET framework which allows the two application programs E and F to be run.

The other is VM4 and is the Java Virtual Machine that allows the Java applications G and H to be executed.

Benefits and limitations of virtual machines

Benefits of using VM

VM software makes it possible to run earlier versions of an OS. A programmer needs to test a new application under development. He might need to ensure the application will run perfectly on computers using an earlier version of the OS.

Conversely: A new release of the host OS operating system is available and developers will need to confirm that their existing software will execute using the new OS.

To solve this, install the VM software. Install this new release of the host OS so that the new release is running as a guest OS. Test all the existing applications programs bearing in mind that the developer could have several earlier versions of the OS each running under a VM.

Two different operating systems can be run on the same hardware so old application programs that will only run on an earlier OS version can be retained. This is not affected if the hardware is upgraded

Limitations of using VM

There is an overhead in installing and maintaining this 'extra layer' of VM software because it is added on top of the host OS rather than completely replacing it. The VM software running can degrade the performance of the PC hence response times will be slower.

15.03 Logic circuits

The half adder

An 'adder' is an electronic circuit that performs the addition of bit patterns. Adder circuits are a component of the **arithmetic and logical unit** in the processor.

A half adder is a circuit that behaves as follows:

- The two inputs are binary digits, about to be added together
- Two outputs show the value of the addition (Sum) and the carry bit (Carry).

A half adder circuit is constructed using an XOR gate and an AND gate as shown in Figure 15.04.

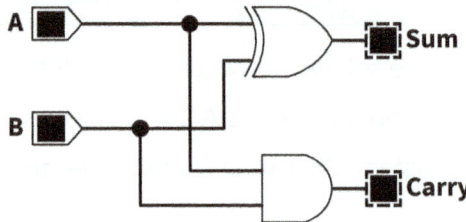

Figure 15.04 Half-adder circuit.

The truth table will show the results for these four additions.

```
                 0       0       1       1
                 0 +     1 +     0 +     1 +
    Sum    >     0       1       1       1
    Carry  >     0       0       0       1
```

Note that this addition was for two bits only.

> ### Progress check A
> Draw the truth table for this half-adder circuit.

Worked example 15.04

Consider the task of adding together the contents of two bytes.

The addition of the two bits in bit position zero might produce a carry bit. The carry bit must then be included in the calculation for the next bit in bit position 1.

This is repeated for the whole byte. Each carry must be included when adding the bits in the next bit position.

This is implemented in the circuit called a **full adder**.

Progress check B

Do you agree with the Sum and Carry values in Table **15.03**?

The full-adder circuit is constructed using five gates.

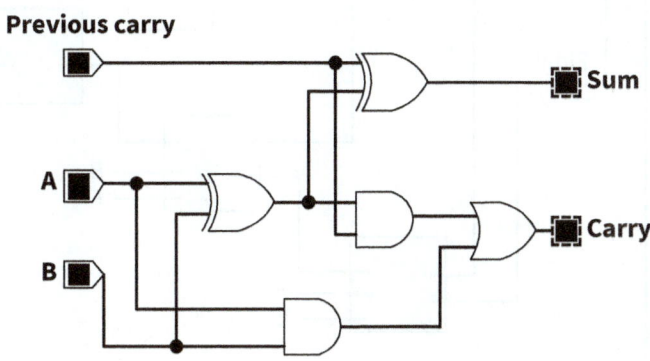

Figure 15.05 Full-adder circuit.

The full adder

The full-adder circuit will have three inputs: A and B (as before) and a previous carry, PC. It will also have two outputs: the Sum and Carry

Input			Output	
PC	A	B	Sum	Carry
0	0	0	0	0
0	0	1	1	0
0	1	0	1	0
0	1	1	0	1
1	0	0	1	0
1	0	1	0	1
1	1	0	0	1
1	1	1	1	1

Table 15.03 Full-adder truth table.

Worked example 15.05

Add two 4-bit numbers

Figure **15.06** shows how four full-adder circuits are used to add bit pattern ABCD to bit pattern EFGH.

(Continued)

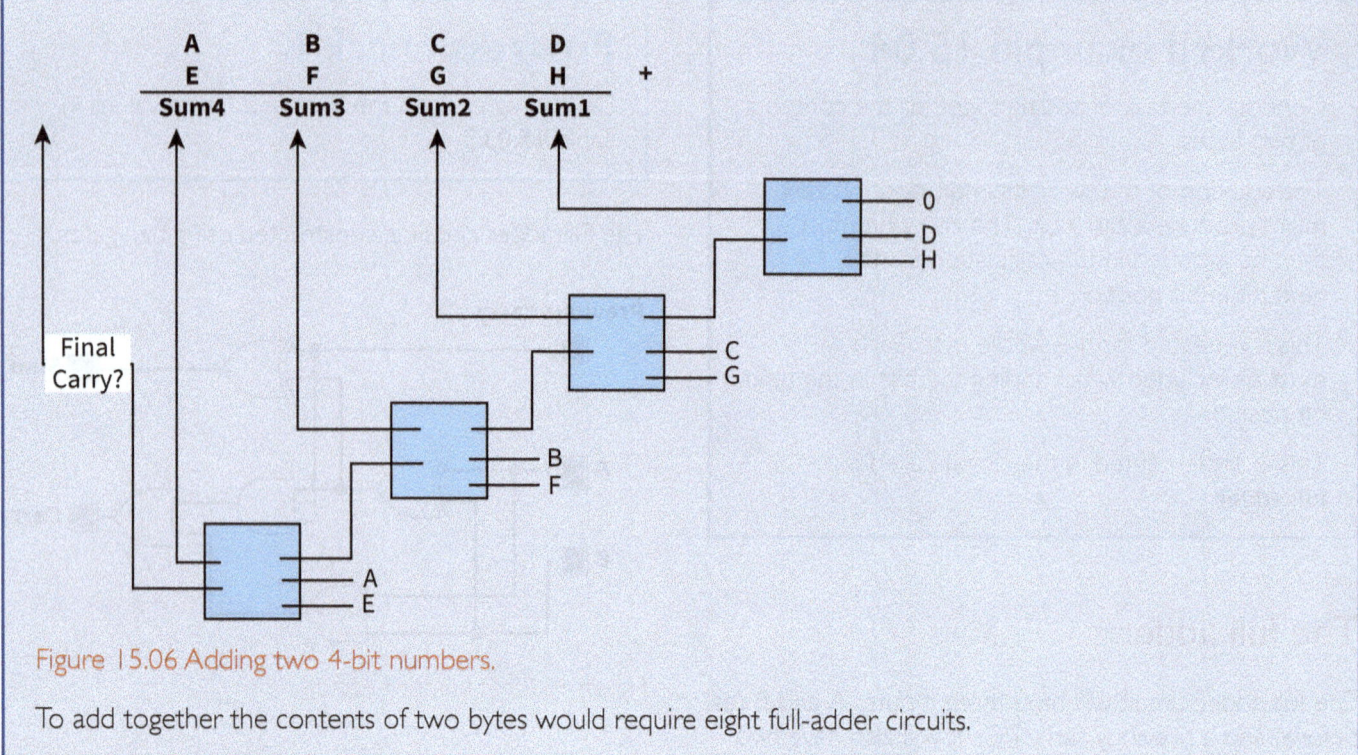

Figure 15.06 Adding two 4-bit numbers.

To add together the contents of two bytes would require eight full-adder circuits.

15.04 Flip-flops

The logic circuits we have studied are combinational circuits. Their output(s) is dependent only on the inputs being applied <u>at that time</u>.

Flip-flops, by contrast, use sequential logic.

Sequential logic circuits are the basic building blocks for storage registers, shift registers and other memory devices. Output is dependent on current inputs and a further input remembered from some previous input combination. This implies that a sequential circuit must have some form of memory.

A sequential logic circuit is said to be a **bistable** or a **two-state device**. Output will be one of two basic states (represented by a 1 or 0 value). The device is said to be **latched** in this state. The state remains until a signal is applied which causes the state to change. The timing of a change is determined by a clock cycle.

A sequential logic circuit can be made to change state by the application of some **asynchronous communication**, or by a **synchronous communication** (that is, a clock driven signal).

The SR flip-flop

The SR flip-flop is a one-bit memory device with two inputs. The S input (SET) causes the output to be set to 1. The R input (RESET) produces an output of 0.

The SR flip-flop is constructed from two cross-coupled NAND gates as shown on the left in Figure 15.07. In a circuit diagram containing a SR flip-flop, the detail of the NAND gates would not be shown. The flip-flop would be shown as on the right of Figure 15.07.

It is a convention in electronics that, if it is the 'low' (zero) state which is significant, then the inputs are labelled $\overline{R}$ and $\overline{S}$.

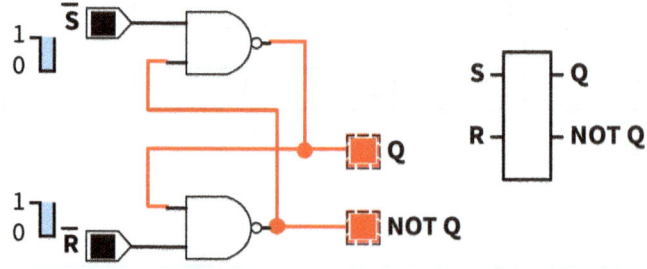

Figure 15.07 SR flip-flop.

We have labelled the 'SET' state to indicate Q=1 and the 'RESET' state to indicate Q=0.

The following combinations of R and S show the changes to the output.

State	Inputs		Output		Action
	S	R	Original Q	Final Q	
SET	1	0	0	1	Sets Q to 1
	1	1	0	1	No change
RESET	0	1	1	0	Resets Q to 0
	1	1	1	0	No change

Table 15.04 SR flip-flop states changes.

Note that when S=1 and R=1, output Q can be either 0 or 1 depending of the state of R and S before this current state existed. Therefore S=1 and R=1 will not change the Q output.

Note also that S=0 and R=0 is an undesirable state and must be avoided. It will cause both Q and NOT Q to be set high at 1 and cause the flip-flop to become unstable. If this state is reached the future behaviour of the flip-flop becomes unpredictable.

A sequence of signal changes is shown in Figure **15.09**. You should trace the changing values of R and S and see how they determine the changed state of the output.

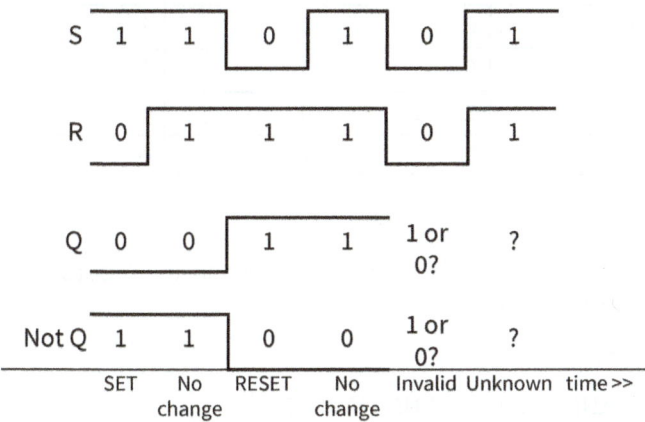

Figure 15.08 Signal change sequence.

SR flip-flop using NOR gates

An SR flip-flop is constructed using two cross-coupled NOR gates.

The differences are that the inputs are active HIGH and that the invalid state exists when both inputs (S and R) are at 1.

Using an SR flip-flop for storage

When the circuit is retaining some binary value it will have R=1 and S=1. The circuit can behave as a store for a single bit.

The above discussion shows there is one signal (R=1) that will cause the bit stored (Q) to be set to 1. The signal (S=1) causes the bit stored to be set to 0.

Several flip-flops together would be used to store the data value for a byte.

The JK flip-flop

The JK flip-flop solves the issue of the invalid condition of the SR NAND gate flip-flop when R and S are both 0. This is now avoided by the addition of an **input clock** signal to the SR flip-flop circuit.

Two additional 3-input NAND gates are added to the SR flip-flop. The clock signal acts as an input to each of the additional NAND gates.

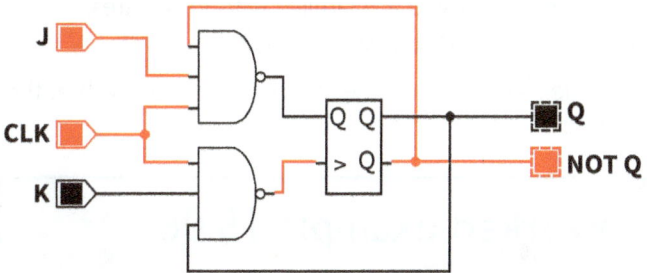

Figure 15.09 JK flip-flop.

State	Inputs		Output		Action
	J	K	Original Q	Final Q	
All of these combinations are as for the SR flip-flop (with inputs now labelled J and K)	0	0	0	0	Memory no change
	0	0	0	1	
	0	1	1	0	Resets Q to 0
	0	1	0	1	
	1	0	0	1	Set Q to 1
	1	0	1	0	
Toggle	1	1	0	1	Toggles Q setting

Table 15.05 JK flip-flop states.

Assume the starting point is that J=1 and K=1. A clock pulse then causes output Q to change state.

If a sequence of clock pulses is sent, the output on Q will toggle: 1, 0, 1, 0, 1, 0, 1, 0, etc. This circuit construction could therefore be used for a simple 'Toggle switch' in electronics.

If J=1 and K=0, and a clock signal is sent, Q is SET to 1. If J=0 and K=1, and a clock signal is sent, Q is RESET to 0. If J=1 and K=1, the Q output is toggled.

Tracing these actions and monitoring the settings of the S and R input to the SR flip-flop within the circuit confirms that only one of either SET or RESET can be set active at the same time. This solves the problem of the invalid state of the SR flip-flop.

15.05 Boolean algebra

From Chapter 3 you are familiar with logic gates, Boolean expressions and truth tables.

Consider, A and B are the inputs to a circuit with X the output:

> ### Worked example 15.06
>
> X = NOT(A OR B)
>
> This means:
>
> X = 1 when neither (A is 1) NOR (B is 1)

> ### Worked example 15.07
>
> X = (A OR B) OR (A AND C)
>
> This means X = 1 when, either (A is 1 OR B is 1) or (A is 1 AND C is 1) or both.

Boolean algebra notation

Boolean algebra is used to describe a logic expression/circuit.

	Boolean algebra notation	Example
OR	+	X OR Y
AND	Period/full stop	X AND Y
NOT	'bar' on top	NOT X

Table 15.06 Boolean algebra notation.

> ### Progress check C
>
> The following are three logic expressions:
>
> a   A AND NOT B
>
> b   NOT(C AND D) OR NOT D
>
> c   NOT(P OR Q OR R) AND R
>
> Rewrite each expression using Boolean algebra.

Forming a Boolean expression from a given truth table

Input			Output
A	B	C	X
0	0	0	0
0	0	1	0
0	1	0	0
0	1	1	0
1	0	0	1
1	0	1	1
1	1	0	0
1	1	1	0

Table 15.07 Truth table.

Look for the combination(s) that produce a 1 output. There are two rows.

These are:

A AND NOT B AND NOT C

A AND NOT B AND C

So, the output X is 1 if either the first combination or the second or both combination occurs.

So, the Boolean algebra expression is:

$X = (A.\bar{B}.\bar{C}) + (A.\bar{B}.C)$

Forming the Boolean expression for a given circuit

There is nothing new here. We write on the diagram the output expression from each gate, until we have the expression for the final output.

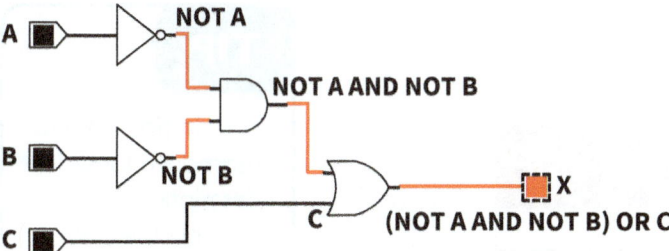

Figure 15.10 Logic circuit.

The Boolean expression is: $X = \bar{A} \cdot \bar{B} + C$

Simplification of Boolean expressions

One of the first uses of algebra you will have come across is for the simplification of expressions.

The approach is to look for common elements and add brackets where required to make the order of precedence clear.

Given	Simplification
2X + 6Y	2(X+3Y)
PQ + PQR	PQ(1+R)
AC+BC+AD+BD	C(A+B) + D(A+B) = (C+D)(A+B)

We need to study some **identities** that are used to simplify expressions.

The identities that follow can all be confirmed by considering the appropriate logic gate where one of the inputs is either 0 or 1.

> ## Progress check D
>
>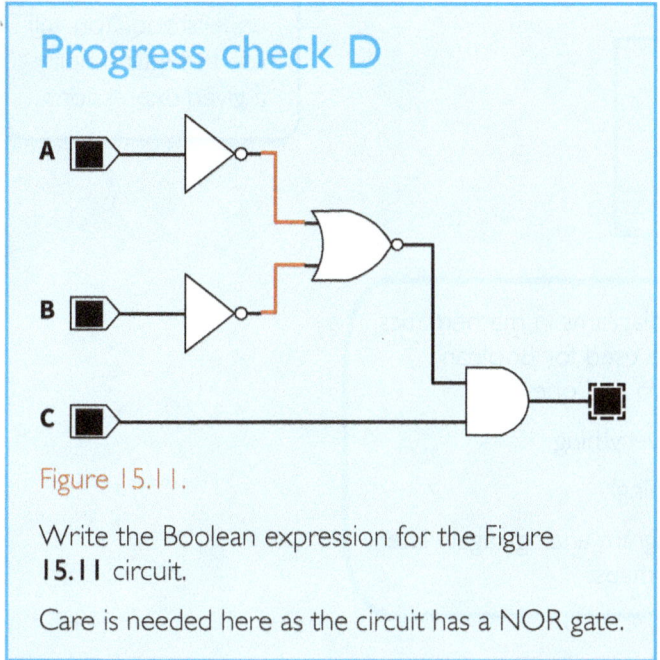
>
> Figure 15.11.
>
> Write the Boolean expression for the Figure 15.11 circuit.
>
> Care is needed here as the circuit has a NOR gate.

1 AND gate

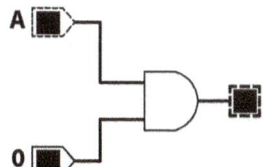

Input		
A	0	Output
1	0	0
0	0	0

Figure 15.12 AND gate, inputs A and 0.

The truth table tells us whatever the value of A, the output from the AND gate is always 0.

The identity is: $A \cdot 0 = 0$

2 Consider this second AND gate:

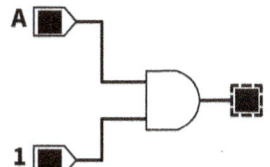

Input		
A	1	Output
1	1	1
0	1	0

Figure 15.13 AND gate, inputs A and 1.

The identity is: $A . 1 = A$

3 Consider inputs A and NOT A

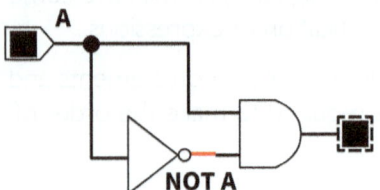

Input		Output
A	NOT A	
1	0	0
0	1	0

15.14 AND gate, inputs A and NOT A.

The identity is: $A . \overline{A} = 0$

> ## Progress check E
> Draw the truth table for an OR gate with inputs A and 1.
> Deduce the identity for $A + 1$.

TIP

You do not need to reproduce these law descriptions, only to apply the law to a given Boolean expression.

These identities need to be understood. You will use them to simplify a given expressions.

Identities summary

$A . A = A$
$A + A = A$
$A . \overline{A} = 0$
$A + \overline{A} = 1$
$A . 1 = A$
$A + 1 = 1$
$A . 0 = 0$
$A + 0 = A$

> If you have studied Venn diagrams in mathematics, the same principles can be used for Boolean expressions containing zero and one.
> - Think of a 1 value as 'everything'
> - zero as the set of 'nothing'
>
> We shall use this Venn diagram analogy again later when we study Karnaugh maps.

There are more identities:

Commutative law	$A + B = B + A$
	$A . B = B . A$
Associative law	$A + (B + C) = (A + B) + C$
	$A . (B . C) = (A . B) . C$
Distributive law	$A . (B + C) = A . B + A . C$
	$A + (B . C) = (A + B) . (A + C)$

The second distributive law identity, given above, is less obvious. It can be proved by the expansion of the right-hand side.

$(A + B) . (A + C)$
$A . A + A . C + B . A + B . C$
$A + A . C + A . B + B . C$
$A . (1 + C) + A . B + B . C$
$A + A . B + B . C$
$A . (1 + B) + B . C$
So, $A + (B . C) = (A + B) . (A + C)$

We have in fact simplified our first expression, using the identities involving 0 and 1.

> ### Progress check F
> Simplify these Boolean expressions.
> a   A.B.C + A.B
> b   A.B.($\bar{B}$ + D)
> c   A.(B.C + 1).C
> d   P.(Q + $\bar{P}$)
> e   A.B.$\bar{C}$ + A.B.C + A.$\bar{B}$
> f   B.(A + C) + A + A.(A + B)

De Morgan's laws

De Morgan's laws are used with the logic functions NAND and NOR.

A NAND gate behaves as two inputs to an AND gate, followed by output into NOT gate.

A NOR gates behaves as two inputs to an OR gate, followed by output into a NOT gate.

A	B	NOT A	NOT B	A NAND B NOT (A AND B)	NOT A OR NOT B
0	0	1	1	1	1
0	1	1	0	1	1
1	0	0	1	1	1
1	1	0	0	0	0

Table 15.08 NAND logic.

The fifth column is A NAND B.

The final column has the same outputs.

The identity for NAND $\overline{A.B} = \bar{A} + \bar{B}$

> ### Progress check G
> Construct a similar truth table showing the result of A NOR B.
>
> What operation between NOT A and NOT B gives the same outputs?

De Morgan's laws summary
$\overline{A.B} = \bar{A} + \bar{B}$
$\overline{A + B} = \bar{A}.\bar{B}$

Simplification of expressions using De Morgan's law
Simply the expression: $(\overline{\bar{A} + \bar{B}}).(A + C)$
$= (A.B).(A + C)$
$= A.B.1$
$= A.B$

> ### Progress check H
> Use De Morgan's laws to simplify these expressions.
> a $\overline{A + B}$
> b $A.\bar{B}$
> c $\overline{\bar{A} + B}$

15.06 Karnaugh maps (K-map)

Drawing a grid, called a **Karnaugh map**, is a tool to simplify a Boolean expression.

Consider a logic expression involving the values A and B.

The headings for the rows and columns represent A and B with a 1 and $\overline{A}$ and $\overline{B}$ with a 0.

Each of the four cells in the Karnaugh map shows the relevant expression.

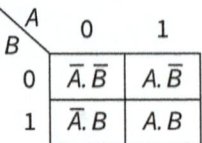

Figure 15.15 Two-variable Karnaugh map.

If we extend this to a map designed for four variables:

$\overline{AB}$ / $\overline{CD}$	00	01	11	10
00				
01				
11				
10				

> The order of the bit pairs for the columns and rows is important. They use a system called **Gray Code** – each bit pair differs by only <u>one bit</u> change from the previous pair in the row and column.

Figure 15.16 Four-variable Karnaugh map.

Worked example 15.08

Consider the expression: $\overline{C}.D.\overline{A}.\overline{B} + \overline{C}.D.\overline{A}.B + \overline{C}.D.A.B + \overline{C}.D.A.\overline{B}$

This original expression is called the **sum of products**.

Put 1 bits in the cells corresponding to each of the four terms.

Put 0 bits in all other cells.

Put a sausage, called a **minterm**, around any complete rows or columns.

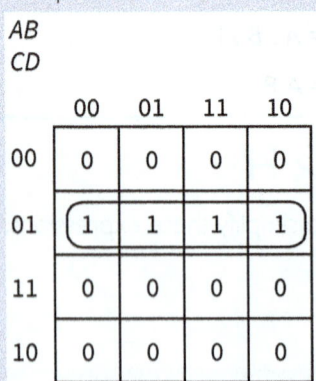

Figure 15.17 Minterm.

For the given expression, the conclusion is that the 1 bit positions do not depend on A or B.

The expression therefore simplifies to $\overline{C}.D$.

Worked example 15.09

There can be more than one minterm. Consider the expression:

$\overline{AB}$ / $\overline{CD}$	00	01	11	10
00	1	0	0	0
01	1	1	1	1
11	1	0	0	0
10	1	0	0	0

Figure 15.18 Two minterms.

The vertical minterm is: $\overline{A}.\overline{B}$

The horizontal minterm is: $\overline{C}.D$

So, the simplified expression is: $\overline{A}.\overline{B} + \overline{C}.D$

Worked example 15.10

Consider the expression: $\bar{A}.\bar{B}.\bar{C} + \bar{A}.B + A.B.\bar{C} + A.C$

This is different as it only uses three variables and so the Karnaugh map has a different dimension.

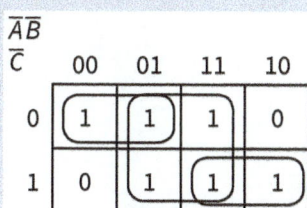

Figure 15.19 Three minterms.

Note that we need not group an entire row or column but the group will have a 'powers of 2' (2, 4, 8) number of minterms.

Working from the left: The first minterm is: $\bar{A}.\bar{C}$, the second minterm is: B and the third minterm is: $A.C$.

This gives the logic expression: $\bar{A}.\bar{C} + B + A.C$

Progress check 1

a Draw the Karaugh map for this expression and use it to simplify the expression.

Past paper questions

1 a Complete the truth table for this NAND gate.

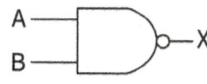

A	b	x
0	0	
0	1	
1	0	
1	1	

[1]

A SR flip-flop is constructed using two NAND gates.

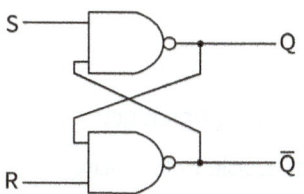

b i Complete the truth table for the SR flip-flop.

	S	R	Q	$\bar{Q}$
Initially	1	0	0	1
R changed to 1	1	1		
S changed to 0	0	1		
S changed to 1	1	1		
S and R changed to 0	0	0		

[4]

ii One of the combinations in the truth table should not be allowed to occur.
State the values of S and R that should not be allowed. Justify your choice.
S =   R =   [3]

Another type of flip-flop is the JK flip-flop.

c i   Give one extra input present in the JK flip-flop.   [1]
   ii Give **one** advantage of the JK flip-flop.   [1]

d Describe the role of flip-flops in a computer.   [2]

Cambridge International AS & A level Computer Science 9608 paper 32 Q5 June 2016

2 a i Complete the Boolean function that corresponds to the following truth table.

INPUT			OUTPUT
P	Q	R	Z
0	0	0	0
0	0	1	0
0	1	0	0
0	1	1	0
1	0	0	1
1	0	1	1
1	1	0	0
1	1	1	1

$Z = P.\overline{Q}.\overline{Q} +$ [3]

The part to the right of the equals sign is known as the sum-of-products.

ii For the truth table in part a i complete the Karnaugh Map (K-map)

	PQ			
	00	01	11	10
R 0				
1				

The K-map can be used to simplify the function in part (a) (i).

iii Draw loop(s) around appropriate groups of 1's to produce an optimal sum-of-products. [2]

iv Using your answer to part (a) (iii), write the simplified sum-of-products Boolean function.
Z =   [1]

b   The truth table for a logic circuit with four inputs is given below:

INPUT				OUTPUT
P	Q	R	S	Z
0	0	0	0	0
0	0	0	1	0
0	0	1	0	0
0	0	1	1	0
0	1	0	0	0
0	1	0	1	1
0	1	1	0	0
0	1	1	1	1
1	0	0	0	0
1	0	0	1	1
1	0	1	0	0
1	0	1	1	0
1	1	0	0	0
1	1	0	1	1
1	1	1	0	0
1	1	1	1	1

i   Complete the K-map corresponding to the truth table.

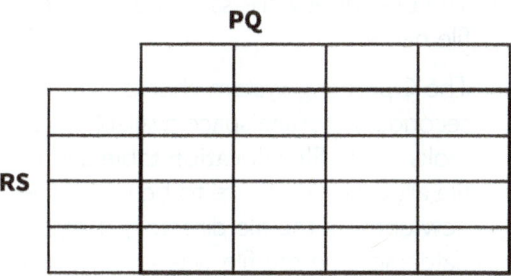

[4]

ii   Draw loop(s) around appropriate groups of 1's to produce an optimal sum-of-products. [2]

iii   Using your answer to part (b) (ii), write the simplified sum-of-products Boolean function.

Z =   [2]

Cambridge International AS & A level Computer Science 9608 paper 32 Q5 November 2015

Chapter 16: System software

Learning Objectives:

Purposes of an operating system:

- Understand the need for an operating system
- Understand the role of the user interface
- Understand the role of the memory manager
- Processor management
- Understand the issues with a multi-access operating system
  - Process states: running, ready and blocked (or suspended)
  - Understand the benefits of different low-level scheduling algorithms
  - Round-robin, shortest job first, first come-first served, shortest remaining time
- Understand how the kernel acts as the interrupt manager
- Understand different memory management techniques
- Paging and segmentation.

Translation software:

- Understand how an interpreter executes program code
- Understand the stages of compilation
- Write language grammar using Backus-Naur Form (BNF)
- Understand the use of a syntax diagram
- Understand and evaluate expressions using Reverse Polish Notation (RPN).

16.01 Purpose of an operating system (OS)

Maximising resources

Chapter 5 introduced the operating system.

The OS is software that manages the use of the available resources of the computer system.

Consider a PC. There is only one processor, a limited number of USB ports, RAM memory of (say) 4GB and a limited amount of secondary storage. These 'resources' must be managed to get an acceptable level of performance.

The user interface

The user interface hides the complexities of the hardware from the user.

Consider the end of a word processing session.

The user does a file-save and then keys in the file name.

The Operating System checks that there is sufficient secondary storage space available to save the file. It looks at the **file allocation table** and decides which file allocation units are to be used. Then it makes a new entry in the file directory. It records the file name, date and time the file was saved. It records the first file **allocation unit** used for this file.

A **command line interface** needs the user to trigger events by keying in one-line commands. This will require the user to have a detailed knowledge of the available commands.

A **graphical user interface (GUI)** will be very different. The user uses a pointing device such as a mouse or trackpad, or for a touch-screen, a stylus or finger, to point to icons or text on the screen. The user has several windows visible that each display one of the processes currently loaded.

16.02 Process management

Multi-tasking and processes

Modern PC computers have sufficient primary memory to allow several programs to be loaded into memory.

The program, once loaded into memory, is ready to be executed but there is only one processor, so at any instant in time the processor is executing one program only.

Consider a session where four simultaneous file downloads are taking place. Each download is being done by a **process**. Four different processes are each using the same program.

The OS is said to be '**multi-tasking**'.

If this is a GUI interface, the user will see several other processes that are currently running, namely the date and time clock display, the spreadsheet software which was loaded earlier, etc.

It is the role of the OS to make the most efficient use of the computer system in managing all the processes that are currently running.

Process states

All processes in main memory will be in one of three states: 'Ready', 'Suspended' or 'Running':

- **Running:** a process that has current use of the processor is said to be 'running'
- **Ready** (or 'runnable'): a process that is capable of use of the processor, but is having to wait
- **Suspended:** a process might not be able to make use of the processor for some reason:
  - The process does not have the various resources available in order to continue executing
  - It could be waiting for a signal from some other process before it can move to the ready state
  - In a paging system, the process is waiting for new pages to be loaded from secondary storage. (Paging is discussed in Section 16.03.)

The need for low-level scheduling

One of the OS program modules is the low-level scheduler.

Low-level scheduling means the management of processor usage. To do this, the OS must know the current state of all processes.

A **Process Control Block (PCB)** stores data about the current state of each process. These PCBs are used by the low-level scheduler software.

Strategies for low-level scheduling

Which process will execute next?

If there are one or more processes in a runnable state, the algorithms below may be used by the low-level scheduler to decide what process will get next use of the processor.

Round-robin

Give all the runnable processes in sequence a fixed amount of time, called a **time-slice**. When the current running process exhausts its time slice, it moves to the ready state. The processor is given to the next process, until its time-slice is over. This repeats and all processes in the ready state get their time-slice in sequence.

First come, first served

All processes in the ready state form a queue. The processor is given to the process that is at the head of the **'ready' queue**. The current process continues execution until it must move to the suspended state.

Processes can have priorities

A process can be given a priority. When a process is loaded, the OS will take note of its priority. The OS will maintain a **priority queue**. The process at the head of the queue will get the next use of the processor.

Shortest job first

Always give the processor to the process with the shortest estimated run-time.

Shortest remaining time

Always give the processor to the process with the shortest estimated remaining run time. This strategy should see a fast throughput of processes.

> ### Progress check A
> During its execution a process will change state many times.
>
> Consider each of the following and state the original state and the new state of the process.
>
> a A process is interrupted as its time slice has expired.
>
> b A process now completes a sequence of disk-read operations.
>
> c A process is given the use of the processor.
>
> d A process is executing, but now has to wait for some input from the keyboard by the user.

> ### Progress check B
> If the scheduling algorithm is based on allocating a priority to each process, two possible strategies are 'shortest job first' and 'shortest remaining time'.
>
> Suggest a third possible strategy.

The kernel and interrupts

An **interrupt** is a signal to the processor to indicate that some event has occurred.

The low-level scheduler is repeatedly starting one process and 'parking' another. The starting and suspension of processes will be controlled with the use of interrupt signals.

The operating system module that does this is the kernel. The **kernel** acts as a low-level interrupt handler.

> ### Worked example 16.01
> Consider, a round-robin strategy. PROCESS-A currently has the processor:
>
> - PROCESS-A is executing
> - Interrupt signal sent from the KERNEL
> - Interrupt Service Routine (ISR) code is executed
> - PROCESS-A is returned to the tail of the Ready queue
> - PROCESS-X (head of the ready queue) starts executing

16.03 Memory management

The OS must have a strategy for management of the available memory space.

For example, what happens when a program finishes its execution?

Memory is managed by the OS module called the **memory manager**.

Key roles of the memory manager will be to maintain a map of the memory that is currently used and the unused memory, ensure the security of any process, i.e. a process must not reference any memory locations used by other programs.

A memory manager sub-program is the **loader**. The task of the loader software is to allocate memory for each process.

The memory manager must then track where in primary memory the program and its data are currently stored. This is important as we shall see later that parts of a process can be moved in memory during the course of its execution.

Relative addresses and physical addresses

When a program is compiled, memory addresses are expressed as relative to the address of the first instruction.

The memory manager must continually map all relative addresses to their physical memory address.

The mapping is simple:

Physical instruction address = Start address of the process + the relative address.

Relative addressing was one of the modes of addressing discussed in Chapter 4.

Dividing up the memory

The memory manager will divide the available RAM into fixed size chunks of memory called **allocation units**.

There are two different strategies: **segmentation**, which uses large size allocation units called segments and **paging**, which uses small size allocation units, called **page frames**.

Segmentation

An applications program is divided into fixed sized **segments** when the program is compiled.

The loader will then calculate that (say) applications program X, requires five segments.

Programmers write program code that minimises the movement of code and the data it will use. The larger the size of a segment the better chance that a particular routine can be achieved with code that takes up only one segment.

Paging

The main memory is divided into the same sized units called **page frames**.

Programs/processes are divided into fixed sized units - of the same size - called **pages**.

The implication of this is that the process pages might be scattered throughout the available page frames, the memory manager must manage which (process) pages are allocated to which page frames (done by maintaining a page-map or **page-frame table**) and the **logical address** of a program instruction is expressed as (`PageNumber, Offset`. As an example, an address (2, 518) represents the 518th byte from the start address of page 2.

Using paging, not all the pages of the program need to be loaded to start execution. There might be insufficient page frames available for the whole of the program to be loaded.

Virtual memory

Not having all the pages of the process loaded gives rise to virtual memory.

This means there is no restriction on the size of a process that can be scheduled and start its execution.

A process will continue to execute until an instruction is met that is in a page that is not currently loaded. This new page must then be swapped into memory, possibly at the expense of another page that is swapped out.

This is called **page swapping**.

How does the memory manager choose which page to swap out? The Memory Manager will maintain a page table for each loaded process. This will show the page number, the page frame number into which the page has been loaded and a time stamp for when it was loaded.

The strategy for deciding which page to swap out when required could be to swap out the page that has been loaded into memory for the longest time.

Alternatively, if there was a second time stamp showing the time at which the page was last accessed, the strategy could be to swap out the page that has not been recently accessed.

Some operating systems will periodically scan for pages that have not been recently accessed and maintain this list of page frames. This way there is always a page available when needed.

One possible problem is that too much page swapping will lead to a degradation in performance. This is called **disk thrashing**. In this situation, the Memory Manager spends almost all of its time swapping pages in and out of memory and little time in the execution of the process.

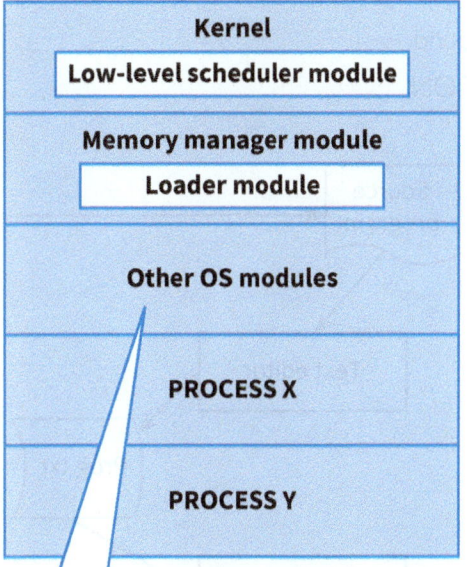

This shows primary memory with:
- the OS modules
- two application processes currently loaded.

Note: The diagram has omitted other modules which form part of the OS which you don't need to know at this level but which are covered in Chapter 5.

Figure 16.01 Memory map.

16.04 Translation software: the interpreter

Using a programming language interpreter, the programmer will write the **source code** and is then able to attempt to execute the code at any stage.

Here is the sequence of operations:

The interpreter software is loaded

The application program is loaded

The user tells the program to run
REPEAT
   The interpreter software considers the next statement in sequence
     If the syntax is fine
        Execute the statement
     Else
        Statement error found
        Report to the user
UNTIL error found
END EXECUTION

16.05 Translation software: the compiler

A compiler translates a program written in a particular high-level language into machine code. A program written in Language-X would require the use of the Language-X compiler.

The compiler software looks at all the source code statements in sequence (checking for errors) and only produces the final **object (machine code)** file when no errors are found.

Compilation is a repetitive process, continuing until all errors are eliminated. See Figure **16.02**.

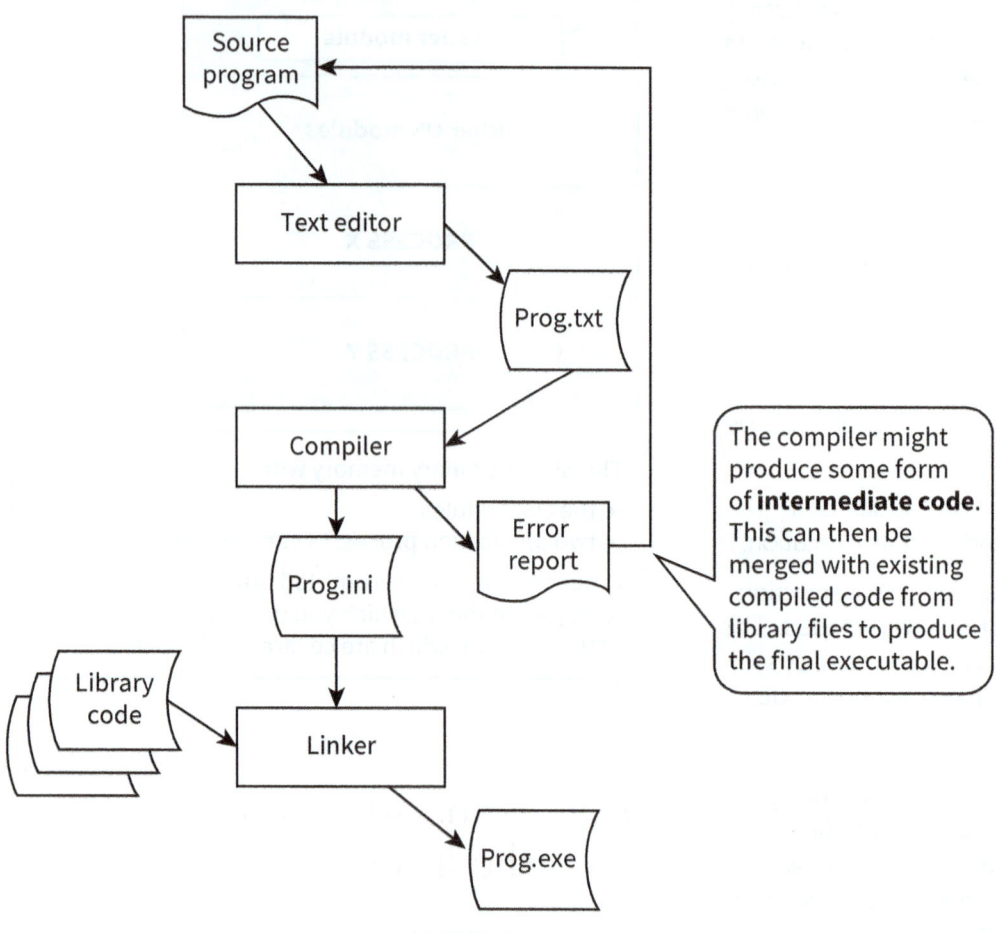

Figure 16.02 The compilation process.

> **TIP**
>
> Chapter 5, section 5.04 studied a two-pass assembler.
>
> The compiler works in a similar way.
>
> The compiler must also make two passes through the source code in order to complete the symbol table entries.
>
> The first pass inserts each new variable/constant name.
>
> The second pass through the source code can establish the actual memory address to be used for that identifier.

Traditionally the source code was produced using text editor software, then the compiler was a separate software program. Modern software called an **Integrated Development Environment (IDE)** does the program creation and compilation using the same software.

Key points about the use of a compiler are that the program can only be executed once all errors have been found at which point this final compilation will report 'No errors found' and once the object file has been created the compiler software and the source code are both no longer needed.

Compilation stages

The compiler software will work through a sequence of stages.

Lexical analysis

Lexical analysis is the first stage of the compilation process.

It will refer to a **keyword table** and will create a **symbol table**.

The keyword table lists all the language keywords (if, then, else, repeat, until, etc.) with **a token** that is used to represent each word.

The lexical analyser will look at the source code:

- remove any whitespace from the source file
- remove any comment statements
- check for obvious errors in the use of identifier names, for example, that they do not exceed 64 characters
- Replace each language keyword with its token, for example, the sequence of characters P, R, I, N and T will be identified as the keyword PRINT and replaced by the token for PRINT
- All identifier names are replaced in the source code by a **pointer to an address** in memory which links to an entry in the symbol table.

The symbol table is then built. The lexical analyser will build up a symbol table which contains all the identifiers found in the source code and, if applicable, their data type. Constants have their value stored. An array would have its lower and upper bound stored.

For a large source code program the symbol table will contain hundreds of entries so it is important that fast access to any identifier entry is possible.

This can be done by constructing the symbol table as a **hash table** with a hash key generated for each entry. Hashing was discussed in Chapter 13 Section 13.02.

Consider the following program statement:

```
// Calculate discount rate
IF Discount = True THEN
    DiscountRate = 5
ELSE
    DiscountRate = 0
END IF
```

Symbol table

Identifier	Token	
	Value	Data type
`Discount`	300	BOOLEAN
`DiscountRate`	301	INTEGER
5	302	CONSTANT
0	303	CONSTANT

Table 16.01 The symbol table.

Assume addresses 300 onwards are used for the program variables and constants. What will the lexical analyser produce from this statement?

Keyword table

Keyword	Address
REPEAT	100
UNTIL	101
IF	150
THEN	151
ELSE	152
END IF	153
True	200
False	201
=	250

Table 16.02 Keyword table.

The source code is scanned and the lexical analyser produces the following output string:

| 150 | 300 | 250 | 200 | 151 | 301 | 250 | 302 | 301 | 250 | 303 | 152 |

The comment statement is removed.

All 'whitespace' has been removed.

The two variable identifiers and two constants are added to the symbol table.

The keywords have been looked up in the keyword table and replaced by their matching address.

Source code errors that will be identified at the lexical analysis stage include:

- Use of invalid identifier names
- A keyword may have been spelt incorrectly – e.g. Cnsole
  - The lexical analyser will fail to find this as an entry in the keyword table
  - The analyser could think it is an identifier
  - It will (wrongly) insert it as an identifier entry in the symbol table
- However, for a strongly typed language, the compiler would then realise that there was not a matching declaration statement for this identifier.

Syntax analysis

Most syntax errors will be identified in the IDE with careful checking by the developer and using the various aids that the IDE provides. This is **dynamic syntax checking** (see section 5.02).

However, some syntax errors might not be identified early. In this case, it is the task of the compiler's **syntax analyser** to identify any remaining errors.

Syntax checking establishes if a sequence of input characters matches the rules of the language.

The **language grammar rules** must be available to the compiler.

As we shall see shortly, language grammar rules can be documented using either **Backus Naur Form (BNF)** sentences or rules, or visually using a **syntax diagram**.

For example, the Visual Basic.NET compiler will check the statement:

```
Console.Writeline("My best score was ..." & MyScore
```

and report that the statement has a missing closing bracket.

All syntax errors will be reported by the compiler. The programmer must then return to the source code, make the changes and re-compile the code. See Figure 16.01.

Code generation

This is the third stage of the compilation process.

Once the source code is compiled and no errors are found, the compiler can generate the object file or 'executable' file.

The code generation process will need to make reference to the information stored in the symbol table as illustrated in Table 16.01 and to code contained in various program libraries.

This will be statements that have used the (public) built-in functions of the language, or (private) program modules previously written by the programmer.

Code optimisation

This is the final stage of the compilation process. The code, as it has been compiled, might not be in its most efficient form for execution.

The compiler might recognise final changes that can be made to make the code execute in less time or to use less memory for the final object file.

Progress check C

Which of these are true statements?

a   A compiler must be present in primary memory every time we run a program.

b   An interpreter produces an object file.

c   Using an interpreter will use more primary memory at run-time.

d   A compiler will attempt to find all errors in the source code.

e   An interpreter attempts to find all errors in the source code.

f   An interpreter runs the program until the first error is found.

g   The same compiler can be used to translate a Visual Basic.NET program and a Java program.

Progress check D

Consider these program statements.

The code is run through the lexical analyser.

Show:

- the contents of the symbol table
- the output character string produced.

```
FOR Index = 1 To 20
    Product = Index * Index
NEXT
```

Symbol table

Identifier	Token	
	Value	Type
⋮		

Table 16.03 Symbol table.

Assume addresses 300 onwards are used for the program variable and constants.

a   Show the contents of the Table **16.03** produced by the lexical analyser.

b   Show the output string produced by this statement.

Keyword table

Keyword	Address
REPEAT	100
UNTIL	101
FOR	102
TO	103
NEXT	104
⋮	
=	250
+	251
-	252
*	253
/	254

Table 16.04 Keyword table.

Progress check E

When we say code should be 'optimised' what does this mean in practice?

16.06 Programming language grammar

Syntax diagrams

A syntax diagram describes one structure of the programming language grammar.

The following examples illustrate the diagrams needed to define various syntax.

A syntax diagram is always read from left to right.

Worked example 16.02

Define a 'digit' character.

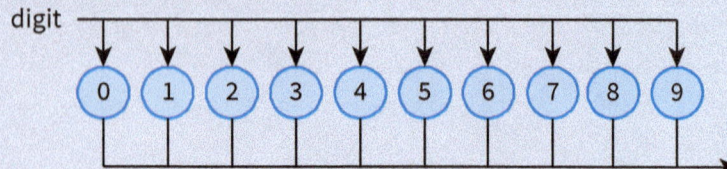

Figure 16.03 Defining a 'digit'.

This diagram shows that a digit is always exactly one of the ten digit characters shown.

Define a 'letter'.

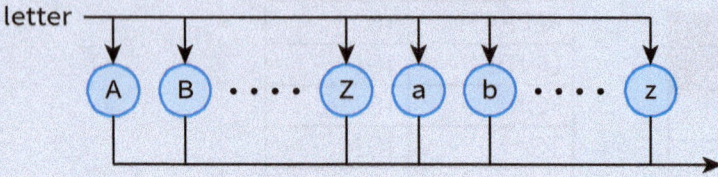

Figure 16.04 Defining a 'letter'.

We conclude a letter is always exactly one of the upper or lower case letters.

These previous two definitions can then be used to define an 'identifier'.

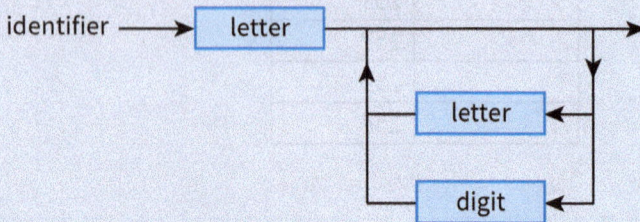

Figure 16.05 Defining an 'identifier'.

Progress check F

Copy and complete the table below.

Use Figures **16.03**, **04** and **05** to decide if these suggested identifiers are VALID or INVALID.

Suggested Identifier	VALID/INVALID	Explanation (If invalid)
P		
MyObject		
8index		
Count		
My_Object		
Loop5times		

> **Progress check G**
>
> Show what new/amended syntax diagrams are needed if the language allows the use of the underscore character anywhere within an identifier name.

Backus-Naur notation (BNF)

Backus-Naur Form (BNF) is a special language called a **meta-language** that is used to describe the syntax and composition of statements that make up a high-level programming language.

A syntax element is enclosed between the < > characters and a typical statement would be:

```
<digit> ::= 0 | 1 | 2 | 3 | 4 | 5 | 6 | 7 | 8 | 9

<binarydigit> ::= 0 | 1
```

This first statement reads as `<digit>` 'is defined as' **0 or 1 or 2 or .... 8 or 9**.

Since each of the terms on the right-hand side of each rule cannot be broken down further 0, 1, 2, etc. are called **terminal symbols**.

A rule definition may be **recursive**. Recursion is discussed at length in Chapter 19. In this BNF context, recursion means that the definition makes a reference to itself.

Consider this definition to describe identifier names for a programming language.

```
<letter> ::= A|B|C .... |Z|a|b|c| .... |z

<digit> ::= 0|1|2|3|4|5|6|7|8|9

<identifier> ::= <letter>|
                 <identifier><letter>|
                 <identifier><digit>
```

The third rule states that a valid identifier name can be either:

A single letter character,

or a letter followed by one or many letter characters,

or a letter followed by one or more digit characters.

The process of analysing whether or not a given identifier is valid (following the given rules) is called **parsing the expression**.

Example 1 - Identifier name `She`

Is this valid?

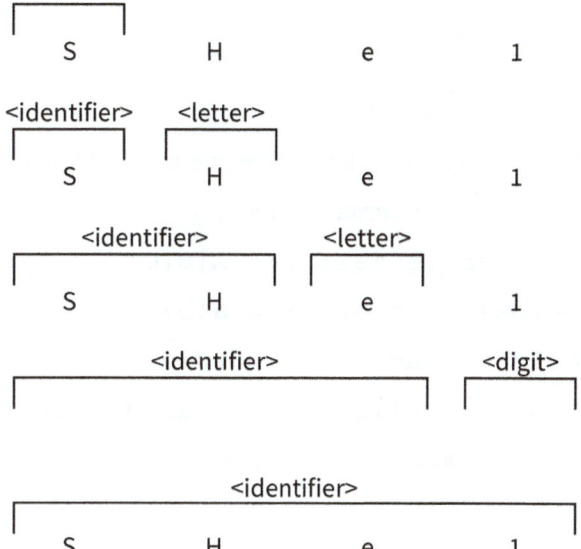

Figure 16.06 Parsing an expression.

This demonstrates that the expression _is_ a valid identifier name.

Example 2 - Identifier name `1he`

Is this valid?

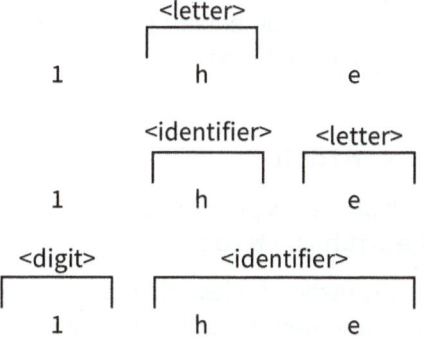

Figure 16.07 Parsing an expression.

The parsing of BNF expressions is best illustrated by practice examples.

Progress check H

```
<product_code> ::= <letter> | <letter><letter> | <letter><letter><letter>
      <letter> ::= A|B|C| .... |Z|a|b|c ....   |z
```

Which of the following product codes are valid?

a   AJA
b   D5R
c   SA

Progress check I

The following set of rules defines the format for a list of letters.

```
        <comma> ::= ,
   <cap_letter> ::= A|B|C|D|E | ... |X|Y|Z
 <lower_letter> ::= a|b|c|d|e| ..... |x|y|z
<valid_character> ::= <digit> | <lower_letter>
         <list> ::= <valid_character> | <valid_character><comma><list>
```

Which of the following are valid lists ?

a   s
b   p
c   s,y,u,
d   s,h,y,4,6

Reverse Polish notation (RPN)

Infix notation

When we were taught the fundamentals of maths we wrote expressions using infix notation.

Typically:

`Area = Length x Width`

The operator, the multiply sign, is positioned between the two operands `Length` and `Width`.

The meaning for this expression is clear. However, some expressions will require the use of brackets to convey the order in which the component parts must be evaluated.

`Z = (x + y) / 5`

The brackets are needed here to make it clear that the sum of `x + y` must be worked out first.

Reverse Polish (or postfix notation)

The operand for the expression is written following the two operands.

`Area = Length Width x`

And for the second expression above:

`x y + 5 /`

Reverse Polish notation has the major advantage over infix in that the meaning for any expression is clear without the use of brackets.

Study carefully the examples in Table 16.01.

Infix expression	Postfix expression
(8 - 4) * 5	8 4 - 5 *
(3p + 5) / (p - z)	3 p * 5 + p z - /
2*7 - 8/4	2 7 * 8 4 / -
7^4 - 9/3	7 4 ^ 9 3 / -

Table 16.01 Infix-reverse Polish expressions.

Convert between reverse Polish notation and infix form

A **binary tree** can be used to represent expressions both in infix and reverse Polish notation.

Consider the expression: (3p + 5) / (p - z)

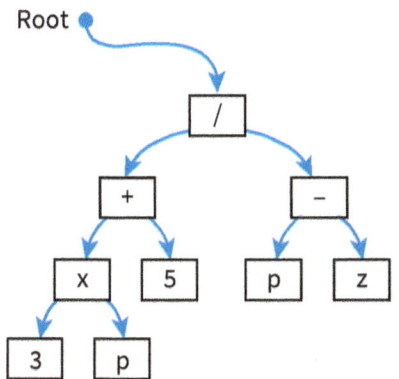

Figure 16.08 Expression as a binary tree.

In Chapter 19, Section 19.01 we shall develop a recursive algorithm for traversing a binary tree.

If we use an **in-order traversal** algorithm, the values in the expression will be output in the order that gives the infix expression.

> ## Progress check J
>
> Here is the in-order traversal algorithm.
>
> | |
> |---|
> | InOrderTraversal(Root) |
> | IF Root.LeftPointer <> Null |
> | THEN |
> | // move left |
> | InOrderTraversal(Root.LeftPointer) |
> | ENDIF |
> | OUTPUT Root.Data |
> | IF Root.RightPointer <> Null |
> | THEN |
> | // move right |
> | InOrderTraversal(Root.RightPointer) |
> | ENDIF |
> | ENDPROCEDURE |
>
> Which statements make it clear that the `InOrderTraversal` procedure is recursive?

Post-order traversal

If we simply change the order of doing things for the traversal algorithm we will traverse the tree in a different order.

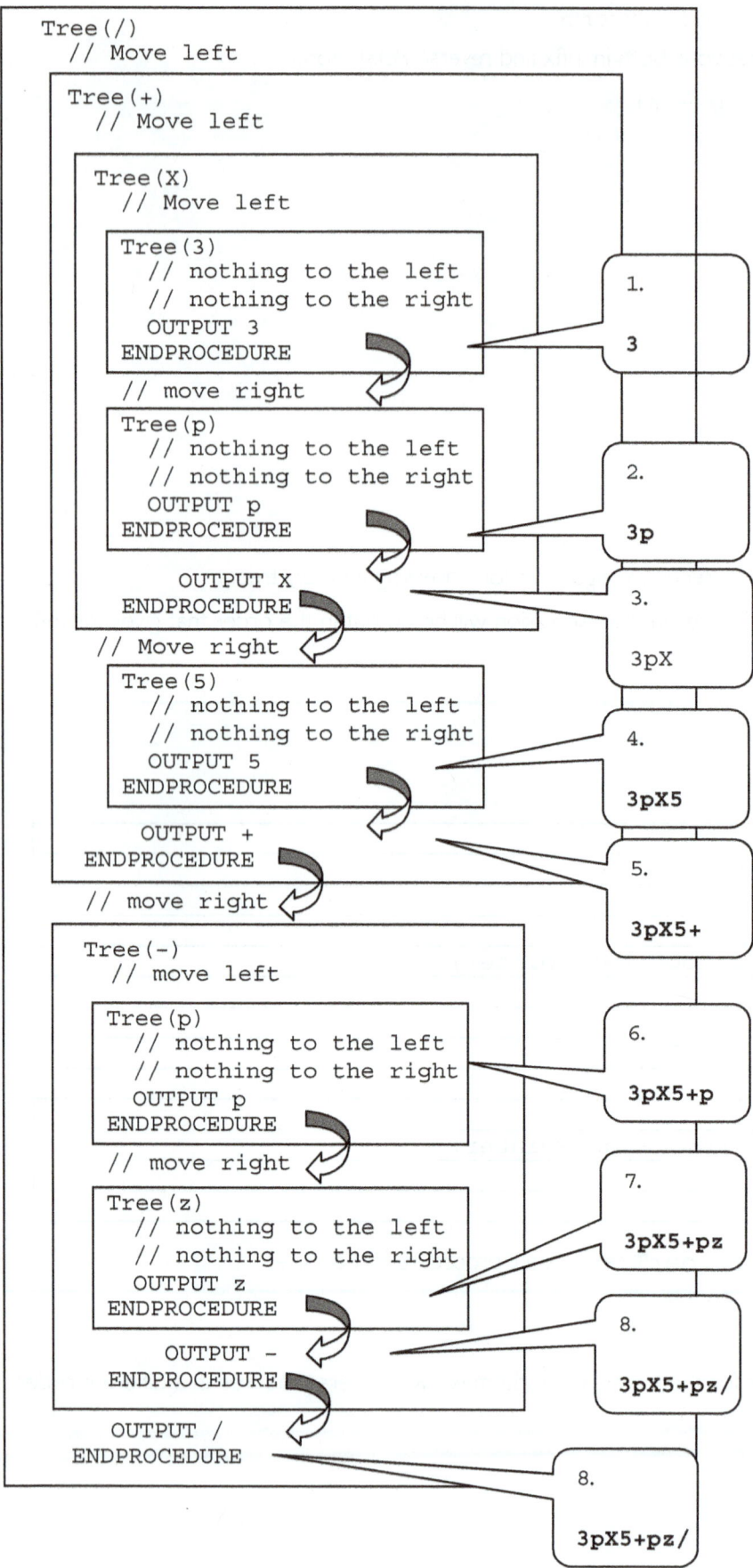

Figure 16.09 Traversing the expression tree in Figure 16.08

```
PostOrderTraversal(Root)
    IF Root.LeftPointer <> Null
        THEN
            InOrderTraversal(Root.LeftPointer)
    ENDIF
    IF Root.RightPointer <> Null
        THEN
            InOrderTraversal(Root.RightPointer)
    ENDIF
        OUTPUT Root.Data
ENDPROCEDURE
```

We have effectively changed the order to 'left – right – root'. The traversal of the given tree will produce the following traversal and output.

The trace confirms that for the `PostOrderTraversal` algorithm, the expression is output in reverse Polish.

Progress check K

Evaluate the following reverse Polish expressions:

a   11 6 – 5 *

b   3 4 ^ 9 / 3 + 4 /

c   14 6 – 8 *

Write these expressions in reverse Polish.

d   (a + b) / 6

e   (2a + b)³

Evaluating a reverse Polish expression

This will demonstrate another advantage of the use of reverse Polish. The elements that make up the expression can be processed using a **stack data structure**.

Consider the evaluation of the expression: (9 * 7 + 2) / 5

In reverse Polish this becomes: 9 7 * 2 + 5 /

The method will be to push operands onto the stack in sequence and then, when an operator is met: pop two values, evaluate and push the result onto the stack.

Trace the evaluation of: 9 7 * 2 + 5 / gives:

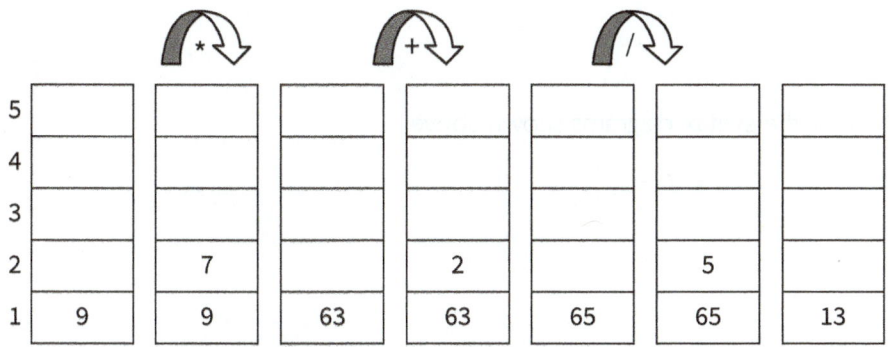

Figure 16.10 Stack used for evaluating reverse Polish expression.

Progress check L

Trace the changing contents of a stack when it is used to evaluate the reverse Polish expression:

`2 4 ^ 5 - 2 /`

Past paper questions

1. The following syntax diagrams, for a particular programming language, show the syntax of:
   - An assignment statement
   - A variable
   - A letter
   - An operator

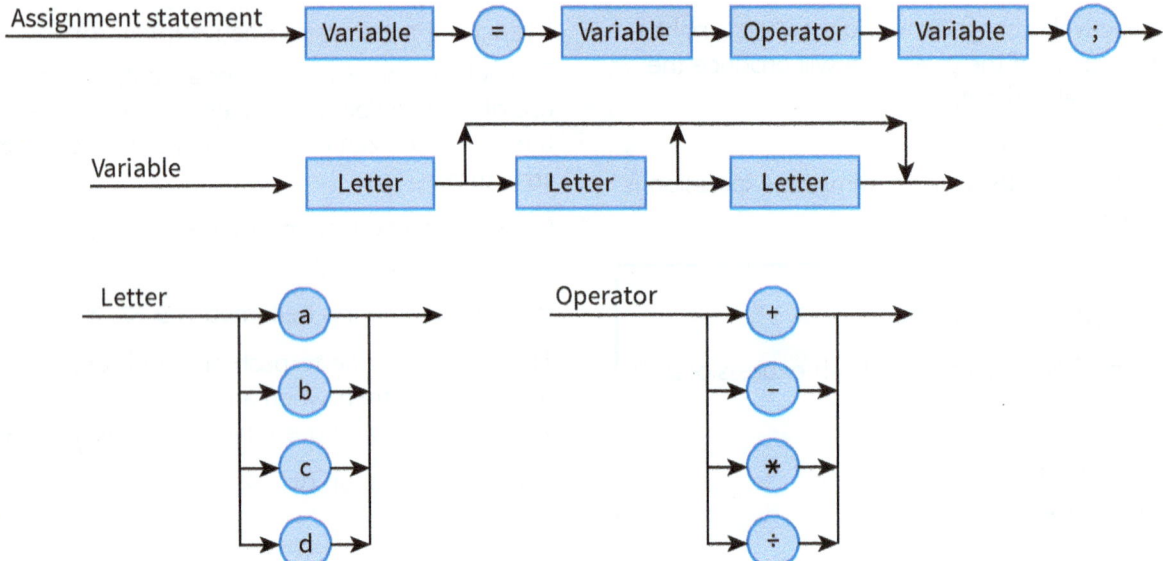

   a. The following assignment statements are invalid.

   Give the reason in each case.

   i. `a = b + c` [1]

   ii. `a = b - 2;` [1]

   iii. `a = dd - cce;` [1]

   b. Write the Backus-Naur Form (BNF) for the syntax diagrams shown above.

   `<assignment statement> ::=`

   `<variable> ::=`

   `<letter> ::=`

   `<operator> ::=` [6]

   c. Rewrite the BNF rule for a variable so that it can be any number of letters.

   `<variable> ::=` [2]

d Programmers working for a software development company use both interpreters and compilers.

   i   The programmers prefer to debug their programs using an interpreter.

       Give one possible reason why. [1]

   ii The company sells compiled versions of its programs.

       Give a reason why this helps to protect the security of the source code. [1]

Cambridge International AS & A level Computer Science 9608 paper 32 Q1 June 2015

2 In this question, you are shown pseudocode in place of a real high-level language. A compiler uses a keyword table and a symbol table. Part of the keyword table is shown below.

Tokens for keywords are shown in hexadecimal.

All the keyword tokens are in the range 00 to 5F.

Keyword	Token
←	01
+	02
=	03
⋮	⋮
IF	4A
THEN	4B
ENDIF	4C
ELSE	4D
FOR	4E
STEP	4F
TO	50
INPUT	51
OUTPUT	52
ENDFOR	53

Entries in the symbol table are allocated tokens. These values start from 60 (hexadecimal).

Study the following piece of code:

```
Start ← 0.1
// Output values in loop
FOR Counter ← Start TO 10
     OUTPUT Counter + Start
ENDFOR
```

a Complete the symbol table below to show its contents after the lexical analysis stage.

Symbol	Token	
	Value	Type
Start	60	Variable
0.1	61	Constant

[2]

b   Each cell below represents one byte of the output from the lexical analysis stage. [2]

Using the keyword table and your answer to part (a), complete the output from the lexical analysis.

60	01											

The compilation process has a number of stages. The output of the lexical analysis stage forms the input to the next stage.

  i   Name this stage. [1]

  ii State two tasks that occur at this stage. [2]

c   The final stage of compilation is optimisation. There are a number of reasons for performing optimisation. One reason is to produce code that minimises the amount of memory used.

  i   State another reason for the optimisation of code. [1]

  ii What could a compiler do to optimise the following expression?

      A ← B + 2 * 6   [1]

  iii These lines of code are to be compiled :

      X ← A + B

      Y ← A + B + C

Following the syntax analysis stage, object code is generated. The equivalent code, in assembly language, is shown below :

```
LDD 436     //loads value A
ADD 437     //adds value B
STO 612     //stores result in X
LDD 436     //loads value A
ADD 437     //adds value B
ADD 438     //adds value C
STO 613     //stores result in Y
```

  iv Rewrite the equivalent code, given above, following optimisation. [3]

Cambridge International AS & A level Computer Science 9608 paper 32 Q2 November 2015

3   There are four stages in the compilation of a program written in a high-level language.

  a   Four statements and four compilation stages are shown below.

Draw a line to link each statement to the correct compilation stage.

Statement	Compilation stage
This stage removes any comments in the program source code.	Lexical analysis
This stage could be ignored.	Syntax analysis
This stage checks the grammar of the program source code.	Code generation
This stage produces a tokenised version of the program source code.	Optimisation

[4]

Cambridge International AS & A level Computer Science 9608 paper 33 Q2a November 2016

4. A computer operating system (OS) uses paging for memory management. In paging:
   - Main memory is divided into equal-size blocks, called page frames
   - Each process that is executed is divided into blocks of the same size, called pages
   - Each process has a page table that is used to manage the pages of this process

   The following table is the incomplete page table for a process X.

Page	Presence flag	Page frame address	Additional data
1	1	132	
2	1	245	
3	1	232	
4	0	0	
5	1	542	
6	0	0	
⋮	⋮	⋮	⋮
135	0	0	

When a particular page of the process is currently in main memory, the Presence flag entry in the page table is set to 1.

If the page is not currently present in memory, the Presence flag is set to 0.

a. The page frame address entry for Page 2 is 245.

   State what the value 245 could represent. [1]

b. Process X executes until the next instruction is the first instruction in Page 4. Page 4 is not currently in main memory.

   State a hardware device that could be storing this page. [1]

c   When an instruction to be accessed is not present in main memory, its page must be loaded into a page frame. If all page frames are currently in use, the contents of a page frame will be overwritten with this new page.

The page that is to be replaced is determined by a page replacement algorithm.

One possible algorithm is to replace the page that has been resident in main memory for the longest time.

   i   Give the additional data that would need to be stored in the page table. [1]

   ii Complete the table entries below to show what happens when Page 4 is swapped into main memory. Assume that Page 5 is the one to be replaced.

   In the final column, give an example of the data you have identified in part (c) (i).

Page	Presence flag	Page frame address	Additional data
∫	∫	∫	∫
4			
∫	∫	∫	∫

An alternative algorithm is to replace the page that has been used least.

   iii Give the different additional data that the page table would now need to store. [1]

   iv   In the following table, complete the missing data to show what happens when Page 3 is swapped into main memory. Assume that Page 1 is the one to be replaced. [3]

   In the final column, give an example of the data you have identified in part (c) (iii).

Page	Presence flag	Page frame address	Additional data
∫	∫	∫	∫
3			
∫	∫	∫	∫

d   Explain why the algorithms given in part (c) may not be the best choice for efficient memory management.

Cambridge International AS & A level Computer Science 9608 paper 33 Q3 November 2016

Security

Learning Objectives:

- Understand the need for encryption
- Use the terminology associated with encryption
- Understand symmetric encryption
- Understand the operation of asymmetric encryption
- Describe how a secure communication is made with asymmetric encryption
- Understand the use of a digital certificate
- Describe how a communication is made which includes a digital signature
- Understand the use of the Secure Socket Layer (SSL) protocol
- Understand the basic technology of quantum encryption.

17.01 Encryption

Encryption

Encryption is not specific to computing. It has been used for thousands of years for the sending and receiving of messages. Encryption is not designed to stop a third party having access to data, but to ensure that they are unable to understand the data if it is intercepted.

Data that is sent over a communication link is susceptible to interception.

Emails and other data might pass through many computers, routers and networks before they reach their destination, therefore the data could be intercepted and read by a third party.

Symmetric encryption

Symmetric encryption uses the same algorithm and key for the encryption and the **decryption** process.

The rows/columns example that follows uses symmetric encryption.

Consider a message which is to be sent and received.

'ILL MEET YOU AT 6 OCLOCK'

The user writes the message into a (say) 5 × 5 grid.

The message characters are rearranged in column sequence order:

I	L	L	Δ	M
M	E	E	T	Δ
U	Δ	A	T	Δ
6	Δ	O	C	L
O	C	K	Δ	Δ

Δ is used to represent a <Space> character.

In summary:

- The **plain text** is the message – ILLΔMEETΔUΔATΔ6ΔOCLOCKΔΔ
- Decide on the encryption key - the number of characters on each row (5)
- The encryption algorithm is: "Write the message into a grid starting with the first row"
- The **cipher text** is: IMU6OLRΔΔCLEAOKΔTTCΔMΔΔLΔ

A recipient of the cipher text would only be able to decrypt this message if they knew the **encryption algorithm** and the **encryption key**.

> **Progress check A**
>
> A simple text message is encrypted with symmetric encryption.
>
> Your algorithm is to replace each character by the character three places further on in the alphabet. If necessary, the transposition is cyclic e.g. 'Y' is replaced by 'B'.
>
> Decrypt the cipher text: **CHEUDKRXVHDWRQH**

Encryption algorithm example

Many encryption algorithms use the 'Exclusive OR' operator in the following way:

The encryption process is:
Plain text (ASCII character code)   0100 1111
Encryption Key   0101 0011 XOR
Cipher text   0001 1100

The decryption process is:
Cipher text   0001 1100
Encryption Key   0101 0011 XOR
Result (original plain text)   0100 1111

The Exclusive OR operator will reproduce the original text when the same key is used both for encryption and for decryption.

17.02 Encryption protocols

Asymmetric encryption (Public key cryptography)

A much more secure technique is to use asymmetric encryption. A secure technique is one that is impossible to decipher or one where the decryption cannot be achieved within a realistic time. Two keys are used, called the **public key** and **private key**.

The plain text is encrypted with the sender's private key. The recipient must be in possession of the sender's public key, so that this public key can used to decrypt the cipher text.

> **TIP**
>
> An 8-bit key is unrealistic in practice.
>
> Asymmetric encryption keys are typically 1024 or 2048 bits. 2048-bit keys are more than sufficient for security. It would take an average computer more than 14 billion years to crack a 2048-bit key!

The golden rule is that the private key is only ever in the possession of its owner. Ideally, it is generated automatically and is unknown to the staff who work at the company that provides the key.

Public-key encryption algorithms

The creation and use of asymmetric encryption keys is complex and outside the syllabus. Asymmetric encryption assumes that, with a knowledge of the public key, it is impossible, in a reasonable time-frame, to generate the matching private key.

The method calculates the public key as the product of two large prime numbers. The private key is then derived from calculating the prime factors of this large number. The private key stores this data, but this calculation is impossible to compute in a reasonable amount of time.

17.03 Encrypted communications

Once the users each have a **digital certificate**, they must give their public key to the intended correspondent. This is done when each user sends an email to the other user.

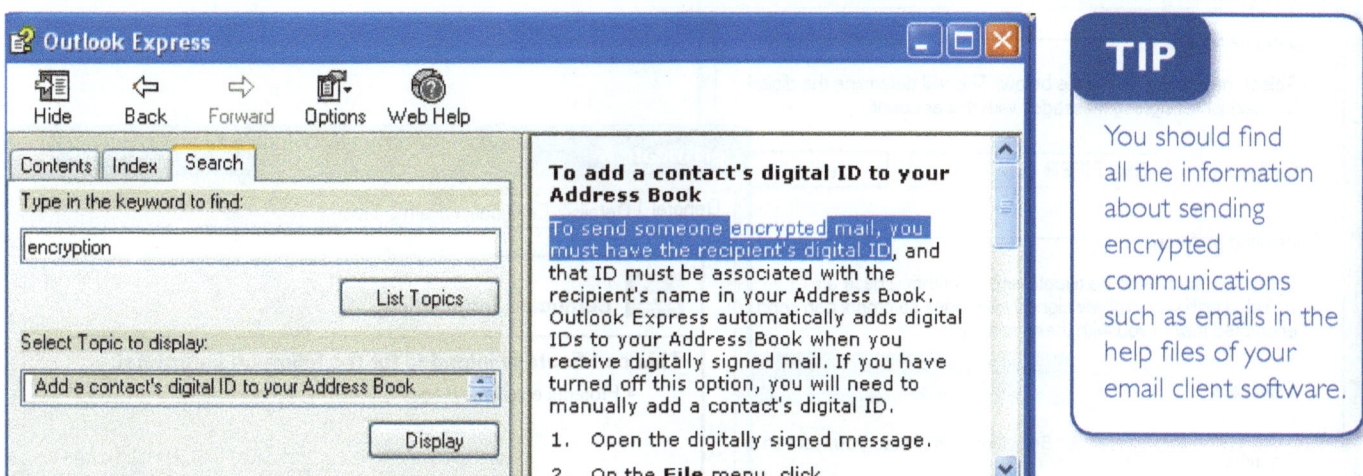

Figure 17.01 Outlook screenshot on handling digital IDs.

> **TIP**
>
> You should find all the information about sending encrypted communications such as emails in the help files of your email client software.

The ownership and knowledge about keys is illustrated in Figure **17.02**.

In this situation, A is to send an encrypted email to B.

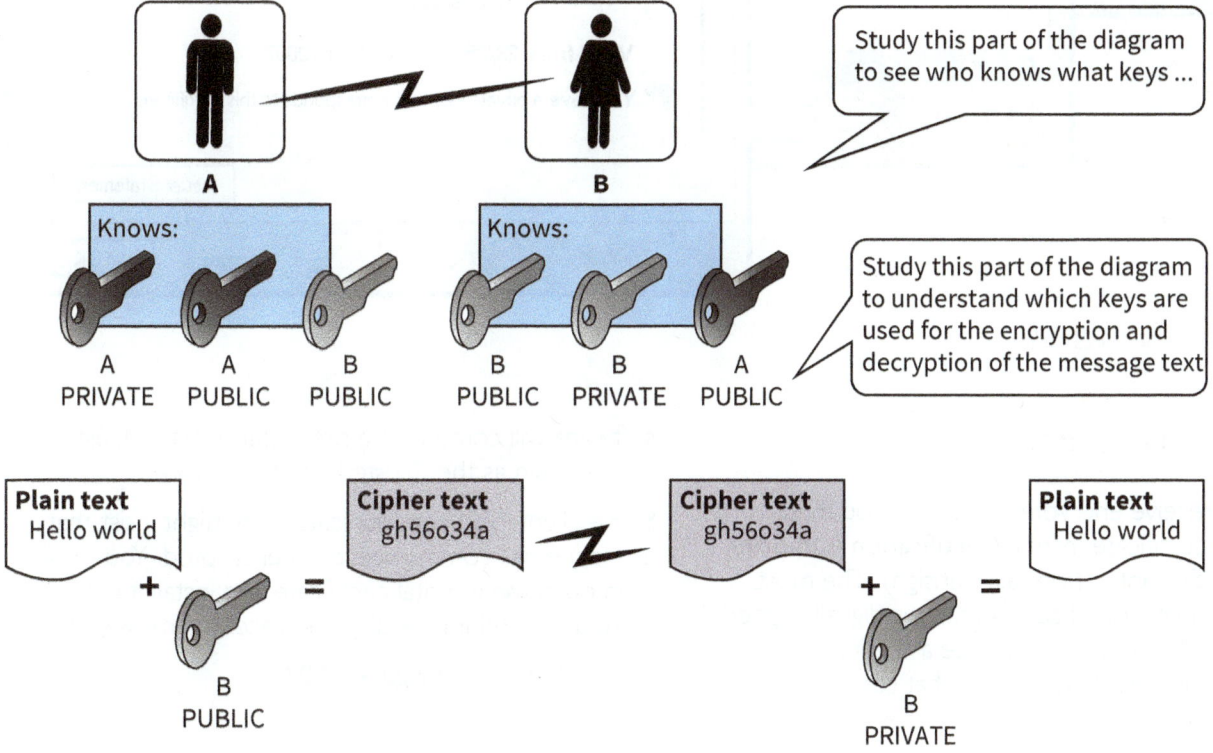

Figure 17.02 Sending an encrypted email.

17.04 Digital certificates

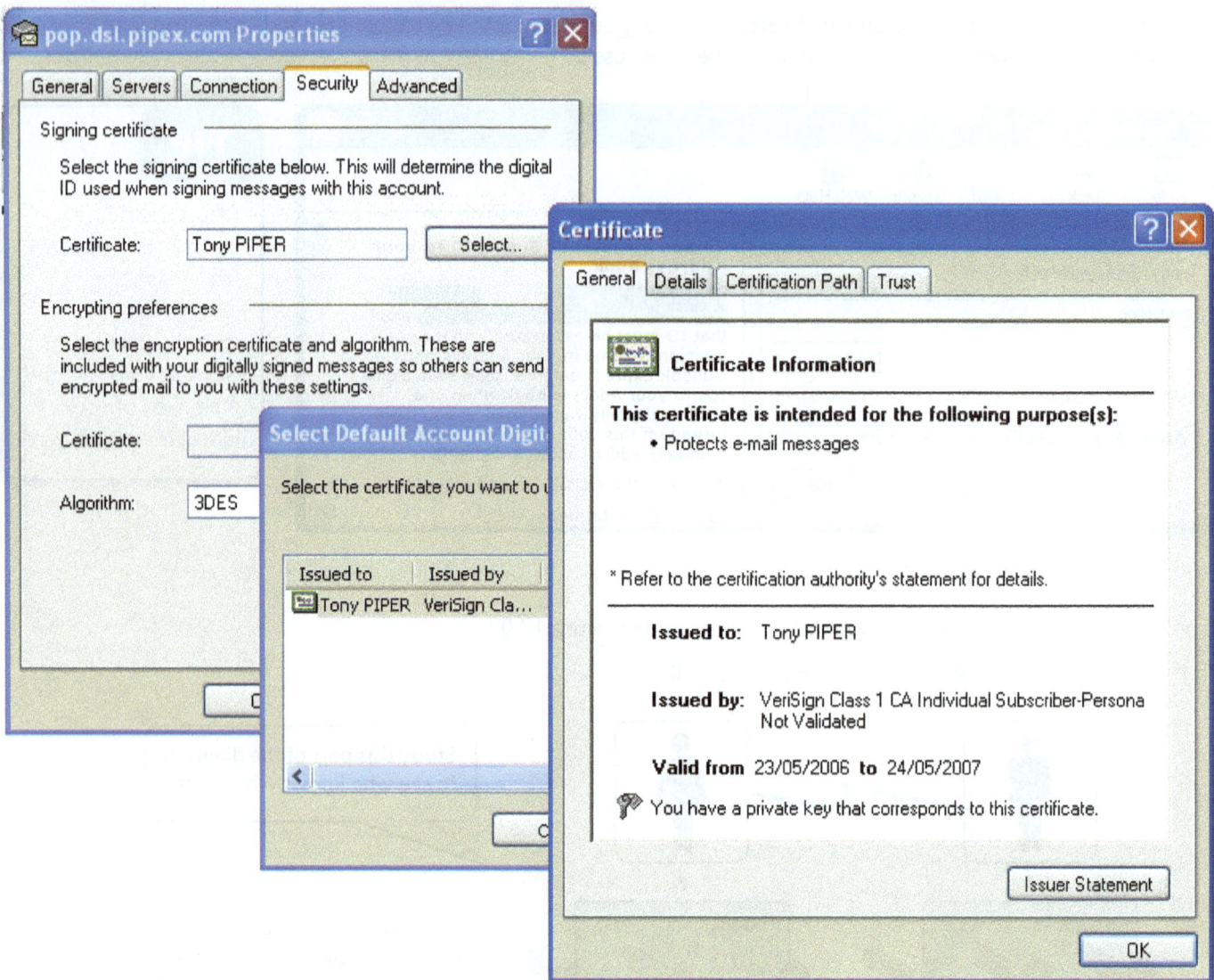

Figure 17.03 Digital certificate.

Getting a digital certificate

To send and receive encrypted messages you must have a digital certificate from a **Certification Authority (CA)** such as Symantec (formally Verisign). The most important part of a certificate is that it is digitally signed by a trusted CA. Anyone can create a certificate, but browsers only trust certificates that come from an organisation on their list of trusted CAs. Browser software will come with a pre-installed list of trusted CAs, known as the Trusted Root CA store.

Some clients you communicate with might insist that all (say) email communication is encrypted. You must then purchase a digital certificate and install it on the computer used for sending and receiving messages.

This is illustrated in Figure **17.03**.

Digital signatures

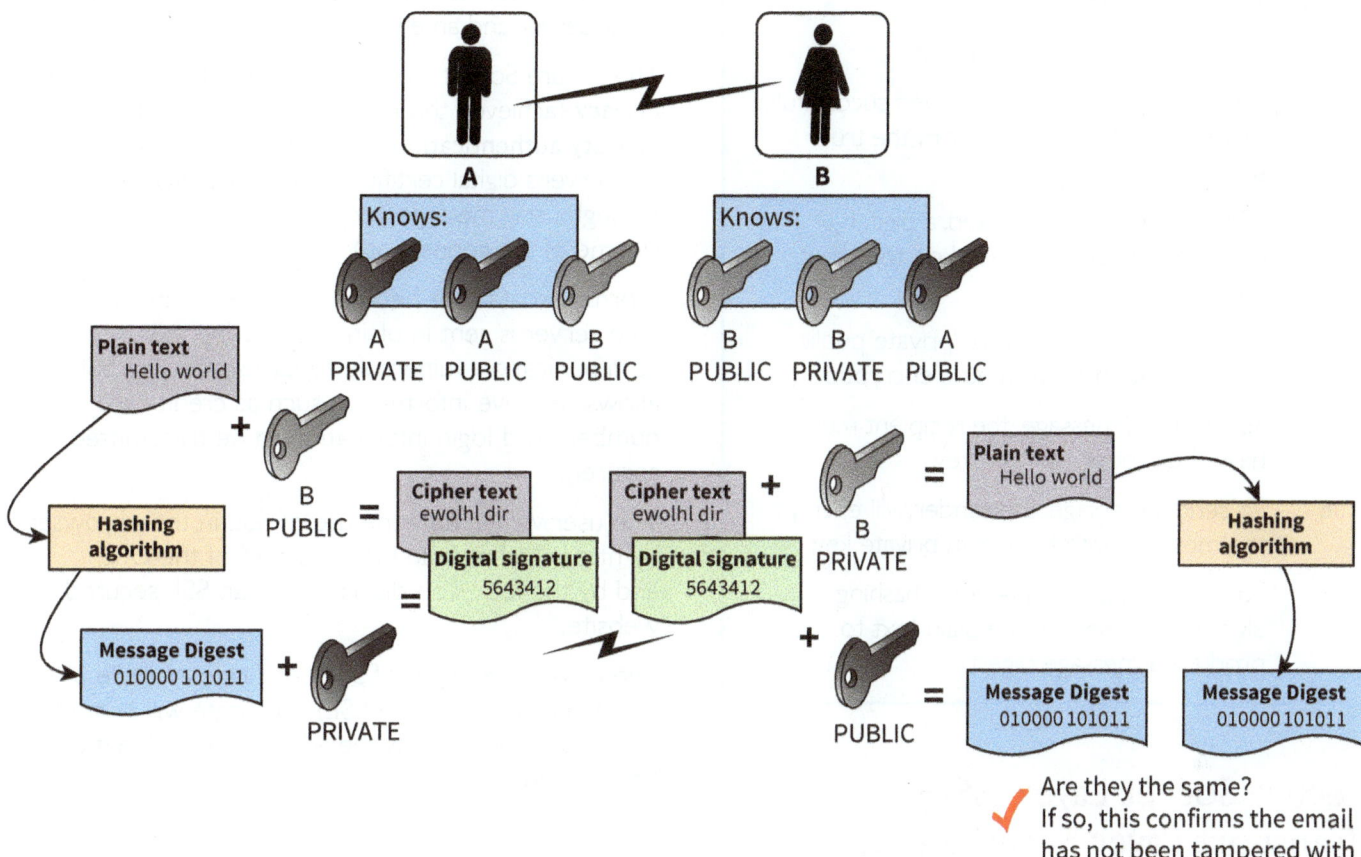

Figure 17.04 Adding a digital signature.

The encryption stage:

Step 1 – The diagram looks complex at first, but appreciate that the first stage, producing the cipher text, is identical to Figure **17.02**. That is, as if no digital signature were to be added.

The hashing algorithm will be provided as part of the digital certificate. When recipient B comes into possession of A's public key, they will also be provided with the hashing function of A's certificate.

Step 2 – The hashing function is used on the plain text to produce a **message digest**.

Step 3 – The message digest is encrypted with A's private key.

The cipher text with the digital signature is communicated to recipient B.

The decryption stage:

Step 1 – Exactly as in Figure **17.02**. The cipher text is decrypted using A's public key.

> **TIP**
>
> When we produce our 'signatures' on paper documents, the appearance of the signatures will be roughly the same. This analogy does not hold for digital signatures. The string of binary digits that make up a digital signature will be different each time, even though the same certificate is being used.

Step 2 – The **hashing algorithm** is used on the decrypted text to produce the message digest.

Step 3 – A second copy of the message digest is produced by using A's public key on the digital signature received. The question is then asked, do the two message digests match?

A match between the two message digests confirms that neither the cipher text nor the digital signature were changed in transit.

Progress check B

Which of these are true statements?

a If an encrypted email is received successfully, that is proof that it came from the true sender.

b After it has been purchased, a digital certificate must be installed on the client email software.

c The other terminology for 'private-public key encryption' is symmetric encryption.

d To receive a message, the recipient must have the sender's private key.

e To send a message, the sender will encrypt the message with their own private key.

f To create a digital signature, a hashing algorithm is used on the plain text to produce a message digest.

Secure Socket Layer (SSL) – Transport Layer Security (TLS)

SSL is an example of a handshaking protocol. The two end-points exchange messages until they agree that they are ready to communicate.

TLS is an updated and more secure version of SSL. Providers, such as Symantec, still refer to the purchase of an SSL certificate (even though the technology now used is TLS).

SSL is used when a user needs to be assured that a communication over the internet is secure. SSL will secure a communication using the internet's TCP.

SSL (Secure Socket Layer) is a standard security protocol for establishing an encrypted link between a server and a client. This is typically communication between a web server (website) and a browser, or an email server and an email client.

The Secure Socket Layer protocol has three objectives, **Privacy** (achieved through the use of encryption), **identity authentication** (achieved through the use of the server's digital certificate) and **reliability** (achieved through using message integrity checking during the lifetime of the connection).

Normally, data sent between a browser and a web server is sent in plain text, leaving the communication vulnerable to eavesdropping. SSL allows sensitive information such as credit card numbers and login information to be transmitted securely.

The user will identify the use of SSL in their browser by https: (rather than http:) as part of the URL and by the lock icon displayed for an SSL secured website.

There are three types of SSL certificate available. An 'extended validation (EV SSL) certificate will in most recent browsers display the address bar with a green background.

How is an SSL connection established and used?

The SSL protocol creates a **session key** that is used for two-way communication for the duration of the session.

> **TIP**
>
> The server is in possession of the digital certificate. The web browser has access to a large list of trusted certificates.

Worked example 17.01

The client browser is to connect to a web server secured with SSL.

The detailed steps are listed below and are also shown in Figure 17.05.

1. The browser requests that the server identify itself.
2. The server sends a copy of its SSL certificate, which includes the server's public key.
3. The browser checks the certificate against a list of trusted CAs stored by the browser.

   It must check that the certificate is unexpired, correctly valid, and that its name is valid for the website that it is connecting to.
4. If the browser trusts the certificate, it creates, encrypts, and sends back a symmetric session key using the server's public key.

   The session key is only active for the duration of this SSL communication session. The word 'symmetric' means the same key is used by both client and server for encryption and decryption.
5. The server decrypts the symmetric session key using the server's private key.
6. The web server sends back an acknowledgement encrypted with the session key to start the encrypted session.
7. Server and browser now encrypt all transmitted data with the session key.

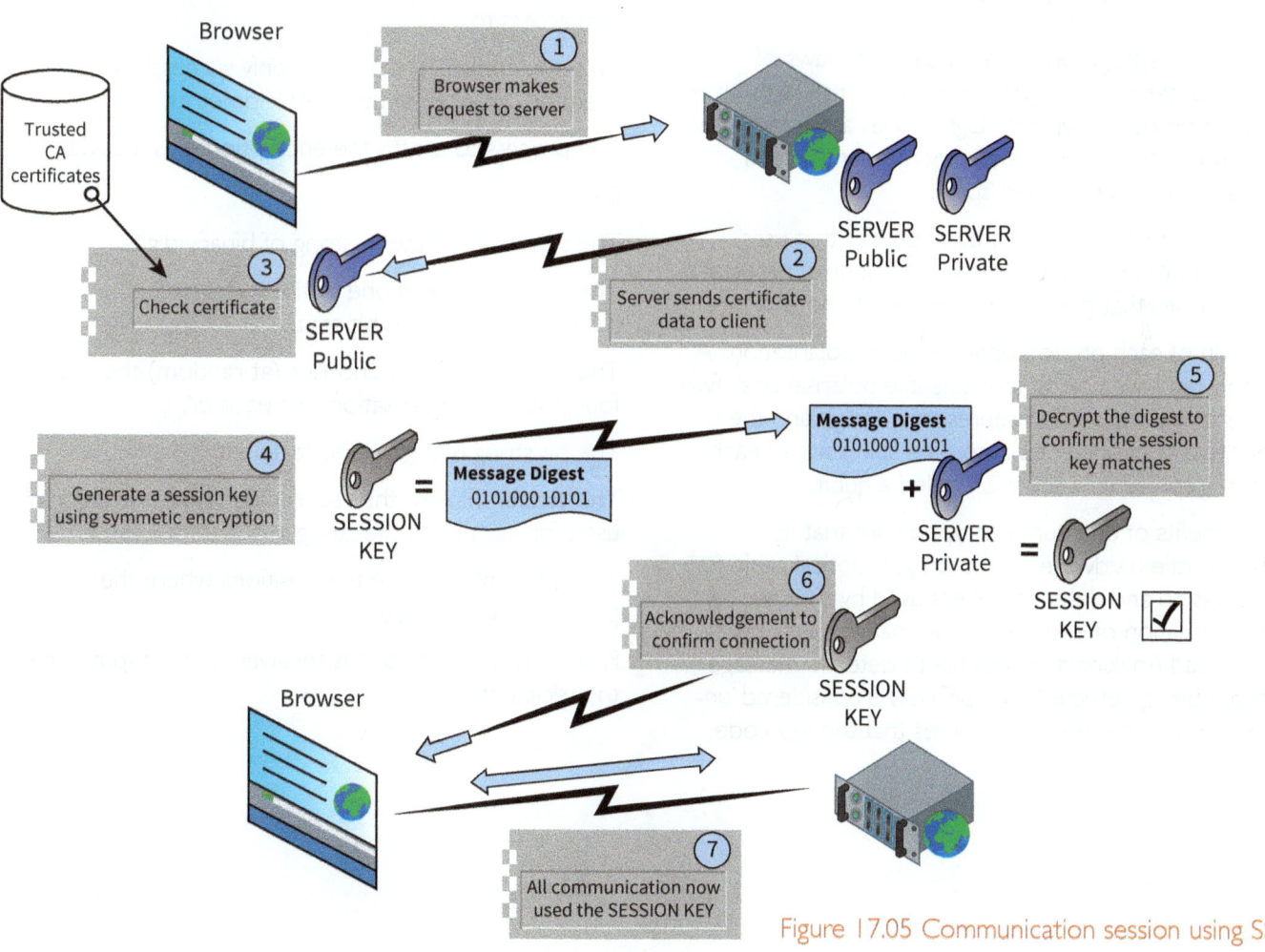

Figure 17.05 Communication session using SSL.

> ## Progress check C
>
> The seven steps below (1 to 7) describe a communication session using SSL.
>
> a   What is the missing text (a) and (b)?
>
> b   Put the statements (A, B and C) in their correct positions
>
>   A – The server sends the browser an acknowledgement – encrypted with the session key.
>
>   B – The browser checks the certificate against a list of trusted Certificate Authorities.
>
>   C – The server decrypts the symmetric session key using its private key.
>
> 1 Browser asks the server to identify itself.
> 2 The servers sends a copy of its .... (a) ....
> 3 A / B / C?
> 4 The browser creates an encrypted symmetric session key using the server's .... (b) ....
> 5 A / B / C?
> 6 A / B / C?
> 7 The browser and server communicate with encrypted communications using the session key.

Quantum cryptography

Quantum cryptography uses fundamental laws of physics rather than the present mathematical algorithms for asymmetric encryption. Light waves are transmitted as photons. A photon has energy, momentum and angular momentum (called 'spin').

Quantum mechanics is an area of physics that uses fundamental laws applied to the behaviour of particles. The particles that give us light are called photons.

The spin of each photon determines its polarisation. A photon can have one of four possible polarisations. Two polarisations are used to represent a 1 digit and the other two to represent a zero. The spin state of each photon represents a single bit called a qubit.

The benefits of quantum encryption are that it requires little hardware (a photon gun, optical cable for transmission and detection filters used by the receiver), the polarisation of each photon is changed as soon as it is read (making it impossible to detect a message without being detected), the process is considered 'un-hackable' and the method assumes that the key code generated between sender and receiver is impossible to gain access to.

The drawbacks are that it has only successfully been used for distances of up to 80 kilometres.

The process to create the encryption is as follows:

Begin

The sender generates a string of binary digits.

The sender chooses one of the two possible polarisations for each bit sent.

The receiver similarly chooses (at random) the – one of four possible - polarisations for each bit.

The bit string is sent to the recipient.

The sender informs the recipient of the polarisations used for each bit in the string.

The recipient will note the positions where the polarisations matched

From this, a secret code is received and computed by the recipient.

Past paper questions

1. a Explain the following terms:

   Encryption

   Public key [2]

   b A user downloads software from the internet.

   i State what should be part of the download to provide proof that the software is authentic. [1]

   ii Describe the process for ensuring that the software is both authentic and has not been altered. [4]

Cambridge International AS & A level Computer Science 9608 paper 32 Q2c, d June 2015

2. Digital certificates are used in internet communications. A Certificate Authority (CA) is responsible for issuing digital certificates.

   a Name three data items present in a digital certificate. [3]

   b The method of issuing a digital certificate is as follows:

   1 A user starts an application for a digital certificate using their computer. On this computer a key pair is generated. This key pair consists of a public key and an associated private key.

   2 The user submits the application to the CA. The generated ….. (i) ….. key and other application data are sent. The key and data are encrypted using the CA's ….. (ii) ….. key.

   3 The CA creates a digital document containing all necessary data items and signs it using the CA's ….. (iii) ….. key.

   4 The CA sends the digital certificate to the individual.

   In the above method there are three missing words. Each missing word is either 'public' or 'private'.

   i

   Justification [2]

   ii

   Justification [2]

   iii

   Justification [2]

   c Alexa sends an email to Beena. Alexa's email program:

   - Produces a message digest (hash).
   - Uses Alexa's private key to encrypt the message digest.
   - Adds the encrypted message digest to the plain text of her message.
   - Encrypts the whole message with Beena's public key.
   - Sends the encrypted message with a copy of Alexa's digital certificate.

   Beena's email programme decrypts the encrypted message using her private key.

   i State the name given to the encrypted message digest. [1]

   ii Explain how Beena can be sure that she has received a message that is authentic (not corrupted or tampered with) and that it came from Alexa. [2]

   iii Name two uses where encrypted message digest are advisable. [2]

Cambridge International AS & A level Computer Science 9608 paper 32 Q2 June 2016

3. Katarina works for a company specialising in the sale of computer parts and accessories. She works in the London office and her colleague Lucy works in the Hong Kong office. Katarina emails confidential information to Lucy so that only Lucy can read the information.

   a. Explain how public and private keys are used to ensure that only Lucy has a readable copy of the confidential information. [4]

   b. Julio is buying items from the online shop. He already has an account with the shop.

   Explain how the use of Secure Socket Layer (SSL) or Transport Layer Security (TLS) helps to keep Julio's confidential information secure. [3]

Cambridge International AS & A level Computer Science 9608 paper 32 Q5a, b June 2018

Artificial Intelligence

Learning Objectives:

- Understand how graphs can be used in AI:
  - Understand Dijkstra's algorithm for finding the shortest path from one node of a graph to all the others
  - Understand the A* algorithm for finding the shortest path from one node of a graph to a given second node
- Understand the methods used with:
  - Deep learning
  - Machine learning
  - Reinforcement learning
- Understand how artificial neural networks are used in machine learning
  - Understand the back propagation of errors
- Show how regression analysis methods are used in machine learning.

18.01 Graphs and AI

We will study the graph data structure in Chapter 19. Graphs are of interest in AI.

Remind yourself of the terms used with a graph.

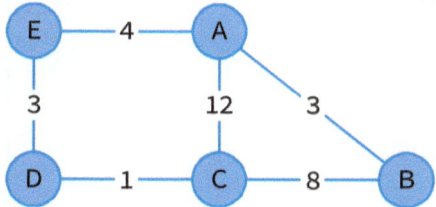

Figure 18.01 A weighted graph.

The graph shown has five **nodes** (labelled A, B, C, D and E). For this graph, the nodes represent five towns.

The lines drawn to connect the nodes are called **edges**. For this graph each edge represents a route that connects two towns.

This is a weighted graph. Each path in the graph has a **weight**. For this graph, the weight represents the distance between each town.

18.02 Dijkstra's algorithm

The algorithm is concerned with the shortest path and shortest distance between a node and each of the other nodes.

Progress check A

Study Figure **18.01**.

List the possible routes from A to C.

What is the distance covered by the shortest route between A and C?

For this graph the calculation is straightforward, but for applications of graphs in computer science we could be dealing with graphs with hundreds of nodes.

The basis of **Dijkstra's algorithm** is as follows:

- Maintain a list showing, for each node, the currently known shortest path and its distance
- When a possible shortest path for a node is found, that node is added to the list
  - In the example which follows, the list is called `PathKnown` and is initially empty
  - Shortest path values are updated when necessary
- At the start, none of the paths or distances are known, so the distances are all initialised to infinity
- Dijkstra's algorithm will iterate until the `PathKnown` list contains every node.

Worked example 18.01

Find the shortest path and distance from node A to the other nodes in the Figure 18.02 graph.

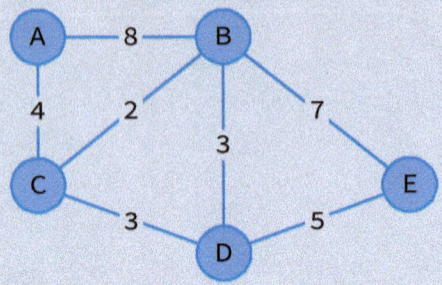

Figure 18.02 Example graph.

Step 1 – Initialisation

	A	B	C	D	E
PathKnown= []	∞	∞	∞	∞	∞

Step 2 – Choose A as the start node

Since we are starting at A, update the table to show:

	A	B	C	D	E
PathKnown= [A]	0	∞	∞	∞	∞

Step 3 – Consider neighbours of A (the last node to be added to **PathKnown**).

Start at the base node A

Reachable/Neighbours of A are nodes B distance 8 and C distance 4, so add this data (distance and path) to the table.

C has the shortest path, so add C to **Pathknown**.

	A	B	C	D	E
PathKnown= [A, C]	0	8 A – B	4 A – C	∞	∞

Further steps …

The algorithm must then iterate, taking the starting point each time as the node which has just been added to **PathKnown**.

The complete trace is shown in Table 18.01.

There are some things to note:

The changing values for the shortest path to each node are recorded in the Table 18.01 trace table.

The Shortest path column shows the changing contents of the array/list **PathKnown** ('Shortest path known').

Since none of the shortest paths to any of the nodes is initially known, the contents of **PathKnown** are initially an empty list.

In the trace table – Table 18.01 – when a set of values for a node are recorded for the first time or updated, the cell is bordered.

Also in the trace table, when the shortest path values for a node are finalised the cell is greyed out.

Each of the numbered steps in the trace table is an iteration of a loop in the algorithm.

The algorithm will stop when the `PathKnown` list contains every node.

	Shortest path	A	B	C	D	E
1	Initialise: `PathKnown=[]`	∞	∞	∞	∞	∞
2	Set node A as the start: `PathKnown = [A]`	0	∞	∞	∞	∞
3	Neighbours of A are C=4 and B=8. Add the data for nodes B and C.					
		0	8 A – B	4 A – C		
	Shortest path is B, so add B to the shortest path list `PathKnown = [A, B]`					
4	Neighbours of B are C = 10, D = 11 and E = 15. Add the data for nodes C, D and E.					
		0	8 A – B	4 A – C	11 A – B – D	15 A – B – E
	Shortest path is C, so add C to shortest path list `PathKnown = [A, B, C]`					
5	Neighbours of C is D = 7 only, but no change to the node D data.					
		0	8 A – B	4 A – C	11 A – B – D	15 A – B – E
	Only path is to D, so add D to `PathKnown`. `PathKnown = [A, B, C, D]`					
6	Neighbours of D is E = 7 only so update the node E data.					
		0	8 A – B	4 A – C	7 A – C – D	12 A – C – D – E
	Add E to `PathKnown` `PathKnown = [A, B, C, D, E]`					
7	Stop	0	8 A – B	4 A – C	7 A – C – D	12 A – C – D – E

Table 18.01 Dijkstra's algorithm trace table.

The final contents of the table shows the shortest distance to the nodes (B, C, D and E) from A.

Here is the pseudocode for Dijkstra's algorithm.

> **TIP**
>
> You won't need to write algorithms to set up, access or perform searches on a graph. However, you need to know how to comment on a given algorithm.

Identifier	Description
`TheGraph`	The given graph – this would have data for each node, the list of neighbours and their edge weights.
`Source`	The 'base' vertex.
`PathKnown`	List/array of all the vertices where the shortest path has been finalised.
`Vertex`	The 'current vertex' being considered.
`Neighbour`	A node which is a neighbour of `Vertex`.
`NextNode`	Temporary variable to store the next node to be added to the `PathKnown` list.
`ShortestPath`	List/array of the calculated shortest path for each node.
`ShortestWeight`	List/array of the calculated weight of shortest path for each node.

Table 18.02 Dijkstra algorithm identifier table.

> **TIP**
>
> This is a complex algorithm. However, if you have first studied carefully the Figure 18.02 graph, you should be able to follow the basic structure of the algorithm.
>
> A variety of data structures could be used for the `ThisGraph` graph data.
>
> If you want to study this further, search the web for 'Dijkstra algorithm'. You will find code for an implementation of the algorithm in various programming languages.

```
PROCEDURE Dijkstra(TheGraph, Source)
    // initialise
    FOR EACH Vertex IN TheGraph
        ShortestPath[Vertex] ← ∞
    ENDFOR
    ShortestPath[Source] ← 0  //Weight from source to source is set to 0
    Vertex ← Source
    WeightFromSource ← 0
    WHILE PathKnown list is not empty     //Main loop
        FOR EACH Neighbour OF Vertex
            Add the weight for this node to WeightFromSource
            IF WeightFromSource is empty or less that the node's current value
                THEN
                    Update or add Neighbour weight to ShortestWeight[Neighbour]
                    Update or add Neighbour path to ShortestPath[Neighbour]
            ENDIF
            Calculate NextNode - the neighbour with the smallest weight
            from Source
        NEXT Neighbour
        Add NextNode to PathKnown list
    ENDWHILE
END PROCEDURE
```

18.03 The A* algorithm

The **A* algorithm** (pronounced 'a star') is a second algorithm for path finding and graph traversal.

The algorithm uses a technique we have not studied elsewhere called a **heuristic function**. A heuristic approach is one that is designed to arrive at a solution faster than by following the steps in a more rigorous algorithm.

A heuristic approach will <u>not</u> explore all possible states of the problem but it will begin by exploring the most likely ones.

Consider this example from playing chess or drafts. You could try every possible next move and then apply some evaluation of each possible move. A heuristic would initially exclude routes that begin with an apparently bad move. A grid is an example that can be conceptualised as a graph. Each grid on the board is a node and nodes will have a number of neighbours.

If the task was to find the shortest route from the top of the board to the bottom, then obvious moves to ignore would be moves that are sideways or upwards.

> ### Progress check B
>
> A chess board, 8 rows and 8 columns, is to be represented as a graph.
>
> a How many nodes are there?
>
> b The number of edges for each square will vary. What values are possible for the number of edges from any given node?

Using the Dijkstra algorithm to find the shortest route between two squares on a given grid would require many, many calculations and comparisons. However, it is always guaranteed to find the shortest route.

This idea can be demonstrated by considering the following example. Consider this small grid where the task set is to find the shortest route from node A to node B.

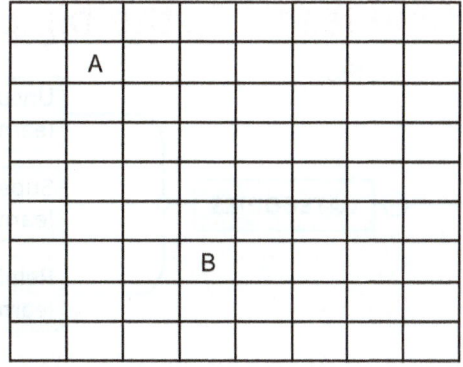

Figure 18.03 Using the A* algorithm.

Consider using Dijkstra's algorithm to find the shortest path and route. The algorithm will know from the stored data that square A has eight neighbours and so all possible routes will be tried. But we can see that five of the possible 'next squares' would be a bad choice.

From a knowledge of the coordinates of node A and node B, the A* algorithm can compute that sensible initial moves will include: diagonal right, down or right. So, the algorithm is able to made a good heuristic guess at the next path move.

The A* algorithm requires maths that is constantly calculating the difference between the Dijkstra calculation and an estimated heuristic value. In this example it is the distance 'as the crow flies'.

> ### Progress check C
>
> For the grid shown in Figure **18.03**, assuming horizontal, vertical and diagonal moves are all allowed.
>
> a Calculate the weight of the shortest path from node A to node B.
>
> b How many different 'shortest path routes' are possible?

18.04 Machine learning: the big picture

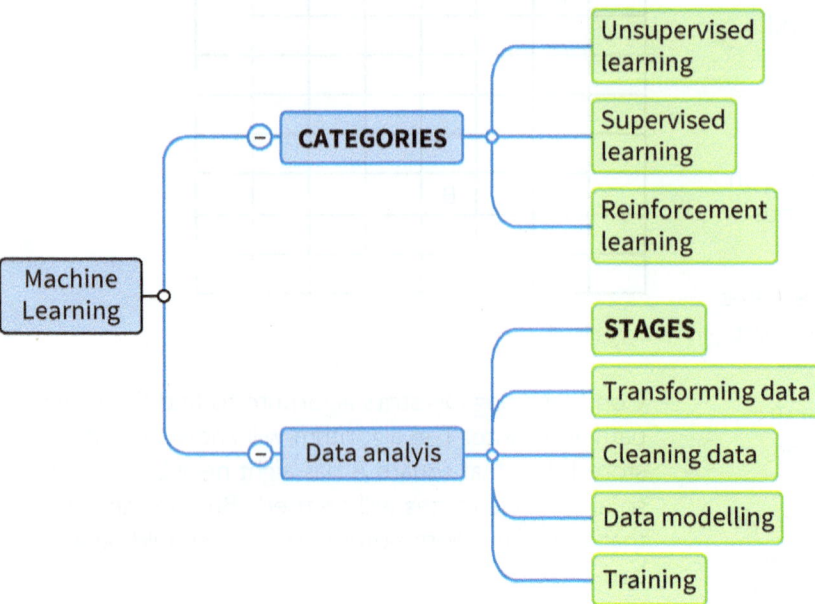

Figure 18.04 Machine learning – overview.

18.05 Before machine learning: data analysis

We as humans have always used data to understand and make sense of the world we live in. Hence data has a value and is a key component of learning and decision making.

In the modern world, data often has a wider value than the purpose for which it was generated. Transaction payment data is generated as a record of the transaction: who ordered what, the cost, the despatch date, method of payment and more. But this data, when collected in large volumes, will yield other even more useful information for the company that can be used for other aspects of the company's operation. It will show purchasing trends and customer preferences and could therefore be the source from which targeted marketing is done.

Remember that, in the AS work in Chapter 7, we introduced the term **big data**.

Data analysis

Consider how a company/organisation might have to use machine learning. This processing of the data will be done by mathematical and statistical techniques (that are not new). What is new is the use of machine learning algorithms that will include predicting future behaviour, classifying information and data and allowing the company/organisation to make informed decisions.

To make raw data useful, the starting point for the use of machine learning techniques is **data analysis**. Four key stages make up data analysis.

Transforming the data

This can be as simple as organising the data into rows and columns. For an examination of transaction data, we could group all the transactions for (say) each customer under a single header.

We will also want to analyse unstructured data in the form of email messages, video, sound and images that cannot be organised into this structured rows/columns transformation.

It might be possible to convert some text values into a numeric representation. For example, eight different colour names that form the raw data could be transformed for data analysis with the use of a number code for each colour.

Cleansing the data (Data scrubbing)

Data might be incomplete, or known to contain rare and extreme values. Data values might not be available in some cases or simply known to be incorrect.

The data analysis would want to exclude these data values.

Data modelling

This is where statistical techniques play their part. Techniques such as **regression analysis** (discussed later in this chapter) will confirm if there is a correlation between variables, or if a dataset can be classified in some way.

Machine learning in action

The basis of machine learning in some real world activity is represented by a mathematical function where the algorithm is not known in advance. The algorithm is established after data analysis.

Hence the term '**training**' is sometimes used to describe the first stage of machine learning. The process is trained to match given input(s) to the known output(s).

This approach is very different to the approach used when programming a task using a procedural language.

Given the tasks of multiplying two numbers, their comparison is shown here:

1. Procedural programming approach:
   - The algorithm/function to do this is <u>known</u>.
   - The user will give two inputs to the known algorithm.
   - The process outputs the result.
2. Machine learning approach:
   - The algorithm/function to do the computation is <u>unknown</u>.
   - Supply several data sets: pairs of numbers with the answer for each pair and data modelling tries to arrive at the function that produced the answer.
   - Machine learning will deduce the function.

18.06 Supervised learning

This form of machine learning is similar to a student learning something new under the supervision of a teacher. The teacher will present lots of examples to the student (the 'training data'). The student can then attempt to derive specific rules from the examples. The student will attempt the output for some given outputs. The teacher will feed back to the student whether or not they gave the correct response.

Supervised learning always has a set of independent, labelled input variables (A, B, C, etc.) and a dependent output variable (X). The task of machine learning is to deduce an algorithm or mapping function that could predict an output (X) from a given set of input data. This is called 'supervised learning' since the **known input and output data** must be made available, just as a teacher would present their student with examples. Learning will end when the model produces an acceptable level of performance.

A problem to attempt recognition of a particular item, such as a door, would be appropriate for this model of learning. The input data would consist of training examples for doors of different sizes, in different buildings, different colours and made from different materials. This training data would also have examples of (say) windows and other items that use the same materials and are roughly the same size, and the learning must decide which ones do not match.

Supervised learning could be used for both types of problem.

There are **regression-type problems** where the target will be to predict a quantitative value such as the number of items of an article to store in the warehouse (see later).

There are **classification-type problems** where the target is a qualitative value such as whether a particular customer is one to whom it is worth continuing to send marketing emails.

18.07 Unsupervised learning

With **unsupervised learning** there is only a measured set of input values (A, B, C, etc.) but no corresponding output. The task for an unsupervised learning model is to identify some underlying structure or distribution of the dataset.

The model is having to calculate and to discover any patterns/structures in the data.

Unsupervised learning falls into two categories.

One of these is **clustering** where the data is shown to have groupings, such as data for a large number of internet users. Their predominant use was analysed and found to fit into three categories: online purchases, research and leisure.

The other of these is **association**, for example, where the structure algorithm discovers that there is an association between clients' purchasing habits: customers who bought product A also tended to buy product D.

18.08 Reinforcement learning

This is analogous to a human learning by trial and error. A number of situations are presented and each one generates some form of response. Some situations will effectively get a penalty or a reward. This reward/penalty will then influence the generation of the algorithm.

> **TIP**
>
> There is an analogy here with our definition of real-time processing studied in Chapter 3, where feedback always influenced the next state of the system.

Worked example 18.02: Learning to play 'bat-and-ball'/'pong'

This was one of the very first Atari computer games. The user batted a ball back to the opponent (the computer). The user response is continually to move the bat either up or down to intercept the ball.

This is the 'Hello World' of **reinforcement learning**!

With a supervised learning model such as a neural network, the training data would consist of hundreds of action frames taken from actual game-play (the input) <u>and</u> the user response to each frame (that is move up or move down: the output).

With reinforcement learning, we do <u>not</u> know the actual response to any frame (unlike supervised learning). Hence, we do not have a set of 'training data' as we needed for supervised learning.

The key components and the working of the network model for reinforcement learning are shown in Figure **18.04**:

The **Agent** is the human player or machine.

The **Environment** is the console display that shows rewards/feedback in the form of an increasing points score and also the current state of the game.

A network that learns in this way is called a **policy network**.

Figure **18.05** shows that every action by the agent is the result of the current state and any reward that was generated.

(Continued)

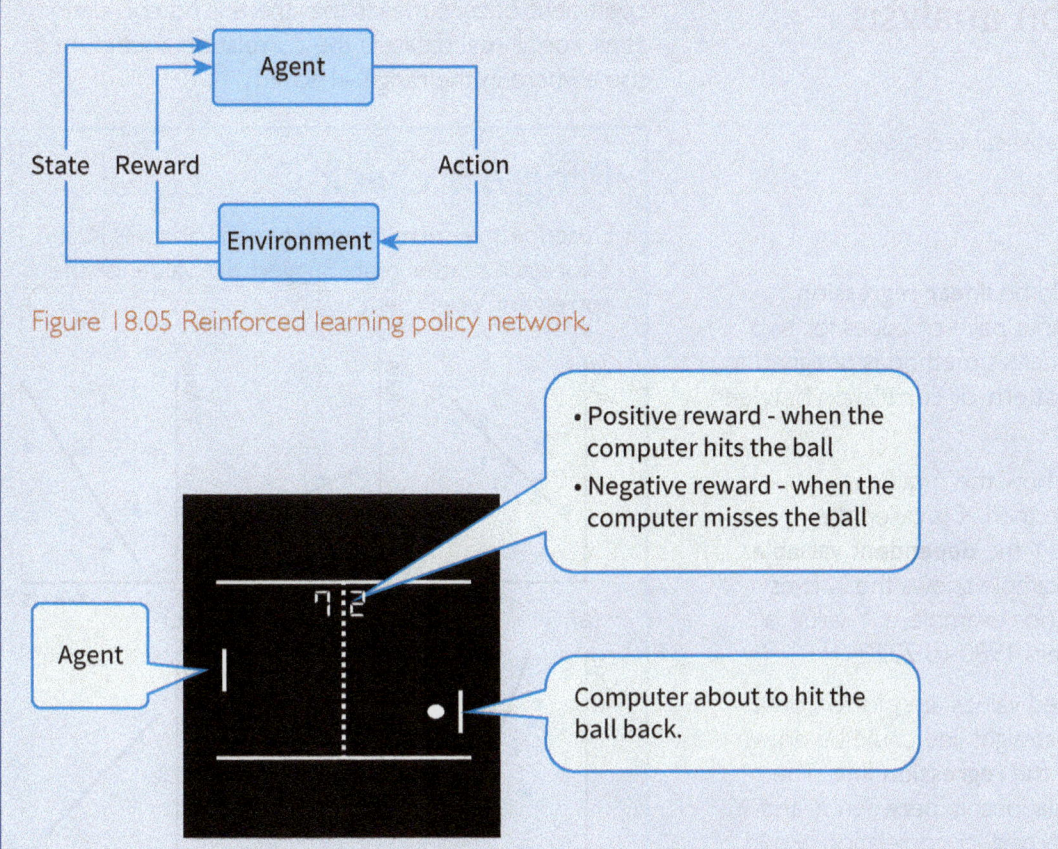

Figure 18.05 Reinforced learning policy network.

Figure 18.06 Atari pong screen display.

The network calculates for any frame the probability of making the move, up or down.

The aim of the policy network will be to generate as many positive rewards as possible.

The working of the model uses maths but the underlying principle is simple. All successful responses by the agent are given a positive reward. Conversely, all wrong responses get a negative reward. This should ensure that with time the negative responses will get less frequent and the success of the agent will increase.

Other applications where a policy network with rewards could be used are in a marketing scenario where a cost is added if some condition is met or with a robot, that when traversing an area, will get a penalty when it collides with an obstacle.

Machine learning tools

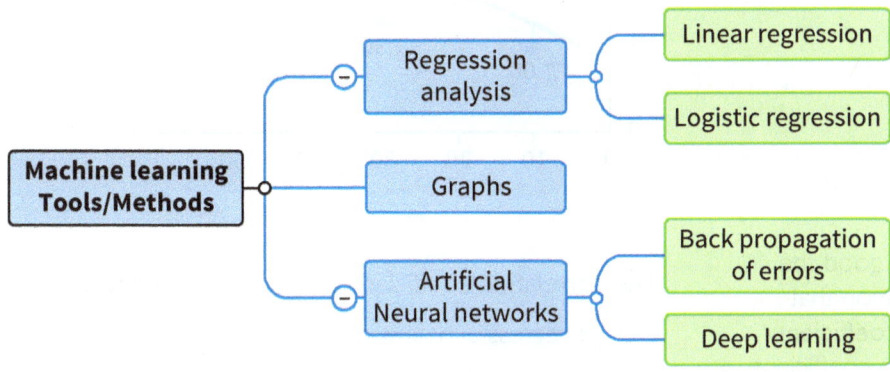

Figure 18.07 Machine learning tools.

18.09 Regression analysis methods

Regression analysis is a statistical technique.

Linear regression

The simplest pattern would be **linear regression**. The method takes as its input pairs of values for two variables (X and Y). The analysis method is designed to find out if there exists a 'pattern' or correlation between the two values (X and Y).

If the intention is to study how the Y value is determined by the X value then X is called the **independent variable** and Y the **dependent variable**. A common **scatterplot** example shows the X axes as some measure of time (for example, a Y value is plotted for each of the years 1980 to 2020).

This means when the paired values are plotted, on a grid called a scatterplot, a straight line could be drawn between the points called the **regression line**. The strength of the possible relationship between X and Y is called the **correlation**. A perfect correlation would mean that every pair of (X, Y) values would lie exactly on the regression line. Figure **18.08** would suggest that there is a pattern: low values for X tend to produce a low Y value and high X values produce a high Y value.

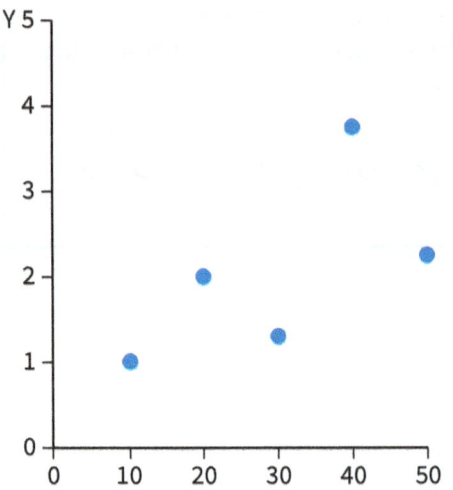

Figure 18.08 Scatterplot.

There is maths that can be applied. How good the pattern is can be expressed with a calculation that returns a number called the **correlation coefficient**. A perfect correlation reflects a correlation coefficient value of exactly either −1 or +1. A correlation coefficient of zero means that there is no correlation at all. For all real datasets the correlation coefficient is somewhere in the range −1 to +1.

Progress check D

Describe the correlation between variables X and Y for each scatter plot. Suggest the value for the correlation coefficient.

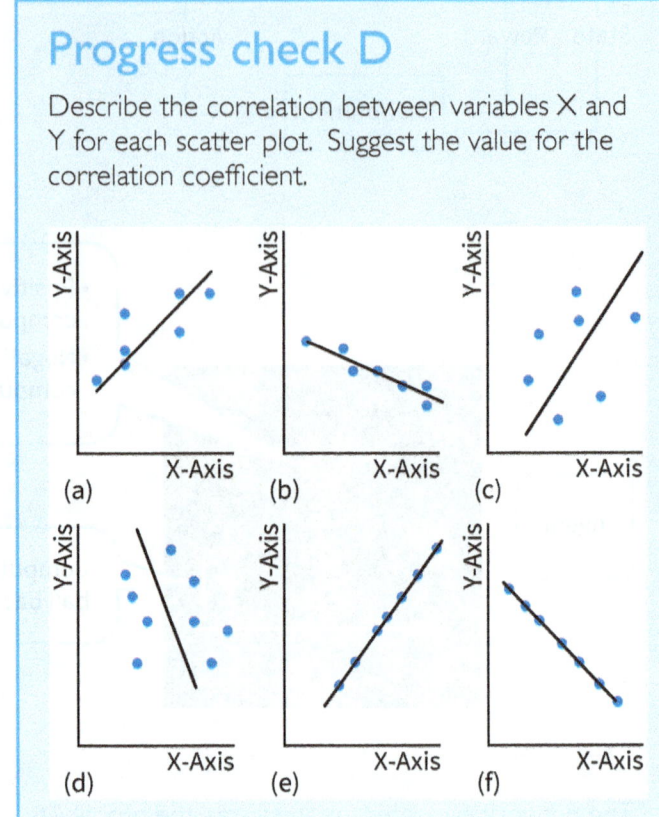

Figure 18.09.

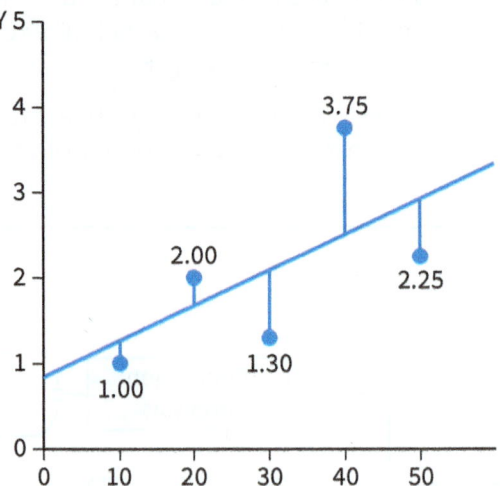

Figure 18.10 Scatterplot with regression line.

The correlation coefficient is calculated as follows:

- a regression line is drawn
- a vertical line is imagined from each data point to the line

- this distance is calculated
- the average of all these distances is computed

The regression line, or 'line of best fit', is the one drawn such that this average distance has the lowest possible value.

The regression trend line for the dataset can be used to predict a single Y value for a single given X value.

Progress check E

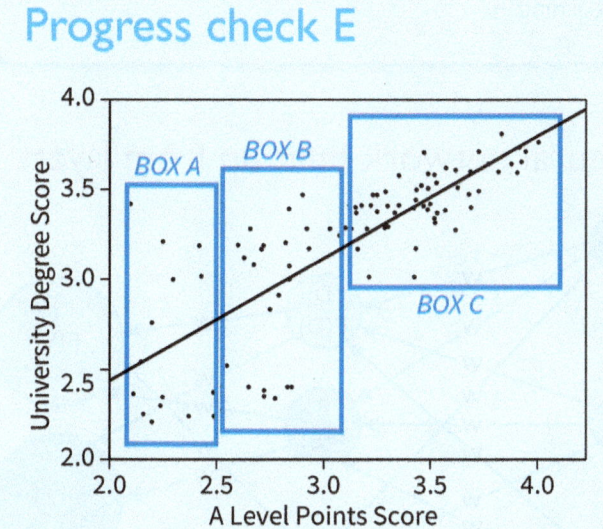

Figure 18.11 Regression line.

Each plot point represents a student who studied Computer Science at a university. The scatterplot shows a score (Y) in one of their final university exams measured against their average point score for A Level attainment (X) before attending university.

a   Is there positive or negative correlation between X and Y?

b   Make a guess at the value for the correlation coefficient.

c   Three groups of students have been selected, shown in Box A, Box B and Box C.

Which group of students is the one where the X score appears the most reliable predictor of the Y score?

Logistic regression

This technique uses a different mathematical calculation. The independent variable X is used to calculate a probability value (between 0 and 1) for each X value.

The maths then, similarly to regression analysis, calculates a regression line based on the minimum average distance between each point and the regression line.

The method is well suited to the classification of values into one of two possible classes.

TIP

You do not need to know the maths that is used to make all this happen.

Worked example 18.03

The task is the analysis of 200 emails. Each email is given a point score calculated from a number of different factors, such as, the quality of the language, its source and many others. The probability score is calculated for each of the 200 emails and their values displayed on a scatterplot.

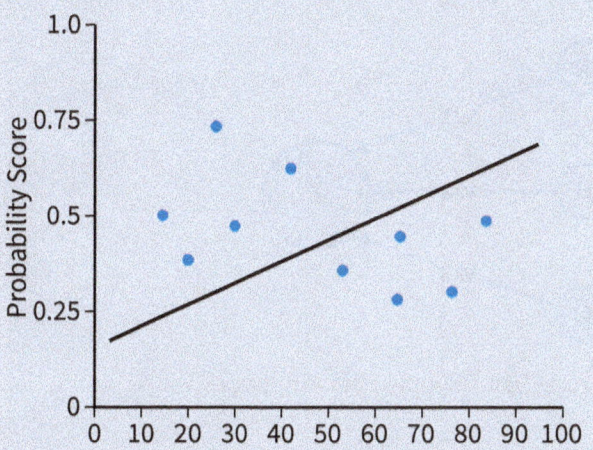

Figure 18.12 Logistic regression.

The scatterplot is shown as Figure 18.12. This suggests the maths has identified that there are two clear categories into which the emails fall. From the indicators chosen, the user concludes that these are 'spam' and 'non-spam'. Therefore, a **logistic regression** scatterplot can be used to predict the category (on the Y-axis) for a single email from its calculated score (on the X-axis).

A logistic regression AI model deals with binary values restricted to 0 and 1 representing True/False, Above/Below etc.)

18.10 Artificial neural networks

Neural networks occur naturally in the human brain. One branch of AI attempts to copy the behaviour of a neural network.

- An artificial network is built up from neurons
- Each neuron is always in one of two states, 'activated' or 'not activated'
- The neurons are organised into layers
- The neurons are connected such that:
  - a neuron never connects to another neuron in the same layer
  - each neuron connects to all other neurons in the next adjacent layer (to the right)

The connections are used to send messages from an activated neuron to all connected neurons to the right.

Study the neural network in Figure 18.13. It has three inputs and a single output. Each connection can be allocated a weight. The weight (or 'influence') of each input can be changed by altering its weight value.

> **TIP**
>
> You do not need to know the maths that is used to make all this happen for a neural network. Study the practical example of image recognition that follows shortly.
>
> You only need to show understanding of how neural networks have helped with machine learning.

Neural network built up from layers

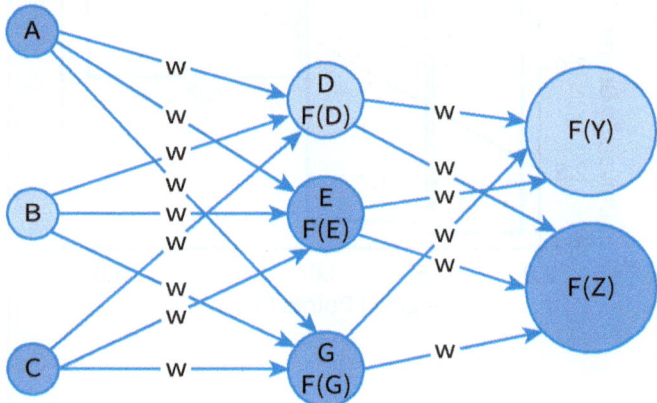

Figure 18.14 Neural network with layers.

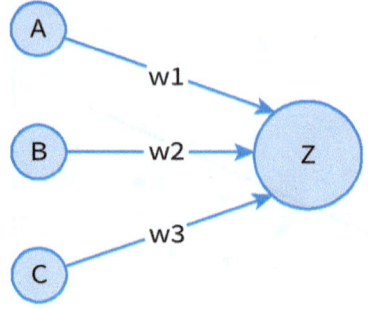

Figure 18.13 Simple neural network.

A neural network functions as follows. The final output Z will work as a function. The function F(Z) used for neuron Z has a critical threshold value at which the function is triggered and the node activated. A value below the threshold causes no output to be produced.

The Z() function performs the calculation:

(A value * w1 + B value * w2 + C value * w3) then determines if it is above or below the critical value.

In fact, it is not quite as simple as that. A factor called the **bias** (it will be different for each node) is also used to ensure that the function will generate a number between 0 and 1.

The three inputs (A, B and C) are each connected to an intermediate layer (nodes D, E and G). Each node in the intermediate layer has its own activation threshold.

At present there is no signal received from B.

- At D, there is a signal from A + No signal from B + signal from C = Threshold function F(D) not triggered
- At E, there is a signal from A + No signal from B + signal from C = Threshold function F(E) is triggered
- At G, there is a signal from A + No signal from B + signal from C = Threshold function F(G) is triggered
- At the final layer F(Z) is triggered but F(Y) is not.

This network design is called a **multilayer perceptron**.

Training the network and back propagation

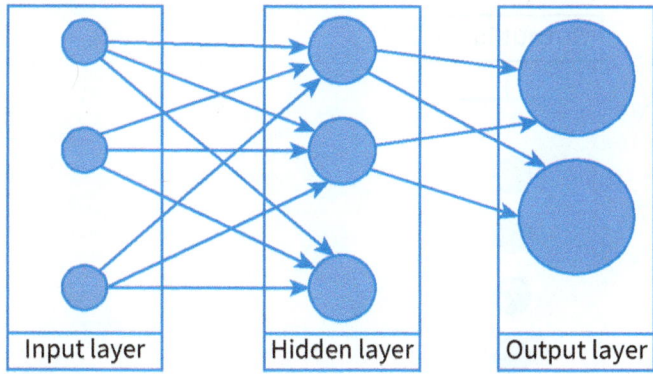

Figure 18.15 Neural network terminology.

Figure 18.15 shows the terminology used for the various layers. The hidden section may consist of more than one layer. The hidden layer(s) can be visualised as inside a black box.

The model is built from known (and therefore accurate) outputs based on the input variables. The intermediate layers are built up from patterns which are detected from the input data. The learning is essentially empirical, in that the strength of the weights can be changed. A small weight value means the data travelling on this route can be ignored as it has been proven to have little or no influence on the final result. Conversely a large positive or negative weight will influence the data received by the next layer.

The model is sequentially processing the data provided by the neurons in the previous layer together with the weight values present in the current layer.

The network can be trained using supervised learning. The weights of the connections can be 'tweaked' by small incremental amounts until the network's predicted output(s) matches closely with the known correct output(s).

The process of training the network is called **back propagation**. The term comes from the process where navigation starts from the output layer on the right and works back towards the input layer on the left. Back propagation is the application of an algorithm which changes parameters associated with a node. So, changes to the weights and /or biases reduce the error between the output value calculated and the known real output value. Back propagation will be an iterative process.

18.11 Deep learning

Deep learning is the term given to a neural network made up of many layers. It will be employed for complex problems where there are over five hidden layers. Object recognition is one of the major current applications of deep learning where there can be over 100 layers. As the number of layers increases so does the amount of computer processing power required. This is one of the drivers in the recent interest in deep learning, that the amount of the processing power required is now widely available.

Software is now available in popular programming languages such as Python, which provide libraries for work with machine learning. The libraries will include the statistical methods for linear regression and logistic regression. The libraries will also have modules for carrying out a 'black box approach' for setting up and then using a neural network.

Worked example 18.04

A practical example of deep learning.

The task is to present the computer with an image of a hand-drawn digit – each one is a 28 by 28 pixel image. Machine learning is to be used to identify the digit in the image.

This example is the 'Hello World' of neural networks!

The scanned image will form the input for the task, and the scan identifies separately a grey-scale value for each of the 784 pixels.

(Continued)

The network structure.

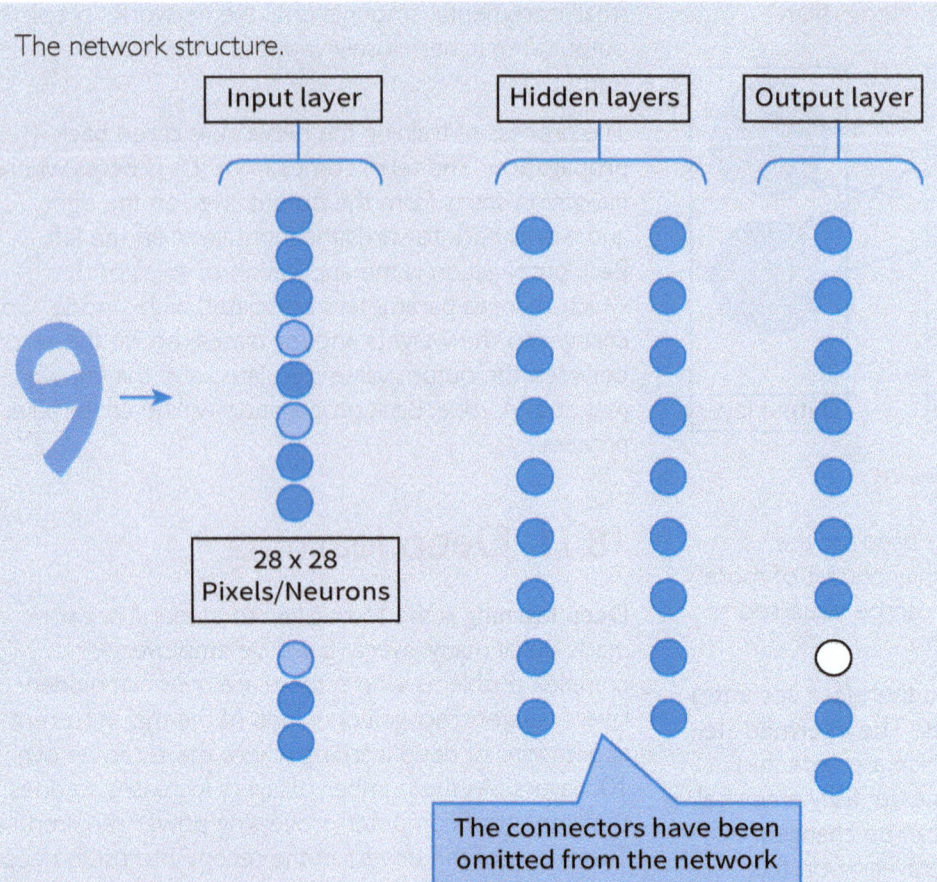

Figure 18.16 Neural network for image processing.

The neural network software then forms the new model as follows:

- The input layer will have a neuron for each of the 28 by 28 (784) pixels - 784 neurons
- The output layer has ten neurons each representing the digits 0,1,2, …9
- The number of hidden layers and neurons for each is a bit of guess …

  We will show 2 hidden layers each with 16 neurons. An experienced AI specialist would intuitively think that the first hidden layer could be used to identify 'edges' of the image – for example, a short straight horizontal line near the top middle of the image (that could be one of the building blocks of a '7' digit). So, an intuitive guess by the AI analyst is that all of the possible digits are made up from a total of nine sub-shapes. Therefore, the AI design has nine neurons for each of the nine possible small shapes in the hidden layer.

  - The second layer will then try combinations of neurons from the first layer to identify a shape. For example, a combination of five small shapes in the top half of the image (indicated by the particular five neurons which are activated) might suggest a loop shape.
  - If a different neuron in the second hidden layer was suggesting a loop in the bottom part of the image then,
  - The final layer would trigger the neuron representing digit 8.

Functioning of the network:

- Each neuron will hold a number value between 0 and 1
- At the input layer this represents a grey-scale value for the pixel
- Each neuron has its own **activation function** and threshold value – determined by the weighting of the edges for the other nodes which connect to it. In fact, each neuron has a second number associated with it, called

(Continued)

its **bias**. The bias number is used to set the **threshold level**. The calculation function applied to each neuron determines whether or not each neuron is activated.

- The activation function for each node in the output layer generates a number between 0 and 1. The number is the network's calculation of the probability of the image representing this number.

Training the network:

The whole process of the neural network 'learning' is to find the particular set of values, the weight and its bias for each of the neurons in the hidden layers, which minimise a calculated value called **the cost**. The algorithm that does this calculation is called back propagation.

For a single training data input image, the back propagation algorithm calculates the cost value by comparing each of the output node values generated with the known value. It is known since, for a particular image, it is known that the digit was (say) a '7'.

The algorithm will conclude that a hidden layer node which generates a function value of (say) 3.2 is having a significantly greater influence on the final cost value than a node with a value of only (say) 0.2.

We can describe this in the form of an algorithm.

```
// The biases and weights are set up at random for all nodes.
REPEAT
    Next training data image is presented to the network
    The network calculates the value(s) for all neurons in the output layer
    // For the early iterations of the loop, the predicted output will be
    'rubbish'
    // The network then does a calculation called the 'Cost'
    CostValue ← 0
    FOR EACH Neuron in the output layer
        // Compare the generated  value with the known result
        NeuronDifference ← Known value - Generated value
        CostValue ← CostValue + NeuronDifference
    NEXT Output layer neuron
    // Cost value now known
    // The maths is actually a little more complex than this …
    // The cost number is small when the generated result is close
    // to the true result
UNTIL No more training data examples
Calculate the average Cost value for all the training data
```

This is what the back propagation algorithm is doing. Maths takes over at this point and uses matrices and calculus to find the minimum of this cost value.

The maths calculates **what weight and bias changes to which neurons will cause the average cost value to be minimised**. When the cost value is small, the neural network is consistently finding that the difference between the predicted value and the known digit value are minimal.

Exam-style questions

1 The graph shown in **Figure 18.17** shows five towns and the roads and distances which connect them.

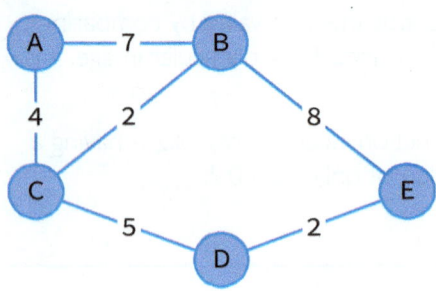

Figure 18.17 – Example graph.

The data for the graph is to be stored as a record data structure. The **record structure** will store the data for one town: its name, the other towns which can be visited and the distances.

```
TYPE TownData
DECLARE ..................................................................................
DECLARE Neighbour :   ARRAY[1..4] OF CHAR
DECLARE NeighbourDistance : ..........................................

..................................................

DECLARE ThisMap : ARRAY[1..5] ........................................
```

a   Complete the pseudocode to implement the data design for this graph. [4]

b   Suggest a data structure which could be used for the calculated shortest path for the five nodes. [1]

c   Use Dijkstra's algorithm to complete **Table 18.03** to trace the calculated shortest paths from Town A to each of the other towns.

   • Use list `PathKnown[]` to show the order in which nodes are visited.
   • Show at each stage any newly calculated distances. [8]

	Shortest path	A	B	C	D	E
1	Initialise: PathKnown=[]	∞	∞	∞	∞	∞
2	Set node A as the start: PathKnown= [A]	0 Empty	∞	∞	∞	∞
3	Neighbours of A are B = 7 and C = 4					
4						
5						
6						
8						

Table 18.03 – Dijkstra's algorithm trace table.

2 Put a tick in either the True/False column for each of these statements. [4]

		True	False
a	A linear regression analysis has paired values (X, Y) for its dataset.		
b	A logistic regression analysis has paired values (X, Y) for its dataset.		
c	The value calculated for the correlation coefficient always computes a value between 0 and 1.		
d	A linear regression analysis will show whether the data-points fall into two (or more) categories.		
e	For a regression analysis scatterplot it is a convention to plot the independent variable on the X axis and the dependent variable on the Y axis.		
f	A calculated correlation coefficient of +0.85 suggests that high values of the independent variable produce high values of the dependent variable.		
g	Deep learning is a technique using regression analysis.		
h	A popular application of regression analysis is image recognition.		

3   Put a tick in either the True/False column for each of these statements. [3]

		True	False
a	All AI models need training data.		
b	A neural network is made up of many neurons. Each neuron is given a weight and a bias.		
c	All neurons in a neural network have a threshold value above which the neuron is activated.		
d	The inputs to a single neuron are the connecting neurons from the adjacent layer on the right.		
e	Deep learning is a technique using neural networks.		
f	Back propagation is an algorithm used to refine the weights and biases of neurons in a neural network.		

Computational thinking and problem solving

Learning Objectives:

Algorithms:

- Write the pseudocode for a linear search
- Write pseudocode for a binary search
- Compare the efficiency of searching algorithms
- Understand the pseudocode for an insertion sort
- Understand the pseudocode for a bubble sort
- Compare the efficiency of these sort algorithms
- Understand the binary tree data structure
- Understand the algorithms for the following:
- Stack
  - Insert an item
  - Remove an item
- Queue
  - Insert an item
  - Remove an item
- Linked list
  - Search for an item
  - Insert an item
- Binary tree
  - Find an item
  - Insert an item
- Write arithmetic expressions in infix and postfix notation
- Understand how a post-order traversal of a binary tree produces postfix representation.

Recursion:

- Understand recursion and the need for the use of a stack
- Write and trace recursion algorithms
- Understand the use of recursion in the process followed by a compiler.

19.01 Searching algorithms

Linear search

Now we have studied arrays and loops, we shall use both structures in a problem.

> **Worked example 19.01**
>
> A program stores 20 surnames in a 1D array. The user inputs the surname to be found. The program will output the array position at which the item is found, or the message 'Item NOT FOUND'. The algorithm required is a linear search.

(Continued)

> Input the item to find
> REPEAT
> Compare the next array item with the required value
> 		IF they match:
> 			Output the array position
> 			Stop searching
> 		Else:
> 			Move to the next array item
> UNTIL found or end of the array already reached

The variables needed are:

Identifier	Data type	Description
SearchName	STRING	The data find to search for
Surname	ARRAY [1:20] OF STRING	The surname data
Index	INTEGER	Index position in the surname array
IsFound	BOOLEAN	Flags whether or not the requested surname has been found

Table 19.01 Identifiers for the linear search algorithm.

```
INPUT SearchName
IsFound ← FALSE
Index ← 1
REPEAT
    IF Surname[Index] = SearchName
        THEN
            IsFound ← TRUE
            OUTPUT "Surname was FOUND - at position", Index
        ELSE
            Index ← Index + 1
    ENDIF
UNTIL (IsFound = TRUE) OR (Index = 21)
IF IsFound = FALSE
    THEN
        OUTPUT  "Surname was NOT FOUND"
ENDIF
```

The choice of loop structure was a `REPEAT – UNTIL` loop, as we might not need to consider all items in the array.

The algorithm will only find and report the first occurrence of the requested surname.

How many comparisons?

When carrying out a linear search, if there are N values in the dataset, on average the program will have to compare N/2 values in the array before the required item is found.

> ## Progress check A
> Rewrite the pseudocode for the REPEAT loop above using a WHILE-ENDWHILE loop structure.

> ## Progress check B
> Describe how the linear search algorithm can be modified, so that multiple occurrences of the value would be found and output and so that the number of occurrences is calculated.

Binary search

When can we use a binary search?

The data items must be stored in the array in order.

The algorithm is essentially:

> Input the value to find
>> REPEAT
>>> Find the middle value
>>>
>>> compare the required value with this middle value.
>>>
>>> IF not found:
>>>> Discard either the top half or bottom half of the current list
>>>
>>> The new middle value is calculated and another comparison made.
>>
>> UNTIL found

The algorithm is also called a 'binary chop'. We are successively reducing the size of the list by a half, before the next sub-list and new middle value is calculated.

The algorithm will search the array `ThisArray` (upper bound `N`) for the value `ThisValue`.

Identifier	Data type	Description
`ThisArray`	`ARRAY[1..N] OF STRING`	The array of data items
`N`	`INTEGER`	Upper bound of `ThisArray`
`ThisValue`	`STRING`	The value to search for
`Found`	`BOOLEAN`	Flags to TRUE when `ThisValue` is found
`Top`	`INTEGER`	Index to the current list
`Bottom`	`INTEGER`	Index to the current list
`Middle`	`INTEGER`	Index to the current list
`NotInList`	`BOOLEAN`	Flags to TRUE when the list to consider is empty

Table 19.02 Identifiers for the binary search/chop algorithm.

```
Found ← FALSE
NotInList ← FALSE
Top ← N
Bottom ← 1
REPEAT
    Middle ← Integer value of (Top + Bottom)/2 )
    IF ThisArray[Middle] = ThisValue
```

```
            THEN
                Found ← TRUE
                OUTPUT "Value is FOUND"
            ELSE
                IF Bottom > Top
                    THEN
                        NotInList ← TRUE
                    ELSE
                        IF ThisArray[Middle] < ThisItem
                            THEN
                                // Retain the top half of the current list ...
                                Bottom ← Middle + 1
                            ELSE
                                // Retain the bottom half of the currentlist ...
                                Top ← Middle - 1
                        ENDIF
                ENDIF
        ENDIF
    UNTIL (Found = TRUE) OR (NotInList = TRUE)
    IF NotInList = TRUE
        THEN
            OUTPUT "Requested item was NOT FOUND"
    ENDIF
```

Progress check C

Do you understand the binary search algorithm?

a   What is the condition that compares the requested value with the middle value of the current list?

b   When a new sub-list is about to be set up, is the current middle value included?

c   What condition in the algorithm tests for a new list with no values?

d   When the top half of the current list is retained, which pointer value(s) are changed: `Top` or `Bottom` or both?

Binary search performance

The algorithm is a very efficient one for finding a particular value, since the size of the list is halved on every iteration. This results in a logarithmic relationship between the size of the list and the number of comparisons, so that for a list with 128 items it would take at worst, 7 comparisons, i.e. forming seven sub-lists in order to find the value. Compare this algorithm with a linear search where, on average, it would take 64 comparisons for a list with 128 data items.

The main control structure in the binary chop algorithm is a loop. Every time a new sub-list is considered the algorithm carries out the next iteration. The binary chop algorithm is said to have an iterative solution.

When we introduce the topic of recursion later in this chapter, we will show a recursive solution that does not use a loop.

19.02 Sorting algorithms

The two algorithms that we will develop could be used to sort either string, integer or real number values.

Insertion sort

The insertion sort algorithm works as follows, each item in the list is considered in sequence starting with the second, a sub-list of sorted items is formed on the left-hand side and the right-hand sub-list increases by one as each new data value is considered.

An example of this is:

The integers in the `MyData` array are to be sorted using the insertion sort algorithm.

The original list is:

MyData

1	2	3	4	5	6	7
6	3	11	4	9	2	7

Figure 19.01 Unsorted list.

The trace table shows on row 1 the list after the second item (3) has been considered.

The next item to be processed is 11.

Figure **19.02** shows the changing position of the items.

MyList

1	2	3	4	5	6	7
3	6	11	4	9	2	7
3	6	11	4	9	2	7
3	4	6	11	9	2	7
3	4	6	9	11	2	7
2	3	4	6	9	11	7
2	3	4	6	7	9	11

The diagram shows the changing contents of the array:
- The circles show the value which was last considered
- The rectangles shows the increasing size of the sorted sub-list.

Figure 19.02 Insertion sort trace.

The insertion sort algorithm.

Identifier	Data type	Description
`MyArray`	`ARRAY[1..N] OF INTEGER`	The array of data items
`N`	`INTEGER`	Upper bound of `ThisArray`
`CurrentValue`	`INTEGER`	The 'circled value' in the diagram
`SortedListPosn`	`INTEGER`	Loop counter for moving through the sub-list
`InsertPosn`	`INTEGER`	Index of the insert position in the sub-list
`ShufflePosn`	`INTEGER`	Loop counter for the sub-list when all values to the right have to be shuffled up one place
`Index`	`INTEGER`	Index of the current item considered
`InsertPosnFound`	`BOOLEAN`	Flags to TRUE when the position in the sub-list is found

Table 19.03 Identifiers for the insertion sort.

```
    FOR Index 2 TO N           // consider all items starting with the second
        CurrentValue ← MyList[Index]
        // find the position in the sorted list to insert
        SortedListPosn ← 1
        InsertPosnFound ← FALSE
        REPEAT
            IF CurrentValue > MyList[SortedListPosn]
                THEN
                    SortedListPosn ← SortedListPosn + 1
                ELSE
                    InsertPosn ← SortedListPosn
                    InsertPosnFound ← TRUE
            ENDIF
        UNTIL InsertPosnFound = TRUE
        // current value will move to InsertPosn
        // and all others on the right shuffle to the right one place
        FOR ShufflePosn ← Index TO [InsertPosn + 1] STEP -1
            MyList[ShufflePosn] ← MyList[ShufflePosn - 1]
            MyList[InsertPosn] ← CurrentValue
        ENDFOR
    ENDFOR
```

Progress check D

Complete the trace table showing the changing contents of the array **MyAnimals** as an insertion sort is applied.

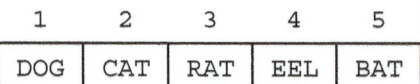

Figure 19.03 Insertion sort trace table.

TIP

You have already studied the bubble sort in Chapter 10. It is repeated here as we now have to compare this algorithm with a second sorting method – the insertion sort.

Bubble sort

A bubble sort requires that the data values are stored in an array.

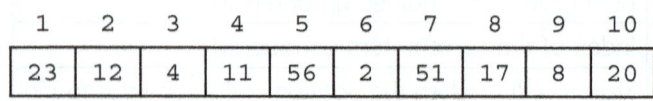

Figure 19.04 Bubble sort data.

The outline algorithm is as follows:

```
Compare adjacent items starting with cells 1 and 2
    that is compare 23 with 12
    if the first item is larger:
    then swap the items in the array
        So MyArray[1] now stores 12
        MyArray[2] stores 23.
```

Repeat comparing adjacent items until finally we compare `MyArray[9]` with `MyArray[10]`.

1	2	3	4	5	6	7	8	9	10
12	4	11	23	2	51	17	8	20	56

Figure 19.05 Bubble sort, first pass.

The first pass:

This is called one pass up through the data items. At this point we are certain that the largest value is in the final array position.

Subsequent passes:

We now start a second pass. The final comparison made will be between items 8 and 9.

The third pass will do a final comparison between items 7 and 8 and the 9th and last pass will compare items 1 and 2 only.

This suggests that if there are N data items, the total number of passes needed is (N-1).

Swapping two items

This needs some thought. If we action

```
MyArray[1] ← MyArray[2]
MyArray[2] ← MyArray[1]
```

the result is that both array cells contain the same value.

The solution is to use a temporary variable to store one of the values.

```
Temp       ← MyArray[1]
MyArray[1] ← MyArray[2]
MyArray[2] ← Temp
```

Identifier	Data type	Description
MyArray	ARRAY[1:10] OF INTEGER	The array storing the data items
Temp	INTEGER	Stores one of the data values when a swap is made
Pass	INTEGER	Loop counter for the outer loop
UBound	INTEGER	The upper bound of the array
I	INTEGER	Index value for the array
Swapped	BOOLEAN	Set to FALSE at the start of each pass. Set to TRUE when a swap occurs.

Table 19.05 Bubble sort identifier table.

```
Pass ← 1
REPEAT
    Swapped ← FALSE
    For i ← 1 TO  (UBound - Pass)
        // the comparisons loop
        IF MyArray[i] > MyArray[i + 1]
            THEN
                // swap
                Swapped ← TRUE
                Temp ← MyArray[i]
                MyArray[i] ← MyArray[i + 1]
                MyArray[i + 1] ← Temp
        ENDIF
    ENDFOR
    Pass ← Pass + 1
UNTIL (Pass = UBound) OR (Swapped = FALSE)
```

The **outer REPEAT loop** starts a new pass

The **inner FOR loop** repeats the comparison of adjacent items

Note: The use of boxes drawn onto the pseudocode helps to see where each loop starts and ends

Check: The first iteration of the outer loop (`Pass=1`) uses i values 1 to (10-1), i.e. 9 for the inner loop.

The Boolean variable `Swapped` is used to check after each pass whether any values were swapped on that pass. If there were no swaps, the array items must already be in order and so no more passes are required.

> ## Progress check E
>
> Use the bubble sort algorithm to sort the array `Animal`.
>
> Draw up and complete a trace table with the following headings. Add as many rows as necessary.
>
> | Pass | i | UBound |
> |------|---|--------|
> | 1 | 1 | 5 |
>
> | Animal | | | | |
> |--------|-----|-----|-----|-----|
> | 1 | 2 | 3 | 4 | 5 |
> | CAT | ANT | COW | RAT | BEE |
>
> Figure 19.06 Bubble sort trace table.
>
> You will need around 10 blank rows for the trace table.
>
> Were the items sorted before all possible iterations of the outer loop?

Sorting algorithms: performance criteria

Different sorting algorithms can be compared in terms of their efficiency. An algorithm's efficiency can be measured in terms of an '**order of complexity**' using the **big-O notation**, which is discussed later in the chapter.

The number of items to be sorted will be a factor in the total sort-time taken. Efficiency can be measured in terms of the total number of comparisons needed to complete the sort.

A second criterion for judging algorithms is their space requirement: does the algorithm require memory space in addition to the memory containing the array elements?

Study the quick sort and bubble sort algorithms. The insertion sort used no additional memory and the bubble sort required temporary memory for only a single data item.

Also, the efficiency should be considered in terms of the worst case (completely unsorted), best case (the original list is already in sort order) or an average case.

Consider the 'best case' when the original list is already sorted. The bubble sort algorithm can recognise that, with a single pass through the list, the list is completely sorted and will stop. The insertion sort requires that all loop iterations be carried out.

Hence the conclusion is that, for a best-case scenario, the bubble sort is more efficient that the insertion sort.

19.03 Abstract data types (ADT)

Binary trees

A **binary tree** is a data structure consisting of a number of **nodes** that are linked together.

Each node in the binary tree consists of the data value, a left pointer (to link to a descendant node) and a right pointer (to link to a **descendant** node).

All nodes, except the **root** node, are a descendant of a parent node.

The binary tree shown in Figure **19.07** has five nodes and the values were inserted to the tree in the order:

COURGETTE, SWEDE, PARSNIP, ARTICHOKE and TURNIP.

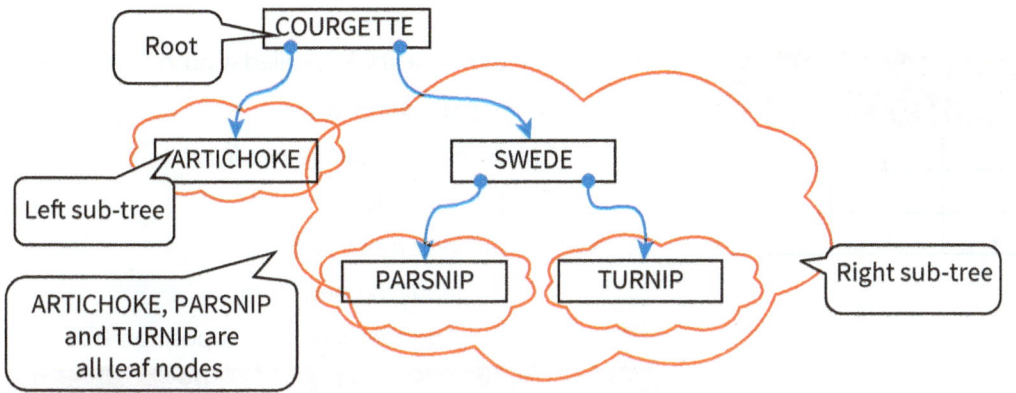

Figure 19.07 Binary tree terminology.

Root: 1

	LeftPointer
1	4
2	3
3	0
4	0
5	0

	TreeData
1	COURGETTE
2	SWEDE
3	PARSNIP
4	ARTICHOKE
5	TURNIP

	RightPointer
1	2
2	5
3	0
4	0
5	0

Figure 19.08 Binary tree array data.

The tree was formed as follows:

- Add COURGETTE - is the first item, so becomes the root
- Add SWEDE
  - compare SWEDE with COURGETTE and place to the right
  - link from COURGETTE
- Add PARSNIP
  - compare with COURGETTE and move right
  - then compare with SWEDE and place to the left
  - link from SWEDE
- Add ARTICHOKE
  - compare with the root COURGETTE – place to the left
  - link from COURGETTE
- Add TURNIP
  - compare with COURGETTE and move right
  - compare with SWEDE – place to the right
  - link from SWEDE

The tree data is to be stored in three 1D arrays with a root value. This is shown in Figure **19.08**.

Progress check F

The following values form a binary tree data structure in the order shown.

ROME, BRUSSELS, AMSTERDAM, TORONTO, WARSAW, JAKARTA

a   Draw the conceptual tree.

b   The tree data is stored in three 1D arrays: `Data`, `LeftP` and `RightP`.

Show the contents of the three arrays and the root value.

Using the data structures

Remember, a stack, queue and linked list were all introduced in Chapter 10.

Syllabus summary:

	Stack	Queue	Linked list	Binary tree
Find an item			√	√
Insert an item	√	√	√	√
Delete an item	√	√	√	

Table 19.06 Syllabus summary.

Stack

A stack is a dynamic data structure that operates on the principle 'last item added will be the first to leave'. This is often abbreviated to 'last in – first out' or, turned the other way around "First in – last out".

To implement a stack we shall use an array with lower bound 1 and upper bound N to store the data items. The stack is controlled by a single pointer, the index position of the item that is currently at the 'top of stack' position.

Identifier	Data type	Description
MyStack	ARRAY[1:20] OF INTEGER	Data values in MyStack
TOS	INTEGER	Index position of the MyStack array for the item currently at the top of the stack

Table 19.07 Identifier table for a stack.

Figure **19.09** shows the stack after the three items 106, 57 and 44 are added in that order.

The first item to leave will be 44.

If no items leave, the next new item will be stored at position 4.

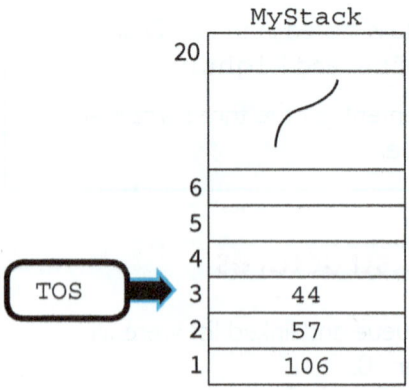

Figure 19.09 Item added to a stack.

Stack: insert an item

Inserting an item to a stack is called a 'push' to the stack. The algorithm is straightforward.

    Check that the stack is not full

    IF space available, then

        Increment TOS

        Input the new item

        Add the new item at position TOS

Identifier	Data type	Description
NewItem	INTEGER	New data item to be added

Table 19.08 Identifier table: add item for the stack.

```
IF TOS = 21
    THEN
        OUTPUT 'Stack is full'
    ELSE
        TOS ← TOS + 1
        INPUT NewItem
        MyStack[TOS] ← NewItem
ENDIF
```

Stack: delete an item

Removing an item from the stack is called a 'pop' from the stack. The algorithm is straightforward.

    Check if the stack is empty

    IF NOT empty

        THEN Output the item at position 'top of stack'

        Decrement the stack pointer

> ### Progress check G
> Write the pseudocode for the 'remove from stack' algorithm.

Queue

A queue is a dynamic data structure that operates on the principle 'first item added will be the first to leave. This is often abbreviated to 'first in – first out'.

To implement a queue we shall use an array with lower bound 1 and upper bound N to store the data items.

The queue is controlled by two pointers. A 'head pointer' points to the item that is currently at the head of the queue. A 'tail pointer' points to the item that is currently at the rear of the queue.

Queue: insert an item

Consider the queue `MyQueue` that has 10 cells. The current state of the queue shows that seven items have joined the queue and four have already left. The current queue occupies cells 5 to 7 (that is, length 3 items).

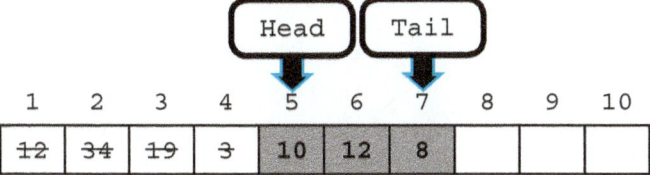

Figure 19.10 Items added and removed on a queue.

The stage will soon be reached where, once three more items have joined the queue, the queue will run out of space.

The solution is to make a queue behave as a 'circular queue'. That is, once the `Tail` pointer reaches value 10 and a new value is to be added, `Tail` will be re-set to index 1.

> ## Progress check H
>
> Starting with the queue shown in Figure 19.10.
>
> An item is about to leave the queue:
>
> a   Which item is this?
>
> b   What pointer change is required?
>
> A new item joins the queue.
>
> c   How will the algorithm know the position at which to store the item?

Figure 19.11 shows the queue after more values have left and three new values join.

All the storage space is now used up.

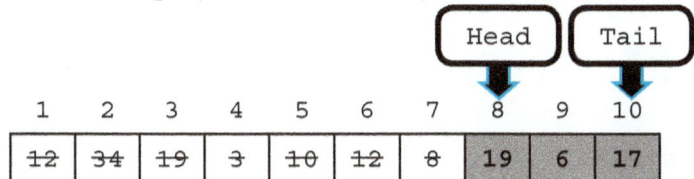

Figure 19.11 More queue changes.

If a new value now attempts to join, we could store this at position 1.

After three more items join – 23, 89 and 41, the state of the queue will be:

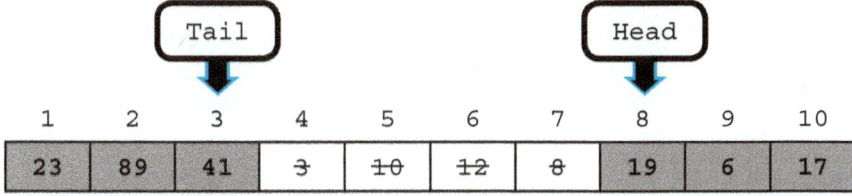

Figure 19.12 More changes: the queue is now 'circular'.

The queue is effectively now the list of values: 19, 6, 17, 23, 89 and 41 (in that order).

We now have a situation where `Tail > Head`. This will indicate that the queue is currently in a circular state.

Add item to the queue

```
1    IF (Head = 1 AND Tail = 10) OR (Head = Tail + 1)
2        THEN
3            OUTPUT "Queue is already full"
4        ELSE
             IF Tail = 0
5                THEN
6                    Head ← 1
7                    Tail ← 1
8                ELSE
9                    IF Tail = 10
10                       THEN
11                           Tail ← 1
12                       ELSE
13                           Tail ← Tail + 1
14                   ENDIF
15           ENDIF
16       INPUT NewItem
17       Queue[Tail] ← NewItem
18   ENDIF
```

The lines have been numbered as they are referred to in PROGRESS CHECK 1.

Remove item from the queue

```
1    IF Head = 0
2        THEN
3            OUTPUT "Queue is EMPTY"
4        ELSE
5            OUTPUT "Removed was ", Queue[Head]
6            IF Head = Tail
7                THEN
8                    Head ← 0
9                    Tail ← 0
10               ELSE
11                   IF Head = 10
12                       THEN
13                           Head ← 1
14                   ENDIF
15           ENDIF
     ENDIF
```

> **Progress check 1**
>
> Do you understand the queue algorithms?
>
> For the 'Add item to Queue' algorithm:
>
> a   What line number tests for a full queue?
>
> b   Describe the condition which tests for a full queue.
>
> For the 'Remove from Queue' algorithm:
>
> c   Which line number tests for the queue 'going circular'?
>
> d   What condition tests for an empty queue?

Linked list

A linked list is a data structure consisting of a set of nodes. Each node consists of the data value and a link pointer to one of the other nodes.

The purpose of the linked list structure is to link the nodes in some particular order, for example, the data items are linked in alphabetical order.

Implement a linked list where the data and link values are stored as two 1D arrays.

Identifier	Data type	Description
Data	ARRAY[1..20] OF STRING	The data value for the nodes
Link	ARRAY[1..20] OF INTEGER	The link pointer value for the nodes
Start	INTEGER	The index of the node which is at the start of the linked list

Table 19.09.

To implement our linked list we would like a 'type of data' that consists of a string value (for the data values) + an integer value (for the link pointers).

We introduced a 'user-defined data type' in Chapter 13. This problem needs a data type made up of a string value and an integer.

```
TYPE    LinkedList
    DECLARE Data : STRING
    DECLARE Link : INTEGER
ENDTYPE
```

Note: We won't use the data structures suggested earlier in Table 19.09 (separate 1D arrays for the data, left and right pointers).

This list provides us with as many as 20 node values. Declare an array `Node` of data type `LinkedList`.

Identifier	Data type	Description
Node	ARRAY[1..20] OF LinkedList	The data value for the nodes

Table 19.10.

Start: 3

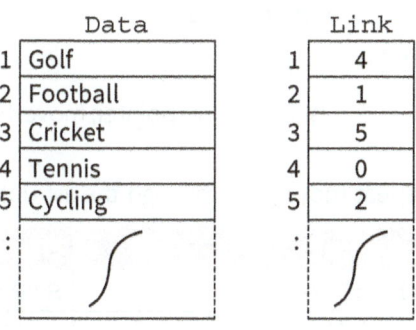

Figure 19.13 Items added to the linked list.

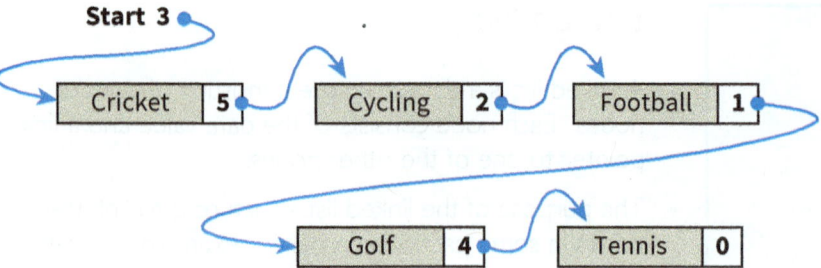

Figure 19.14 Conceptual linked list.

Figure 19.13 shows the data values stored in the arrays. Figure 19.14 shows the conceptual linked list which is created by the link pointers.

There is some detail needed here. The program would need to know at this stage that the next available 'free' array position is 6.

One strategy for this is to initialise the linked list as a linked set of nodes with the start point initially showing zero.

> ## Progress check J
> The following values join a linked list data structure in the order shown.
>
> LONDON, AMSTERDAM, NEW DELHI, DHAKA, SINGAPORE and NEW YORK.
>
> Form the linked list that maintains the list in alphabetical order.
>
> Show the conceptual linked list.

Linked list: find an item
Input the required value

Look at the node pointed to by the start pointer

IF found THEN

    output found

ELSE

    Using the link pointer, move to the next node

Repeat moving up through the list until found OR we have reached the end of the list (Link = 0).

Identifier	Data type	Description
ThisItem	STRING	The item to search for
Found	BOOLEAN	Flags to TRUE when found
Current	INTEGER	Index of the current node considered

Table 19.11 Linked list identifier table.

Note: The algorithm uses the `Node` array defined in Table 19.10.

```
INPUT ThisItem
Found ← FALSE
Current ← Start
IF Current <> 0
    THEN
        REPEAT
            IF ThisItem = Node[current].Data
                THEN
                    Found ← True
                    OUTPUT "Found ... at position ", Current
                ELSE
                    Current ← Node[current].Link
            ENDIF
        UNTIL Found = True OR Current = 0
ENDIF
IF Current = 0 THEN
    OUTPUT "Item was NOT FOUND"
END IF
```

- The first item to consider is at position `Start`
- Test for 'empty list'
- Note, the 'dot notation' used to refer to the data part of the node
- Ready to move to the next node in the linked list

Linked list: insert an item

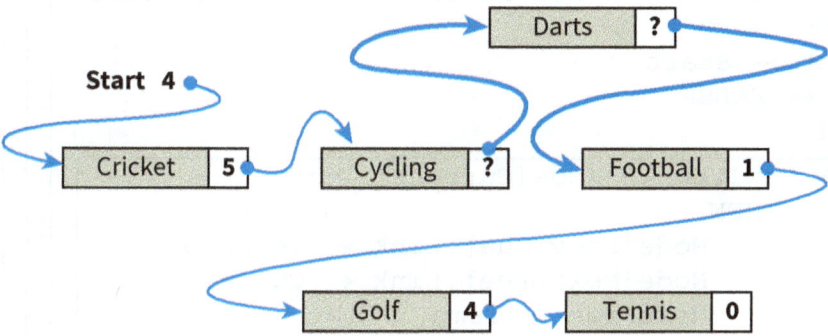

Figure 19.15 Item added to a linked list.

The insert algorithm will be:

- Traverse the list until we find the first node which is greater than the insert item (Football).
- That would establish the new item is inserted between Cycling and Football.
- The new value becomes part of the linked list by:
- Storing the data value (Darts) at the next free location (6)
- Adjusting the link pointers:
  - Dart's pointer will be the current Football pointer
  - Cycling's pointer will change to 6

There are special cases that must be considered, the linked list could be empty or the new node could become the new start of the list.

```
IF NextFree = 0                           ← Is the linked
    THEN                                      list full?
        OUTPUT "REFUSED - list is full"
    ELSE
        INPUT NewItem
        Node[NextFree].Data ← NewItem
        IF Start = 0                          ← Is the linked list empty?
            THEN
                Start ← NextFree
                Temp ← Node[NextFree].Link
                Node[NextFree].Link ← 0       ← NextFree is the index of
                NextFree ← Temp                  the next available cell
            ELSE
                // traverse the list - starting at Start to find
                // the position at which to insert the new item
                Temp ← Node[NextFree].Link
                IF NewItem < Node[Start].Data
                    THEN
                        // new item will become the start of the list
                        NodeNext[Free].Link ← Start
                        Start ← NextFree
                        NextFree ← Temp
                    ELSE
                        // the new item is not at the start of the list
                        Previous ← 0
                        Current ← Start
                        Found ← FALSE
                        REPEAT
                            IF NewItem <= Node[Current].Data
                                THEN
                                    Node[Previous].Link ← NextFree
                                    Node[NextFree].Link ← Current
                                    NextFree ← Temp
                                    Found ← TRUE
                                ELSE
                                    // move to the next node
                                    Previous ← Current
                                    Current ← Node[Current].Link
                            ENDIF
                        UNTIL Found = True OR Current = 0
                        IF Current = 0                            ← New item is at the
                            THEN                                     end of the linked list
                                Node[Previous].Link ← NextFree
                                Node[NextFree].Link ← 0
                                NextFree ← Temp
                        ENDIF
                ENDIF
        ENDIF
ENDIF
```

Linked list: delete an item

Consider the original items. The task is to delete Golf from the linked list.

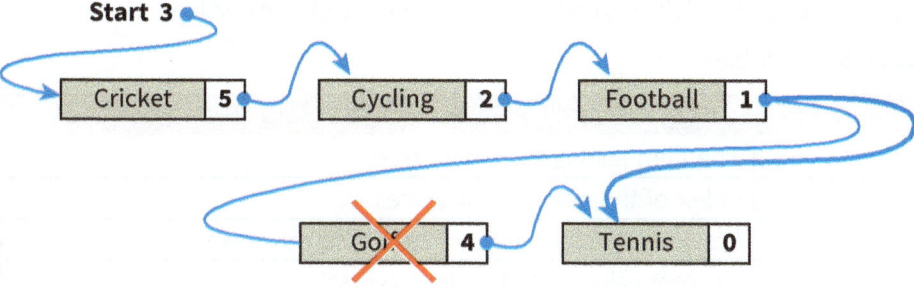

Figure 19.16 Delete an item from a linked list.

A change will be made to the pointers as shown in Figure **19.16**.

The algorithm will be:

- Input the item to delete
- Traverse the list until found
- Make the pointer change:
  - The pointer of the previous node (Football's pointer) will now point to the node pointed to by the deleted item (Tennis).

A special case will be the item to delete is the first in the list.

Binary tree

We introduced the terminology used for a binary tree earlier in the chapter.

Binary tree: find an item

The algorithm is straightforward:

    Input the search Item
    Assign the Current node as the Root
        REPEAT
            IF Current value = Search item
                THEN Found
            ELSE
                IF search Item < Current value THEN
                    (if possible …) 'move left'
                    to a new Current node
                ELSE
                    (if possible …) 'move right'
                    to a new Current node
                END IF
            END IF
        UNTIL found or there are no descendants to consider

Binary tree: insert an item

We shall need to check for the special cases, i.e. the tree is empty or there is space available for a new item.

The algorithm will traverse the tree to locate the right or left position at which to insert the new value.

The algorithm will need the following additional variables:

Identifier	Data type	Description
NewTreeItem	STRING	The item joining the binary tree
NextFree	INTEGER	Index of the next free array cell
Previous	INTEGER	Previous array position visited in the traversal
Current	INTEGER	Current value visited in the traversal
LastMove	CHAR	Indicates the last move in the traversal: • L – left • R – right • X – no previous move

Table 19.12 Identifier table for insert item to binary tree.

```
IF NextFreePosition >100              ← Test for binary tree full
    THEN
        OUTPUT "No more values can be added"
    ELSE
        INPUT NewTreeItem
        IF Root = 0                   ← Test for linked list is empty
            THEN
                Root ← NextFree
            ELSE
                // traverse the tree to find the position for the new value
                Current ← Root
                LastMove ← 'X'
                REPEAT
                    Previous ← Current
                    IF NewTreeItem < TreeData[Current]
                        THEN
                            // move left
                            LastMove ← 'L'
                            Current ← LeftPointer[Current]
                        ELSE
                            // move right
                            LastMove ← 'R'
                            Current ← RightPointer[Current]
                    ENDIF
                UNTIL Current = 0
```

(Continued)

```
        IF LastMove = 'R'
            THEN
                RightPointer[Previous] ← NextFree
            ELSE
                IF LastMove = 'L'
                    THEN
                        LeftPointer[Previous] ← NextFree
                ENDIF
        ENDIF
    NextFree ← NextFree + 1
  ENDIF
ENDIF
```

Hash tables

The technique called 'hashing' is used to get fast access to some item of data from a dataset.

When we use an array, the program code accesses a data item by using the array index.

For example, with an array of names, to get access to the name HARRIS we need to know that HARRIS is at index position 39.

The user of the application would not know the value 39, they know they want to search for HARRIS.

Hashing is a technique that will use some formula, usually coded as a function, to calculate the index value from the name.

Problems with hashing

The formula must be chosen so that the appropriate range of address is calculated.

The programmer will know we need to store 150 data items, so the **hashing function** must generate numbers in the range 01 to 150 (or close to this).

Two or more data items could generate the same storage address, called a **collision**. There is a possible solution to this: if the key generated is N and there is already a data item stored here, store the new item at the first unoccupied location after N. This is called **open hashing**.

> **TIP**
>
> Visual Basic has an advanced array data type called an `ArrayList`. Items can referenced by the data item or the index position.

Hashing is used later in Chapter 23 when we create a direct access file.

A dictionary

Using a paper dictionary, we have 'data pairs'; the word together with its description.

We search for an entry to find its description. Programming languages have code equivalents.

| Visual Basic | ```
Dim ClubDictionary As New Dictionary(Of String, String)
'Add four entries.
ClubDictionary.Add("Real Madrid", "Spain")
ClubDictionary.Add("Liverpool", "England")
ClubDictionary.Add("Barcelona", "Spain")
ClubDictionary.Add("Juventus", "Italy")

If ClubDictionary.ContainsKey("Barcelona") Then
    'Write value of the key.
    Dim Country As String = ClubDictionary.Item("Barcelona")
    Console.WriteLine(Country)
End If
``` |
|---|---|

Note that Visual Basic has a class `Dictionary`.

`Add` and `ContainsKey` are methods of the `Dictionary` class

When a new club is added, Visual Basic, behind the scenes, will 'hash' the value, so that it can be retrieved later from the entry of the club name.

| Python | ```
ClubDictionary = {"Real Madrid" : "Spain",
                  "Liverpool" : "England",
                  "Barcelona" : "Spain",
                  "Juventus" : "Italy"
                  }
print(ClubDictionary)
ThisCountry = ClubDictionary.get("Barcelona")
print(ThisCountry)
``` |
|---|---|

Note that:

Python has a class `dictionary`

The `dictionary` class has a `get` method

Java	`Not available`

Graphs

Graphs are a useful tool for the computer scientist. They are used as an abstraction to describe real-life scenarios and data. A graph uses two fundamental principles of computer science, 'abstraction', where unnecessary detail is discarded and the graph then provides a model of the problem and 'automation', where the issue then is: how can we represent the graph data in a form that can be stored and processed by a computer?

As an example, a graph could represent a road map.

The nodes (A to F) are towns - the connecting lines represent a road between them.

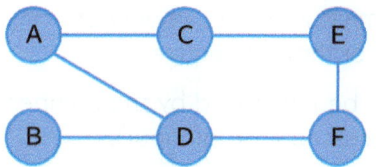

Figure 19.17 A simple graph.

Conclusions that result include:

- There is a direct route from C to E which does not pass through any of the other towns
- There is no direct road from A to B
- To get to B from A, we must drive via town D
- A is a neighbouring town to D
- We can get directly to two other towns (C and D) from A
- There are two ways (paths) to get from B to F – the route B-D-F or the route B-D-A-C-E-F.

The **graph** is made up of a number of **vertexes** (or **nodes**). The nodes are joined with lines called **edges** (or **arcs** where each edge connects exactly two vertices. The visual nature of graphs simplifies the process of understanding and leads to better problem solving. Vertices connected directly are called **neighbours**. The **degree** of a vertex or node is the number of other nodes that are directly connected to it.

Progress check K

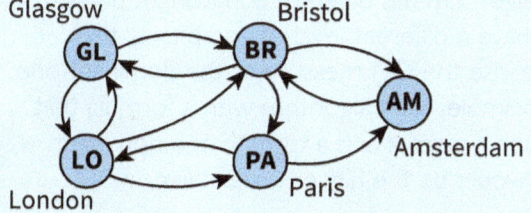

Figure 19.18 Airport routes graph.

Flights are available between airports. Some flights are available in one direction only.

a Someone flies from Bristol to Amsterdam. Is a return flight available from this airline?

b What is the degree of the London vertex?

c Is a direct flight available from London to Amsterdam?

Weighted graphs

A weighted graph is one where the edges are labelled with some value.

An example would be, to show on the graph the distance between the towns.

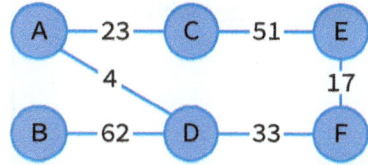

Figure 19.19 Weighted graph.

Directed graph

A directed graph shows an arrow in one direction on each of the edges (to convey some meaning).

An example of this is on a map, when a road is one way and the arrow indicates the direction of travel.

If the road were 'two-way', two edges would be drawn between the vertices.

A further example is when the vertices represent teams and each edge represents a match played between those teams. In this case the arrow indicates the winner with a direction from the winner to the loser.

Adjacency matrix: Undirected graph

The graph data can be represented in the form of a matrix. A matrix looks like a two-dimensional array.

	A	B	C	D	E	F
A	0	0	1	1	0	0
B	0	0	0	1	0	0
C	1	0	0	0	1	0
D	1	1	0	0	1	1
E	0	0	1	0	0	1
F	0	0	0	1	1	0

Figure 19.20 Adjacency matrix.

Progress check L

Draw the adjacency matrix for the Figure **19.18** air routes graph.

Adjacency matrix: directed weighted graph

The matrix cells show either the weight or 'infinity' for no edge.

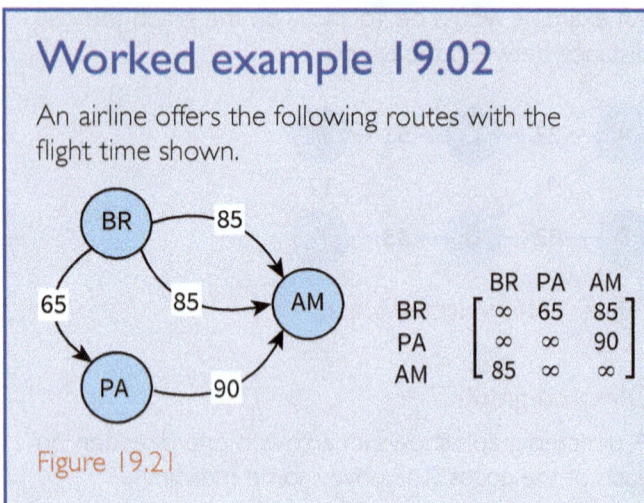

Worked example 19.02

An airline offers the following routes with the flight time shown.

Figure 19.21

Adjacency list

An adjacency list is an alternative to using an adjacency matrix. It shows, for each vertex in the graph, the adjacent vertices with their weights.

Initial vertex	Terminal vertex
BR	PA:65, AM:85
PA	AM:90
AM	BR:85

Table 19.13 Adjacency list.

19.04 The performance of algorithms

For any algorithm that we design we must consider a number of factors:

- **Correctness:** the algorithm must product the right result, i.e. the correct output(s) for given input(s).
- **Speed of computation:** this is not a factor of the algorithm itself but, will also be influenced by the tool that is used to implement it, for example, the processing power of the computer.
- **Time complexity:** a measure of how long the algorithm takes to complete. The size of the input will be a factor is determining the execution time.
- **Space complexity:** a measure of the amount of memory space the algorithm will require.

All factors will generally be influenced by the number of data items to be processed (size of input).

Big O notation

'Big O' notation is used to describe the complexity of an algorithm. It is expressed for a given algorithm using a measure called the **order of growth**.

Order of growth

The 'order of growth' is designed as a measure of how fast the algorithm computes.

The symbol O is used to stand for 'order of growth'.

This is a simple idea. If, in a problem, the data items were doubled, would the completion time double, or perhaps increase fourfold, or increase by a larger factor?

We must be clear that other factors that could influence the execution time should be eliminated.

For most algorithms, a small number of data inputs are likely to compute quickly. Therefore, the order of growth discussion will take into account a large number of data inputs only.

> **TIP**
>
> If an algorithm has different component parts that each have a different level of complexity, then summarise the O() measure as the dominant one. For example, in an algorithm with a formula that included a term x and a term x^2, the dominant term would be the higher order term, x^2.

Linear time complexity

Dataset size is n.

If n doubles and the algorithm's time complexity at most doubles there is a linear increase in time complexity. The complexity of the algorithm is stated as **O(n)**.

This is called the '**Big-O**' notation – where the O stands for 'order of growth'.

Some worked examples will serve to explain this further.

Worked example 19.03

Consider searching an array `MyArray` of size `n` for a particular value.

The worst case scenario is that all values need to be considered.

```
INPUT RequiredValue
FOR i ← 1 TO n
        Consider the next value of the array
NEXT i
OUTPUT "Found / Not Found"
```

If n doubles, the number of comparisons doubles.

Conclusion: The algorithm has linear time complexity $O(n)$.

Worked example 19.04

Consider this pseudocode procedure.

```
PROCEDURE MyFunction (AnArray() : INTEGER, n : INTEGER)
    DECLARE i AS INTEGER
    OUTPUT  i
    FOR i ← 1 TO n
        OUTPUT AnArray[i]
    NEXT i
    OUTPUT  "End of function"
ENDPROCEDURE
```

The two outputs outside the loop do not depend on the size of the data set n.

They are said to have a **constant time complexity**, $O(i)$.

The loop has a number of steps equal to the size of n and so this has complexity $O(n)$.

The algorithm's complexity is expressed as $O(1) + O(n)$.

BUT, since for a large value of n the $O(n)$ term will become dominant, the algorithm's complexity is simplified to $O(n)$, i.e. the dominant term.

Conclusion: This procedure has linear time complexity $O(n)$.

Worked example 19.05

Consider the algorithm to calculate the sum of the integers starting at 1, up to value **n**.

This 'sum of the integers' algorithm will compute faster for the input of 100 numbers rather than 1000000. There is a formula that calculates this sum.

$$\tfrac{1}{2} n(n+1)$$
$$\text{i.e. } (n^2 + n) / 2$$

For a large n, the dominant term is the n^2

As this expression has dominant term n^2, the algorithm is stated to have order of growth **O(n^2)**

Consider the situation where, for the sum 1 ... 1000, the completion time T is calculated.

If the algorithm is used a second time for integers 1 to 3000 (that is the size of the dataset increased by factor 3), then the completion time would increase by factor 3^2, i.e. 9 times T.

Conclusion: The algorithm has **polynomial time complexity : O(n^2)**.

Worked example 19.06

Consider the binary search algorithm to find a particular value from the array `MyArray()` of size **n**.

The outline algorithm was:

> Input the value to find
>
> Calculate the median value
>
> Compare:
>
>> If required value is after the median, discard the top half
>>
>> If required value is before the current median, discard the bottom half
>
> Re-calculate the median
>
> Repeat until value found

The list is reduced in size by half each time.

E.g. An array of size 1024 would require (at worst) 11 steps to locate the value.

$\log_2 1024 = 10$

So, the number of comparisons is $\log_2 n$.

Conclusion: The binary search algorithm has **logarithmic time complexity - O($\log_2 n$)**.

19.05 Recursion

A binary tree illustrates the basic idea of recursion. We can think of the structure as a number of trees that are contained as part of a biggest tree at a higher level. Hence think of the Figure 19.22 tree in this way. The **leaf nodes** should be thought of as a tree with no **left or right sub-tree**. Recursion can be a powerful technique to use in many algorithms.

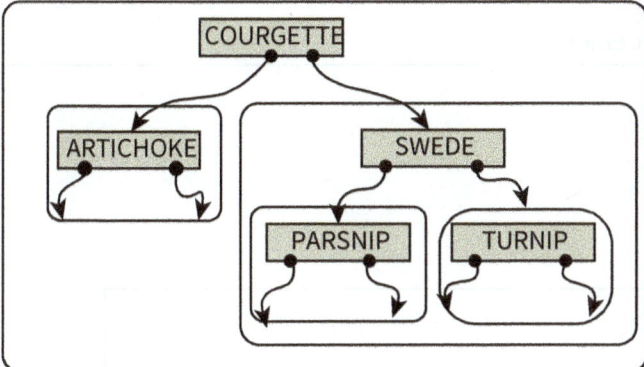

Figure 19.22 Binary trees and recursion.

Recursion is not an easy concept to grasp.

A recursive procedure is one that is defined in terms of itself, one that calls itself and, if coded as a function, there must be a stopping condition to make the recursion terminate.

A recursive rule in Backus-Naur Form is a rule that is defined in terms of itself.

For example, in maths, the 'factorial of number N' is defined thus:

Factorial N (written as N!) = N × (N-1) × (N-2) × .... × 3 × 2 × 1

This means that Factorial 5 = 5 × Factorial 4.

This fits with the definition 'defined in terms of itself'.

Designed as a function `Factorial` it would have a single parameter, the number, and will be defined as follows:

```
FUNCTION Factorial(ThisNumber)
    IF ThisNumber = 1
        THEN
            RETURN 1
        ELSE
            RETURN ThisNumber x Factorial(ThisNumber - 1)
    ENDIF
ENDFUNCTION
```

Note the **stopping condition** is met when `ThisNumber = 1`.

The compiler and recursive code

The compiler does not know whether or not a function is recursive. Every time the function name is met in the source code, the address of the function entry point is recorded and the compiler continues to translate instructions.

The compiler can deal with a function call even if all the statements in its definition have been scanned. Every time a function call is made the compiler will need to store the context and the function parameters on the stack, so that it can recover these values at a later stage in the compilation process. If the function calls itself many times there is the risk of 'stack overflow' where the memory space allocated for the stack becomes full.

Some functions are written with the recursive call statement as the final statement in the function definition and this gives rise to what is called 'tail recursion'. If the function call is the last statement in the function definition, then there is no necessity to save the context in the stack, and we can just overwrite it. Here there is no possibility of 'stack overflow' even if the function was to call itself indefinitely.'

Binary search: recursive solution

A binary search can have a recursive solution since we are repeatedly searching a new (smaller) sub-list formed from the current list.

The stopping condition is that the search item is found or the item is not in the list.

The algorithm uses the identifiers shown in Table 19.02.

```
PROCEDURE BinarySearch
    INPUT ThisValue
    Found ← FALSE
    NotInList ← FALSE
    // flags if the required value is not found
    Top ← N
    Bottom ← 1
    REPEAT
        Middle ← Integer value of (Top + Bottom)/2 )
        IF ThisArray[Middle] = ThisValue
            THEN
                Found ← TRUE
                OUTPUT "Value is FOUND"
        ELSE
            IF Bottom > Top
                THEN
                    NotInList = TRUE
                ELSE
                    IF ThisArray[Middle] < ThisItem
                        THEN
                            // retain the top half of the list
                            Bottom ← Middle + 1
                        ELSE
                            // retain the bottom half of the list
                            Top ← Middle - 1
                    ENDIF
            ENDIF
        ENDIF
    UNTIL (Found = TRUE) OR (NotInList = TRUE)
    IF NotInList = TRUE
        THEN
            OUTPUT "Requested item was NOT FOUND"
    ENDIF
ENDPROCEDURE
```

Binary tree traversal: recursive solution

To output the values in order from a binary tree required that we visit the nodes in some defined order.

Consider the following tree.

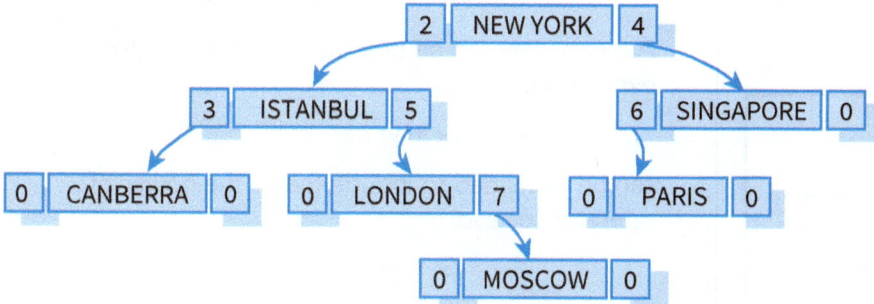

Figure 19.23 Binary tree data.

The outline algorithm is:

    Go to the root

    IF there is a left node THEN move left

    REPEAT moving left until the left pointer is Null

    OUTPUT the current value

    Move back to the Root – OUTPUT, the root of this subtree

    IF there is a right node THEN move right …

We can visualise this as moving through a sequence of subtrees. Each subtree is dealt with in the order: move left (if possible….), OUTPUT the root and then move right (if possible….).

The algorithm is recursive as we are continually dealing with a subtree, and often have to leave the completion of the current tree (left – root – right) until later when we return to this tree.

The algorithm for the tree traversal follows as a pseudocode procedure.

The root of each tree/subtree is passed as parameter `Root`.

```
PROCEDURE InOrderTraversal(Root)
    IF Root.LeftPointer <> Null
        THEN
            // move left
            InOrderTraversal(Root.LeftPointer)
    ENDIF
    OUTPUT Root.Data
    IF Root.RightPointer <> Null
        THEN
            // move right
            InOrderTraversal(Root.RightPointer)
    ENDIF
ENDPROCEDURE
```

> These are the lines which show the procedure is recursive.
>
> The procedure is calling itself.

> And again …

The algorithm is elegant, requiring very few statements.

Visiting the nodes in this order, which outputs the data values in order, is called an **in-order tree traversal**. The order of the procedure calls is illustrated with the next diagram. The arrows show when a call is completed and the algorithm returns to a previous call. This process is called **unwinding**.

```
Tree(NEW YORK)
    // Move left
    Tree(ISTANBUL)
        // Move left
        Tree(CANBERRA)
            // nothing to the left
            OUTPUT CANBERRA
            // nothing to the right
        ENDPROCEDURE
        OUTPUT ISTANBUL
        // Move right

        Tree(LONDON)
            // nothing to the left
            OUTPUT LONDON
            // Move right
            Tree(MOSCOW)
                // nothing to the left
                OUTPUT MOSCOW
                // nothing to the right
            ENDPROCEDURE
        ENDPROCEDURE
    ENDPROCEDURE
    OUTPUT NEW YORK
    // Move right
    Tree(SINGAPORE)
        // Move left
        Tree(PARIS)
            // nothing to the left
            OUTPUT PARIS
            // nothing to the right
        ENDPROCEDURE
        OUTPUT SINGAPORE
        // nothing to the right
    ENDPROCEDURE
ENDPROCEDURE
```

Infix expressions

A binary tree can be used to represent an infix expression.

$$(x + y) / z^3$$

can be expanded to include the 'to the power of' operator to read:

$$(x + y) / z^3$$

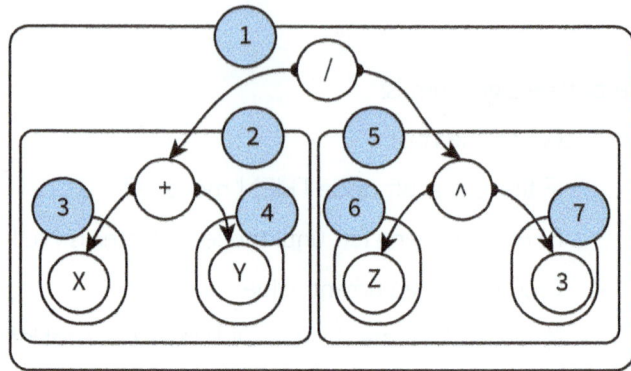

Figure 19.24 Infix expression as a binary tree.

Use the in-order traversal algorithm to trace the above tree.

New Tree() call		Tree root	OUTPUT
1		/	
2		+	
3		X	X
	Unwind to tree 3	+	+
4		y	Y
	Unwind to tree 1	/	/
5		^	
6		z	Z
	Unwind to tree 5	^	^
7			3

Table 19.13 In-order traversal trace table.

Post order traversal

The traversal order can be changed. Consider a traversal of the tree in the order move left (if possible), move right (if possible) and then OUTPUT the root.

This is called a post order traversal.

> **TIP**
>
> The general advantage of a recursive method is that recursive solutions tend to require fewer steps for the algorithm and therefore less code than an alternative iterative solution.

Progress check M

Draw the binary tree for the expression:

$$a \times t + 1/2 \times t^2$$

Past paper questions

1 The array `ItemList[1:20]` stores data. A **bubble sort** sorts these data.

   a Complete the pseudocode algorithm for a bubble sort.

   ```
   01  MaxIndex ← 20
   02  NumberItems ← ..................................................................
   03  FOR Outer ← 1 TO ..................................................................
   04      FOR Inner ← 1 to NumberItems
   05          IF ItemList[Inner] > ..................................................................
               THEN
                   Temp ← ItemList[..................................]
                   ItemList[Inner] ← ItemList[..............................]
   09              ItemList[Inner + 1] ← ..................................................
   10          ENDIF
   11      ENDFOR
   12      NumberItems ← ..................................................................
   13  ENDFOR
   ```
   [7]

   b The algorithm in **part a** is inefficient.

   i   Explain why the algorithm in **part a** is inefficient. [2]

   ii Explain how you would improve the efficiency of this algorithm. [3]

   c An insertion sort is another sorting algorithm.

   State **two** situations when an insertion sort is more efficient than a bubble sort. Give a reason for each.

   [4]

Cambridge International AS & A level Computer Science 9608 paper 41 Q2 June 2018

2. An Abstract Data Type (ADT) is used to create a linked list. The linked list is created as an array of records. The records are of type `ListNode`.

An example of a record of `ListNode` is shown in the following table.

Data Field	Value
Player	"Alvaro"
Pointer	1

a i Use **pseudocode** to write a definition for the record type, **ListNode**.

[3]

ii An array, `Scorers`, will hold 10 nodes of type ListNode. Use **pseudocode** to write an array declaration for this array. The lower bound subscript is 0.

[2]

b The linked list stores `ListNode` records in alphabetical order of player. The last node in the linked list always has a `Pointer` value of -1. The position of the first node in the linked list is held in the variable `ListHead`.

After some processing, the array and variables are in the state as follows:

ListHead
0

Scorers

	Player	Pointer
0	"Alvaro"	1
1	"Antoine"	3
2	"Dimltri"	7
3	"Crisciano" 1"	2
4	"Gareth"	5
5	"Graziano" 1	6
6	"Olivier"	8
7	"Erik"	4
8	"Yaya"	9
9	"Zoto"	-1

A **recursive** function traverses the linked list to search for a player.

An example of calling the function, using pseudocode, is:

```
Position ← SearchList("Gareth", ListHead)
```

Complete the following **pseudocode** to implement the function SearchList ().

The function will return a value of 99 when a player is not found.

```
FUNCTION SearchList(Find : STRING, Position : INTEGER) RETURNS INTEGER
    IF Scorer[Position].Player = ............................................................................................
        THEN
            RETURN ............................................................................................
        ELSE
            IF Scorer[Position].Pointer <> -1
                THEN
                    Position ← SearchList(Find, ............................................................................................)
                    RETURN ............................................................................................
                ELSE
                    RETURN ............................................................................................
            ENDIF
    ENDIF
ENDFUNCTION
```
[5]

3 A linked list abstract data type (ADT) is created. This is implemented as an array of records. The records are of type `ListElement`.

An example of a record of `ListElement` is shown in the following table.

Data Item	Value
Country	"Scotland"
Pointer	1

a i Use **pseudocode** to write a definition for the record type, `ListElement`. [3]

  ii Use **pseudocode** to write an array declaration to reserve space for only 15 nodes of type `ListElement` in an array, `CountryList`. The lower bound element is 1. [2]

b The program stores the position of the last node in the linked list in `LastNode`. The last node always has a `Pointer` value of `-1`. The position of the node at the head of the list is stored in `ListHead`.

After some processing, the array and variables are in the following state.

CountryList

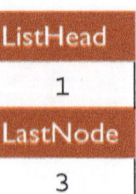

	Country	Pointer
1	"Wales"	2
2	"Scotland"	4
3		-1
4	"England"	5
5	"Brazil"	6
6	"Canada"	7
7	"Mexico"	8
8	"Peru"	9
9	"China"	10
10		11
11		12
12		13
13		14
14		15
15		3

A **recursive** algorithm searches the list for a value, deletes that value, and updates the required pointers. When a node value is deleted, it is set to empty "" and the node is added to the end of the list.

A node value is deleted using the pseudocode statement

```
CALL DeleteNode("England", 1, 0)
```

Complete the following **pseudocode** to implement the `DeleteNode` procedure.

```
PROCEDURE DeleteNode(NodeValue: STRING, ThisPointer : INTEGER, PreviousPointer : INTEGER)

IF CountryList[ThisPointer].Value = NodeValue
  THEN
    CountryList[ThisPointer].Value ← ""

    IF ListHead = ............................................................................
    .....


    THEN
      ListHead ← ............................................................................
      ..............
```

```
    ELSE
       CountryList[PreviousPointer].Pointer ←
     CountryList[ThisPointer].Pointer ENDIF
       CountryList[LastNode].Pointer ← ..................................................................
...................................................

    LastNode ← ThisPointer
ELSE
  IF CountryList[ThisPointer].Pointer <> -1
    THEN
       CALL DeleteNode(NodeVal
ue, ............................................................................, ThisPointer)
    ELSE
      OUTPUT "DOES NOT EXIST"
  ENDIF
ENDIF
    ENDPROCEDURE                                            [5]
```

Cambridge International AS & A level Computer Science 9608 paper 41 Q6 June 2018

Chapter 20

Further programming: fundamentals of practical coding

Learning Objectives:

- Describe, in overview, the various paradigms used for programming.

Low Level:

- Familiarise yourself with the pseudocode used for assembly language instruction (in Chapter 4)
- Understand the various modes of addressing
- Trace an assembly language program
- Write an assembly language program
- Understand and apply how the constructs used in high-level programming are applied in assembly language.

Declarative:

- Understand the structure of a declarative program

- Use the data and rules to formulate a decision for a set goal.
- Understand the concept of backtracking.

Imperative (Procedural):

- Understand the use of the procedural paradigm for program code.

  The writing of procedural code in the three supported languages is studied in detail in Chapter 21

Object-oriented programming (OOP):

- Understand the use of OOP.

  The writing of OOP code is studied in detail in Chapter 22

20.01 Programming paradigms: overview

A 'paradigm' is a set of concepts, theories, methods and standards for doing something. A paradigm is a 'school of thought'. A programming paradigm is the way of building the structure and elements of a computer program. Certain types of problem will be better suited to the adoption of one paradigm than to another.

Low-level programming: overview

A low-level paradigm means programming using the basic machine operations of the processor.

Programming using machine code, even if the codes could be written in hexadecimal, not binary, would be extremely tedious.

Hence the use of assembly language where mnemonics can be used for the different instructions. This approach could be appropriate for a program where there was a need to directly address the various processor registers, for example, in the coding of a device driver.

Each instruction written in assembly language always translates to exactly one instruction in machine code.

Various addressing modes

This was studied in Chapter 4 Section 4.02. The various modes of addressing were covered: immediate, direct,

> **TIP**
>
> For AS Level you are asked only to trace a given program.
>
> For A Level the syllabus states 'the ability to write low-level code ....' So now, you need to know how to write a simple program from scratch.

indirect, indexed and relative. The list to be covered here for the A Level paper is the same.

Imperative programming: overview

Imperative programming is studied in detail in Chapter 21.

It is also called procedural programming, which is a huge clue!

'First do this, next do that' describes the spirit of the imperative paradigm.

The computational steps in an imperative language are called statements or commands. Program statements/commands are executed in the order shown by control structures (loops and selection). Typical commands offered by imperative languages include assignment, input/output and procedure calls.

Data is represented using variables and, as the program executes, the value stored by these variables can change.

Using the imperative programming paradigm, the natural abstraction is the procedure.

A complete program can be designed in a modular way as a series of procedures. One or more actions are carried out by a procedure, which can be triggered as a single command (usually a 'call' statement).

Object-oriented programming (OOP): overview

OOP is studied in detail in Chapter 22.

The object-oriented paradigm adopts a bottom-up approach and defines first the 'things' or objects that are at the core of the task specification. The definition of a type of object is coded as a class definition.

Declarative programming: overview

The declarative (or 'logic' or 'rule-based') paradigm is very different from other programming paradigms. The declarative paradigm fits extremely well when used for problems that deal with the extraction of knowledge from basic facts and rules.

Execution of the 'program' involves setting a query (or setting a goal). The program then searches for a solution. Execution is a systematic search of a set of facts making use of a given set of inference rules.

> **TIP**
>
> Don't confuse 'declarative programming paradigm' with the 'declaration of variables' in a high-level language.

20.02 Low-level programming in practice

We shall illustrate each mode of addressing with a program. Familiarise yourself again with the assembly language instruction set given in Chapter 4.

Direct addressing

The operand address is the actual address to be used. The op code for direct addressing is `LDD`.

Worked example 20.01

Numbers 6 and 3 are stored in memory at locations N1 and N2. Write code to multiply 6 by 3 and store the answer at location ANSWER.

```
LOOP:   LDD   ANSWER
        ADD   N1
        STO   ANSWER
        LDD   COUNT
        INC
        STO   COUNT
        CMP   N2
        JNE   LOOP
        END

N1:     6
N2:     3
COUNT:  0
ANSWER: 0
```

Figure 20.01 Program using direct addressing.

(Continued)

Tracing the execution of the code gives:

ACC	Address			
	N1	N2	COUNT	ANSWER
	6	3	0	0
0				
6				
0				
1			1	
6				
12				12
1				
2			2	
12				
18				18
2				
3			3	

Figure 20.02 Trace of the Figure **20.01** program.

There is no 'multiply' instruction in this instruction set, so the calculation is done by adding 6 three times.

The program illustrates setting up a loop in assembly language.

The `LDD` and `STO` instructions both use direct addressing.

The programmer has used symbolic addresses – `N1`, `N2`, `COUNT` and `ANSWER`.

The same program, without the use of symbolic addressing, is shown in Figure 20.03.

It shows the program is loaded to main memory with the first instruction at address 100.

100	LDD	113
101	ADD	110
102	STO	113
103	LDD	112
104	INC	
105	STO	112
106	CMP	111
107	JNE	100
108	END	
109		
110	6	
111	3	
112	0	
113	0	

Figure 20.03 Direct addressing with absolute addresses.

Note that although all the addresses are shown as absolute addresses the instructions are still the same. They use direct addressing. Direct addressing can use either an absolute address or a symbolic address as the operand.

Immediate addressing

The address is not really an address at all, the operand is an actual value. The op code for the load instruction in our instruction set is LDR.

This is the same problem: calculate 6 × 3

LOOP:	LDD	ANSWER
	ADD	#6
	STO	ANSWER
	LDD	COUNT
	INC	
	STO	COUNT
	CMP	#3
	JNE	LOOP
	END	

COUNT:	0
ANSWER:	0

Figure 20.04 Program using immediate addressing.

Three of the instructions have 'hard coded' the number to be used. It will not be retrieved from a memory address as in the two previous programs. The instructions have used the 'immediate values', 6 and 3.

Relative addressing

Addresses are expressed relative to the start address of the program. For example, if the first program instruction is at address 100, we would reference address 109 with an operand of +9.

100	LDD	+12
101	ADD	+9
102	STO	+12
103	LDD	+11
104	INC	
105	STO	+11
106	CMP	+10
107	JNE	100
108		
109	6	
110	3	
111	0	
112	0	

Figure 20.05 Program using relative addressing.

Indirect addressing

The operand is an address that holds the address to be used in the instruction. The op code for indirect addressing is `LDI`.

This program displays four characters stored at location 120 onwards.

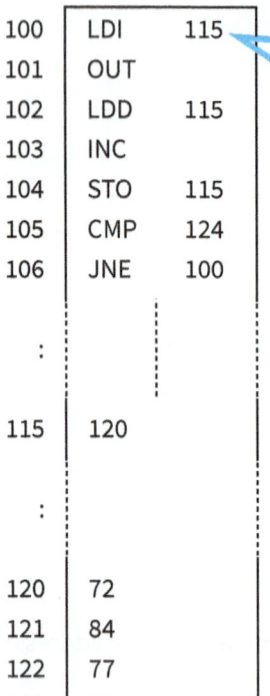

100	LDI	115
101	OUT	
102	LDD	115
103	INC	
104	STO	115
105	CMP	124
106	JNE	100
⋮		
115	120	
⋮		
120	72	
121	84	
122	77	
123	76	

- Inspect address 115
- Find the forwarding address 120
- Load the contents of address 120 to ACC

Figure 20.06 Program using indirect addressing.

A trace of the program gives:

ACC	Address					OUTPUT
	115	120	121	122	123	
72						ASCII 72 = H
120						
121	121					
84						ASCII 84 = T
121						
122	122					
77						ASCII 77 = M
122						
123	123					
76						ASCII 76 = L
123						
124	124					

Figure 20.07 Trace of Figure 20.06 program.

Indexed addressing

Indexed addressing uses the value found in the Index Register. The op code for indexed addressing is `LDX`.

This gives the same output as earlier. The program displays four characters stored at location 120 onwards.

This time the loop counter is being controlled by the value at address 114 (as before).

The memory address holding the output character is calculated as (120 + the offset value stored in index register IX).

100	LDR	#0	// IX Stores the memory offset from 120
101	LDX	120	// indexed addressing
102	OUT		
103	INC	IX	
104	LDD	114	
105	INC	ACC	
106	STO	114	
107	CMP	#4	
108	JNE	101	
114	0		// loop counter
120	72		
121	84		
122	77		
123	76		

Figure 20.08 Indexed addressing.

A trace of the program gives:

ACC	IX	114	OUTPUT
	0		
72			ASCII 72 = H
	1		
0			
1		1	
84			ASCII 84 = T
	2		
1			
2		2	
77			ASCII 77 = M
	3		
2			
3		3	
76			ASCII 76 = L
	4		
3			
4		4	

Figure 20.09 Trace of Figure 20.08 program.

Common constructs in assembly language

All the constructs we are familiar with in our high-level language programming – selection with If statements, loops – can be implemented in assembly language.

Some examples follow.

Assignment

> ### Worked example 20.02
>
> Add two numbers and store the answer at location RESULT.
>
> Visual Basic equivalent:
>
> ```
>     Result = NUMB1 + NUMB2
>  START:   LDD NUMB1
>           ADD NUMB2
>           STO RESULT
>           END
>  NUMB1:   7
>  NUMB2:   15
>  RESULT:  0
> ```
>
> Figure 20.10 Assignment equivalent code.

Selection

> ### Worked example 20.03
>
> If the number loaded is 100 then output "Y", otherwise output "N".
>
> Visual Basic equivalent:
> ```
>  7   If Numb = 100 Then
>  8      Console.WriteLine("Y")
>  9   Else
> 10      Console.WriteLine("N")
> 11   End If
> ```
>
> ```
>  START:   LDD NUMB
>           CMP #100
>           JPE TRUE
>  FALSE:   LDD N
>           OUT
>           JMP END         The JMP is needed to stop the control
>  TRUE:    LDD Y           going into the 'TRUE' action
>           OUT
>  END:     END
>
>  NUMB:    100
>  Y:       89       // ASCII code for 'Y'
>  N:       78       // ASCII code for 'N'
> ```
>
> Figure 20.11 Selection equivalent code.

Post-condition loop

Worked example 20.04

The text CAT is to be output COUNTER times.

Visual Basic equivalent:

```
 7  Do
 8      Counter = 5
 9      Console.WriteLine("CAT")
10      Counter = Counter - 1
11  Loop Until Counter = 0
```

```
        START:  OUT CHAR1
                OUT CHAR2
                OUT CHAR3
                OUT
                LDD COUNTER
                DEC ACC
                CMP #0
                JPN START
          END:  END

      COUNTER:  5
        CHAR1:  67       // ASCII code for 'C'
        CHAR2:  65       // ASCII code for 'A'
        CHAR3:  84       // ASCII code for 'T'
```

Figure 20.12 Assignment equivalent code.

Progress check A

Write an assembly language program that is equivalent to the following pre-condition loop:

```
 6      Counter = 5
 7      Do While Counter <> 0
 8          Console.WriteLine("CAT")
 9          Counter = Counter - 1
10      Loop
```

Progress check B

Six numbers are stored at location NUMBER, NUMBER+1 and NUMBER+2, etc.

Write a program to count how many of the numbers match with 42.

20.03 Declarative programming

Given the necessary facts and rules, declarative programming will use deductive reasoning to solve a problem. Prolog is a declarative language. Prolog stands for Programming in Logic. Prolog is a very important tool in programming artificial intelligence applications and in the development of expert systems.

Using a procedural language, on the other hand, the programmer must provide step-by-step statements that tell the computer exactly how to solve a given problem. In other words, the programmer must know how to solve the problem before the computer can do it.

Compare this to the Prolog programs that follow. We only need to supply a description of the problem and the ground rules for solving it. Prolog is then left to determine how to go about finding a solution.

A Prolog program is not a sequence of actions, it is a collection of facts with rules for drawing conclusions from those facts.

A Prolog program arrives at a solution by logically inferring one thing from something already known.

Prolog statements use predicate logic. Predicate logic is simply a way of making it clear how reasoning is done. Predicate logic puts the relationship first, followed by one or more objects. The object(s) then become argument(s) that the relationship acts upon.

Facts

For example, the following natural language sentences are transformed into predicate logic syntax.

Natural Language	Predicate Logic
Tom is a member of Team X	`teamX(tom).`
Tom is currently fit (and so available to play)	`fit(tom).`
Ali can play in midfield.	`position(ali, midfield).`

Table 20.01 Facts using predicate logic.

The three statements in Table 20.01 are facts.

Rules

A rule enables the program to infer one fact from other facts.

Here are some rules concerning a "likes" relation:

Natural Language	Predicate Logic
Cindy likes everything that Bill likes.	`likes(cindy, Something):-likes(bill, Something).`
Hilary likes everything that is green.	`likes(hilary, Something):-green(Something).`

Table 20.01 Rules using predicate logic.

The use of `Something` is like using a variable in a procedural high-level language.

The :- symbol is read as 'if', and it serves to connect the two parts of a rule.

A rule can require two or more conditions, we then use the comma to read as 'and'.

Queries or setting a goal

Once we give Prolog a set of facts, we can proceed to ask questions concerning these facts. This is known as querying the Prolog program, or setting a 'goal'.

The Prolog programming environment includes an inference engine. The inference engine includes a pattern matcher, which retrieves stored (known) information by matching answers to questions. Prolog tries to infer that a goal is true (in other words, answer a question) by questioning the set of facts and rules.

Worked example 20.05

Setting a goal.

Consider the following list of facts:

`teamA(tom).`

`teamA(ali).`

`teamA(mohammed).`

`teamA(luke).`

`fit(tom).`

`fit(luke).`

`fit(mohammed).`

(Continued)

```
position(tom, goalkeeper).
position(ali, defender).
position(ali, midfield).
position(luke, forward).
position(luke, forward).
position(mohammed, forward).
position(luke, forward).
```

There might be multiple solutions to the set goal.

Prolog always looks first at the start of the fact list. It looks at each fact until it reaches the bottom, **backtracking** each time to its previous reference point in the list of facts.

Study the list of facts above and then,

Set the goal: `position(ali, Where)`

The inference engine of Prolog will process the query as follows:

- Look for the first occurrence of `position` – the argument does not match with `ali`
- Move to the next occurrence of `position` – finds a match with `ali`
  - `Where = defender`
- Move to the next `position` clause – finds a second match with `ali`
  - `Where = midfield`
- Prolog must consider all the `position` clauses as there is no ordering for the data items
- No more matches are found

Backtracking with rules

Worked example 20.06

A goal where the solution requires backtracking.

The manager needs to know who is available to play for the next match in each position.

The knowledge base needs the rule:

`available_to_play(X, Y):-teamA(X),position(X, Y), fit(X).`

'The player is available to play in the stated position if they are a Team A player <u>and</u> they can play in this position <u>and</u> they are currently fit'.

```
teamA(tom).
teamA(ali).
teamA(mohammed).
teamA(luke).
```

(Continued)

```
fit(tom).
fit(luke).
fit(mohammed).
position(tom, goalkeeper).
position(ali, defender).
position(ali, midfield).
position(luke, forward).
position(luke, forward).
position(mohammed, midfield).
position(luke, forward).
```

Worked example 20.07

Who is currently fit to play in midfield?

Set the goal:

```
available_to_play(X, midfield):-teamA(X), fit(X),
                                 position(X, midfield).
```

The backtracking process:
- The first clause used in the goal set is `teamA` - so bind `tom` to `X`
- Put `X` in the fit clause and search ... a match is found in the first `fit` clause
- Now search the `position` clause with `tom` bound to `X`
- This fails to find a match in the seven `position` clauses
- So, `tom` is not a possible
- Backtrack to the `teamA` clause list and bind `ali` to `X`
- Search the three `fit` clauses fails to match `X` with `ali`
- So, `ali` is not a possible... (There is no need to consider the `position` clauses)
- Backtrack to the `teamA` clause list and bind `mohammed` to `X`
- Search the `fit` clauses finds an `X=mohammed` match
- Search the position clauses finds a match with `X=mohammed` and `midfield`
  - Prolog outputs: `available_to_play(X, midfield)= mohammed`
- A final backtrack to the `TeamA` list for `X=luke`
- Finds an `X=luke` match for the `fit` clause
- Backtracks, but does not find a match in the `position` clauses
- So, `luke` is not a possible.

Worked example 20.08

A program gives advice on whether a person may legally drive a certain class of vehicle.

The following partially completed knowledge base has some of these facts and rules. They have been numbered for easy reference.

```
01 age(edward,20).
02 age(robert,19).
03 age(flora,17).
04 age(emma,17).
05 age(andrew,16).
06 minimum_age(motor_cycle,16).
07 minimum_age(car,17).
08 minimum_age(heavy_goods_vehicle, 20).
09 passed_test(edward, heavy_goods_vehicle).
10 passed_test(andrew, motor_cycle).
11 passed_test(emma, car).
12 hasprovisional_licence(andrew).
13 hasprovisional_licence(robert).
14 permitted_to_drive(X,V) :- passed_test(X,V).
15 permitted_to_drive(X,V) :- hasprovisional_licence(X)
                             And age(X,A)
                             And minimum_age(V,L) And A >= L.
```

Figure 20.13 'Permitted to drive' program.

Facts:

Fact 1 means that Edward is 20 years old.

Fact 6 means the minimum age for driving a motor-cycle is 16.

Fact 10 means Andrew has passed the driving test for a motor-cycle.

Fact 12 means that Andrew has a provisional driving licence.

Rules:

Rule 14 means that person X may drive a vehicle V if person X has passed the test for a vehicle of class V.

Rule 15 means that person X may drive a vehicle V if person X has a provisional licence and is old enough to drive a vehicle of class V.

Consider the query:

Is Flora permitted to drive a car?

`? permitted_to_drive(flora, car).`

The inference engine would do the following:

First look at rule 14 and then scan the facts to see if Flora has passed the test for a car.

The answer is 'no', so rule 15 is examined.

The facts are scanned again to check if Flora has a provisional licence.

No relevant fact is found so the program returns 'no'.

Consider these queries:

`? permitted_to_drive(robert, motor_cycle)` — Returns the answer 'yes' using rule 15 and facts 2, 6 and 13.

`? permitted_to_drive(emma, V)` — Returns 'car' using rule 14 and fact 11

Progress check C

Study the knowledge base on the right.

a   Explain in words 16.

What is the output from the following goals?

b   `plays(tansy, Y)`

c   `likes(yenene, A)`

Write a new rule which states:

d   'Ken likes all females, or males who like golf'.

```
01  male(kai).
02  male(john).
03  male(ken).
04  female(tansy).
05  female(tadi).
06  female(natene).
07  female(yenene).
08  plays(yenene, tennis).
09  plays(tadi, tennis).
10  plays(tadi, golf).
11  plays(ken, rugby).
12  plays(natene, hockey).
13  plays(natene, golf).
14  plays(tansy, golf).
15  plays(ken, football).
16  plays(natene, tennis).
17  likes(yenene, X) :- female(X), plays(X, golf).
18  likes(natene, X) :- male(X), plays(X, rugby).
19  likes(tansy, X) :- male(X), plays(X, tennis).
```

The comma is read as 'and'

Figure 20.14 'Who likes what' program.

Past paper questions

1   A declarative language is used to represent facts and rules about flights.

```
01  direct(edinburgh, paris) .
02  direct(palma, rome) .
03  direct(glasgow, palma) .
04  direct(glasgow, vienna) .
05  direct(glasgow, salzburg) .
06
07  flies(paris, fly_jet) .
08  flies(mumbai, british_air) .
09  flies(palma, ciebe) .
10  flies(vienna, fly_jet) .
11  flies(salzburg, ciebe) .
12
13  can fly(x, y) if direct(x, y) and direct(z, y) .
```

These clauses have the following meaning:

Clause	Explanation
01	There is a direct route from Edinburgh to Paris.
07	Fly Jet operates flights to Paris.
13	It is possible to fly from X to Y if there is a direct flight from X to Z and a direct flight from Z to Y.

a   More facts need to be included.

   There is a direct flight from London to Rome and British Air flies to Rome.

   14

   15   [2]

b   Using the variable Q, the goal

   ```
   flies(Q, fly_jet) .
   ```

   Returns

   ```
   Q = paris, vienna
   ```

   Write the result returned by the goal

   ```
   flies(K, ciebe) .
   ```

   K =   [2]

c   Use the variable M to write the goal to find where you can fly direct from Glasgow.   [2]

d   If an airline flies to an airport, that airline also flies every direct route out of that airport.

   Write a rule to represent this condition.

   ```
   flies(Y, X)
   ```
                                                                                                                         [3]

e   State what the following goal returns.

   ```
   can_fly(glasgow, rome).
   ```
                                                                                                                         [1]

Cambridge International AS & A level Computer Science 9608 paper 41 Q1 June 2018

2   An intruder detection system for a large house has four sensors. An 8-bit memory location stores the output from each sensor in its own bit position.

   The bit value for each sensor shows:

   - 1 – the sensor has been triggered
   - 0 – the sensor has not been triggered

   The bit positions are used as follows:

   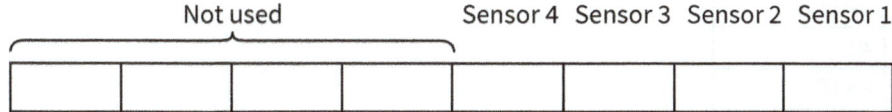

   The output from the intruder detection system is a loud alarm.

   The intruder system is set up so that the alarm will only sound if two or more sensors have been triggered.

   An assembly language program has been written to process the contents of the memory location.

The table show part of the instruction set for the processor used.

Instruction		Explanation
Op code	Operand	
LDD <address>		Direct addressing. Load the contents of the given address to ACC
STO <address>		Store the contents of ACC at the given address
INC <register>		Add 1 to the contents of the register (ACC or IX)
ADD <address>		Add the contents of the given address to the contents of ACC
AND <address>		Bitwise AND operation of the contents of ACC with the contents of <address>
CMP #n		Compare the contents of ACC with the number n
JMP <address>		Jump to the given address
JPE <address>		Following a compare instruction, jump to <address> if the compare was True
JGT <address>		Following a compare instruction, jump to <address> if the content of ACC is greater than the number used in the compare instruction
END		End the program and return to the operating system

Part of the assembly code is:

	Op code	Operand
SENSORS :		B00001010
COUNT :		0
VALUE :		1
LOOP :	LDD	SENSORS
	AND	VALUE
	CMP	#0
	JPE	ZERO
	LDD	COUNT
	INC	ACC
	STO	COUNT
ZERO :	LDD	VALUE
	CMP	#8
	JPE	EXIT
	ADD	VALUE
	STO	VALUE
	JMP	LOOP
EXIT :	LDD	COUNT
TEST :	CMP	…
	JGT	ALARM

i   Dry run the assembly language code. Start at **LOOP** and finish when **EXIT** is reached.

BITREG	COUNT	VALUE	ACC
B00001010	0	1	

[4]

ii The operand for the instruction labelled **TEST** is missing.

State the missing operand. [1]

iii The intruder detection system is improved and now has eight sensors.

One instruction in the assembly language code will need to be amended.

Identify this instruction. [2]

Cambridge International AS & A level Computer Science 9608 paper 32 Q6c June 2016

Chapter 21: Further programming: imperative

Learning Objectives:

You will have started by studying how pseudocode can be used to describe the steps for the solution of a given problem. The aim of this chapter is to show how all of the ideas and statements you have used in pseudocode can be translated into practical programming using your chosen language i.e. Visual Basic, Python or Java.

Chapter 20 gave an overview of the three different programming paradigms on which particular programming languages are based. Chapter 20 also gave a more detailed study of low-level language programming and declarative programming.

By the time you read this you should have done a considerable amount of practical programming using your chosen language.

In this part of the Revision Guide, we take you through the fundamentals of practical coding with the syntax used for each language.

The chapter is putting into practice what was covered for the AS syllabus in Chapters 9, 10, 11 and 12:

- Declaration and assignment of variables and constants
- Built-in functions
- Arithmetic expressions
- Arrays
- If structures
- CASE structure
- Count-controlled loop
- Post-condition loop
- Pre-condition loop
- Procedures
- Functions.

What software to use?

The code extracts in this book were produced using the following software:

- Visual Basic: Visual Studio 2017, Visual Basic Express edition (free)
- Python: Python Integrated Development and Learning Environment (IDLE) version 3.7 (free)
- Java NetBeans 8.2 (free).

General points: the development process:

- Python programs are interpreted in the IDLE environment
- Using Visual Studio or Visual Basic, the program code must first be 'built' (that is compiled) and then it can be executed
- Using Java with NetBeans, the source code is compiled into a form called bytecode. This bytecode is then run using the Java Virtual Machine software. All of these features are within the NetBeans IDE. Refer back to Chapter 5 where the translation process for Java using bytecode was discussed.

21.01 Variables and constants

Good practice is to use meaningful variable names and always state their data type.

Pay attention to use of whitespace and indentation. Indentation in Python is part of the code structure and its correct use is essential.

Data types

Data	Language data types		
	VB	Python	Java
Signed integer	Integer 4 bytes	int	Int 4 bytes
Real number – with a decimal part	Single – 4 bytes Double – 8 bytes	float	Float – 4 bytes Double – 8 bytes
Single character	Char 2 bytes in Unicode	Not available	Char – 2 bytes in Unicode
String of characters	String 2 bytes per character	Str stored as ASCII characters	String
Date	Date 8 bytes	Uses the datetime class	Uses the date class Import to the program with: Java.util.Date ;
Boolean logical value (True or False)	Boolean	bool	Boolean

Table 21.01 Summary of language data types.

Declaration and assignment of variables

Visual Basic	`Dim StudentName As String`
	`Dim StudentFullTime As Boolean`
	
	`StudentName = "Lewis" ;`
	`StudentFullTime = False ;`
		• Variables <u>must</u> be declared
		• Identifiers are not case sensitive
		Convention :
		• use CamelCaps /CamelCase for identifiers

Python	`StudentName = 'Rosari'`
	`StudentFullTime = False`
	
	Variables are not declared before assigned a value.
		• Every statement must be on a new line
		• Uses lower case for keywords
		• Identifiers are case sensitive

Java	`String studentName ;`
	`Boolean studentFullTime ;`
	
	`studentName = 'Lewis' ;`
	`studentFullTime = False ;`
		• Variables <u>must</u> be declared
		Convention :
		• camelCaps for identifiers
		• Lower case for keywords
		• All caps for class identifiers
		• Identifiers <u>are</u> case sensitive
		• All statements end with a semi-colon

> **TIP**
>
> Python only: The data type intended for each variable does not have to be formally declared. A comment (see following page) could be useful to clarify what data type was intended for each variable.

21.02 Arithmetic operators and functions

Operation	VB	Python	Java
Add	a + b	a + b	a + b
Subtract	a – b	a – b	a – b
Multiply	a * b	a * b	a * b
Divide	a / b	a / b	a / b • a and b are both type float or double
Integer division	a \ b	a // b	a / b • a and b are both type integer
Exponent	a ^ b	a ** b	Use Math method Math.pow(a, b)
Modulus	a Mod b	a % b	a % b
Equals	=	==	==
Greater than (or equal to)	> or >=	> or >=	> or >=
Less than (or equal to)	< or <=	< or <=	< or <=
Not equal	a <> b	a != b	a != b
AND operator	a > b And c <> 0	a > b and c <> 0	a > b && c <> 0
OR operator	a> b Or c <> 0	a > b or c <> 0	a > b || c <> 0

Table 21.02 – Language operators.

Declaration and assignment of a constant

Visual Basic	`Const Pi = 3.142`	Each constant and declaration starts with keyword `Const`
Python	`Pi = 3.142`	
Java	`Static Final Double pi = 3.142 ;`	Each declaration starts with keyword `Static`

Code comments

Comments will be useful for stating the date you created the program, what version it is and other useful information.

Visual Basic	`' This is the comment text` `' and this is the comment continued`
Python	`# This is the comment text` `# and this is the comment continued`

Java	`// This is the comment text`
	`// and this is the comment continued`
	
	Or,
	
	`/* This starts a multi-line comment`
	`    and this is the comment continued`
	`*/`

21.03 Input from the user

Visual Basic	`Console.write("Enter the name: ")` `StudentName = Console.Readline`	
Python	`StudentName = input ("Enter the name: ")`	– The text prompt is a parameter of the input function – All input data is read as a string

Java	`import java.util.Scanner ;`
	 `Scanner console= new Scanner(System.in) ;`
	 `System.out.print("Enter the name: ") ;`
	 `studentName = console.next() ;`
		– Scanner class is imported to the program
		 – A scanner object is created
		 – The scanner object reads the input string
		 – The output prompt is a separate statement

> **TIP**
>
> Good practice is to provide the user with a text prompt that makes clear the input expected.

21.04 Output from the program

Output will be the value of a variable, an expression, some text, or a combination.

Visual Basic	`Console.Writeline("The name was " & StudentName)` – When Console.Write( ) was used earlier the cursor remained on the same line.
Python	`print("The name was ", StudentName, end = '')` – Omit the final term to move to a new line.
Java	`System.out.println("The name was " + studentName)` – Using print instead of println, the cursor remains on the same line.

21.05 Built-in functions

In Chapter 11 Table 11.01 and Table 11.02 gave examples of built-in functions in pseudocode used with strings, characters and numbers. Here we summarise how these pseudocode functions are implemented by each programming language.

Manipulation of strings

Visual Basic	Python	Java
Access a single character in the string		

`x = "Covent Garden"`
`x(7) returns "<Space>"`
First char is position 1
	`x = "Covent Garden"`
	`x(7) returns "G"`
	First char is position 0
		`String x = "Covent Garden";`
		`char y = x.charAt(7);`

A sub-string from the left		

`x = ""`
`Left(x, 6)`
Returns "Covent"
	`x = "Covent Garden"`
	`x(0, 6) returns "Covent"`
		`String x = "Covent Garden";`
		`String y = x.substring(0,6)`
		returns "Covent"

A sub-string from the right ...		

`x = "Covent Garden"`
`Right(x, 6)`
Returns "Garden"
	`x = "Covent Garden"`
	`y = x(-6,:)`
	Returns "Garden"
		`String x = "Covent Garden";`
		`String y = x.substring`
		`(7,x.length());`

A sub-string from anywhere within the string...		

`x = "Covent Garden"`
`y = Mid(x, 8, 4)`
Returns "Gard"
	`x = "Covent Garden"`
	`y = x(7, 4)`
	Returns "Gard"
		`String x = "Covent Garden";`
		`String y = x.substring(7, 11)`
		returns "Gard"

The length of a string		

`x = "Covent Garden"`
`l = Len(x)`
Returns 13
	`x = "Covent Garden"`
	`l = len(x)`
	Returns 13
		`String x = "Covent Garden";`
		`int y = x.length();`

Changing the string to 'all upper case'		

`x = "Covent Garden"`
`x.ToUpper`
returns "COVENT GARDEN"
	`x = "Covert Garden"`
	`x.upper()`
	Returns "COVENT GARDEN"
		`x = "Covent Garden"`
		`x.toUpperCase()`
		Returns "COVENT GARDEN"

Changing the string to 'all lowercase'		

`x = "Covent Garden"`
`x.ToLower`
Returns "covent garden"
	`x = "Covent Garden"`
	`x.lower()`
	Returns "covent garden"
		`x = "Covent Garden"`
		`x.toLowerCase()`
		Returns "covent garden"

The character for a given ASCII value		
`Chr(68) returns "D"`	`chr(68) returns "D"`	`(char) 68 returns "D"`
The ASCII value for a given character		
`Asc("4") returns 52`	`ord("4") returns 52`	`(int) "4" returns 52`
Changing the case of a character		

`UCase("g") returns "G"`
`LCase("Q") returns "q"`
	`Char1 = "g"`
	`Char1.upper() returns "G"`
	`Char2 = "Z"`
	`Char2.lower() returns "z"`	

Concatenate strings		
`String1 & String2`	`String1 + String2`	`string1 + string2`

Table 21.03 Language built-in functions for strings/characters.

String manipulation in Python ('Slicing')
Built-in functions for numbers

Visual Basic	Python	Java
Changing a string to a number		

`x = "121.73"`
`CInt(x)` returns 121
	`x = "85.78"`
	`y = int(x)`
	returns 85
		`x = "4.81"`
		`integer.valueOf(x)`
		returns 4

Integer part only of a number		

`x = 12.87`
`Math.Truncate(x)`
returns 12
	`X = 12.87`
	`x = int(x)`
	returns 12
		`x = "12.87"`
		`int(x)` returns 12

Table 21.04 Languages built-in functions for numbers.

> **TIP**
> The first four examples for Python code in Table **21.03** use the technique called 'slicing'. This means isolating a sub-string from a string.

21.06 Selection

In Chapter 11 Section 11.02 we studied the pseudocode for selection, using an IF statement and using a CASE structure.

> **TIP**
> If you are creating the program code with an IDE, the software will carry out the appropriate indentation for you.

IF – THEN structure

Note that the code uses the same scenario for which the pseudocode was developed in Chapter 11.

Visual Basic	`If Mark >= 40 Then`
	    `Console.WriteLine("PASS")`
	`End If`	

Python	`Mark = int(input('Enter the mark: '))`
	`if Mark >= 40:`
	    `print("PASS")`
		– Indentation is all important with Python.
		– There is no 'end if'
		– The colon replaces the 'then'
		– The indented statement belongs with the 'if'

Java	`if (mark >= 40)`
	    `{`
	    `System.out.println ("PASS") ;`
	    `}`
		– The condition is contained inside brackets
		– The action statements are in a 'braces sandwich'
		– The positioning of the braces is a convention you need to adopt and then stick to.

IF – THEN – ELSE structure

Use when there are two possible actions for the condition.

Note that the code uses the same scenario for which the pseudocode was developed in Chapter 11.

| Visual Basic | ```
If Mark >= 40 Then
    Console.WriteLine("PASS")
Else
    Console.WriteLine("FAIL")
End If
``` | |
| Python | ```
if Mark >= 40:
    print("PASS")
else:
    print("FAIL")
``` | – Note again the indentation must be used. |
| Java | ```java
import java.util.Scanner ;
public class JavaTestBed
{
public static void main(String[] args)
    {
    Scanner obj = new Scanner(System.in) ;
    System.out.println("Enter the mark:") ;
    int mark = obj.nextInt() ;
    if (mark >= 40)
    {
        System.out.println("PASS") ;
    }
    else
    {
        System.out.println("FAIL") ;
    }
    }
}
``` | |

Nested IFs structure

This is used when there are many possible actions following the condition. Note that the code is for the same scenario for which the pseudocode was developed in Chapter 11.
```

| Visual Basic | ```
If Mark < 40 Then
    Console.WriteLine("FAIL")
ElseIf Mark >= 40 And Mark < 75 Then
    Console.WriteLine("MERIT")
Else
    Console.WriteLine("DISTINCTION")
End If
``` | Indentation <u>must</u> be used |
| Python | ```
Mark = int(input('Enter the mark: '))
if Mark < 40:
    print('FAIL')
elif Mark >= 40 and Mark < 75:
    print('MERIT')
else:
    print('DISTINCTION')
``` | – Note again, indentation <u>must</u> be used.<br>– Elif reads as 'Else if' |
| Java | ```
    System.out.println("Enter the mark:") ;
    int mark = obj.nextInt() ;
    if (mark < 40)
        {
        System.out.println ("FAIL") ;
        }
    else if (mark < 75)

/* This could have been
  "else if (mark >= 40 && mark < 75)"
  but "mark >= 40"
  has already been catered for */
        {
        System.out.println("MERIT") ;
        }
    else
    /* We fall through to here if
      mark >= 75 */
        {
        System.out.println("DISTINCTION") ;
        }
``` | |
```

Case structure

This is used when there are many possible actions for the condition. Note that the code below is for the same scenario for which the pseudocode was developed in Chapter 11.

| Visual Basic | ```
Select Case Mark
    Case < 40
        Console.WriteLine("FAIL")
    Case 40 to 49
        Console.WriteLine("Grade E")
    Case 50 To 59
        Console.WriteLine("Grade D")
    Case 60 To 69
        Console.WriteLine("Grade C")
    Case 70 To 79
        Console.WriteLine("Grade B")
    Case >= 80
        Console.WriteLine("Grade A")
End Select
``` | |
|---|---|---|
| Python | A 'case structure' is not available in Python.
Use nested Ifs instead. | |
| Java | ```
Scanner input = new Scanner(System.in);
System.out.print("Enter the mark: ");
int mark = input.nextInt();
if (mark<40)
    {
    System.out.println("FAIL");
    }
if (mark>=40 && mark<=50)
    {
    System.out.println("Grade E");
    }
if (mark>=50 && mark<=60)
    {
    System.out.println("Grade D");
    }
//     etc....
    }
}
``` | Note:<br>• && is used for the 'and' operator in Java<br>• The condition after the if must be enclosed using brackets |

The 'switch' statement in Java

This behaves like a case structure in Visual Basic. However it will not cater for conditional expressions. The following example illustrates the syntax.

```java
public static void main(String[] args)
    {
Scanner input = new Scanner(System.in);
System.out.print("Enter the test score: ");
int testScore = input.nextInt();
switch (testScore)
    {
case 0: case 1: case 2: case 3: case 4: case 5:
System.out.println("Please do the test again");
break;
case 6: case 7: case 8: case 9: case 10:
System.out.println("Please study your wrong answers");
break;
case 11: case 12: case 13: case 14: case 15:
System.out.println("Well done - take the next test when you are ready");
break;
    }
```

21.07 Iteration

In Chapter 11 Section 11.02 we studied the pseudocode for three different ways to create a loop.

Count-controlled loop

Input seven marks.

| Visual Basic | ```Dim Index As Integer
Dim Mark As Integer
For Index = 0 To 6
    Console.write("Enter mark " & Index+1 & ": ")
    Mark = console.readline
Next Index``` | <ul><li>Index acts as the 'loop counter'</li><li>The loop counter is used in the prompt for the user</li><li>The marks are not retained</li><li>Hence the need to store the marks in an <u>array</u></li></ul> |
|---|---|---|

Note that start value 0 with end value 6 does 7 iterations.

The incremental step can be changed as follows:

To count backwards: `For Index = 6 To 0 Step -1`

To increment in steps other than 1: `For Index = 0 To 6 Step 2`

Python	```
	`for Index in range (5):`
	`    # the Index value starts at 0 and ends at 4`
	`    Mark = int(input('Enter the mark: '+`
	`                     str(Index+1) + ": "))`

Note that the single parameter 5 above sets the first loop counter value of 0 and the final iteration has value 4 (not 5).

Range(0, 1, 5) produces the same result.

The second parameter is the 'increment step'.

Java	Code	Notes:
	`for (int counter = 1; counter < 7; counter++)`	• This loop does six iterations
	`{`	• The first parameter initialises the loop counter
	`    System.out.print("Enter the mark: ");`	• The second parameter is the stopping condition
	`    int mark = input.nextInt();`	• the third parameter is the loop increment; ++ indicates steps of +1
	`    System.out.println(counter);`	
	`    System.out.println(mark);`	
	`}`	

Pre-condition loop

Since the condition is at the start of the loop, it is possible, if the condition is initially true, that the loop statements are never executed.

(same task …) Input six marks.

Visual Basic	Code	Notes
	`Dim Index As Integer`	• The pseudocode syntax was
	`Dim Mark As Integer`	`WHILE - ENDWHILE`
	`Index = 0`	• The Visual Basic keywords are
	`Do While Index < 7`	`Do While - Loop`
	`    Console.Write("Enter mark " & Index + 1 & ": ")`	
	`    Mark = Console.ReadLine`	
	`    Index = Index + 1`	
	`Loop`	

Python	Code	Notes
	`# Index is Integer`	Indenting must be used to mark the start and end of the statements inside the loop.
	`# Mark is Integer`	
	`Index = 0`	
	`while Index < 7:`	
	`    Mark = int(input('Enter the mark: '+ str(Index+1) + ": "))`	
	`    Index = Index + 1`	

Java	```	

	int counter = 1;
	while (counter < 7)
	{
	    System.out.print("Enter the mark: ");
	    int mark = input.nextInt();
	    System.out.println(counter);
	    System.out.println(mark);
	    ++counter;
	} // effectively the 'end while' line
		• The stopping condition is at the start of the loop
		• There is no matching 'end while' statement for the 'while'
		• The braces indicate where the loop begins and ends

Post-condition loop

Since the condition is at the end of the loop, the loop statements will be executed at least once.

(same task …) Input seven marks.

Visual Basic	Dim Index As Integer
	Dim Mark As Integer
	Index = 0
	Do
	    Console.Write("Enter mark " & Index + 1 & ": ")
	    Mark = Console.ReadLine
	    Index = Index + 1
	Loop Until Index = 7
		• the pseudocode syntax was
		  REPEAT - UNTIL
		• The Visual Basic keywords are
		  Do - Loop Until

Python	Post-condition loops are not available in Python. They can always be emulated using a pre-condition loop.	

Java	int counter = 1;
	do
	    {
	    System.out.print("Enter the mark: ");
	    int mark = input.nextInt();
	    System.out.println(counter);
	    System.out.println(mark);
	    ++counter;
	    }
	while (counter < 7);
		• The Scanner object for keyboard input has variable name input
		• Variations for data input are:
		  • For a string - console.nextLine
		  • For an integer – console.nextInt
		• with the condition test at the end of the loop, there will be at least one iteration

21.08 Arrays

Arrays were discussed in Chapter 10. We studied a one-dimensional (1D) array and a two-dimensional (2D) array.

Visual Basic and Java support arrays.

The array subscripts start (lower bound) at 0.

All items in the array must be of the same data type.

Python does not have arrays. it has a data structure called a 'list'.

The list subscripts start at 0.

A list has an identifier.

A list is an ordered sequence of items.

Items do not have to be of the same data type.

The code below uses the 'sales' scenario we studied in pseudocode in Chapter 10.

> ### Worked example 21.01
>
> This code stores the seven salesperson names.
>
> ### Using a 1D array
>
> | Visual Basic | |
> |---|---|
> | | ```
> Dim Person(6) As String
> Dim Index As Integer
> For Index = 0 To 6
>     Console.Write("Person: ")
>     Person(Index) = Console.ReadLine
> Next
> Console.WriteLine("7 names now stored in array")
> ``` |
> | Python | ```
> DummyList = []
> Person = ["P-One", "P-Two", "P-Three", "P-Four", "P-Five", "P-Six"]
> Person.append ("P-Seven")
> print("Two lists created")
> print("1" + Person[0])
> print("2" + Person[1])
> # etc
> ``` |
>
> Note the syntax used to create an empty list: `DummyList`
>
> For a list with six names, the first name is stored with list subscript 0 and the list's append method is used to add a new seventh name.

(Continued)

| Java | ```
String[] person;
person = new String[8];
person[1] = "P-One"; person[2] = "P-Two";
person[3] = "P-Three"; person[4] ="P-Four";
person[5] = "P-Five"; person[6] ="P-Six";
person[7] = "P-Seven" ;
for (int counter=1; counter<8; counter++)
{
    System.out.println(counter);
    System.out.println(person[counter]);
}
``` |
|---|---|

Note that two statements can be written on the same line.

The first two statements declare the data type and size of the array. Java starts with array index = 0 (which has not been used).

Alternatively, values can be assigned when the array is initialised with the statement;

```
String[] person = {"P-One", "P-Two", etc... }
```

Worked example 21.02

Store the salesperson name and the figure for the total sales made in the first quarter of the year.

Data is often organised into two or more separate 1D arrays (or in Python, two separate lists).

The data design will be a 1D array/list storing the salesperson names, and a second array/list storing the seven quarter 1 sales figures.

The following code to input the data illustrates this data design.

| Visual Basic | ```
Dim Person(6) As String
Dim Quarter1Sales(6) As Integer
Dim Index As Integer

For Index = 1 To 6
    Console.Write("Salesperson name: ")
    Person(Index) = Console.ReadLine
    Console.Write("Quarter 1 sales: ")
    Quarter1Sales(Index) = Console.ReadLine
Next
``` |
|---|---|

(Continued)

| Python | ```
Person = ["", "P-One", "P-Two", "P-Three", "P-Four", "P-Five", "P-Six"]
Quarter1Sales = [0, 11, 22, 33, 44, 55, 66]
print("Name and sales figures lists created")
print
# search the list for a person
PersonNumber = input("Which salesperson(1 to ) ? ") - 1
Index = int(PersonNumber)

print(Person[Index])
print(Quarter1Sales[Index])
``` |
|---|---|

Note the 'dummy' data item at the start of each list. This makes the real data start with index value 1.

Two separate lists are created. The user keys in the index position. The data from each list is output for this index position.

| Java | ```
Scanner input = new Scanner(System.in);

String[] person; person = new String[8];
int quarter1Sales[]; quarter1Sales = new int[8];

person[1] = "P-One"; person[2] = "P-Two"; person[3] ="P-Three";
person[4] ="P-Four"; person[5] ="P-Five"; person[6] ="P-Six";
person[7] = "P-Seven" ;
quarter1Sales[1]=11; quarter1Sales[2]=22; quarter1Sales[3]=33;
quarter1Sales[4]=44; quarter1Sales[5]=55;quarter1Sales[6]=66;
quarter1Sales[7]=77;

System.out.print("Enter person number: ");
int personNumber = input.nextInt();
System.out.println(quarter1Sales[personNumber]);
``` |
|---|---|

Using a 2D array

Visual Basic and Java both support two-dimensional arrays.

Python does not have arrays. The equivalent structure to a two-dimensional array is a **'list of lists'**.

Worked example 21.03

Store and display the sales figures for each person for each quarter of the year.

Data design is 1D array for the names: size 6 (as above) with data type String. A 2D array for the sales figures with data type Integer and with 6 rows (for each salesperson) and 4 columns (for each quarter).

Visual Basic	

```
Dim PersonNo As Integer
Dim QuarterNo As Integer

PopulateArray()

For PersonNo = 1 To 6
    Console.WriteLine("Salesperson name: " &
    Person(PersonNo))
    For QuarterNo = 1 To 4
        If QuarterNo = 4 Then
            Console.WriteLine(MonthlySales(PersonNo,
            QuarterNo))
        Else
            Console.Write(MonthlySales(PersonNo, QuarterNo)
            & " ")
        End If
    Next QuarterNo

Next PersonNo
Sub PopulateArray()
    Person(1) = "P-One" : Person(2) = "P-Two" : Person(3) =
"P-Three"
    ' etc. - names of the other salespersons

    MonthlySales(1, 1) = 11 : MonthlySales(1, 2) = 12
    MonthlySales(1, 3) = 13 : MonthlySales(1, 4) = 14
    ' etc. - data for the other salespersons and quarters
        End Sub
```

Note that the basic program design has **'nested loops'**. The outer loop iterates for each salesperson and the inner loop iterates for each quarter.

The use of the colon allows multiple statements on one line.

This code reads and displays the array contents.

The data values are 'hard coded' into the arrays in procedure `PopulateArray`. This avoids having to input the data to test the program code.

Note the choice of test data values used. They help to check the working of the code. For example, the first person has been given name 'Person-1'.

(Continued)

Python	
| | ```python
AllSales = [ [],\
[0,11,12,13,14],\
[0, 21,22,23,24],\
[0, 31,32,33,34],\
[0, 41,42,43,44],\
[0, 51,52,53,54],\
[0, 61,62,63,64] ]
# empty list item makes index start at  1
# zero values makes index for inner lists start at 1
# so, person 1 has index 1
PersonNo = int(input("Person number? : "))
QuarterNo = int(input("Quarter? : "))

print("This is the required data")
print(AllSales[PersonNo][QuarterNo])
# final statement display all the data in list AllSales
``` |

Note the use of the 'backslash (\) character to split the text for a single program statement onto a new line when setting up the list contents.

Java	
| | ```java
Scanner console = new Scanner(System.in);
// four quarterly sales figures for six salespersons
// array subscript zero has dummy values assigned
int [][] allSales =    {
    {0, 0, 0, 0, 0},
    {0, 11, 12, 13, 14},
    {0, 21, 22, 23, 24},
    {0, 31, 32, 33, 34},
    {0, 41, 42, 43, 44},
    {0, 51, 52, 53, 54},
    {0, 61, 62, 63, 64}
                       };
System.out.print("Enter person number: ");
int personNo = input.nextInt();
System.out.print("Enter quarter number: ");
int quarterNo = console.nextInt();
System.out.println(allSales[personNo][quarterNo]);
``` |

Note the single statement to declare and assign values to the 2D array and the use of the dummy person data and dummy (quarter zero) data.

21.09 Functions

Functions fall into two types: built-in functions and user-defined functions. You are already familiar with some of the built-in functions shown in Tables **21.03** and **21.04** earlier in the chapter. Remember that, for a user-defined function, you will decide on the identifier name, so ensure that it is meaningful, just as you would for variables and constants.

This is the example used in Chapter 11.

Worked example 21.4

A function is written to add two numbers and return the answer.

| Visual Basic | ```
Sub Main()
Dim No1, No2, Answer As Integer
Console.Write("First number ? ") : No1 = Console.ReadLine()
Console.Write("Second number ? ") : No2 = Console.ReadLine()
Answer = AddTwoNumbers(No1, No2)
Console.WriteLine("Answer is : " & Answer)
End Sub
Function AddTwoNumbers(Number1 As Integer, Number2 As Integer) As Integer
    Dim FnAnswer As Integer
    FnAnswer = Number1 + Number2
    Return FnAnswer
End Function
``` |
|---|---|

The AddTwoNumbers function has two integer arguments. 'As Integer' in the function header indicates the function will return an integer.

| Python | ```
def AddTwoNumbers(Number1, Number2):
    FnAnswer = Number1 + Number2
    return FnAnswer
No1 = int(input("First number? "))
No2 = int(input("Second number? "))
Answer = AddTwoNumbers(No1, No2)
print("Answer is : " + str(Answer))
``` |
|---|---|

In Python a function is defined *before* it is called.

(Continued)

| Java | ```java
public static int addTwoNumbers(int number1, intnumber2)
    {
    int answer = number1 + number2;
    return answer;
    }
public static void main(String[] args)
{
Scanner input = new Scanner(System.in);
System.out.print("First number: ");
int no1 = input.nextInt();
System.out.print("Second  number: ");
int no2 = input.nextInt();
int finalAnswer= addTwoNumbers(no1, no2);
System.out.println(finalAnswer);
}
``` |

Worked example 21.05

Design a function to calculate how many words are in a string of text input by the user.

| Visual Basic | ```vb
Sub Main()
    Dim MyString As String
    Dim WordCount As Integer
    Console.Write("Text string: ") : MyString = Console.ReadLine
    WordCount = CountWords(MyString)

    Console.WriteLine("Contains " + Str(WordCount))
    Console.ReadLine()
End Sub

Function CountWords(ThisString As String) As Integer
    Dim i As Integer
    Dim SpacesCount As Integer
    Dim WordCount As Integer
    SpacesCount = 0
    For i = 2 To Len(ThisString) - 1
        ' the first and last characters are ignored
        If Mid(ThisString, i, 1) = " " Then
            SpacesCount += 1
        End If
    Next
    WordCount = SpacesCount + 1
    Return WordCount
End Function
``` |

(Continued)

Note the function for the number of characters in a string: Len().

| Python | ```
    RESTART: C:/_____CUP_New/

Text string: Tale of Two Cities
Contains 4
>>>

def CountWords(ThisString):
    # i is Integer
    # SpacesCount is Integer
    # WordCount is Integer
    SpacesCount = 0

    for i in range(2,len(MyString)):
        # the first and last characters are ignored
        if ThisString[i] == " ":
            SpacesCount += 1
            WordCount = SpacesCount + 1
    return WordCount

# Main program starts here
# MyString is String
# NoOfWords is Integer
MyString = input("Text string: ")
NoOfWords = CountWords(MyString)
print("Contains " + str(NoOfWords))
``` |
| Java | ```
public static int countWords(String thisString)
    {
    int spacesCount = 0;
    System.out.println(thisString);
    for (int I = 1; I < thisString.length(); i++)
        {
        // the first and last characters are ignored
        char nextChar = thisString.charAt(i);
        if (nextChar == ' ')
            {
            spacesCount ++;
            }
        }
    return spacesCount + 1;
    }
public static void main(String[] args)
{
Scanner input = new Scanner(System.in);
System.out.print("Text string : ");
String myString = input.nextLine();

int numberOfWords = countWords(myString);
System.out.println("Number of words was ..." + numberOfWords);
}
``` |

Note that delimiters for a char data type literal are single quotes.

21.10 Procedures

We introduced procedures in Chapter 11 Section 11.02. A procedure is a key component for producing a structured program.

Worked example 21.06

Display a program main menu.

Design: a procedure is used to display the menu text.

Visual Basic	
| | ```
Sub MainMenu
Do
    Call MenuText
    Choice = Console.ReadLine
    If Choice = 1 Then Call CreateFile()
    If Choice = 2 Then Call ReadFile()
Loop Until Choice = 3
End Sub

Sub MenuText
    Console.WriteLine("1. Create file")
    Console.WriteLine("2. Read file")
    Console.WriteLine("3. End")
End sub
``` |

Note that the text to display the menu is coded as procedure `MenuText`.

The code to create the file is coded as procedure `CreateFile` (code not shown).

The code to read the file contents is procedure `ReadFile` (code not shown).

Python	
| | ```
def MenuText():
    print("1. Create file")
    print("2. Read file")
    print("3. End")

def CreateFile():
    print ("call to stub Printfile procedure")

def ReadFile():
    print ("call to stub Readfile procedure")

# Main program starts here ...
Choice = 0
while Choice != 3:
    MenuText
    Choice = int(input("Choice: "))
    if Choice == 1:
        CreateFile()
    if Choice == 2:
        ReadFile()
``` |

(Continued)

Java

```java
public static void createFile()
    {
    System.out.print("Call to stub create file procedure");
    }
public static void readFile()
    {
System.out.print("Call to stub read file procedure");
    }
public static void menuText()
    {
    System.out.println("1. Create file");
    System.out.println("2. Read file");
    System.out.println("3. End");
    }
public static void main(String[] args)
{
Scanner console = new Scanner(System.in);
int choice = 0;
while (choice != 3)
{
    menuText();
    choice = console.nextInt();
    if (choice == 1)
        {
        createFile();
        }
    if (choice == 2)
        {
        readFile();
        }
}
```
Note that != is used for 'not equal to' in Java.

When we are testing a program, we want to avoid the keying in of lots of data every time the program is run.

Design: Store the data in array `MyAnimal` inside procedure `PopulateArray`.

Execute the assignment statements with the call to `PopulateArray`.

(Continued)

| Visual Basic | ```
Dim MyAnimal(10) As String
Call PopulateArray
End Sub

Sub PopulateArray
    MyAnimal(1).Animal = "aardvark"
    MyAnimal(2).Animal = "bear"
    MyAnimal(3).Animal = "elephant"
    MyAnimal(4).Animal = "goat"
    MyAnimal(5).Animal = "zebra"
End sub
``` |

Note that the data is 'hard coded' into an array in procedure `PopulateArray`, assigned to the array with the call to `PopulateArray` and can then be used by the program. For example, more program code could write the data items to a file.

| Python | ```
def PopulateArray():
    MyAnimalList = [ "", "aardvark", "bear", "elephant", "goat", "zebra"]

#   Main program starts here ...
PopulateArray
print("List of animals created ...")
``` |
| Java | ```
public static void populateArray()
    {
    String [] myAnimal =
    {"aarvark", "Bear", "elephant", "goat", "zebra"};
    System.out.println("List of animals created");
    }
public static void main(String[] args)
{
populateArray();
}
``` |

Procedures: with parameter passing

Passing parameters by value

This is the example we studied in Chapter 11.
```

Worked example 21.07

Consider a dataset of 200 kitchen stock item prices. The prices are stored in a 1D array `KitchenPrice`. A program inputs the price of a new kitchen. The program displays the price after it has been increased by 15%. Since we do not want the program to permanently change the price, the price is 'passed by value' to a procedure.

Visual Basic

```vb
27      Sub Main()
28          Dim KitchenPriceString As String
29          Dim KitchenPrice As Single
30
31          ' code for passed by value
32          Console.Write("Kitchen price : ")
33          KitchenPriceString = Console.ReadLine()
34          KitchenPrice = Val(KitchenPriceString)
35
36          Console.WriteLine("Check for Current price " & Str(KitchenPrice))
37          Console.WriteLine()
38          Call IncreasePrice(KitchenPrice)
39          Console.WriteLine()
40          Console.WriteLine("Price in the main program is : " & Str(KitchenPrice))
41
42          Console.ReadLine()
43      End Sub
44
45      Sub IncreasePrice(ByVal ThisPrice As Single)
46          ThisPrice = ThisPrice * 1.15
47          Console.WriteLine("Price reported From inside the procedure (ByVal) is : " & Str(ThisPrice))
48          Console.WriteLine("Which demonstrates the price has NOT been permanently changed")
49      End Sub
```

Console output:
```
Kitchen price : 2000
Check for Current price  2000
Price reported From inside the procedure (ByVal) is :  2300
Which demonstrates the price has NOT been permanently changed
Price in the main program is :  2000
```

Python

```python
def IncreasePrice(ThisPrice):
    ThisPrice = ThisPrice * 1.15
    print("Price reported From inside the procedure (by value) is : " \
                                        + str(ThisPrice))
    print("Which demonstrates the price has NOT been permanently changed")

# main program starts here ...
# KitchenPriceString As String
# KitchenPrice As Single

# code for passed by value
KitchenPriceString = input("Kitchen price : ")
KitchenPrice = float(KitchenPriceString)
print("Check for Current price " + str(KitchenPrice))
print()
IncreasePrice(KitchenPrice)
print()
print("Price in the main program is : " + str(KitchenPrice))
```

Note that we have needed to use two methods: `Float()`, to convert a string to a real number and `Str()`, to convert a real number to a string.

(Continued)

Java

```java
package javatestbed;    ;
import java.util.Scanner;

public class JavaTestBed
{
    public static void increasePrice(double thisPrice)
    {
        thisPrice = thisPrice * 1.15;
        System.out.println("Price reported From inside the "
                + "procedure (ByRef) is : " + thisPrice);
    }

    public static void main(String[] args)
    {
    Scanner input = new Scanner(System.in);
    // code for passed by value
    System.out.print("Kitchen price : ");
    String kitchenPriceString = input.next();
    double kitchenPrice = Double.parseDouble(kitchenPriceString);

    System.out.println("Check for Current price " + kitchenPrice);
    System.out.println("");
    increasePrice(kitchenPrice);
    System.out.println("");
    System.out.println("Price in the main program is : " + kitchenPrice);
    System.out.println("Which demonstrates the price has "
                    + "NOT been permanently changed");
    }
}
```

```
run:
Kitchen price : 2000
Check for Current price 2000.0

Price reported From inside the procedure (ByRef) is : 2300.0

Price in the main program is : 2000.0
Which demonstrates the price has NOT been permanently changed
BUILD SUCCESSFUL (total time: 4 seconds)
```

Note that Java treats the parameter as a local variable, so the passing is effectively 'by value'.

Passing parameters by reference

Worked example 21.08

A program inputs the price of a new kitchen. The program will permanently increase the price by 15%.

To permanently change the price, the value is 'passed by reference' to a procedure.

Visual Basic

```vb
3       Sub Main()
4           Dim KitchenPriceString As String
5           Dim KitchenPrice As Single
6
7           ' code for passed by reference
8           Console.Write("Kitchen price : ")
9           KitchenPriceString = Console.ReadLine()
10          KitchenPrice = Val(KitchenPriceString)
11
12          Console.WriteLine("Check for Current price " & Str(KitchenPrice))
13          Console.WriteLine()
14          Call IncreasePrice(KitchenPrice)
15          Console.WriteLine()
16          Console.WriteLine("Price in the main program is : " & Str(KitchenPrice))
17          Console.WriteLine("Which demonstrates the price HAS been permanently changed")
18          Console.ReadLine()
19      End Sub
20
21      Sub IncreasePrice(ByRef ThisPrice As Single)
22          ThisPrice = ThisPrice * 1.15
23          Console.WriteLine("Price reported From inside the procedure (ByRef) is : " & Str(ThisPrice))
24      End Sub
```

Console output:
```
Kitchen price : 2000
Check for Current price  2000

Price reported From inside the procedure (ByRef) is :  2300

Price in the main program is :  2300
Which demonstrates the price HAS been permanently changed
```

Python

```python
def IncreasePrice(ThisPrice):
    ThisPrice = ThisPrice * 1.15
    print("Price reported From inside the procedure (by value) is : " \
                                                    + str(ThisPrice))
    return ThisPrice

# main program starts here ...
# KitchenPriceString As String
# KitchenPrice As Single

# code for passed by value
KitchenPriceString = input("Kitchen price : ")
KitchenPrice = float(KitchenPriceString)
print("Check for Current price " + str(KitchenPrice))
print()
KitchenPrice = IncreasePrice(KitchenPrice)
print()
print("Price in the main program is : " + str(KitchenPrice))
print("Which demonstrates the price HAS been permanently changed")
```

- Behaves as a function with a return value
- Value returned

Note that Python does not support a procedure that uses parameters passed by value. The procedure behaves as a function with the value passed to variable `KitchenPrice` on return to the main program.

(Continued)

```java
Java
 6    public static double increasePrice(double thisPrice)
 7    {
 8        thisPrice = thisPrice * 1.15;
 9        System.out.println("Price reported From inside the "
10                + "procedure is : " + thisPrice);
11        return thisPrice;
12    }
13
14    public static void main(String[] args)
15    {
16    Scanner input = new Scanner(System.in);
17    // code for passed by value
18    System.out.print("Kitchen price : ");
19    String kitchenPriceString = input.next();
20    double kitchenPrice = Double.parseDouble(kitchenPriceString);
21
22    System.out.println("Check for Current price " + kitchenPrice);
23    System.out.println("");
24    kitchenPrice = increasePrice(kitchenPrice);
25    System.out.println("");
26    System.out.println("Price in the main program is : " + kitchenPrice);
27    System.out.println("Which demonstrates the price HAS"
28                      + " been permanently changed");
29    }
30    }
```

```
run:
Kitchen price : 2000
Check for Current price 2000.0

Price reported From inside the procedure is : 2300.0

Price in the main program is : 2300.0
Which demonstrates the price HAS been permanently changed
BUILD SUCCESSFUL (total time: 4 seconds)
```

Exam-style questions

For some programming practice, we have used the four tasks that were studied at the end of Chapter 11. There you studied the pseudocode for each task. We will now write program code for each of the tasks.

1. A program will read an unknown number of ON/OFF values from array Values. Some of the values are "ON" and some are "OFF". There is a final value in the array of "X". [4]

   Count the number of ON values.

   Pseudocode for the problem is given on the next page:

```
        ONCount ← 0            // Variable stores the number
                                  of ON values
        Index ← 1              // loop counter
        REPEAT
            If Values[Index] = "ON"
                THEN
                    ONCount ← ONCount + 1
                    Index ← Index + 1
            ENDIF
        Until Index = -1
        OUTPUT "The number of True values is : ", ONCount
```

Write the program code for this problem. Use as test data nine ON/OFF values.

Candidates using Python should include one or more comment statements at the start of the code to show the data type for all variables used.

2 A user inputs an unknown number of words at the keyboard. Input ends when "END" is keyed. The program counts the number of words which started with letter 'P' (it could be a capital or lower case p).

Incomplete pseudocode for the problem is given below:

```
        PCount ← 0
        INPUT NextWord
        WHILE NextWord <> "END"
            FirstLetter = LEFT(NextWord, 1)
            IF ......................................................................
                THEN
                    PCount ← PCount + 1
            ENDIF
            INPUT NextWord
        ENDWHILE
        OUTPUT "The number of Ps was : ", PCount
```

a Write the one line of pseudocode that is incomplete.   [1]
b Write the program code.   [5]

Candidates using Python should include one or more comment statements at the start of the code to show the data type for all variables used.   [8]

> **TIP**
>
> You should be able to write code to address a range of scenarios:
>
> - Given the problem description and the pseudocode, the task is to write the code
> - Given the problem description and the pseudocode, but with some steps omitted, the task is to write the program code
> - Given the problem description, you are asked to write the code.
>
> There is an increasing level of difficulty for each of these three cases.

3 Three employees are sales staff. A program is to record the number of sales made by each employee over the first six months of the year.

Use the table given below for test data.

	1	2	3	4	5	6
1	0	0	0	3	4	0
2	1	12	12	6	7	8
3	2	4	5	1	2	3

Write program code to calculate and output the total number of sales made for the six employees taken together and the six sales totals for each of the salespersons.

4 A binary tree is to be created to store customer names. The data design is three 1D arrays.

    `NodeData[ ]`   Stores the customer names.

    `NodeLeft[ ]`   Stores the binary tree left pointers.

    `NodeRight[ ]`   Stores the binary tree right pointers.

The following data is used as test data:

Customer names join the tree in the order in which an order is received:
The order was:

HARRIS, ALI, PETERS, WILKES, PATEL, OZAWA, WANG

The names are added to the array in the order they are received.

a Draw the binary tree. [4]

b Now write the following program code: [3]

    A main menu with options:

    A   Create and populate the binary tree

    B   Search for a name

    C   End

    A procedure `CreateTree` showing the data contents for the three arrays. [5]

    A procedure `SearchTree` which is called from the menu. [6]

5 An array/list stores N data items. The data items are in order.

The pseudocode below describes the binary search algorithm with some omissions.

a Write the pseudocode for the omissions (A), (B) and (C).

    PROCEDURE BinarySearch

        INPUT ThisValue

        Found ← FALSE

        NotInList ← FALSE

        // flags whether the required value is not found

        Top ← N

        Bottom ← 1

> **TIP**
>
> You need to be able to write program code based on one of the data structures studied in Chapter 19. Question 4 uses a binary tree data structure.

```
REPEAT
    Middle ← Integer value of (Top + Bottom)/2 )
    IF ThisList[Middle] = ThisValue
        THEN
            Found ← TRUE
            OUTPUT "Value is FOUND"
        ELSE
            IF ...................... (A) ..................................... .
                THEN
                    NotInList = TRUE
                ELSE
                    IF ThisList[Middle] < ThisItem
                        THEN
                            // retain the top half of the list
                            Bottom ← Middle + 1
                        ELSE
                            // retain the bottom half of the list
                            .................. (B) ........................... .
                    ENDIF
            ENDIF
    ENDIF
UNTIL (Found = TRUE) OR (NotInList = TRUE)

IF ...................... (C) ............................ .
    THEN
        OUTPUT "Requested item was NOT FOUND"
ENDIF

ENDPROCEDURE
```

Use the following list as test data:

`ANT, BEE, CAT, DOG, EAGLE, GOAT, HORSE, PARROT, RAT, ZEBRA` [3]

b   Write program code to:

  Set up this test data in the array/list.

  Input an animal name and then search the array/list for this name.

  Output either: 'This name was found after X comparisons' or 'This name was not found'. [8]

Chapter 22

Further programming: object-oriented

Learning Objectives:

- Understand the terminology used for object-oriented design and programming
- In your chosen programming language:
  - define a class
  - define methods within the class including getter and setter methods
  - create an instance of an object
- Understand the concepts of inheritance, polymorphism and containment
- Produce a class diagram for a given problem
  - which includes inheritance and polymorphism
- In your chosen programming language:
  - implement inheritance, polymorphism and containment.

22.01 Object oriented: in practice

Object-oriented programming is referred to as OOP. Before developers write code, they must produce an 'object-oriented design'.

> **TIP**
>
> You do not need to know pseudocode for describing object-oriented design.

22.02 The building blocks of OOP

A class

A **class** is the definition of what an **object** will look like, i.e. the object specification. A class is given an identifier name, for example, `Customer`.

The class acts as the template from which an instance of an object is created.

The class defines the **properties** of the object and the methods used to implement the object's behaviour.

Properties

Think of these as being like the attributes in database modelling.

A `CAR` class could have properties for the make, model, colour, number of seats and other attributes.

> **Progress check A**
>
> A car is purchased by a customer. State which three properties would be recorded about the sale (in addition to the car data).

The member variables are private to the class and hence will be effectively hidden from the programmer.

Methods

Think of a **method** as something we can <u>do</u> with an object.

When we model real-world objects such as a 'product' or 'customer' object, methods will be needed for every action required on that object.

Getter and setter methods

In OOP code, each property of the class must have a 'setter method' and a 'getter' method.

The getter method would include a way to 'set' or assign a value to a particular car `objectmethod` assigns a particular value to a car object.

The setter method would include a method to access and 'get' the value for the make of a particular car `objectmethod` accesses and uses the object's `VehicleMake` value. An example of this is when the object's property value is to be output.

| Visual Basic | ```
Public Class VEHICLE
    Private mMake As String

    Property Make As String
        Get
            Make = mMake
        End Get

        Set(ThisMake As String)
            mMake = ThisMake
        End Set
    End Property
End Class
``` |
|---|---|

Note that the property which is a 'member' of the class is **mMake**.

The lower case 'm' prefix is a convention used to show 'member' of the class. The Make set method assign a value from the main program to **mMake**..

The Make get method uses the existing **mMake** value in some program, for example, in an output statement.in an output statement.

| Python code | ```
class VEHICLE:
    def __init__ (self, Make, RegistrationID):
        self.Make = Make
        self.RegistrationID = RegistrationID
``` |
|---|---|

| Java code | ```java
class VEHICLE
{
    private String mRegistration;
    private String mMake;

    // constructor
    public VEHICLE(String m, String r)
    {   mRegistration = r;
        mMake = m;
    }
    public void setRegistration(String p)
        { mRegistration = p; }

    public String getRegistration()
        { return (mRegistration); }

    public void setMake(String m)
        { mMake = m; }

    public String getMake()
        { return (mMake); }

    public void displayVehicleData(VEHICLE v)
        { System.out.println("Make is : " + v.getMake());
          System.out.println("with registration : " + v.getRegistration());
        }
}
``` |
|---|---|

- The VEHICLE class has two properties.
- Each property has a 'getter' and a 'setter' method.
- For the setter method the data value is passed as a parameter.

Other methods

Objects will 'do' things, such as output to the screen the current properties of an object.

We shall create a method `DisplayData` to show the current make and registration ID of a car object.

| Visual Basic | ```vb
Sub DisplayData()
    Console.WriteLine("Make is: " & Make & "-Registration : " & _
                                                    RegistrationID)
End Sub
``` |
|---|---|

Note that `RegistrationID` has been added to the `VEHICLE` class.

A method is coded as a procedure.

The method name is `DisplayData`.

| Python code | ```python
def dDisplayData(self):
    print ("Make is : ", self.Make, " Registration: ",
                                        self.RegistrationID)
``` |
|---|---|

| Java code | ```java
public void displayVehicleData(VEHICLE v)
    { System.out.println("Make is : " + v.getMake());
      System.out.println("with registration : " + v.getRegistration());
    }
``` |
|---|---|

- The VEHICLE class has a method for outputting the property values.

Note that the 'getter methods are used for output.

The 'dot notation' used: `<object identifier>.<method>`

> **Progress check B**
>
> Explain the difference between a class and an object.

22.03 Create an object

The terminology for this is to "create an instance of the VEHICLE class".

Visual Basic	
| | ```vb
Sub Main()
    Dim MyVehicle As VEHICLE

    ' create the object
    MyVehicle = New VEHICLE

    ' assign values for the object properties
    MyVehicle.Make = "Nissan"
    MyVehicle.RegistrationID = "WJ012HG"

    ' use the methods of the VEHICLE class
    MyVehicle.DisplayData()
    Console.ReadLine()
End Sub
``` |

Note that the identifier used is `MyVehicle` for the instance of the `VEHICLE` class.

Lines 10 and 11 will use the Get method for property `Make` and property `RegistrationID`.

Line 14 uses the `DisplayData` method.

Note the 'dot notation' used throughout for properties and methods.

Look back to the Sub `DisplayData` method code. The `Console.Writeline` statement uses the two property set methods for `Make` and `RegistrationID`.

Python code	
| | ```python
# create the new object with the properties shown
MyVehicle = VEHICLE("Nissan", "WJ012HG")

# use the method of the VEHICLE class
# to display the data
MyVehicle.DisplayData()

Alternatively:

MyCar = VEHICLE
MyCar.Make = "Nissan"
MyCar.RegistrationID = "AB012TR"

# use the method of the CAR class
# to display the data
MyCar.DisplayData(MyCar)
``` |

Java code | Java-21
```
64  public static void main(String[] args)
65  {
66      // seeing how the class definition is used ...
67      // create a vehicle object
68          VEHICLE thisVehicle = new VEHICLE("Nissan", "WJ012HG");
69          thisVehicle.displayVehicleData(thisVehicle);
```

22.04 Inheritance

Worked example 22.01

A garage stores data for all new vehicles (VEHICLE) it sells. Vehicles are classified as either a car (CAR) or commercial (COMMERCIAL) vehicle. A commercial vehicle is either a van (VAN) or a lorry (LORRY).

An object-oriented design gives:

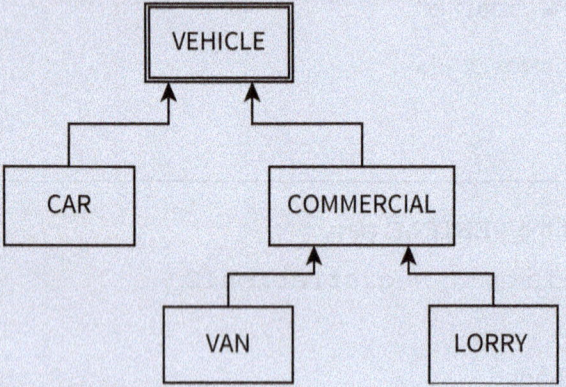

Figure 22.01 Inheritance diagram.

> **TIP**
>
> In an inheritance diagram, the branch arrows always point to the parent class.

Terminology:

VEHICLE is called the superclass.

COMMERCIAL is the parent class of VAN and LORRY.

CAR is a child class or sub-class of VEHICLE.

VAN and LORRY are sub-classes of COMMERCIAL.

Any sub-class can inherit the properties and methods of its parent class.

Inheritance can be clarified by labelling each branch of the inheritance diagram with the term 'is a', for example, a car 'is a' vehicle, a van 'is a' commercial vehicle and others.

Progress check C

A campsite has numbered pitches. The pitches are of two types, for tents or for caravans.

Draw the inheritance diagram for the object-oriented design.

> ## Progress check D
> A library is available for borrowing a large number of resources, which include books, CDs and DVDs. Some books are for reference only and cannot be borrowed. The library has recently started to stock a number of audio-books, which can be borrowed.
>
> Draw the inheritance diagram for the object-oriented class design.

22.05 Class diagram

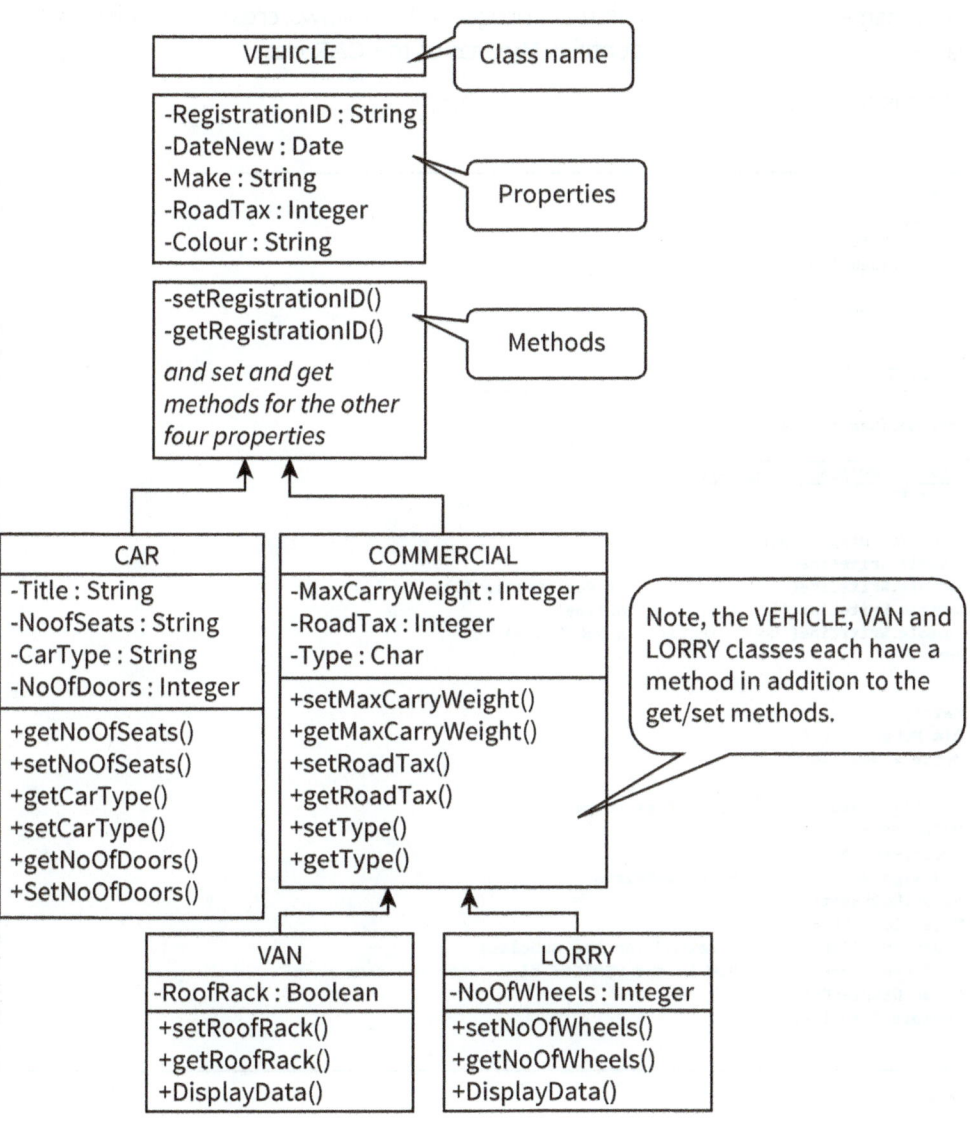

Figure 22.02 Class diagram.

The class diagram shows the object-oriented design.

- The class diagram shows the properties and methods for each object
- It has several instances of inheritance
- In practice this means that, for example, the CAR class will have properties and methods of its own, but also inherits the properties and methods from the VEHICLE parent class
- Different objects can have a method with the same name:
  - There is a method in the VEHICLE superclass DisplayData
  - There is a method with the same name DisplayData in several classes
  - This is called **polymorphism.** This is discussed later.

> ### Progress check E
> Study the Figure **22.01** class diagram to confirm these setter/getter methods for each property.

Child classes and inheritance
The CAR sub-class code below has been coded with properties for the car type and number of seats properties.

An instance of an object
The main program that follows, creates an object with identifier MyCar of the CAR class.

Visual Basic
```
1  Public Class CAR
2      Inherits VEHICLE
3      Private mCarType As String
4      Private mNoOfSeats As Integer
5
6      Property CarType As String
7          Get ...
10         Set(ThisCarType As String) ...
13     End Property
14
15     Property NoOfSeats As Integer
16         Get ...
19         Set(ThisNoOfSeats As Integer) ...
22     End Property
23
24     Overrides Sub DisplayData()
25         Console.WriteLine("Make: " & Make)
26         Console.WriteLine("Registration: " & RegistrationID)
27         Console.WriteLine("Car type: " & CarType)
28         Console.WriteLine("No of seats: " & NoOfSeats)
29     End Sub
30 End Class

3  Sub Main()
4      Dim MyCar As CAR
5      MyCar = New CAR
6
7      ' assign values for parent class properties
8      MyCar.Make = "Nissan"
9      MyCar.RegistrationID = "AB123TR"
10     ' assign values for the CAR subclass
11     MyCar.NoOfSeats = 6
12     MyCar.CarType = "Estate"
13     ' use the DisplayData() method for the subclass
14     ' it overrides the method in the VEHICLE class with the same name
15     MyCar.DisplayData()
16     Console.ReadLine()
17 End Sub
```

Note that this is the CAR class code.

Line 2 - The CAR class will inherit from the VEHICLE parent class.

CAR has two properties of its own and inherits the properties of VEHICLE.

The main program (lines 4 and 5) shows the creation of a new CAR object.

Python code

```python
class VEHICLE:
    def __init__(self, Make, RegistrationID):
        self.Make = Make
        self.RegistrationID = RegistrationID

    def DisplayVehicleData(self):
        print("Make is : ", self.Make, " Registration: ", self.RegistrationID)

class CAR(VEHICLE):
    def __init__(self, CarType, NoOfSeats):
        self.CarType = CarType
        self.NoOfSeats = NoOfSeats

    def DisplayCarData(self):
        self.DisplayVehicleData()
        print("Car type : ", self.CarType, " Number of seats: ", str(self.NoOfSeats))

# Main program starts here ...
MyCar = CAR("Estate", 6)
MyCar.Make = "Nissan"
MyCar.RegistrationID = "AB012TR"
print ("Car object created ...")
MyCar.DisplayCarData()
```

```
RESTART: C:_____CUP_New\TEXT- Ver
itence.py
Car object created ...
Car type : Estate  Number of seats:  6
Make is :  Nissan  Registration: AB012TR
>>>
```

Note that the `DisplayCarData` method in the `CAR` class itself calls the `DisplayVehicleData` method from the parent class

Java code

```java
class VEHICLE
{
    private String mRegistration;
    private String mMake;

    // constructor
    public VEHICLE(String m, String r)
    {
        mRegistration = r;
        mMake = m;
    }
    // getter and setter methods as before ..
}

class CAR extends VEHICLE
{
    private String mCarType;
    private int mNoOfSeats;
    // constructor
    public CAR(String r, String m)
    {
        super(r, m);
        mCarType = "Saloon";
        mNoOfSeats = 4;
    }
    public String getCarType()
    { return (mCarType); }

    public void setCarType(String t)
    { mCarType = t; }

    public int getNoOfSeats()
    { return (mNoOfSeats); }

    public void setNoOfSeats(int n)
    { mNoOfSeats = n; }

    public void displayCarData(CAR c)
    {
        c.displayVehicleData(c);
        System.out.println("Car type : " + c.getCarType() );
        System.out.println("Number of seats : " + c.getNoOfSeats() );
    }
}
public class JavaTestBed
{
    public static void main(String[] args)
    {
        // seeing how the class definition is used ...
        // create a car object
        CAR thisCar = new CAR("Nissan", "WJ012HG");
        thisCar.setCarType("Estate");
        thisCar.setNoOfSeats(7);
        thisCar.displayCarData(thisCar);
        System.out.println("New car object created");
    }
}
```

- VEHICLE is the superclass.
- The 'super' keyword inherits the two properties from the superclass **VEHICLE**.
- Two additional properties.
- New method – displays the properties not displayed by the superclass method.
- The type and number of seats parameter values overwrite the values held in the constructor.

```
Output - JavaTestBed (run)
run:
Make is : Nissan
with registration : WJ012HG
Car type : Estate
Number of seats : 7
New car object created
BUILD SUCCESSFUL (total time: 0 seconds)
```

Note that the CAR class inherits from the VEHICLE class.

CAR has two new properties, the car type and number of seats.

CAR has a new method `displayCarData` to display the new properties.

If we use the VEHICLE class `DisplayData` method, we only show two of the properties (Make and RegistrationID). We need to add a new DisplayData method for the CAR class so that we can show the others (`CarType` and `NoOfSeats`).

22.06 Polymorphism

Polymorphism is the technique by which methods in the class hierarchy with the same name produce a different behaviour. The `DisplayData` method appears in both the VEHICLE, CAR and other classes.

Visual Basic	In the CAR class:

```vb
Overrides Sub DisplayData()
    Console.WriteLine("Make is: " & Make & " - Registration : " & RegistrationID)
    Console.WriteLine("Car type is: " & CarType & " - No of seats : " & NoOfSeats)
End Sub
```

In the VEHICLE class:

```vb
Overridable Sub DisplayData()
    Console.WriteLine("Make is: " & Make & " - Registration : " & RegistrationID)
End Sub
```

Note that the CAR class method will 'override' a method from the parent class with the same name.

The VEHICLE class method has been changed to state it is 'overridable'.

Python code	

```
RESTART: C:/_____CUP_New/TEXT- Ver
itence 3.py
Car object created ...
Make is : Nissan   Registration: AB012TR
Car type : Estate  Number of seats: 6
>>>
```

```python
class VEHICLE:
    def __init__ (self, Make, RegistrationID):
        self.Make = Make
        self.RegistrationID = RegistrationID

    def DisplayData(self):
        print("Make is : ", self.Make, " Registration: ", self.RegistrationID)

class CAR(VEHICLE):
    def __init__ (self, CarType, NoOfSeats):
        self.CarType = CarType
        self.NoOfSeats = NoOfSeats

    def DisplayData(self):
        print("Make is : ", self.Make, " Registration: ", self.RegistrationID)
        print("Car type : ", self.CarType,  " Number of seats: ", str(self.NoOfSeats))

# Main program starts here ...
MyCar = CAR("Estate", 6)
MyCar.Make = "Nissan"
MyCar.RegistrationID = "AB012TR"
print ("Car object created ...")
MyCar.DisplayData()
```

Note that the names of the output method in each class have been changed. Both the CAR and VEHICLE classes now have a method called `DisplayData`.

Running the code confirms the method used is the one from the child CAR class. The method with the same name in the parent class VEHICLE is overridden.

Java code

In the VEHICLE class:

```java
        public void displayData()
28      { System.out.println("Make is : " + getMake());
29        System.out.println("with registration : " + getRegistration());
30      }
```

In the CAR class:

```java
        public void displayData()
56      {
57        System.out.println("Car make : " + getMake() );
58        System.out.println("Car registration : " + getRegistration() );
59        System.out.println("Car type : " + getCarType() );
60        System.out.println("Number of seats : " + getNoOfSeats() );
61      }
```

In the main program:

```java
65      public static void main(String[] args)
66      {
67      // seeing how the class definition is used ...
68      // create a car object
69      CAR thisCar = new CAR("Nissan", "WJ012HG");
70
71      thisCar.displayData();
72      System.out.println("New car object created");
73      }
```

> The thisCar object will use the displayData method in the CAR class.

```
JavaTestBed (debug) ×   JavaTestBed (run) ×

run:
Car make : Nissan
Car registration : WJ012HG
Car type : Saloon
Number of seats : 4
New car object created
BUILD SUCCESSFUL (total time: 0 seconds)
```

Note that in the earlier code there were two separate methods used for the output of the car data. We will now use a better design, where output of the sub-class data is achieved using a single method. This revised code is using polymorphism. The design has a method in the superclass VEHICLE and the inherited class CAR that has the same method name, `DisplayData()`.

> **Progress check F**
>
> There is another example of polymorphism shown in the Figure **22.02** class diagram. What is its main property and what are its associated methods?

22.07 Objects in a different context: designing a GUI form

Here is the use of classes and objects in a very different context.

You should already have some idea about a different use of objects if you have attempted to create a forms-based Windows application in your programming language. The form will typically contain a number of controls, such as a text box and radio buttons, and these behave as 'objects'. The programming environment has a class definition of the properties and methods defined for each of these controls.

22.08 Encapsulation

Encapsulation is the combining together of an object's properties and the methods that access that data. Encapsulation will restrict the programmer's access to the object's data.

The only code that allows the reading or writing of property data values are the getter/setter methods for each property.

Data hiding is a very important concept of OOP and is a feature of data encapsulation. This provides a structure for the validation of data that can be hidden away from the programmer. Code to validate the input of a property value is placed within the setter method for the property within the class. The validation code is therefore coded once only, but is active whenever a program assigns a value to this property. Hence the suggestion that the validation is 'hidden away' from the programmer.

22.09 Containment (or Aggregation)

The idea of **containment** in object-oriented programming is the idea that an outer class contains an instance of another class and allows access to the contained object through its own methods.

Aggregation is one form of containment. The contained object can exist independently from the outer object. For example, a Family object might contain an instance of a Cat object, representing a cat that the family owns. An instance of a Cat object can exist in its own right.

> **Worked example 22.02**
>
> The vehicle data is to include data about the vehicle's engine. The engine data description is already coded in class `ENGINE`.
>
> When you are formulating the object-oriented design for the given problem, aggregation/containment is clarified using the words 'has a'.
>
> In our application each `VEHICLE` 'has a' `ENGINE`.

(Continued)

VISUAL BASIC

```
1   Public Class VEHICLE
2       Inherits ENGINE

1   Public Class ENGINE
2       Private mEngineType As String
3       Private mEngineSize As Integer
4
5       Property EngineType As String
6           Get
7               EngineType = mEngineType
8           End Get
9           Set(ThisEngineType As String)
10              mEngineType = ThisEngineType
11          End Set
12      End Property
13
14      Property EngineSize As Integer
15          Get
16              EngineSize = mEngineSize
17          End Get
18          Set(ThisEngineSize As Integer)
19              mEngineSize = ThisEngineSize
20          End Set
21      End Property
22  End Class
```

Note that to allow containment, the VEHICLE class must inherit ENGINE.

The DisplayData method in CAR now needs to be amended to include the display of the ENGINE properties (code not shown).

PYTHON code

```python
class ENGINE:
    def __init__ (self, EngineType, EngineSize):
        self.EngineSize = EngineSize
        self.EngineType = EngineType

class VEHICLE:
    def __init__ (self, Make, RegistrationID):
        self.Make = Make
        self.RegistrationID = RegistrationID
        self.Engine = ENGINE()

    def DisplayData(self):
        print("Make is : ", self.Make, " Registration: ", self.RegistrationID)

class CAR(VEHICLE):
    def __init__ (self, CarType, NoOfSeats):
        self.CarType = CarType
        self.NoOfSeats = NoOfSeats

    def DisplayData(self):
        print("Make is : ", self.Make, " Registration: ", self.RegistrationID)
        print("Car type : ", self.CarType, " Number of seats: ", str(self.NoOfSeats))
        print("Engine type : ", self.EngineType, " Engine size: ", str(self.EngineSize))

# Main program starts here ...
MyCar = CAR("Estate", 6)
MyCar.Make = "Nissan"
MyCar.RegistrationID = "AB012TR"
MyCar.EngineType = "Diesel"
MyCar.EngineSize = 2500
print ("Car object created ...")
MyCar.DisplayData()
```

(Continued)

Note the new class ENGINE.

A new ENGINE property is added to the VEHICLE class.

The properties of ENGINE are added to the output with the `DisplayData` method.

JAVA code Java-24

> The CAR class is to be changed to 'contain' an ENGINE object.

```
5       class ENGINE
6       {
7       private int mEngineSize;
8       private String mEngineType;
9       // constructor
10      public ENGINE()
11          {
12          mEngineSize = 0;
13          mEngineType = "Diesel";
14          }
15      public int getEngineSize()
16          { return (mEngineSize); }
17      public void setEngineSize(int n)
18          { mEngineSize = n; }
19
20      public String getEngineType()
21          { return (mEngineType); }
22      public void setEngineType(String t)
23          { mEngineType = t; }
24      }
```

```
54      class CAR extends VEHICLE
55      {
56      ENGINE mEngine;
57      private String mCarType;
58      private int mNoOfSeats;
59
60      // constructor
61      public CAR(String r, String m, ENGINE e)
62          {
```

> 'Containment' ...

```
80      public void displayData(CAR c, ENGINE e)
81          {
82          System.out.println("Car make : " + c.getMake() );
83          System.out.println("Car registration : " + c.getRegistration() );
84          System.out.println("Car type : " + c.getCarType() );
85          System.out.println("Number of seats : " + c.getNoOfSeats() );
86          System.out.println("Engsize type : " + e.getEngineType() );
87          System.out.println("Engine size : " + e.getEngineSize() );
88          }
```

(Continued)

```
92      public static void main(String[] args)
93      {
94          ENGINE thisEngine = new ENGINE();
95          thisEngine.setEngineType("Petrol");
96          thisEngine.setEngineSize(2500);
97
98          CAR thisCar = new CAR("WJ012HG", "Nissan", thisEngine);
99          thisCar.setCarType("Estate");
100         thisCar.setNoOfSeats(6);
101
102         thisCar.displayData(thisCar, thisEngine);
103         System.out.println("New car object created");
104     }
```

Note that a new class `ENGINE` is created with its two properties, the constructor and getter/setter methods.

The `CAR` class code is amended to include the `ENGINE` object.

The `displayData` method in the `CAR` class is amended to also output the engine data.

The main program assigns the data values and displays the car and engine properties.

Past paper questions

1. A programmer wants to create a computer simulation of animals searching for food in a desert. The desert is represented by a 40 by 40 grid. Each position in the grid is represented by a pair of coordinates. 'A' represents an animal and 'F' represents food. At the start of the simulation, the grid contains 5 animals and 1 food source.

   The following is an example of part of the grid.

	0	1	2	3	4	...	37	38	39
0	A					..			
1			F			..			
2						..		A	
3				A		..			
...	..	..	..	..	..	..	..	..	..
38				A		..	A		
39						..			

A timer is used. In each time interval, each animal randomly moves 0 or 1 position in a random direction. The program generates this movement by computing two random numbers, each of which can be -1, 0 or 1. The program adds the first random number to the across number and the second random number to the down number representing the animal's position.

For example:

- If 0 and 1 are generated, the across value does not change, the down value increases by 1.
- If -1 and 1 are generated, the across value decreases by 1, and the down value increases by 1.

Each animal has an individual score. If the animal moves to a position in the grid with food ('F'):

- the animal's score increases by 1
- the food disappears
- one new animal ('A') is randomly generated and added to the grid (to a maximum of 20 animals)
- one new food ('F') is randomly generated and added to the grid.

The simulation is to be implemented using object-oriented programming.

The programmer has designed two classes, `Desert` and `Animal`.

The Desert class consists of:

- attributes
    - Grid
    - StepCounter
    - AnimalList
    - NumberOfAnimals
- Methods
    - Constructor
    - IncrementStepCounter
    - GenerateFood
    - DisplayGrid

Each attribute consists of a value and a get and set method that allows access to the attributes.

The following table describes the attributes and methods for the `Animal` class.

Identifier	Data type	Description
`Constructor ()`		Instantiate an object of the `Animal` class • Generate a pair of random numbers between 0 and 39. • Place animal at that random position. • Initialise the animal's score to 0.
`EatFood ()`		• Delete the food. • Increase the score of the animal that called the method. • Call the `GenerateFood` method of the `Desert` class. • Call the `Constructor` method of the `Animal` class.

(Continued)

Identifier	Data type	Description
Move ()		- Call the GenerateChangeInCoordinate method for each coordinate (across or down number) of the animal's position. - Moves the animal to the new space. - If there is food in the new position, call the EatFood method.
Score	INTEGER	Initialise to 0
Across	INTEGER	The across value, between 0 and 39
Down	INTEGER	The down value, between 0 and 39

a   Write program code to declare the attributes and constructor for the Animal class.

You only need to write the set and get methods for the attribute Across.

You should also write:

- The constructor for the class
- Set and get methods for the Across attribute only. [6]

b   The constructor method of the Desert class:

- initialises an empty grid
- creates 5 animal objects which are added to the AnimalList (an array of animal objects currently on the grid)
- generates one food
- sets the StepCounter to 0

Write program code for the Constructor method. [5]

Cambridge International AS & A level Computer Science 9608 paper 41 Q6a and 6b November 2017

Chapter 23

Further programming: files and file processing

Learning Objectives:

File processing:

- Understand the different file organisation methods
  - Serial, sequential and random
- Understand the different file access methods
  - Sequential and direct access
- Write code for file operations
  - Write data, read data, append data
- Understand the difference between a text file and a binary file
- Write code using a 'record' data structure with a binary file
- Write code to add and retrieve records for a random organisation binary file.

Exception handling:

- Understand what is an exception
- State examples of common exceptions
- Understand how error handler code deals with an exception
- Write code which includes an error handler.

23.01 File processing

Basic file operations

We have already studied the pseudocode for basic file operations: open a file in either read mode, write mode or append mode, close the file and test for the end of file.

Create a text file

Serial file organisation

Serial organisation means that data items are written to the file in no particular order and that data items can only be read from the file in sequential order, starting with the first item in the file.

Worked example 23.01

A file stores a list of animals in a text file.

Visual Basic	

```vb
Dim ThisInputFile As System.IO.StreamWriter
ThisInputFile = New IO.StreamWriter("e:\Animals.txt")
PopulateArray()
For Index = 1 To 6
    LineOfText = Animal(Index)
    ThisInputFile.WriteLine(LineOfText)
Next
ThisInputFile.Close()
```

> **Serial file organisation** The records are in no particular order.

(Continued)

Note that data values are read from the array `Animal()` to avoid keying in the animal names.

The key object is a `StreamWriter` object that has the method `WriteLine()`.

Python	

```python
# code reads the items from a list (to avoid keying in ...)
# the 'end of line' (\n) character is added before each file write
Animal = ["ANT","BEE","CAT","DOG","EAGLE", \
         "GOAT","HORSE","PARROT","RAT","ZEBRA","XX"]
AnimalFile = open("f:\Animals.txt","w+")
Index = 1
while Animal[Index] != "XX":
    AnimalFile.write(Animal[Index] + "\n")
    Index = Index + 1

print("Animals file created ...")
AnimalFile.close()
```

Note 'w+' as the file mode will write to the file and create it if it does not exist.

'\n' is the 'end of line' character added to each data item before the file write.

The items are read from the Animal list.

Java	

```java
package javatestbed;
import java.io.FileWriter;
import java.io.IOException;
import java.io.PrintWriter;
public class JavaTestBed
{
public static void main(String args[])throws IOException
    {
    String animal [] = {"ANT", "BEE", "CAT", "DOG", "EAGLE",
    "GOAT", "HORSE", "PARROT", "RAT", "ZEBRA", "XX"} ;

    FileWriter fw = new FileWriter ("J://java/Animals.txt");
    PrintWriter pw = new PrintWriter(fw);

    int index = 0 ;
    while (animal[index] != "XX")
```

(Continued)

| Java | ```
            {
                pw.printf("%s"+"%n", animal[index]);
                index ++ ;
            }
        pw.close();
        fw.close() ;
        System.out.println("File Created ...") ;
    }
}
``` |

Note that three library modules are required:

FileWriter, **PrintWriter** and **IOException**.

File handling in Java can generate exceptions. These are managed in the header for the main program with the addition of '**throws IOException**'.

The **fw** **FileWriter** object maps to the file path.

The **pw** **PrintWriter** object will write the line of text.

Read the contents of the text file

| Visual Basic | ```
Dim NextLineOfText As String
Dim ThisOutputFile As System.IO.StreamReader
ThisOutputFile = New IO.StreamReader("e:\Animals.txt")
Do
    NextLineOfText = ThisOutputFile.ReadLine
    Console.WriteLine(NextLineOfText)
Loop Until ThisOutputFile.EndOfStream
ThisOutputFile.Close()
``` |

The key object is a `StreamReader` object that has the method. `ReadLine()`.

| Python | ```
AnimalFile = open("f:\Animals.txt","r")
for x in AnimalFile:
    NextAnimal = x
    print(NextAnimal)
AnimalFile.close()
OR:
with open("f:\Animals.txt") as AnimalFile:
    for line in AnimalFile:
        print(line)
AnimalFile.close()
``` |

(Continued)
```

Note that file mode is 'r' to read the file contents.

Java	

```java
package javatestbed;
import java.io.FileReader;
import java.io.BufferedReader;      ;
import java.io.IOException;

public class JavaTestBed
{
public static void main(String args[])throws IOException
{
FileReader fh = new FileReader("J://java/Animals.txt");
BufferedReader tr = new BufferedReader(fh);

String lineOfText = tr.readLine();
System.out.println(lineOfText) ;
while (lineOfText != null)
   {
     lineOfText = tr.readLine();
     System.out.println(lineOfText) ;
   }
fh.close();
tr.close() ;
System.out.println("File contents read ...") ;
}
}
```

Note that two libraries are needed, `FileReader` and `BufferedReader`.

The 'end of file' is tested for with the (`lineOfText != null`) condition.

23.02 Using a 'record' structure

In Chapter 10 Section 10.01 we studied the 'record' data structure.

The data items might not all be string values so a text file is not suitable.

Worked example 23.02

A charity stores data about its donors. The name of the donor is recorded and whether or not they make a regular monthly payment, the monthly amount and the number of years they have contributed.

The record type definition in pseudocode is:

```
TYPE DONOR
    DonorName       : STRING
    Monthly         : BOOLEAN
    MonthlyAmount   : REAL
    Years           : INTEGER
ENDTYPE
```

Visual Basic

```vb
Structure DonorData
    Dim DonorName As String
    Dim Monthly As Boolean
    Dim MonthlyAmount As Single
    Dim Years As Integer
End Structure

Sub Main()
    Dim MyDonor As DonorData

    MyDonor.DonorName = "Ali"
    MyDonor.Monthly = True
    MyDonor.MonthlyAmount = 20.0
    MyDonor.Years = 3
    Console.WriteLine("Data values assigned to MyDonor")
    Console.ReadLine()
End Sub
```

Note the 'dot notation' used for each field of the record.

The data for the object has been hard coded for this example.

(Continued)

| Python | ```
class DonorRecord:
    def __init__(self):
        self.DonorName = ""
        self.Monthly = False
        self.monthlyAmount = 0
        self.Years = 0

ThisDonor = DonorRecord
ThisDonor.DonorName = "Ali"
ThisDonor.Monthly = True
ThisDonor.MonthlyAmount = 20.00
ThisDonor.Years = 3

print("One donor object created ...")
``` | Remember that indenting must be present. |

Note that Python does not have a record data type.

We can create the fields of the record as a class constructor with initial default values assigned.

Once the class definition is created, we create an object `ThisDonor` of that class.

| Java | ```
class donorRecord
{
String donorName ;
boolean monthly ;
float monthlyAmount ;
int years ;

public donorRecord()
{
donorName = "" ;
monthly = false ;
monthlyAmount = 0 ;
years = 0 ;
donorRecord thisDonor = new donorRecord();
// instantiates a donor record
thisDonor.donorName = "Ali" ;
thisDonor.monthly = true ;
``` |

(Continued)

Java	`thisDonor.monthlyAmount = 20 ;`
	`thisDonor.years = 3 ;`
	`}`
	`}`

Java does not have a record data type.

We can create the fields of the record as a class with no methods.

Once the class definition is created, we create an object `ThisDonor` of that class.

Progress check A

A program is to store the surname and initials (separately) for a number of employees who each have an employee code (typically D768). The program also stores the number of years of service and whether or not they are a full-time employee.

a   Write pseudocode for an employee record structure.

b   Write a declaration statement for a data structure to store data for 150 employees.

23.04 Binary files

If we use a record type structure then we must create a **binary file** (instead of a text file).

The file organisation for a binary file can be either serial organisation, sequential organisation or random.

For our example, the binary file for the donor data contains a string value, then a Boolean, then a real number and finally an integer.

Visual Basic: Define the 'record' and create the binary file

```
Sub CreateDonorFile()
    Dim DonorFileWriter As BinaryWriter
    Dim DonorFile As FileStream

    DonorFile = New FileStream("F:\DonorFile.dat", FileMode.Create)
    DonorFileWriter = New BinaryWriter(DonorFile)

    DonorArray()

    For Index = 1 To 3
        DonorFileWriter.Write(Donor(Index).DonorName)
        DonorFileWriter.Write(Donor(Index).Monthly)
        DonorFileWriter.Write(Donor(Index).MonthlyAmount)
        DonorFileWriter.Write(Donor(Index).Years)
    Next
    DonorFileWriter.Close()
    DonorFile.Close()
    Console.WriteLine("Donor.dat binary file created ...")
End Sub

Imports System.IO
Module Module1
    Structure DonorData
        Dim DonorName As String
        Dim Monthly As Boolean
        Dim MonthlyAmount As Decimal
        Dim Years As Integer
    End Structure

    Dim Donor(5) As DonorData
```

The donor data — This is read from the Donor array. Code not shown.

Figure 23.01 Add record to a binary file.

Note that a 'record' `DonorData` has been coded and then an array `Donor()` of this data type.

The `Donor()` array contents have been hard coded (the code for this is not shown).

The array then contains the data that is read to the file.

Visual Basic: Read the contents of the binary file

```vb
Sub ReadDonorFile()
    Dim DonorFile As FileStream
    Dim DonorFileReader As BinaryReader
    Dim RecordNumber As Integer
    DonorFile = New FileStream("F:\DonorFile.dat", FileMode.Open)
    DonorFileReader = New BinaryReader(DonorFile)

    ' now loop until the end of the binary file reached ...
    RecordNumber = 1
    Do While DonorFile.Position < DonorFile.Length
        Console.WriteLine("Record: " & Str(RecordNumber))
        Console.WriteLine(DonorFileReader.ReadString)
        Console.WriteLine(DonorFileReader.ReadBoolean)
        Console.WriteLine(DonorFileReader.ReadDecimal)
        Console.WriteLine(DonorFileReader.ReadInt32)
        Console.WriteLine()
        RecordNumber = RecordNumber + 1
    Loop
End Sub
```

Note: We know that the data for each donor record consists of these items in this order:
- Donor name – data type string
- Monthly? – data type Boolean
- Monthly amount – data type Decimal
- Number of years – Data type Integer

Hence the **BinaryReader** object will know what it is about to read from the **FileStream**.

Figure 23.02 Retrieve record from a binary file.

Python: Define the 'record' and create the binary file

```python
import pickle

Donors =[ ["ADAMS",True,15.00,5],["CHI",False, 0.00,1],\
          ["PIPER",True,30.00,3],["SMITH", True,10.00,3], \
          ["WALTERS",True,10.00,3], ["YOO", False, 0.00, 1], [] \
        ]

DonorFile = open("F:\DonorFile.dat", 'wb')

for Index in range(7):
    pickle.dump(Donors[Index], DonorFile)
    print ("Record written")
print ("Binary sequential file created ...")
DonorFile.close()
```

Figure 23.03 Add record to a binary file (PYTHON).

The file mode is 'wb', i.e. write to the binary file.

The last record written is an empty list. We can check for this in the code that follows to read the file contents.

The code uses the `pickle` library.

This allows data in the form of a record to be written with one 'write' operation. The donor records are each a sub-list of the Donors list..

The pickle 'dump' method can write either a class instance or a list.

Python: Read the contents of the binary file

```python
import pickle
DonorFile = open("F:\DonorFile.dat", 'rb')
Donor =[ [] ]

while not(Donor == []):
    Donor = pickle.load(DonorFile)
    print(Donor)
    for Field in Donor:
        print(Field)

DonorFile.close()
```

```
RESTART: C:\                    CUP_New
s sequential file READ v3.py
['ADAMS', True, 15.0, 5]
ADAMS
True
15.0
5
['CHI', False, 0.0, 1]
CHI
False
0.0
1
['PIPER', True, 30.0, 3]
PIPER
True
30.0
3
['SMITH', True, 10.0, 3]
SMITH
True
10.0
3
['WALTERS', True, 10.0, 3]
WALTERS
True
10.0
3
['YOO', False, 0.0, 1]
YOO
False
0.0
1
[]
```

Figure 23.04 Retrieve record from a binary file (PYTHON).

Remember, the data written to the file was seven lists, six donor record lists and an empty list.

The file mode is 'rb', for read binary file.

The pickle 'load' method reads one list from the binary file.

The program print statements show how the records and their fields are accessed.

Java: Define the 'record' and create the binary file

```java
package javatestbed;
import java.io.IOException;
import java.io.FileOutputStream;
import java.io.DataOutputStream;

class donorRecord
    {
    String donorName;
    boolean monthly;
    double monthlyAmount;
    int years;

    public donorRecord()
        {
        donorName = "XX";
        monthly = false;
        monthlyAmount = 0;
        years = 0;
        }
    }
```

```java
24   public static void main(String args[]) throws IOException
25   {
26       try
27       {
28           donorRecord [] thisDonor = new donorRecord[5];
29           thisDonor[1] = new donorRecord();
30           thisDonor[1].donorName = "ADAMS"; thisDonor[1].monthly = true;
31           thisDonor[1].monthlyAmount = 15.00; thisDonor[1].years = 5;
32           thisDonor[2] = new donorRecord();
33           thisDonor[2].donorName = "CHI"; thisDonor[2].monthly = false;
34           thisDonor[2].monthlyAmount = 0.00; thisDonor[2].years = 0;
35           thisDonor[3] = new donorRecord();
36           thisDonor[3].donorName = "PIPER"; thisDonor[3].monthly = true;
37           thisDonor[3].monthlyAmount = 30.00; thisDonor[3].years = 3;

39           // set up the file stream and link to the file name
40           FileOutputStream fos = new FileOutputStream("J:/Java/DonorBINARYfile.DAT");
41               // link file stream to data stream
42           DataOutputStream dos = new DataOutputStream(fos);
43           for (int i = 1; i < 4; i++) // loop for each array element
44           {
45               dos.writeUTF(thisDonor[i].donorName);
46               dos.writeBoolean(thisDonor[i].monthly);
47               dos.writeDouble(thisDonor[i].monthlyAmount);
48               dos.writeInt(thisDonor[i].years);
49           }
50           dos.close(); // close data stream
51           System.out.println("File created with 3 donor records ...");
52       }
53       catch (IOException x)
54       {
55           System.out.println("IO error");
56       }
57   }
58   }
```

Figure 23.05 Add record to a binary file (JAVA).

Two new library files are imported, `FileOutPutStream` and `DataOutputStream`.

Note the class record definition for `donorRecord`.

The 'data output stream' object has methods that write data for each data type, i.e. `writeUTF` for string data, `writeBoolean` for Boolean data, etc.

Java: Read the contents of the binary file

```java
2    package javatestbed;
3    import java.io.EOFException;
4    import java.io.FileInputStream;
5    import java.io.DataInputStream;
6
7    class donorRecord          • As before.
8    {
9        String donorName;

24   public static void main(String args[]) throws Exception
25   {
26       try
27       {
28       // set up file stream and link to file name
29       FileInputStream fis = new FileInputStream("J:/Java/DonorBINARYfile.DAT");
30       // link file stream to data stream
31       DataInputStream dis = new DataInputStream(fis);
32
33       donorRecord[] thisDonor = new donorRecord[10];
34       int i = 1;
35       while (true) // loop for each array element
36       {
37           thisDonor[i] = new donorRecord();
38           System.out.print(thisDonor[i].donorName = dis.readUTF()); System.out.print(" ");
39           System.out.print(thisDonor[i].monthly = dis.readBoolean()); System.out.print(" ");
40           System.out.print(thisDonor[i].monthlyAmount = dis.readDouble()); System.out.print(" ");
41           System.out.println(thisDonor[i].years = dis.readInt() );
42
43           i += 1;
44       }
45       }
46       catch (EOFException x)
47       { System.out.println("End of File reached"); }
48       }
49   }
```

```
run:
ADAMS true 15.0 5
CHI false 0.0 0
PIPER true 30.0 3
End of File reached
BUILD SUCCESSFUL (total time: 0 seconds)
```

Figure 23.06 Retrieve record from a binary file (JAVA).

The two new library imports are `FileOutputStream` and `DataOutputStream`.

The code must know the order in which the data was written to the file, i.e. String, Boolean, Double and Integer in that order.

Serial file organisation

In the case of serial file organisation, data items are written into the binary file in no particular order.

Sequential file organisation

In the case of sequential file organisation, the file is created with the records ordered in some way, for example, stored in donor name order.

The file is said to be a sequentially organised file, with donor name chosen as the key field.

> ### Progress check B
> Study this file of cricketers with their highest score this season.
>
> | | |
> |---|---|
> | Adams | 34 |
> | Chi | 45 |
> | Lewis | 45 |
> | Kelly | 121 |
> | Davies | 103 |
> | Morris | 4 |
> | Patel | 23 |
>
> a What is the file organisation?
> b What is the key field?
> c Searching the file to find 'Davies' requires five 'read' operations. True or false?

The program code for this is identical to that shown in section 23.02. The donor names must be stored in the array in alphabetical order. The data items are then read and stored in the file in the same order.

Sequential file access

The program code for this is identical to Figure **23.02**. The donor names are stored and displayed in alphabetical order.

Limitations for sequential access

Data values can only be read from the file in sequence (i.e. 'sequentially'). A file with N items will require on average, N/2 items to be read before the required one is found. Searching for a data item will be inefficient when compared to random organisation with direct access to a particular record.

23.05 Random files

If our donor file contained thousands of records, we would need fast access to individual records. Using random file organisation, we can do this.

> **TIP**
>
> Before you study the code which follows, look back to Chapter 13 where random organisation files with direct access were introduced.

Write a record	Read a record

`OPENFILE "Donor.rnd" FOR RANDOM`
`RecordAddress ← File pointer`
`SEEK "Donor.rnd", RecordAddress`
`PUTRECORD  "Donor.rnd",`
`             new record data`
`CLOSEFILE "Donor.rnd"`
	`OPENFILE "Donor.rnd" FOR RANDOM`
	`RecordAddress ← File pointer`
	`SEEK "Donor.rnd", RecordAddress`
	`GETRECORD  "Donor.rnd", Record data`
	`CLOSEFILE "Donor.rnd"`

Table 23.01 Pseudocode for random files.

A **file pointer** value is set.

The `SEEK` command moves the file pointer to this **address** in the file.

The record's data is written.

To retrieve this record: The file pointer value is set, the `SEEK` command moves the file pointer to this address in the file and the data values are read.

Visual Basic: Add a record to a random file

```vb
1       Imports System.IO
2       Module Module1
3           Dim FilePointer As Integer
4           Dim DonorFile As FileStream
5           Dim DonorFileWriter As BinaryWriter

7           Sub Main()
8               Dim Choice As Integer
9
10              FilePointer = 0

24          Sub AddDonorRecord()
25              Dim NewName As String
26              Dim NewMonthly As Boolean
27              Dim NewMonthlyAmount As Decimal
28              Dim NewYears As Integer
29
30              DonorFile = New FileStream("F:\DonorFile.rnd", FileMode.OpenOrCreate)
31              DonorFileWriter = New BinaryWriter(DonorFile)
32
33              Console.Write("Name: ") : NewName = Console.ReadLine
34              Console.Write("Monthly: ") : NewMonthly = Console.ReadLine
35              Console.Write("Monthly amount: ") : NewMonthlyAmount = Console.ReadLine
36              Console.Write("Years: ") : NewYears = Console.ReadLine
37
38              DonorFile.Position = FilePointer
39              DonorFileWriter.Write(NewName)
40              DonorFileWriter.Write(NewMonthly)
41              DonorFileWriter.Write(NewMonthlyAmount)
42              DonorFileWriter.Write(NewYears)
43
44              FilePointer = FilePointer + 100
45
46              DonorFileWriter.Close()
47              DonorFile.Close()
48              Console.WriteLine("New record written ...")
49          End Sub
```

- The first record is written at the start of the file.
- Subsequent records are written at byte position 100, 200, etc.

Figure 23.07 Write record to random file.

Visual Basic: Retrieve a record from the direct access file

```vb
51          Sub ReadDonorRecord()
52              Dim DonorFileReader As BinaryReader
53              Dim FilePointer As Integer
54
55              DonorFile = New FileStream("F:\DonorFile.rnd", FileMode.Open)
56              DonorFileReader = New BinaryReader(DonorFile)
57
58              Console.Write("File pointer: ") : FilePointer = Console.ReadLine
59              DonorFile.Position = FilePointer
60              Console.WriteLine("file pointer: " & Str(FilePointer))
61              Console.WriteLine(DonorFileReader.ReadString)
62              Console.WriteLine(DonorFileReader.ReadBoolean)
63              Console.WriteLine(DonorFileReader.ReadDecimal)
64              Console.WriteLine(DonorFileReader.ReadInt32)
65              Console.WriteLine()
66
67              DonorFile.Close()
68              Console.ReadLine()
69          End Sub
```

A record is retrieved by knowing its file pointer position.

Figure 23.08 Retrieve a record from the random file.

Python: Add a record to a random file

The basic design is similar to Visual Basic. Python has a seek method that sets up the file pointer before a read or write operation.

A careful calculation could work out exactly how many bytes are used to store a single record. This can be avoided if, as we did for the Visual Basic code, we simply write each new record with an offset from the start of the file as a multiple of 100. We would need to be certain that the data for one record is less than 100 bytes.

A better solution would be to 'hash' the file position from (say) the donor name. This is covered in the next section.

```python
import pickle

Donors =[ ["ADAMS",True,15.00,5],["CHI",False, 0.00,1],\
          ["PIPER",True,30.00,3],["SMITH", True,10.00,3], \
          ["WALTERS",True,10.00,3], ["YOO", False, 0.00, 1], [] \
        ]
# each record is written with an offest of 0, 100, 200, etc
# from the start of the file

DonorFile = open("F:\DonorFile.RND", 'wb')
FilePointer = 0
for Index in range(7):
    DonorFile.seek(FilePointer)
    pickle.dump(Donors[Index], DonorFile)
    print ("Record written")
    FilePointer = FilePointer + 100
print ("Binary random file created ...")
DonorFile.close()
```

Figure 23.09 Add a record to random file (PYTHON).

Python: Retrieve a record from the direct access file

```python
import pickle
DonorFile = open("F:\DonorFile.RND", 'rb')
Donor =[ [] ]

FilePointer = 0
while not(Donor == []):
    DonorFile.seek(FilePointer)
    Donor = pickle.load(DonorFile)
    print(Donor)
    for Field in Donor:
        print(Field)
    FilePointer = FilePointer + 100
DonorFile.close()
```

Figure 23.10 Retrieve a record from the file (PYTHON).

> **TIP**
>
> **'Pickling with Python'** is an extremely useful library for file handling. Anything can be written to the file: strings, numbers, Booleans, records, objects. The Pickle code will simply write the data with a single serial read line of code, and later make sense of the data with a single write line of code.

Java: Add a record to a random file

Worked example 23.03

Create a random file of 100 dummy records.

```java
package javatestbed;
import java.io.IOException;
import java.io.RandomAccessFile;

public static void main(String args[]) throws Exception
{
int recordSize = 50;
try // set up a file with 100 dummy records
    {
    RandomAccessFile raf = new RandomAccessFile("J:/Java/DonorBINARYfile.RND", "rw");
    for (int i = 0; i < 100; i++)
        // loop for each array element
        {
        int filePointer = i * recordSize;
        raf.seek(filePointer);
        raf.writeUTF("XXXXXXXXXXXXXXXXXXXX") ;
        raf.writeBoolean(true) ;
        raf.writeDouble(0.00) ;
        raf.writeInt(0) ;
        System.out.println(filePointer);
        }
    raf.close();
    System.out.println("Random file created with 100 dummy records ...");
    }
catch (IOException x)
    { System.out.print("Problem creating the file ..."); }
}
```

Note that the code sets up a random access file with 100 dummy records each of 50 bytes.

The library file needed is `RandomAccessFile`.

The 'random access file' object has the 'seek' method that positions the file pointer.

The `writeUTF`, `writeBoolean` methods are the same as used earlier.

Add a new record at file pointer position 2.

```java
public static void main(String args[]) throws IOException
{
int recordSize = 50;
try
    {
    RandomAccessFile raf = new RandomAccessFile("J:/Java/DonorBINARYfile.RND", "rw");
    raf.seek(2 * recordSize);
    raf.writeUTF("CHI");
    raf.writeBoolean(false) ;
    raf.writeDouble(0.00) ;
    raf.writeInt(1) ;
    raf.close();
    System.out.println("New record created at file pointer position 2 ...");
    }
catch (IOException x)
    { System.out.print("Problem creating the file ..."); }
}
```

```
run:
New record created at file pointer position 2 ...
BUILD SUCCESSFUL (total time: 0 seconds)
```

Figure 23.11 Add a record to random file (Java).

Java: Retrieve a record from the direct access file

```java
public static void main(String args[]) throws IOException
{
Scanner input = new Scanner(System.in);
int recordSize = 50;
try
    {
    RandomAccessFile reader = new RandomAccessFile("J:/Java/DonorBINARYfile.RND", "r");
    System.out.print("Enter the record number: ");
    int recNumber = input.nextInt() ;
    reader.seek(recNumber * recordSize);

    donorRecord thisDonor = new donorRecord();
    thisDonor.donorName = reader.readUTF();
    thisDonor.monthly = reader.readBoolean() ;
    thisDonor.monthlyAmount = reader.readDouble() ;
    thisDonor.years = reader.readInt() ;
    reader.close();
    System.out.println(thisDonor.donorName);
    System.out.println(thisDonor.monthly) ;
    System.out.println(thisDonor.monthlyAmount) ;
    System.out.println(thisDonor.years );
    }
catch (IOException x)
    { System.out.print("Problem reading the file ..."); }
}
```

Figure 23.12 Retrieve a record from the file (Java).

Note that the reader `randomAccessFile` object has methods, `readUTF`, `readBoolean`, etc.

Any attempt to display a record will show the dummy data.

Progress check C

Which of these are true statements?

a A random file must use fixed length records.

b The position of each record is calculated using a file pointer.

c Records can only be sequentially accessed from a random file.

d The file pointer or the record address can be calculated from one of the data items.

Hashing

Hashing calculates in some way, the file pointer position <u>from</u> (for example) the name of the donor. This is a better solution than allocating file positions in sequence. A record is retrieved by keying in the name and does not require a knowledge of the file position for that record.

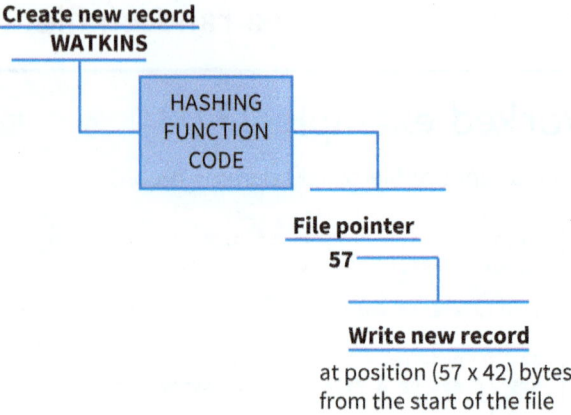

Figure 23.13 Hashing the file pointer.

Each donor name will be saved as a fixed length string, hence **all records will be stored using a fixed length number of bytes**. Assume each record takes up 42 bytes.

The name WATKINS hashes to 57.

Therefore, the WATKINS record will start at file pointer position (57 × 42).

Progress check D

Look back to Table **20.01** in Chapter 20.

The three fields for each donor record stored were donor name (a fixed length string of 20 characters), monthly payment (Boolean) and monthly amount (real number (use Single)).

Calculate exactly how many bytes are used for the Donor records if coded in Visual Basic.

23.06 Exception handling

An **exception** is a problem that arises during the execution of a program. An exception can occur for many different reasons. These include the following:

- A user has entered invalid data which has caused the program execution to halt, for example, the program has tried to assign a string value to an Integer variable
- Attempt to use an invalid array index
- A file in the program code does not exist
- A file directory in the program code does not exist
- Attempt to access a file without the permissions to do so
- A network connection has been lost.

In summary, exceptions can be caused by user error, program code error or a physical resource that has failed.

Exceptions can be either **checked exceptions** or **runtime exceptions**.

Checked exception

This is caused by a user error or a problem that cannot be foreseen by the programmer. For example, a 'file open' statement has hard coded the name of a file or directory that does not exist.

This type of error cannot be flagged at compile time.

Runtime exception

A runtime exception is an exception that the programmer will attempt to foresee could happen when the program is run. An example would be an arithmetic calculation that "attempts to divide by zero".

Code examples

Figure 23.14 and Figure 23.15 that follow are examples of 'checked exceptions'.

File does not exist

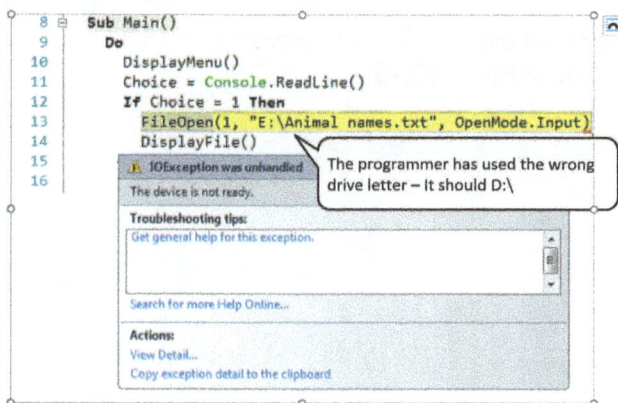

Figure 23.14 File does not exist: No exception hander code.

Data entry does not match declared data type

Figure 23.15 Incorrect data for data type: No exception handling code.

This is an example of a runtime exception error.

See the code example later, for Visual Basic, Python and Java, that addresses this issue.

Handling errors

Exceptions that can be anticipated by the programmers will be 'caught' or 'trapped'. **Catching and trapping** then results in the exceptions being 'resolved' with code called an **exception handler**.

In Visual Basic the basic structure that allows the programmer to 'catch' errors is illustrated with the following suggested pseudocode:

```
TRY
    // main program contains
    // statement(s) here which might cause an error
    //
CATCH
    // code to handle an exception that occur within
    // the TRY block
FINALLY
    // perform clean-up code in here
    //
ENDTRY
```

Figure 23.16 File does not exist (with error handler code).

What type of error caused the exception?

Visual Basic has a class `Exception`, so the solution is to create a variable that is an instance of it. The source of the error can be reported.

```vb
3   Sub Main()
4       Dim e As Exception
5       Try
6           FileOpen(1, "FileXYZ", OpenMode.Input)
7           ' do something ...
8           FileClose(1)
9       Catch e
10          Console.WriteLine(e.Message)
11      End Try
12      Console.WriteLine()
13      Console.WriteLine("But, program continues to execute")
14      Console.WriteLine("after the statement which caused the error")
15      Console.ReadLine()
16  End Sub
```

> You might want to refer back to the work on OOP. The Exception class has a method Message.
>
> The execution reports the Exceptioin object's message as shown.

```
Could not find file 'C:\Users\Tony\AppData\Local\Temporary Projects\Exception Divide by zero\bin\Debug\FileXYZ'.
But, program continues to execute
after the statement which caused the error
```

Figure 23.17 Uses the exception object message property.

Exception handler code: Visual Basic – Python – Java

The general issues have been illustrated earlier with code examples in Visual Basic.

Worked example 23.04

A program is to input an integer value. It will output the number multiplied by 5. If the user keys in a value that is not an integer, we do not want the program to crash. Look back to Figure **23.15**.

Visual Basic

```vb
1   Module Module1
2       Sub Main()
3           Dim ThisInteger As Integer
4           Dim Answer As Integer
5
6           Console.Write("Enter an integer: ")
7           Try
8               ThisInteger = Console.ReadLine()
9
10              Answer = ThisInteger * 5
11              Console.WriteLine("Answer is :" & Str(Answer))
12
13          Catch
14              Console.WriteLine("That was not an integer")
15          End Try
16          Console.ReadLine()
17      End Sub
18
19  End Module
```

Figure 23.18 Error handler with Visual Basic.

(Continued)

Python

Each different exception in Python has a name. Two examples are where an incorrect data value is recognised as a '`ValueError`' and where there is a failure to read input from a file is recognised as an '`IOError`'.

In the Figure 23.19 code we repeatedly ask the user to key in an integer, until Python recognises an integer input.

```python
while True:
    try:
        ThisInteger = int(input("Enter an integer: "))
        break
    except ValueError:
        print("Thta not an integer  - please enter again...")

Answer = ThisInteger * 5
print("Answer is :" + str(Answer))
```

Figure 23.19 Error handler with Python.

Java

```java
public static void main(String args[]) throws IOException
{
Scanner input = new Scanner(System.in);
try
    {
    System.out.print("Enter an integer: ");
    int thisInteger = input.nextInt();
    System.out.println(thisInteger); }
catch(Exception e) // catches any exception
    {
    System.out.println("This was not an integer");
    }
}
```

Figure 23.20 Error handler with Java.

We have already used error trapping in the previous file handling examples.

Other exceptions include `ArithmeticException` and `ArrayIndexOutOfBoundsException`. An arithmetic exception is an arithmetic error such as an attempted division by zero. An array index out of bounds error is an attempt to reference an array element outside the upper or lower boundary value.

Exam-style questions

1 A text file Takings.TXT contains the daily takings (to the nearest dollar) at a shop for a 14-day period. Each figure is stored on a new line in the file.

Assume that the first figure in the file is the takings for day 1 – the 14th figure is the takings for day 14.

Use the identifiers shown in the pseudocode below in your program code. [8]

Identifier	Data type	Description
`NextValue`	`STRING`	The current figure read from the file
`Biggest`	`STRING`	The current largest takings figure
`BiggestDayNumber`	`INTEGER`	The day number with the biggest takings
`Counter`	`INTEGER`	The takings number

Table 23.02 Identifier table.

```
OPEN "Takings.Txt" FOR READ
Biggest ← 0
Counter ← 1
REPEAT
    READFILE NextValue
    IF TONUM(NextValue) > Biggest
        THEN
            Biggest ← TONUM(StringNextValue)
            BiggestDayNumber ← Current
    ENDIF
    Counter ← Counter + 1
UNTIL EOF("Takings.txt")
CLOSEFILE ("Takings.txt")
OUTPUT BiggestDayNumber, Biggest
```

Things to note:

The pseudocode uses the built-in functions:

- `EOF( )` to test for "has the end of the file been reached"
- Assumes a built-in function `TONUM( )` to change the string value read from the text file to a number.

Use the given pseudocode to **write program code** to:

- Create the Takings.TXT file (you should read the fourteen numbers from an array or list).
- Output the largest figure with the corresponding day number.

2 Jim collects books. He will write a program to store data about his books.

The program design has a 'record' type data structure with five fields for each book.

Table **23.03** shows the information to be stored about each book.

Field name	Description
`Title`	Title of the book
`Author`	Author name
`RefNo`	A four digit reference code
`Fiction`	True or False
`LastRead`	Date when the book was last read

Table 23.03 Book data fields.

a Write pseudocode to design an Abstract Data Type (ADT) with identifier `Book`.

b The records are to be stored in a random access file.

A function `Hash()` takes, as a single parameter, the reference number. It returns a hash value. [3]

This hash value is the disk address of the record in the file and is calculated as follows:

Hash value = (`RefNo` Modulus 2000) + 1. [4]

Write the `Hash()` function program code. [3]

c We shall add three book records to the file MyBooks.RND.

Show the code for test data for three books – title and reference number only – which is originally stored in an array/list. [3]

d Write program code to write the data for the three books from the array/list to the file. [4]

e Write program code to: [6]

- prompt the user for a book reference number, then
- output: the disk address where the book was stored AND the title and reference number of the book.

Answers

All sample answers to past exam paper questions have been written by the authors. In examinations, the way marks are awarded may be different.

All exam-style questions and sample answers in this title were written by the authors. In examinations, the way marks are awarded may be different.

Chapter 1

Progress Checks

Progress Check A
a 65
b 170
c 255

Progress Check B
3 = 0000 0011
31 = 0001 1111
96 = 1100 0000

Progress Check C
a 137
b 518
c 0000 0011 1111
d 0001 1110 1010
e 1100 1010 1011

Progress Check D
Size A is 2048 bytes, Size B is 2100 bytes so File B has the larger size.

Progress Check E

+13	0	0	0	0	1	1	0	1	
+78	0	1	0	0	1	1	1	0	+
Carries					1	1			
Answer	0	1	0	1	1	0	1	1	

Which checks to give answer +91 denary.

+90	0	1	0	1	1	0	1	0	
+92	0	1	0	1	1	1	0	0	−
Carries					1	1			
Answer	1	1	1	1	1	1	1	0	

Which checks to give answer (−128 + 126) = −2 denary.

Progress Check F
0001 1000 0100

Progress Check G
16 colours so 4 bits so 0.5 of a byte so number of bytes = 1024 × 64 × 0.5.

Progress Check H
Would include: Line thickness, line colour, centre coordinates, radius, shaded (yes/no), shade style/colour.

Progress Check I
130,000 samples.

Progress Check J
Row 2: 4w5g5b8r8w.

Row 3: 14w8r8w.

Row 4: 30w.

Past paper questions

Q1 This is **Question 1 in 9608 Paper 11 June 2015**. The mark scheme is available on the Cambridge International School Support Hub (requires registration). At the time of writing the published mark scheme is available on the Cambridge International School Support Hub. The Examiner's Report for the June 2015 series is also available there and this may contain comments specific to this question.

The following are what the author of the Revision Guide would suggest as reasonable answers, with alternatives suggested where appropriate.

a B 8 [1]
b 0110 0001 [1]
c i 114 = 0111 0010 [1]
   ii −93 = 1010 0011 [1]

Note: Where an 8-bit binary pattern is written a gap has been left between the two nibbles, to make the binary more readable.

Q2
a

Term	Definition
Bitmap graphic	Measured in dots per inch (dpi); this value determines the amount of detail an image has
Image file header	Picture element
Image resolution	Image made up of rows and columns of picture elements
Pixel	Image made up of drawing objects; the properties of each object determine its shape and appearance
Screen resolution	Specifies the image size, number of colours, and other data needed to display an image
Vector graphic	Number of samples taken per second to represent some event in a digital format
	Value quoted for a monitor specification, such as 1024 x 768; the larger the numbers, the more picture elements will be displayed

[6]

b i $\dfrac{512 \times 256}{8 \times 1024} = 16$ KB

1 mark for numerator and 1 mark for denominator [2]

ii So that it is possible to estimate how many images can be stored, or to decide if it can be sent as an email attachment. [1]

Q3
a 0011 0111 [1]
b 131 [1]
c 1001 1010 [1]
d 78 [1]

Q4

This is **Question 4 in 9608 Paper 11 June 2016**. The mark scheme is available on the Cambridge International School Support Hub (requires registration). At the time of writing the published mark scheme is available on the Cambridge International School Support Hub. The Examiner's Report for the June 2016 series is also available there and this may contain comments specific to this question.

The following are what the author of the Revision Guide would suggest as reasonable answers, with alternatives suggested where appropriate.

a All analogue sound samples must each be converted to a digital value. Each recorded sample is encoded as a binary pattern.

When performing a sound recording, there will be software settings for:
- the sample resolution, i.e. how many bits are used to store each sample
- the sampling rate – e.g. samples taken every $1/1000^{th}$ of a second. [3]

b i The important word in the question stem is to **_justify_** your choice [3]

Lossy compression: three points from the following:
- The human ear will not notice that the decompressed stream will not be identical to the orifinal file / that parts of the original data have been discarded, removed or deleted.
- File size reduction is greater than using lossless.
- Email has limits on sizes for attachments / a smaller file will take less time to transmit via email.
- The file may not need to be of high precision or accuracy.
- The producer has requested an MP3 file.

Lossless compression: three points from the following:
- The file to be high precision and accuracy.
- None of the original data is lost / the decompressed files will be identical to the original.
- The producer has requested a flac file.

ii Three points from the following: [3]
- Lossless method of compression.
- Reduces the physical size of a string of adjacent, identical characters / pixels etc.
- The repeating string of a run is encoded into two values.
- One value represents the number of identical characters in the run (the run count).
- The other value is the code of the character / colour code of the pixel etc. in the run (the run value).
- The run value and the run count combination may be preceded by a control character.
- Any valid example given.

iii Row 1: 153 10 255 3 153 3 [2]
Row 2: 153 9 255 6 153 1
Row 3: 153 7 255 9

Alternative correct answer:
Row 1: 153 9 255 2 153 2
Row 2: 153 8 255 5 153 0
Row 3: 153 6 255 8

Chapter 2

Progress Checks

Progress Check A
Unicast (the data will use the address of the email server).

Progress Check B
Network cards in each computer; Ethernet copper cabling with terminators; a file server.

Progress Check C
Network could be a wireless network so: WNIC cards in each computer; router for wireless network.

Progress Check D
On-demand.

Progress Check E
2^{32} (Don't try to work this out ...).

Progress Check F
168.13.11.229 is an address on segment A. The new address must start 168.13.13.

Progress Check G
Each group is 4 Hex digits = 16 bits.
IPv6 has 8×16 = 128 bits.

Progress Check H
118A:77FF:F::342B:DC::11CC or
118A:77FF:F:0:342B:DC:0:11CC

Progress Check I
(1) 168.13 and (2) 168.13.13

Past paper questions

Q1

a   This is **Question 5 in 9608 Paper 11 June 2015**. The mark scheme is available on the Cambridge International School Support Hub. (requires registration). At the time of writing the published mark scheme is available on the Cambridge International School Support Hub. The Examiner's Report for the June 2015 series is also available there and this may contain comments specific to this question.

The following are what the author of the Revision Guide would suggest as reasonable answers, with alternatives suggested where appropriate. [2]

Description	Conventional telephone using PSTN	Internet-based systems
Connection only in use while sound is being transmitted		X
Dedicated channel used between two points for the duration of the call	X	
Connection maintained throughout the call	X	

Description	Conventional telephone using PSTN	Internet-based systems
Encoding schemes and compression technology used		X
Lines remain active even when a power outage	X	

b   The internet is made up of a large number of inter-connected networks. The networks will use a variety of communications methods to communicate. The internet uses the TCP/IP protocol. [3]

The World Wide Web is a vast collection of web pages and other resources which are made available from various websites. Web pages are constructed using the HTML markup language. To gain access to a particular resource the user must know the Universal Resource Locator (URL) for that resource. Resources are accessed using browser software.

Web page data is transmitted over the internet using the HTTP protocol.

c   Note: The keyword in the stem of the question is 'Name' – so one word answers are fine.

   i   router [1]
   ii   gateway [1]
   iii server [1]

Q2

a   This is **Question 3 in 9608 Paper 11 November 2015.** The mark scheme is available on the Cambridge International School Support Hub. (requires registration). At the time of writing the published mark scheme is available on the Cambridge International School Support Hub. The Examiner's Report for the November 2015 series is also available there and this may contain comments specific to this question. [2]

The following are what the author of the Revision Guide would suggest as reasonable answers, with alternatives suggested where appropriate.

Statement	True (√)
The IP address consists of any number of digits separated by single dots.	
Each number in an IP4 address can range from 0 to 255	√
IP addresses are used to ensure that messages and data reach their correct destinations	√
Public IP addresses are considered to be more secure than private IP addresses	

b   i

http	Enables browser to know what protocol is being used to access information in the domain
cie.org.uk	cie.org.uk is the domain name
computerscience.html	actual web page / file being viewed

[3]

   ii
   - %20 – because the space character is not allowed in a URL, or
   - %20 is the coding for a space (32 in denary). [1]
   - ? – separates the URL from any parameters or variables [1]

Q3

This is **Question 6 in 9608 Paper 11 November 2015.** The mark scheme is available on the Cambridge International School Support Hub (requires registration). At the time of writing the published mark scheme is available on the Cambridge International School Support Hub. The Examiner's Report for the November 2015 series is also available there and this may contain comments specific to this question. [4]

The following are what the author of the Revision Guide would suggest as reasonable answers, with alternatives suggested where appropriate.

Benefits of copper cabling:

Copper cabling is relatively inexpensive to purchase and install.

Copper cabling has been extensively used for many years – hence it is a reliable and a widely used technology with widespread expertise in its usage.

Benefits of fibre-optic:

Optical cables have greater bandwidth.

Optical cables are immune to electromagnetic interference and other effects.

Other relevant points could be made (especially for fibre-optic).

Q4

This is **Question 7 in 9608 Paper 11 June 2016**. The mark scheme is available on the Cambridge International School Support Hub. (requires registration). At the time of writing the published mark scheme is available on the Cambridge International School Support Hub. The Examiner's Report for the June 2016 series is also available there and this may contain comments specific to this question.

The following are what the author of the Revision Guide would suggest as reasonable answers, with alternatives suggested where appropriate.

a   Internet Protocol   [1]

b

Address	Denary Hexadecimal	Valid/ Invalid	Reason
33.2A.6AA.BBBB	Hex	Invalid	There are more than 32 bits, or The 3rd and 4th group use more than one byte
2.0.255.1	Denary	Valid	There are four bytes – each byte is in the range 0 to 255
6.0.257.6	Denary	Invalid	The third group is a value greater than 255
0A.78.F4.J8	Hex	Invalid	J is an invalid hex digit

[1] per row for correct Valid/Invalid + Reason.

c   A public IP address must be used to access a resource over the internet.

A private address can only be reached internally across a LAN.

Public addresses are provided by the ISP.

Private addresses are assigned by the Network Manager for the router and all the devices connected to the organisation's LAN. These private addresses are unique only within their LAN. A different organisation will use the same private addresses for their LAN (typically starting 192. ...).
[2]

Chapter 3

Progress Checks

Progress Check A

Pressure: pressure pad in the road approaching a set of traffic control signals

Temperature: computer-controlled oven. Temperature is continually sensed in order to feedback to actuators with will switch on/off a heating circuit.

Wind speed/flow measurement: a wind speed over some threshold value might trigger an actuator that closes the windows of a computer-controlled greenhouse.

Light intensity: when the intensity reaches a low threshold, this triggers the switching on of lights to illuminate the vicinity.

Progress Check B

Electric current: open/close doors on a train.

Hydraulic (fluid) pressure: power steering, braking system on a car.

Pneumatic (air) pressure: moving parts on heavy plant machinery such as a digger or fork-lift truck.

Progress Check C

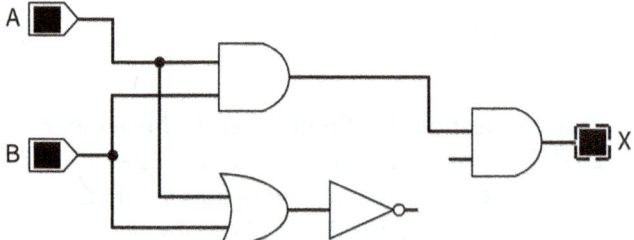

Figure 3.14 Circuit solution.

Progress Check D

> **TIP**
>
> The solution uses two intermediate points (P and Q) before the final AND gate.

Inputs			Intermediate		Output
A	B	C	P	Q	X
0	0	0	0	0	0
0	0	1	0	0	0
0	1	0	0	0	0
0	1	1	0	1	1
1	0	0	0	0	0
1	0	1	0	0	0
1	1	0	1	0	1
1	1	1	1	1	1

Table 3.10 Truth table solution.

Progress Check E

(NOT A AND B AND C) OR (A AND B AND NOT C) OR (A AND B AND C)

Progress Check F

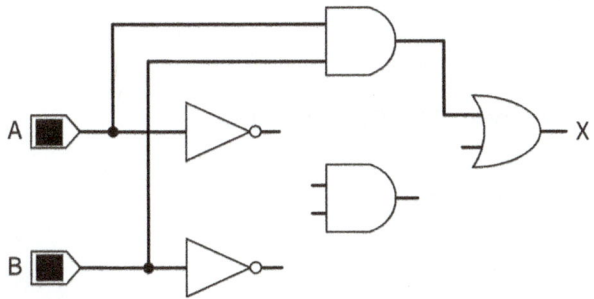

Figure 3.15 Derived circuit.

Past paper questions

Q1

This is **Question 7 in 9608 Paper 11 June 2015**. The mark scheme is available on the Cambridge International School Support Hub (requires registration). At the time of writing the published mark scheme is available on the Cambridge International School Support Hub. The Examiner's Report for the June 2015 series is also available there and this may contain comments specific to this question.
The following are what the author of the Revision Guide would suggest as reasonable answers, with alternatives suggested where appropriate.

a [5]

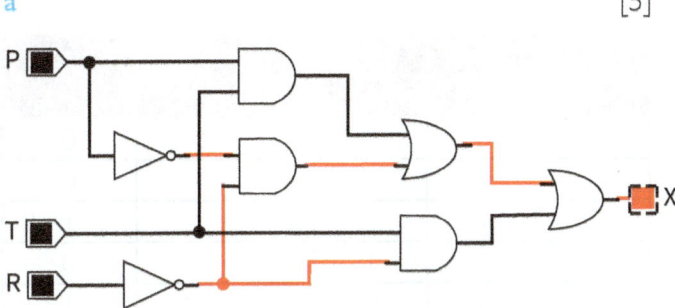

Other circuits are possible for a correct answer depending how the logic expression is simplified.

b [4]

P	T	R	Workspace	X
0	0	0		1
0	0	1		0
0	1	0		1
0	1	1		0
1	0	0		0
1	0	1		0
1	1	0		1
1	1	1		1

Q2

This is **Question 5 in 9608 Paper 11 November 2016**. The mark scheme is available on the Cambridge International School Support Hub (requires registration). At the time of writing the published mark scheme is available on the Cambridge International School Support Hub. The Examiner's Report for the November 2016 series is also available there and this may contain comments specific to this question.

The following are what the author of the Revision Guide would suggest as reasonable answers, with alternatives suggested where appropriate.

a [5]

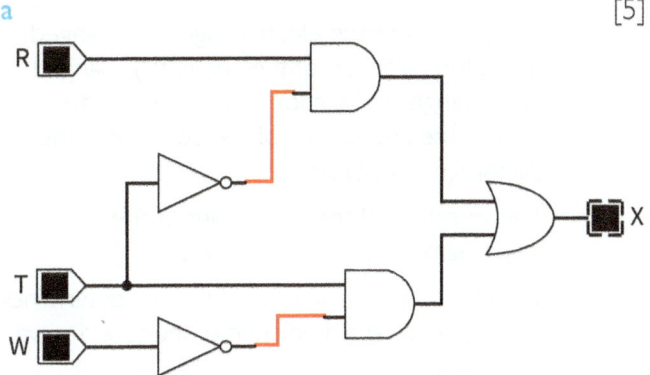

b (R AND NOT T) OR (T AND NOT W) [2]

c

INPUT			Working Space	Output
R	T	W		X
0	0	0		0
0	0	1		0
0	1	0		1
0	1	1		0
1	0	0		1
1	0	1		1
1	1	0		1
1	1	1		0

[4]

Q3

This is **Question 5 in 9608 Paper 11 November 2017.** The mark scheme is available on the Cambridge International School Support Hub (requires registration). At the time of writing the published mark scheme is available on the Cambridge International School Support Hub. The Examiner's Report for the November 2017 series is also available there and this may contain comments specific to this question.

The following are what the author of the Revision Guide would suggest as reasonable answers, with alternatives suggested where appropriate.

a i
- Diaphragm [3]
- (Voice) coil of wire
- (Permanent) Magnet

ii A loudspeaker converts electrical current into sound waves. [4]

An electric current in the coil creates an electromagnetic field and changes in the audio signal causes the direction of the electric current to change.

The polarity of the electromagnet is changed when the direction of the current is changed. This change of direction causes the coil to move. The movement of the coil causes the diaphragm to vibrate.

The vibration of the air in front of the diaphragm create the sound wave.

The amount of movement of the coil determines the frequency and amplitude of the sound wave produced.

b i External hard disk drive or a pen drive. [4]

ii It could be used for: [2]

Additional secondary file storage for the backup (or archiving) of files.

The transfer of files to another computer.

Chapter 4

Progress Checks

Progress Check A

2^{16} different addresses = 2097152.

Progress Check B

12 clock cycles × 3 microseconds = 36 microseconds.

Progress Check C

0011 1010$_2$ = 58 ✓.

Progress Check D

There are three - `IN`, `OUT` and `END`

Progress Check E

90

Progress Check F

64

Progress Check G

Before – 0011 0100, After – 0000 0110, Denary 6.

Progress Check H

`LDD NUMBER`

OR `#B0010 0000`

`STO NUMBER`

Past paper questions

Q1

This is **Question 3 in 9608 Paper 11 June 2015.** The mark scheme is available on the Cambridge International School Support Hub. (requires registration). At the time of writing the published mark scheme is available on the Cambridge International School Support Hub. The Examiner's Report for the June 2015 series is also available there and this may contain comments specific to this question.

The following are what the author of the Revision Guide would suggest as reasonable answers, with alternatives suggested where appropriate.

Direct	The operand is the address of the value to be used.
Immediate	The operand is the value to be used.
Indexed	The operand plus the contents of the Index Register (IX) is the address of the value to be used.
Indirect	The operand is the address of the address of the value to be used.
Relative	The operand is the offset from the current address where the value to be used is stored.

[4]

Q2

This is **Question 8 in 9608 Paper 11 June 2015**. The mark scheme is available on the Cambridge International School Support Hub (requires registration). At the time of writing the published mark scheme is available on the Cambridge International School Support Hub. The Examiner's Report for the June 2015 series is also available there and this may contain comments specific to this question.

The following are what the author of the Revision Guide would suggest as reasonable answers, with alternatives suggested where appropriate.

a [3]

The data bus width:

The width of the data bus determines the number of bits that can be simultaneously transferred

If we design a data bus with more bits this will increase the number of bits that can be moved at one time. Transferring more bits at the same time will allow for instructions which consist of more bits. This means that fewer clock cycles will be needed to execute an instruction.

The clock speed:

Each instruction in the processor's instruction set has a stated number of clock cycles taken for its execution.

The clock speed sets the number of cycles the CPU executes each second.

If we increase the clock speed all instructions take less time to execute.

If is usually possible to change the clock speed setting. But a higher clock speed will generate more heat so there will be a practical upper limit on the clock speed setting.

b *Two points needed for the 2 marks ...*

USB is supported by all popular operating systems.

USB devices are advertised as called 'plug and play' – the device will be automatically detected and configured when first attached.

c The sequence order is - 2, 6, 5, 1, 4, and 2 [6]

1. The address contained in the Program Counter (PC) is copied to the Memory Address Register (MAR)
2. The value in the Program Counter (PC) is incremented so that it points to the next instruction to be fetched
3. The instruction is copied from the memory location contained in the Memory Address Register (MAR) and copied to the Memory Data Register (MDR)
4. The instruction is copied from the Memory Data Register (MDR) and placed in the Current Instruction Register (CIR)
5. The instruction is decoded
6. The instruction is executed

Q3

a   A = control bus.

B = address bus.

C = data bus. [3]

b *This is 'bookwork' – these definitions should be learnt...*

Program Counter	stores the address of next instruction to be executed
Memory Data Register	stores the data in transit between memory and other registers, or
	holds the instruction before it is passed to the CIR
Current Instruction Register	stores the current instruction being executed
Memory Address Register	stores the address of the memory location which is about to be accessed

[4]

Q4

a *Little different from the previous question BUT you must be clear the order in which each register plays its role in the fetch-execute cycle.*

- The Program Counter (PC) holds the address of the next instruction to be fetched
- The address in the Program Counter (PC) is copied to the Memory Address Register (MAR)
- The Program Counter (PC) is incremented
- The instruction is copied to the Memory Data Register (MDR) from the address held in the Memory Address Register (MAR)
- The instruction from the Memory Data Register (MDR) is copied to the Current Instruction Register (CIR). [4]

b One mark for each statement or letter in the correct place. Order is B, D and A and finally C.

At the end of the cycle for the current instruction (B) the processor checks if there is an interrupt. If the interrupt flag is set, (D) the register contents are saved, (A) the address of the Interrupt Service Routine (ISR) is loaded to the Program Counter (PC) and when the ISR completes, (C) the processor restores the register contents. [4]

Chapter 5

Progress Checks

Progress Check A

System software.

Progress Check B

Processor, primary memory, secondary storage, input/output devices, the user interface.

Progress Check C

Object file	
1.1. 1000 1000	1.2. 01011100
1.3. 1000 1111	2.1 +4
1.5. 0000 1111	2.2 +5
1.9. 1111 1111	

Symbol table	
Label	Address
1.4. PATTERN	1.7. +4 (153)
1.6. ANSWER	1.8. +5 (154)

Note that the numbering is used as follows: 1.3 the 'third entry on the first pass'; 2.1 the' first entry on the second pass'.

Progress Check D

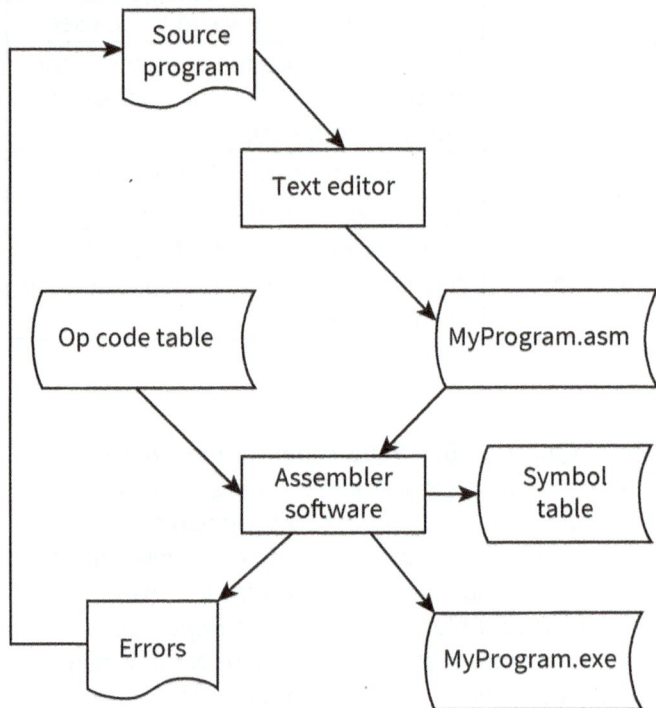

Figure 5.17 The assembler translation process.

Past paper questions

Q1

This is **Question 11 in 9608 Paper 11 November 2015**. The mark scheme is available on the Cambridge International School Support Hub. (requires registration). At the time of writing the published mark scheme is available on the Cambridge International School Support Hub. The Examiner's Report for the November 2015 series is also available there and this may contain comments specific to this question.

The following are what the author of the Revision Guide would suggest as reasonable answers, with alternatives suggested where appropriate.

Statement	Interpreter	Compiler
The translator creates an executable file		√
When the translation encounters a syntax error, game execution will halt	√	
The translator analyses and checks each line just before executing it	√	
The translator will produce faster execution of the game program		√
Use of this translator method makes it more difficult for the user to modify the code of the game supplied to the user		√

[5]

Q2

This is **Question 11 in 9608 Paper 11 November 2015.** The mark scheme is available on the Cambridge International School Support Hub. (requires registration). At the time of writing the published mark scheme is available on the Cambridge International School Support Hub. The Examiner's Report for the November 2015 series is also available there and this may contain comments specific to this question.

The following are what the author of the Revision Guide would suggest as reasonable answers, with alternatives suggested where appropriate.

Term	Definition
Compiler	The software reads the source code and reports all errors. The software produces an executable file.
Interpreter	The software reads each statement and checks it before running it. The software halts when it encounters a syntax error.
Compiler + Interpreter	The software translates a high level language program into machine code for the processor to execute.
Assembler	The software translates low-level statements into machine code for the processor to execute

[3]

Q3

This is **Question 2 in 9608 Paper 11 November 2016.** The mark scheme is available on the Cambridge International School Support Hub (requires registration). At the time of writing the published mark scheme is available on the Cambridge International School Support Hub. The Examiner's Report for the November 2016 series is also available there and this may contain comments specific to this question.

The following are what the author of the Revision Guide would suggest as reasonable answers, with alternatives suggested where appropriate.

a   i   The hardware is unusable without an OS.   [2]

The OS provides an interface between the user and the hardware and so the OS hides complexity of hardware from user.

The OS must be present – otherwise applications programs will not run.

ii   Management tasks carried out by the OS are; [2]

- The management of all the processes (programs) which are currently available to be executed by the processor
- Management of the main memory – do we have enough available free memory to load another process? Make sure the memory freed up when a process finishes execution is made available
- Management on all peripherals attached
- Management of the secondary store. Is there enough disk space to download and store a file?
- Security management – privileges and rights associated with different users of the computer system
- Provision of a user interface.

b   Consider a speller-checker DLL which is available to be used by the word processor, the spreadsheet software and other apps. [2]

The .DLL file is a library file may be used by many application programs.

The code for the DLL is saved separately from the main .EXE file.

The DLL code is only loaded into main memory when required at run-time.

Q4

This is **Question 7(a) in 9608 Paper 11 November 2016**. The mark scheme is available on the Cambridge International School Support Hub (requires registration). At the time of writing the published mark scheme is available on the Cambridge International School Support Hub. The Examiner's Report for the November 2016 series is also available there and this may contain comments specific to this question.

The following are what the author of the Revision Guide would suggest as reasonable answers, with alternatives suggested where appropriate.

a *Marks awarded Name of utility [1] + description [1] × 3*

All of the items of software below would be relevant for the scenario given in the question.

Disk formatter	Prepares a hard disk to allow data to be stored on it.
Virus checker	Checks for viruses and then quarantines or removes any virus found
File compression	Reduces file size by using a compression algorithm.
Backup software	Makes copy of files on another medium to be stored away from the computer. In the event of data corruption or loss of data the backup files will be used following a 'restore' procedure.
Firewall	Designed to prevent unauthorised access to the computer system from some external source such as the internet.

Q5

This is **Question 4(c) in 9608 Paper 11 November 2017**. The mark scheme is available on the Cambridge International School Support Hub (requires registration). At the time of writing the published mark scheme is available on the Cambridge International School Support Hub. The Examiner's Report for the November 2017 series is also available there and this may contain comments specific to this question.

The following are what the author of the Revision Guide would suggest as reasonable answers, with alternatives suggested where appropriate.

This is bookwork, but the question has asked you to use the sample program to establish the processor. Study this question — it neatly illustrates in detail the working of a two-pass assembler.

The assembler software scans the program instructions in sequence.

- When it meets a symbolic address it checks to see if this address has already been entered to the symbol table.
- If not, it adds it to the symbol table in the symbolic address column,
- If it is already in symbol table, check if the matching absolute address is present (i.e. known).
- If the absolute address is known, it is entered alongside the name.
- If the absolute address is not known, enter 'unknown' to the table (It will be worked out on the second pass and then entered)

Note, the question only asked for the detail about what is happening on the first pass. A second pass must be carried out — using this newly constructed symbol table and the table of op codes — to produce the object/ executable file. [3]

Chapter 6

Progress Checks

Progress Check A

Check digit is X.

The complete employee code: 9437X.

Progress Check B

Member Data	From a list	Range	Format	Length	Presence	Check digit
Family Name				√	√	
Forenames				√	√	
DateOfBirth	√	√	√		√	
Address				√		
Email			√		√	
MemType	√				√	
NoOfVisits	√	√				
Before	√					

Progress Check C

Passwords: When you set up a password for the first time, or when you change your password, you are asked to key in the new password twice.

Progress Check C

You should have checked that for each row, the total number of 1 bits is an even number and that, for each column, the total number of 1 bits is an even number.

Progress Check D

One error.

0	0	0	0	1	1	1	1
1	1	1	0	0	0	0	0
1	0	1	1	0	0	0	1
0	1	1	1	1	0	0	0
0	0	1	1	0	1	1	0

The error <u>can</u> be identified:

The parity bit for byte 2 would be calculated as 1.

The parity bit in column 4 of the would be calculated a zero.

Therefore byte 2 – column 4 is the error – change the bit to a 1.

Past paper questions

Q1

This is **Question 9 in 9608 Paper 11 November 2015**. The mark scheme is available on the Cambridge International School Support Hub (requires registration). At the time of writing the published mark scheme is available on the Cambridge International School Support Hub. The Examiner's Report for the November 2015 series is also available there and this may contain comments specific to this question.

The following are what the author of the Revision Guide would suggest as reasonable answers, with alternatives suggested where appropriate.

a [2]

Validation:

A validation check is designed to check whether the data is 'reasonable'. This could mean the data meets some given criteria.

Maybe give an example?

The number of items sold must be in the range 1 to 100.

Verification:

When some form of transfer of data takes place, a verification check checks if the data which is transferred is the same as the original.

Or, in a different context ...

Consider when entering a datum value to a screen capture form. The software will require that the data value is entered twice. The software checks that the two entries match – if not, then the user will be required to re-enter the data.

b *Write sentences and they should include most of the key points below. Giving an example is a good idea.* [4]

Parity checks are a done when data is transferred to detect and possibly correct data corruption.

A parity check will calculate the number of 1 bits in each byte. The system will use either 'even parity' or 'odd parity'. Even parity means the total number of 1 bits in a byte must total to an even number (0, 2, 4, 6 or 8).

The parity bit is the 8th bit in the byte.

Immediately the data transfer is completed, the parity of each byte is checked.

Example: the character with 7-bit ASCII code 1001 001 is to be transmitted. The transfer software is using 'even parity' so the parity bit added is a 1 - to make the complete byte transmitted 1001 0011.

Q2

This is **Question 10 in 9608 Paper 11 November 2015**. The mark scheme is available on the Cambridge International School Support Hub (requires registration). At the time of writing the published mark scheme is available on the Cambridge International School Support Hub. The Examiner's Report for the November 2015 series is also available there and this may contain comments specific to this question.

The following are what the author of the Revision Guide would suggest as reasonable answers, with alternatives suggested where appropriate.

a A virus is malicious code / software / program – that is designed to cause harm to a computer system. The effect of a virus could be to: [2]

- cause loss of data or the corruption of data on the computer, e.g. deletion of all the files on the secondary storage device.
- cause the computer system to crash completely or run very slowly.

b Note: *The keyword in the question is 'when?'* [2]

The virus checker will perform a check when:

- the computer is first turned on. It checks for corruption of the boot sector software.
- a file is downloaded to the computer.

Q3

This is **Question 7(c) in 9608 Paper 11 November 2016**. The mark scheme is available on the Cambridge International School Support Hub (requires registration). At the time of writing the published mark scheme is available on the Cambridge International School Support Hub. The Examiner's Report for the November 2016 series is also available there and this may contain comments specific to this question.

The following are what the author of the Revision Guide would suggest as reasonable answers, with alternatives suggested where appropriate.

a If the data is encrypted, a hacker may still get access to the data. However, the data will not be intelligible to the hacker as they will not have the decryption key. The decryption key is essential in order to decrypt the data. [2]

b The statement describes data verification (not validation). [2]

Data validation is a procedure to ensure that data is reasonable / sensible / that it satisfies some required criteria. For example software will check that a gender value entered to a data entry form may only have the value 'M' or 'F'.

c A password can be guessed (if weak). The password can be fraudulently obtained; for example, by a person looking over the shoulder of the user keying in the password. Or, the password could be 'captured' using data logging software. [2]

Q4

This is **Question 5 (a) only in 9608 Paper 11 June 2017**. The mark scheme is available on the Cambridge International School Support Hub (requires registration). At the time of writing the published mark scheme is available on the Cambridge International School Support Hub. The Examiner's Report for the June 2017 series is also available there and this may contain comments specific to this question.

The following are what the author of the Revision Guide would suggest as reasonable answers, with alternatives suggested where appropriate.

a i Count the number of one bits in the first seven bit positions. [2]

Add a 0 or 1 to bit position 0, to make the count of one bits an odd number (as the question states the system is using odd parity).

   ii A = 1 [2]

   B = 1

   iii The parity bit is worked out for each vertical row – the system counts the number of 1 bits for each of the first seven columns. [2]

The computer checks the parity of each bit position in the parity byte.

If the parity is incorrect, then there is an error in the data received.

If there was no parity error, there is no error in the data received.

Chapter 7

Progress Checks

Progress Check A

1 Keep the client informed about progress and an possible slippage.

2 Keep the user informed when Business A staff will need to interview certain Business B staff.

3 Make them aware of any legislation must comply with, for example, registration of application to comply with the Data Protection Act.

4 Ensure the privacy and security of any personal data made available to Business A during the development of the software.

Progress Check B

Run the software.

Copy the software.

Distribute the software to other users.

Study the code and change and improve the software.

Past paper questions

Q1

This is **Question 6 in 9608 Paper 11 November 2017.** The mark scheme is available on the Cambridge International School Support Hub (requires registration). At the time of writing the published mark scheme is available on the Cambridge International School Support Hub. The Examiner's Report for the November 2017 series is also available there and this may contain comments specific to this question.

The following are what the author of the Revision Guide would suggest as reasonable answers, with alternatives suggested where appropriate.

a   *This is asking for a 'bookwork definition' of ethics.*   [2]

Ethics are a system of moral principles that are a framework for guiding a person's behaviour.

A set of ethics will be based on philosophical guidelines.

Ethics are relevant to the computer scientist as they will guide the employer and an employee's behaviour in the workplace.

b   *The question here has stated the eight principles – so the employee's behaviours must be matched to three of these. For other questions – see Q2 below - on this topic, the principles will not be given in the stem of the question – so they need to be memorised.*   [2]

Marks awarded as follows:

issue [1] + correct principle [1] + possible action [1] = 2 × [3]

I   Raj is uncomfortable with one of his colleagues:

- This is clearly an issue with one of his work colleagues. It will need to be addressed by management – in the first instance Raj's Line Manager.
- Possible action: Talk the issue through with Raj's Line Manager to establish the precise reason for Raj's issue. The Line Manager will also want to speak with the colleague. Strategy could be some team building exercises.

ii   Raj is unfamiliar with programming language:

- This is an issue particular to Raj ('Self' principle) and also specific to the role he asked to perform (so 'Profession').
- Possible action: Undergo training.

iii   Visit to unfamiliar workplace:

- This will impact on the client so, 'Client and employer'. Also 'Management' as action needs to be taken to reassure Raj.
- Possible action: He should speak to his Line Manager to make them aware of his anxiety. Manager should ensure that, for the first series of visits, Raj always visits the workplace with a colleague.

Q2

This is **Question 6 in 9608 Paper 11 June 2016.** The mark scheme is available on the Cambridge International School Support Hub (requires registration). At the time of writing the published mark scheme is available on the Cambridge International School Support Hub. The Examiner's Report for the June 2016 series is also available there and this may contain comments specific to this question.

The following are what the author of the Revision Guide would suggest as reasonable answers, with alternatives suggested where appropriate.

The question describes a 'team of software engineers' and the task is 'an e-commerce development' – so choose three principles which address these two issues.

Principle: 'CLIENT AND EMPLOYER'

At various times the programmers will be using sensitive data of the client. Confidentiality should be followed at all times. The data should never be disclosed to anyone outside of the team.

Principle: 'PRODUCT'

Testing should be undertaken which follows the highest possible standards. The team should follow closely the programme of development and methodology as set out by the Team Leader. There may be existing standards for the display of forms, etc. for this particular client which must be followed.

Principle: 'COLLEAGUES'

Each member of the team should be supportive of all the other team members – always willing to share expertise and advice.

++++++++++++++++++++++++++++++++++++

The other five principles are listed below. A good extension exercise would be to describe a workplace issue where each of these principles should be followed.

PUBLIC - Software engineers shall act consistently with the public interest.

JUDGEMENT - Software engineers shall maintain integrity and independence in their professional judgment.

MANAGEMENT - Software engineering managers and leaders shall subscribe to and promote an ethical approach to the management of software development and maintenance.

PROFESSION - Software engineers shall advance the integrity and reputation of the profession (consistent with the public interest).

SELF - Software engineers shall participate in lifelong learning regarding the practice of their profession and shall promote an ethical approach to the practice of the profession. [6]

Chapter 8

Progress Checks

Progress Check A

Primary key: `StudentNumber`.

Index also the `StudentName` attribute, we will frequently search the database for a pupil using their name.

Progress Check B

If there is a tuple in the `ORDER` table with a `ProductID` value absent from the `PRODUCT` table.

Progress Check C

a `CourseCode`.

b Address and the course(s) on which they can teach, although this second suggestion presents a problem as some data might need to be stored in a new table.

c `TrainerName` (as there will not be too many trainers and it is highly unlikely that we shall have two trainers with the same name).

d Note: It cannot be just `CourseDate` (as we have two different courses scheduled for the same date).

So, it will be a composite key of `CourseDate` + `CourseCode`.

e One TRAINER will deliver many COURSEDIARY sessions.

One COURSE is offered many times in the COURSEDIARY table.

f `TrainerName` to link back to the `TrainerName` attribute in table TRAINER.

`CourseCode` to link back to `CourseCode` in table COURSE.

g

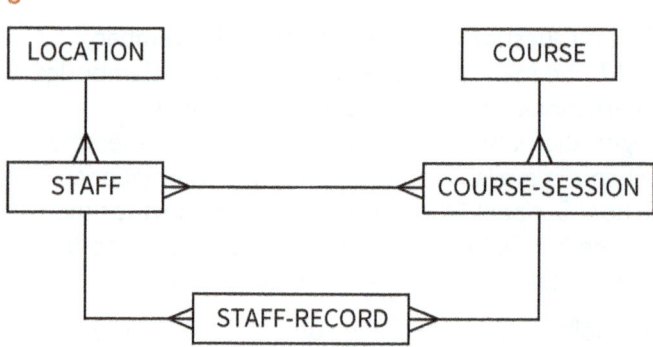

Figure 8.07.

Progress Check D

Foreign key Table – Attribute	Links to
STAFF.City	LOCATION.City
STAFF-RECORD.StaffID	STAFF.StaffID
STAFF-RECORD.CourseTitle	COURSE.CourseTitle
COURSE-SESSION.CourseTitle	COURSE.CourseTitle

Progress Check E

1 a No, that statement is First Normal Form.

b True

c True

d No, if it has a composite primary key we need to look carefully at the non-key attributes.

e True

Progress Check F

a i True

ii True, i.e. if we know the tutor's initials, we will automatically know the tutor name.

iii True, i.e. if we know the tutor's initials, we will automatically know the tutor room.

iv No, 3NF is concerned with non-key attributes.

b i `TutorInitials`.

ii "One tutor will be responsible for many students".

Progress Check G

a YES.

b YES.

c NO.

d NO.

e YES.

Progress Check H

Table	Primary key	Foreign Key(s)
BAND	BandName	None
AGENT	AgentName	None
BAND-TOUR	TourName	BandName links to primary key BAND.BandName.
BAND-TOUR-GIGS	TourName + GigDate (Could also have been BandName + GigDate)	• BandName links to primary key BAND.BandName • TourName links to primary key BAND-TOUR.TourName • VenueName links to primary key VENUE.VenueName
VENUE	VenueName	None

Progress Check I

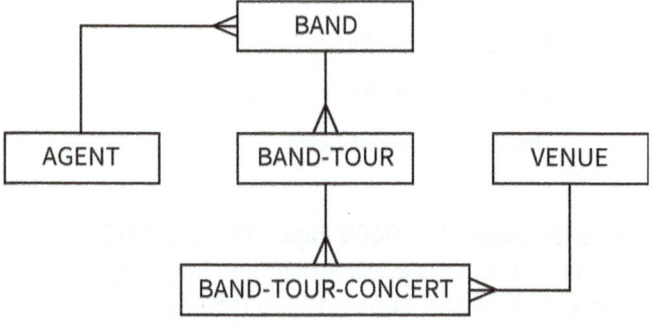

Figure 8.08.

Progress Check J

a
```
SELECT BandName
FROM BAND
WHERE AgentName = 'Maximum Exposure'
```

b
```
SELECT BandName
FROM BAND-TOUR-CONCERT
WHERE StartDate >= #01/01/2022#
```

c
```
SELECT TourName
FROM BAND-TOUR-CONCERT
WHERE StartDate > #01/06/2022# AND MaxNoOfConcerts > 10
```

d
```
SELECT BAND-TOUR-CONCERT.BandName,
BAND-TOUR-CONCERT.TourName,
              VENUE.VenueName
WHERE VENUE.Location = 'Paris'
```

e
```
SELECT ConcertDate
FROM BAND-TOUR-CONCERT
WHERE TourName = 'Back to the future'
ORDER BY ConcertDate
```

Past paper questions

Q1

This is **Question 7 in 9608 Paper 11 November 2017**. The mark scheme is available on the Cambridge International School Support Hub (requires registration). At the time of writing the published mark scheme is available on the Cambridge International School Support Hub. The Examiner's Report for the November 2017 series is also available there and this may contain comments specific to this question.

The following are what the author of the Revision Guide would suggest as reasonable answers, with alternatives suggested where appropriate.

a i [2]

PATIENT(**PatientID**, PatientName, Address, Gender)

DOCTOR(**DoctorID**, Gender, Qualification)

APPOINTMENT(**AppointmentDate**, **AppointmentTime**, DoctorID, PatientID)

a ii

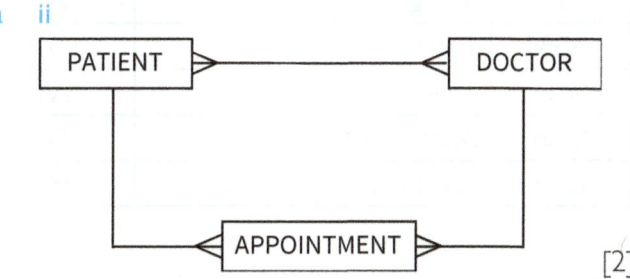

[2]

Once you have labelled the E-R diagram – describe each relationship line to confirm your understanding …

Many PATIENTs are seen by many DOCTORs

Note: the many-to-many relationship between PATIENT and DOCTOR was not needed for the strongest answer.

One PATIENT attends for many APPOINTMENTs.

One DOCTOR takes many APPOINTMENTs.

This is a good example where the initial many-to-many relationship is solved by the inclusion of the third table APPOINTMENT.

b Add an attribute (for example Attended to the appointments table. [2]

Q2

This is **Question 9 in 9608 Paper 11 June 2015**. The mark scheme is available on the Cambridge International School Support Hub (requires registration). At the time of writing the published mark scheme is available on the Cambridge International School Support Hub. The Examiner's Report for the June 2015 series is also available there and this may contain comments specific to this question.

The following are what the author of the Revision Guide would suggest as reasonable answers, with alternatives suggested where appropriate.

a The `ShopSales` table has repeated group (of attributes). [1]

There are a number of products for each sales person.

b Table: `SalesPerson` [2]

FirstName	Shop
Nick	TX
Sean	BH
John	TX

Table: `SalesProducts` [3]

FirstName	ProductName	NoOfProducts	Manufacturer
Nick	television set	3	SKC
Nick	refrigerator	2	WP
Nick	digital camera	6	HKC
Sean	hair dryer	1	WG
Sean	electric shaver	8	BG
John	television set	2	SKC

FirstName	ProductName	NoOfProducts	Manufacturer
John	moblie phone	8	ARC
John	digital camera	4	HKC
John	toaster	3	GK

c i Any two from: [2]

The primary key of the `SalesPerson` table is `FirstName`

This primary key links to the `FirstName` attribute in the `SalesProducts` table – this makes `FirstName` in the `SalesProducts` table a foreign key.

ii *This is a challenging question – it is wanting you to recognise that the given table is not in Third Normal Form.* [2]

There are two non-key attributes which are dependant - a non-key dependency.

`Manufacturer` is dependent on `ProductName`, (which is not the primary key of the `SalesProducts` table.

iii SalesPerson (`FirstName`, Shop) [2]

SalesProducts (`FirstName`, `ProductName`, NoOfProducts)

OR

SalesProducts (SalesID, FirstName, ProductName, NoOfProducts)

Product (`ProductName`, Manufacturer)

Marks awarded for:

The correct attributes in each table.

The correct primary keys.

Q3

This is **Question 1 in 9608 Paper 11 June 2017**. The mark scheme is available on the Cambridge International School Support Hub (requires registration). At the time of writing the published mark scheme is available on the Cambridge International School Support Hub. The Examiner's Report for the June 2017 series is also available there and this may contain comments specific to this question.

The following are what the author of the Revision Guide would suggest as reasonable answers, with alternatives suggested where appropriate.

a   Many-to-one.   [1]
b   i   `A-NURSE(NurseID, FirstName, FamilyName, WardName)`   [1]
    ii The primary key `WardName` in the `A-WARD` table, links to the foreign key `WardName` in the `A-NURSE` table.   [2]
c   i   Many-to-many relationship   [1]
    ii `B-WARD-NURSE(WardName, NurseID)`   [2]

    A mark will be awarded for the correct attributes and the second mark for recognising the composite primary key.

    iii

```
  ┌─────────┐              ┌─────────┐
  │ B-NURSE │              │ B-WARD  │
  └────┬────┘              └────┬────┘
       │                        │
       │   ┌───────────────┐    │
       └──<│ B-WARD–NURSE  │>───┘
           └───────────────┘
```
   [2]

Again an example where the many-to-many relationship between B-NURSE and B-WARD (not shown) must be replaced by the two one-to-many relationships shown.

d   i   `SELECT NurseID, FamilyName`
        `FROM B-NURSE`
        `WHERE Specialism = 'THEATRE';`   [3]
    ii `UPDATE B-NURSE`
        `SET FamilyName = 'Chi'`
        `WHERE NurseID = '076';`   [3]

Q4

This is **Question 1 in 9608 Paper 11 November 2016.** The mark scheme is available on the Cambridge International School Support Hub. (requires registration). At the time of writing the published mark scheme is available on the Cambridge International School Support Hub. The Examiner's Report for the November 2017 series is also available there and this may contain comments specific to this question.

The following are what the author of the Revision Guide would suggest as reasonable answers, with alternatives suggested where appropriate.

a   One mark for each correct line.

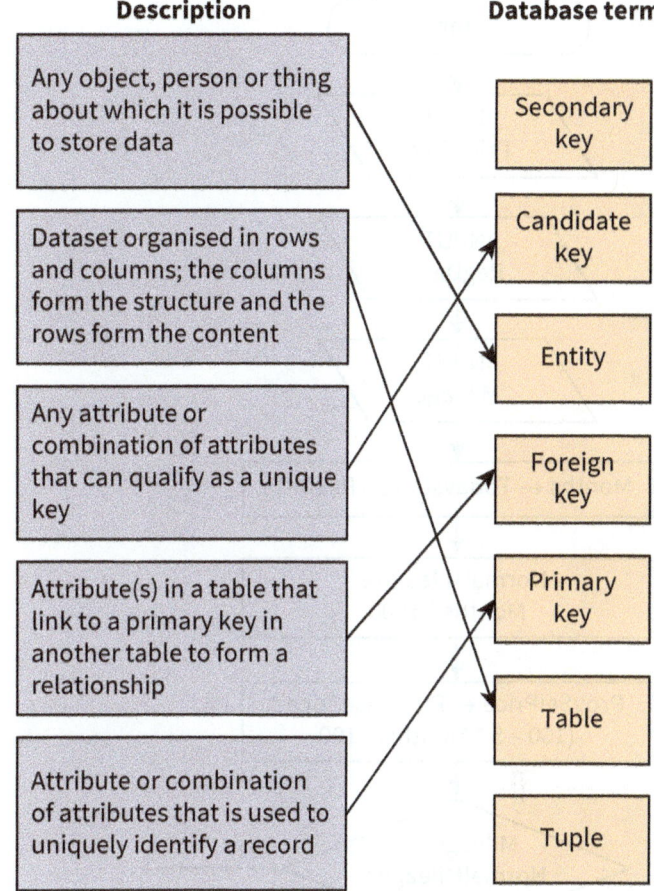

b   Referential integrity is an issue when there is a relationship between two tables.

Every record in the 'many side table' must have a matching record in the 'one side table'. In practice this means that the primary key attribute must be present in each of the 'many side' records.

Referential integrity is a particular issue if we attempt:

- to update a record in the one side table – if we change the primary key value, there may be orphaned records in the many side table.
- to delete a record from the one side table – there may be records in the many side table which now do not have a matching primary key value.   [3]

Chapter 9

Progress Checks

Progress Check A

a   PASS.
b   RETAKE (care needed with a value right on the boundary).

Progress Check B

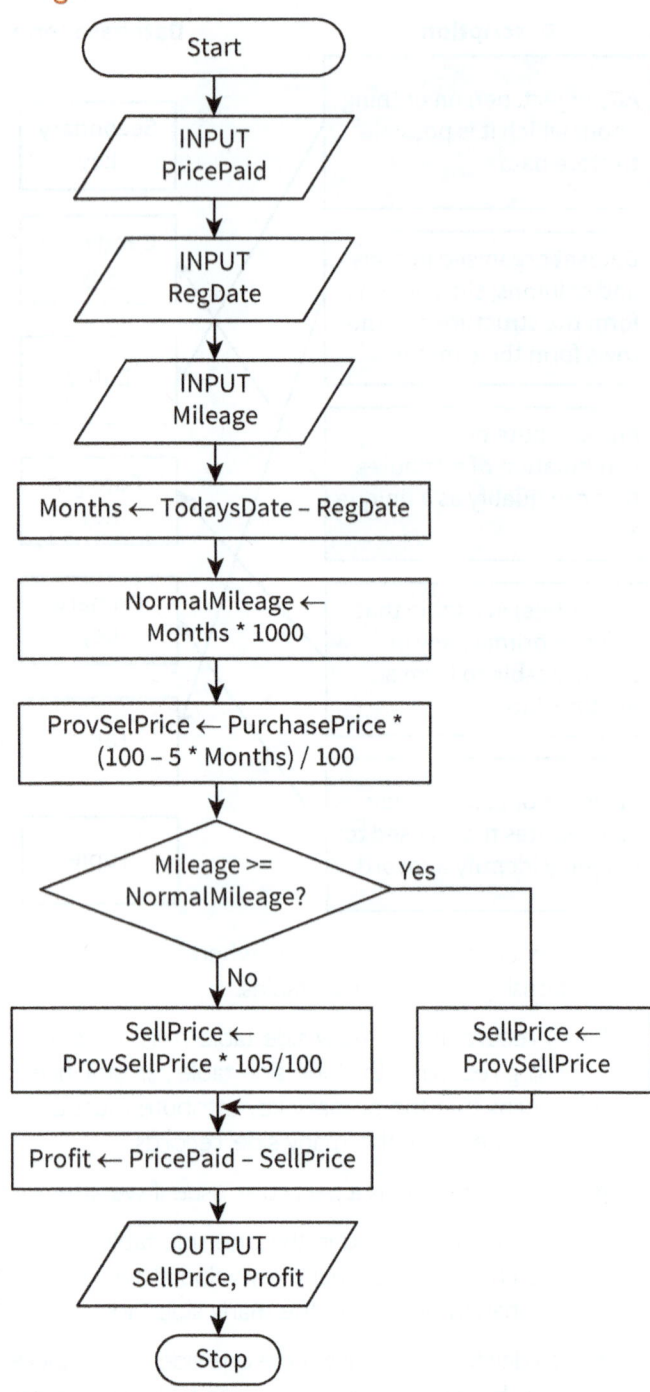

Figure 9.06.

Progress Check C

A: Year ← 1
B: Value ← Value *1.1
C: Value >= Amount * 2
D: OUTPUT Year

Past paper questions

Q1

This is **Question 4 in 9608 Paper 21 November 2015**. The mark scheme is available on the Cambridge International School Support Hub. (requires registration). At the time of writing the published mark scheme is available on the Cambridge International School Support Hub. The Examiner's Report for the November 2015 series is also available there and this may contain comments specific to this question.

The following are what the author of the Revision Guide would suggest as reasonable answers, with alternatives suggested where appropriate.

Remember the fundamental points when drawing a program flowchart.

The chart will have a 'Start' and 'End' box.

Use the correct shape boxes for input, output, processing and a decision box.

A decision box must have two outcomes labelled 'True' and 'False'.

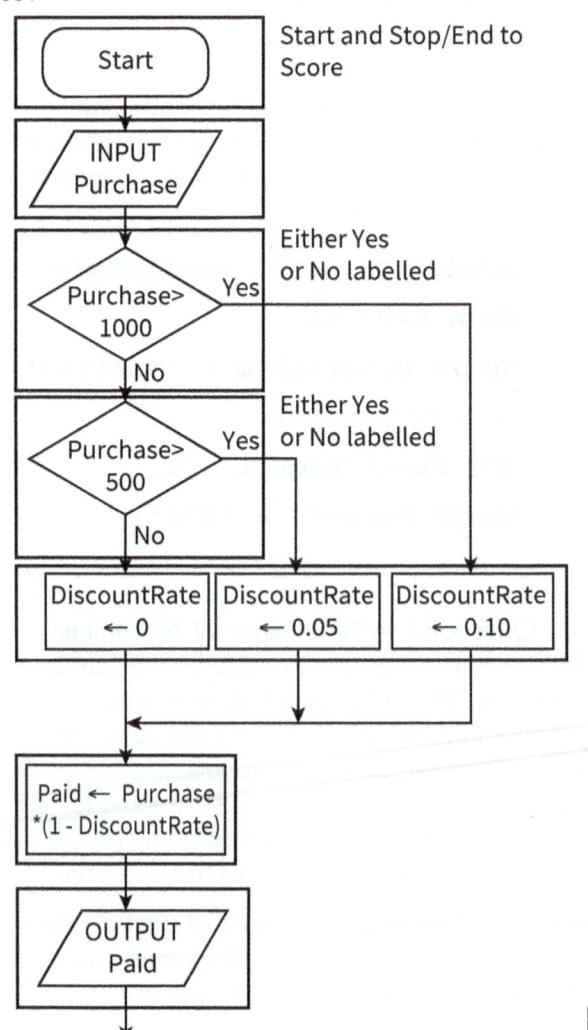

[6]

Q2

This is **Question 3(b)(i)** in **9608 Paper 21 November 2016**. The mark scheme is available on the Cambridge International School Support Hub. (requires registration). At the time of writing the published mark scheme is available on the Cambridge International School Support Hub. The Examiner's Report for the November 2016 series is also available there and this may contain comments specific to this question.

The following are what the author of the Revision Guide would suggest as reasonable answers, with alternatives suggested where appropriate.

```
INPUT TicketType
WHILE NOT (TicketType = 'E' OR TicketType = 'S')
    INPUT TicketType
ENDWHILE
```

1 mark for the `loop`.
1 mark for the condition.
1 mark for INPUT before and inside the `loop`.

Chapter 10

Progress Checks

Progress Check A

8 will be recognised as the integer value eight.

"8" will be recognised as a <u>string</u> value with a single character the digit 8.

'8' will be recognised as <u>character</u> value of eight.

Progress Check B

FamilyName	STRING
Forenames	STRING
DateOfBirth	DATE
Address	STRING
Email	STRING
MemType	CHAR
NoOfVisits	INTEGER
MemberBefore	BOOLEAN

Progress Check C

3 sales.

January

Progress Check D

a 4

b `Sales[1,7]`

Progress Check E

Solution 1: Two separate arrays:

`Name      : ARRAY[1,203] OF STRING`

`JoinDate  : ARRAY[1,203] OF DATE`

Solution 2: Define a 'record', then an array of this record type.

```
TYPE EmployeeData
DECLARE Name     : STRING
DECLARE JoinDate : DATE
END TYPE
DECLARE Employee : EmployeeData
```

Progress Check F

File has three lines of text.

Screwdriver
Hammer
Saw

Progress Check G

File has one line of text

Saw

Progress Check H

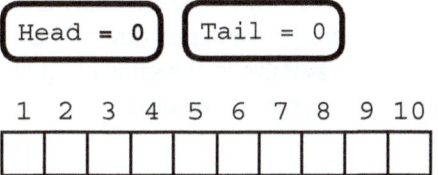

Progress Check I

a 10

b Head ← Head + 1

c A new item always added at index position Tail + 1

Progress Check J

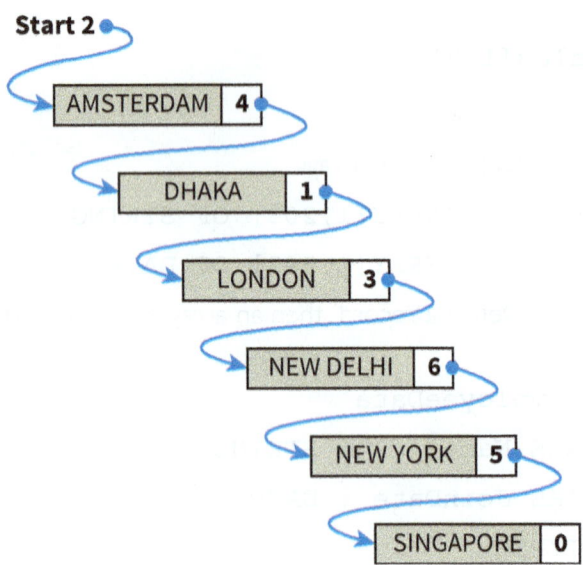

Past paper questions

Q1

This is **Question 5(a) in 9608 Paper 22 June 2016**. The mark scheme is available on the Cambridge International School Support Hub (requires registration). At the time of writing the published mark scheme is available on the Cambridge International School Support Hub. The Examiner's Report for the June 2016 series is also available there and this may contain comments specific to this question.

The following are what the author of the Revision Guide would suggest as reasonable answers, with alternatives suggested where appropriate.

a i The data needs to be permanently available to the application programs(s). Therefore the data must be saved before a program is closed down. This data must be made available to the same program the next time the program is executed. [1]

   ii Problem: [5]

   When a line of text is read from the file there is nothing to indicate where the title ends and the artist name begins.

   Solution 1:

   Add a 'separator character' between each data item – This would need to be a character which never occurs in the data.

   For example using '$' as the separator character.

   The text line would be: `Kind of Green$Miles Coltrane$Rack1-5`

Solution 2:

The design which follows is called using 'fixed length records'.

Use a fixed number of characters for each data item – Where necessary the artist name and title are padded out with trailing <Space> characters.

The text line would be: `Kind of Green       Miles Coltrane      Rack1-5`

The design here has used a total of 20 characters for both the title and artist data.

Marks would be allocated as follows - Two marks for description of problem + Two marks for description of solution.

Q2

This is **Question 4(c) in 9608 Paper 21 November 2016**. The mark scheme is available on the Cambridge International School Support Hub (requires registration). At the time of writing the published mark scheme is available on the Cambridge International School Support Hub. The Examiner's Report for the November 2016 series is also available there and this may contain comments specific to this question.

The following are what the author of the Revision Guide would suggest as reasonable answers, with alternatives suggested where appropriate.

a [2]

```
OPEN "PRODUCTS" FOR READ
i ← 1
WHILE NOT EOF ("PRODUCTS")
    READIFLE ("PRODUCTS" , PCode[i]
    READIFLE ("PRODUCTS" ,
PDescription[i]
    READIFLE ("PRODUCTS" , Temp
    PRetailPrice[i] ← TONUM(Temp)
    i ← i + 1
ENDWHILE
CLOSE ("PRODUCTS")
OUTPUT "PRODUCTS file contents written to arrays"
```

b The alternative suggested is using fixed length records. [5]

   Benefit – There is now only one read operation needed to read the complete data for one record. This will be read to the program as a single string.

Drawback – Additional program code must be written to isolate each data item from the string.

Chapter 11

Progress Checks

Progress Check A

`1FaultTotal`	X	Starts with a digit character
`NoOfFaults`	√	
`Number Of Faults`	X	Contains characters
`NumberofFaults`	√	
`Number_Of_Faults`	√	Underscore allowed
`Number-Of-Faults`	X	Dash character not allowed

Progress Check B

a `DECLARE` keyword missing.

b Used 'equals sign' – should be the assignment symbol (←).

c The statement is 'the wrong way around' – should be:

   `PayRate ← YearsEmployed * 5.50`

d Not using camel case or meaningful variable names.

Progress Check C

1 "slow"
2 "DOWN"
3 "NOT"
4 "VERY F"
5 "doFAST"
6 "slow/fast"
7 43.96
8 40

Progress Check D

```
FOR Index ← 1 TO 7
    OUTPUT StudentMark[Index]
NEXT Index
```

Progress Check E

```
Index ← 1
REPEAT
    NextMark ← StudentMark[Index]
    IF NextMark <> -1
        THEN
            OUTPUT NextMark
            Index ← Index + 1
    ENDIF
UNTIL NextMark = -1
```

Progress Check F

Pass	i	UBound	Swapped
1		5	FALSE
	1		TRUE
	2		
	3		
	4		TRUE
2			FALSE
	1		
	2		
	3		TRUE
3			FALSE
	1		
	2		TRUE
			FALSE
4	1		

Animal				
1	2	3	4	5
CAT	ANT	COW	RAT	BEE
ANT	CAT			
			BEE	RAT
ANT	CAT	COW	BEE	RAT
		BEE	COW	
ANT	CAT	BEE	COW	RAT
	BEE	CAT		
ANT	BEE	CAT	COW	RAT
ANT	BEE	CAT	COW	RAT

Table 11.07 Bubble sort trace. The items were sorted before the final pass was made.

Progress Check G

a   17, 24 and 28

b   04

c   We cannot determine that. The menu will continue to be displayed until the user enters choice 3.

Progress Check H

Add a third parameter to the procedure header.

```
PROCEDURE IncreasePrice(PriceArray :
ARRAY OF REAL, UBound : INTEGER,
PriceIncrease : INTEGER)
```

13 becomes `PriceArray[Item] ← PriceArray[Item] * (1 + PriceIncrease/100)`

Call the procedure with:

```
CALL IncreasePrice(Electricals, 550, 20)
```

Progress Check I

Variable	Data type	Description
Values	ARRAY [1..200] OF INTEGER	The stored data
Index	INTEGER	The loop counter/ array index
ONCount	INTEGER	Stores the total for the number of TRUE values

Table 11.08 Identifier table.

Past paper questions

Q1

This is **Question 2(a) and (b) in 9608 Paper 22 June 2015**. The mark scheme is available on the Cambridge International School Support Hub (requires registration). At the time of writing the published mark scheme is available on the Cambridge International School Support Hub. The Examiner's Report for the June 2015 series is also available there and this may contain comments specific to this question.

The following are what the author of the Revision Guide would suggest as reasonable answers, with alternatives suggested where appropriate.

a   i   Displays a menu with 4 choices to the user. The software prompts the use for the input of a number for their menu choice.

If the number input is 1, 2, 3 or 4 the program continues to the next stage.

If the number is invalid, the user is prompted again.

This continues until the user response is valid.

Maximum 3 marks for each point

ii The input number from the user is being validated. It may require several attempts before a valid number is entered. Each attempt is one iteration of the loop.

Must use the term 'validated' to score the mark.

b   i   3 – 1 mark

ii This new design limits the number of attempts. – 1 mark

Q2

This is **Question 5(c) in 9608 Paper 22 June 2015**. The mark scheme is available on the Cambridge International School Support Hub (requires registration). At the time of writing the published mark scheme is available on the Cambridge International School Support Hub. The Examiner's Report for the June 2015 series is also available there and this may contain comments specific to this question.

The following are what the author of the Revision Guide would suggest as reasonable answers, with alternatives suggested where appropriate.

a   2 – 1 mark

b

Tick or Cross	Explanation
X	The second parameter should be data type CHAR – the double quote delimiters implies this is a STRING
X	Should have only two parameters
√	

1 mark for each row

Q3

This is **Question 3 (a) and (b) in 9608 Paper 21 November 2015**. The mark scheme is available on the Cambridge International School Support Hub (requires registration). At the time of writing the published mark scheme is available on the Cambridge

International School Support Hub. The Examiner's Report for the November 2015 series is also available there and this may contain comments specific to this question.

The following are what the author of the Revision Guide would suggest as reasonable answers, with alternatives suggested where appropriate.

a

Test case	Inputs		Output
	InA	InB	OutZ
1	TRUE	TRUE	FALSE
2	TRUE	FALSE	TRUE
3	FALSE	TRUE	TRUE
4	FALSE	FALSE	TRUE

[4]

b

```
IF InA = TRUE AND InB = TRUE
    THEN
        OutZ ← FALSE
    ELSE
        OutZ ← TRUE
ENDIF
```

Marks awarded:

1 mark for a correct IF – THEN - ELSE – ENDIF structure

1 mark for the correct condition – InA = TRUE AND InB = TRUE

1 mark for the correct Logic: OutZ ← FALSE when the condition is true

Alternative answer could be:

```
OutZ←NOT(InA AND InB)
OutZ← NOT InA OR NOT InB
```

Q4

```
TotalSales ← 0
FOR SalesPerson ← 1 TO 6
    FOR MonthNumber ← 1 TO 12
        TotalSales ← TotalSales + Sales[SalesPerson, MonthNumber]
        PersonTotal ← PersonTotal + Sales[SalesPerson, MonthNumber]
    NEXT MonthNumber
    OUTPUT "Person ",SalesPerson, "-", PersonTotal
    PersonTotal ← 0
NEXT SalesPerson
OUTPUT TotalSales
```
[5]

Chapter 12

Progress Checks

Progress Check A

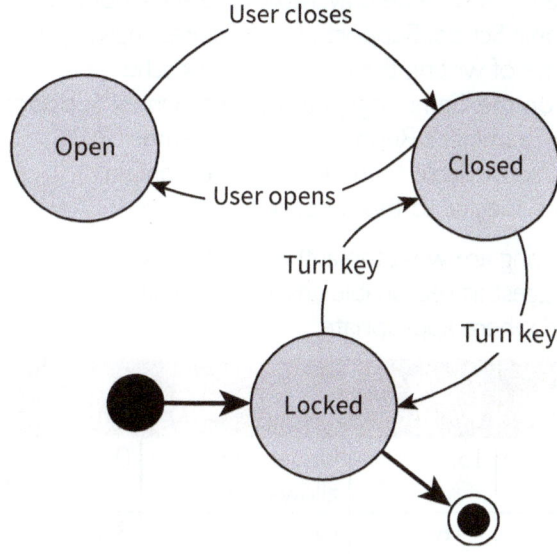

Figure 12.13.

Progress Check B

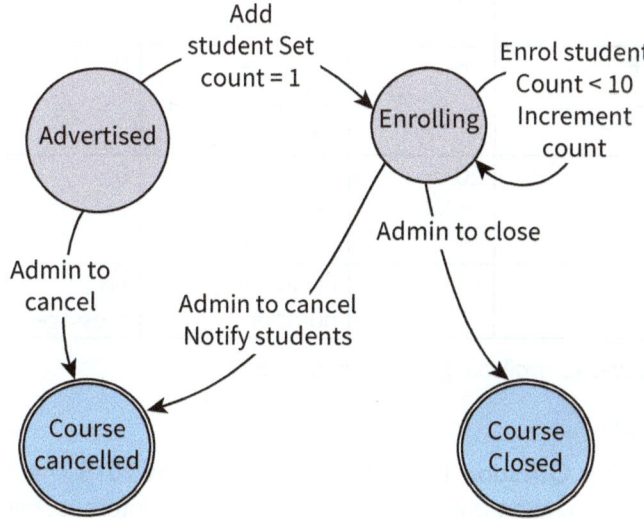

Figure 12.14

Progress Check C

```
i ← 0
REPEAT
    OUTPUT i
    i ← i + 1
UNTIL i = 10
```

Past paper questions

Q1

This is **Question 1(b) in 9608 Paper 21 November 2016**. The mark scheme is available on the Cambridge International School Support Hub (requires registration). At the time of writing the published mark scheme is available on the Cambridge International School Support Hub. The Examiner's Report for the November 2016 series is also available there and this may contain comments specific to this question.

The following are what the author of the Revision Guide would suggest as reasonable answers, with alternatives suggested where appropriate.

TicketType	Baggage Weight	Explanation	Expected output
E	15	Under the allowance	0
E	>16	Over the allowance	3.50
S	<=20	Under the allowance	0
S	>20	Over the allowance	5.75
E	16	16 is the boundary for a type E ticket	0
S	20	20 is the boundary for a type S ticket	0
E or S	<0	Invalid weight number	Error message

5 marks available for each correct row

Q2

This is **Question 1(a) in 9608 Paper 43 Nov 2016**. The mark scheme is available on the Cambridge International School Support Hub (requires registration). At the time of writing the published mark scheme is available on the Cambridge International School Support Hub. The Examiner's Report for the June 2015 series is also available there and this may contain comments specific to this question.

The following are what the author of the Revision Guide would suggest as reasonable answers, with alternatives suggested where appropriate.

1 mark for both 'Set code entered' correct.
1 mark for each label.

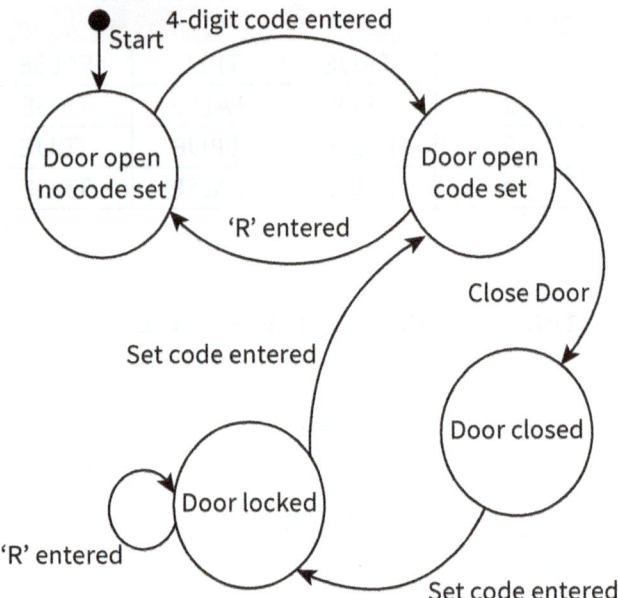

Q3

This is **Question 4(d) in 9608 Paper 21 Nov 2016**. The mark scheme is available on the Cambridge International School Support Hub. (requires registration). At the time of writing the published mark scheme is available on the Cambridge International School Support Hub. The Examiner's Report for the November 2016 series is also available there and this may contain comments specific to this question.

The following are what the author of the Revision Guide would suggest as reasonable answers, with alternatives suggested where appropriate.

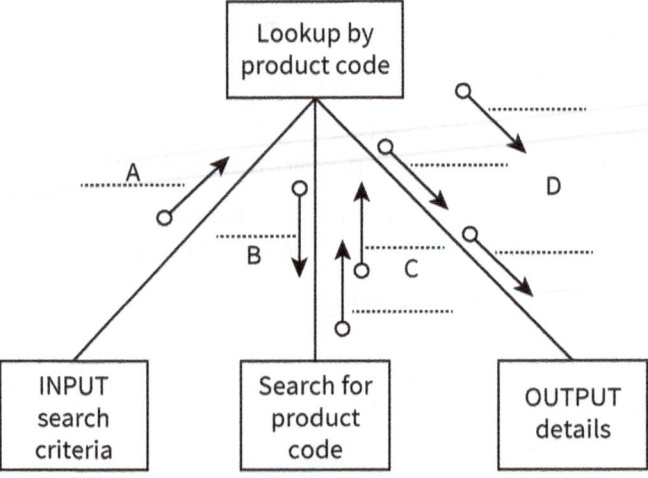

One mark per group (one or more names) as follows:

A: SearchCode

B: SearchCode // ThisIndex

C: ThisRetailPrice, ThisDescription

D: SearchCode, ThisDescription, ThisRetailPrice   [4]

Chapter 13

Progress Checks

Progress Check A

```
TYPE
    DECLARE ProductCode : (A, B, C, D)
ENDTYPE
.
DECLARE ThisProductCode :
ProductCode

ThisProductCode ← C
```

Progress Check B

```
DECLARE ShoeSize : SET OF (38, 39,
40, 41, 42, 43, 44)

IF ThisSize = 44
    THEN
        OUTPUT "Out of stock"
ENDIF
```

Progress Check C

```
TYPE NurseData
    DECLARE NurseID              : STRING
    DECLARE FamilyName           : STRING
    DECLARE FirstNames           : STRING
    DECLARE RegistrationDate     : DATE
    DECLARE HeathAndSafetyCourse : CHAR  (will store value 'Y' or 'N')
    DECLARE WardName             : STRING
ENDTYPE
```

Alternatively a BOOLEAN variable …

Progress Check D

a We need fast access to individual customer accounts.

b Account number.

Progress Check E

a 17 ¾   0100 0111 0000 0101

b 3 3/16   0110 0110 0000 001

c -9 ½   1110 1000 0100

Progress Check F

The mantissas all begin with digits 01 or 10.

a Mantissa: 7/8
   Exponent: +1
   Number: 1.75

b Mantissa: -15/16
   Exponent: +7
   Number: -120

c Mantissa: -3/4
   Exponent: -119
   Number: -3×2^{-121}

Progress Check G

Mantissa: ½ + ¼ + 1/8 + 1/16 = +15/16

Exponent: 15

Number: $+15/16 * 2^{15}$

             $= +15 * 2^{11}$

             $= +15 * 2048 = +3720$

Past paper questions

Q1

This is **Question 1 in 9608 Paper 32 June 2018**. The mark scheme is available on the Cambridge International School Support Hub (requires registration). At the time of writing the published mark scheme is available on the Cambridge International School Support Hub. The Examiner's Report for the June 2018 series is also available there and this may contain comments specific to this question.

The following are what the author of the Revision Guide would suggest as reasonable answers, with alternatives suggested where appropriate.

a `CollegeStudent.StudentID ← 6539` [1]

b i 1 mark per point

   `StudentCourse: ARRAY[1:6] OF`

   All valid strings from:

   `DECLARE StudentCourse: ARRAY[1:6] OF ("Computer Science", "Engineering", "Science", "Maths", "Physics", "Chemistry", "Music", "Drama", "English Language")`

   ii `DECLARE StudentID: 1..8000` [1]

c i 1 mark per point.

   Type declaration `TYPE` and `ENDTYPE`

   Declaring `Code` as `STRING`

   Declaring `Mark` as ARRAY [1:6] OF INTEGER

   `AverageMark` as REAL

   For example:

   `TYPE StudentAssessment`
   `  DECLARE Code : STRING`
   `  DECLARE Mark : ARRAY[1:6] OF INTEGER`
   `  DECLARE AverageMark : REAL`
   `ENDTYPE`

   ii Any 3 from the following. 1 mark for each point.

   `StudentID` key field is hashed to produce home location

   If home location is free, insert record/data

   Else use overflow method to find free location to store record/data

   If no free location is available, then file is full and record/data cannot be stored.

Q2

This is **Question 1 in 9608 Paper 31 Nov 2016**. The mark scheme is available on the Cambridge International School Support Hub (requires registration). At the time of writing the published mark scheme is available on the Cambridge International School Support Hub. The Examiner's Report for the November 2016 series is also available there and this may contain comments specific to this question.

The following are what the author of the Revision Guide would suggest as reasonable answers, with alternatives suggested where appropriate.

a +2.5

   = 0101000000000010 [3]

   Give marks for correct answer (normalised or not normalised) [1]

   = 10.1 [1]

   = 0.101×2^2 // evidence of shifting binary point appropriately [3]

   [Max 3]

b −2.5

   1011000000000010

   Give marks for correct answer

   One's complement of 12-bit mantissa of +2.5 <u>101011111111</u> – allow f.t. [1]

   +1 to get two's complement <u>101100000000</u> [1]

   [Max 3]

c 3 [3]

   Give marks for correct answer

   = 0.011×2^3 // exponent is 3 [1]

   11.0 // (1/4 + 1/8) * 8 [1]

   [Max 3]

d i Not normalised [1]

   ii First two bits should be different for normalised number // because the number starts with 00 [1]

e reduced accuracy [1]

   increased range [1]

Chapter 14

Progress Checks

Progress Check A

a Transport Communication Protocol, Internet Protocol.

b Application layer, Transport layer, Network layer, Link layer.

c Any 3 of HTTP, FTP, POP3, SMTP.

Progress Check B

Internet Protocol address: the source and destination address given to every data packet on a packet-switched network.

Socket: a socket is formed when a connection is made by the transport layer. The socket is the IP address and the port number.

Port number: the transport layer sends packets to a from a process using a socket number. The popular standard port numbers are allocated to server applications, for example, port 80 for a web server. Port numbers above 1046 are allocated dynamically for the client computer process.

Progress Check C

Tracker computer: the computer that keeps a mapping of all the swarm hosts and what pieces of the file they are in possession of.

Seed: the computer that has the entre file contents.

Swarm: the collection of participating computer hosts.

Past paper questions

Q1

This is **Question 3 in 9608 Paper 32 November 2015**. The mark scheme is available on the Cambridge International School Support Hub (requires registration). At the time of writing the published mark scheme is available on the Cambridge International School Support Hub. The Examiner's Report for the November 2015 series is also available there and this may contain comments specific to this question.

The following are what the author of the Revision Guide would suggest as reasonable answers, with alternatives suggested where appropriate.

a *One mark for one point below:*
In circuit switching a dedicated circuit (or channel or pathway) is created. This circuit is maintained continuously for the duration of connection.

b *6 marks.*
Circuit switching creates and uses a dedicated circuit.
Using circuit switching the whole is bandwidth available for the communication. Using all the available bandwidth should mean faster data transfer.
Data arrives in order it is sent. Data should not be lost.
Therefore – for all of the points above – circuit switching is better suited for real-time applications such as video conferencing.

c *3 marks for three points from:*
The web page content is organised into packets for data transfer.
Each packet is labelled with its destination address.
The router uses this IP address to decide which is to be the most efficient route to direct the packet.
Packets – which make up the is web page - can take different routes to reach their final destination.

Q2

This is **Question 5 in 9608 Paper 31 November 2016**. The mark scheme is available on the Cambridge International School Support Hub (requires registration). At the time of writing the published mark scheme is available on the Cambridge International School Support Hub. The Examiner's Report for the November 2016 series is also available there and this may contain comments specific to this question.

The following are what the author of the Revision Guide would suggest as reasonable answers, with alternatives suggested where appropriate.

a i *One mark for each missing layer in the correct order.*

Application
Transport
Internet
Network/Link

   ii Each layer in implemented with program code. – *1 mark*

b i *Note: The stem keyword is 'describe' – so a good answer will state what the Transport layer is doing and then expand on this stating its purpose.* [4]

   Check the port on which data is being received – this is to identify the application protocol being used.

   Check the packet's destination socket - so that packets will be sent to the correct application.

   Note the packet sequence number – this is needed to reassemble the packets in the correct order.

   Calculate the checksum datum for each packet – this is checked against the datum embedded as part of the packet data. If they match, the data integrity is OK.

   If the checksums do not match, request that the packet data is re-sent.

   ii HTTP/HTTPS – *1 mark*

   iii POP3 – *1 mark*

Q3 a [5]

Responsibility	TCP	IP
Correct routing		√
Host to host communication	√	
Communication between networks		√
Retransmitting missing packets	√	
Reassembling packets into the correct order	√	

b 1 mark for name, 1 mark for matching use, maximum of 4 marks for 2 protocols.

   POP3/IMPA [1] receiving emails / download emails from a server

   SMTP [1] sending emails [1]

   FTP [1] allows files to be transferred from one computer to another [1]

   HTTP/HTTPS [1] transfer of web pages/hypertext [1]

   Bit Torrent [1] used for peer-to-peer file sharing

c Internet / Network (layer) [1]

d i 1 mark per point to a maximum of 4:

   Message data / payload

   IP version number

   Internet header length

   Type of service

   Explicit congestion notification

   Totla length / size of packet in bytes

   Identification / sequence / packet number

   Fragmentation flags

   Fragmentation offset

   Time to live / number of hops

   Protocol

   Header checksum

   Source IP address

   Destination IP address

   ii 1 mark per benefit, 1 mark per expansion, maximum 4 marks for 2 benefits. For example:

   Alternative route available …

   In case of network problem …

   If packet fails to arrive …

   Then only that packet has to be resent

   iii 1 mark per point to a maximum of 2.

   Network ID / IP address of network destination [1] Subnetmask [1]

   Routing metric / data to decide best route

   IP addresses of possible next hop / gateway

   Interface

Chapter 15

Progress Checks

Progress Check A

Input		Output	
A	B	Sum	Carry
0	0	0	0
0	1	1	0
1	0	1	0
1	1	1	1

Progress Check B

Required you to check the Sum and Carry bits on each of the eight rows.

Progress Check C

a $A.\overline{B}$
b $\overline{C.D} + \overline{D}$
c $\overline{P + Q + R.R}$

D CHECK D

$(\overline{A} + \overline{B}) + C$

Progress Check E

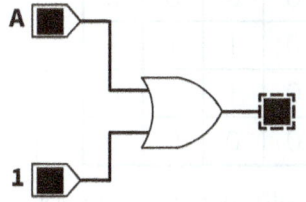

Input		Output
A	1	
1	1	1
0	1	1

Figure 15.20.

So, $A + 1 = 1$

Progress Check F

a $A.B$
b $A.B.D$
c $A.C$
d $P.Q$
e A
f $A + B.C$

Progress Check G

A	B	NOT A	NOT B	NOT(A OR B) = A NOR B	NOT A AND NOT B
0	0	1	1	1	1
0	1	1	0	0	0
1	0	0	1	0	0
1	1	0	0	0	0

Which suggests the second form of De Morgan's law:

$\overline{A + B} = \overline{A} . \overline{B}$

Progress Check H

1 $\overline{A} . \overline{B}$ 2 $\overline{A} + B$ 3 $A . B$

Progress Check I

a $B + A . \overline{C}$

AB C	00	01	11	10
0	0	1	1	0
1	0	1	1	1

Figure 15.21.

ii $C.D + B.D$

Since this can be written as: $\overline{\overline{C.D} . \overline{B.D}}$ using De Morgan's law.

iii

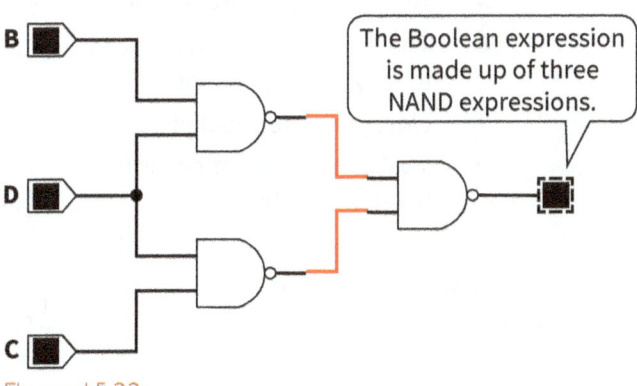

The Boolean expression is made up of three NAND expressions.

Figure 15.22.

Past paper questions

Q1

5 a

A	B	X
0	0	1
0	1	1
1	0	1
1	1	0

[1]

b i

S	R	Q	$\overline{Q}$
1	0	0	1
1	1	0	1
0	1	1	0
1	1	1	0
0	0	1	1

[4]

ii

S = 0 R = 0

Produces Q = 1, $\overline{Q}$ = 1 //

Q and $\overline{Q}$ have same value

Q and $\overline{Q}$ should be complements of each other

It also becomes unstable [3]

c i

Clock (pulse) [1]

ii

- A mark could be awarded for any of the following answers:
- All four possibilities are valid
- The 1-1 combination changes output to logical complement
- Unstable state avoided
- Invalid state cannot occur // the flip-flop is stable [1]

d

Memory // data storage

Stores a single bit [1]

Q2

a i

Z = P.$\overline{Q}$.$\overline{R}$ + [1]

P.$\overline{Q}$.R + [1]

P.Q.R [1]

ii

[1]

		PQ			
		00	01	11	10
R	0	0	0	0	1
	1	0	0	1	1

iii 1 mark each loop

		PQ			
		00	01	11	10
R	0	0	0	0	1
	1	0	0	1	1

Allow f.t. from (ii) [2]

iv

Z =

P.$\overline{Q}$ [1]

+ P.R [1]

Allow f.t. from (iii)

b i 1 mark row headings. 1 mark column headings. 1 mark per 2 correct rows (based on headings)

		PQ			
		00	01	11	10
RS	00	0	0	0	0
	01	0	1	1	1
	11	0	1	1	0
	10	0	0	0	0

[4]

ii 1 mark for loop with two 1s; 1 mark for loop with four 1s

		PQ			
		00	01	11	10
RS	00	0	0	0	0
	01	0	1	1	1
	11	0	1	1	0
	10	0	0	0	0

Allow f.t. from (i)

−1 for each incorrect grouping, max. 2 errors [2]

iii Z =

Q.S [1]

+ P.$\overline{R}$.S [1]

Allow f.t. from (ii). −1 error if more than 2 terms

Chapter 16

Progress Checks

Progress Check A

a A process is interrupted as its time slice has expired
- RUNNING and then changes to RUNNABLE

b A process now completes a sequence of disk read operations
- SUSPENDED and changes to RUNNABLE

c A process in given the use of the processor
- RUNNABLE and changes to RUNNING

d A process is executing but now has to wait for some input from the keyboard from the user
- RUNNING and changes to SUSPENDED

Progress Check B

A user priority.

A priority based on the resources the process will use.

Progress Check C

a FALSE: an interpreter has better diagnostic features.

b FALSE: no object code is produced by an interpreter.

c TRUE: the interpreter software and the source code program are in memory.

d TRUE

e FALSE: it only finds the first error is comes across and then stops.

f TRUE

g FALSE: compiler software is language specific. The compiler for a Language-X program is different software to the compiler used for a program written in any other high-level language.

Progress Check D

Symbol table

Identifier	Token Value	Token Type
`Index`	300	INTEGER
`1`	301	CONSTANT
`20`	302	CONSTANT
`Product`	303	INTEGER

Output string is:

| 102 | 300 | 250 | 301 | 103 | 302 | 303 | 250 | 300 | 253 | 300 | 104 |

Progress Check E

Minor changes made after compilation so that the code runs with maximum efficiency.
The code is changed so that it will execute in the shortest possible time and use the minimum amount of primary memory.

Progress Check F

Suggested Identifier		Explanation
`P`	VALID	
`MyObject`	VALID	
`8index`	INVALID	Must start with at least one letter character
`Count`	VALID	
`My_Object`	INVALID	Contains the underscore character which has not been defined
`Loop5times`	VALID	

Progress Check G

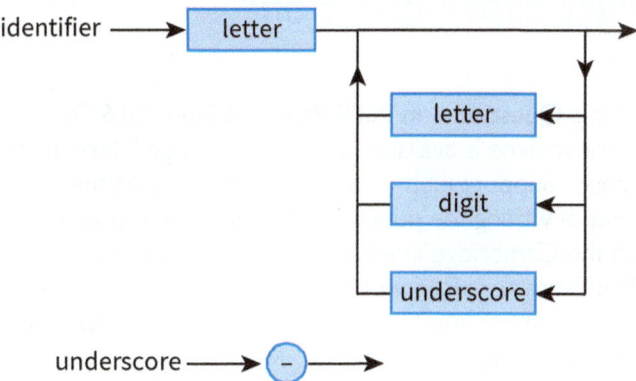

Figure 16.11.

Progress Check H

a Valid.

b Invalid (there is no definition for digit 5).

c Valid.

Progress Check I

a Valid.

b Valid.

c Invalid (a list cannot end with a comma character).

d Invalid (no definition for the digit 4).

Progress Check J

InOrderTraversal(Root.LeftPointer)
InOrderTraversal(Root.RightPointer)
On both these lines the procedure is calling itself.

Progress Check K

a 25

b 3

c 64

d a b + 6 /

e 2 a * b + 3 ^

Progress Check L

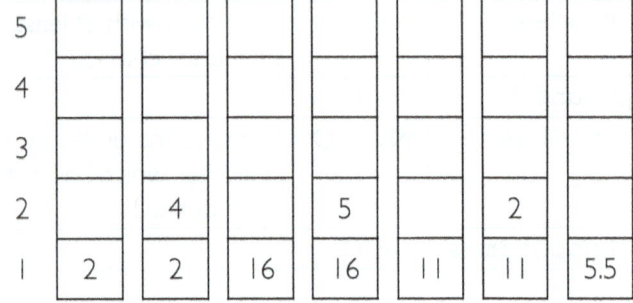

Past paper questions

Q1

This is **Question 1 in 9608 Paper 32 June 2016**. The mark scheme is available on the Cambridge International School Support Hub (requires registration). At the time of writing the published mark scheme is available on the Cambridge International School Support Hub. The Examiner's Report for the June 2016 series is also available there and this may contain comments specific to this question.

The following are what the author of the Revision Guide would suggest as reasonable answers, with alternatives suggested where appropriate.

a 1 mark each

   i ';' missing

   ii '2' is not a variable

   iii 'e' is not a valid letter

b 6 marks

```
<assignment statement> ::=
<variable> '=' <variable>
<operator><variable>';'

<variable> ::=
<letter>|<letter><letter>
|<letter><letter><letter>

<letter> ::= 'a'|'b'|'c'|'d'

<operator> :: '+'|'-'|'*'|'÷'
```

c 2 marks

```
<variable> :== <letter> |
<letter><variable>
```

OR

```
<variable> :== <letter> |
<variable><letter>
```

d i 1 mark for one point from:

   Using an interpreter debugging is faster.

   An interpreter can be used to debug code before all the code is written.

   An interpreter will provide better diagnostics.

  ii 1 mark for one point from:

   A compiler produces executable version of the code. Once this object file is available the source code is not required.

   Once the object file has been created, it is a difficult task to attempt to create the original source file by reverse-engineering.

Q2

This is **Question 2 in 9608 Paper 32 November 2015**. The mark scheme is available on the Cambridge International School Support Hub (requires registration). At the time of writing the published mark scheme is available on the Cambridge International School Support Hub. The Examiner's Report for the November 2015 series is also available there and this may contain comments specific to this question.

The following are what the author of the Revision Guide would suggest as reasonable answers, with alternatives suggested where appropriate.

a   3 marks for the final two rows:

Symbol	Token	
	Value	Type
Counter	62	Variable
10	63	Constant

b   2 marks

| 60 | 01 | 61 | 4E | 62 | 01 | 60 | 50 | 63 | 52 | 62 | 02 | 60 | 53 |

   i   Syntax analysis – 1 mark   [1]
   ii   2 marks for two points from:

        Syntax analysis will construct a parse tree for the expressions that makes up each statement.

        The parse tree is used to check the syntax of each statement. If a statement is incorrect, the error is reported.

c   i   1 mark

        Code is optimised to minimise the execution time.

   ii   The compiler could calculate 2*6 and replace it with the value 12.

   iii 3 marks

        LDD 436
        ADD 437
        STO 612
        ADD 438
        STO 613

Q3

This is **Question 2(a) in 9608 Paper 31 November 2016**. The mark scheme is available on the Cambridge International School Support Hub. (requires registration). At the time of writing the published mark scheme is available on the Cambridge International School Support Hub. The Examiner's Report for the November 2016 series is also available there and this may contain comments specific to this question.

The following are what the author of the Revision Guide would suggest as reasonable answers, with alternatives suggested where appropriate.

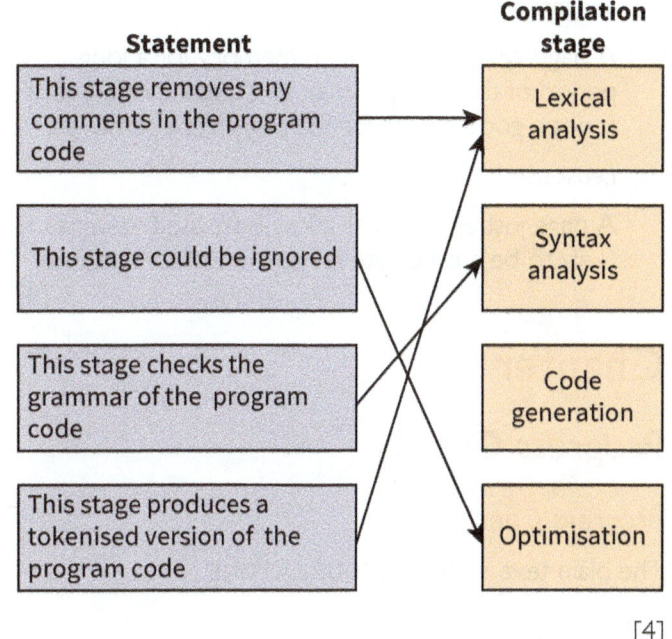

[4]

Q4

This is **Question 3 in 9608 Paper 31 November 2016**. The mark scheme is available on the Cambridge International School Support Hub. (requires registration). At the time of writing the published mark scheme is available on the Cambridge International School Support Hub. The Examiner's Report for the November 2016 series is also available there and this may contain comments specific to this question.

The following are what the author of the Revision Guide would suggest as reasonable answers, with alternatives suggested where appropriate.

a   The 245th page frame from the start of memory [1]
    or the 245th page frame from some base address.

b   Flash memory or magnetic disk or hard drive. [1]

c   i   Time of page load.   [1]

    ii
Page	Presence Flag	Page frame Address	Additional data
4	1	542	12:07:34:49

[1 + 1 + 1]

    iii Number of times the page has been accessed.
                                                     [1]

    iv
Page	Presence Flag	Page frame Address	Additional data
3	1	132	1

[1 + 1 + 1]

d *Longest resident*:

A page which has stayed in memory for a long period of time of time may be accessed often; so, it is not a good choice for the page to be removed.

Least used:

A page just entered has a low least used value; so, is likely to be a candidate for an immediate swap out.

[4]

Chapter 17

Progress Checks

Progress Check A

The plain text is: ZEBRAHOUSEATONE

Progress Check B

a False: Only the use of a digital signature provides proof of authenticity.

b False: A digital certificate must be purchased.

c False: Private-public key encryption is asymmetric encryption.

d False: 3 The recipient has the sender's public key.

e True

f True

Progress Check C

a SSL Certificate.

b Public key.

Step 3 – B

Step 5 – C

Step 6 – A

Past paper questions

Q1

This is **Question 2(c) and (d) in 9608 Paper 32 June 2015**. The mark scheme is available on the Cambridge International School Support Hub (requires registration). At the time of writing the published mark scheme is available on the Cambridge International School Support Hub. The Examiner's Report for the June 2015 series is also available there and this may contain comments specific to this question.

The following are what the author of the Revision Guide would suggest as reasonable answers, with alternatives suggested where appropriate.

a Encryption is the process of converting the original plain text into cipher text - 1 mark

2 marks for two points from:

Public key is used in a system of asymmetric encryption. The public key is made available to a third party with whom you intend to communicate. The sender will use the recipient's public key to encrypt the message. The recipient is the only holder of the matching private key – and so is the only person who is able to decrypt the message.

b i Digital signature - 1 mark

ii 4 marks for four points from:

The original software file is put through a hashing algorithm. This generates a hash total (the sender's hash) which is encrypted with the software house private key. This together forms the digital signature.

The software file + the digital signature is transmitted.

The receiver is in possession of the software house public key,

So the digital signature can be decrypted using the public key.

The receiver hashes the received software file to generate the receiver' hash.

If this matches with the sender hash then the software is authentic and the file has not been altered.

Q2

a *1 mark for each correct data item, to a maximum of 3. For example:*

Serial number

Certification authority that issued the certificate

CA digital signature

Name of cmpany, organisation, indidivual, subject or owner that owns the certificate

'Subject' public key

Period during which certificate id valid / other relevant date

b   i   *One mark for* Public.

        Maximum 1 mark for the following points:

        The individual keeps their private key private

        The public key can be known by (others) the public

   ii   *One mark for* Public.

        Maximum 1 mark for the following points:

        The individual does not know the private key of the CA

        The individual only knows the public key of the CA

        Only the CA can decrypt the packaged information

   iii *One mark for* Private.

        Maximum 1 mark for the following points:

        Only the CA's public key will allow decryption of the certificate

        Proving the certificate was issued by the A

c   i   Digital signature

   ii   1 mark for each point, to a maximum of 2.

        Alexa's digital certificate.

        Includes Alexa's public key

        Used to hash messages received or used to produce message digest

        Generated hash compared to digital signature

   iii 1 mark for each point, to a maximum of 2. For example:

        Financial transcation

        Legal document

        Software distribution

Q3

a   Four points from:
- Katarina's computer/software encrypts the email before she sends it
- using Lucy's public key
- Lucy's computer/software decrypts the email when it is received
- using Lucy's private key. As the private key is known only to Lucy, only she can understand the email. [4]

b   1   for each of three points:
- Julio's computer/software checks the digital certificate of the online shop's website
- If digital certificate is invalid his computer/software rejects website
- If valid a session is created/the transaction can continue
- The encryption algorithms to be used are agreed
- The session keys to be used are generated
- The (session) key is used to encrypt the data sent. [3]

Chapter 18

Progress Checks

Progress Check A

There are three possible paths:

A to C has distance 12.

A to B to C has distance 3 + 8 = 11.

A to E to D to C has distance 4 + 3 + 1 = 8.

Therefore, the shortest path between A and C is 8.

Progress Check B

a   64 nodes.

b   Possible weights are:

    8: the square is not on a horizontal or vertical border.

    5: the square is on a border.

    3: the square is one of the four corner squares.

Progress Check C

a   Shortest path is weight 4.

b   There is only one path.

Progress Check D

a Strong positive correlation: Correlation coefficient 0.7.

b Strong negative correlation: Correlation coefficient –0.8.

c Weak positive correlation: Correlation coefficient 0.3.

d Weak negative correlation: Correlation coefficient –0.3.

e Perfect positive correlation: Correlation coefficient +1.0.

f Perfect negative correlation: Correlation coefficient –1.0

Progress Check E

a Positive correlation.

b Answer close to +0.7.

c The closer the values are to the regression line the more accurate any prediction would be, so it's Box C.

Exam-style questions

1 a [4]

```
TYPE TownData
DECLARE TownName : CHAR
DECLARE Neighbour :  ARRAY[1..4] OF CHAR
DECLARE NeighbourDistance : ARRAY[1..4] OF INTEGER
END TYPE


DECLARE ThisMap : ARRAY[1 ..5] OF TownData
```

b Many solutions would work. The two possible data structures below show stored data for this graph.

Solution 1: An array of strings: [1]

	NodePath
1	""
2	"ACB"
3	"AC"
4	"ACD"
5	"ACDE"

Solution 2: Using a list:

```
NodePath = ["", "ACB", "AC", "ACD", "ACDE"]
```

c [8]

	Shortest path	A	B	C	D	E
1	Initialise: `PathKnown=[]`	∞	∞	∞	∞	∞
2	Set node A as the start: `PathKnown= [A]`	0 Empty	∞	∞	∞	∞
3	Neighbours of A are B = 7 and C = 4					
		0 Empty	7 A – B	4 A – C		
	Shortest path is C, so add C to `PathKnown` `PathKnown= [A, C]`					
4	Neighbours of C are B = 6, D = 9: update B data and add the D data					
		0 Empty	6 A – C – B	4 A – C	9 A – C – D	
	Shortest path is B, so add B to `PathKnown` `PathKnown = [A, C, B]`					
5	Neighbour of B is E = 14 only, so add E data					
		0 Empty	6 A – C – B	4 A – C	9 A – C – D	14 A – C – B – E
	Only path is to E, so add E to the `PathKnown` **`PathKnown= [A, C, B, E]`**					
6	Neighbour of E is D = 16; do <u>not</u> update D data.					
		0 Empty	6 A – C – B	4 A – C	9 A – C – D	14 A – C – B – E
	Add D to `PathKnown` **`PathKnown= [A, C, B, D]`**					
7	Neighbour of D is E = 11: Update the E data					
	Add E to `PathKnown` **`PathKnown= [A, C, B, D, E]`**	0 Empty	6 A – C – B	4 A – C	9 A – C – D	11 A – C – D – E
8	Stop					

2

		True	False
a	A linear regression analysis has paired values (X,Y) for its dataset.	√	
b	A logistic regression analysis has paired values (X,Y) for its dataset.	√	
c	The value calculated for the correlation coefficient always computes a value between 0 and 1.		√
d	A linear regression analysis will show whether the data points fall into two (or more) categories.		√
e	For a regression analysis scatterplot it is convention to plot the independent variable on the X axis and the dependent variable on the Y axis.	√	
f	A calculated correlation coefficient of +0.85 suggests that high values of the independent variable produce high values of the dependent variable.	√	
g	Deep learning is a technique using neural networks	√	
h	A popular application of regression analysis is for image recognition.		√

[4]

3

		True	False
a	All AI models need training data.	√	
b	A neural network is made up of many neurons, each neuron is given a weight and a bias.	√	
c	All neurons in a neural network have a threshold value above which the neuron is activated.	√	
d	The inputs to a single neuron are the connecting neurons from the adjacent layer on the right		√
e	Deep learning is a technique using neural networks.	√	
f	Back propagation is an algorithm used to refine the weights and biases of neurons in a neural network.	√	

[3]

Chapter 19

Progress Checks

Progress Check A

Loop statements change as shown. All other statements unchanged.

```
DO WHILE (IsFound = FALSE) AND Index < 21)
...
ENDWHILE
```

Progress Check B

Change the loop structure to `FOR-NEXT` as all items in the array must be considered.

Initialise a counter to zero before the loop starts.

Add one to a counter each time a match is found.

Progress Check C

a `ThisArray[Middle] = ThisValue`

b No.

c `Bottom > Top`

d `Top` only.

Progress Check D

MyAnimals

1	2	3	4	5
DOG	CAT	RAT	EEL	BAT
(CAT)	DOG	RAT	EEL	BAT
CAT	DOG	(RAT)	EEL	BAT
CAT	DOG	(EEL)	RAT	BAT
(BAT)	CAT	DOG	EEL	RAT

Progress Check E

Pass	i	UBound	Swapped
1		5	FALSE
	1		TRUE
	2		
	3		
	4		TRUE
2			FALSE
	1		
	2		
	3		TRUE
3			FALSE
	1		
	2		TRUE
			FALSE
4	1		

Animal				
1	2	3	4	5
CAT	ANT	COW	RAT	BEE
ANT	CAT			
			BEE	RAT
ANT	CAT	COW	BEE	(RAT)
		BEE	COW	
ANT	CAT	BEE	(COW	RAT)
	BEE	CAT		
ANT	BEE	(CAT	COW	RAT)
(ANT	BEE	CAT	COW	RAT)

Progress Check F

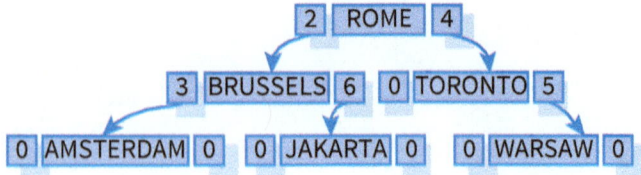

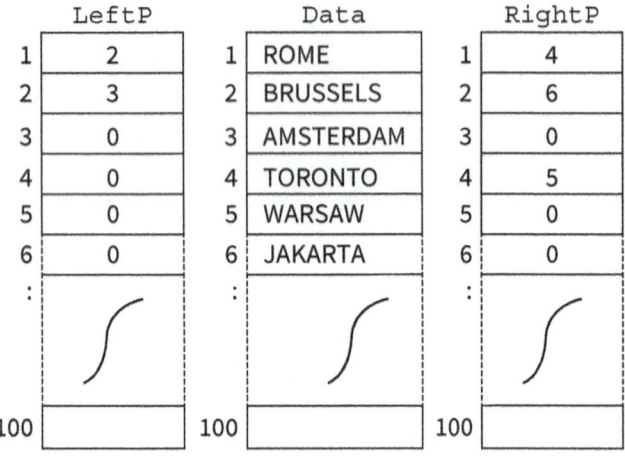

Figure 19.25.

Progress Check G

Remove item from stack:

```
IF TOS = 0
    THEN
        OUTPUT 'Stack is empty'
    ELSE
        OUTPUT MyStack[TOS]
        TOS ← TOS - 1
ENDIF
```

Progress Check H

1. a Item 10 (at index position 5).

   b Head ← Head + 1

2. Stored at MyQueue[Tail + 1]

Progress Check I

a 1

b (Head=1 AND Tail=10) OR (Head = Tail + 1)

c 6

d 1

Progress Check J

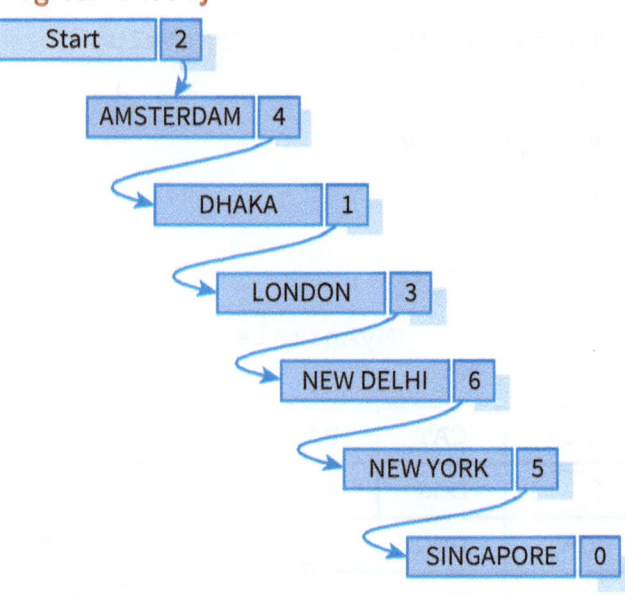

Figure 19.26.

Progress Check K

a Yes

b 5

c No

Progress Check L

	GL	BR	LO	PA	AM
GL	0	1	1	0	0
BR	1	0	0	1	1
LO	1	1	0	1	0
PA	0	0	1	0	1
AM	0	1	1	0	0

Progress Check M

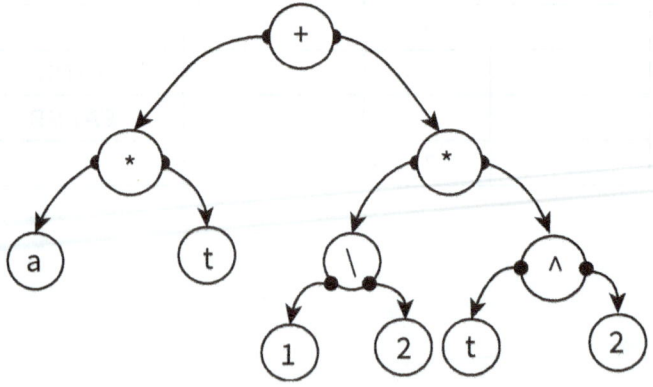

Figure 19.27.

Past paper questions

Q1

This is **Question 2 in 9608 Paper 41 June 2018**. The mark scheme is available on the Cambridge International School Support Hub (requires registration). At the time of writing the published mark scheme is available on the Cambridge International School Support Hub. The Examiner's Report for the June 2018 series is also available there and this may contain comments specific to this question.

The following are what the author of the Revision Guide would suggest as reasonable answers, with alternatives suggested where appropriate.

a   7 marks - a mark for each completed statement:

```
01   MaxIndex ← 20
02   NumberItems ← MaxIndex - 1
03   FOR Outer ← TO MaxIndex - 1
04       FOR Inner ← 1 to NumberItems
05           IF ItemList[Inner] > ItemList[Inner + 1]
06               THEN
07                   Temp ← ItemList[Inner]
08                   ItemList[Inner] ← ItemList[Inner + 1]
09                   ItemList[Inner + 1] ← Temp
10           ENDIF
11       ENDFOR
12       NumberItems ← NumberItems - 1
13   ENDFOR
```

b   i   1 mark for each point:

Iterations continue ...

after the array is already sorted.

b   ii   3 marks – three points from:

A flag variable is used to indicate if a swap has occurred.

If the inner loop completes all comparisons with no swaps, then the flag variable is set to indicate this.

On completion of each iteration of the inner loop the value of the flag variable is inspected.

If the variable is set so that the list is completely sorted the program terminates.

c   Insertion sort - 4 marks:

Situation: When the original list of data items is almost sorted.

Reason: Because the algorithm finishes as soon as it is sorted.

Situation: When there are a large number of data items.

Reason: Because the insertion sort algorithm performs fewer comparisons.

Q2

This is **Question 6 in 9608 Paper 41 June 2018**. The mark scheme is available on the Cambridge International School Support Hub (requires registration). At the time of writing the published mark scheme is available on the Cambridge International School Support Hub. The Examiner's Report for the June 2018 series is also available there and this may contain comments specific to this question.

The following are what the author of the Revision Guide would suggest as reasonable answers, with alternatives suggested where appropriate.

a   i   *3 marks:*

```
TYPE List
    DECLARE Player : String
    DECLARE Pointer : INTEGER
ENDTYPE
```

   ii   *2 marks:*

```
DECLARE Scorers : ARRAY[0:9] OF ListNode
```

b   *5 marks – one for each completed statement:*

```
FUNCTION SearchList (Find, Position) RETURNS INTEGER
    IF Scorer [Position] . Player = FInd
        THEN
            RETURN Position
        ELSE
            IF Scorer(Position).Player <> -1
                THEN
                    Position ← SearchList (Find,
                                  Scorer[Position].Pointer)
                    RETURN Position
                ELSE
                    RETURN 99
            ENDIF
    ENDIF
ENDPROCEDURE
```

Q3

This is **Question 6 in 9608 Paper 42 November 2018**. The mark scheme is available on the Cambridge International School Support Hub (requires registration). At the time of writing the published mark scheme is available on the Cambridge International School Support Hub. The Examiner's Report for the November 2018 series is also available there and this may contain comments specific to this question.

The following are what the author of the Revision Guide would suggest as reasonable answers, with alternatives suggested where appropriate.

a ii 2 marks

```
DECLARE CountryList : ARRAY[1 : 15] OF ListElement
```

b 5 marks - one mark for each completed statement:

```
PROCEDURE DeleteNode(NodeValue : STRING, ThisPointer : INTEGER,
                                         PreviousPointer : INTEGER)
    IF CountryList[ThisPointer].Value = NodeValue
        THEN
            CountryList[ThisPointer].Value ← ""
            IF ListHead = ThisPointer
                THEN
                    ListHead ← CountryList[ThisPointer].Pointer
                ELSE
                    CountryList[PreviousPointer].Pointer ←
                                CountryList[ThisPointer].Pointer
            ENDIF
            CountryList[LastNode].Pointer ← ThisPointer
            LastNode ← ThisPointer
            CountryList[ThisPointer].Pointer ← -1
        ELSE
            IF CountryList[ThisPointer].Pointer <> -1
                THEN
                    CALL DeleteNode(NodeValue,
                        CountryList[ThisPointer].Pointer, ThisPointer)
                ELSE
                    OUTPUT "DOES NOT EXIST"
            ENDIF
    ENDIF
ENDPROCEDURE
```

Chapter 20
Progress Checks

Progress Check A

```
START:          LDD     COUNTER
                CMP     #0
                JPE     END
                LDD     C_LOC
                OUT
                LDD     A_LOC
                OUT
                LDD     T_LOC
                OUT
                LDD     COUNTER
                SUB     #1
                STO     COUNTER
                JMP     START
END:            END

COUNTER:        5       // loop counter
   C_LOC:       67      ASCII code for C
   A_LOC:       65      ASCII code for A
   T_LOC:       84      ASCII code for T
```

Progress Check B

```
                LDR     #0
NEXT_NUMBER:    LDD     COUNTER
                CMP     #0
                JPE     PRINTOUT
                LDX     NUMBER
                CMP     #42
                JPE     ADD_1
                JMP     GET_READY
ADD_1           LDD     TOTAL
                INC     ACC
                STO     TOTAL
GET_READY:      INC     IX
                JMP     NEXT_NUMBER
PRINTOUT:       LDD     TOTAL
                OUT
END:            END

COUNTER:        6
NUMBER:         42
```
                3
                43
                16
                42
                42
```
TOTAL:          0
```

Note the use of indexed addressing. The next number to be considered is at address NUMBER + the contents of the index register (IX).

Progress Check C

a Natene plays tennis (a 'fact').

b Y = golf.

c A = natene, tadi

d This needs two rules ...

likes(ken, P) :- female(P).

likes(ken, P) :- male(P), plays(P, golf).

Past paper questions

Q1

This is **Question 1 in 9608 Paper 41 June 2018**. The mark scheme is available on the Cambridge International School Support Hub (requires registration). At the time of writing the published mark scheme is available on the Cambridge International School Support Hub. The Examiner's Report for the June 2018 series is also available there and this may contain comments specific to this question.

The following are what the author of the Revision Guide would suggest as reasonable answers, with alternatives suggested where appropriate.

a 2 marks – one mark per fact:

14 `direct(london, rome).`

15 `flies(rome, british_air).`

b 2 marks:

K = Palma, Salzburg

c 2 marks:

`direct(glasgow, M).`

d 3 marks:

`flies(Z,X) AND direct(Z, Y)`

e YES – 1 mark

Q2

This is **Question 6(c) in 9608 Paper 32 June 2016**. The mark scheme is available on the Cambridge International School Support Hub. (requires registration). At the time of writing the published mark scheme is available on the Cambridge International School Support Hub. The Examiner's Report for the June 2016 series is also available there and this may contain comments specific to this question.

The following are what the author of the Revision Guide would suggest as reasonable answers, with alternatives suggested where appropriate.

i   [4]

BITREG	COUNT	VALUE	ACC
B00001010	0	1	B00001010
			B00000000
			1
		2	2
			B00001010
			B00000010
			0
	1		1
			2
		4	4
			B00001010
			B00000000
			4
		8	8
			B00001010
			B00001000
			1
	2		2
			8

ii   2   [1]

iii   CMP #8 changes to CMP #128   [2]

Chapter 21

Exam-style questions

1 [4]

Visual Basic

```
Module      Module1
    Dim     Values(10) As String
    Sub     Main()
        Dim OnCount As Integer
        Dim Integer As Integer
        OnCount = 0
        Call PopulateArray
        Index = 1
        Do
            IF Values(Index) = "ON" THEN
                OnCount = OnCount + 1
            End If
            Index = Index + 1
        Loop until  Values(Index) =  "X"
        Console .Writeline("Number of ON values was:  " & OnCount)
        Console .Readline()
    End Sub
    Sub PopulateArray()
        Values (1) = "ON" : Values (2) = "ON" : Values (3) = "OFF"
        Values (4) = "OFF" : Values (5) = "ON" : Values (6) = "OFF"
        Values (7) = "ON" : Values (8) = "ON" : Values (9) = "ON"
        Values (10) = "X"
    End Sub
```

Python

```python
# ONCount is Integer
# Index is Integer
Values = ["","ON", "ON","OFF", "OFF", "ON", "OFF", "ON", "ON", "ON", "X"]
OnCount = 0
Index = 1
while Values[Index] != "X"
```

```
        if Values[Index] == "ON"
            OnCount += 1
        Index += 1
print ("Number of ON values was: " + str (OnCount))
```

```java
public static void main(String[] args)
{
String values [] = {"ON", "ON", "OFF", "OFF", "ON",
                    "OFF", "ON", "ON", "ON", "X" };
int onCount = 0;
int index = 0;
while (values[index] != "X")
    {
    if (values[index] == "ON")
        {
        onCount ++;
        }
    index ++;
    }
System.out.println("Number of ON values was : " + onCount);
}
```

2

a   Incomplete Pseudocode line: several possibilities would work: [1]

```
IF TO_UPPER(FirstLetter) = "P" THEN or
IF TO_LOWER(FirstLetter) = "p" THEN or
IF FirstLetter = "P" OR FirstLetter = "p" THEN
```

b   [5]

Visual Basic

```vb
Sub main()
    Dim PCount As Integer
    Dim NextWord As String
    Dim FirstLetter As String
    PCount = 0
    Console.Write("Next word:  ") : NextWord = Console.Readline()
    While NextWord <> "END"
        FirstLetter = Left(NextWord, 1)
```

```vb
            If   UCase(FirstLetter) = "P" Then
                PCount = PCount + 1
            End If
            Console.Write("Next word: ") : NextWord =  Console.Readline()
        End While
        Console.Writeline("The number of words starting with p was:    " & PCount)
        Console.Readline()
End Sub
```

Python

```python
# PCount As Integer
# NextWord As String
# FirstLetter As String
PCount = 0
NextWord = input("Next word:   ")
while NextWord != "END" :
    FirstLetter = NextWord[0]
    if   FirstLetter.upper() == "P":
            PCount += 1
    NextWord = input("Next word:   ")
print("The number of words starting with p was:   "  +  str(PCount))
```

Java
```java
public static void main(String[] args)
{
Scanner input = new Scanner(System.in);
int pCount = 0;
System.out.print("Next word : ");
String nextWord = input.nextLine();
while (!nextWord.equals("END"))
{
    char firstLetter = nextWord.charAt(0);
    if (firstLetter == 'P')
    {
        pCount ++;
    }
    System.out.print("Next word : ");
    nextWord = input.nextLine();
}
```

> ```
> System.out.println("Number of words starting with P were : " +
> pCount);
> }
> }
> ```
> Note that strings cannot be compared with the usual =, <, > operators
>
> Use the equals function: `string1.equals(string2)` returns a Boolean value:
>
> The condition used in the code above asks if the strings are 'not equal': `(!nextWord.equals("END"))`

3 [8]

Visual Basic

```vb
    Dim Sales(3, 6) As Integer
    Sub Main()
        Dim Person As Integer : Dim MonthNo As Integer
        Dim PersonTotal(3) As Integer : Dim GrandTotal As Integer
        Call PopulateSalesArray()
        GrandTotal = 0
        For Person = 1 To 3
            For MonthNo = 1 To 6
                GrandTotal = GrandTotal + Sales(Person, MonthNo)
            Next
        Next
        Console.WriteLine("Total sales made were:   " & str(GrandTotal))
        Console.WriteLine()
        For Person = 1 To 3
            PersonTotal(Person) = 0
            For MonthNo = 1 To 6
                PersonTotal(Person) = PersonTotal(Person) + Sales(Person, MonthNo)
            Next
            Console.WriteLine("Person   " & Person & " made " & PersonTotal(Person) & " sales. ")
        Next
        Console.ReadLine()
    End Sub
    Sub PopulateSalesArray()
        Sales (1, 1) = 0 : Sales (1, 2) = 0 : Sales (1, 3) = 0
        Sales (1, 4) = 3 : Sales (1, 5) = 4 : Sales (1, 6) = 0
```

```
            Sales (2, 1) = 1 : Sales (2, 2) = 12 : Sales (2, 3) = 12
            Sales (2, 4) = 6 : Sales (2, 5) = 7  : Sales (2, 6) = 8
            Sales (3, 1) = 2 : Sales (3, 2) = 4  : Sales (3, 3) = 5
            Sales (3, 4) = 1 : Sales (3, 5) = 2  : Sales (3, 6) = 3
    End Sub
```

Python
```python
# Person is Integer
# MonthNo is Integer
# GrandTotal is Integer
Sales = [[0, 0, 0, 0, 3, 4, 0], [0, 1, 12, 12, 6, 7, 8], [0, 2, 4, 5, 1, 2, 3]]
PersonTotal = 0
GrandTotal = 0
for Person in range (0, 3) :
    for MonthNo in range (0, 6) :
        GrandTotal = GrandTotal + Sales[Person][MonthNo]
print("Total sales made were:  " + str(GrandTotal))
print("")
for Person in range (0, 3) :
    PTotal = 0
    for MonthNo in range (0, 6)
        PTotal = PTotal + Sales[Person] [MonthNo]
    PersonTotal.append(PTotal)
    print ("Person " + str(Perso + 1) + " made " + str(GrandTotal))
```

Java
```java
public static void main(String[] args)
{
int sales [] []= {
    {0,0,0,3,4,0}, {1,12,12,6,7,8}, {2,4,5,1,2,3}
                };
int [] personTotal;  personTotal = new int[3];
int grandTotal = 0;
for (int person = 0; person < 3; person++)
{
    for (int month = 0; month < 6; month++)
    {
```

```
        grandTotal = grandTotal + sales[person][month];
      }
  }

    System.out.println("Total sales made " + grandTotal);
    System.out.println("");

for (int person = 0; person < 3; person++)
{
    personTotal[person] = 0;
    for (int month = 0; month < 6; month++)
    {
        personTotal[person] = personTotal[person] + sales[person][month];
    }
    System.out.println("Person number: " + (person + 1) + " made "+
                                        personTotal[person] + " sales.");
}
```

4 a   [4]

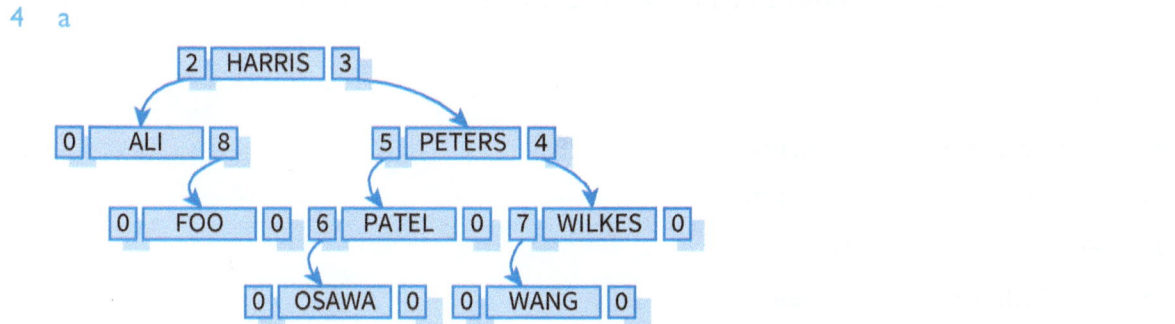

Figure 21.01.

b   [3]

Visual Basic

```
Dim NodeData(20) As String
Dim NodeRight(20) As Integer
Dim NodeLeft(20) As Integer
Dim Root As Integer
Sub  Main()
    Dim Choice As Char
    Do
        Call DisplayMenu()
        Console.Write("Choice?  "  : Choice = Console.ReadLine ()
```

Note: This is the binary tree search algorithm that was studied in Chapter 10.

[5]

```vbnet
            If UCase (Choice) = "A" Then CreateTree()
            If UCase (Choice) = "B" Then SearchTree()
        Loop until UCase(Choice) = "C"
End Sub
Sub DisplayMenu()
    Console.WriteLine("A.  Create and populate the binary tree")
    Console.WriteLine("B. Search for a name")
    Console.WriteLine("C. End")
End Sub
Sub CreateTree()
    Root = 1
    NodeData(1) = "HARRIS" : NodeLeft(1) = 2 : NodeRight(1) = 3
    NodeData(2) = "ALI" : NodeLeft(1) = 0 : NodeRight(2) = 8
    NodeData(3) = "PETERS" : NodeLeft(3) = 5 : NodeRight(3) = 4
    NodeData(4) = "WILKES" : NodeLeft(4) = 7 : NodeRight(4) = 0
    NodeData(5) = "PATEL" : NodeLeft(5) = 6 : NodeRight(5) = 0
    NodeData(6) = "OSAWA" : NodeLeft(6) = 0 : NodeRight(6) = 0
    NodeData(7) = "WANG" : NodeLeft(7) = 0 : NodeRight(7) = 0
End Sub
    Sub SearchTree()
        Dim SearchName As String                                           [6]
        Dim CurrentPosn As Integer
        Dim Found As Boolean
        Dim NotInList As Boolean
Console.Write("Name?  ") : SearchName = Console.ReadLine()
Found = False
NotInList = False
CurrentPosn = Root
Do
    If SearchName = NodeData (CurrentPosn) Then
        Found = True
        Console.Write("Found at Position  " & CurrentPosn)
    Else
        If SearchName < NodeData(CurrentPosn) Then
            ' If possible move left
```

```
                    If NodeLeft(CurrentPosn) <> 0 Then
                        CurrentPosn = NodeLeft(CurrentPosn)
                    End If
                Else
                    ' If possible move right
                    If NodeRight(CurrentPosn) <> 0 Then
                        CurrentPosn = NodeRight(CurrentPosn)
                    End If
                End If
            End If
Loop Until Found = True Or CurrentPosn = 0
End Sub
End Module
```

Python Code

```python
def DisplayMenu():
    print("A. Create and populate the binary tree")
    print("B. Display tree contents")
    print("C. Search for a name")
    print("X. End")

def DisplayTree():
    print ("Root: " + str(Root))
    for i in range(1, 6):
        print(str(NodeLeft[i]) + "   " + NodeData[i] + "   " + str(NodeRight[i]))

def SearchTree():
    # SearchName is String
    # CurrentPosn is Integer
    # Found is Boolean
    # NotInList is Boolean
    SearchName = input("Name ? ")
    Found = False
    NotInList = False
    
    CurrentPosn = Root
    Found = False
    while not(Found == True or CurrentPosn == 0):
        if SearchName == NodeData[CurrentPosn]:
            Found = True
            print("Found at position " + str(CurrentPosn))
        else:
            if SearchName < NodeData[CurrentPosn]:
                # if possible - move left
                CurrentPosn = NodeLeft[CurrentPosn]
            else:
                # if possible - move right
                CurrentPosn = NodeRight[CurrentPosn]
        if CurrentPosn == 0:
            print("Name was not found")
```

```python
# Main program starts here
Root = 1
NodeData = ["", "HARRIS", "ALI", "PETERS", "WILKES", "PATEL"]
NodeLeft = [0, 2, 0, 5, 7, 6]
NodeRight = [0, 3, 8, 4, 0, 0]
print("Tree now created ...")

Choice = ""
while Choice != "X":
    DisplayMenu()
    Choice = input('Choice? ')
    if Choice.upper() == "A":
        CreateTree()
    if Choice.upper() == "B":
        DisplayTree()
    if Choice.upper() == "C":
        SearchTree()
    if Choice.upper() == "X":
        exit
```

Java Code

```java
package chapter.pkg21.exam.q4;
import java.util.Scanner ;

public class CHAPTER21EXAMQ4
{
public static Scanner input = new Scanner(System.in);
public static String nodeData [] = {
                    "", "HARRIS", "ALI", "PETERS",
                    "WILKES", "PATEL", "OZAWA", "WANG", "FOO"};
public static int nodeRight [] = {0,3,8,4,0,0,0,0,0} ;
public static int nodeLeft [] = {0,2,0,5,7,6,0,0,0} ;
public static int root = 1;

public static void displayMenu()
{
    System.out.println("A. Display tree");
    System.out.println("B. Search for a name");
    System.out.println("X. End");
    System.out.println("");
}
public static void displayTree()
{
    System.out.println("Root: " + root);
    for (int index = 1; (index < 9);  index++ ) {
        System.out.print(index + ":  ");
        System.out.print(nodeLeft[index] + "  ");
        System.out.print(nodeData[index] + "  ");
        System.out.println(nodeRight[index] + "  ");
        System.out.print("");
    }
```

```java
    }
    public static void searchTree()
        {
        System.out.print("Enter person name: ");
        String searchName = input.next();
        boolean found = false;
        int currentPosn = root;

        while (!(found == true || currentPosn == 0))
            {
            if (searchName.equals(nodeData[currentPosn]))
                {
                found = true;
                System.out.println("Found at position "+ currentPosn);   }
            else
                if (searchName.compareTo(nodeData[currentPosn]) < 0)
                    {
                    // if possible - move left
                        currentPosn = nodeLeft[currentPosn];            }
                else
                    {
                    // if possble - move right
                    currentPosn = nodeRight[currentPosn];               }
            } // end of the while loop
        if (currentPosn == 0)
        {
        System.out.println("This name was NOT FOUND");
        System.out.print("");
        }
        }

public static void main(String[] args)
{
System.out.println("Binary tree with eight nodes created ... ");
System.out.println("");
String choice = "";
while (!choice.equals("X"))
    {
    displayMenu();
    System.out.print("Choice ? ");
    choice = input.next();
    if (choice.equals("A"))
        {
        displayTree();
        }
    if (choice.equals("B"))
        {
        searchTree();
        }
    }
}
}
```

5 a The missing pseudocode is: [3]

   (A) `Bottom > Top`

   (B) `Top ← Middle - 1`

   (C) `NotInList = TRUE`

   b The code: [8]

Visual Basic

```vb
Dim Animal(20) As String
Sub  Main()
    Animal(1) = "ANT"   : Animal(2) = "BEE"    Animal(3) = "CAT"   :
    Animal(4) = "DOG"   : Animal(5) = "EAGLE"  : Animal(6) = "GOAT"   :
    Animal(7) = "HORSE" : Animal(8) = "PARROT" : Animal(9) = "RAT"   :
    Animal(10) = "ZEBRA"
    Call BinarySearch()
End Sub
Sub  BinarySearch()
    Dim  ThisName As String
    Dim NotInList, Found  As Boolean
    Dim Bottom, Middle, Top As Integer : Dim NoOfComparisons As Integer
    Console.Write( "Which name?  " ) : ThisName = Console.ReadLine
    Found = False : NotInList = False
    ' flags if the required value Is Not found
    Top = 10 : Bottom = 1
    NoOfComparisons = 0
    Do
        NoOfComparisons = NoOfComparisons + 1
        Middle = Int((Top + Bottom) / 2)
        If Animal(Middle) = ThisName Then
            Found = True
            Console.WriteLine( "Value is FOUND after  " &
            Str(NoOfComparisons) & "  comparisons"
        Else
            If Bottom > Top Then
                NotInList = True
            Else
                If Animal(Middle) < ThisName Then
                    ' retain the top half of the list
```

Note: This is the binary tree search algorithm which was studied in Chapter 10

```
                        Bottom = Middle + 1
                    Else
                        ' retain the bottom half of the list
                        Top = Middle - 1
                    End If
                End If
            End If
        Loop until (Found = True) Or (NotInList = True)

        If NotInList = True Then
            Console.WriteLine("Requested item was NOT FOUND")
        End If
    End Sub
```

Python Code

```python
def BinarySearch():
    # ThisName As String
    # NotInList, Found As Boolean
    # Bottom, Middle, Top, NoOfComparisons - Integer

    ThisName = input("Which name? ")
    Found = False
    NotInList = False
    # flags if the required value Is Not found
    Top = 10
    Bottom = 1
    NoOfComparisons = 0

    while not(Found == True or NotInList == True):
        NoOfComparisons = NoOfComparisons + 1
        Middle = int((Top + Bottom) / 2)
        if Animal[Middle] == ThisName:
            Found = True
            print("Value is FOUND after " + str(NoOfComparisons) + " comparisons")
        else:
            if Bottom > Top:
                NotInList = True
            else:
                if Animal[Middle] < ThisName:
                    # retain the top half of the list
                    Bottom = Middle + 1
                else:
                    # retain the bottom half of the list
                    Top = Middle - 1
    if NotInList == True:
        print("Requested item was NOT FOUND")

# Main program starts here
Animal = ["ANT", "BEE", "CAT", "DOG", "EAGLE", "GOAT", "HORSE", "MOUSE", "PARROT", "RAT"]
BinarySearch()
```

Java Code

```java
1     package chapter.pkg21.exam.pkg5;
2     import java.util.Scanner ;
3     public class CHAPTER21EXAM5 {
4     public static Scanner input = new Scanner(System.in);
5     public static String animal [] = {
6                       "", "ANT", "BEE", "CAT", "DOG", "EAGLE",
7                       "GOAT", "HORSE", "PARROT", "RAT", "ZEBRA"};

10    public static void binarySearch()
11    {   int noOfComparisons;
12      int top = 10, bottom = 1, middle ;
13      System.out.print("Which animal ? ");
14      String thisName = input.next();
15      noOfComparisons = 0;
16      boolean notInList = false;
17      boolean found = false;
18      while (!(found == true || notInList == true))
19         { noOfComparisons = noOfComparisons + 1;
20           middle = (top + bottom) / 2;
21           if (animal[middle].equals(thisName))
22               {found = true;
23                System.out.println("Name found after " +
24                       noOfComparisons + " comparisons");   }
25           else
26              if (bottom > top)
27                  { notInList = true; }
28              else
29                  if (animal[middle].compareTo(thisName) < 0)   {
30                     // retain the top half of the list
31                     bottom = middle + 1;                        }
32                  else
33                  { // retain the bottom half of the list
34                     top = middle - 1;     }
35           if (notInList == true)
36              { System.out.print("Requested item was not found");  }
37      } }
38    public static void main(String[] args)
39    {   binarySearch() ;    }   }
```

Chapter 22

Progress Checks

Progress Check A

The customer name, the price paid, the data of the sale (and many others …).

Progress Check B

A class is the definition of what an object will look like, i.e. the object specification.

The class acts as the template or 'blueprint' from which an instance of an object is created.

Progress Check C

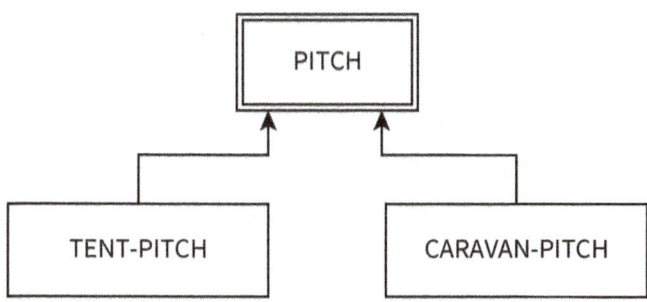

Figure 22.03.

Progress Check D

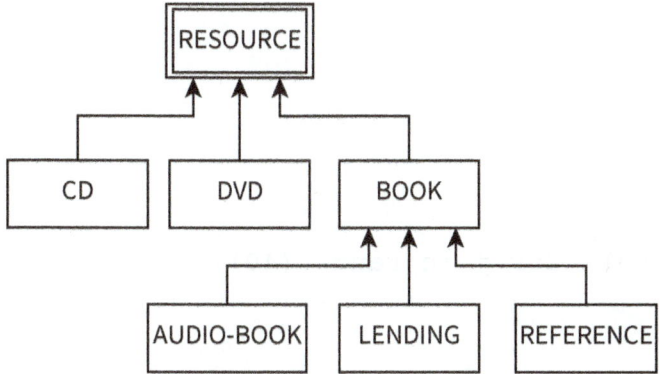

Figure 22.04.

There is no 'correct' answer here.

An alternative design would be to have the class `LENDING`, with sub-classes `BOOK` and `AUDIO-BOOK`.

Alternatively, there could be a single class for `BOOK` with an additional property `Reference` of data type Boolean.

Progress Check E

Make sure you are clear about the difference between a property and a method.

Past paper questions

Q1

This is **Question 6 (a) and (b) in 9608 Paper 41 November 2017**. The mark scheme is available on the Cambridge International School Support Hub. (requires registration). At the time of writing the published mark scheme is available on the Cambridge International School Support Hub. The Examiner's Report for the November 2017 series is also available there and this may contain comments specific to this question.

The following are what the author of the Revision Guide would suggest as reasonable answers, with alternatives suggested where appropriate.

a   1 mark per bullet to max 6

- Declaring a class with the name animal
- Declaring variables for across, down and score (all integers)
- … as private//protected
- Correct constructor header and ending
- Randomly generating an across between 0-39 inc. in constructor
- Randomly generating a down between 0-39 inc. inconstructor
- Initialising Score to zero in constructor.
- Correct get for `Across`
- Correct set for `Across`

VB example: [5]

```
Class Animal
      Private Across As Integer
      Private Down As Integer
      Private Score As Integer
      Function GetAcross()
            Return Across
      End Function
```

```
        Sub SetAcross(Value As Integer)
            Across = Value
        End Sub

        Sub New ()
            Randomize ()
            Across = randomnumber.Next(0, 40)
            Down = randomnumber.Next(0, 40)
            Score = 0
        End Sub
End Class
```

Python example:
```
class Animal   :
      def _init_(self)   :
            x = random.Randint(0, 39)
            y = random.Randint(0, 39)
            self.Across = x
            self.Down = y
            self.Score = 0
      def SetAcross(A)  :
            self.Across = A
      def GetAcross()   :
            return self.Across
```

Python example:
```
def   _init_ (self  :
      self.grid = [[' ' for i in range (40)] for j in range (40)]
      self.AnimalList = []
      self.StepCounter = 0
      for i in range(5)   :
            newAnimal = Animal ()
            self.AnimalList.append(newAnimal)
            self.GenerateFood()
```

VB example:

```
Sub New()
    For x = 0 to 39
        For y = 0 to 39
            grid (x, y) = ""
        Next
    Next
    For z = 0 To 4
        AnimalList(z) = New
        Animal
    Next
    Call GenerateFood ()
End Sub
```

Chapter 23

Progress Checks

Progress Check A

```
TYPE EmployeeData
DECLARE EmployeeCode  : STRING
DECLARE Surname       : STRING
DECLARE Initials      : STRING
DECLARE YearsService  : INTEGER
DECLARE FullTime      : BOOLEAN
ENDTYPE
DECLARE Staff : ARRAY[1..150] OF EmployeeData
```

Progress Check B
a   Serial organisation.
b   There is no key field.
c   True.

Progress Check C
a   True.
b   True.
c   False.
d   True.

Progress Check D

We need to know that in Visual Basic

— Each character in a string uses 2 bytes

— A Boolean value takes up 2 bytes

— A real number data type Single uses 4 bytes

so:

$(2 \times 20) + 2 + 4 = 46$ bytes

Exam-style questions

Q1 [8]

Visual Basic:

```vb
Module Module1
    Dim Take(14) As Integer
    Sub   Main()
        Takings()
        CreateFile()
        ReadFileAndAnalysis()
    End Sub
    Sub   Takings()
        Take(1) = 101 : Take(2) = 231 : Take(3) = 98 : Take(4) = 100
        Take(5) = 0 : Take(6) = 0 : Take(9) = 106
        Take(8) = 209 : Take(9) = 274 : Take(10) = 202 : Take(11) = 231
        Take(12) = 188 : Take(13) : = 197 : Take(14) = 203
    End Sub
```

```vb
Sub CreateFile()
    Dim LineOfText
    Dim Index As Integer
    Dim TakingsFile As System.IO.StreamWriter
    TakingsFile = New IO.StreamWriter("F:\Takings.TXT")
    For Index = 1 To 14
        LineOfText = Str(Take(Index))
        TakingsFile.WriteLine(LineOfText)
    Next
    Console.Writeline("File created …")
    TakingsFile.Close()
End Sub

Sub ReadFileAndAnalysis()
    Dim TakingsFile As System.IO.StreamReader
    Dim Biggest, BiggestDayNo, NextFigure As Integer
    TakingsFile = New IO.StreamReader("F:\Takings.TXT")
    Biggest = Int(TakingsFile.ReadLine)
    BiggestDayNo = 1
    For Index = 2 To 14
        NextFigure = Int(TakingsFile.ReadLine)
        If NextFigure > Biggest Then
            Biggest = NextFigure
            BiggestDayNo = index
        End If
    Next
    Console.Writeline("Day    :    " & Str(BiggestDayNo) & "had takings of " & Str(Biggest))
    TakingsFile.Close()
    Console.Readline()
End Sub
```

Python:

```python
Def CreateFile() :
    # LineOfText As String, Index As Integer
    TakingsFile = open("F:\Takings.PYI", "w+")
    Index = 0
```

```
        while Take[Index] != -1:
            LineOfText = str (Take[Index])
            TakingsFile.write(LineOfText + "\n")
            Index = Index + 1
        print ("File created ... ")
        TakingsFile.close()
Def  ReadFileAndAnalysis() :
        # Biggest, BiggestDayNo, NextFigure As Integer
        TakingsFile = open("F:\Takings.TXT", "r")
        Biggest = 0
        BiggestDayNo = 1
        Index = 1
        for x in TakingsFile:
            if NextFigure > Biggest :
                Biggest = NextFigure
                BiggestDayNo = Index
            Index = Index + 1
            print("Day : " + str(BiggestDayNo) + " had takings of")
TakingsFile.close
# Main program starts here ...
Take = [0, 101, 231, 98, 100, 0, 0, 106, 209, 274, 202, 231, 188, 197, 203, -1]
CreateFile()
ReadFileAndAnalysis()
```

Note the use of the dummy value at the end of the list.

It is used in the While statement to terminate the loop

Q2

a   [3]

```
TYPE Book
        DECLARE Title    : STRING
        DECLARE Author   : STRING
        DECLARE ISBN     : STRING
        DECLARE Fiction  : BOOLEAN
        DECLARE LastRead : DATE
ENDTYPE
```

b [4]

Visual Basic:

```vb
Function Hash(RefNo As Integer) As Integer
    Dim Address As Integer
    Address = (RefNo Mod 2000) + 1
    Return Address
End Function
```

Python:

```python
import pickle

def Hash(RefNo):
    Address = (int(RefNo) % 2000) + 1
    return Address
```

Java:

```java
class Book
{
    String title;
    int refNumber;

    public Book(String t, int r)
    {
        title = t;
        refNumber = r;
    }
}
public class JavaTestBed
{
    public static int hash(int recNumber)
    {   return(recNumber % 2000 + 1); }
```

c [3]

Visual Basic:

```vb
Sub Main()
    PopulateArray()
    Console.ReadLine()
End Sub

Sub PopulateArray()
    MyBook(1).Title = "Jazz highlights" : MyBook(1).RefNo = 4563
    MyBook(2).Title = "Under the light" : MyBook(2).RefNo = 6751
    MyBook(3).Title = "Murder at the mill" : MyBook(3).RefNo = 7865
End Sub
```

Python:

```python
# Main program starts here ...
# ThisRefNo is String
# ThisTitle is String
# ThisAddress is Integer
TitleList = ["", "Jazz highlights", "Under the light", "Murder at the mill"]
RefNoList = ["0", "4563", "6754", "7865"]
```

Java:

The test data used is show in the part (d) Java code which follows.

d [3]

Visual Basic:

```vb
Sub Main()
    PopulateArray()
    WriteToFile()
    Console.ReadLine()
End Sub

Sub WriteToFile()
    Dim BookFileWriter As BinaryWriter
    Dim BookFile As FileStream
    Dim ThisAddress As Integer
    BookFile = New FileStream("E:\BookFile.RND", FileMode.OpenOrCreate)
    BookFileWriter = New BinaryWriter(BookFile)

    For Index = 1 To 3
        ThisAddress = Hash(MyBook(Index).RefNo)
        BookFile.Position = ThisAddress
        BookFileWriter.Write(MyBook(Index).Title)
        BookFileWriter.Write(MyBook(Index).RefNo)
        Console.WriteLine("New record written")
    Next
    Console.WriteLine("File with three records now created")
    BookFile.Close()
End Sub
```

Python:

```python
def WriteToFile():
    BookFile = open("E:\BookFilePY.RND", "wb")
    for Index in range (1,4):
        ThisAddress = Hash(RefNoList[Index])
        BookFile.seek(ThisAddress)
        pickle.dump(TitleList[Index], BookFile)
        pickle.dump(RefNoList[Index], BookFile)
        print("New record written")
    print("File with three records now created")
    print ("")
    BookFile.close
```

Java:

```java
22  public static void main(String args[]) throws IOException
23  {
24      int recordSize = 50;
25      try
26          {
27          RandomAccessFile reader = new RandomAccessFile("J:/Java/23-Exam-Q2.RND", "rw");
28          String bookTitle [] = {"Jazz hightlights", "Under the lights", "Murder at the mill"};
29          int bookRefNumber [] = {3451, 8895, 1329};
30          int recNumber;
31          for (int i = 0; (i < 3); i++)
32              {
33              Book thisBook = new Book(bookTitle[i], bookRefNumber[i]);
34              recNumber = hash(bookRefNumber[i]);
35              int filePointer = recNumber * recordSize;
36              System.out.println("Record number : "
37                      + recNumber + " filePointer : " + filePointer );
38              reader.seek(filePointer);
39              reader.writeUTF(thisBook.title);
40              reader.writeInt(thisBook.refNumber);
41              }
42          reader.close();
43          System.out.println("Random access file with three records created...");
44          }
45      catch (IOException x)
46          { System.out.print("Problem writing to the file ..."); }
47  }
48  }
```

```
New record written
New record written
New record written
File with three records now created
Reference number? :6751

Disk address used was :   752
Under the light
6751
```

e   [4]

```vb
Sub SearchForBook()
    Dim RefNo As Integer
    Dim ThisAddress As Integer
    Dim BookFileReader As BinaryReader
    Dim BookFile As FileStream
    BookFile = New FileStream("E:\BookFile.RND", FileMode.Open)
    BookFileReader = New BinaryReader(BookFile)

    Console.Write("Reference number? :")
    RefNo = Console.ReadLine

    ThisAddress = Hash(RefNo)

    BookFile.Position = ThisAddress
    Console.WriteLine()
    Console.WriteLine("Disk address used was : " & Str(ThisAddress))
    Console.WriteLine(BookFileReader.ReadString)
    Console.WriteLine(BookFileReader.ReadInt32)
    Console.ReadLine()
End Sub
```

Python:

```python
def SearchForBook():
    BookFile = open("E:\BookFilePY.RND", "rb")
    ThisRefNo = int(input("Reference no? "))

    ThisAddress = Hash(ThisRefNo)

    BookFile.seek(ThisAddress)
    ThisRefNo = pickle.load(BookFile)
    ThisTitle = pickle.load(BookFile)

    print("Disk address is ... " + str(ThisAddress))
    print("Book reference number is  ... " + ThisRefNo)
    print("Book title is   ... " + ThisTitle)
    BookFile.close
```

```
 RESTART: C:_____CUP_New\SUPPORT FILES
xam Q2.py
New record written
New record written
New record written
File with three records now created

Reference no? 6754
Disk address is ... 755
Book reference number is  ... Under the light
Book title is   ... 6754
```

Java:

```java
22    public static void main(String args[]) throws IOException
23    {
24    Scanner input = new Scanner(System.in);
25    int recordSize = 50;
26    try
27        {
28        RandomAccessFile reader = new RandomAccessFile("J:/Java/23-Exam-Q2.RND", "r");
29        System.out.print("Reference number : ");
30        int refNumber = input.nextInt();
31        int recNumber = hash(refNumber);
32        int filePointer = recNumber * recordSize;
33
34        reader.seek(filePointer);
35        String thisTitle = reader.readUTF();
36        int thisRefNumber = reader.readInt();
37        System.out.println("Record number : " + recNumber);
38        System.out.println( "FilePointer : " + filePointer );
39        System.out.println( "Title : " + thisTitle + "  with Reference number : " + thisRefNumber) ;
40        reader.close();
41        }
42    catch (IOException x)
43        { System.out.print("Problem reading the random access file ..."); }
44    }
45    }
```

```
run:
Reference number : 8895
Record number : 896
FilePointer : 44800
Title : Under the lights  with Reference number : 8895
BUILD SUCCESSFUL (total time: 6 seconds)
```

Glossary

abstraction in computer science abstraction is used to reduce complexity of the problem to facilitate the design and implementation of a complex software system

accumulator (ACC) single general purpose register inside the processor

accuracy the accuracy of the sound is a measure of how close the recorded sound playback is to the original sound

actuator hardware to convert a form of energy into the motion of some component

allocation units fixed-sized chunks RAM is divided into file allocation units

argument the argument of a function will take none, one or more values of a particular data type

analogue-to-digital converter hardware that converts an analogue signal to a digital value

arithmetic shift when bits are shifted the sign of the number is always retained

authorisation granting of permissions to users or groups of users to access files and procedures

back propagation algorithm used to compute changes to the weights/biases of individual neurons in the hidden layers

big data dataset that, due to its size, variety and the speed at which new data is generated, is impossible for a human to process without machine learning technology

bit rate number of bits transmitted per second along the communication channel

bus width number of lines used on the communication channel

cache memory temporary, high-speed memory

case structure selection structure used when the logic requires many possible outcomes

class description of the properties and methods for a given 'thing'

command line interface user interaction done with one-line commands

condition expression that returns a TRUE or FALSE value

containment when a class definition contains a property that is already designated as a separate class

control system receives data from sensors and acts on the data with hardware that can change the state of the system. There is continual feedback

cyclic shift bits are shifted from one end and reappear at the other end

datagram an alternative to the term 'packet'

data integrity the maintenance of, and the assurance of the accuracy and consistency of, data over its entire life-cycle

data type specifies which type of date will appear in a given field

data validation checks are implemented with software to ensure that data is reasonable and meets some criteria

data verification for data entry by the user, the datum is entered twice and the software will compare, and if a match is not established the user is prompted for the process of data entry to be repeated. For an electronic data transfer, the data received is checked byte by byte against the original data. If it does not match then the data must be re-sent until a match is established

decryption process of converting the cipher text back to plain text

digital data data stored as a sequence of binary numbers

digital-to-analogue converter hardware that converts a digital value to an analogue signal

properties drawn objects have properties. For example, a straight line would have start point coordinates, end-point coordinates, colour, thickness, etc

fetch when a program instruction or a data value is retrieved from some form of storage before it is given to the processor

field single data value

file allocation table map of the usage of the file allocation units

file organisation how data is written to and stored in the file

file pointer pointer to the byte number within a binary file

file session duration of the use of a file between the point in time at which it is 'opened' (by program code) and the later point in time when the file is 'closed' (with program code)

flag value that is used to indicate that some event did/did not occur

graph diagram consisting of vertices connected by lines called edges

graphical user interface (GUI) user interacts with the OS using a pointing device

guard the transition may be conditional on some condition being met. This is called the guard. If so, it can also be labelled on the connecting line

hashing function calculation to compute the storage address of an item from its data value

hashing algorithm/function (hash value) calculation performed on the original plain text to produce the message digest hashing function

host sender and recipient of the communication

identifier name used by the programmer to represent a particular data item

index number that identifies an element of the array

Internet Service Provider (ISP) an organisation that provides a communication service for a business, institution or individual to connect to the internet

interrupt signal sent to the processor to indicate that an event has occurred that needs its attention. An interrupt can originate from a device (hardware interrupt) or from the program execution (software interrupt)

interrupt service routine (ISR) software that is loaded and run to deal with the interrupt

iterative repeated over and over again

logical address address that appears to the application software, as opposed to the real address, called the physical address

logical drives typically, the computer system has one physical disk drive for its secondary storage. The available space is 'partitioned' into logical drives each referenced by a drive letter (C:, D:, etc.)

logistic regression suitable for classification problems where the target is a qualitative value (such as 'spam'/'non-spam')

logical shift when bits are shifted (left or right) the empty bit positions are filled with zero bits

machine code binary patterns for the machine operations carried out by the processor

malicious program code section of a program that is designed to do harm to a computer system

method something that can be done to the object

Multiple Instruction Multiple Data Stream (MIMD) a number of processors function asynchronously and independently. At any time, different processors might be executing different instructions on different pieces of data

Multiple Instruction Stream Multiple Data Stream (MISD) individual data streams are processed in parallel but with different instructions for each data stream

node general term used to describe any item of hardware used on the network

object one instance of a class

one's complement the one's complement of a binary pattern is created by changing all 1 bits to zeros and all zero bits to 1s. This is called 'flipping' the bits

order of growth measure of how fast an algorithm's execution time increases when the size of the input increases

parameter actual data value given to the procedure at 'call time'

passing parameter(s) when a procedure is called and the parameters are described as 'passed' to the procedure header

path sequence of vertices connected by edges

pattern matching looking for similarities or patterns in the decomposed tasks that help solve complex problems more efficiently

port logical address of the interface that directs data from the Application layer and indicates its origin

primary key attribute chosen to make the tuples unique

private network network that is typically in an office or the home.

procedure header information inside the procedure brackets, following the identifier

process program which is loaded to main memory and is being executed

program instruction every program instruction has one or two parts: the op code, usually followed by the operand

program library library of precompiled program code that is written to enable particular features of a program to be implemented

property an attribute of the class. All of the data about each object is held in a drawing list or property list for the object.

pseudocode 'pseudo' program code. It is made up of statements for all the structures permitted by a programming language

record/record structure collection of fields for one customer

regression line line drawn on the scatterplot. The line will indicate if there appears to be a relationship between Y and X. The line is called the 'line of best fit'

relationship link between two entities

reverse engineering an attempt to produce the original source code from the object code

RISC processor each stage is done with one instruction, with each use taking exactly one clock cycle to execute

sample measurement of the sound at a constant time interval

sampling the process of recording a measurement of the sound at a constant time interval

sampling rate the agreed time interval at which samples are taken. Typically expressed as 'the sampling rate of 1000 samples per second' or 'one sample is taken every 1/000 th of a second'

secondary storage any form of data storage that will preserve the data after the power to the computer is removed

serial a file where the records are not organised in any pre-defined order. An exception to this is the chronological order in which new records are added to the end of the file

Single Instruction Stream Multiple Data Stream (SIMD) individual data streams are processed in parallel using the same instruction

Single Instruction Stream Single Data Stream (SISD) sequential processing

socket 'address' needed for each data packet, its IP address and port number

solid state (flash) memory constructed entirely from electronic components

source code program code statements as written by the programmer

symmetric encryption both the sender and receiver have knowledge of the same encryption algorithm and key

syntax error error in the source code that does not obey the grammar of the programming language

text file file that stores a sequence of binary data, containing one or more lines of text each containing characters from the character set

topology physical layout of the cabling and the connection of the devices or nodes to the cable

two's complement the two's complement of a binary pattern is done by writing the one's complement and adding 1

unicode an alternative coding system to ASCII

unsupervised learning occurs when the dataset is unlabelled and the machine learning algorithm attempts to find a structure such as clustering of items or an association between items

Acknowledgements

The authors and publishers acknowledge the following sources of copyright material and are grateful for the permissions granted.

Cover image Westend61/Getty Images; Fig 3.03 Georges Mir/EyeEm/Getty Images; Fig 3.04 PeopleImages/Getty Images

All past exam paper questions are reproduced by permission of Cambridge Assessment International Education.

Index

A
A* algorithm, 237
abstract data types (ADT), 124–127
    binary tree, 215, 258–259, 267–269
    dictionary, 269–270
    hash tables, 209, 269
    linked lists. see linked lists
    queue, 124–125, 260–262
    stacks, 124, 260
abstraction, 106–108
access rights, 97
accumulator (ACC), 42, 43, 46
activation function, 246
activity, state-transition diagram, 159
actuators, 36
adaptive maintenance, 164
ADC. see analogue-to-digital converter (ADC)
addition of binary numbers, 6–7
address bus, 44, 45
addressing modes, 48
address (pointer), memory, 146
adjacency list, 272
adjacency matrix
    directed weighted graph, 272
    undirected graph, 271
ADT. see abstract data types (ADT)
agent, 240
aggregate functions, 100
aggregation, 340–343
AI. see artificial intelligence (AI)
algorithms, 108–110
    Big O notation, 272–274
    defined, 108
    Dijkstra's, 233–236
    encryption, 223, 224
    hashing, 172–173, 227
    identifier names, selection of, 110
    in-order traversal, 215
    performance of, 272–274
    program flowchart, 111
    pseudocode, 113–114
    searching. see searching algorithms
    sorting. see sorting algorithms
    stepwise refinement, 110–111
    Structured English and, 109–110
    traversal, 215–217
allocation units, 204, 206
ALU. see Arithmetic Logic Unit (ALU)
analogue data, 12
analogue-to-digital converter (ADC), 12, 36
analysis, program development life cycle stage, 154–155
AND gate, 37, 197
AND operator, 55, 132
application layer, TCP/IP protocol, 181
application protocols
    FTP (File Transfer Protocol), 183
    HTTP (HyperText Transfer Protocol), 182–183
    POP3 (Post Office Protocol version 3), 183–184
    SMTP (Simple Mail Transfer Protocol), 183–184
application virtual machines, 191–192
arcs, graphs, 271
arithmetic expressions, 132
Arithmetic Logic Unit (ALU), 43, 44, 192
arithmetic operations, 47
arithmetic operators, 132, 302
arithmetic shift, 52
    left, 55
    right, 54
array processing, 190
arrays, 312–316
    assigning values to, 121
    bubble sort, 121
    defined, 119
    element of, 120
    index, 120
    linear search, 121
    one-dimensional, 120
    of records, 121
    systolic, 190
    two-dimensional, 120–121
artificial intelligence (AI), 86–88, 233–248
    applications of, 87
    defined, 86
    graphs and, 233
    A* algorithm, 237
    Dijkstra's algorithm, 233–236
    impact of, 87–88
    machine learning. see machine learning
    neural networks, 244–245
    regression analysis methods. see regression analysis
artificial neural networks, 244–245
ASCII (American Standard Code for Information Interchange), 9, 14
assembler, 63–65
assembly language, 46–47
    addressing modes, 48
    Boolean operators, 55
    constructs in, 290–291
    instructions. see instructions, assembly language
    programs, sample, 48–50
    shift instructions, 52–55
assignment operator, 131
'assign' operator, 51
association, unsupervised learning, 240
asymmetric encryption, 224
asynchronous communication, 194
attenuation, 21
attribute, 90
audio data, 14
authentication, user
    with passwords, 74–75
    terminal restrictions, 75
    using biometric techniques, 75
    using digital signatures, 75
authentication certificates, 75
authorisation, 76

B
back propagation, 245
backtracking, prolog, 293–295
backup, database, 97
back-up software, 63
Backus Naur Form (BNF), 210, 213
base, number system, 1
    conversion between different, 2–4
base 2 number system. see binary numbers
base 10 number system. see denary numbers
base 16 number system. see hexadecimal numbers
BCS (British Computer Society) code of conduct, 83–85
bias, 244, 247
big data, 87, 238
Big O notation, 258, 272–274
    linear time complexity, 272
    order of growth, 272
binary coded decimal (BCD), 8
binary files, 352–356
binary numbers, 2
    addition, 6–7
    conversion
        to denary number, 2
        to hexadecimal number, 3
    denary number conversion to, 2
    hexadecimal number conversion to, 4
    one's complement, 6
    subtraction, 7–8
    two's complement, 5
binary search, 253–254
    and recursive solution, 275–276
binary tree, 215, 258–259, 267–269
    infix expressions, 278
    post order traversal, 279
    and recursion, 275–279
    traversal, 275–276
biometric techniques, user authentication with, 75
BIOS (Basic Input-Output System), 60
bistable, sequential logic circuit, 194
bit depth, 9
bitmaps, 9–11
    applications of, 12
    calculations, 10
    drawbacks, 11
    encodings used for, 10
    run-length encoding and, 13
bit rate, 23
bits, 1, 43
    allocation to mantissa and exponent, 176
    least significant, 4
    manipulation, 52–56, 57
    most significant, 4
    parity, 79
bit streaming
    issues with, 24
    on-demand, 24
    real-time, 23
BitTorrent, 184
BNF. see Backus Naur Form (BNF)
Boolean algebra
    expression
        creation from truth table, 196
        formation for given circuit, 196–197
        simplification of, 197–199
    identities, 197–198
    notation, 196
BOOLEAN data type, 117
Boolean operators, 55
booting-up, 60
boot program code, 35
breakpoints, 70
bridge, 23
broadband router, 75
bubble sort, 121, 141–142, 256–258
buffers, 24, 34
built-in functions, 132–134, 303–305
    manipulation of strings, 304
    maths functions, 132, 133
    string handling functions, 132, 133
    terminology, 132–133
buses (communications channel). see system bus
bus topology, 19
bytes, 1, 9
    parity, 79

C
CA. see Certification Authority (CA)
cables, 22
    coaxial, 21
    copper, 21
    fibre-optic, 21
    twisted-pair, 21
cache memory, 35, 45
candidate key, 90
capacitive technology, touchscreen, 34
Carrier Sense Multiple Access/Collision Detection (CSMA/CD), 23
carry bit, 43, 54
Carry Flag, 52
case structure, 136–137, 308
cell phone networks, 26
central processing unit (CPU)
    architecture, 42–46
    registers, 42–43
Certification Authority (CA), 226
characters, representation of, 8
    ASCII coding system, 9
    Unicode, 9
CHAR data type, 118
check digit method, data validation, 77
checked exception, 361
checksum check, 80–81
cipher text, 223
CIR. see Current Instruction Register (CIR)
circuit switching, 184
circular queue, 125
CISC. see Complex Instruction Set Computer (CISC)
classes, in OOP, 169, 330
    child, 336
    diagram, 335–338
classification-type problems, 239
client-server model, 18
cloud computing, 20
clustering, unsupervised learning, 240
coaxial cable, 21
coding, program development life cycle stage, 156
collisions, 23, 269
colour depth, 10
command line interface, 61, 204
comma separator, 170
commercial software, 86
compare instructions, assembly language, 48
compilers, 66, 208–210
    benefits of, 67
    code generation, 210
    lexical analysis, 209–210
    process of compilation, 208
    and recursive code, 275
    syntax analysis, 210
Complex Instruction Set Computer (CISC), 187
    instruction execution, 188–189
    interrupt handling on, 189
composite data types, 169
compression software, 63
compression techniques, 13–14
    lossless encoding, 13
    lossy encoding, 13–14
    run-length encoding, 13
computational thinking
    abstraction, 106–108
    algorithms, 108–110
    constructs, 110
    decomposition, 108
    pattern recognition, 108
    searching algorithms. see searching algorithms
    sorting algorithms. see sorting algorithms
computer program, 43
computer system
    central processing unit. see central processing unit (CPU)
    components of, 31
    control system, 36
    data storage, 34
    fetch-execute (F-E) cycle, 51–52
    memory. see memory
    monitoring system, 35
    performance, factors affecting, 45–46
    ports, 46
    security of, 74
    system bus. see system bus
    system software. see system software
    Von Neumann model, 34
condition, 110, 134
console, output to, 132
constants, 300
    assignment, 131, 302
    declaration, 131, 302
constant time complexity, 273
constructs, 134–142
    in assembly language, 290–291
    case structure, 136–137
    for computing algorithms, 110
    IF structure, 134–136
        IF-THEN-ELSE-ENDIF, 135
        IF-THEN-ENDIF, 134
        nested **IF**, 135–136
    loops. see loops
    problems using, 140–142
containment/aggregation, 340–343
control bus, 44
control characters, 9
control system, 36
copper cables, 21
copyright law, 86
cores, processor, 45
corporate spyware, 75
corrective maintenance, 164
correlation, 242
correlation coefficient, 242–243
count controlled loops, 138, 309–310
CPU. see central processing unit (CPU)
CSMA/CD. see Carrier Sense Multiple Access/Collision Detection (CSMA/CD)
Current Instruction Register (CIR), 43
cybersecurity, 74
cyclic shift, 52
    left, 54
    right, 54

D
data
    cleansing, 239
    concurrent access to, 95
    dependency, 189
    duplicated, 92, 97
    hiding, 340
    integrity, 76–80, 97
    modelling, 239
    redundant, 92
    representation. see data representation
    security. see data security
    storage, 34. see also memory
    transforming, 238
    validation, 77–79
data analysis, 238–239
Database Administrator (DBA), 97
database management system (DBMS), 95–97
    business, 96
    duplicated data, 97
    software tools within, 95–97
databases, 89–102
    backup, 97
    file based approach, 89
    locking, 96
    relational. see relational databases
database server, 18
data bus, 44, 45
data definition language (DDL), 98–99
data dictionary, 90, 95
data entry
    data verification for, 79
    tools for, 78–79
datagrams, 185
data maintenance, data manipulation for, 100–101
data manipulation language (DML), 99–101
data modelling, 95
data movement instructions, assembly language, 47
data representation, 168–178
    data types. see data types
    file organisation and access, 170–173
data scrubbing, 239
data security, 20, 74–76, 97
    authorisation, 76
    encryption, 76
    password protection, 76
    protection measures, 74–75
data types, 301
    BOOLEAN, 117
    character, 118
    composite, 169
    DATE, 117
    enumerated, 168
    non-composite, 168–169
    numbers, 117–118
    standard, 117
    string, 118
    TIME, 117
    user-defined, 168–170
data values, 125
    fixed length, 171
data verification
    for data entry, 79
    during data transfer, 79
DATE data type, 117
DBMS. see database management system (DBMS)

DDL. see data definition language (DDL)
debugging, 69–70
declaration statement, 117
declarative programming, 291–295
  overview, 285
decomposition, computational thinking, 108
decryption, 223
dedicated lines, 25
deep learning, 245–248
defragmentation software, 62
degree of vertex, 271
delimit, 170
De Morgan's laws, 199
denary numbers, 1
  binary number conversion to, 2
    floating-point real numbers, 174–175
  conversion
    to binary number, 2
    to hexadecimal number, 4
  conversion real numbers
    to floating point representation, 175
  hexadecimal number conversion to, 2, 4
dependent variable, 242
descendant node, 258
design, program development life cycle stage, 155–156
  equivalent pseudocode, 159
  state-transition diagram, 159–161
  structure chart, 158–159
diaphragm, 33
dictionary, 173, 269–270
digital certificate, 225, 226–229
  digital signatures, 227
  getting, 226
digital data, 12
digital signatures, 227
  user authentication with, 75
Dijkstra's algorithm, 233–236
direct access, 171
  random file, 172
  sequentially organised file, 171–172
direct addressing, 48, 285–286
directed graphs, 271
directed weighted graph, 272
disk contents analysis, 62
disk formatter, 62
disk recovery, 62
disk thrashing, 207
DLL files. see Dynamic Link Library (DLL) files
DML. see data manipulation language (DML)
DNS. see Domain Name Service (DNS)
domain controller server, 18
Domain Name Service (DNS), 25, 185
double entry, 79
double quotes, 118
DRAM. see dynamic RAM (DRAM)
drivers, 62
duplicated data, 92, 97
dynamic IP address, 28
Dynamic Link Library (DLL) files, 63
dynamic memory allocation, 169
dynamic microphone, 32
dynamic RAM (DRAM), 35
dynamic syntax checking, 162, 210

E
each possible state, state-transition diagram, 159
edges, graphs, 233, 271
EEPROM. see Electronically Erasable Programmable ROM (EEPROM)
electromagnetic spectrum, 21–22
Electronically Erasable Programmable ROM (EEPROM), 35
element, of arrays, 120
email server, 18
embedded systems, 31–32
emulation, 190
encapsulation, 340
encodings
  ASCII, 9
  for bitmaps, 10
  Unicode, 9
encryption, 76
  algorithm, 223, 224

asymmetric, 224
  defined, 223
  public key, 224
  symmetric, 223
encryption key, 223
entity, 90
entity-relationship (E-R) diagram, 91
enumerated data type, 168
environment, 240
errors
  handling, 361–362
  logic, 162
  rounding, 178
  run-time, 162
  source code, 208
  syntax, 162
Ethernet, 23
even parity, 79
ethics, 83–85
  BCS code of conduct, 83–85
  and role of computing professional, 83
  software-developer workplace-scenarios, 85
event-driven control system, 36
exception
  checked, 361
  defined, 360
  handling, 360–363
  runtime, 361
exception handler, 361
exclusive OR (EOR) gate, 37
execution, program, 43
existence check method, data validation, 78
exponent, 174
  allocation of bits to, 176
extended character set, 9

F
FAT. see File Allocation Table (FAT)
FDM. see fused depositional modelling (FDM)
feedback, 36
fetch-execute (F-E) cycle, 51–52
  interrupts and, 51–52
fibre-optic cable, 21
fields, 89
File Allocation Table (FAT), 61, 204
file allocation unit, 61
file compression utility software, 63
file directory, 61
file header data, 10
file mode, 122
file organisation, 122, 170–173
  random organisation, 171
  selection, and access method, 173
  sequential organisation, 171
  serial organisation, 170
file pointer, 171, 357
file processing, 346–349
  operations for, 346
  serial, 346
files, 121–123
  access methods, 171–172
  binary, 352–356
  need for, 121–122
  organisation. see file organisation
  processing. see file processing
  sharing, 17
  sound, compression of, 14
  text. see text files
file server, 18
file session, 171
file system, 60–61
File Transfer Protocol (FTP), 183
FILO (First In – Last Out), 124
firewalls, 75
first normal form (INF), 93
fixed length data values, 171
flag register, 43
flash memory, 33
flip-flops
  JK flip-flop, 195–196
  SR flip-flop, 194–195
floating-point real numbers, 173–178
  binary
    approximation, 177–178
    conversion into denary, 174–175
    format of, 173–174
  denary real number, conversion of, 175
  normalised, 175–176

flowchart, 111
foreign key, 91
format check method, data validation, 77
FOR-NEXT loop, 138
free software foundation (FSF), 85
FSF. see free software foundation (FSF)
FTP (File Transfer Protocol), 183
full adder logic circuit, 193–194
functions, 143, 317–319
  built-in. see built-in functions
  user-defined, 146–148
fused depositional modelling (FDM), 32

G
getter method, 330–331
graphical user interface (GUI), 61, 204, 340
graphics
  bitmap, 9–11
  vector, 11–12
graphs, 270–272
  and artificial intelligence, 233
  A* algorithm, 237
  Dijkstra's algorithm, 233–236
  directed, 271
  undirected, 271
  weighted, 233, 271
Gray Code, 200
GUI. see graphical user interface (GUI)

H
hackers, 75
half adder logic circuit, 192
hard disks, 33
  formatter, 62
hardware, 31–39
  devices, operation of, 32–34
  embedded systems, 31–32
  internet, 25–26
  LAN, 22–23
  management for input/output, 61–62
hashing, 360
  algorithms, 172–173, 227
  function, 171, 269
hash tables, 209, 269
HDMI. see High Definition Multimedia Interface (HDMI)
header section, 181–182
head pointer, queue, 261
heuristic function, 237
hexadecimal numbers, 2
  binary number conversion to, 3
  conversion
    to binary number, 4
    to denary number, 2, 4
  denary number conversion to, 4
High Definition Multimedia Interface (HDMI), 46
hosts, 180
HTTP (HyperText Transfer Protocol), 182–183
Huffman compression, 14
hybrid topology, 20

I
IAS. see immediate access store (IAS)
IDE. see Integrated Development Environment (IDE)
identifiers, 117
  for binary search/chop algorithm, 253
  for bubble sort, 257
  for insertion sort, 255
  for linear search algorithm, 252
  names, 110, 130–131
identities, Boolean algebra, 197–198
identity authentication, 228
IF structure, 134–136
  IF-THEN-ELSE-ENDIF, 135
  IF-THEN-ENDIF, 134
  nested IF, 135–136, 306–307
IF-THEN-ELSE-ENDIF statement, 135
IF-THEN-ELSE statement, 305–306
IF-THEN-ENDIF statement, 134
IF-THEN statement, 305
image resolution, 11
IMAP (Internet Message Access Protocol), 184
immediate access store (IAS), 43

immediate addressing, 48, 287
imperative programming, 285, 300–326
independent variable, 242
indexed addressing, 48, 288–289
index file, 171
indexing, 90
index register (IX), 43
indirect addressing, 48, 288
infix notation, 214, 215
inheritance, 334–338
  child classes and, 336
initial seeder, 184
initial state, state-transition diagram, 159
in-order traversal algorithm, 215
in-order tree traversal, 276
input, algorithm design stage, 113
input devices, 31
  microphone, 32
  touchscreen, 34
input/output instructions, assembly language, 47
input variables, 36
insertion sort, 255–256
Institute of Electrical and Electronics Engineers (IEEE), 83
  ethics principles, 84
instructions, assembly language
  arithmetic operations, 47
  compare, 48
  data movement, 47
  input/output, 47
  jump, 48
instruction set, 45, 46
INTEGER data type, 118
Integrated Development Environment (IDE), 67–71, 208
  debugging, 69–70
  prettyprint, 69
  reporting variables, 70
  report window, 70–71
  text editor, 68
internal clock, 45–46
internet, 24
  bit streaming, 23
  hardware, 25–26
internet layer, TCP/IP protocol, 181–182
internet protocol (IP), 26–28
Internet Service Provider (ISP), 18, 24, 185
interpreter, 66, 207–208
  benefits of, 67
interrupt register, 51, 189
interrupts, 51, 189
  and fetch-execute cycle, 51–52
  kernel and, 206
Interrupt Service Routine (ISR), 51, 189
IP. see internet protocol (IP)
IP addresses, 26–28
  classes, 27
  dynamic, 28
  IPv4, 26–27
  IPv6, 27
  private, 28
  public, 28
  static, 28
  subnetting, 28
IP addresses, TCP/IP protocol, 181
IPv4 addresses, 26–27
IPv6 addresses, 27
ISP. see Internet Service Provider (ISP)
ISR. see Interrupt Service Routine (ISR)
iteration. see loops
iteration construct, 110
iterative model, in program development life cycle, 157–158
IX. see index register (IX)

J
Java, 67
  arithmetic operators and functions, 302
  arrays, 121, 312–316
  binary files
    adding records to, 354–355
    reading contents of, 355–356
  built-in functions, 304–305
  case structure, 308
  class object, creation of, 333

code comments, 302
containment/aggregation, 342–343
count-controlled loop, 310
data types, 301
exception handler, 363
functions, 317–319
IF-THEN-ELSE structure, 306
IF-THEN structure, 305
inheritance, 336
methods, 332
nested IF structure, 307
polymorphism, 339
post-condition loop, 311
pre-condition loop, 311
procedures, 321, 322, 324, 326
program output, 303
random files
  adding records to, 359
  retrieving record from, 360
record structure, 351–352
'switch' statement in, 309
text file
  creation of, 347–348
  reading content of, 348
user input, 303
variables, declaration and assignment of, 301
Java Virtual Machine (JVM), 67, 192
JK flip-flop, 195–196
jump instructions, assembly language, 48
just-in-time (JIT) compilation, 67
JVM. see Java Virtual Machine (JVM)

K
Karnaugh maps (K-map), 200–201
kernel, 206
keyboard, input from, 131
key field, 171
key number, 171
keyword table, 209
kilobytes, 4, 5
knowledge engineering, 87

L
LAN. see local area network (LAN)
language grammar rules, 210
language translators
  assembler software, 63–65
  compiler, 66, 67
  interpreter, 66, 67
  Java, 67
laser printer, 32
latched state, 194
leaf nodes, 274
least significant bit, 4
leeches, 184
left subtree, 275
length check method, data validation, 77
lexical analysis, 209–210
licensing, software. see software licensing
LIFO (Last In – First Out), 124
limit check method, data validation, 77
linear regression, 242–243
linear search, 121, 140–141, 251–253
linear time complexity, 272
linked lists, 263–267
  data, visualising, 125–126
  defined, 125
  deletion of items, 127, 267
  implementation, 125
  insertion of items, 127, 265–266
  nodes, 125
  searching an item, 264–265
link pointer, 125
lists
  linked. see linked lists
  Python, 121, 312, 314, 316
loader, 206
local area network (LAN)
  characteristics of, 17
  hardware to support, 22–23
  and IP addressing. see IP addresses
  topologies. see topologies, network
local variable, 145
logarithmic time complexity, 274
logical address, 207
logical drive areas, 60–61
logical operators, 132
logical schema, 95

logical shift, 52–53
  left, 53–54
  right, 53
logic circuits, 36
  constructing truth table from, 38–39
  construction of, 38
  full adder, 193–194
  half adder, 192
logic errors, 162
logic gates, 36
  AND gate, 37
  NAND gate, 37–38
  NOR gate, 38
  NOT gate, 37
  OR gate, 37
  XOR (EOR) gate, 37
logistic regression, 243
loop counter, 138
loops, 110, 138
  count controlled, 138, 309–310
  post-condition, 139, 311
  pre-condition, 139, 310–311
lossless encoding, 13
loss of accuracy, 176, 178
lossy encoding, 13–14
low-level programming
  direct addressing, 285–286
  immediate addressing, 287
  indexed addressing, 288–289
  indirect addressing, 288
  overview, 284–285
  relative addressing, 287
low-level scheduler, 205

M
MAC address (media access control address), 23, 182
machine code, 46
machine learning
  in action, 239
  data analysis, 238–239
  overview, 238
  reinforcement learning, 240–241
  supervised learning, 239
  tools, 241
  unsupervised learning, 240
magnitude, of numbers, 4–5
maintenance, program development life cycle stage, 156
malware, 62, 75
mantissa, 174
  allocation of bits to, 176
many-to-many relationship, 91
MAR. see Memory Address Register (MAR)
masking operation, logical operators and, 57
massively parallel computer system, 190
matching operation, logical operators and, 56–57
maths functions, 132, 133
MDR. see Memory Data Register (MDR)
megabytes, 4, 5
memory
  address (pointer), 146
  buffers, 34
  cache, 35, 45
  management, OS and, 206–207
  map, 207
  primary, 31, 61
  random-access, 34
  read only, 35
  secondary. see secondary storage/memory
  segmentation, 206–207
  virtual, 207
Memory Address Register (MAR), 43
Memory Data Register (MDR), 43, 44
memory manager, 206
mesh topology, 20
message digest, 227
meta-language, 213
methods, OOP, 330–332
microcontroller, 32
microphone, 32
microwaves, 22
MIMD. see multiple instruction, multiple data (MIMD)
MISD. see multiple instruction, single data (MISD)
modem, 25–26
monitoring system, 35
most significant bit, 4

MP3 (audio format), 14
multilayer perceptron, 244
multiple instruction, multiple data (MIMD), 190
multiple instruction, single data (MISD), 190
multitasking, 61, 205

N
NAND gate
  and De Morgan's laws, 199
  JK flip-flop, 195
  SR flip-flop, 194
NAT. see Network Address Translation (NAT)
negative bit, 43
neighbour vertices, 271
nested IF statement, 135–136, 306–307
Network Address Translation (NAT), 28
Network Interface Card (NIC), 22
network/link layer, TCP/IP protocol, 182
network/networking
  benefits of, 17
  cell phone, 26
  client-server model, 18
  Ethernet, 23
  and file sharing, 17
  IP addresses and. see IP addresses
  local area. see local area network (LAN)
  peer-to-peer, 18, 184
  private, 23, 75
  threats, 75–76
  topologies. see topologies, network
  wide area. see wide area network (WAN)
  wired, 20–21
  wireless, 21–22
neural networks
  deep learning, 245–248
  defined, 244
  with layers, 244
  simple, 244
  terminology, 245
nibble, 3
NIC. see Network Interface Card (NIC)
nodes, 19
  binary tree, 258
  descendant, 258
  graphs, 233, 271
  linked list, 125
  root, 258
non-composite data types, 168–169
NOR gate, 38
  and De Morgan's laws, 199
  SR flip-flop with, 195
normalisation, 92–94
normalised floating-point real numbers, 175–176
NOT operator, 132
NTFS (file system), 62
numbers
  built-in functions for, 305
  data types, 117–118
number systems, 1–5. see also binary numbers; denary numbers; hexadecimal numbers

O
object code, 63
object (machine code) file, 208
object-oriented programming (OOP), 330–343
  building blocks, 330–332
  classes. see classes, in OOP
  containment/aggregation, 340–343
  encapsulation, 340
  inheritance, 334
  methods, 330–332
  objects. see objects
  overview, 285
  polymorphism, 338–339
objects, 169, 330
  creation of, 333–334
  designing, 340
  properties of, 330
odd parity, 79
on-demand bit streaming, 24

one-dimensional (1D) array, 120
one's complement, 6, 7
1-to-many relationship, 91
1-to-1 relationship, 91
OOP. see object-oriented programming (OOP)
op code, 46
open hashing, 269
open source software, 85
operand, 46
operating system (OS)
  file system, 60–61
  hardware management, 61–62
  and memory management, 206–207
  multi-tasking, 205
  need for, 60
  primary memory, 61
  process management, 61
  purpose of, 204
  resources managed by, 60–62
  security management, 61
  user interface, 61, 204
  utility software. see utility software
operators
  arithmetic, 132, 302
  Boolean, 55
  logical, 132
optical disk reader/writer, 33
order of complexity, 258
order of growth, 272
OR operator, 55, 132
OS. see operating system (OS)
output, algorithm design stage, 113
output devices, 31
  printers, 32
  speakers, 32–33
  touchscreen, 34
  virtual headset, 34
overflow, 7, 177
overflow bit, 43

P
packet switching, 185
page frames, 206, 207
page-frame table, 207
pages, 207
page swapping, 207
paging, 206, 207
parallel processing architectures
  multiple instruction, single data, 190
  single instruction, multiple data, 190
  single instruction, single data, 189
parameters, 132
  passing
    by reference, 325–326
    by value, 322–324
  procedures with, 144–145
parity bit, 79
parity block check, 79–80
parity byte, 79
parity check, 79
parsing, expression, 213
partitions, 60–61
passwords
  protection, 76
  user authentication with, 74–75
pattern matching, 190
pattern recognition, computational thinking, 108
PC. see program counter (PC)
PCB. see Process Control Block (PCB)
peers, 18
peer-to-peer (P2P) networking, 18, 184
perfective maintenance, 164
permissions, 76
pharming, 76
phishing, 76
photons, 230
physical addresses, 206
pipelining, 188–189
'pixellation,' 11
pixels, 9, 10
place values, 1
plain text, 223
platters, hard disks, 33
pointer data type, 169
pointers, 209
  file, 171
  link, 125
policy network, 240, 241

polymorphism, 336, 338–339
polynomial time complexity, 274
POP3 (Post Office Protocol version 3), 183–184
ports, 46, 181
post-condition loop, 139, 311
pre-condition loop, 139, 310–311
presence check method, data validation, 77
prettyprint, 69
primary key, 90
primary memory, 31, 61
printer
  laser, 32
  3D, 32
print server, 18
priority queue, 205
privacy, 228
private cloud, 20
private IP address, 28
private key, 224
private network, 23, 75
procedures, 143–145, 320–326
  calling, syntax for, 143
  defining, syntax for, 143
  header, 144
  with parameters, 144–145
  passing parameters
    by reference, 325–326
    by value, 322–324
process
  defined, 205
  states, 205
Process Control Block (PCB), 205
processing, algorithm design stage, 113
processors, 31
  Arithmetic Logic Unit, 43
  buses, 43–44
  CISC-based, 187–188
    instruction execution, 188–189
    interrupt handling on, 189
  cores, 45
  internal clock, 45–46
  RISC-based, 187, 188
    instruction sequence, 189
    interrupt handling on, 189
process virtual machines, 191–192
program counter (PC), 43
program-data independence, 90
program development life cycle
  analysis stage, 154–155
  coding stage, 156
  design stage. see design, program development life cycle stage
  iterative model, 157–158
  maintenance stage, 156
  RAD model, 157
  testing stage. see testing, program development life cycle stage
  waterfall model, 156–157
program instructions, 46
program libraries, 63
programmable ROM (PROM), 35
programming paradigms
  declarative, 285
  imperative, 285
  low-level, 284–285
  object-oriented, 285
  overview, 284
programming/programming language, 130
  arithmetic expressions, 132
  built-in functions. see built-in functions
  console, output to, 132
  constants, 131
  constructs. see constructs
  functions. see functions
  grammar, 211–217
  identifier names, 130–131
  Java. see Java
  keyboard, input from, 131
  loops. see loops
  paradigms. see programming paradigms
  procedures. see procedures
  Python. see Python
  structured. see structured programming
  variables
    assignment, 131
    declaration, 131

Visual Basic. see Visual Basic (VB)
Prolog (Programming in Logic), 291–292
  backtracking with rules, 293–295
  facts, 292
  queries/goal setting, 292–293
  rules, 292
PROM. see programmable ROM (PROM)
properties
  of objects, 330
  vector graphics, 11
property list, 11
protocols
  application. see application protocols
  defined, 180
  Secure Socket Layer, 228–229
  stack, 180
  TCP/IP. see TCP/IP protocol stack
  Transport Layer Security, 228
pseudocode, 50, 113–114, 130. see also programming/programming language
  arrays in. see arrays
  data types. see data types
  examples, 148–150
PSTN. see Public Switched Telephone Network (PSTN)
public cloud, 20
public IP address, 28
public key encryption, 224
Public Switched Telephone Network (PSTN), 25
Python, 300
  arithmetic operators and functions, 302
  binary files
    adding records to, 353–354
    reading contents of, 354
  built-in functions, 304–305
  case structure, 308
  class object, creation of, 333
  code comments, 302
  containment/aggregation, 341
  count-controlled loop, 310
  data types, 301
  exception handler, 363
  functions, 317–319
  hash table data structure, 173
  IF-THEN-ELSE structure, 306
  IF-THEN structure, 305
  inheritance, 336
  lists, 121, 312, 314, 316
  methods, 331, 332
  nested IF structure, 307
  polymorphism, 338–339
  post-condition loop, 311
  pre-condition loop, 310
  procedures, 320, 322, 323, 325
  program output, 303
  random files
    adding records to, 358
    retrieving record from, 358
  record structure, 351
  text file
    creation of, 347
    reading content of, 348
  user input, 303
  variables, declaration and assignment of, 301

Q
quantum cryptography, 230
queries, 100
query processor, 95, 96
queues, 124–125, 260–262

R
radio waves, 21–22, 26
RAD model. see Rapid Applications Development (RAD) model
RAM. see random-access memory (RAM)
random-access memory (RAM), 34
  dynamic, 35
  static, 35
random files, 356–360
  direct access to, 172
  organisation, 171
range check method, data validation, 77
Rapid Applications Development (RAD) model, 157

read only memory (ROM), 35
   Electronically Erasable Programmable, 35
   programmable, 35
ready, process state, 205
'ready' queue, 205
REAL data type, 118
real numbers, floating-point. *see* floating-point real numbers
real-time bit streaming, 23
Real Time Operating system (RTOS), 31
record key number, 171
record locking, 96
records, 118, 169
record structure, 89, 349–352
recursion, 213, 275–279
reduced instruction set computers (RISC), 187
   instruction sequence, 189
   interrupt handling on, 189
redundant data, 92
referential integrity, 91
registers
   general purpose, 42
   special purpose, 42–43
register transfer notation, 51
regression analysis, 239
   linear regression, 242–243
   logistic regression, 243
regression line, 242, 243
regression-type problems, 239
reinforcement learning, 240–241
relational databases, 90
   entity-relationship (E-R) diagram, 91
   foreign key, 91
   indexing, 90
   normalisation process, 92–94
   primary key, 90
   referential integrity, 91
   relationships, 91
   secondary key, 90
   table notation, 90
   terminology, 90
relationships, 91
relative addresses, 206
relative addressing, 48, 287
reliability, 228
repeater, 21, 23
REPEAT-UNTIL loop, 139
report window, IDE, 70–71
requirements specification, 154
resistive technology, touchscreen, 34
re-usable program code, 145
reverse engineer, 86
Reverse Polish Notation (RPN), 214–217
right subtree, 275
RISC. *see* reduced instruction set computers (RISC)
ROM. *see* read only memory (ROM)
root node, 258
rounding error, 178
router, 23
   broadband, 75
   role of, 185
routing tables, 23, 185
RPN. *see* Reverse Polish Notation (RPN)
RTOS. *see* Real Time Operating system (RTOS)
run-length encoding (RLE), 13
running, process state, 205
run-time errors, 162
runtime exception, 361

S
satellite communication, 22
scalable vector graphics, 11, 12
scatterplot, 242
Schmit, Eric, 87
scope, of variable, 145
screen resolution, 11
searching algorithms
   binary search, 253–254
   linear search, 121, 140–141, 251–253
secondary key, 90
secondary storage/memory, 31
   hard disks, 33
   optical disk reader/writer, 33
   solid state (flash) memory, 33
second normal form (2NF), 93–94

Secure Socket Layer (SSL) protocol, 228–229
security, 223–230
   of computer system, 74
   data. *see* data security
   digital certificate, 225, 226–229
   encryption. *see* encryption
   quantum cryptography, 230
seeder, 184
segmentation, 206–207
selection construct, 110
   case structure, 308
   IF-THEN-ELSE structure, 305–306
   IF-THEN structure, 305
   nested **IF** structure, 306–307
sensors, 35, 36
sequence construct, 110
sequential files
   access, 356
   direct access to, 171–172
   organisation, 171, 356
   sequential access for, 171
sequential logic circuits
   JK flip-flop, 195–196
   SR flip-flop, 194–195
serial files
   organisation, 170, 346, 356
   sequential access for, 171
server, 22
   database, 18
   domain controller, 18
   email, 18
   file, 18
   print, 18
   web, 18
session key, 228
sets, data type, 169
setter method, 330–331
shareware, 85–86
shift instructions, assembly language, 52–55
SIMD. *see* single instruction, multiple data (SIMD)
single instruction, multiple data (SIMD), 190
single instruction, single data (SISD), 189
single quotes, 118
single-step mode, 70
SISD. *see* single instruction, single data (SISD)
SMTP (Simple Mail Transfer Protocol), 183–184
socket, 181
software
   development. *see* software/program development
   licensing. *see* software licensing
   translation. *see* translation software
   virtual machines, 190–192
software licensing
   commercial software, 86
   copyright law, 86
   free software foundation, 85
   open source initiative, 85
   shareware, 85–86
software/program development
   iterative model, 157–158
   life cycle. *see* program development life cycle
   RAD model, 157
   system maintenance, 164
   waterfall model, 156–157
solid state (flash) memory, 33
sorting algorithms, 254
   bubble sort, 121, 141–142, 256–258
   insertion sort, 255–256
sound, 12–13
   file, compression of, 14
source code, 63, 207
   errors, 208
speakers, 32–33
spyware, 75
SQL. *see* Structured Query Language (SQL)
SRAM. *see* static RAM (SRAM)
SR flip-flop, 194–195
SSL protocol. *see* Secure Socket Layer (SSL) protocol
stacks, 51, 124, 217, 260
'staircase effect,' 11
star topology, 19–20

state-transition diagram, 159–161
static IP address, 28
static RAM (SRAM), 35
status register, 43
stepwise refinement, 110–111
stopping condition, 275
STRING data type, 118
string handling functions, 132, 133
strongly typed languages, 131
structure charts, 158–159
Structured English, 109–110
structured programming, 143–148
   passing values by reference, 146
   passing values by value, 146
   procedures, 143–145
   user-defined functions, 146–148
Structured Query Language (SQL), 98
   data definition language, 98–99
   data manipulation language, 99–101
subnetting, 28
subprograms, 143
subroutines, 143
subtraction of binary numbers, 7–8
supervised learning, 239
suspended, process state, 205
swarm, 184
switch, 22
'switch' statement, in Java, 309
symbol table, 209
symmetric encryption, 223
synchronous communication, 194
syntax analyser, 210
syntax analysis, 210
syntax diagrams, 210, 211–213
syntax errors, 66, 162
system bus, 43, 45
   address, 44
   control, 44
   data, 44
   width, 45
system maintenance, 164
system software, 60–71, 204–218
   language translators. *see* language translators
   operating system. *see* operating system (OS)
   process management, 205–206
   program libraries, 63
   utility software. *see* utility software
system virtual machines, 190–191
systolic arrays, 190

T
table, 90
table-level locking, 96
tail pointer, queue, 261
TCP/IP protocol stack, 180
   application layer, 181
   internet layer, 181–182
   IP addresses, 181
   network/link layer, 182
   transport layer, 181
TCP/IP protocol suite, 180
telecommunications, 21–22
terminal symbols, 213
testing, program development life cycle stage, 156
   data, selection of, 164
   error types, 162
   methods, 162–163
text editor, 66, 68
text files, 121
   compression of, 14
   creation of, 346–348
   opening, 122
   organisation, 122
   reading from, 123, 348–349
   writing to, 122–123
thermoplastics, 32
thick-client computing, 19
thin-client computing, 19
third normal form (3NF), 94
threats, network, 75–76
   hackers, 75
   malware, 75
   pharming, 76
   phishing, 76
   spyware, 75
   virus, 75
3D printer, 32
TIME data type, 117
time (data type), 117
time-driven control system, 36

time-slice, 205
TLS protocol. *see* Transport Layer Security (TLS) protocol
token, 209
topologies, network, 19–20, 26
   bus, 19
   hybrid, 20
   mesh, 20
   star, 19–20
torrent descriptor file, 184
tracker computer, 184
transition, state-transition diagram, 159
translation software
   compiler, 208–210
   interpreter, 207–208
Transmission Control Protocol (TCP), 180
transmission speeds, cables, 21
transport layer, TCP/IP protocol, 181
Transport Layer Security (TLS) protocol, 228
truth tables
   construction from circuit, 38–39
   full-adder, 193
   AND gate, 37
   logic expression construction from, 39
   NAND gate, 38
   NOR gate, 38
   NOT gate, 37
   OR gate, 37
   XOR (EOR) gate, 37
tuple, 90
twisted-pair cables, 21
two-dimensional (2D) arrays, 120–121
two's complement, 5, 7

U
UDP. *see* User Datagram Protocol (UDP)
underflow, 177
undirected graphs, 271
Unicode, 9
Uniform Resource Locator (URL), 25
uniqueness check method, data validation, 78
Universal Serial Bus (USB), 46
unsupervised learning, 240
unwinding process, 276
URL. *see* Uniform Resource Locator (URL)
USB. *see* Universal Serial Bus (USB)
user accounts, 74
User Datagram Protocol (UDP), 181
user-defined data types, 168–170
user-defined functions, 146–148
user interface, 61
UTF-8 (Unicode), 9
utility software
   back-up software, 63
   defragmentation software, 62
   disk contents analysis, 62
   disk formatter, 62
   file compression, 63
   virus checker, 62

V
values
   data. *see* data values
   passing by reference, 146
   passing by value, 146
variables, 300
   assignment, 131, 301
   declaration, 131, 301
   dependent, 242
   independent, 242
   input, 36
   local, 145
   reporting, 70
   scope, 145
vectored interrupts, 189
vector graphics, 11–12
   applications of, 12
vector processing, 190
vertexes, graphs, 271
VGA. *see* Video Graphics Array (VGA)
Video Graphics Array (VGA), 46
views, database, 95
virtual headset, 34
virtual machines (VMs)
   benefits of, 192
   defined, 190

   limitations of, 192
   process, 191–192
   system, 190–191
virtual memory, 207
Virtual Private Network (VPN) software, 28
virus, 62, 75
virus checker, 62
virus database, 62
Visual Basic (VB)
   arithmetic operators and functions, 302
   arrays, 121, 312–316
   binary files
      adding records to, 352–353
      reading contents of, 353
   built-in functions, 304–305
   case structure, 308
   class object, creation of, 333
   code comments, 302
   constant, declaration and assignment of, 302
   containment/aggregation, 341
   count-controlled loop, 309–310
   data structure, 173
   data types, 301
   exception handler, 362
   functions, 317–319
   IF-THEN-ELSE structure, 306
   IF-THEN structure, 305
   inheritance, 336
   methods, 331, 332
   nested **IF** structure, 307
   polymorphism, 338
   post-condition loop, 311
   pre-condition loop, 310
   procedures, 320, 322, 323, 325
   program output, 303
   random files
      adding records to, 357
      retrieving record from, 357
   record structure, 350
   text file
      creation of, 346
      reading content of, 348
   user input, 303
   variables, declaration and assignment of, 301
visual check, 79
VMs. *see* virtual machines (VMs)
voice coil, 33

W
WAN. *see* wide area network (WAN)
WAP. *see* Wireless Access Point (WAP)
waterfall model, in program development life cycle, 156–157
web server, 18
weighted graphs, 233, 271
   directed, 272
WHILE-ENDWHILE loop, 139
wide area network (WAN)
   characteristics of, 18
WiFi, 22
wired networks, 20–21
Wireless Access Point (WAP), 22
Wireless Network Interface Card (WNIC), 22
wireless networks, 21–22
WNIC. *see* Wireless Network Interface Card (WNIC)
wordline, 35
World Wide Web (WWW), 24
WWW. *see* World Wide Web (WWW)

X
XOR (EOR) gate, 37
XOR operator, 55

Z
zero bit, 43, 53